Teaching Students with Moderate to Severe Disabilities
An Applied Approach for Inclusive Environments

Lee B. Hamill
Xavier University, Cincinnati, Ohi

Caroline Everington
Winthrop University, Rock Hill, South Carolina

D1306662

Merrill
Prentice Hall

Upper Saddle River, New Jersey
Columbus, Ohio

Library of Congress Cataloging in Publication Data

Hamill, Lee B.
    Teaching students with moderate to severe disabilities : an applied approach for
inclusive environments/by Lee B. Hamill and Caroline T. Everington.
    p. cm.
Includes bibliographical references (p.) and index.
ISBN 0-13-020573-7
    1. Handicapped students–Education—United States. 2. Inclusive education—United
States. 3. Curriculum planning—United States. I. Everington, Caroline T., II, Title.

LC4031 .H355 2002
371.9'046—dc21

2001040931

Vice President and Publisher: Jeffery W. Johnston
Executive Editor: Ann Castel Davis
Editorial Assistant: Keli Gemrich
Production Editor: Sheryl Glicker Langner
Production Coordination: Holly Henjum, Clarinda Publication Services
Design Coordinator: Diane C. Lorenzo
Photo Coordinator: Nancy Harre Ritz
Cover Designer: Ali Mohrman
Cover Art: Suzy Turley, Southeast School—Franklin County BMR/DD
Production Manager: Laura Messerly
Director of Marketing: Kevin Flanagan
Marketing Manager: Amy June
Marketing Coordinator: Barbara Koontz

This book was set in Minion by The Clarinda Company. It was printed and bound by R. R. Donnelley &
Sons Company. The cover was printed by The Lehigh Press, Inc.

Photo Credits: Scott Cunningham/Merrill, pp. 3, 81, 123, 131, 26; Lee B. Hamill, pp. 8, 21, 56, 85, 93, 114, 172,
198, 223, 231, 253, 291, 301, 311, 332, 341, 400; Barbara Schwartz/Merrill, p. 25; Tom Watson/Merrill, pp. 36, 51,
161; Todd Yarrington/Merrill, pp. 105, 183, 241; Anne Vega/Merrill, pp. 213, 347, 379; PH College, p. 297.

Pearson Education Ltd., *London*
Pearson Education Australia Pty. Limited, *Sydney*
Pearson Education Singapore, Pte. Ltd.
Pearson Education North Asia Ltd., *Hong Kong*
Pearson Education Canada, Ltd., *Toronto*
Pearson Educación de Mexico, S.A. de C.V.
Pearson Education—Japan, *Tokyo*
Pearson Education Malaysia, Pte. Ltd.
Pearson Education, *Upper Saddle River, New Jersey*

10 9 8 7 6 5 4 3 2 1
ISBN: 0-13-020573-7

Preface

In *Teaching Students with Moderate to Severe Disabilities,* we introduce preservice educators to classroom and community-based curricular strategies and materials for teaching preschool, elementary, and secondary students with moderate to severe disabilities. We describe the underlying structure and process for developing and implementing applied curricula and show you how applied curricula can support learning in the general education classroom, the school, and the community. We also teach you how to level materials and activities to provide the instructional support that allows students with moderate to severe disabilities and their non-disabled peers to participate together in those inclusive learning environments.

The present emphasis on instruction for skill development through adaptation in the general education classroom has replaced the 1980s focus on segregated classes that offered a functional community-based curriculum for students with moderate to severe disabilities. Because we believe it is important for instruction in inclusive classrooms to focus on meaningful activities that further the ability of *all* students to function outside the classroom, the goal of this text is to combine *both* community and general education approaches with an emphasis on the application of academic content. Consequently, this text takes the approach that most instruction for all students occurs in general education settings and, beginning with the academic content of typical students, uses applied connections and the concept of leveling to provide adaptation strategies.

 **TEXT PREVIEW**

The text is divided into three sections. Section I presents a general overview of the curriculum for students with moderate to severe disabilities. Section II describes methods of assessment, curricular options, and professional interactions in the various learning environments for these students. Section III provides information on implementing appropriate instruction at both the elementary and secondary education levels for the three environments: general education classroom, school, and community.

Section I: Foundations of Curriculum

Section I consists of four chapters. Chapter 1, "Establishing the Context," provides the theoretical framework and philosophical perspective of the text. It builds a context for the framework and perspective of the text by giving a brief history of the attitudes and treatment of people with moderate to severe disabilities and the various approaches to curriculum development.

Chapter 2, "Characteristics and Strategies for Support," describes the characteristics and educational needs of students with moderate to severe disabilities. The chapter considers relevant characteristics that affect learning in the following areas: physical and health, cognitive, and social development. It also addresses adaptations and supports to facilitate learning.

Chapter 3, "Communication and Technology Supports," introduces strategies for enhancing communicative abilities and personal independence through assistive technology. The chapter begins with an overview of the recent legislation on assistive technology. It then presents a model for considering assistive technology and making informed selections. Enhancement of daily performance through assistive technology is discussed. Finally, the chapter addresses alternative and augmentative communication for persons with moderate to severe disabilities.

Chapter 4, "The Learning Environment," provides perspectives on applied curriculum models and inclusive practice. The chapter begins with an exploration of some of the issues regarding the implementation of inclusive classrooms. Next, it examines theoretical perspectives on functional and applied curricula for persons with disabilities. Finally, strategies for implementing applied curricula for *all* students in general education environments are presented.

Section II: Implementation of Curriculum

Chapter 5, "Authentic Assessment in Inclusive Environments," considers approaches to authentic assessment and presents strategies for referencing both the student's environment and the standard curriculum of the classroom. Strategies for monitoring student performance are presented.

Chapter 6, "Designing the Instructional Program: The IEP," presents strategies for developing an individual educational plan. Strategies for student and parent participation in identifying goals and services are provided. The chapter also discusses the development and implementation of the IEP document itself.

Chapter 7, "Supporting Inclusive Environments Through Collaboration," addresses strategies for working jointly with others to provide instruction and support. The chapter details the interactions of special education teachers with other teachers, administrators, paraprofessionals, parents, community members, and students. This chapter also addresses collaborative relationships that provide teacher support.

Section III: Instructional Environments

Section III addresses the implementation of appropriate instruction for students with moderate to severe disabilities in the three environments they encounter: classroom, school, and community.

Chapter 8, "Positive Behavioral Supports in Inclusive Environments," addresses classroom organization and proactive approaches to behavior management. The chapter provides positive strategies for building new behaviors that more effectively meet the individual's needs.

Chapter 9, "The Preschool Classroom," provides strategies for addressing the needs of persons with moderate to severe disabilities in typical preschool settings.

Chapter 10, "The Elementary Classroom," discusses adaptations to the standard elementary school curricula and strategies for creating alternative or parallel curricula and offers strategies for providing peer support.

Chapter 11, "The Secondary Classroom," discusses academic adaptations to the general education curriculum as well as applied and parallel curricula. The chapter also addresses other instructional needs of secondary education students, including interpersonal skill development in the areas of communication, behavior, and social adjustment.

Chapter 12, "The Elementary School Environment," presents a model of applied curricula for all students at the elementary level. The chapter describes an applied program in which all students can participate, including general education students. In addition, the chapter presents models in which general objectives in the areas of communication, behavior, and social adjustment can be addressed in all settings.

Chapter 13, "The Secondary School Environment," is a companion chapter to Chapter 12 that discusses applied curricula for all students at the secondary education level. The chapter covers appropriate nonacademic and extracurricular activities for students with disabilities, such as school clubs, lunch, and special events.

Chapter 14, "Community-Based Instruction," addresses community instruction for both elementary and secondary students with moderate to severe disabilities. The chapter covers instructional adaptations that provide adjunct activities to the general education curriculum. This chapter also addresses the development of employment opportunities.

Chapter 15, "Educational Transitions," the concluding chapter in the text, brings closure to the preceding chapters on instruction by addressing educational transitions. It presents approaches for helping students transition smoothly into school and from the elementary school to secondary education programs. The chapter also discusses transition from high school to adulthood, including postsecondary education programs, employment options, lifestyle options, and adult services.

 ## ACKNOWLEDGMENTS

We want to thank a number of people who have contributed to this book. We are grateful to Joy Garand-Nichols, Elizabeth Lahm, Laura Owens-Johnson, and Tom Pierce who co-authored several of the chapters with us. We also want to thank Ann Dunlevy for the material she wrote for *The Breakfast Place,* some of which is included in this book, as well as Suzanne Killy and Diane Perry for sharing their expertise and outstanding instructional programs. Their contributions have greatly enhanced the text. In addition, we want to thank our many colleagues and students who offered their ideas and insights. Their supportive comments and suggestions have added greatly to the content you will read. We particularly want to thank our colleagues, Cynthia Geer, Debora Hess, and Jennifer Kinney, who looked over our shoulders and shared their own insights as well as expert knowledge of general education curricula. We also want to acknowledge the valuable contributions of Jane Rawls, Administrative Specialist, Winthrop University, and our graduate students at Xavier and Winthrop Universities, Debby Abitz, Victoria Haygood, Lenita Knight, Sheila Sherwood, Carrie Tolford, Donna Leiter, and Sara Young, who eagerly pitched in to help us complete this project. We thank the following reviewers: Pamela J. Gent, Clarion University; Christine Givner, California State University, Los Angeles; Deborah Peters Guessling, Providence College; and Tony Russo, Marywood University. Finally, we want to thank our husbands, Jim and Bob, for their patience and support throughout the writing of this text. Their encouragement saw us through the hours of work.

Discover the Companion Website
Accompanying This Book

THE PRENTICE HALL COMPANION WEBSITE: A VIRTUAL LEARNING ENVIRONMENT

Technology is a constantly growing and changing aspect of our field that is creating a need for content and resources. To address this emerging need, Prentice Hall has developed an online learning environment for students and professors alike—Companion Websites—to support our textbooks.

In creating a Companion Website, our goal is to build on and enhance what the textbook already offers. For this reason, the content for each user-friendly website is organized by topic and provides the professor and student with a variety of meaningful resources. Common features of a Companion Website include:

FOR THE PROFESSOR—

Every Companion Website integrates **Syllabus Manager™**, an online syllabus creation and management utility.

- **Syllabus Manager™** provides you, the instructor, with an easy, step-by-step process to create and revise syllabi, with direct links into

Companion Website and other online content without having to learn HTML.
- Students may log on to your syllabus during any study session. All they need to know is the web address for the Companion Website and the password you've assigned to your syllabus.
- After you have created a syllabus using **Syllabus Manager™**, students may enter the syllabus for their course section from any point in the Companion Website.
- Clicking on a date, the student is shown the list of activities for the assignment. The activities for each assignment are linked directly to actual content, saving time for students.
- Adding assignments consists of clicking on the desired due date, then filling in the details of the assignment—name of the assignment, instructions, and whether or not it is a one-time or repeating assignment.
- In addition, links to other activities can be created easily. If the activity is online, a URL can be entered in the space provided, and it will be linked automatically in the final syllabus.
- Your completed syllabus is hosted on our servers, allowing convenient updates from any computer on the Internet. Changes you make to your syllabus are immediately available to your students at their next logon.

FOR THE STUDENT—

- **Topic Overviews**—outline key concepts in topic areas
- **Characteristics**—general information about each topic/disability covered on this website
- **Read About It**—a list of links to pertinent articles found on the Internet that cover each topic
- **Teaching Ideas**—links to articles that offer suggestions, ideas, and strategies for teaching students with disabilities
- **Web Links**—a wide range of websites that provide useful and current information related to each topic area
- **Resources**—a wide array of different resources for many of the pertinent topics and issues surrounding special education

- **Electronic Bluebook**—send homework or essays directly to your instructor's email with this paperless form
- **Message Board**—serves as a virtual bulletin board to post—or respond to—questions or comments to/from a national audience
- **Chat**—real-time chat with anyone who is using the text anywhere in the country—ideal for discussion and study groups, class projects, etc.

To take advantage of these and other resources, please visit the *Teaching Students with Moderate to Severe Disabilities: An Applied Approach for Inclusive Environments* Companion Website at

www.prenhall.com/hamill

Contents

Chapter 4
The Learning Environment 81

SECTION II
Implementation of the Curriculum for Students with Moderate to Severe Disabilities 103

Chapter 5
Authentic Assessment in Inclusive Environments 105

Chapter 6
Designing the Instructional Program: The IEP 131

SECTION III
*Instructional Environments
181*

Chapter 8
*Positive Behavioral Supports in
Inclusive Environments 183*

Chapter 9
The Preschool Classroom 213

Chapter 10
The Elementary Classroom 241

*Caroline Everington, Lee B. Hamill, and Joy D.
Garand-Nichols*

Chapter 11
The Secondary Classroom 265

Chapter 12
The Elementary School Environment 295

Chapter 13
The Secondary School Environment 321

Chapter 14
Community-Based Instruction 347

Laura Owens-Johnson and Lee B. Hamill

Chapter 15
Educational Transitions 379

Foundations of Curriculum for Students with Moderate to Severe Disabilities

chapter 1

Establishing the Context

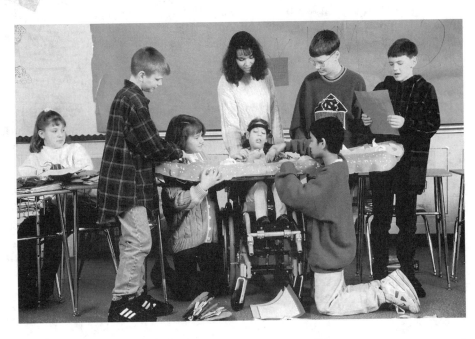

The title of this book tells you it is about teaching persons with moderate to severe disabilities. However, it is more than that. As you can see from the story of Cara, it is about finding creative and meaningful approaches to ensure that all students reach their maximum potential. It is about the curriculum we choose to teach, the process of teaching, and the values of teaching that influence those decisions.

When we examine the curriculum used and the process of teaching, we must address (a) *what* constitutes an appropriate curriculum, (b) *how*

A PARENT'S PERSPECTIVE

Cara, a woman who has Down syndrome and a moderate to severe disability, graduated from high school in 1998. She has been working and taking classes at a local college for 2 years. She takes the bus independently, transferring downtown amid the hustle and bustle of rush hour commuters. She works all day and then hurries to class, finding her way without any assistance. She buys her bus card at the office in town. Her parents couldn't be prouder.

Cara spent her school years in a variety of settings with varying degrees of *inclusion*. Because her parents are strong advocates, she was luckier than most. She was fully included in grade school, rather segregated in middle school, and included again in high school. Regardless of the setting, however, there was a common thread throughout: She never had an IEP that was implemented in the spirit in which it was written, and she never had an annual review where anyone could share meaningful data on the attainment of IEP goals. She graduated without a transition plan. Although she was in general education classes in high school, no one really tried to teach her much. Everyone was nice to her, but no one thought she could learn very much.

With the 1997 amendments to Individuals with Disabilities Education Act (IDEA), things should be better for students. There is now a mandate that learners who receive special education services participate and make progress in the general curricula. (No more segregated field trips to the bowling alley for the special education class instead of attending math class.) Measures of student progress must be given. General education teachers must help design and implement IEPs for all students in their classrooms. The bar has been raised and schools must now make certain that *every* child learns.

Cara has accomplished a lot since she has been out of school. She can count money and make change, which she could never do with those worksheets and plastic coins the teachers used. She orders pizza on the phone when her friends are over and even knows how much to tip the driver. She leaves her parents notes if she goes out.

Cathy, Cara's mother, knows her daughter is a remarkable young woman who has accomplished things others never thought she could. But Cathy says her heart aches when she thinks of the lost possibilities. What could Cara do if someone had really tried to teach her the things other children were learning? What would she know if the instructional activities had been more applied? What would she know if the appropriate accommodations had been made in the regular classroom? Who could she be? Cathy hopes in the future that parents will not have to look back and say, "*what if?*"

Source: Adapted with permission from Heizman, C. (1998). *Parent to Parent 22* (1). Cincinnati, OH: Child Advocacy Center.

the curriculum will be taught, and, in the case of persons with moderate to severe disabilities, (c) *where* the teaching will occur (Knowlton, 1998). We make assumptions and hold values that influence our decisions on each of these aspects.

We will first examine the notion of an appropriate curriculum. Appropriate curricula for students with moderate to severe disabilities who are in inclusive settings presents a complex problem for teachers (Bricker, 1997). For typically functioning school-aged students, the primary source of curricula is generally the standard curricula adopted by the school district and/or state. Curricular development for persons with disabilities should start with the standard curricula (Knowlton, 1998), but the instructional needs of Cara and other individuals with moderate to severe disabilities often do not fall neatly under this umbrella. Frequently, we may need to adapt the curricula. In other cases, we may need to alter the curricula to match the content with individuals' functional needs, particularly in the areas of vocational and life skills (Polloway, Patton, Epstein, & Smith, 1989). **An applied curriculum that connects the general education concepts being taught with the context where those concepts are utilized in managing one's everyday life is key to making the standard curriculum accessible for students with moderate to severe disabilities. This is the central thread that guides our descriptions of appropriate curriculum and adaptations throughout the book.**

The second aspect is *how* we teach, the methods, materials, and activities we use (Clark, 1994). There is a long and rich history of research on instructional methodology for persons with moderate to severe disabilities (Wolery, Ault, & Doyle, 1992). We have developed many successful strategies for teaching persons with moderate to severe disabilities that we present throughout this book. **The hands-on nature of an applied curriculum and the accompanying increased opportunity for au-** **thentic assessment of student progress contributes to the accessibility of the general education curriculum for students with moderate to severe disabilities.**

We also know it is important to use materials and activities that are meaningful to the students and allow them to transfer that knowledge to situations outside of the school setting (Helmke, Havekost, Patton, & Polloway, 1994). This is true for *all* students and is the central concept that provides the framework for this text. **Throughout the book, you will discover how many classroom materials and activities can be developed at several different levels to meet the different educational needs of a group of students with widely diverse abilities and allow those students to learn together.**

A related issue regarding *how* we teach is that of access. All students must be provided with access to the standard curriculum of the classroom as much as possible. This underscores the importance of assistive technology and natural supports. Throughout this book, we weave these concepts into each chapter.

The third aspect of teaching we must address is *where* instruction takes place. We are firmly committed to the assumption that instruction must be delivered in inclusive environments in neighborhood schools with same-aged peers (Lipsky & Gartner, 1997; Sapon-Shevin, 1999; Stainback & Stainback, 1992; Villa, Thousand, Stainback, & Stainback, 1992). It is our position that the general classroom is the least restrictive environment for *all* students, including those with identified disabilities. This is important for the first two aspects discussed, *how* and *what* we teach, because activities that take place in interactive, inclusive settings can help meet the interpersonal development needs of all students, including students with disabilities (Diem & Katims, 1991).

As a result of social, legal, and political movements (discussed later), students with moderate to severe disabilities are being placed in the general classroom in increasing numbers.

Although we strongly support this movement, as Cara's mother noted in the vignette, frequently it is for social reasons only and very little actual instruction and skill acquisition occurs (Bricker, 1997). Further, the instruction offered to students with moderate to severe disabilities in inclusive settings may not be appropriate for their needs (Ferguson, 1997). Part of the issue is that teachers often experience great difficulty in determining what and how to teach persons with moderate to severe disabilities in these settings. This may become more problematic as the focus on proficiency and standards-based assessment forces general education teachers to increase their efforts on academics for the typical population in their class (Clark, 1994).

As previously stated, we have a good knowledge base in curricula and instruction for persons with moderate to severe disabilities. However, much of the research and models supporting those strategies is based on instruction in segregated special education classroom or community settings, not the general education classroom. Our knowledge base regarding curriculum and teaching strategies for persons with moderate to severe disabilities in inclusive settings is in its infancy.

To date, much of the literature on inclusive practice focuses on students with mild disabilities and addresses adaptations to the standard curricula, such as books on tape and study guides (Blenk & Fine, 1995; Hoover & Patton, 1997; Kochhar, West, & Taymans, 2000; Wood, 1998). For many students with moderate to severe disabilities, adaptations to the standard curriculum may be insufficient because they have more extensive needs requiring more alteration of the content, resulting in a different curriculum. For students with moderate to severe disabilities, we see two instructional issues: (1) teachers are often unable to provide the amount of support that students need, and (2) they are having difficulty matching students' needs within the standard curricula. In these cases, teachers have to be much more creative. Many

are realizing that because of these curriculum challenges, inclusion is more complex than we originally thought (Ferguson, 1997).

This text addresses these issues in some new ways. Regarding identification and delivery of curricula within the general classroom, we look at ways that teachers can identify meaningful curricula within that context. In addition, we operate under the premise that curricula relevant for students with moderate to severe disabilities is *also relevant to typical students.* That is, adopting a more functional and community-oriented curricula approach can be relevant to *all* students in the classroom (Field, LeRoy, & Rivera, 1994). We discuss this in greater detail in this chapter and later chapters.

Regarding how we teach, we can enhance the learning experiences of *all* students by emphasizing nontraditional modes of curriculum delivery. For example, the traditional approach to instruction of lecture and seatwork may not prepare students to be functional adults. Students who spend the majority of their day sitting in rows doing isolated tasks and taking written tests may not learn how to make decisions for themselves or how to get along with others. This book emphasizes learning approaches that employ real-life contexts and examples and that encourage cooperation among peers in delivery of instruction.

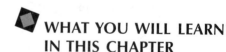 **WHAT YOU WILL LEARN IN THIS CHAPTER**

This book is not just about addressing curricular needs for students with moderate to severe disabilities. Rather, it is about making curriculum and instruction more relevant and accessible for *all* students. To understand the context of these approaches, we must first look at our past. Having a solid understanding of attitudes and assumptions regarding the curriculum and services for persons with moderate to severe disabilities in the past will assist us in making better teaching decisions in the present.

First we survey the history of curricula for persons with moderate to severe disabilities. We see how our values and assumptions regarding persons with disabilities have influenced our curriculum and instruction and, as a result of these values and assumptions, how persons with moderate to severe disabilities have learned and progressed.

Next we examine some of the history regarding attitudes, treatment, and services for persons with moderate to severe disabilities. In this section, we see how our values and assumptions regarding the capabilities of persons have influenced where and how they have received services. We also examine the effect of different service delivery models on the persons with disabilities.

We must reach some shared understandings of the population we are referring to when we use the phrase "moderate to severe disabilities." We offer definitions for various groups that may fall within the classification "moderate to severe disabilities": mental retardation, developmental disabilities, autism, and severe handicaps.

HISTORY OF CURRICULUM FOR PERSONS WITH MODERATE TO SEVERE DISABILITIES

As stated previously, we are currently faced with a dilemma regarding curriculum and instruction of persons with moderate to severe disabilities in inclusive settings. We have much to learn from our past. Through the research and practice of the past 30 years, we have learned a great deal about teaching persons with moderate to severe disabilities. In this section, we compare and contrast four approaches to the curriculum in our field: developmental, functional, community based, and applied.

Developmental Approaches

Up to the 1980s, teachers of persons with moderate to severe disabilities used a developmental approach to curriculum development. This ap-

FIGURE 1–1   Infant Skill Sequence in Fine Motor Development

1. Attempts to imitate scribble.
2. Holds crayon.
3. Pushes car along.
4. Puts three or more cubes in a cup.
5. Opens box and takes out object.
6. Turns pages of book.
7. Puts beads in box.
8. Places one peg in pegboard.
9. Places round block in form board.
10. Builds tower of two cubes.

Source: Adapted from Bayley, N. (1969). *Bayley scales of infant development.* San Antonio, TX: The Psychological Corporation.

proach was termed *developmental* because it referenced curricula and skills of typically developing infants and young children. Scales of normal infant and childhood development such as those developed by Gesselle (1940) and Bayley (1969) were often used to identify skills for instruction. In some cases, curriculum guides were developed for persons with moderate to severe disabilities based on these skills (Everington, 1982).

The idea for using infant skill sequences was based on the notion that individuals with cognitive disabilities learn the same way as typical children, and it is merely a problem of needing more time (Beirne-Smith, Ittenbach, & Patton, 1998). For the person with disabilities, skills in such curricula include infant developmental milestones such as stacking blocks or completion of puzzles or preschool preacademic skills such as color identification, sorting, and matching (see Figure 1–1). Students were taught skills geared to their "developmental age." For example, a 10-year-old who functioned at the level of a 2-year-old was given infant materials typical of a 2-year-old (Falvey, Grenot-Scheyer, Coots, & Bishop, 1995).

During this time, classrooms for school-aged persons with moderate to severe disabilities included a plethora of items used in preschool programs: form board puzzles, lacing shoes, wooden cubes, pegboards with pegs, stacking rings, and so on. It was thought that by using these items the individuals would learn on-task and fine motor behavior that would be helpful in later employment and school settings.

There were several problems with this approach. First, increased research on persons with cognitive disabilities indicated that they do not necessarily follow a "slowed-down" version of typical development in all areas (Beirne-Smith, Ittenbach, & Patton, 1998). Further, the developmental orientation led to what was termed by many as the "readiness model" (Luckasson & Spitalnik, 1994). The readiness model operated under the assumption that basic skills had to be mastered before moving to more complex skills or, more important, before moving into community or less restrictive settings. For example, before moving to a general education classroom or before taking a job in the community, the individual had to complete the program curriculum. Thus people with disabilities had to earn the right to community membership (Luckasson & Spitalnik, 1994). This orientation has been responsible for many students with moderate to severe disabilities not being permitted to receive instruction in inclusive settings—the general classroom, a community living arrangement, or a competitive job site (Brown et al., 1979).

Second, this type of instruction did not appear to enhance the performance of persons with disabilities in critical life skill areas (Siegal-Causey & Allinder, 1998). That is, a curriculum that consisted of working puzzles and stacking blocks did not transfer to essential skills needed for independence, socialization with nondisabled peers, communication, self-care, domestic, or work skills. The research also indicated that instruction occurring in the classroom on unrelated skills did not generalize to settings where the individual needed to use them: home and community (Stokes & Baer, 1977). For a skill to be useful, a person must be able to use it in the intended setting at the time it is needed.

However, note that developmental scales may still be useful for infants or very young children (Brown & Snell, 2000). In such cases, you may wish to reference curriculum guides such as *Hawaii Early Learning Program* (HELP) or *Assessment, Evaluation, Program System (AEPS) for Infants and Children* (Bricker, 1993). Although these are based on typical developmental sequences, they contain skills that are functional for infants and young children with disabilities.

Functional and Age-Appropriate Curricula

As we learned more about skill development for persons with moderate to severe disabilities, a shift began in the early 1980s from the models based on normal child development to models referenced to skills needed in the environment in which the individual presently functions and

Math manipulatives can be used to help students master fine motor skills.

those needed in future environments (Falvey, 1989). The emphasis on skill selection has concentrated on those perceived to be the most functional, that is, those that contribute the most to the individual's independence (Brown, Branston, Hamre-Nietupski, Pumpian, Certo, & Gruenewald, 1979). The emphasis was on skills that enhanced functioning in adult life, particularly work and independent living. The notion was that an educational program that includes functional curriculum provides students with an opportunity to develop competencies important for independent living and success in the work environment (Wehman, Kregel, & Barcus, 1985).

Along with the notion of functionality came the concept of age appropriateness. That is, curricula should be referenced to the activities and routines of the individual's same-aged peers. This stems from the concept of normalization, which was grounded in the notion that the lives of persons with disabilities should reflect the culture and values of persons without disabilities as much as possible (Nirje, 1969; Wolfensberger, 1970). That is, the lives of persons with disabilities should be like those of persons without disabilities. For schools, this meant the materials and activities that teachers used in special education classrooms should be as close to those of the same-aged peers as possible.

Another aspect of functional curricula is the deemphasis on academics (Weaver, Adams, Landers, & Fryberger, 1998). Many functional curricula guides stress decreasing academic instruction as the students get into the middle and secondary grades (Kokaska & Brolin, 1985). When academics are addressed, a "functional academic approach" is used. This represents a departure from the standard academic curricula and emphasizes only "survival" curricula (Clark, 1994). For example, this approach would imply teaching only those reading vocabulary words considered essential (sign for rest room or danger) or the minimal mathematical skills necessary to survive.

Community-Based Instruction

Functional curriculum is still relevant and continues to play an important role in instruction for persons with moderate to severe disabilities, but this approach is not sufficient for enabling individuals with disabilities to become fully functioning individuals. Research has taught us that maximal generalization occurs when training occurs in a setting most like the setting where the skill will be used (Gee, Graham, Sailor, & Goetz, 1995; Stokes & Baer, 1977).

The case of Cara is an example. Cara's mother mentioned that her daughter's teachers attempted to teach her money management skills by using worksheets. Although money management meets the criteria as a functional skill and worksheets as an age-appropriate teaching approach, the teaching context was inappropriate for her to generalize. When Cara's parents taught her those skills using real transactions that were meaningful—ordering pizza, for example—Cara quickly acquired those skills. Thus we learned that teaching is most effective if the setting and circumstances resemble the present and future environments (Beck, Broers, Hogue, Shipstead, & Knowlton, 1994).

As we learned the importance of the teaching context on generalization, the community-based instructional (CBI) approach gained prominence as a primary mode. CBI refers to teaching students skills in practical settings where those skills will be used (Beck et al., 1994). Those environments are thought to be more authentic.

Authentic learning environments are those environments outside of the classroom or school building, such as the grocery or local hospital. Instruction that occurs in community-based settings takes advantage of natural cues and consequences as the individual participates in expected routines (Goetz, Gee, & Sailor, 1985). Research has documented that skill acquisition, maintenance, and generalization are all enhanced when instruction occurs in these natural settings (Gee et al., 1995). With the success of this model for instruction, schools have increasingly implemented community-based instruction, some with significant portions of the school day spent in community settings such as groceries, banks, work sites, and shopping malls.

Although there is little argument regarding the effectiveness of this approach with persons with moderate to severe disabilities, the problem with this model is that instruction is occurring outside of the school environment, thus isolating the students with disabilities from their same-aged typical peers. Some have gone so far as to advocate that community-based instruction not occur during the school day because it separates the individual with disability from his or her same-aged typical peers (Stainback & Stainback, 1996).

Applied Curricula

In general education, we have similar movements in curricula in the form of school-to-work (Brolin, 1995), vocational education (Beck, Copa, & Pease, 1991), and applied curricula (Hamilton, 1980). Applied curricula is instruction that attends to vocational and consumer life skills as well as the social needs of all students and creates links between school and adult life. It assumes that students engaged in instructional activities that are meaningful to them have the best chance of developing school competencies (Simon & Dippo, 1987). Emphasizing academic skill acquisition in a practical context and encouraging students to generalize the information they learn to nonacademic or nonschool environments may be more motivating and relevant than traditional or remedial approaches. This is not a new concept. John Dewey supported "learning by doing" in 1937. However, the recent emphasis on academics has resulted in many general education teachers devoting less time to applied curricula.

Our Contemporary Dilemma

The advent of inclusive practice has brought a new dilemma for curriculum and instruction for persons with moderate to severe disabilities. Using community-based instructional approaches, we have made significant gains in the quality of lives for persons with disabilities as evidenced by their increased independence. However, CBI as it is presently configured is a special education program. As such, it does not provide integration with typical school-aged peers. We face a significant puzzle in how to facilitate maximum independence while at the same time maximizing inclusive opportunities. This is the challenge this book addresses.

HISTORY OF SERVICES FOR PERSONS WITH DISABILITIES

In the previous section, we presented an historical overview of curriculum development for persons with moderate to severe disabilities. Curriculum and instruction are central to our work, but as educators we must be mindful of the bigger picture—the social and historical context and its influence on our services.

In recent decades we have made great gains in enacting federal legislation and creating social policies that have enabled persons with disabilities to be included in school and community settings. This section briefly traces our history with regard to attitudes and treatment and provides a context for the contemporary approaches this text promotes. We explore our values and assumptions regarding services for persons with moderate to severe disabilities and the influence of these services on the personal independence and quality of life of the people with disabilities.

Our History

Much of the history of services for persons with disabilities is a history of exclusion from the mainstream of society (Smith, 1998). This

TABLE 1-1   Evolution of Services and Supports

Focal Questions	Era of Institutions	Era of Deinstitutionalization	Era of Community Membership
Who is the person of concern?	The patient	The client	The citizen
What is the typical setting?	An institution	Group home, special classroom, workshop	A person's home, general classroom, local business
How are services organized?	In facilities	Continuum of options	Supports tailored for the individual
What is the model?	Custodial/Medical	Behavioral	Individual
What are the services?	Care	Programs	Supports
Who controls the planning?	A professional	Interdisciplinary (IEP) team	The individual
What is the planning context?	Standards of professional practice	Team consensus	A circle of friends
What has the highest priority?	Basic needs	Skill development	Self-determination and relationships
What is the objective?	Control or cure	Changed behavior	Changes in environment and attitudes

Source: Lipsky, D.K., and Gartner, A. (1997), *Inclusion and school reform: Transforming America's classrooms* (p. 81). Baltimore: Paul H. Brookes. Adapted with permission.

exclusion is deeply rooted in our society and our values and therefore is something we as educators and service providers must examine. In many ways we have come a long way from the turn of the last century; in many ways we have not. Although not as prevalent, the same prejudicial and stereotypical attitudes that existed 100 years ago in the institutional era coexist with more progressive mindsets today. Table 1–1 outlines three major eras we have passed through during the past 100 years. These periods are important for us to examine and remember because many attitudes and treatment patterns remain with us today, impeding the

inclusion and personal independence of persons with disabilities. We discuss each of these eras in this section.

Era of Institutions

The beginning of the 20th century was one of the darkest periods of the history of persons with cognitive disabilities. This era was dominated by the eugenics movement, which focused on eradicating the condition of mental retardation through enforced sterilization, marriage prohibitions, and institutionalization (MacMillan, 1982). Mental retardation was thought to be the cause of many of our social ills. By segregating persons with mental retardation into institutions and preventing them from having children, people believed the condition would be eliminated (Beirne-Smith, Ittenbach, & Patton, 1998). Persons with mental retardation were treated as subhuman without, in many cases, adequate housing, clothing, or care (Gerry & Mirsky, 1992).

During this era, professionals and teachers used approaches that could be best described as either "medical" or "custodial" (Blatt, 1987). The term *medical* was used because disability was commonly viewed as a disease and the individual with the disability as a patient. When we view people from the medical model, we think of the condition in terms of a "cure" or whether it can be "fixed" (Lehr & Brinkerhoff, 1996). In most cases, no "cure" or "easy fix" was available for persons with moderate to severe disabilities. As a result, many individuals with cognitive disabilities were determined to be unfit for education (Lehr & Brinkerhoff, 1996).

Medical attitudes still prevail today. For example, when we consider medication as our only means of intervention with a child who may be hyperactive, we may be using a medical approach. When we look at intervention from only this perspective, we have limited expectations for what people can do to change this condition themselves or for what others can do to help them change.

The failure of the medical approach gave way to what might be termed a *custodial* approach. Because there was no "cure," people with moderate to severe disabilities were considered hopeless. The approach was merely to care for the individuals in the most efficient and cost-effective way—custodial. For these individuals, there were no expectations (Wolfensberger, 1983). Unfortunately, this approach is still present in our classrooms today. Even though our field may be progressive in our attitudes and treatment of persons with disabilities, there are still individuals working with this population who display custodial attitudes. The example of Nor-

ton is a contemporary example of a custodial attitude in an inclusive classroom. As you can see, including Norton in the general class does not guarantee that he will flourish and learn. As this example shows, the teacher's and caregiver's attitudes are important in this process.

NORTON HAS NO CHANCE TO GROW AND TO LEARN

Norton is in a general education classroom all day. The school district pays for an instructional assistant, Donna, to provide support for Norton. Because the teacher is busy, she relies on Donna for all instruction. Donna does not believe Norton can do anything on his own, and thus she does everything for him. This prevents Norton from acquiring skills and demonstrating competence. Donna sits next to him and follows him to all activities, thus preventing him from interacting with peers in an meaningful way. When IEP review time comes, Norton has shown little progress. The team decides to continue working on the same skills.

Donna likes Norton and is well intentioned, but her attitude and treatment reflect a custodial attitude. Because the classroom teacher permits this, it could be assumed she has no expectations for Norton either. This treatment differs little from the institutions of the past.

Era of Deinstitutionalization

The era of deinstitutionalization began in the 1970s and brought many shifts in thinking that resulted in changes in services and expectations. At the beginning of this era, numerous court cases affirmed the civil rights of persons with mental retardation and legislated appropriate treatment and training (Hickson, Blackman, &

Reis, 1995). The courts mandated special education services in the schools and stated that persons with disabilities should live in the community whenever possible. We began to move people from institutions to homes in local communities and to special classes in local schools. To meet the needs of persons with disabilities, it was thought they needed to be served in specialized programs where they would receive intensive attention and instruction (Bradley, 1994). The special education class developed in the schools. The group home was developed for people to live in the community and the sheltered workshop for employment.

During this time, the most important change that occurred was the change in viewpoints toward disabilities. We began to humanize our attitudes toward persons with disabilities (Gerry & Mirsky, 1992). Our attitudes and expectations toward learning changed greatly. In place of the hopelessness of the previous era, we adopted a developmental attitude that promoted the assumption *everyone could learn* (Bradley, 1994). Leaders in the field such as Mark Gold (1980) began to change the way we looked at persons with disabilities. Disability was thought of as a mismatch between the person's ability and his or her environment, rather than a permanent condition (Apter, 1982). The idea was that if we increase the competence of the individual, we will decrease the image and impact of the disability (Gold, 1980). These ideas were important because they provided optimism and spurred the growth of services and research. During this time, we demonstrated we could teach individuals many skills to make them successful, and, as a result, services and social integration increased.

As you can see from Table 1–1, skill development for the individual was the highest priority. This assumption, of course, continues to be important in our instruction and our teaching today. However, there are weaknesses in this model. Some have indicated this model has too strong a focus on limitations of the individual (Karagiannis, Stainback, & Stainback, 1996).

That is, the emphasis is sometimes more on what the person *cannot do* rather than what he or she *can do.*

During this time, we began to gain greater insight into the sociological impact of disability. We began to look at the discriminatory way in which society treats persons with disabilities and the devastating impact of prejudice and stereotypical treatment on the individual (Bogdan & Knoll, 1995). Our primary means to address prejudice and stereotype was by attempting to develop skills in each individual to the maximum degree possible and, at the same time, attempting to change the attitudes of society by increasing awareness of disability issues. We have succeeded in both areas to some degree.

Era of Community Membership

The movement beginning in the late 1980s and continuing to the present could be called the era of community membership (Bradley, 1994). Three main aspects characterize this movement: inclusion, advocacy, and empowerment (Lipsky & Gartner, 1997). It is important to highlight the differences between this movement and the deinstitutionalization movement and to emphasize that both are still occurring.

Regarding inclusion, the focus of our efforts today is full community membership for all persons with disabilities. Much discussion has centered on what it means to be a community member. Being a community member does not imply that being physically present in the community is sufficient. Instead, a community member is someone who not only takes part in activities, but who also receives needed assistance and support from community members (Baumgart & Giangreco, 1996). We have begun to realize that community membership is not an objective that can be reached merely by increasing the individual's competence through instruction. It implies the community must take responsibility for all its members and must provide the types of support they need (McKnight, 1989). Community membership is a major focus of this book. In each chapter we explore ways to include persons with disabilities into school communities and look at strategies for enhancing interaction with and acceptance from typical peers.

Advocacy and empowerment are key aspects of contemporary programs. To become fully functioning community members, persons with disabilities must learn to speak for themselves, make their own decisions, create options, and make choices in their lives (Wehmeyer, 1996; Williams & Shoultz, 1982). Central to developing self-advocacy and empowerment is the way we make decisions on educational goals and services the person needs. As you can see from Table 1–1, the emphasis is shifting from the process in which the team makes the decision on services and goals for the person to what is called "person-centered planning" (Forest & Lusthaus, 1992). In the past, the teacher or the team was thought to be responsible to fit the person to the environment. The idea was that we had to make them "ready" or to change them in some way for the environment. In the past model, the emphasis was on the teacher to make the individual fit in. Although this is important, *the idea the environment could change to match the individual did not often occur to teachers or service providers.*

In contrast, in the community model, the control for decisions shifts from the team of professionals to the individual with disabilities (see Figure 1–2). To the degree possible, the person with disabilities makes decisions regarding goals and services. This requires teaching specific skills in self-advocacy and self-determination. In this book, we will address person-centered planning approaches as well as the development of skills for self-determination and advocacy.

A final and significant aspect of the community era is the method of service delivery. In the past, we addressed the needs of persons with disabilities through the efforts of professionals in specialized programs. If a person had a need—for example, housing, transportation, or communication—we sought to find the special

service that would meet this need. Over time, we began to realize that these specialized services, although helping the individual, increased the isolation of the individual with disabilities from the community at large (McKnight, 1989). The more services the person used, the more excluded from the community he or she became.

To address this dilemma, we have embraced the notion of "natural supports," defined as what people do for each other naturally for exchange of knowledge, information, emotional assistance, and help (Drew & Hardman, 2000). Supports are resources and strategies that result in enhanced independence, productivity, and satisfaction (Luckasson & Spitalnik, 1994).

Think about your own life, and you will realize you rely on others for many things: to discuss your problems, pick up your mail when you are away, run errands for you, share recreational activities, and help with study or work. As you can see from the example of Jennie, we all need assistance from others, and most persons have a community (group of friends and/or family members) that provides needed supports. At the present time, for many persons with moderate to severe disabilities, these supports are more likely to be provided by paid individuals.

The concept of natural supports assumes the individual with disabilities will have supports like Jennie. The example of Oscar displays a model of natural community supports for an individual with disabilities. This is not to imply that persons with disabilities no longer need specialized services. On the contrary, Oscar would also need the specialized services of a job coach and assistive technologist for help with his employment. He might also need a case manager to assist with other services, such as money management, on an as-needed basis.

 DEFINITIONS

Before we survey the contents of this text, we must establish an understanding of the meaning of *moderate to severe disabilities.* In this section, we review definitions.

FIGURE 1–2

In the past, we tried to fit the person to the services.

In the present, we attempt to match the services to the needs of the individual.

EXAMPLE OF NATURAL SUPPORTS FOR JENNIE, A COLLEGE STUDENT

Jennie is a typical college student. Although she lives independently, she depends on others for support in many ways. Here are some examples of support she used when she graduated from college:

a. Her friend Dedra went with her to help her buy a used car and to negotiate the deal;

b. Her friend Nan went with her to look at apartments, and Dedra and Nan helped her make the final decision;

c. Four friends, Brian, Dedra, Niles, and Juan, helped her move;

d. Her parents gave her some money to assist with all the expenses of getting started;

e. She talks to three friends weekly—Brian, Dedra, and Nan—about personal aspects of her life and depends on their opinions;

f. She had car trouble two weeks ago and a co-worker, Mark, gave her a ride to work;

g. Many of her friends accompany her on social outings to movies, dance clubs, and restaurants.

EXAMPLE OF NATURAL SUPPORT FOR OSCAR, AN INDIVIDUAL WITH A DISABILITY

Like Jennie, Oscar is a young adult. Oscar has been living at home until recently. Oscar works at Pizza Hut. Here are examples of natural supports Oscar has in his life:

a. Marie, another employee at Pizza Hut, gives him a ride to work;

b. Oscar shares an apartment with a friend from church—Matt—who helps him to get to work on time and helps sometimes with shopping;

c. Dana, a friend who lives in the apartment complex, takes Oscar shopping and on errands as well;

d. Oscar spends social time with his girlfriend Mandy, as well as with Matt and members from his church;

e. Oscar's parents help with transportation and his expenses, if he needs extra help;

f. For support or advice on personal aspects of his life, he talks to Dana, Matt, or Mandy;

g. Oscar belongs to a hiking club that provides support for leisure and social needs.

All persons with moderate to severe disabilities can be classified as having one or more of the following disabilities: mental retardation, a developmental disability, or autism. Many special education programs have abandoned the use of categorical labels in favor of more generic terminology, such as mild/moderate and moderate/severe disabilities, but future teachers must still understand the definitions for mental retardation, developmental disabilities, and autism. Labels are used to qualify persons for research and for many services. We discuss each group separately, even though the three groups are not mutually exclusive. Because there is a good deal of overlap, some students may be identified as having mental retardation, a developmental disability, *and* autism.

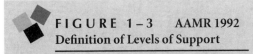

FIGURE 1–3   AAMR 1992 Definition of Levels of Support

Intermittent: Supports on an as-needed basis. Characterized by episodic nature, person not always needing support(s), or short-term supports needed during life-span transitions (e.g., job loss or an acute medical crisis). Intermittent supports may be high or low intensity when provided.

Limited: Intensity of supports characterized by consistency over time, time limited but not of an intermittent nature. May require fewer staff members and less cost than more intense levels of support.

Extensive: Supports characterized by regular involvement (e.g., daily) in at least some environments (such as work or home) and not time limited (e.g., long-term support and long-term home living support).

Pervasive: Supports characterized by their constancy, high intensity; provided across environments; potential life-sustaining nature. Pervasive supports typically involve more staff members and intrusiveness than do extensive or time-limited supports.

Source: Adapted with permission from Luckasson, R., et al. (1992). *Mental retardation: Definition, classification, and systems of supports* (p. 26). Washington, DC: American Association on Mental Retardation.

Mental Retardation

The American Association on Mental Retardation (AAMR) develops the definition of *mental retardation* used nationally and internationally for categorization. According to the most recent (1992) AAMR definition of mental retardation,

Mental retardation refers to substantial limitations in present functioning. It is characterized by significantly subaverage general intellectual functioning, existing concurrently with related limitations in two or more of the following adaptive skill areas: Communication, Self-Care, Home Living, Social Skills, Community Use, Self-Direction, Health and Safety, Functional Academics, Leisure

and Work. Mental retardation manifests before age 18. (Luckasson et al., 1992, p. 1)

According to the AAMR definition, to be classified as having mental retardation three conditions must be met. First, the person must have significantly subaverage intellectual functioning. This means he or she must have a Full Scale IQ score on an individually administered intelligence measure (IQ test) of 70 to 75 or below (Luckasson et al., 1992).

Second, he or she must have limitations in 2 or more of the 10 adaptive skill areas listed in the definition. We discuss adaptive behavior later in the text.

The third and final condition is that the evidence of intellectual or adaptive skill deficits must occur before the individual turns age 18. This implies mental retardation is a disorder that affects the cognitive and emotional growth of the person during critical years of development.

The 1992 AAMR mental retardation definition represents a significant change from previous AAMR definitions and is relevant to teaching and instructional planning. For the first time, the severity of mental retardation is categorized by the level of supports a person needs to participate in daily activities and to function independently (Schalock et al., 1994). In the past, mental retardation was classified by levels derived from IQ tests: mild, moderate, severe, and profound.

As we discussed earlier, the presence or absence of support can influence how a person functions in a given environment. The current AAMR definition has replaced the IQ-based levels of mild, moderate, severe, and profound of previous definitions with the following four levels of support: intermittent, limited, extensive, and pervasive (see Figure 1–3). The introduction of the levels of support in this definition attempts to move the field from labeling of individuals (e.g., severe mental retardation) to describing the person and the supports needed (Schalock et al., 1994). This is in keeping with the contemporary era of community membership we discussed earlier.

FIGURE 1–4   **The 1994 Federal Definition of Developmental Disability**

A developmental disability is a severe, chronic disability of an individual 5 years of age or older that:
- (A) is attributable to a mental or physical impairment or combination of mental and physical impairments;
- (B) is manifested before the individual attains the age of 22;
- (C) is likely to continue indefinitely;
- (D) results in substantial functional limitations in three or more of the following areas of major life activity—
  - (i) self-care; (ii) receptive and expressive language; (iii) learning; (iv) mobility; (v) self-direction; (vi) capacity for independent living; and (vii) economic and self-sufficiency; and
- (E) reflects the individual's need for a combination and sequence of special, interdisciplinary, or generic services, supports, or other assistance that is of lifelong or extended duration and is individually planned and coordinated, except that such term, when applied to infants and young children, means individuals from birth to age 5, inclusive, who have substantial developmental delay or specific congenital or acquired conditions with a high probability of resulting in developmental disabilities of services or not provided. [102(7)]

Source: Reprinted with permission from Smith, T. E. C. (1998). Developmental disability: Definition, description, and directions. In A. Hilton & R. Ringlaben (Eds.), *Best and promising practices in developmental disabilities* (p. 9). Austin, TX: ProEd.

MARIE IS A STUDENT WITH A DEVELOPMENTAL DISABILITY

Marie is 13 and in eighth grade. She is taking language arts, science, social studies, physical education, pre-algebra, music, and introduction to computers. Marie needs support in three areas: communication, mobility, and independent living. Although she cannot speak or sign, she communicates well using an electronic system that is activated by a micro switch pad she touches. Marie cannot walk, but she has a motorized wheelchair that enables her to move about school. She needs assistance from others in self-care (dressing and hygiene) and in feeding. Although adaptations have enabled her to function more independently, she still qualifies for services under the umbrella of developmental disabilities.

The intensity of support needed by a particular individual varies according to the task and environment. For example, some individuals need limited support in a given area (self-feeding) and extensive support in others (communication).

In addition, the presence or absence of support can influence how the person functions in a particular environment. With appropriate supports, an individual can become a full participant in a given environment. This text encourages the providing of the full range of supports in integrated settings—classroom, school, and community—and emphasizes the use of many natural supports, including peers and community members.

In addition to profiling the intensity of needed support in intellectual and adaptive skill areas, the 1992 AAMR definition requires that the strengths and weaknesses and supports be identified in the following areas: (1) psychological/emotional considerations, (2) physical and health considerations, and (3) environmental considerations (Luckasson et al., 1992). This multidimensional approach is important be-

MATT IS A STUDENT WITH A DEVELOPMENTAL DISABILITY AND MENTAL RETARDATION

Matt is a 6-year-old first grader. He is nonverbal and communicates with gestures and manual signs. He is friendly with other students and is learning to form friendships. He has difficulties in several adaptive skill areas. He has difficulty communicating verbally and needs supports to complete self-care skills such as brushing his teeth and community skills such as street crossing. Unlike Marie, Matt also has a cognitive disability and does not function at grade level on academic tasks. Thus he also needs support in learning.

cause many persons with moderate to severe disabilities have complex needs. As you will learn in Chapter 2, many persons with mental retardation have psychological/emotional problems as well as physical and health considerations. The focus on these issues helps us design more holistic interventions.

Developmental Disability

The term *developmental disability* is more functional in nature than the definition of mental retardation. It can include both persons with mental retardation and those who do not have a cognitive disability (Smith, 1998). This definition differs from that of mental retardation in that it (a) does not require a cognitive impairment, but it (b) does require a substantial limitation in three or more areas of major life activity (see Figure 1–4). In contrast, the AAMR definition requires a deficit in only two adaptive skill areas.

For example, a student with cerebral palsy who is functioning in the typical range cognitively may need support in the areas of language, mobility, independent living, and/or self-direction. Consider the case of Marie, who has significant deficits in several adaptive skill areas. Because her cognitive skills are on grade level, she probably does not have "significantly subaverage general intellectual functioning" as required for the diagnosis of mental retardation. Thus she has a developmental disability but not mental retardation.

In contrast, a student such as Matt could have the classification of developmental disability and mental retardation.

Autism

Many persons who need moderate to severe supports may also be classified as having autism. Leo Kanner first identified autism in 1943 and described the condition as having the following characteristics:

> Difficulty developing relationships with people; delayed speech acquisition and inability to use speech; repetitive and stereotypical behavior; lack of imagination; good rote memory; obsessive insistence on the sameness of routine; normal physical appearance. (Kanner [1943] as cited in Turnbull, Turnbull, Shank, & Leal, 1999, p. 405]

In 1991 Congress identified autism as a separate IDEA disability area (Turnbull et al., 1999). The following is the IDEA definition for autism:

> Autism means a developmental disability significantly affecting verbal and nonverbal communication and social interactions, generally evident before age 3, that adversely affects educational performance. Other characteristics often associated with autism are engagement in repetitive activities and stereotyped movements, resistance to environmental change or changes in daily routines, and unusual responses to sensory experiences. The term does not apply if a child's educational performance is adversely affected primarily because the child has a serious emotional disturbance. (34 CER, part 300, S 300, 7[b] [1])

SEAN IS A STUDENT WITH AUTISM

Sean is a very attractive 5-year old. He appears very happy as he laughs and skips down the hall of the school. Sean has exceptional motor abilities. He can run swiftly and throw a ball accurately. He has some verbal language. He repeats commercials and jingles with complete accuracy. However, he does not use this language to communicate with others. He has learned to communicate his needs to family, peers, and others using a combination of pictures and gestures. Sean does not make eye contact and has been described by others as being in a world of his own. He needs support in self-care areas of toileting and dressing. When in the community or out in his yard, he must be supervised at all times because he runs away or darts into oncoming traffic.

He has strengths in spatial skills. For example, he can put together fairly complex puzzles. He was recently given an intelligence test and his full scale IQ score was 58.

To sum up, four core features appear to be hallmark characteristics for persons with autism (Sturmey & Sevin, 1994): (a) social skill deficits, (b) severe problems with social interactions, (c) an insistence on sameness, and (d) disturbances in responses to sensory stimuli. Regarding the insistence for sameness, many persons with autism exhibit a strong need for routines. Changes in routines can result in behavior difficulties. They often react to sensory stimuli (touch, noise) differently than typical persons. These reactions can result in behavioral issues (screaming when the class bell rings or striking out when touched). We discuss approaches for these challenges in Chapter 8.

The interests of persons with autism are often severely restricted (Mesibov, Adams, & Klinger, 1997). For example, a child with autism may be intensely interested in playing and arranging geometric forms and display little interest in other toys or in communicating with persons in his or her surroundings.

In comparing the definition of autism with mental retardation and developmental disabilities, there is significant overlap. First, autism is a developmental disorder. It is generally thought to be identified by age 3 years (Mesibov et al., 1997). As you can see from the description of autism, most persons with this condition have deficits in several adaptive skills. Thus most are likely to have a diagnosis of developmental disability. In addition, approximately 70% of persons with autism have mental retardation (Beirne-Smith, Ittenbach, & Patton, 1998). Therefore, they have a diagnosis of both mental retardation and autism.

As you can see from the example of Sean, he meets the criteria for the three categorical definitions of autism, mental retardation, and developmental disabilities. Because Sean is 5 years old, he meets the developmental requirement for both a developmental disability and mental retardation. Regarding developmental disabilities, Sean has skill deficits in at least three areas: language, independent living, and self-care. He meets the definition of mental retardation because he has an IQ below 70 to 75 and he has deficits in two or more areas of adaptive skills. However, as previously mentioned, not all persons with autism have mental retardation.

TASH Definition of Severe Disabilities

Not all definitions refer to a categorical label of the disability. The Association for Persons with Severe Handicaps (TASH), one of the leading professional organizations in the field of disabilities, developed a definition for people who have severe disabilities. The TASH definition is useful for two reasons: (1) it concentrates on identifying supports needed to function in community settings; and (2) it defines disabilities in terms of the fit between the person and the environment (McDonnell, Hardman, McDonnell, & Kiefer-O'Donnell, 1995). Unlike the definitions for mental retardation and developmental disabilities, no mention is made of intelligence or performance on adaptive skill tests. As you can see from this definition, persons with moderate disabilities (also addressed in this text) may not need the extensive level of support and thus would not qualify for this definition.

> These people include individuals of all ages who require extensive ongoing support in more than one major life activity in order to participate in integrated community settings and to enjoy a quality of life that is available to citizens with fewer or more disabilities. Support may be required for life activities such as mobility, communication, self-

care, and learning as necessary for independent living, employment, and self-sufficiency. (Meyer, Peck, & Brown, 1991, p. 19)

 ## CONCEPTUAL FRAMEWORK OF THIS TEXT

We believe instruction for persons with moderate to severe disabilities should occur in the environments of their same-aged peers, with their peers whenever possible. However, for this population, skill needs may differ within each environment as well as the time spent there. Although educating students with moderate to severe disabilities in general education settings is a major focus in this text, we believe using only the general education classroom as a reference for curriculum limits skill development and generalization for students with disabilities.

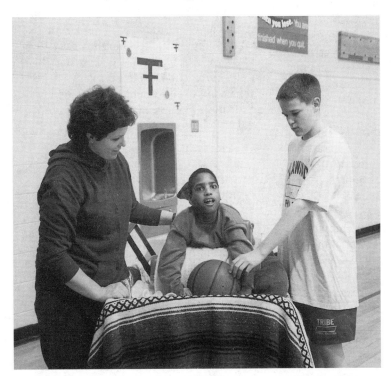

Extracurricular activities provide an excellent opportunity for developing social skills.

Furthermore, the instruction taking place in inclusive classrooms should focus on meaningful activities that further the ability of *all* students to function outside the classroom. It is the goal of this text therefore to combine *both* community and general education approaches. That is, we reference three learning environments: the general education classroom, the school, and the community.

We believe there are important differences in curricular content and social development issues in preschool, elementary, and secondary settings. Therefore, we address these learning environments separately.

The General Education Classroom

Our assumption here is that for all students most instruction occurs within the general education classroom. In this environment, we begin by referencing the standard curriculum of typical students. For students needing assistance in participating, we present curriculum adaptations. Applied activities and materials are emphasized.

For individuals with more significant disabilities who do not have requisite skills for direct adaptation of content, we present strategies for altering the activity or for creating a "parallel curricula." For example, in a fourth-grade geography lesson, many participation skills can be targeted to enable the individual to take part in the lesson, such as sitting in the group, turn taking, and pointing to designated areas of a wall map (direction following). Related, parallel activities may be designated for this individual, such as tracing letters for the country names or verbalizing the names of countries in the lesson. When altering curriculum, the text attempts to balance the use of age-appropriate materials and developmentally appropriate instruction.

The School Environment

Because of the importance of developing independent living and self-determination skills, other environments of the school must be referenced in curricula. Examples include the cafeteria where feeding and language skills can be addressed or the rest room where personal hygiene skills could be learned. Extracurricular activities, such as school clubs and athletic events, provide an excellent opportunity for developing communication and social skills. We present methods of ecological assessment and use opportunities present in the natural environment to support instruction.

Applied curricula, such as budgeting and cooking, are important for mentally typical students of all ages as well. Generating an applied curriculum for all students offers one way to address these critical needs for persons with disabilities. For secondary education students, the text highlights the "Breakfast Place," which is a model of a restaurant started in a school (Hamill & Dunlevy, 1993). For elementary students, the "Kid's Kitchen" offers a curriculum that includes various activities from daily breakfast preparation to a monthly bakery business in the school. Both the "Breakfast Place" and the "Kid's Kitchen" teach a variety of community skills to all students, such as food preparation, money management, and appropriate social interaction.

Community Environments

Finally, the text addresses models of community-based instruction and presents sample training environments for employment, community mobility, and independent living skills (e.g., shopping, banking). We use ecological assessment to generate objectives for students at a variety of ability levels. Concrete suggestions are offered on logistics: scheduling, staffing, transportation, and funding of such programs. Once again, the text emphasizes ways community instruction can be implemented within the standard curricula of mentally typical students so all students may benefit.

 SUMMARY

In conclusion, this book is about change in the way we view curriculum and instruction for persons with moderate to severe disabilities. It is about a vision for *all* learners that embraces curriculum that is meaningful and instructional strategies that enable all learners to have access to the curriculum.

This text provides a format for evaluating programs and student accomplishments, an understanding of the purpose for developing and implementing an applied approach to instructional activities and materials, and the interdisciplinary nature of instruction in general education environments. To identify appropriate objectives, you will learn to reference the primary environments where instruction takes place: the general education classroom, school, and community. The text also provides strategies for creating natural supports for students with disabilities in these contexts.

 CHAPTER EXTENDERS

Key Terms and Concepts

1. An *applied curriculum* is one that connects the content being taught with the context where that content is used in managing everyday life.
2. *Community-based instruction* takes place in the natural setting where the skill will be used.
3. *Deinstitutionalization* is the change in service delivery from large residential settings to homes in the community.
4. A *developmental approach* to curriculum references typically developing children to identify the skills for instruction.
5. *Functional curriculum* emphasizes the development of skills that enhance functioning in adult life, particularly in work and independent living, and de-emphasize academics.
6. *Moderate to severe disabilities* is a generic term used to identify students who have

been classified with one or more of the following disabilities: mental retardation, development disabilities, or autism.
7. *Natural supports* are the resources and strategies people in the community naturally use to assist each other to enhance independence and productivity.

Study Guide

1. Define the following key terms:
   a. developmental approach,
   b. functional curriculum,
   c. age-appropriate instruction and materials,
   d. applied curriculum,
   e. community-based instruction,
   f. mental retardation,
   g. developmental disability,
   h. autism, and
   i. severe disabilities.
2. Compare and contrast the era of institutionalization, era of deinstitutionalization, and era of community membership.
3. Discuss the similarities and differences between the terms *mental retardation* and *developmental disabilities*.
4. Identify your natural supports. Who do you go to when you have a problem? Who helps you when you need to take your car in for repair? Who could you turn to for financial problems? Who provides companionship? How many people are in your network? How can we build similar communities of support for people with disabilities?
5. Describe the four levels of support identified in the 1992 AAMR definition of mental retardation.
6. Discuss the similarities and differences between developmental disabilities and mental retardation.
7. List and describe the core features of autism.
8. Discuss the differences in support needs between individuals who have moderate disabilities and those with severe disbilities.
9. Define age appropriate instruction and materials.

Group Activity I

Look again at the description of the custodial treatment of Oscar, the student with autism who was included in the general classroom. Imagine Oscar is your child. You are very concerned about the minimal expectations the assistant and teacher have for Oscar. How will you address this? (Note: Changing classes is not an option.) What might you ask the professionals to do differently? How might you attempt to change their opinion?

Group Activity II

In most places in the United States, we are very far from what we might call "community acceptance" for persons with moderate to severe disabilities. Brainstorm ways that you can create systems change in your local community.

Field Experience I

Spend a day in an inclusive classroom that has at least one person with moderate to severe disabilities. Observe the curriculum and teaching strategies you see used with this person with moderate to severe disabilities. How much actual instruction is occurring? How much is the person doing for him or herself versus how much is being done for the person? Does the instruction occur within the context of the general lesson or is the person pulled aside or pulled out of the class? Do the skills appear to be age appropriate and functional? Is the instruction presented in a way that appears to be meaningful to the person with disabilities?

Observe the curriculum and instruction for the typical students in this setting as well. Does the curriculum appear to be meaningful for the students? Is the instruction presented in a way that engages the learners?

Field Experience II

Spend a day observing or volunteering in a setting that serves persons with moderate to severe disabilities—classroom, community living arrangement, or supported employment setting. As you spend time in this setting, observe how the persons with disabilities are treated. Are they treated with respect? Does the individual with disabilities appear to be part of the greater community? If it is an inclusive setting, is the individual with disabilities accepted by his or her peers? What are the expectations for the person with disabilities in this setting? What evidence do you have of expectations? You may need to interview one of the caretakers in the setting to determine answers to some of these questions. Which of the three eras (institutions, deinstitutionalization, or community membership) does this setting reflect? Write up your reactions and provide suggestions for change.

chapter 2

Characteristics and Strategies for Support

Oscar is in a fourth-grade class. He is very verbal but has difficulty responding appropriately in conversations. His reading skills are on a first-grade level. He has established friendships with many of the students in his class. He is friendly and has a good sense of humor. He has problems staying on task and remembering what he has learned. He has been described as being hyperactive. Oscar has been identified with Fragile X syndrome.

Jasmine is a pretty 17-year-old junior in high school. This term she is taking public speaking, health, home economics, current events, consumer math, and art. She does volunteer work in the community as a member of Key Club. Jasmine's reading skills are at the second-grade level and her math skills are at the third-grade level. She is friendly and outgoing although she is somewhat immature in her interactions with peers. Jasmine has been identified with mental retardation.

Marie is 13 and in eighth grade in the middle school. This term she is taking language arts, social studies, physical education, pre-algebra, music, science, and introduction to computers. Marie is not ambulatory, but she has a motorized wheelchair that enables her to get around the school independently. She can use a few words to communicate but she relies primarily on an assistive device, which she can activate using a touch pad. She is popular with the other students and is a member of the group that works on the school yearbook. Marie has been identified with cerebral palsy.

Matt is a 6-year-old first grader. He is nonverbal and communicates with gestures and signs. He is learning to form friendships with the other students in his class. He has difficulty staying in his seat, and his attention span is very brief. Matt has been identified with autism.

Like students found in any classroom, students identified as having moderate to severe disabilities represent a very heterogenous group of individuals with strengths and needs in a variety of areas. As the descriptions at the beginning of the chapter illustrate, Oscar is verbal, but Matt is nonverbal. Marie has cerebral palsy, but can function close to grade level in academics. Oscar is very outgoing and friendly, and Matt has difficulty forming friendships and communicating with others.

As we learned in Chapter 1, the term *moderate to severe disabilities* has been used to refer to individuals who may have a variety of labels such as mental retardation, severe and profound handicaps, autism, deaf and blind, and severe emotional disturbance (Alper, 1996). The predominant characteristics of this group are that they have complex needs and frequently require support from others to function independently (Falvey, 1989). Most, but not all, members of this group of individuals are likely to have cognitive impairments as well as one or more additional disabilities such as a medical issue or motor, vision, or hearing impairment. Thus as a teacher of persons with moderate to severe disabilities you must have some basic understanding of various conditions that may affect learning so you can provide the maximum educational experience for all your students.

WHAT YOU WILL LEARN IN THIS CHAPTER

Three major issues are relevant for teachers of persons with moderate to severe disabilities:

(a) cognition and learning, (b) motivation and behavior, and (c) physical and medical impairments. For each of these areas this chapter offers some suggestions for addressing the issues in your instruction and for arranging your classroom environment.

This chapter surveys the various conditions that might affect learning and highlights major approaches to instruction. Although diagnosis of various conditions is important for guiding educators to more appropriate teaching approaches, the primary focus of this text is strategies for support. First we address issues important to delivery of effective instruction. Then we discuss issues important for creating a positive learning and classroom environment. The chapter concludes with a review of physical and medical impairments that describes some of the more common health and medical needs and ways to work with therapists and health care professionals to provide support in inclusive settings. Many of the characteristics we discuss in this chapter are displayed by many children in your classroom who do not have identified disabilities, and the strategies we review in this chapter will be useful for them as well.

◆ CHARACTERISTICS RELATED TO COGNITION AND LEARNING

Like many children in any classroom, students with moderate to severe disabilities frequently have problems with attention, memory, and generalization that make it difficult for them to acquire information, retain learned material, and transfer learned material to new situations. These are problems that require some level of support in almost all learning situations. Thus when presenting instruction on a given skill, use strategies that maximize the students' acquisition, retention, and generalization of the material you teach. We begin our discussion with the issue of generalization.

Generalization

One of the most significant difficulties students with moderate to severe disabilities face is the issue of generalization. *Generalization* can be defined as "when a response that has been trained in a specific setting with a specific instructor occurs in a different setting or with a different instructor" (Alberto & Troutman, 1995, p. 398). This aspect of teaching is critical to the ultimate success of our students because the true purpose of teaching is to give students individual skills they can use in different settings or in novel situations (Rosenthal-Malek & Bloom, 1998). For students with moderate to severe disabilities, this means using a skill learned in the classroom, such as following directions, in other school settings, at home, or in the community. It can also mean responding in the same manner—giving eye contact to the speaker—to different persons in the environment—caregivers, parents, employers, and/or peers.

Strategies for Enhancing Generalization. As you can see from the description of Oscar, with prompting from his teacher Ms. Perez, he began to respond with eye contact to other persons and in other settings. Ms. Perez implemented a fairly simple strategy of verbal reminders or prompts to accomplish this. Often, simple strategies such as verbal reminders are not sufficient to accomplish generalization of the behavior. Or the student may become dependent on the verbal reminders, thus defeating the purpose of the instruction, which is independent behavior in the new settings. There are many approaches to enhance generalization for all students. We suggest you use more than one to increase your likelihood of success.

One of the more effective methods of teaching generalization strategies is to teach the skills in the setting where students will use them, such as the general classroom of the student's same-aged peers and/or the community where he or she lives (Gee et al., 1995). When training is provided in the context of the classroom or the

A GENERALIZATION EXAMPLE FOR OSCAR

Oscar has difficulty answering questions appropriately. For example, on Monday mornings when Oscar's teacher, Ms. Perez, asked him about his activities over the weekend, he would stare at the floor and tell her that he went to his grandmother's house or he had lunch at McDonald's. Every Monday, she would remind him to look at her while he told her about his weekend. After being reminded, Oscar began looking at her while he talked.

After several weeks of reminders, Oscar has learned to look at Ms. Perez most of the time when he talks to her. Ms. Perez has begun to expect Oscar to transfer this behavior to other persons and settings. With prompts from Ms. Perez, he is starting to look at Mr. Farmer, the classroom aide, when he speaks to him. Oscar even is beginning to look directly at Ms. Brown, the bus driver, when she stops at his house each morning, and he says "good-bye" as he gets off the bus at his destination.

FIGURE 2–1
Generalization Examples for Matt

1. **Use multiple examples in teaching.** When teaching Matt to identify the men's room, four different public rest rooms—two in the school building and two in the community—were targeted for training.
2. **Teach relevant/functional skills.** The first words that Matt learned to sign were chosen from those items/activities determined to be his favorites—toy car, potato chips, and listening to music.
3. **Teach the student to self-monitor generalization.** To assist Matt in staying in his seat on the bus, he was given a picture of himself seated in the bus and an accompanying short story to carry with him.
4. **Implement the same strategy across settings.** The family, general education teacher, special education teacher, and language pathologist all have agreed to use the same approach to increase Matt's in-seat behavior and decrease his running around the room.
5. **Program for generalization.** Matt's classroom peers have been trained to reinforce Matt for appropriate social behaviors through compliments.

community during routines and typical activities, the student learns to respond to the natural cues present in the environment (King-Sears, 1997). You will see many examples of natural cues in Chapters 8 through 14, which address teaching skills in the classroom, school, and community.

In contrast, when instruction is provided in a segregated setting, such as a self-contained special class, or when instruction requires many artificial cues or sequences, such as using play money in a make-believe store, generalization is more difficult and may require more direct programing (Gee et al., 1995). This text addresses instruction in naturalistic contexts in the classroom, school, and community in the hope that this strategy will enhance generalization.

However, instruction in the naturalistic setting does not always result in generalization to other settings/persons, especially if the conditions between settings differ on several dimensions (Sprague & Horner, 1984). Therefore, as a teacher, you must plan for generalization. The following five strategies will help you plan for generalization. Examples of these strategies for Matt illustrate how they can be used with a particular student (see Figure 2–1).

Five Specific Generalization Strategies:

1. **Use multiple examples in your instruction.** Teach your students in more than one setting, with more than one person, or with a set of similar objects (Stokes & Baer, 1977;

Stokes & Osnes, 1988). For example, when teaching use of vending machines, use several machines that differ in format in your instruction.

2. **Teach relevant/functional behaviors.** Relevant or functional skills are those skills that have meaning for the student and are useful for gaining mastery/control of his or her environment (Stokes & Osnes, 1988). Teach skills with "high purchase power" because they are more likely to be maintained and generalized. High purchase power skills are skills that enable students to get what they want. For example, for communication training, choose vocabulary reflecting important needs for the student.

3. **Teach students to self-monitor for generalization.** Mediation strategies are techniques to teach students to control their own generalization (King-Sears, 1997). Teach students to remind themselves through self-talk or to carry reminders of the desired behavior, such as pictures of themselves performing the task, audiotape reminders, or scripted stories.

4. **Implement the same strategy across settings.** Multiple teaching environments and the team approach advocated throughout this text are important factors in ensuring that learned skills are transferred across settings and persons. When multiple settings contain the common elements (stimuli), generalization will be more likely to occur (Stokes & Baer, 1977; Stokes & Osnes, 1988).

5. **Program for generalization.** In the student's IEP, write generalization objectives and develop a plan for determining if generalization has occurred (Matlock, Lynch, & Paeth, 1990). This plan might consist of observing the student in other settings and with other people. If the observations indicate the student is not performing the skill in the new setting, subsequent instruction may be needed in that setting. Peers can be important in promoting generalization. However, in some cases, particularly if the student with disabilities is nonverbal, peers may need to be trained in how to interact (Mundschenk & Sasso, 1995).

Memory and Attention.   Learning new material can be challenging for many students, particularly for those with moderate to severe disabilities. One reason is that students with disabilities have problems in discrimination. That is, they experience difficulty in attending to the important aspects of the task (Koegel & Koegel, 1995). Discrimination learning occurs in all types of tasks from academics to social skills. Two examples of this are problems Oscar has on two very different tasks. He has difficulty in (a) determining the difference between the letter "p" and the letter "b" and in (b) remembering not to talk when the teacher or others are talking.

When beginning teaching on new tasks, make adaptations in your teaching strategies and the materials to enhance discrimination for many of the students in your classroom. The three strategies listed here will be helpful and should enhance your effectiveness with all students in your classroom.

Three Strategies for Enhancing Discrimination:

1. **Reinforce the correct response.** Students must be given specific feedback on their performance (Malott, Whaley, & Malott, 1997). Direct and immediate reinforcement of correct responses calls attention to the correct response in a positive way. This is preferable to calling attention to the incorrect response. An example is to reinforce class members (including Oscar) when they are paying attention rather than punishing individuals for not paying attention. To enhance discrimination, provide the positive feedback at the moment the behavior is occurring.

2. **Use strategies to highlight the desired response.** Color coding, auditory cues, and picture prompts are all examples of ways you can highlight the correct response. For example, to help Oscar with letter discrimination, you might initially highlight the tail of the "p" in a contrasting color. The key is to emphasize

the difference between the correct response and other responses or answers.

3. **Teach responses to natural cues.** Teach students to respond to cues in the environment rather than prompts or instructions supplied by you (Snell & Brown, 1993). Teach Oscar to watch other students for cues. When they are quiet, he should not talk. (This works if the other students in your room are good models of appropriate behavior.)

Chapters 8 through 14 provide many other examples of approaches for enhancing discrimination when teaching specific skills in classroom, school, and community settings.

A DISCRIMINATION STRATEGY FOR OSCAR

Oscar's teacher uses highlighting to help Oscar focus on the written directions for his seatwork. He uses a marker to highlight the key words in the directions. This way, Oscar can work on his own without asking the teacher what to do next. The teacher found this strategy worked with many other students as well.

Retention (Maintenance). Like many students in any classroom, students with cognitive disabilities have difficulty retaining the material they learn. Maintenance of learned skills is important because learned behaviors must be maintained before more advanced skills can be taught (Wolery, Ault, & Doyle, 1992). In addition, for skills to be generalized, they must be maintained.

For many tasks, the memory of students with cognitive disabilities may not be as efficient as their mentally typical peers (J.D. Smith, 1998). Students with a cognitive disability may need repeated demonstrations to learn a simple response, and once they learn the task, they may not be able to maintain the response. This is a problem teachers face regularly with all students, and thus they need to incorporate strategies for facilitating maintenance into instruction with all students.

Two Strategies for Facilitating Retention:

1. **Use repetition.** Repetition enhances memory and retention. Arrange for your student to perform the skill several times a day in different settings. For example, when Matt was learning the sign for "toy," his teacher set up many situations where he would have to use that sign every day (Beirne-Smith et al., 1998; Polloway & Patton, 1997).

2. **Use self-instruction.** You can teach your students ways to help remember desired behavior. There are many strategies. One way is for students to set a goal for themselves (Polloway & Patton, 1997). For example, you might help Oscar to set a goal to listen and not talk during whole class instruction. To help him succeed, you and Oscar prepare a reminder card: "I will listen and not talk when Ms. Perez is talking." The reminder card is placed on his desk and he is instructed to refer to it during the day. A more advanced approach would be to use self-talk. In this case, students learn to remind themselves of what they need to do prior to the event.

A MEMORY STRATEGY FOR MATT

Matt has difficulty remembering his daily job—wiping the chalkboard at the end of the day. The teacher has prepared a schedule that contains pictures of each of the primary activities he does each day in the order in which they occur—individual reading time, recess, lunch, library, *cleanup job,* and bus. Because he has been using his picture schedule, he no longer needs verbal reminders from his teachers.

◆ MOTIVATIONAL AND BEHAVIORAL CHARACTERISTICS

Effective classroom teachers facilitate caring and supportive environments for all students (Sapon-Shevin, 1999). This section addresses psychological and motivational issues that are important considerations for teachers. First we discuss the impact of the learning climate itself on the student. Students who have cognitive and learning problems frequently experience failure in instructional settings. As a result, some develop behaviors that prevent them from achieving maximum independence and cause them to be dependent on others in problem-solving situations. Although not all persons with disabilities develop these behaviors, teachers must understand these characteristics so they can prevent them from developing in any of their students (Beirne-Smith et al., 1998). Three of these characteristics—failure expectation, outerdirectedness, and acquiescence—are discussed in this section. All students are at risk for failure and many display these characteristics, but students with moderate to severe disabilities are more likely to develop these problems.

Ways to overcome these problems—creating successful learning, decreasing dependence on others, and promoting self-determination—are presented. Because this text emphasizes instruction in inclusive settings, keep in mind that these issues are relevant to *all* students who experience learning difficulties.

As we know, many other things influence student learning that are independent of the control of the teacher. These aspects include psychological and biological states that may influence the student's availability to learn and perform in the classroom. We discuss these aspects in the later part of this section.

Create Success and Minimize Failure

Several researchers who have compared individuals with mental retardation to typically functioning individuals found that persons with mental retardation have a greater tendency to approach new situations with an expectation of failure (Zigler & Hodapp, 1986). Persons who expect to fail tend to set lower goals, reduce the amount of effort they extend in a given task, and fail to attempt new tasks. These characteristics can create a condition called *learned helplessness* (Seligman, 1975). For the teacher, this can be a very frustrating experience because many of his or her students may not appear to even try new tasks or will quit after the first failure.

We outline three strategies for maximizing success. You will find these helpful with any student in your class who displays learned helplessness or failure expectation.

Three Strategies for Maximizing Student Success in Learning Situations:

1. **Minimize the chance of errors.** Apply the principles of *errorless learning* whenever possible. Attempt to arrange the materials and instruction so the student will make only correct responses (Alberto & Troutman, 1999). Break down the task into small steps to minimize the student's experience of failure. For example, begin word identification with a picture of the object paired with the word on a card. As the student begins to respond correctly, the picture becomes more faded with each version of the card until it finally disappears with the last card containing only the word (Snell & Brown, 1993).

2. **Frequently use descriptive praise and reinforcement for correct responses and attempts.** The student must have a clear understanding of the correct response. Direct reinforcement of correct responses provides immediate validation. Students who have experienced frequent failure need a higher rate of reinforcement. Descriptive praise is one of the most effective and easiest ways to do this. When giving feedback, try to describe the exact behavior the student has done correctly. For example, say, "I like the way you kept your hands to yourself in group today." This provides the learner with

a model of the desired response. We discuss the use of reinforcement in greater detail in Chapter 8.

3. **Promote positive attitudes in others regarding student abilities.** Educators, peers, and family members who are in the individual's environment must truly believe the individual is capable of learning and achieving independence (Falvey & Grenol-Scheyer, 1995). Attitudes of others are important for motivation. Sometimes, you may need to work actively with peers to ensure that cooperative and group experiences involving students with disabilities are positive.

For example, Jones and Carlier (1998) describe an approach for promoting supportive peer groups in cooperative learning situations. They suggest creating evaluation criteria for group work that rates students on the amount of positive feedback they provide to each other and the amount of participation the group allows each member.

You may also need to work actively to promote positive attitudes and expectations with other professionals, administrators, and parents. Showcasing student accomplishments and giving visible responsibilities to persons with disabilities are two approaches.

4. **Employ multileveled instruction.** Leveling classroom materials and activities allows you to individualize instruction. Leveled materials permit a group of students with different degrees of skill to work together on the same activity while each student simultaneously performs tasks at his or her own ability level (Hamill & Dunlevy, 1994). When materials are leveled, all the students in the group are working on the same activity, but each student's tasks are individualized. This allows students the opportunity to learn the concepts targeted for them and also the chance to learn ancillary material that has been assigned to others in the group. Materials presented in this manner can maximize the

amount of time each student is engaged in learning and allows you to address all the students' individual needs at one time.

Leveling not only gives equal academic opportunity to an academically diverse group of learners but it also provides opportunities for peer teaching. This can increase participation and social skills development for every student in the group. You also can use the leveling process to reinforce previously learned skills. To enhance the generalizability of school information to real-life situations, leveled materials could use authentic items and be designed to create practical learning activities in the classroom when teaching in the authentic environments is not feasible (Hamill & Dunlevy, 1999; Nietupski, Hamre-Nietupski, Clancy, & Veerhusen, 1986). Information Words Bingo is one example of a multilevel language arts activity (see pp. 34-35). You will find many other examples of specific leveled materials throughout the chapters of this text.

JASMINE FOLLOWS THE WRONG CUE

Mr. Schwartz, Jasmine's art teacher, asked several of his students to help get the room ready for the day's watercolor class. He asked Jasmine to get all the paints on the bottom shelf out of the supply closet. As Jasmine approached the closet, she looked around the room to see what other students were doing. Pete, a student who liked to play jokes on his friends, noticed her confusion and told her to get only the red paint jars. Jasmine followed Pete's instruction instead of Mr. Schwartz's and received a correction from Mr. Schwartz. Jasmine was confused by this because she did not understand why Pete would tell her to do the wrong thing.

Decrease Dependence on Others

Related to the failure experience is the tendency for students with cognitive disabilities to demonstrate a characteristic termed *outerdirectedness,* which refers to the individual's reliance on social and linguistic cues provided by others in a problem-solving situation (Bybee & Zigler, 1992). In other words, when presented with a problem they cannot solve, students with learning problems are more likely to look to others for the answer. In addition to relying on others, they are less likely to discriminate helpful cues from misleading cues when they look to others for those signals (Bybee & Zigler, 1992).

In addition to providing opportunities for success and positive feedback as previously discussed, build the student's skills in empowerment and self reliance. You will learn more about building these skills in future chapters. However, here are two suggestions that can be useful with many students:

1. **Teach students strategies in problem solving.** Teaching students to solve their own problems can decrease dependence on others. However, in many cases, independent problem solving must be systematically trained. For example, problem-solving training sequences frequently involve the following: (a) identify the problem, (b) generate alternatives, (c) identify potential consequences, (d) choose a solution, and (e) evaluate results (Harris, 1982; Zirpoli & Meloy, 2001). When choosing a solution, it is important for students to be able to tell others why that was the best option for them (Khemka, 2000). Problem-solving instruction can be woven into daily routines. The textbox provides examples of aspects of problem solving for Oscar and Jasmine.
2. **Encourage peers and other adults to provide positive support for self-reliance and independent problem solving.** Peers and others must strike a balance between providing help and allowing the person to solve

EXAMPLES OF GOALS FOR INDEPENDENT PROBLEM SOLVING

Oscar will:

1. Try things on his own first several times before asking for help from peers or others.
2. Tell himself when he is feeling discouraged that he is smart and can do things.

Jasmine will:

1. Identify her own preferences in activities and items.
2. Learn to say "no" to family and friends when her preferences are different.

problems on his or her own (Perske, 1972). Whenever possible, allow students with disabilities to take the same risks as their peers.

Increase Self-Determination Skills

A final characteristic related to repeated failure is the strong desire to please others, particularly those in authority (Shaw & Budd, 1982). This bias toward providing a "socially desirable" response is so strong that many students with cognitive disabilities will tell the questioner whatever they think the person wants to hear. When students with a cognitive disability are asked a yes/no question, they more likely to acquiesce— answer "yes"—regardless of the appropriateness of that response (Sigelman, Budd, Spanel, & Schoenrock, 1981). Acquiescence increases as the linguistic difficulty of the question increases. This tendency makes it difficult to determine students' preferences and feelings. It may yield incorrect information regarding students' understanding because they may not understand even though they indicate they do. In addition, it hinders independent thinking and

Example of a Bingo Game for Practicing Information Words for Middle School Students

Each bingo card should be created on a square piece of paper that is divided by lines into 16 equal squares. Write a different word from one of the word lists below in each of the squares. The set of call cards should contain all the words or phrases for each of the levels to give all students an equal chance of winning the game. (Be careful not to create two cards with the same set of words.)

For some students, the bingo card contains pictures like these:

For students with first- to second-grade skills, the bingo card contains words from the following list:

1. go	11. fire	21. off
2. stop	12. police	22. push
3. in	13. poison	23. pull
4. out	14. danger	24. office
5. up	15. keep out	25. hot
6. down	16. open	26. cold
7. Men	17. closed	27. for sale
8. Women	18. enter	28. mix
9. wait	19. exit	29. don't walk
10. walk	20. on	30. sell by

For students with fifth- to sixth-grade skills, the bingo card contains words from the following list:

1. caution	11. ring for service	21. please pay when served
2. information	12. grocery	22. waiting room
3. emergency exit	13. restrooms	23. keep off grass
4. private	14. do not handle	24. no fishing
5. hospital	15. open other end	25. do not disturb
6. cashier	16. watch your step	26. thin ice
7. elevator	17. ladies	27. store in dry place
8. handle with care	18. park closes at dark	28. chill
9. ticket office	19. wet paint	29. fire alarm
10. entrance	20. wrong way	30. order here

For students with seventh- to eighth-grade skills, the bingo card contains words from the following list:

1. artificially sweetened
2. contains no cholesterol
3. wash in lukewarm water
4. flame retardant
5. non-chlorine bleach
6. concentrated
7. pasteurized
8. explosives
9. physician
10. construction entrance

11. prohibited
12. enriched
13. escalator
14. no preservatives
15. veterinarian
16. fragile
17. no hitchhiking
18. pharmacy
19. receptionist
20. high voltage

21. nonprescription medication
22. no loitering
23. fire extinguisher
24. discontinue if symptoms persist
25. alcohol prohibited
26. imitation flavoring
27. baste often
28. child-resistant
29. trespassers will be prosecuted
30. avoid prolonged or excessive exposure

NOTE: You can modify the game for students who require more support by repeating several words on the same card for a student who is learning only a few words or pairing a student who needs additional cues with a peer buddy.

Also, you can expand this activity by asking students to give definitions or use the words correctly in sentences either verbally during the game or later as written seat work.

Adapted from: Hamill, L. B., & Dunlevy, A. (1994). *Playing to learn: Classroom games for content area, social, and living skills.* Portland, ME: J. Weston Walsh.

JASMINE GETS INVOLVED WITH THE WRONG PEER GROUP

Jasmine is very eager to make friends. A group of students in her neighborhood invited her to go out late one night. They went to a house down the street where all the lights were out and asked her to climb in the window and take the stereo. They told her that the people were friends and had given permission to borrow the stereo. When she hesitated, they called her "chicken," and said they would not be her friend if she did not go in. When Jasmine climbed in the window, she knocked down a lamp and was discovered by the people. The friends ran away, and Jasmine was arrested and charged with breaking and entering.

fosters dependence on others. Students who are anxious to please others may be more vulnerable to peer pressure and display decreased decision-making skills (Khemka, 2000). In the extreme, these characteristics can lead persons with cognitive disabilities to become victimized by others (Khemka, 2000; Luckasson, 1992) and to be led into criminal activities (Everington & Fulero, 1999; Everington & Luckasson, 1989).

There are several avenues for addressing this problem. One way is to teach students skills in self-determination (Wehmeyer, 1996) and self-advocacy (Miller & Keys, 1996). Although these approaches are presented in greater detail in Chapter 15, here are a few general guidelines:

1. **Be mindful that control should reside with the student.** Whenever possible, students should be involved in all decisions that have a direct impact on them. For example, Marie can decide what goals are most important to emphasize on her IEP.

2. **Provide students with opportunities to make choices and to identify and voice their preferences.** Presenting options can begin in early childhood and can increase in complexity as the student gains experience in expressing preferences. For example, Matt's teacher presents choices to Matt in the form of pictures or actual objects several times a day. At lunch, she holds up two types of drinks and asks him to pick the one he wants. For activity time, she shows him three pictures of the available activities for the day (computer, drawing, reading) and asks him to point to the one he wants.

3. **Foster reciprocal friendships.** Too often, relationships with peers are not reciprocal. That is, the peer functions as a teacher rather than as a friend. Encourage and reinforce peer relationships involving reciprocity. Encouraging typical peers to value positive attributes of the individual with disabilities is a start. For example, the sunny disposition of

the person with Down syndrome and the joy that person can bring to any relationship should not be discounted (Robinson, 2000). Teaching others to value personal attributes is important.

4. **Use appropriate questioning techniques.** In the instructional setting, be mindful of the questioning techniques you use to determine the student's level of understanding. When comprehension is critical, choose open-ended questions over questions requiring yes/no responses (Everington & Fulero, 1999). When possible, ask students to give explanations in their own words. For example, instead of asking the student if she understands the rules for the lunchroom, ask her to tell you the rules for the lunchroom. Asking students to answer questions in their own words increases expressive language and conversational skills as well.

Encourage and reinforce peer relationships involving reciprocity.

Provide Support for Psychological and Emotional Issues

Thus far, we have been discussing the influence of the learning environment on student pro-gress. As we know, many influences on student learning are independent of the control of the teacher (Wolery, Ault, & Doyle, 1992). These aspects include psychological and biological states that may influence any student's availability to learn and to perform in the classroom. Student learning is also subject to influences from environments outside of the school setting such as the home environment or peer groups. In Chapter 8, we discuss in depth how you can use this information for behavioral intervention. In this section, we provide an overview of general issues regarding student mental health that may affect the classroom environment and learning situation.

Many persons with cognitive disabilities have what is termed *dual diagnosis,* the presence of identified psychopathology (mental illness) and mental retardation. Individuals with mental retardation and cognitive disabilities have a higher prevalence of mental illness than the general population (Galligan, 1990; Menolascino, Wilson, Golden, & Ruedrich, 1986; Myers, 1987; Reiss, 1982; Rutter, Tizard, & Whitmore, 1970). Depending on the types of psychiatric problems being considered, estimates of the prevalence of mental illness in persons with mental retardation range from 30% to 60%. Types of disorders that have been diagnosed in persons with mental retardation are bipolar disorders (mania and depression); schizophrenia; major depression; obsessive-compulsive disorders; delirium and dementia; attention deficit hyperactivity disorder; anxiety disorders; and substance abuse (Beirne-Smith, Ittenbach, & Patton, 1998).

There may be a number of reasons for this higher prevalence. Richardson, Koller, and Katz (1985) found that instability in environment (family discord, abuse, neglect, and changes in caretakers) is related to emotional disturbance in both children with cognitive disabilities and typical children. However, they found that children with cognitive disabilities were significantly more likely to have unstable home environments. This finding and the fact that persons with cognitive disabilities have difficulty in problem solving and in coping with stress in their environment makes mental health an important issue for educators and service providers. This highlights the critical need for creating environments that are nurturing and positive.

Research indicates that persons with cognitive disabilities are more prone to psychiatric problems, but frequently these problems go unnoticed or are attributed to other causes. For example, Reiss, Levitan, and Szyszko (1982) indicate that (1) the same emotional problem appears less important when it occurs in the person with mental retardation as opposed to the intellectually average person, and (2) there is a tendency for emotional problems to be viewed as a consequence of the mental retardation, even when they are not.

Strategies for Promoting Mental Health:

1. **Work closely with mental health professionals such as school counselors, psychologists, and psychiatrists.** Be sensitive to mental health issues and refrain from assuming that all behavioral problems are due to classroom events such as desiring attention from you. This is not to dismiss the critical importance of the behavioral interventions you will learn more about in Chapter 8. However, when a student does have a behavioral issue that is long standing and difficult to address with conventional behavioral interventions, you will need to seek a referral for a psychiatric or psychological evaluation. In addition, it may be important you to be an advocate in attaining psychological or counseling services.

2. **Provide positive support for emotional issues and provide instruction in methods for coping with emotional problems.** Also make sure the student has a positive support network of friends and others across settings who can provide assistance.

3. **Be aware of the issues students may be facing outside of the school domain, and, when appropriate, work with the student to find strategies for coping and adjusting.** This highlights the critical importance of partnering with parents and caregivers. In Chapter 7, you will learn more about strategies for collaboration and teaming with other professionals and parents. You must create an environment in which there is trust and ongoing communication with your students. Your role can be critical in this regard because you may be the only person your student can confide in.

◆ MEDICAL AND PHYSICAL CHARACTERISTICS

The prevalence of medical and physical involvements is higher for persons with moderate to severe disabilities than for the general population. These involvements include but are not limited to epilepsy, cerebral palsy and other orthopedic impairments, and health impairments. Teachers, peers, and caregivers must have at least a rudimentary understanding of the student's physical or medical condition and strategies for support. Some of the more common sensory and motor involvements are highlighted in this section, but you may need to seek additional information on conditions relevant to the particular students you teach. Parents may be a source of information. Others include therapists and medical professionals.

Cerebral Palsy

Students with moderate to severe disabilities may have many types of movement difficulties, but by far the most common cause is a central nervous system disorder known as *cerebral palsy* (Bigge, 1990). Persons with cerebral palsy compose a very heterogeneous group. Persons with cerebral palsy have problems in movement and posture and often display additional impairments. However, the degree of impairment can vary greatly among individuals. Approximately 50% to 60% of individuals with cerebral palsy have mental retardation (Beirne-Smith, Ittenbach, & Patton, 1998). They also may have visual and hearing disorders, speech and language difficulties, and seizures (Pellegrino, 1997). In Chapter 3, you will learn specific strategies for addressing students' alternative and augmentative communication needs.

Individuals with cerebral palsy develop abnormal posture and movement patterns that cannot only result in inefficient movement but can also cause increased and sometimes permanent deformities. Joints and muscles can become stiff and range of movement can become permanently restricted (Bobath, 1963; Dunn, 1991). The focus of treatment is to not only stop the progression of abnormal patterns, but, more important, to teach the student more normal movement patterns. The person providing support identifies posture and movement problems and implements procedures for normalizing the student's muscle tone and establishing proper alignment. This instruction should occur in the context of the student's daily routine of dressing, ambulation, feeding, and other activities.

Cerebral palsy causes abnormal muscle tone, which in turn affects movement and postural control. There are three primary types of abnormalities in muscle tone: high tone (spasticity/hypertonicity), low tone (hypotonia), and fluctuating tone (mixed tones in different areas of the body). To address abnormalities in tone, you must have some understanding of strategies for normalizing muscle tone. For example, take care to use positioning and handling techniques that decrease or relax the muscle tone for the student with high tone (hypertonicity) (Inge, 1996; Rainforth & York, 1991). If this is not done, muscle tone and involuntary movements will increase (Finnie, 1975). In addition to using positioning and handling techniques, strategies such as slow rocking or rolling can be effective in decreasing muscle tone (Everington, 1982). On the other hand, a student with insufficient tone (hypotonicity) may not have sufficient postural control for independent head or trunk control and may need equipment for support and prescribed therapeutic activities to increase muscle tone. Because many students may exhibit mixed tonality—high tone in some areas of the body and low in others—the physical or occupational therapist will be your best resource in suggesting specific activities.

Six Strategies for Addressing Cerebral Palsy:

1. **Use a team approach.** Because of the complex needs of students with moderate to severe disabilities, work with occupational and physical therapists to learn proper handling and positioning strategies for each of the children with cerebral palsy in your class. In addition to working with occupational and physical therapists, work closely with language pathologists and assistive technology personnel (Leppert & Capute, 1996). Although there are general approaches to treatment of this condition, each child will need individualized adaptations. Further, because consistency is critical, all team members, including peers who spend time with the student, should make every effort to implement these strategies.

2. **Maintain postural alignment.** Establishing and maintaining good postural alignment assists in normalizing muscle tone. Work with the therapist to provide supports for seating and for wheelchairs so maximum alignment can be maintained (Inge, 1996). When the student is in a seated position, the pelvis should be at 90 degrees, head and trunk should be in alignment, and the feet flat on the floor or on a supportive surface (Finnie, 1975) (refer to Figure 2–2). Note that not all persons with cerebral palsy use wheelchairs. Regardless, most will need some form of seating support to maintain alignment.

3. **Use adaptive equipment.** Positioning devices such as sidelyers, prone wedges, and standers are helpful for providing alignment

FIGURE 2–2   Proper Positioning

(Pellegrino, 1997) and encouraging appropriate movements. Figure 2–3 displays the use of each of these types of equipment. Combine the time a student spends in the classroom in therapeutic equipment with other activities. For example, the student can participate in independent reading or in a cooperative group activity while he or she is positioned on a sidelyer or a wedge.

Positions should be changed regularly throughout the day. Take students who are in wheelchairs out several times a day and place them on mats with pillows or specific equipment provided for support. This prevents skin breakdown and the development of bedsores as well as easing the strain on particular muscle groups. Refer to Figures 2–4 and 2–5.

Use equipment that maximizes social integration opportunities with typical peers in

FIGURE 2–3   **Examples of Adaptive Equipment**

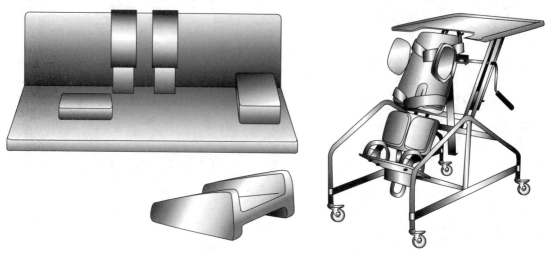

the classroom (Campbell, 2000). When positioning a student in equipment, take care to ensure the student is on the same eye level as his or her peers.

4. **Teach new movement patterns.** To the extent possible, encourage maximum participation (Campbell, 2000). Expectations are

often lowered for persons with physical disabilities, and tasks they could participate in are completed for them by caregivers. Independence is important not only for self-determination but also for skill acquisition and development of motor competence. The occupational and physical therapist can as-

 FIGURE 2–4   **Example of Positioning Enhancing Peer Integration**

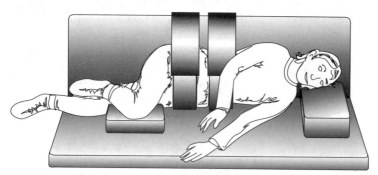

Marie is placed in a sidelyer in her language arts class during independent reading time. Placing a stand equipped with a page turner in front of her would enable her to read independently.

FIGURE 2–5   Combining Instructional Goals and Positioning Needs

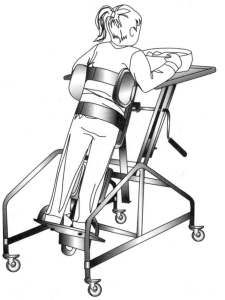

Marie has a job of washing equipment in science class. She is in a prone stander to do this.

sist you in determining ways to increase participation in all routines. For example, the student may not be able to dress independently but can assist in this process by extending arms into shirtsleeves.

5. **Use proper positioning and adaptive equipment for feeding.** Because many students have difficulty in jaw and lip control and other movements necessary for eating and drinking, work closely with therapists in positioning the student and using proper adaptive equipment (Campbell, 2000). As in other activities, it is essential to achieve proper alignment through positioning during all feeding. Many types of adaptive equipment such as modified eating utensils and cups enable greater independence. Work closely with a therapist in learning approaches to assist the student in accomplishing feeding skills such as swallowing, lip closure, and chewing. Most students with disabilities can achieve independence on many feeding skills and should be given maximum opportunities to do so.

6. **Address abnormal reflexes.** In addition to difficulties in movement, students with cerebral palsy often display primitive, infant reflexes (Pellegrino, 1997). These *reflexes,* such as the *startle reflex* or the *asymmetrical tonic neck reflex* (ATNR), are present in typically developing infants but normally integrate (disappear) by the age of 12 months (Pellegrino, 1997). The startle reflex is often observed in newborn infants and consists of total body movement to a change in stimulus. The ATNR is sometimes called the fencer's pose. This reflex is elicited by turning the individual's head to one side. When the head is turned, the arm extends involuntarily on the chin side and the arm on the opposite side flexes. This reflex is disruptive because it prevents voluntary arm movements when the head is turned to the side.

You need to have some understanding of these reflexes because they can interfere with many movement patterns and prevent the acquisition of higher order skills such as locomotion (Everington, 1982). These reflexes can be stimulated or inhibited depending on the position or handling procedure used. When primitive reflexes are present, use positions or handling procedures that inhibit the reflex.

For example, Marie exhibits an ATNR reflex every time her head turns to the left. That is, when her head turns, her left arm extends and her right arm flexes. To prevent this, her teacher can present material at midline. In addition, placing Marie on a prone wedge with arms extended will enable her to move her head without eliciting the reflex and can facilitate the development of new patterns (Everington, 1982). The sidelyer shown in Figure 2–4 with Marie is another piece of equipment that assists in inhibiting this reflex because it enables her to work at midline (Heller, Forney, Alberto, Schwartzman, & Goeckel, 2000).

As with positioning, adaptive equipment enables the student to accomplish motor movements without the interference of the primitive reflexes. Just as you must work closely with the therapist to address abnormalities in movement and muscle tone, the therapist must collaborate with you to provide appropriate strategies for inhibiting abnormal reflexes.

Visual Impairments

Persons with moderate to severe disabilities frequently display difficulties with vision and hearing. Vision impairments can range from problems in acuity (the individual needs glasses or contact lenses) to legal blindness. Legal blindness typically is defined as either (a) 20/200 in the better eye with correction or (b) a severely constricted visual field of less than 20 degrees in the better eye (Levin, 1996). You should have access to visual assessment information. If a severe impairment is present, consult with the certified vision teacher, orientation and mobility specialist, and the optometrist concerning functional use of residual vision and appropriate visual aids and supports. The certified vision teacher can provide direct service (i.e., Braille instruction, computer instruction, and practice in the use of magnification). He or she can act as a resource in gaining free materials for instruction and assisting in adapting materials for classroom instruction. The orientation and mobility specialist is an important resource for teaching travel skills. Peers can also assist in teaching individuals to orient themselves in their environment. The low vision specialist can assist in preplanning for community trips and devising strategies for new environments.

The optometrist can provide information on the functional use of vision and aids as well. Remember that many persons who are classified as

legally blind have some residual vision. Levin (1996) suggests if the corrected vision (with glasses) is worse than 20/60 or 20/80, visual aids will be necessary. Resources for students with visual impairments are available through the American Printing House for the Blind and other organizations.

Three Strategies for Addressing Visual Impairments:

1. **Use visual aids.** Many visual aids are available that enable visually impaired students to function well in the classroom. Appropriate visual accommodations need not be costly or involve sophisticated apparatus. In some cases, you only need to modify the task (enlarged print or highlighting) (Sobsey & Wolf-Schein, 1991). Multisensory approaches such as tactile illustrations or raised-line drawings are helpful (Salend, 2001). More significant visual impairments will require the student to have adaptive equipment such as magnifiers or Braille materials.

2. **Make environmental accommodations.** Whenever possible, make environmental arrangements such as seating in the front of the room and providing additional lighting (Sobsey & Wolf-Schein, 1991). It is also helpful for you and the class members to assist students in orienting themselves using oral directions (Salend, 2001). For example, a peer might assist the student in getting to the workstation by using cues involving a clock face: "Joan, the workstation is located to your right at 3 o'clock."

3. **Teach students to use their residual vision.** For some students, this strategy may involve learning to track an object such as a bell in music class or to focus briefly on an object such as a spoon or glass during mealtimes. Peers can provide good support for reinforcing these type of activities.

Hearing Impairments

Hearing loss can vary from a mild loss to persons who are classified as "hard of hearing" or "deaf." A person is usually classified as deaf when he or she has a hearing loss in the profound range (greater than 90 dB). Persons who are deaf are unable to understand conversational speech without the use of some form of amplification (hearing aid). Persons with less severe losses than that are classified as hard of hearing or hearing impaired (Steinburg & Knightly, 1997).

Hearing loss in children is more common than many people realize. Approximately 10% to 15% of school-aged children fail hearing tests yearly (Steinburg & Knightly, 1997). The cause for many of these problems may be inner ear infections. It is critical for you to have copies of current audiological evaluations and, if there is any hearing loss, to work very closely with the audiologist in designing environmental modifications to maximize hearing and in selecting assistive devices. You need an understanding of the type of hearing loss your student has and the implications of the loss for daily activities. The audiologist can give you information on the degree of loss and sounds that the student may still be able to hear.

Many students with hearing losses may have hearing aids or utilize a *frequency modulated radio amplifying system* (FM) system. The FM system consists of a radio/receiver worn by the student and a microphone and transmitter worn by the speaker, who may be the teacher or a peer (Wehman, 1997) (see Figure 2–6). An FM system can be useful for students who cannot tolerate wearing a *hearing aid*. Note that some students with moderate to severe disabilities may not adapt readily to wearing an aid or using an FM system and may have to be taught to tolerate their aid (Smith, D.D., 2001).

Unfortunately, aids do not completely correct for some types of loss, such as sensorineural impairment. In this type of loss, the problem is in the inner ear and involves transmission of impulses along the auditory nerve. With this type of loss, the student may have a decreased ability to hear certain frequencies of sound. For the sensorineural loss, the aid may make speech louder, but not clearer (Papaioannou, 1996). These problems can be even greater if the speaker is further away or if the student is in a noisy environment such as a classroom. Therefore, the student with this type of loss may continue to experience problems in hearing and may express irritation and discomfort with the aid.

 FIGURE 2–6   **An FM System**

On the other hand, a conductive loss involves a problem in the outer or middle ear which involves perception of sound loudness. For this student, an aid may provide the needed support. However, if this type of loss appears in childhood, frequently it is due to a medical problem such as an infection and can be corrected. Therefore, most of the permanent hearing losses you encounter as a teacher will be sensorineural.

Five Strategies for Addressing Hearing Impairments:

1. **Understand basic care and maintenance of hearing aids.** You not only need to have some understanding of the capabilities of the given device, but you also must be versed in issues of care and maintenance. Some students with moderate to severe disabilities may not wear their aids because they are not functioning properly or because the batteries may be too low. Many of these students do not have the communication skills to inform you about the exact problem; so you should have some information on the device and be aware of changes in the students' behavior that would indicate an equipment problem.

2. **When appropriate, work with students to increase residual hearing.** Just as you would with a student who is classified as blind, you need to work with students who are deaf or hard of hearing on auditory localization or auditory awareness in the context of the school or community environment (Sobsey & Wolf-Schein, 1991). An example of teaching an auditory awareness skill in context would involve teaching the student to respond to the bell between classes. An example of auditory localization would be to teach the student to turn when his or her name is spoken.

3. **Make sure you have the student's attention when delivering instructions.** Because a good deal of classroom instruction is delivered through auditory modalities, be sure you have the student's attention. When giving instructions, face the student, make eye contact, and support verbal instruction with

visual and gestural cues (Papaioannou, 1996). Many students with moderate to severe disabilities will not learn to lip read, but they can be taught to respond to gestural and nonverbal cues given by others when they are speaking. Classroom peers can be encouraged to assist with these cues.

4. **Make environmental accommodations.** Make sure to seat the student in the front of the room or near where you deliver instruction. Try to reduce background noise by installing carpeting, partitions, and/or drapery.

5. **Use interpreters when appropriate.** Educational interpreters can enhance the student's participation in the classroom environment as well as improve academic performance (Salend, 2001). Having an interpreter in the classroom takes some adjustment because you must be sensitive to the time delay in transmitting of information. You and the students should talk to the student and not to the interpreter (Salend, 2001).

Health Impairments and Medication

Many students with more severe disabilities have epilepsy as well as problems with bowel and bladder control, respiration, and feeding. For a student who has one or more of these or other medical or health-related problems, you must work closely with health professionals, such as the school nurse and the student's physician, to provide appropriate supports. In addition, many students will be taking medication for medical, behavioral, and/or emotional problems. In most states, the school nurse administers medication as well as the specific health care procedures discussed in this section (Sobsey & Cox, 1991). However, this is not always the case. Therefore, be aware of the guidelines and procedures for your district.

Seizures. Many of the students you will work with will have a seizure disorder. A seizure can be defined as a "temporary change in behavior resulting from sudden, abnormal bursts of electrical activity in the brain" (Sternberg, 1994, p.

252). There are two types of seizures—partial and generalized. Partial seizures can be classified as either simple or complex. *Simple partial seizures* do not result in a loss of consciousness and consist of involuntary movements of the face or an extremity (Sternberg, 1994). A *complex partial seizure* is brief, but can result in a period of altered consciousness. For example, the person may stare blankly for a period of seconds. This kind of seizure can result in repetitive motor movements that are involuntary. Examples include lip smacking, rubbing objects, or pulling clothing or buttons (Haslam, 1996). As you can surmise, this type of seizure can be hard to diagnose without testing brain functioning. If you have a student you believe has this type of seizure disorder, refer him or her to a physician for administration of an electroencephalogram (EEG) and other tests of brain functioning.

The second type of seizure is the *generalized seizure,* sometimes known as grand mal or tonic-clonic. This is the type of seizure you may be more familiar with. A generalized seizure affects the entire body and results in loss of consciousness. Typically, the individual displays stiffening or jerking of limbs. Involuntary urination may occur. The face or lips may turn a bluish color (cyanosis). After the seizure, some individuals sleep and many experience disorientation. Because this type of seizure involves the total body and a rapid loss of consciousness, some students may injure themselves when they fall. Before a seizure occurs, some individuals experience an aura that may assist them in anticipating the occurrence. The aura may consist of a smell, taste, or visual distortion that appears immediately before the seizure. Because of the likelihood of having students with seizure disorders in your classroom, you will need strategies for monitoring and handling seizures.

Six Strategies for Addressing Seizures in the Classroom:

1. **Ensure student comfort and safety.** Do not insert anything into the student's mouth. Try to move him or her gently to the floor. If possible, arrange the student so he or she is lying on his or her side.

2. **Time the seizure and record behavior.** Supply an accurate and complete record of each seizure to parents and/or medical professionals. Most schools have a form for recording and reporting seizure activity. If not, you will need to develop one. Time the seizure and report as many behavioral changes as you can, including behaviors occurring before and after the seizure. Also record other observations such as changes in skin coloration or any injuries. In some cases, your student may have several seizures in one day. Record all instances.

3. **Notify others of the seizure.** For seizure management and control, medical professionals need as much information as possible. Knowing the duration and frequency of seizures is important in regulating of seizure medication.

4. **Seek emergency assistance when appropriate.** Discuss with your nurse or physician when it is appropriate to seek emergency assistance. This will vary with the student. For example, it is common to call for emergency assistance if the student's seizure lasts for more than 2 minutes.

5. **Make the student as comfortable as possible.** After the seizure, the student may need to sleep for a few hours, so arrange a comfortable place. The student may also need a change of clothing. It is always prudent to ask parents for extra clothes when you have students who are likely to have generalized seizures in the classroom.

6. **Educate peers and classmates on the disorder.** Students should understand the nature of seizure disorders and ways they can provide support.

Seizure Management. Medications (anticonvulsants) are the most common strategy for managing seizure activity. Table 2–1 lists some of the more common medications and their uses and side effects. Three commonly prescribed drugs for seizures are phenobarbital, Dilantin,

TABLE 2–1 Medication Summary

Category	Indication of Use	Trade Name	Side Effects
Anticonvulsant	Manages seizure activity.	Phenobarbital Dilantin Tegretol Depakene Zarontin	Hyperactivity, irritability, sedation, drowsiness. Dilantin can cause enlarged gums and anemia.
Antipsychotic	Treats psychosis in adults. Reduces aggression and hyperactivity in children.	Thorazine Mellaril Haldol	Excessive sedation, Parkinson-like movements (tremors) or restlessness.
Stimulant	Increases attention and decreases hyperactivity.	Ritalin Dexedrine Cylert	Decreased appetite, insomnia, anxiety, headaches, stomachaches.
Antidepressant	Balances depression and mood disorders. Reduces obsessions.	Tofranil Elavil Prozac Zoloft Paxil Desyrel	Dry mouth, tremors, dizziness, nausea, fatigue, constipation.
Antianxiety	Decreases anxiety.	Xanax Valium Ativan Buspar	Drowsiness, fatigue, mental slowness, possible dependence with all but Buspar.

Sources: Haslam, (1996); Heller et al. (2000); Sternberg, (1994); Tsai, (1998).

and Tegretol. Because it is necessary for some students to be on rather high dosages to control their seizures, you should understand the side effects and communicate any behavioral changes to caregivers and health care professionals. For many students, medication successfully controls their seizures with minimal side effects. For others, the physician will need to find the right balance of medication that manages seizures with minimal side effects. For example, a high medication dosage may result in undesirable side effects of drowsiness, inattention, and irritability. A lower dosage may result

in more seizures. The physician may need to work with you and others to find the therapeutic dosage.

For a few students, medication may be unsuccessful in managing their seizures. For some individuals, surgery has been a successful alternative for seizure management (Haslam, 1996).

Some students may need to wear protective headgear such as helmets. In such a case, it is important to balance safety with the need for social integration. Helmets are stigmatizing and should only be used when necessary. When they are used, make attempts to minimize stigmatization. For example, there are hats that can be worn over the helmet (Heller et al., 2000). Further, the student should have input into any decision regarding headgear.

Health Issues. As we noted with sensory impairments, students with moderate to severe disabilities are at greater risk for health impairments. Some students may have ongoing health care needs that affect their educational programming and require attention during the schoolday (Sobsey & Cox, 1991). Some of these conditions require special procedures that involve the assistance of a school nurse. Two special procedures that are of lower frequency than seizures are *clean intermittent catheterization* (CIC) and *tube feeding.*

CIC is a procedure for individuals who are unable to empty their bladders. A hollow tube is inserted into a cavity several times a day to provide drainage (Sobsey & Cox, 1991). Frequently, CIC is used with students who have spina bifida. If you are administering this procedure, you must receive training from a school nurse or other medical professional.

Another health care procedure that is becoming increasingly more common in classrooms is nasogastric tube feeding, used with persons who are unable to take adequate amounts of food and liquids orally. Cerebral palsy is one condition that can require tube feeding. A feeding tube is placed by medical professionals through the nose, the mouth, or directly into the stomach (gastrostomy tube). The gastrostomy tube is used for more permanent conditions, so it is encountered more frequently in the classroom. For a gastrostomy, the student may have a device called a button implanted in the abdomen. When feeding occurs, the tube is inserted into the button and liquified food is poured into a receptacle attached to the tube. As with CIC, it is critical that you receive training on this procedure.

Medication. Many students with moderate to severe disabilities take prescription medications.

Even if your students do not receive their medication at school, you should have a basic understanding of the purpose and side effects of all their medications. In this section, we review common classes of medications used for medical, behavioral, and/or emotional problems. However, be aware that your students' medications are likely to change frequently, underscoring the importance of communicating with health care professionals and caregivers on a regular basis.

Some of the more common groups of medications students with moderate to severe disabilities take are anticonvulsants, antipsychotics, antianxiety agents, antidepressants, and stimulants. As we discussed in the previous section, anticonvulsants are medications used to manage seizure activity. The remaining four groups of drugs are frequently used for students who have behavioral and/or emotional problems (Harper & Wadsworth, 1993; Howell, Evans, & Gardiner, 1997; Sturmey, 1995). Three of these drugs— antipsychotics, antianxiety agents, and antidepressants—are often used with persons who have dual diagnosis (Harper & Wadsworth, 1993). These drugs may be overused with persons with mental retardation (Sturmey, 1995). Further, it is strongly recommended that none of these drugs be used without behavioral intervention and/or therapy. Pharmacological intervention can be effective in making some students more available for learning. However, they still need to learn new behavioral patterns.

SUMMARY

In this chapter, you learned that students with moderate to severe disabilities have complex needs, requiring you to work closely with many other professionals in designing programs. In the areas of cognition and learning, students with moderate to severe disabilities have problems with attention, memory, and generalization. These problems require teaching adaptations in most learning situations.

The cognitive and learning problems many students with moderate to severe disabilities experience can result in high expectancy for failure, dependence on others, and acquiescence. Teachers and peers need to provide positive learning environments to address these issues.

Persons with moderate to severe disabilities have a higher incidence of mental illness. You must be aware of this and work closely with mental health professionals if you have a student with emotional/behavioral problems.

Many persons with moderate to severe disabilities may have medical and physical issues. Teachers who work with persons with cerebral palsy must work closely with physical and/or occupational therapists in providing appropriate positioning and handling procedures. Students with moderate to severe disabilities also may have impairments in vision or hearing. In such cases, you need to work with the audiologist and/or low vision specialist to implement appropriate accommodations. Finally, some students with moderate to severe disabilities have health impairments and take medication. For these students, you must work closely with the school nurse and/or other health care professionals.

 ## CHAPTER EXTENDERS

Key Terms and Concepts

1. *Acquiescence* refers to responding in whatever way pleases the other person regardless of the appropriateness of the response.
2. *Asymmetrical tonic neck reflex* consists of involuntary flexing of the arm on the opposite side when the head is turned to one side.
3. *Dual-diagnosis* is the term used in reference to individuals identified with both mental retardation and mental illness.
4. *Frequency Modulated Radio Amplifying System (FM)* is an assistive device for hearing loss that consists of a radio/receiver worn by the student and a microphone and transmitter worn by the speaker.

5. *Generalization* occurs when a response that has been taught by a teacher in one setting occurs in a different setting or with a different teacher.
6. *Hypotonia* refers to abnormally low muscle tone.
7. *Multi-leveled instruction* refers to a strategy that allows a diverse group of students to work together on the same activity but at their individual skill levels.
8. *Outerdirectedness* refers to reliance on others for direction in problem-solving.
9. *Self-determination* refers to an individual participating in decision making by having opportunities to make choices and expressing preferences.
10. *Spacicity/Hypertonicity* refers to abnormally high muscle tone.

Study Guide

1. Give two examples of generalization.
2. Explain the consequences of hypotonia and hypertonicity in persons with cerebral palsy.
3. Define legal blindness and deafness.
4. Name and describe the different types of seizures.
5. List the five types of drugs used with persons with disabilities.
6. What are CIC and gastrostomy?
7. Name two strategies for addressing students with visual impairments. Describe each one.
8. Provide two strategies for enhancing each of the following: generalization, attention, and memory.
9. Describe each of the following and its effect on learning: failure expectancy, outerdirectedness, and acquiescence.
10. Name two strategies for addressing students with hearing impairments. Describe each one.
11. Discuss the importance of muscle tone and positioning for persons with cerebral palsy.
12. What are important strategies for monitoring and handling seizures in the classroom?

13. Discuss the importance of the teacher's and peers' attitudes and expectations in working with students who have moderate to severe disabilities. What examples have you seen of negative attitudes (demeaning, belittling)? Impersonal treatment (treating the person as if he or she was an object)? Overprotection (doing everything for the person)? How do teacher/peer attitudes like these affect the student?

14. Examine your own attitude toward individuals who have moderate to severe disabilities. How did you feel the first time you interacted with a person with moderate to severe disabilities? How do you feel now? If your attitude has changed, explain why.

Class Debate

Many people believe that too many students are taking medication to address behavioral and emotional problems. Debate the pros and cons of medications for behavioral control. Be sure you address the following medication categories: stimulants (e.g., Ritalin), antidepressant agents (e.g., Prozac), and antipsychotic medications (e.g., Haldol, Mellaril). In your discussion, make certain you consider the effectiveness of each of these three options: behavioral intervention alone, medication alone, and a combination of both.

Small Group Activities

Activity I

Shawanda has a problem with inappropriate hugging with both strangers and friends. She has two problems with discrimination: (a) She does not know the setting or appropriate time for close physical contact (she hugs when people are engaged in conversation with others), and (b) She treats strangers with the same level of intimacy as close friends (she gives everyone a hug).

1. Design a teaching program to help Shawanda discriminate appropriate times to hug others. Describe the cues that you will teach her to help her determine when to act appropriately.

2. Design a method to teach Shawanda to generalize this behavior to a setting outside of the school.

Activity II

Identify a situation when you have experienced one or more of the following: failure expectancy, outerdirectedness, and acquiescence. What were the circumstances? Did you overcome it? If so, how? If not, why? How might this be similar for persons with disabilities? Brainstorm positive teaching approaches for use with all students in your classroom for each of the following: failure expectancy, outerdirectedness, and acquiescence.

Field Experience

Spend a day observing a student with moderate to severe disabilities in a school setting. Look for the characteristics discussed in this chapter. Write down all the instructional and support strategies that you see peers and adults using with the student. What are the attitudes others in this environment convey to the student? What changes might you suggest for the people working with this student?

chapter 3

Communication and Technology Supports

Elizabeth A. Lahm and Caroline Everington

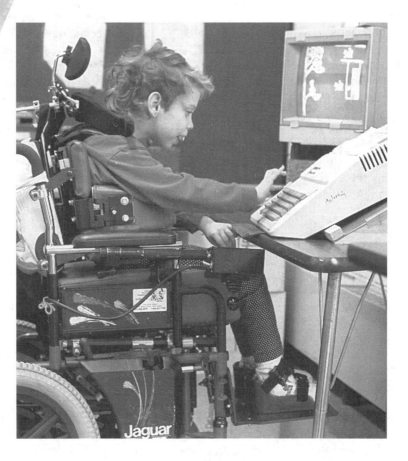

Today's available technologies offer students with moderate and severe disabilities numerous opportunities that were previously not available. The potential to assist them in performing daily living skills, communicating and socializing with peers, and completing vocational tasks are but a few of these. Many issues surround the provision of assistive technology (AT) services and devices. The two most pressing are financial considerations and training direct service providers (Smith & Jones, 1999). With legislative mandates, however, the disability field must resolve these barriers and move toward integrating AT into educational settings.

◆ WHAT YOU WILL LEARN IN THIS CHAPTER

This chapter examines recent legislation and the consequent responsibilities of schools for providing AT devices and services. AT devices are defined in the Individuals With Disabilities Education Act (IDEA) as "Any item, piece of equipment, or product whether acquired commercially off the shelf, modified, or customized that is used to increase functional capabilities of individuals with disabilities." Assistive technology services are defined in the same legislation as "Any service that directly assists an individual with a disability in the selection, acquisition, or use of an assistive technology device." First we present a model for considering AT and making informed selections. Without a good match of the technology to the student's needs, successful implementation is not possible. This model also emphasizes the need for ongoing evaluation as the student progresses in his or her skills and the educational demands change. Second, we review areas of daily performance in which AT can assist individuals with moderate and severe disabilities and provide vignettes of students successfully using AT. The third section of the chapter builds a taxonomy of AT to help understand the broad range of AT available. Finally we address strategies for

achieving the integration of AT into inclusive classrooms.

As the field strives for improved education through educational reform, it looks to "best practices" for guidelines for change. Although many argue about what is "best practice," all agree that reform is necessary to keep up with the ever-changing world. In special education, there has been a major shift toward including children with exceptional learning needs in general education classes with their peers. This shift requires that special education professionals understand the general education curriculum so appropriate links can be made for students with special needs to facilitate their success in those settings.

The general education curriculum is rapidly changing to prepare students for a dynamic, information-based world heavily impacted by technology (National Commission on Excellence in Education, 1983; Office of Technology Assessment, 1995). The field recognizes that discrete skills in a few areas of learning will not be sufficient for success in today's society. Instead, students must learn to use higher order thinking skills across curricular areas and develop strategies for locating and analyzing needed information quickly to use in decision making (SRI International, 1995). This changing focus impacts the curriculum for students with moderate and severe disabilities with greater magnitude.

In analyzing the educational settings in which students with moderate and severe disabilities find themselves, we can identify numerous barriers. For example, the general education setting requires more reading because the environment and tasks have not been modified to the extent they were in self-contained classrooms. It also requires more ability to sequence tasks because the teacher-student ratio is so much larger and the availability of a teacher to frequently prompt a student through a sequence is diminished. Inclusion in the community and work setting places many more demands on these students. It is no longer sufficient to know how to wash tables and floors in restaurants after closing. They must make judgments about what to clean, the tools to use, how to interface with customers, and where basic supplies are kept to refill the condiments table. Each of these demands requires a different type of training and/or modifications that can be easily applied to multiple settings and tasks.

AT can provide students with many more options in these changing environments. For example, the sequencing of tasks can be augmented with a memory aid that allows students to access auditory or visual prompts when they are having trouble with a task. Instead of training students to wash tables at McDonald's, they can be taught to use the memory aid, which will guide them through the steps required to wash the tables in McDonald's or in Denny's or most other places.

THE CALL FOR ASSISTIVE TECHNOLOGY SUPPORT

Recent legislation changes the responsibilities of educators to seek out such assistive devices so their students can be successful in multiple settings. The 1997 amendments to IDEA require assistive technology to be considered for every student receiving special education services. With this legislation, special educators can no longer use lack of knowledge as an excuse for not pursuing AT. Their "consideration" of AT for every student must be documented.

Unfortunately, the regulations for IDEA 1997 do not define *consideration,* so IEP teams are still without guidance on the process of considering assistive technology. In a recent survey of state directors of special education, a wide variety of approaches were identified (Bell, Blackhurst, & Lahm, 1999). Many states have changed their IEP form to include a check box or other short form of notation to show AT was considered. Very few included any record of how consideration was conducted, leaving little data to verify the process.

A simple check-off system does not assure adequate consideration and allows the IEP team to make this judgment without any expertise in assistive technology. Certainly, if the team only has cursory knowledge of AT they will not give AT full consideration. This can lead to under-identification and overidentification of AT. A child who could benefit from a light touch switch, for example, may not have one identified if the team does not know they exist. Similarly, a student who could benefit from a voice output communication aid may have a device recommended that is too sophisticated for the functioning level of that student. Thousands of dollars could be wasted and the student would still be without a means to communicate.

Human Function Model

With a focus on human performance, many researchers are describing models that help conceptualize the relationship between the technology and its user. Three examples are the Human Performance Model (Bailey, 1989), the Human Activity Assistive Technology (HAAT) Model (Cook & Hussey, 1995), and the Human Function Model (Berdine & Blackhurst, 1993). This last model is the one we describe in this chapter. The Human Function Model is a systematic way of considering assistive technology focusing on human functions instead of disabilities. It is based on a model of service delivery developed by Melichar and Blackhurst (1993).

Understanding the function or task a student is expected to do is paramount. It is only through the analysis of function and the interrelationships of the various aspects of the function that decisions can be made about technology. Figure 3–1 illustrates the elements of this model.

The model begins at the bottom with *environment and context.* The environments in which the student must perform the task are identified. Similarly, the context in which it must be performed is identified. For example, a student needs to make a choice from the lunch

F I G U R E   3 – 1   Human Function Model

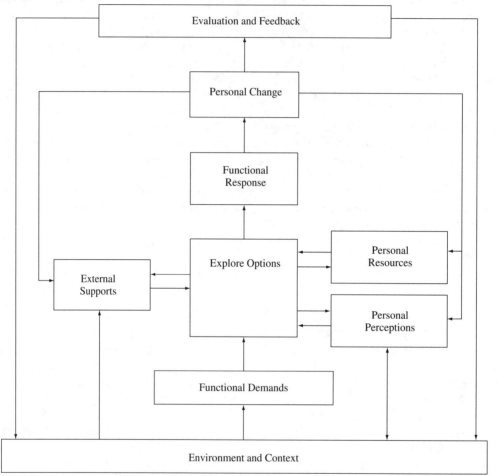

menu. The environment is the cafeteria and the context is choices presented verbally.

The environment and context place *functional demands* on the student. For this student, the demands include listening to the options, communicating a choice, and doing this in a large, noisy room with many other students present. The speed at which the choice must be made and communicated is an additional demand.

In preparing to make responses to environmental demands, you *explore options* that will

enable the student to respond to those demands. Based on what is known about the student, solutions are suggested and tried. These may include adapting the current task, environment, or context, or identifying other materials that can be used to facilitate successful task performance. In this example, some options include the following:

• Making the choice in a one-on-one situation in a quiet classroom before proceeding to the cafeteria;

- Making a picture card or note that indicates the choice, which can be handed to the cafeteria worker;
- Presenting the lunch options either in text or pictures;
- Providing a speech output device that is programmed with the options and will speak the choice to the cafeteria worker; or
- Providing a voice output communication aid that allows the student to construct his or her own response.

It may be more efficient to experiment with these options and adaptations before moving to a more formal assessment. The purpose of the assessment is to identify which part of the task presents the barrier and what abilities the student has that may be alternatively used to complete the task successfully.

As part of the exploring options stage, collect and consider information about the student. The student's *personal perceptions* play a big part in making a decision about which option to accept. For example, this student might be too self-conscious to use a device of any kind. If an assistive device is tried, it is bound to fail.

A second factor in making decisions about response strategies relates to the *personal resources* that people have available to them. Personal resources include abilities in areas such as physical functioning, cognitive ability, intelligence, motivation, speech, and other personal dimensions that can be used in producing actions. To perform the cafeteria task, it is important to know that the student can cognitively make a choice and could carry a picture or word board or carry an alternative communication device as long as it does not weigh more than 2 pounds.

A third factor is the *external supports* available. These include the many resources available to assist individuals in responding to environmental demands. For example, family members can provide both emotional and physical support. They also may be able to provide interpretations of their child's or sibling's personal perceptions when a disability interferes with his or her ability to communicate reactions and preferences. Social service agencies can provide supportive services, such as instruction about ways to cope with environmental pressures. Health insurance agencies can sometimes provide financial support for the purchase of assistive and adaptive devices. Special education and related services are another major form of external support, as are the use of technology devices and the delivery of various technology services.

Of critical concern is the absence as well as the presence of external supports. The lack of sufficient support will result in the abandonment of the AT. A family unwilling or incapable of providing support is detrimental and should impact the type of AT recommended by the IEP team. Finances, however, have the biggest impact. By law, the school district is required to provide recommended AT devices and services. However, reality tells us that only limited funds are available.

The *functional response* is the result of the assessment, experimentation, and decision making. It is the recommended devices and/or adaptations that will facilitate task performance. Ideally several options will be identified so there are other avenues to pursue if the first choice does not work as well as expected.

As a result of the functional response to the environmental demand, *personal changes* occur. Such changes may be dramatic or subtle, depending on the nature of the environmental demand, the decision making that was done, and the nature of the resources that were expended and the supports provided.

Just as personal change is expected, that the student can perform the goal task, continuing advancement of abilities in other areas is also expected. The dynamics of change beg for continuing *evaluation and feedback* so the student does not get stuck at any one stage. Achievement in one area also may lead to the selection of additional technologies or more sophisticated solutions that allow the student the opportunity for continued growth. Once students are successfully communicating their lunch choice, they will discover other areas they want to have a voice in. New solutions will be needed to promote continued achievement.

AREAS OF HUMAN FUNCTION

To assist with the identification of functions, several categories are used to help pinpoint technology applications and services (Blackhurst & Berdine, 1993; Blackhurst & Lahm, 2000; Blackhurst, Lahm, Harrison, & Chandler, 1999). Each category is defined in Figure 3–2.

Existence

Functions associated with existence are those needed to sustain life. They include such tasks as feeding, elimination, bathing, dressing, grooming, and sleeping. Special education services, particularly those for preschool children and those with severe disabilities, may focus on teaching children to perform these functions. Button hooks, weighted eating utensils, and combs with long handles are examples of devices used to assist children in performing existence functions (Blackhurst & Lahm, 2000).

Communication

The reception, internalization, and expression of information are functions included in the second category. Communication aids, speech synthesizers, telephone amplifiers, hearing aids, and the services of speech/language pathologists and audiologists might be appropriate to support communication functions (Blackhurst & Lahm, 2000).

Body Support, Protection, and Positioning

Some children need assistance to maintain a stable position required to attend and learn. King

(1999) uses a modified Baker's basic ergonomic equation to illustrate the importance of positioning and the impact of physical effort on successful use of AT (Figure 3–3). Braces, support harnesses, slings, and furniture adaptations are examples of useful devices in this functional category, as would be the services of a physical therapist and other medical personnel (Blackhurst & Lahm, 2000).

Travel and Mobility

Functions in this category include the ability to move horizontally, vertically, or laterally.

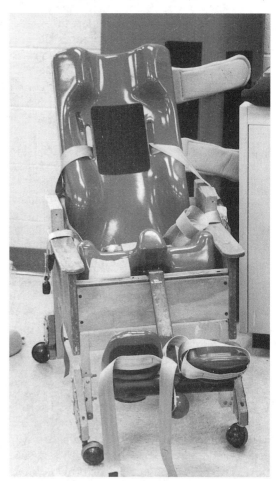

Some children need assistance to maintain a stable position required to attend and learn.

Wheelchairs, special lifts, canes, walkers, specially adapted tricycles, and crutches can be used to support these functions. Some functions, for example navigating within the school by a student who is blind, require the services of a mobility specialist (Blackhurst & Lahm, 2000).

Environmental Interaction

It is easy to overlook this category, but interactions with the environment cannot be avoided. The environment can be adapted or the person can adapt to the environment to accommodate a person with disabilities. Students with moderate and severe disabilities often have less ability to adjust their performance according to the environment; thus the only option is changing the environment. Examples can be found in activities of daily living such as food preparation or arranging classroom space to facilitate learning. Some examples include enlarged doorknobs, special switches for controlling computers, grabbers to reach items on high shelves, and chalkboards and desks that can be raised so a student in a wheelchair can use them. Often assistive technology specialists are called on to provide help with environmental adaptations (Blackhurst & Lahm, 2000).

Education and Transition

Functions associated with school activities and various types of therapies are included in this category. Special education teachers and regular class teachers, speech/language pathologists, rehabilitation counselors, psychologists, and others may be involved in providing direct services to students. In addition, numerous technologies also may be used within the context of schools. These include computer-assisted instruction, audio instructional tapes, print magnifiers, book holders, and other materials and equipment that can facilitate learning (Blackhurst & Lahm, 2000).

Sports, Fitness, and Recreation

Functions associated with group and individual sports and productive use of leisure time are included in the final category. The services of a person trained in adapted physical education may provide a valuable resource in this area. Numerous pieces of equipment and devices that can facilitate functions in this category include balls that emit audible beeps so children who are blind can hear them, specially designed bowling ramps for persons who cannot hold or roll a bowling ball, and audio prompting devices for basketball players who cannot remember the rules (Blackhurst & Lahm, 2000).

Applying the Human Function Model

To demonstrate the use of the human function model and its categories of human function, we provide several vignettes of students with moderate and severe disabilities. Meet Teresa, Jeremy, and Abdulah. For each child, one area of function is identified and illustrated. In reality, these students would most likely have more than one area they would need addressed in their educational program.

> Teresa is a 4-year-old girl with Down syndrome. Her teachers would like her to move about in play areas so she can play more independently. However, Teresa has very low muscle tone and has difficulty moving around on the floor. When playing with toys, they often roll out of her reach and she needs assistance to retrieve them.

Using the human function model to analyze the situation, the following things are noted.

| Environment and context | At school while playing on the floor. The entire classroom is carpeted. |

F I G U R E 3 – 2 UKAT II Consideration Form

ASSISTIVE TECHNOLOGY CONSIDERATION FORM

Student Name: DOB: Date:

FUNCTIONAL PROBLEMS	Problems in this area?	IEP objectives in this area?	AT currently being used	AT needed?	EXPLANATION	*
EXISTENCE Eating; grooming; dressing; elimination; hygiene	Y N	Y N		Y N U		–
COMMUNICATION Oral and written expression; visual and auditory reception; social interaction . . .	Y N	Y N		Y N U		–
BODY SUPPORT, PROTECTION AND POSITIONING Standing; sitting; alignment; stabilizing; preventing injuries . . .	Y N	Y N		Y N U		–
TRAVEL AND MOBILITY Crawling; walking; using stairs; lateral and vertical transfers; navigating	Y N	Y N		Y N U		–
ENVIRONMENTAL INTERACTION Operating equipment; accessing facilities . . .	Y N	Y N		Y N U		–
EDUCATION AND TRANSITION Assessment; learning; access to general curriculum; creative and performing arts; using instructional materials; preparing for new environments . . .	Y N	Y N		Y N U		–
SPORTS, FITNESS, AND RECREATION Individual and group play; leisure activities; sports; exercise; games; hobbies . . .	Y N	Y N		Y N U		–

ACTIONS TAKEN

– Assistive technology has been considered. Current interventions are working and no new assistive technology is needed at this time.
– Assistive technology is needed and should be implemented on a trial basis. Outcomes to be reviewed by __/__/__
– Assistive technology is needed and will be implemented as specified in the IEP.
– Insufficient information to make assistive technology recommendations; refer for additional assessment.

| Directions on the Reverse Side | Key: | Y = Yes | N = No | U = Unsure | AT = | Assistive Technology |

The University of Kentucky Assistive Technology Toolkit -- Department of Special Education and Rehabilitation Counseling, Lexington, KY 40506-0001 © 1999
Developed by A. Edward Blackhurst, Margaret E. Bausch, Jennifer K. Bell, Rebecca B. Burleson, Justin T. Cooper, Linda J. Gassaway, Nancye E. McCrary, and Joy S. Zabala
• **Permission is granted to reproduce this form for non-commercial purposes** •

ASSISTIVE TECHNOLOGY CONSIDERATION FORM

DIRECTIONS	DEFINITIONS
THE INDIVIDUALS WITH DISABILITIES EDUCATION ACT (IDEA, P. L. 105-17), requires that assistive technology be considered for every student who has an IEP. This form can be used by IEP planning teams when addressing this federal mandate. It also can be used when determining whether assistive technology is needed to ensure that students are educated in the least restrictive environment. **The IEP team should complete the reverse side of this form during a scheduled meeting to document that assistive technology has been considered. Examples provided on both sides of the form are illustrative only, and are not meant to be exhaustive.** **FUNCTIONAL PROBLEMS** Examine each area of human function to determine if any problems exist for the student. Circle **Y** (yes) or **N** (no) in the first column to indicate if problems exist. - Circle **Y** (yes) or **N** (no) in the second column to indicate if IEP objectives have been developed to address those problems. - List assistive technology devices or services currently being used by the student. - Circle **Y** (yes), **N** (no), or **U** (unsure) in the fourth column to indicate if assistive technology is needed to accomplish the IEP objectives. - Provide an explanation in the last column for decisions or recommendations made for each functional problem identified. - Place a checkmark in the appropriate box at the end of each row as each area is considered. **ACTIONS TAKEN** Analyze the information in the **"AT NEEDED"** and **"EXPLANATION"** columns. Document the actions taken by the IEP team by checking one or more of the corresponding boxes. - Check the first box if assistive technology has been considered for each problem area and no new AT is needed at this time. - Check the second box if assistive technology is needed for any problem area and a trial period should be implemented. - Check the third box if assistive technology is needed for any problem area and verify that plans for its implementation are in the IEP. - Check the fourth box if there is insufficient information to make an assistive technology recommendation and refer the student for additional assessment.	Problems in **EXISTENCE** are associated with the functions needed to sustain life. Solutions may include adapted utensils, dressing aids, adapted toilet seats, toilet training, and occupational therapy services. Problems in **COMMUNICATION** are associated with the functions needed to receive, internalize, and express information, and to interact socially. Solutions may include, hearing amplifiers, captioned video, speech aids, sign language training, magnifiers, picture boards, writing and drawing aids, pointers, alternative input and output devices for computers, augmentative communication services, social skills training and speech/language pathology services. Problems in **BODY SUPPORT, ALIGNMENT AND POSITIONING** are associated with the functions needed to stabilize, support, or protect a portion of the body. Solutions may include prone standers, furniture adaptation, support harnesses, stabilizers, slings, head gear, and physical therapy services. Problems in **TRAVEL AND MOBILITY** are associated with the functions needed to move horizontally or vertically. Solutions may include, wheelchairs, scooters, hoists, cycles, ambulators, walkers, crutches, canes and orientation and mobility training services. Problems in **ENVIRONMENTAL INTERACTION** are associated with the functions needed to perform activities across environments. Solutions may include the use of switches to control equipment, remote control devices, adapted appliances, ramps, automatic door openers, modified furniture, driving aids and rehabilitation engineering services. Problems in **EDUCATION AND TRANSITION** are associated with the functions needed to participate in learning activities and to prepare for new school settings or post-school environments. Solutions may include adapted instructional materials, educational software, computer adaptations, community-based instruction, creative arts therapy, assistive technology, and other related services. Problems in **SPORTS, FITNESS AND RECREATION** are associated with the functions needed to participate in individual or group sports, play, hobby and craft activities. Solutions may include modified rules and equipment, Special Olympics, adapted aquatics, switch-activated cameras, Braille playing cards, and adapted physical education services.

FIGURE 3–3   Baker's Basic Ergonomic Equation as modified by King (1999)

$$\frac{\text{Motivation of AT user to pursue and complete a given task (M)}}{\text{Physical effort (P) + Cognitive effort (C) +Linguistic effort (L) + Time load (T)}} = \text{Successful AT use . . . or not}$$

Source: Baker, B. (1986). Using images to generate speech. *IEEE Biomedical Conference Proceedings,* Fort Worth, Tx. Cited in King, T.W. (1999). *Assistive technology: Essential human factors.* Needham Heights, MA: Allyn & Bacon.

Functional demands	Reaching her toys when they are out of her immediate range (mobility).
Explore options	Use only toys that will not move; have someone periodically retrieve the toys for her; adapt a scooter for her to self-propel her to the toys.
Personal perceptions	Teresa cries when her toys are out of reach and she has no way to get them.
Personal resources	Teresa can sit independently because she has good upper trunk muscle tone. Her arms are strong and could be used to pull her body if there was less friction as she scooted across the floor. She has some success on floors without carpet.
External supports	Parents, physical therapist, and special education teachers are available to teach and monitor her use of an assistive device.
Functional response	Using a scooter, Teresa pulls herself to out-of-reach toys and cries very little. She is happily babbling most of the time.
Personal changes	Teresa independently explores the whole classroom and explores her house as well. She explores more toys and textures and has begun to verbalize any words.
Evaluation and feedback	Following a 6-month evaluation by the physical therapist, it is decided to try Teresa in a manual wheelchair for added independence and mobility.

Jeremy is a 10-year-old boy with cerebral palsy and severe developmental disabilities. He has moderate coordination in his arms and upper body. He is learning to feed himself with a fork and spoon. He has learned to use the fork, but cannot use a spoon for liquid or semisolid foods without spilling. His teacher is beginning to think Jeremy will need to first learn to eat with a spoon using one that is modified so as not to spill, then transfer to using a regular utensil when he has developed his eating skills more.

Environment and context	At school and home during a meal.
Functional demands	Eating liquid or semisolid foods without spilling (existence).
Explore options	Change foods, adapt a spoon, feed him until he develops the necessary skills.

Personal perceptions	Adapting a spoon is more independent and cost effective—limiting food options is unrealistic and undesirable and an attendant is costly.
Personal resources	Motivation, moderate physical coordination.
External supports	Occupational therapy, AT specialist, teacher, parents, and an older sibling.
Functional response	Use of a swivel-handle spoon that remains upright regardless of the hand and wrist position.
Personal changes	Jeremy can independently eat liquid and semisolid foods with a spoon.
Evaluation feedback	Jeremy smiles a lot while eating independently, eats more of his lunch, and has become very social during the lunch hour.

Abdulah is a 15-year-old boy with severe cognitive and physical disabilities. He is classified as a quadriplegic, with little controlled movement in either his upper or lower extremities. He currently has no reliable mode of communication; however, parents and teachers agree he is communicative, expressing likes and dislikes through body language. Due to his severe physical involvement and no communication, no one is really sure what his cognitive abilities are. Abdulah uses slight head movements to activate a pressure switch, which is connected to a toy, turning it on and off. He enjoys this most of the time but is stuck at that level. He needs a more sophisticated system for making and communicating his choices and needs. The teacher would like to have him use a four-cell communication device, at a minimum.

Environment and context	At school during classroom activities.
Functional demands	Communicating a choice; communicating relevant ideas during classroom activities.
Explore options	Have the choices presented to him serially using either the real object or a quality photograph, requesting he "tell" the teacher which item he wants. Initially, the choices should include high and low preferences so he can easily make a choice. Have the photographed choices presented on a dial scan communication system that is controlled by his switch. Use an expandable *digital communication device* that can scan four or more choices that he can select from using his switch. Implement the chosen activity for a brief period of time.
Personal perceptions	Abdulah smiles, vocalizes, and gets excited when the digital communication device is presented to him and he hears it talk.
Personal resources	Abdulah is motivated; he already knows how to use a switch and enjoys numerous activities.
External supports	Abdulah's father is a photographer. The speech therapist is willing to explore new options.
Functional response	Initially Abdulah randomly selects items from the communication device, but over time they appear to be much more deliberate.

| Personal changes | Abdulah demonstrates definite preferences and expands his repertoire of choices significantly. |
| Evaluation and feedback | Abdulah consistently uses the four-choice system and is ready to advance to eight options. |

These vignettes illustrate the importance of attending to human functions when planning and implementing technology applications in special education. Applying the human function model moves the focus to positive aspects of the child's situation. It gathers information about the resources a child has and explores many options. The IEP team is less likely to default to a "can't do" conclusion with this information in front of them. By removing the focus from the diagnostic label or disability category, teachers and related service providers are enabled to address a child's need more directly.

A Systematic Approach to Consideration

With a systematic framework available, AT can truly be considered. Figure 3–2 illustrates a form that could be used for documenting the process of consideration and decisions made. In each of the eight areas of function, the IEP team reviews abilities and identifies tasks that cannot be performed by the student. For each task identified, they must consider whether the task is achievable, what strategies have been tried, what assistive technology has been used, and if the student is making sufficient progress toward the goal without changes. If the team concludes that progress is not sufficient, then AT should be considered. At the bottom of the form, the team records its next action steps. This may include obtaining some AT devices and trying them with the student before a formal goal is included on the IEP. Specific review dates are set to ensure that the strategy will be reviewed by the team within a reasonable amount of time. In some cases, this trial stage may be bypassed and a more complete AT evaluation scheduled.

A TAXONOMY OF AVAILABLE ASSISTIVE TECHNOLOGIES

The universe of assistive technologies available to consider can be overwhelming. (To access a database of available assistive technology, go to http://www.abledata.com and http://www.closingthegap.com.) It is helpful to have a system to consider them. Think of a continuum of AT ranging from no tech to low tech to medium tech and finally to high tech (Figure 3–4). As a rule of thumb, start with "no-tech." Using the definition of assistive technology in its broadest sense, very few adaptations would not be considered AT. For example, no-tech solutions do not require devices or equipment. These might involve the use of very systematic teaching procedures, service dogs, environmental adaptations, or the services of related services personnel such as physical therapists, occupational therapists, speech/language pathologists, or AT specialists.

Moving up the continuum, consider low-tech solutions that are more sophisticated than no-tech ones but still very simple or commonly available. Many are do-it-yourself adaptations. Some low-tech options are not even considered technology by the general population. They include things such as Velcro fasteners, raised desks that accommodate a wheelchair, or adapted spoon handles.

Medium-tech solutions include the use of simple or commonly available electronic or mechanical devices such as videocassette players and wheelchairs. Up to this point on the continuum, the operation or use of the AT is simple and straightforward. No special training is needed for Velcro. Wheelchairs need some training on all of the features of the chair, especially as they become more complex, but do not need a highly skilled person to operate them after orientation.

FIGURE 3–4   **Examples on the Continuum of Assistive Technologies**

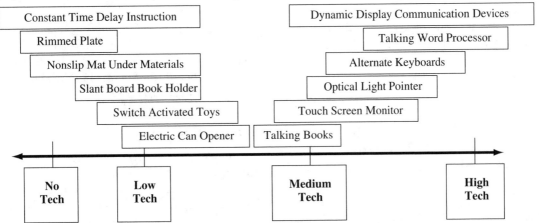

At the top of the continuum are high-tech solutions. A more sophisticated wheelchair may be considered high tech; for example, the power wheelchair that reclines or stands the user. Generally speaking, high-tech solutions involve the use of sophisticated devices, such as computers and interactive multimedia systems. Many high-tech items use computer-based technology that is somewhat invisible to the consumer. One example is the WatchMinder. It can be set to vibrate or beep at set fixed or random intervals to prompt the user to pay attention or be preset with a sequence of tasks in its reminder mode. The technology behind this watch is certainly more sophisticated than a standard watch, but the brains of the watch are not obvious to the user. High-tech devices tend to be more expensive than lower tech ones, so give ample thought to the situation before recommending the high-tech device.

Where a particular device falls on the continuum is irrelevant. The categories are not fixed. What the continuum does is give the service provider a framework to seek solutions, always starting at the bottom and working up. The lower on the continuum a device falls often correlates with the least intrusive ap-

proach or the process of providing natural supports.

Inclusion of AT in the IEP

Teachers and related service providers often find themselves in the dilemma of how to include AT in the IEP. Assistive technology can be costly, and educators feel pressure (often unspoken) to not include it in the IEP because once in the IEP, the district must provide it. It is no secret that today's school districts do not have an abundance of funds. It is often hard to choose between what will benefit a child and what is affordable. For this reason, it is critical to have someone on the IEP team with expertise in AT to help identify the most cost-effective solution for a child.

IDEA 1997 identifies three places in the IEP that AT can be included. It can be written in as a related service. This might include designating the speech therapist as the person who will work with the child on selecting appropriate vocabulary for an alternative communication device. A second place is in the modifications and accommodations section. An example here might be designating a raised desk to accommodate a wheelchair. The third place it can be included is as specially designed instruction. For example, the student may require computer-based instructional activities because he or she can work independently using a switch to interact with the instruction. It is feasible to include it in all three areas because they are interrelated.

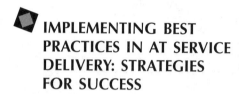

IMPLEMENTING BEST PRACTICES IN AT SERVICE DELIVERY: STRATEGIES FOR SUCCESS

Teaming

Teaming is probably the single most important element of successful use of AT in schools (Parette, 1997). Active teaming is the concurrent activities of all key people in the student's life. It is not sufficient to have multiple disciplines conduct separate assessments and submit a report to the team leader (Basham, Appleton, & Dykeman, 2000). As we discuss throughout this book, the team must collaborate and discuss the student together, sharing insights and analyzing the available information to determine a strategy for considering and implementing AT.

Each person on the interdisciplinary team holds distinct responsibilities for bringing expertise to the team. Figure 3–5 shows a form to track and systematize team participation and responsibilities. It can also serve as a framework for completing the AT service delivery process. It prompts for names of the person responsible and the time line for tasks.

Training

A second critical element of success is training. It does not matter if the AT identified is low tech or high tech. Each person expected to work with the student while the technology is being used must be trained on the use of the device. This includes parents, siblings, and peers, as well as school-based professionals. For the lower tech

items, training may only consist of a demonstration and a review of the purposes of the device. Higher tech devices that are programmable could involve several days of training. If all members of the implementation team cannot support the student in the use of the device, chances of the device failing are escalated (Batavia, Dillard, & Phillips, 1991; King, 1999; McGregor & Pachuski, 1996).

Technical Support

Training is not the only type of support required for successful implementation. Ongoing support is also critical. This includes technology maintenance, repair, upgrades, and programming. Remember, as demonstrated in the Human Function Model (Figure 3–1), the student is expected to change over time. The device must change too.

To see that the training and ongoing support are in place, one person should be assigned the responsibility of overseeing its implementation. This would logically be the AT specialist, if one is available in the district. A school-based technology coordinator could also serve in this role even if he or she does not have AT expertise. This person would serve as coordinator or overseer and possibly provide the maintenance services. In the absence of these types of support personnel, one member of the IEP team will need to assume that role.

With the emphasis on inclusion today, you must know all the tools that can help make inclusion successful for a particular student. Persons with moderate and severe cognitive disabilities are frequently the hardest to place in a general education classroom because the culture of segregated special education classrooms is so different from general education (Goessling, 1998). The misalignment of the terminology and traditions makes it difficult to blend the two. Educational goals differ greatly. For example, students with moderate and severe disabilities often have goals in the existence functional area, requiring more personal assistance,

FIGURE 3–5   Interdisciplinary Team Form

		Team Members															
In the spaces to the right, record the name of each team member. Place a check in the box for each person on the team who is responsible for each task.	Student	Parents	Special Ed.	General Ed.	General Ed.	General Ed.	Instruc. Assist.	AT Specialist.	Rehab. Eng.	S.L.P.	O.T.	P.T.	Adaptive P.E.	School Psyc.	School Nurse	Medical Spec.	Admin.	Peer
I. Functional Problem Identification																		
Referral																		
Screening																		
Assessment																		
Responsibilities																		
Team Function																		
Recommendations																		
II. Implementation																		
Acquisition																		
Training																		
Management																		
Technical Assistance																		
III. Evaluation																		
Student Outcomes																		
AT Program																		
Revisions																		

Student: _____ Date: _____

District: _____ Team Leader: _____

making their presence in the classroom high profile. A better understanding between special educators and general educators on their respective programs and collaboration to achieve mutual benefit would facilitate inclusion in the general education classroom (Goessling, 1998; Turnbull et al., 1999). Communication, social interactions, and academic levels are frequently barriers to participation. Without the support of the collaborative team, it is difficult to implement meaningful instruction in the general education classroom. Technology can be used to improve access to the general education curriculum by facilitating the skills that separate these students from the rest of the student body (Merbler, Hadadian, & Ulman, 1999; Pratt, 1999). The remainder of this chapter examines the state of practice in the areas of existence, communication, and learning, the areas most likely to be the responsibility of classroom teachers. Related service providers frequently oversee the other functional areas.

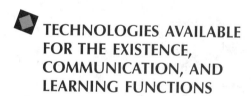

TECHNOLOGIES AVAILABLE FOR THE EXISTENCE, COMMUNICATION, AND LEARNING FUNCTIONS

Existence

Existence is a very important area for students with moderate and severe disabilities that has no parallel in the general education curriculum. For students to approach independence they need to be taught many daily living skills such as hygiene and eating. To be successful, many of these skills do not primarily rely on AT devices but rather on the technology of teaching. The various strategies for teaching are covered elsewhere in this book. AT devices that may facilitate independence in these skill areas are addressed here.

Much of the AT for existence falls in the no-tech and low-tech range on the continuum of technologies. There is considerable overlap with the environmental interaction area of function as well.

Hygiene. Barriers to independence in hygiene are often related to the ability to manipulate the hygiene tool. For example, brushing teeth can be hampered by the narrow handle of the toothbrush. Toothbrushes with built-up handles are available from several commercial sources, but adapting a standard toothbrush is a relatively simple task. In addition to the handle adaptations, straps made of Velco can be attached to keep the toothbrush in the hand if the student's grip is not sufficient to hold it in place during use. Similar adaptations can be purchased or made to hairbrushes, combs, and deodorant containers.

Bathing can be facilitated by using a washcloth mitt that goes over the hand, keeping it in place. The mitt can also include a pocket for the bar of soap. If the student's motor ability prevents reaching certain parts of the body, reachers and extenders can be purchased or made.

Adaptations to the bathroom can facilitate movement within the bathroom and obtaining the proper position to perform the hygiene skills. Most of these adaptations can be found in public bathrooms already, as a result of meeting building requirements of the Americans With Disabilities Act. They include bars on the walls near the toilet and the bathtub. A lowered sink, mirrors, hand dryers, and paper towel dispensers to accommodate wheelchairs are other examples.

Eating. Many educational goals include independent eating skills and food preparation. Utensils shaped differently than standard utensils are often needed. This includes built-up handles and spoons that swivel to keep the bowl of the spoon parallel to the table to prevent spilling. Plate guards, a plastic ridge snapped on one side of a plate, provide a surface to help the user push the food onto the utensil. Plates and bowls with suction cups on the bottom help prevent their movement out of reach of the student. Nonskid materials such as those used for mats for under rugs can help stabilize plates. Weighted cups and cups with handles are two common adaptations as well (DATI, 2000).

Food preparation tools can be adapted much like the eating utensils. Built-up handles are commonly used. Adaptations that help stabilize tools and food during preparation are useful. Cutting boards with prongs can prevent an apple from rolling around the board while trying to cut it. Clamps can be mounted to hold tools, such as peelers, so the student is only required to manipulate the food. Jar and can openers are available in any kitchen appliance department (DATI, 2000). The list goes on and on. Products not available in stores can be ordered through specialty companies, but with the aging of the general population and their acquired disabilities, many can be found in local medical and home-health equipment stores.

Communication

Communication needed for school success can be categorized according to two dimensions: vocal and verbal (Millikin, 1997). Vocal communication can either be verbal or nonverbal (e.g., speech vs. crying), and verbal communication can be vocal or nonvocal (e.g., speech vs. sign language). Spoken communication is verbal and vocal; written communication is verbal and nonvocal. Augmentative and alternative communication can be categorized in the same way. A device that produces speech is an example of verbal and vocal communication; however, in this case it is aided by the device. If the student points to indicate a need or wish, this communication is unaided nonverbal and nonvocal. An issue in the field of moderate and severe retardation is the awareness and utilization of all types of communication.

Students with moderate and severe disabilities typically have significant deficits in communication and do not develop an effective system of nonvocal or nonverbal communication (Wetherby, Schuler, & Prizant, 1997). What abilities they have, however, can be nurtured

through early intervention (Dexter, 1998) and supplemented with the use of AT and augmentative and alternative communication systems (AAC) (Romski, Sevick, & Adamson, 1997; Warren & Kaiser, 1986). The American Speech-Language-Hearing Association defines AAC as "an integrated group of components, including the symbols, aids, strategies, and techniques used by individuals to enhance communication. The system serves to supplement any gestural, spoken, and/or written communication abilities" (cited in Weitz, Dexter, & Moore, 1997, p. 396). Augmentative communication is used to supplement existing speech, and alternative communication uses a substitute for speech (Millikin, 1997).

Spoken Communication. Spoken language is the most common and most efficient way of communicating (Cook & Hussey, 1995); however, an estimated 50% of students with moderate and severe cognitive disabilities do not have the ability to communicate functionally through spoken or nonverbal language (Wetherby, Schuler, & Prizant, 1997). To improve on these statistics, researchers advocate early and continued intervention. As previously thought, there is no need to wait for a student to obtain certain prerequisites. The child learns language incidentally across time and exposure (Romski et al., 1997). The impact of environment, context, and listener familiarity on the listener's comprehension of the communicated message is recognized, and alternative strategies for teaching language and communication are being explored. Two examples are aided language stimulation (Dexter, 1998; Gray, 1997) and providing the listener with a semantic category for the message (Dowden, 1997).

A wide range of assistive technologies are available for individuals to augment or produce alternative verbal language. By definition, gesturing and sign language are forms of augmentative or alternative language (Millikin, 1997). Other simple systems use pictures that represent a concept or a word, using one-to-one correspondence of the picture to the word. By selecting a specific picture the student communicates using implied words. Several collections of pictures are available for use in these systems. For example, Mayer-Johnson, Inc. produces a notebook of picture symbols ready to copy and use (PCS Book I, II, and III), as well as an electronic version that can be incorporated into picture overlays or single pictures to use as needed (PCS Metafiles).

Picture-based, low-tech communication systems are easy to create and adapt as needed but require a listener who understands the implied meaning of the pictures. Pictures can mean different things to different people. When possible, the student is advanced to more abstract symbol systems and ultimately words to communicate with. The more advanced symbol systems convey more specific meanings and are less likely to be misinterpreted by an unfamiliar listener.

One way around the problem of misinterpretation is to use a system that produces spoken language, known as a voice output communication aid (VOCA) (Locke & Levin, 1999). As with low-tech picture and/or symbol communication systems, VOCAs come in a wide range of sophistication and complexity. Similar to picture communication boards, a device like the MiniMessage Mate is capable of having eight pictures, symbols, or words on it, but instead of the listener needing to interpret the meaning of those pictures, the device holds a recorded word, phrase, or sentence for each picture (Figure 3–6). When the user presses one of the pictures, the device "speaks" using a digitized voice. This leaves very little for the listener to interpret.

Two types of VOCAs are available. One uses digitized speech, the recording and playing of speech, as the Two Talker does, and one uses synthesized speech, a mathematical conversion of text to produced speech output. Devices that feature the digitized voice are often easier to understand but require two to six times more memory than text to speech systems. They store words, phrases, and sentences in whole chunks, which makes the system less flexible. The user is

FIGURE 3 – 6 Eight-Picture Communication System: MiniMessage Mate from Words+

limited to predetermined messages and cannot create a unique message unless the words are stored individually. This makes voice retrieval slower and somewhat choppy because it does not adjust to the context of the sentence (Venkatagiri & Ramabadran, 1995).

The synthesized voice systems, on the other hand, use phonetic rules to interpret text. Essentially, the system "sounds the word out" as it speaks. The quality of the voice output is governed by the number of rules it has available to apply and the speed of the processor. The English language has so many exceptions to the rules that a limited system has a more difficult time pronouncing irregular words. Consequently, these systems have a "robotic" sounding speech quality, making them more difficult to understand (Koul & Hanners, 1997). The more sophisticated the system the more natural the quality of speech, but limitations of the current technology prevent production of truly natural-sounding speech (Venkatagiri & Ramabadran, 1995). Most systems come with preset voice options, with voices that sound old, young, male, female, and sometimes silly.

Over the years, the AAC field has debated who should use what type of system. The prerequisites for using any system were once proclaimed to be specific cognitive levels such as the ability to demonstrate cause-and-effect relationships, match pictures with objects, and recognize abstract symbols (Locke & Levin, 1999). These cognitive thresholds are now questioned, and supplementing existing communication with augmentative communication systems is believed to be beneficial, promoting further development of cognitive abilities (Calculator, 1997; Dexter, 1998; Romski et al., 1997; Warren & Kaiser, 1986).

Implementing AAC. Through participation in language-based activities, the student develops higher language and social abilities. Areas affected by this participation include turn taking and the positive affects of participating, understanding of the meaning of language, and the relationships of objects, people, and actions in their environment (Locke & Levin, 1999; Romski et al., 1997). Using AAC devices to facilitate participation provides the child with immediate communication options, a mechanism for learning expressive and receptive language, and helps build the foundation for future language (Weitz et al., 1997).

Identifying an appropriate AAC method for any student differs based on the student's abilities, resources available to the service providers, and the knowledge of the service providers. The steps used to identify AAC are similar across individuals. The first step is to conduct an assessment to determine a reasonable match between the student's abilities and available technologies (Locke & Levin, 1999). There are three components of this step: consideration, screening, and assessing. Initially a team of services providers and parents must consider AT and make the determination if AT is potentially beneficial for this student. Gathering available information about the student's needs and abilities then provides additional information so the team can decide if a full assessment is needed. This screening process may indicate that other available strategies have not been adequately tried and additional time is needed before conducting an assessment.

If a full assessment is called for, the team decides what information is still needed and how they can gather that information. At this point the team must have someone on it with AT expertise. The major areas of assessment will be the student's goals (i.e., what current educational tasks are barriers and which one is most critical for the student to become successful) (Calculator, 1997), how the student will access or operate any device(s) chosen, and the physical and feedback features of the device (Locke & Levin, 1999). No standardized tests or commonly used assessment protocol are available for AT assessment, but several are listed in Table 3–1. A framework for planning the assessment is shown in Figure 3–7.

To determine the best way for the student to access a communication device, the student must be observed in many types of activities. If the student cannot directly select items from an array of options with a finger, the assessor must look for the most consistent alternate movement that will not exhaust the student if used repeatedly over a period of time. Some of the most common ways include using a full hand, an elbow, or the head to activate a switch. The size of the "key" or single communication item depends on the speed and accuracy that each item can be selected using the best movement. Here are some questions to ask:

- Does the student hit the switch accurately on the majority of trials?
- Does the student activate the switch in a reasonable amount of time?
- Is the size of the switch a good match with the student's accuracy?
- Does the student have enough strength to activate the switch and activate it over a period of time?
- Can the same switch be used when the student is in a variety of positions?

TABLE 3–1 Available AT Assessment Protocol

AT Assessment Protocol	Source
AAC feature match software	Doug Dodgen & Associates (1996).
Augmentative/alternative technology assessment tool [Computer software].	Doug Dodgen & Associates (1997).
Control of computer-based technology for people with physical disabilities: An assessment manual.	Lee, K. S., & Thomas, D. J. (1990). Toronto: University of Toronto Press.
INCH: Interaction checklist for augmentative communication.	Bolton, S., & Dashiell, S. (1984). Waucouda, IL: Don Johnston Inc.
Lifespace access profile: Assistive technology planning for individuals with severe or multiple disabilities.	Williams, W. B., Stemach, G., Wolfe, S., & Stanger, C. (1995). Sebastopol, CA: Lifespace Access.
Lifespace access profile: Assistive technology planning for individuals with severe or multiple disabilities (Upper Extension)	
Lifespace access profile: Assistive technology planning for individuals with severe or multiple disabilities. (Transition)	
PCA checklist for computer access.	Fraser, B. A., McGregor, G., & Kangas, K. (1994). Volo, IL: Don Johnston Inc.

Product Name	Developer's Address	Other Contact Information
WatchMinder	WatchMinder, PMB #278, 5405 Alton Pkwy #5A, Irvine, CA 92604	Phone: 800/961-0023 Fax: 949/854-1843 E-mail: addhelper@watchminder.com Web: watchminder.com

Consider placement of the switch. If the student activates the switch frequently, determine if the hits are intentional. Unintentional activations can result in the student's misunderstanding of the purpose of the switch. Moving the switch further away from the student or mounting it above the hand or arm can ensure the switch hits are intentional because they take concerted effort. This level of effort, though, may not be able to be sustained over many trials. The selection of a switch or other control device or interface can be a challenge. The assessor must engineer the activities so all potential movements can be observed and considered.

Once the appropriate switch or control interface is identified, the next step is to determine the vocabulary to use with the communication device. When a student is only able to choose from two pictures or communication options, the content of the communication becomes extremely important. These options should result in something very reinforcing to the student and help establish the relationship between the action and the consequence.

Product Name	Developer's Address	Other Contact Information
IntelliTalk Overlay Maker	IntelliTools, Inc., 1720 Corporate Circle, Petaluma, CA 94954	Phone: 707-773-2000 or 800-899-6687 Fax: 707-773-2001 Email: info@intellitools.com Web: www.intellitools.com
Write:OutLoud	Don Johnston Incorporated, 26799 W. Commerce Dr., Volo, IL 60073	Phone: 847-740-0749 or 800-999-4660 Fax: 847-740-7326 Email: info@donjohnston.com Web: www.donjohnston.com
Mini-Message Mate	Words+, Inc., 1220 W. Ave. J, Lancaster, CA 93534-2902	Phone: 661-723-6523 or 800-869-8521 Fax: 661-723-2114 Email: support@words-plus.com Web: www.words-plus.com
Minspeak	Prentke Romich Co., 1022 Heyl Rd., Wooster, OH 44691	Phone: 330-262-1984 or 800-262-1984 Fax: 330-263-4829 Email: info@prentrom.com Web: www.prentrom.com
Boardmaker PCS Books I, II, & III PCS Metafiles	Mayer-Johnson, Inc., P.O. Box 1579, Solana Beach, CA 92075	Phone: 800/588-4548 Fax: 858-550-0449 Email: mayerj@mayer-johnson.com Web: www.mayer-johnson.com
Dynavox	Dyna Vox Systems Inc., 100 Wharton St., Ste. 400, Pittsburgh, PA 15203	Phone: 412-381-4883 or 800-344-1778 Fax: 412-381-5241 Email: sales@dynavoxsys.com Web: www.dynavoxsys.com

The best way to promote this relationship is to select a communication event that is naturally occurring and presents itself frequently so the number of trials in a day are sufficient to allow the student to learn from them. Too often the communication options are related to existence or daily living skills such as going to the bathroom or eating. It would be nice if students communicated those needs and desires, but they are limited to very short periods of time in the schoolday, which make them very difficult to learn, especially as the first topics of communication. It is better to choose vocabulary or phrases around more generic actions and enhance participation in the learning activity such as requesting more or signifying the desire to participate. The student should have the option for refusing something or terminating the activity. It is unnatural to only request the presence or initiation of something and not be able to refuse it. With a little imagination and thoughtful planning, many learning activities can be crafted or scripted to require these types of communication (Elders & Goossens', 1994; Locke & Levin, 1999).

F I G U R E 3 – 7   **Assessment Planning Document**

Priority Objective #_____: _____

_____

Area(s) of function identified in the screening:

☐ Communication   ☐ Existence

☐ Travel & Mobility   ☐ Body Support, Alignment, and Positioning

☐ Learning, Education, and Rehabilitation   ☐ Environmental Adaptations

☐ Sports, Leisure, and Recreation

Functional Area(s) to Be Addressed	What Do I Know? (From the Screening)	What Do I Need to Know?	How Do I Gather that Information? (Number each task)

Assessment to be completed by: _____

Person(s) responsible for assessment components:

      Name/Title Assessment Tasks

_____   _____

_____   _____

_____   _____

Locke and Levin (1999) categorize communication into four types. The "anytime/anywhere" messages are not specific to an activity and can be used across many situations. One example might be "Are we there yet?" "Anytime/anywhere" messages apply to many activities but are specific to a situation, an example being "It's hot outside." "Sequenced" messages are the third type. "It's my turn now!" is one example of a sequenced message and may be used in conjunction with other sequenced messages like "You can be first." Finally, "specific time" messages carry both content- and situation-specific information, like answering a question asked by the teacher (e.g., "Today is Tuesday" in response to the teacher's question, "What day is it today?").

The "anytime/anywhere" messages can be used more frequently throughout the day, offering many opportunities for practice. However, because they are generic, it is more difficult to learn their relationship to the situation or relate their consequence to anything specific. Elders and Goossens' (1994) caution that these messages limit the potential number of communications because they are not specific to a situation, thus reducing the number of different messages available to the student. At the other end of the continuum are the "specific time" or concentrated messages. It is very clear what is being communicated with this type of message but there are far fewer natural opportunities to practice each day unless the communication overlay is changed with each activity.

The amount communicated with each selection must be considered. One picture or cell on a communication board could speak out a sentence, phrase, or a single word (Elders & Goossens', 1994). Speed of communication is in direct conflict with flexibility. If the communicator can construct messages by putting several words or phrases together, the message will be more specific to a situation and yield better understanding. Constructing a message requires more cognitive ability than using whole sentence units. It may also require more physical

stamina than the student has. If too much effort is required for one message, fatigue could become a factor and limit the communication.

The nature of the activity also affects the communicator in training. If the activity is predictable, then the messages can be sequenced to facilitate appropriate message selection. Activities that require random messages will be much more difficult (Elder & Goossens', 1994). Each of these factors becomes very important, depending on the ability of the emerging speaker.

Equally important to the content and context of the message is the symbol or representation of the message on the communication device. Symbols can be described through an iconicity continuum, with transparent as one pole and opaque at the other. Iconicity is the "degree the sign or symbol visually resembles or suggests its referents" (Millikin, 1997, p. 100). "Transparent" is defined as "symbols that are icons and easily recognized by everyone" (Johnson, Baumgart, Helmstetter, & Curry, 1996, p. 107). They define "opaque" as abstract symbols that must be learned to have meaning. Photographs or real objects are transparent and Blissymbols or written words are opaque. Within that continuum fall several specific types of symbols: real objects, color photographs, black and white photographs, miniature objects, color line drawings, black and white line drawings, universal symbols, and text (Johnson et al., 1996; Locke & Levin, 1999; Millikin, 1997). Figure 3–8 provides examples and sources for several commercially available symbol systems.

The third step in the implementation of AAC is training. Goossens', Crain, and Elder (1992) describe training as "the process of acquiring operational, linguistic, and social knowledge" (p. 157), three components necessary for meaningful communication. Elder and Goossens' (1994) identify three major characteristics of good communication training: instruction that focuses on functional skills, taught in community-based settings, with training integrated across the curriculum. As we discussed in Chapter 2, generalization of skills is a particular issue

FIGURE 3–8   Available Picture Symbol Systems

Symbol System	Reference	Examples of "come"
Blissymbols	Bliss, 1965	
DynaSyms	Carlson, 1994	COME
Minspeak	Baker, 1986	+ VERB
Oakland Schools Symbols	Kirstein & Bernstein, 1981	come
Picsyms	Carlson, 1986	
Picture Communication Symbols	Johnson, 1981	
Rebus Symbols	Woodcock & Davies, 1969	
Makaton Symbols	www.makaton.org.	Discussion

Source: Millikin, C.C. (1997). Symbol systems and vocabulary selection strategies. In S.L. Glonnen & D.C. DeCoste (Eds.), *Handbook of augmentative and alternative communication* (pp. 97-148). San Diego, CA: Singular.

in teaching students with moderate and severe disabilities. Contrived settings and meaningless training tasks do not generalize well and it is very difficult for the individual with severe disabilities to grasp the relationship of the message (action) to its meaning (language) (Johnson et al., 1996).

Initial training should use messages that can be used naturally, interactively, and frequently in the daily routine. Opportunities for communication are best when they are predictable and/or controlled by the teacher so meaningful prompts can be provided, thus shaping the communication skill (Elders & Goossens', 1994). To plan ample opportunities, they often must be staged or scripted.

If all that were needed were ample opportunities to communicate, there would be very few noncommunicators. People with moderate and severe disabilities do not learn well through practice alone. They require more direct teaching and teaching steps are broken down into smaller components.

Written Communication. The degree to which students with moderate and severe disabilities will be successful with written communication depends on their level of cognition. Although there is a range of complexity in written communication, most typical tasks require significant cognitive and physical abilities. Some of the less complex tasks that a large percentage of students with moderate and severe disabilities can begin to master include writing their name, copying information from one source to another, and completing simple forms. Without the requisite motor control, however, even these simple writing tasks become difficult.

A computer or other data entry system may provide some students with the means for independence in these tasks, and increase their productivity and ability to perform tasks similar to their peers in the general education classroom. Standard keyboards require a different set of motor abilities than those of handwriting. Adapting the task to a computer-based task and employing this standard equipment may be all a student needs. If motor abilities are still a barrier, there are numerous adaptations to the standard keyboard. Through the control panels on either Windows or Macintosh systems (Figure 3–9), the keyboard can be adjusted to accommodate students in several ways. Adjusting the delay factor before a key repeats itself may provide a "heavy fingered" typist enough of an accommodation to be successful (Anson, 1999). Audible clicks can be added to key presses to provide the user with additional feedback to confirm that the key has been pressed. Similarly,

FIGURE 3–9 Keyboard Control Panels. top) Windows 98 bottom) Macintosh

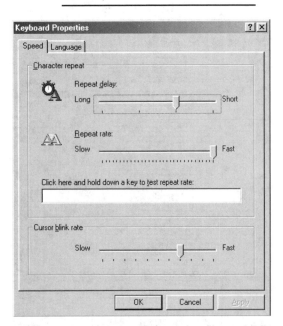

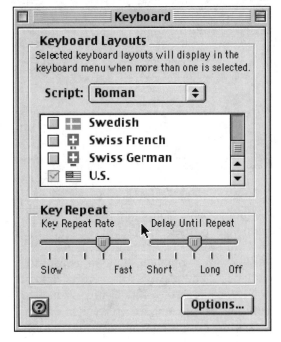

FIGURE 3–10 **Simple and Complex Word Processing Programs.** top) Microsoft Word bottom) Write:OutLoud

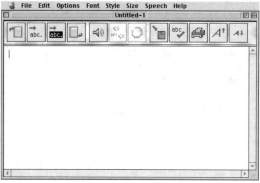

the mouse can be adjusted to fit the needs of a motor-limited user.

Word processors, the most common way of writing with a computer, come in many different levels of complexity. If the student has cognitive limitations, the office or professional versions may be too complex, with a busy, cluttered screen that can distract and take the user away

from the task if a wrong key is pressed (Figure 3–10). Word processors with simple screens, such as IntelliTalk and Write:OutLoud, work better for the student. These two programs can also read the written text back to the user, providing another form of confirmation or feedback.

For most students with moderate and severe disabilities, word processors are beyond their capability and educational tasks never require that level of complexity. The word processor may be used as a vehicle for recording written information, but the student may not actually use its capabilities. For example, using an AAC device or an alternate keyboard, the student may enter text that is preprogrammed in a cell. An example of this is the use of the IntelliKeys keyboard to enter alternate portfolio information into a word processor (Denham & Lahm, 2001).

In addition to using AAC devices and word processsors, several no-tech alternatives are being used. Sign language and facilitated communication are two examples. Facilitated communication can be used for both spoken and written communication. It is a collaborative effort of the student and a trained adult. Students guide the hand of the adult to the message symbol or key on the keyboard to express their thoughts, responses, and requests. The technique is controversial, as many question if the resulting message is the child's or the adult's. For a discussion of the issues surrounding facilitated communication, see a special issue of *Mental Retardation* (Vol. 32), which is a publication of the American Association of Mental Retardation. You can find a bibliography of additional readings on the Web at http://web.syr.edu/~thefci/fcjrnl.htm.

Education and Transition

All IEP goals involve learning and education, so this functional area seems redundant. What is included here, though, are those academic goals such as reading and math. Many students with moderate and severe disabilities have few, if any, goals in the traditional academic areas, but focus on functional, authentic skills that use basic knowledge in these academic areas. Two examples are learning to put coins in a vending machine to purchase a snack or to take inventory of items in the vending machine to determine how many more are needed to fill it. Instructional technologies can be used to teach some of those skills. In the sense that they provide many practice opportunities and use multimodal methods of teaching, they become assistive technologies for these students.

Instructional technologies come in various forms. Categories of software include exploratory, tutorial, drill and practice, educational games, simulations, and problem solving. The design of these programs varies widely and it is important to know the features of instruction that work best for the individual student (Lahm, 1996). For example, if the student is very distractible, selection of programs that have simple screens and minimal extraneous sound is imperative.

The number of instructional programs available is vast and rapidly increasing. However, programs with appropriate content for students with moderate and severe disabilities are limited. Pugliese (1999) identifies seven stages of learning of students with moderate and severe disabilities, and software appropriate for teaching those skills. The stages are cause and effect, language readiness, emerging language, early concepts, advanced concepts and communication, functional learning, and written expression. Specific programs that address these stages are not included here because of the ever-changing market. An excellent resource for locating current software is the Closing the Gap Resource Directory, available online at http://www.closingthegap.com/rd/. Several software development companies that produce products for individuals with moderate and severe disabilities include Broderbund, Don Johnston, IntelliTools, Judy Lynn Software, Laureate

Learning, R. J. Cooper, and SoftTouch/kidTECH (Pugliese, 1999). Getting on the mailing list of these companies is an excellent way to stay current too.

With today's emphasis on alternate portfolio assessments, technology can be used to assist the student with the assessment task. One example is a student who has the job of keeping the vending machine in the school's teachers' lounge full. Using an IntelliKeys alternate keyboard with a custom-designed overlay and a word processor that speaks, the student plans his task by answering the questions like "What is your next job?" and "What do you need to do to complete it?", after the computer reads them aloud to him. The custom overlay provides him with a number of choices related to many tasks he may need to do during the day and he selects the sequence of events for the vending machine task by pressing the appropriate place on the IntelliKeys keyboard. The keyboard sends the corresponding text to the word processor, thus keeping a record of his choices. After the task is completed, he returns to the computer and addresses questions that require him to reflect on his performance and set a goal for the next day (Denham and Lahm, 2001).

 **SUMMARY**

In this chapter, you learned that students with moderate and severe disabilities have numerous assistive technologies available to improve their ability to function independently in daily living skills, communication, and learning. The technologies range from no tech to high tech and vary greatly in cost. Legislation has been passed that requires AT to be considered for all students receiving special education services. We presented a human function framework for considering technology.

Strategies for successful implementation of AT revolve around the supports available to professionals and the families of students with moderate and severe disabilities. Teaming is a critical factor in providing AT services. An interdisciplinary team that shares the responsibilities of assessment and intervention is essential. The expertise of teachers and related service providers in the schools is another major issue. Without proper training, AT will not be adequately considered or matched to the needs of the students. Continuing support to the students and their families, and to the professionals implementing the AT, is essential as well. As we discussed in the human function model, considering AT is an ongoing process. School districts must support continued professional development, staffing, and technical support to be successful.

 CHAPTER EXTENDERS

Key Terms and Concepts

1. An *alternative communication system* is used to enhance communication by supplementing existing speech.
2. *Augmentative communication* uses a substitute for speech to enhance communication.
3. *Assistive technology* is any item, piece of equipment, or product used to increase the functional capabilities of an individual with disabilities.
4. *Assistive technology services* are any services that directly support a person with disabilities in selecting, acquiring, or using an assistive technology device.
5. *Human function model* is a systematic method for considering assistive technology that focuses on the human functions rather than disabilities.

Study Guide

1. What are some advantages of the human function model?
2. Provide examples of functional problems in each of these areas: (a) existence, (b) com-

munication, (c) body support, (d) travel/mobility, (e) education, and (f) recreation.
3. Provide an example for each of the following types of assistive technology: (a) low tech, (b) medium tech, and (c) high tech.
4. Name the three places assistive technology (AT) can be included in the IEP. Provide an example of each.
5. Provide two examples of an alternative communication system and two examples of augmentative communication.
6. Name some considerations for using switches.
7. Define the terms *iconicity* and *transparent*. Discuss the importance of each in designing communication strategies for persons with moderate to severe disabilities.
8. Name two ways computer hardware can be modified for persons with moderate to severe disabilities who are unable to access conventional keyboards.
9. Provide examples of word processing programs that may be appropriate for persons with moderate to severe disabilities.
10. Define the term *VOCA* and provide an example.

Group Activity I

Joanne is unable to communicate choices at mealtimes. Design both a low-tech and a high-tech example of an AT approach for Joanne. What are the advantages and disadvantages for each approach you chose? What other information do you need to know about Joanne before making this decision? How might you gather that information?

Group Activity II

Vocabulary selection is very important for initial communication. Imagine you are limited to only 10 words. What might those words be? How would you choose your vocabulary? List the words for one or two members of the group. Examine the vocabulary. What might be the differences and similarities for person with disabilities?

Group Activity III

Melvin has a great deal of difficulty transitioning and he frequently resists moving from one class activity to the next. His mother has informed you that when he is reminded of the events and their sequence in advance, he is more cooperative. Design both a low- and high-tech communication strategy for Melvin to transition to and from the following activities: reading, language arts, spelling, math, lunch, social studies, library, and physical education. (For a high-tech solution, you may wish to try computer software.)

Field Experience I

Spend a day shadowing an AT specialist or technology coordinator in a school setting.

1. Try to observe at least five students that he or she serves. Observe for function problems and AT solutions. Use Figure 3–2 as a format to track the various function problems and the AT approaches used for each.

2. Interview the technology specialist. How have these AT changes impacted these students? How well are the AT changes working? For approaches that are not as successful as planned, what changes is the AT specialist planning?

Field Experience II

In conjunction with an AT specialist or special education teacher, identify a student in need of AT for a functional problem. Design and implement a low-tech solution. Evaluate its effectiveness. Suggest changes, if appropriate.

Field Experience III

If you are working in a classroom with students who have moderate to severe disabilities, review the students' IEPs in your class. Document all the uses of AT you find in each IEP. Compare your results to what you have learned in this chapter.

chapter 4

The Learning Environment

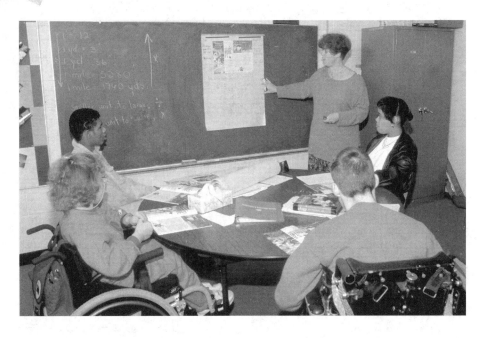

The learning environment provides students with knowledge and skills that allow them to function successfully both in school and in their community. It includes the places where students learn, the things that they learn, and the people with whom they learn. The learning environment begins in the classroom and reaches beyond into school-wide and community-based activities. It is made up of the way we teach curricula. Providing an applied approach to the learning environment lets students directly connect and practice the skills they need to participate effectively in each setting. It also includes all members of the school and community. An inclusive learning environment provides every student with the opportunity to develop both the practical academic and social expertise they need to interact successfully as members of their community while, at the same time, they apply what they are learning to the real world.

WHAT YOU WILL LEARN IN THIS CHAPTER

This chapter explores three key components of the learning environment: (1) where instruction should take place, (2) how instruction should be delivered, and (3) what should be included in the curriculum. We believe instruction must be delivered in an inclusive environment using differentiated and applied approaches. We believe the curriculum should incorporate an applied approach whenever possible. We discuss each of the three aspects in this chapter. First we explore definitions of inclusion, characteristics of inclusive environments, and factors important to implementation of an inclusive model.

Next we explore applied curriculum and school-to-work initiatives. In this section, we discuss the characteristics of applied curriculum and applied curriculum models, including school-to-work models and service learning.

In the last section we link inclusive practice and applied curricula with school reform. We discuss the commonalities between inclusive

practice and applied curricula and contemporary educational issues of equity and access for all learners.

INCLUSIVE PRACTICE

To understand the current context of inclusion, we must first examine the history of special education. Education for persons with disabilities was not mandated until 1975 when the Education for All Handicapped Children Act of 1975 (P.L. 94-142) was passed (Turnbull et al., 1999). The Education for All Handicapped Children Act (EAHCA) of 1975 was one of the most significant pieces of legislation in the 20th century because it ensured public education to *all* school-aged children with disabilities. Prior to that time, many persons with disabilities, especially moderate to severe disabilities, were not provided educational opportunities. If they were, these services were often funded by parents or interest groups and not located in public school settings. In addition, as you will learn in Chapter 6, this law mandated individualized educational plans, parental participation, and due process rights for students and their parents. The subsequent reauthorization of this law, the Individuals With Disabilities Education Act (IDEA) of 1990, ensured those services and added services for early childhood special education and transition.

Because it was thought that students with identified disabilities had to be served by teachers with specialized training, special education evolved from the outset into a different system administered separately with its own teachers, credentialing process, administration, and budgets (Fuchs & Fuchs, 1996). Although EAHCA stated that special education was to be provided in the least restrictive environment (often taken as the general classroom), the primary model was the separate, or "pull-out" approach. From the beginning, professionals questioned the utility of the pull-out approach, and debates raged on the potential harmful effects of giving someone a disability label (Dunn, 1968). Nonetheless, the field continued to develop as a separate and discrete system.

In 1986 Madeleine Will, secretary of the Office of Special Education and Rehabilitative Services, critiqued the state of services at that time. Will noted that during the 10 years of EAHCA, referrals to special education were higher than projected incidence rates for disabilities, many persons referred for special education did not qualify for services, and the pull-out segregated approach did not appear to show the instructional gains hoped for. Will proposed a merger of general, special, remedial, and compensatory programs that was termed the regular education initiative (REI) (Fuchs & Fuchs, 1996).

REI focused on the general classroom. The plan was not merely to place special education students back into the regular class as had been done in what was called "mainstreaming," but rather to create a new system of shared responsibility for *all* students (Lilly, 1988). It was apparent that many students in the general classroom did not qualify for special education services, but nonetheless were experiencing significant problems in learning—often as severe as those receiving services. It appeared to many that the general classroom environment was meeting the needs of few students. By combining the services of all professionals, it was hoped that *all* children with diverse learning needs would receive a better education.

What Is Inclusion?

To arrive at a definition and understanding of inclusion, let's first examine some of the foundations of the movement. Inclusion is the commitment to educate each child in the classroom he or she would otherwise attend (Rogers, 1993). Furthermore, it involves bringing support to the student rather than having the student leave the classroom as in the traditional special education model. In other words, special education teachers and support staff—speech/language pathologists, occupa-

tional therapists, and physical therapists—work collaboratively with the general education teacher to deliver the needed services. It is believed this will make a greater impact on the diverse needs of all students in the classroom, not just those with the identified disabilities (Lipsky & Gartner, 1997). The following definition developed by the National Center on Educational Restructuring and Inclusion (NCERI) (National Study, 1994) encompasses the essential elements of an inclusive environment:

> Providing to all students, including those with significant disabilities, equitable opportunities to receive effective educational services, with the needed supplementary aids and support services, in age-appropriate classrooms in their neighborhood schools, in order to prepare students for productive lives as full members of society. (Lipsky & Gartner, 1997, p. 99)

Sailor's (1991) definition of inclusion adds two more aspects that are important for persons with moderate to severe disabilities. First, Sailor states that a natural proportion of the students with disabilities should be present at each school site. This proportion should be representative of the district at large. For example, if 20% of the district's school-aged population has identified disabilities, then in a class of 20, there should be no more than 4 students who are on IEPs.

Further, the concept of natural proportions implies all students with disabilities for a given grade level should not all be placed in the same classroom. All teachers at that grade level should have students with disabilities in their classes. If this does not happen, you will see certain general education classes become "special classes," and the stigma of segregation will likely continue.

A second important aspect of Sailor's (1991) definition is that a "zero-reject" philosophy should exist. This means no student should be excluded based on the type or extent of his or her disability. Zero reject is particularly important for successful implementation of an inclusive model. Many schools and whole districts have implemented inclusive models, but exclusion is still in effect for persons with moderate to severe disabilities. The majority of students with mental retardation and severe disabilities are still not served in the general classroom (Lipsky & Gartner, 1997). Statistics from 1994–1995 indicate that only 9% to 10% of students classified as having either mental retardation, multiple disabilities, or autism were served in the general classroom (Coutinho & Repp, 1999). This data indicates the strong need for a systems change as well as for advocacy on the part of the professionals who work with students with moderate to severe disabilities (Fiedler, 2000).

As proponents of inclusive practice, we believe that beyond the service delivery issue, inclusion is a moral and a values issue (J. D. Smith, 1998). The fundamental principle of inclusion is the creation of an educational system that values and embraces human diversity (J. D. Smith, 1998). Furthermore, we believe, as many do, that we have a moral imperative to create such a system (Goodlad, Soder, & Sorotnik, 1990). We explore the relationship between inclusive education and issues of equity and access to education later in this chapter when we look at the relationship between inclusive practice and other school reforms.

Characteristics of Inclusive Environments

In order to gain a clearer picture of the inclusive school, this section explores the inclusive school from many different viewpoints—the overall school, the classroom, the role of the teacher, the role of the student, and aspects of the curriculum.

The School Environment. The atmosphere and general philosophy is an important part of the inclusive school environment. A sense of community with shared vision that embraces diversity is a critical part of an inclusive school.

FIGURE 4–1 Aspects Important for Building Community in Schools

- **Security.** Students and teachers know it is safe to be yourself and to take risks.
- **Open communication.** People share what is happening and what they need.
- **Mutual liking.** Students and teachers are encouraged to know and to like their peers.
- **Shared goals and objectives.** The school and the class participate in collective projects.
- **Connectedness and trust.** Students and teachers know they are needed and valued members of the school community.

Source: Sapon-Shevin, M. (1999). *Because we can change the world: A practical guide to building cooperative, inclusive classroom communities.* Boston: Allyn & Bacon.

Figure 4–1 outlines many of the aspects that are important in building a sense of community in the school. Creating an atmosphere of trust and respect is vital for success for any school and particularly for environments that include many diverse learners. In addition, this viewpoint embraces the notion of caring. In a caring environment, students and teachers feel both connected and valued. An inclusive classroom welcomes all learners into the classroom as equally important members of the learning community and allows previously marginalized students to be valued participants (Schniedewind, 1993). As we discuss later in this chapter, inclusion involves collaboration between teacher and students alike. For collaboration to be effective, a trusting community must be established.

The way teachers treat students as well as each other has much to do with forming a sense of community. If teachers are to foster acceptance, they must communicate that they trust their students. They need to assume and to act that students are capable of being responsible, well intentioned, and concerned about others (Solomon,

Schaps, Watson, & Battistich, 1992). They must also assume their colleagues are capable and well intentioned regarding their students.

For inclusive practice to become a reality, *all* staff—administrators, teachers, therapists, assistants—must accept responsibility for education of *all* children. This is difficult because teachers have been socialized to be territorial. The general education teacher (or the administrator) may say, "I only work with *my* children and the child with the identified disability is *your* child." Conversely, the special education teacher or special education administrator may say, "I only work with special education children and cannot address the needs of other children who have learning or behavioral problems." As long as teachers and administrators cling to these outmoded paradigms, inclusive environments cannot develop.

The Classroom Environment. When describing an inclusive classroom, sometimes it is helpful to contrast inclusive models with characteristics of environments that are *not* inclusive. An inclusive classroom is *not* a classroom where all students follow the same text and do the same activity. Inclusive classrooms operate under the assumption that not only is it permissible, but also desirable for students to be working at different paces or levels. Inclusive classrooms accommodate for learner needs and employ differentiated instructional approaches. An inclusive classroom is *not* a homogeneous group of students. Inclusive classrooms embrace and celebrate diversity of all kinds. An inclusive classroom is *not* a classroom based on an individual, competitive model. Cooperation among students is implicit in the model. Finally, an inclusive classroom is *not* a place where the source of all instruction comes from one person (a general education teacher). An inclusive classroom involves other professionals as well as peers in the teaching process.

Role of the Teacher. Because inclusion involves a significant shift in the way services are delivered, the roles of both the general and the special education teachers differ from traditional models. Because inclusive education involves providing services to children when and where they need them, there are no prescribed models. Rather, special and general education teachers collaborate in a variety of ways. Teachers have been socialized to view themselves in a single role, so role changes and ambiguities can cause discomfort. This is true for both general and special education teachers.

One key aspect of inclusive practice is that both general and special education teachers must assume the roles of collaborators. The instructional collaboration between regular and

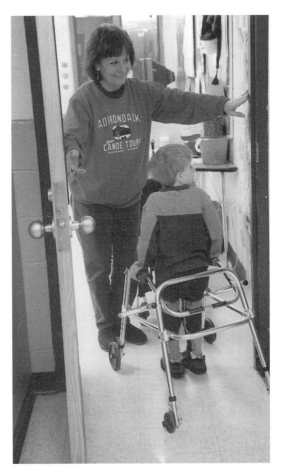

Inclusive classrooms accommodate for learner needs.

special education teachers can take place in many ways (Lipsky & Gartner, 1998). The model the teachers choose is often determined by their personalities and the needs of the students. In fact, it is critical for the model that a "one size fits all" attitude *not* be established (Kochhar et al., 2000). This notion keeps the focus away from adopting one mode as the "correct one" for providing services and toward generating approaches that address the individual needs of both students and the teachers.

In keeping with this notion of individualized needs, many special education teachers report they may have different forms of collaboration with each teacher they work with, as the example of Marge, the intervention specialist, indicates. As the example portrays, teachers work together in different ways and, because we are all individuals, not everyone can collaborate well. True collaboration involves parity, a situation in which each individual's contributions are equally valued by the others (Friend & Cook, 1992). Marge has a different relationship with each of the teachers she works with. She team teaches in one setting and acts as a consultant in another. In one case, with Mr. Crabb, collaboration or parity does not exist. As you can see from the example, the decision making is not shared and there is no joint ownership of the students. The students who have IEPs are Marge's responsibility entirely. It does not appear that Mr. Crabb values Marge's contributions, nor does he see her as an equal contributor.

Establishing and maintaining collaborative relationships is not easy. The structure and philosophy of the school must support this and time must be allocated for ongoing communication (Smith, Gottesman, & Edmundson, 1997). You will learn more in Chapter 7 on the nature of collaboration and approaches for nurturing and fostering collaborative relationships.

As you can see from the example of Marge, one of the ways that regular and special education teachers can provide instruction is through team teaching. There are many ways to team. One teacher may provide instruction on a lesson

while the other circulates assisting students. Often general and special education teachers alternate in the role of the primary teacher, so both have the opportunity to work with students individually.

A second approach for team teaching is to divide the class into two halves and have each teacher provide separate instruction. This can be effective if you are working with students who have a broad range of ability levels. When using this approach, be careful not to use the same groupings consistently. Otherwise, you will be replicating a mini-version of student ability tracking—a practice that is not inclusive.

Often, the special education teacher assumes the role of consultant to the general education teacher. In this model, the special education teacher acts as an expert, providing adaptations for materials, accommodations for tests, and addressing any special needs in the classroom. Being a consultant implies the individual who is the consultant (a special education teacher) may not be directly involved in the process. This can be an effective model as long as both parties participate (Friend & Cook, 1992). Because the special education teacher may not be directly involved in the process of teaching, this requires a role change that may be difficult for a teacher who has been accustomed to direct instruction. Friend and Cook (1992) add that just because a teacher is a consultant does not mean he or she does not collaborate with the other teacher. The planning process the consultant initiates is most effective if it is approached in a collaborative fashion. For example, the special education teacher may bring specific expertise regarding the student with a disability, but planning for that student's needs involves a joint process among all professionals.

As mentioned, for consultation to be effective, both parties must be active participants. The general education teacher must agree to implement programs developed for students with disabilities. In addition, *there must be shared ownership of the students*. That is, the special education teacher cannot make all adaptations for all students who need them. The process of individualized accommodations must be a shared goal and way of teaching for all teachers in the building.

Role of the Students. A sense of collaboration is a critical element not only for the teachers but also for the students. A sense of community must be fostered with *all* students in the building. This must take place on many levels. One level is to foster friendships, which we discuss in depth throughout this book. Another is to encourage cooperation over competition. A cooperative classroom is one in which all members

work together to achieve mutual goals (Sapon-Shevin, 1999). The example about the social studies teacher assignment, adapted from Sapon-Shevin (1999), exemplifies the difference between a cooperative and competitive model for instruction.

As you can see, the outcome of Classroom A, the collaborative approach, is richer and more complex. We presume the students in Classroom A benefited more from the environment that emphasized cooperation and support. The cooperative learning situation allowed all students to take a meaningful part in activities. In an atmosphere of cooperation and support,

---

A DAY IN THE LIFE OF MARGE, THE MIDDLE SCHOOL INTERVENTION SPECIALIST

Social Studies. Marge works with Mr. Crabb, who does not want to share instruction with *any* teacher. Marge assumes the role of consultant here, making accommodations and adaptations for all students who are having problems with the curriculum. She creates study guides and alternative assignments ahead of time and gives those to the students at the beginning of class. During Mr. Crabb's daily lecture, she silently skirts around the room trying to check on student homework and address behavioral issues. Marge is hoping that Mr. Crabb will begin to make some changes for students on his own soon because she feels drained when she leaves.

Science Class. Marge team teaches with Ms. Joy, who loves Marge to collaborate with her on lessons. They often work after school and get energized about the hands-on creative approaches they develop together. While they try to alternate in being lead teacher, they often find that teaming is spontaneous.

They call themselves a "tag team." They have learned much from one another. This class gives Marge her boost for the day.

Math. Marge has a good relationship with Ms. Pickey, but Ms. Pickey prefers that Marge do small group instruction with students who have problems. Usually, Ms. Pickey gives her lecture and Marge pulls a small group to the back of the room for extra help. Marge makes sure the group is not composed of only students with identified handicaps. She notices that Ms. Pickey is beginning to adopt some of her approaches. They seem to be talking more frequently.

English. Mr. Langston seems to enjoy Marge, and she sees that the program is changing as a result of her work in the class. Marge and Mr. Langston work in a variety of ways, depending on the type of assignment and activity. She acts as a consultant and teams with him. For example, for independent reading, Marge has found trade books that are appropriate for her students. She has set up a peer buddy system for language arts writing activities. Marge teams with Mr. Langston when they are introducing a new unit. For example, she may demonstrate in another way what he has just explained to the students.

SOCIAL STUDIES TEACHER ASSIGNMENT: RESEARCH THE APPALACHIAN CULTURE AND MAKE A PRESENTATION TO THE CLASS

Classroom A. Five students work together, meeting during school hours and after school for a period of 2 weeks. They decide to split up the tasks, with some working on research and some making materials for the presentation. José says he would like to gather information on arts and crafts. Mary and Tamminette will look at family values and gender roles. Tamminette comes from an Appalachian family. The group decides it would be great for her to interview her family members. Sherri, the student with a disability, and Fred work on the presentation. They paint a mural depicting arts and crafts and review music to be played in class.

Classroom B. José, Mary, Tamminette, Sherri, and Fred all work separately. Mary is an "A" student who embraces the research portion of the assignment and decides to present a paper to the class. Tamminette decides to bring in some music. José and Fred are confused and do not know how to start the project. They ask Mary and she refuses to help them because she wants to get the best grade in the class. Sherri, the student with a disability, will not be able to participate in this assignment because she cannot do the research or make an individual presentation.

students with disabilities are more likely to experience success, as you can see from the example of Classroom A. In contrast, in the competitive model, Classroom B, Sherri could not

participate and two other students will likely experience difficulty with the assignment.

Cooperative learning groups offer an opportunity for students to take an active role in creating a sense of community in the classroom (Bauer & Sapona, 1991). Interdependence experienced in cooperative learning can empower students by enabling them to recognize their own personal value and can also provide a sense of mutual responsibility (Sapon-Shevin & Schniedewind, 1990). As you can see from the classroom examples, with interdependence, each student's work has importance and is a necessary part of the group project.

Key also for success is for students to have ownership and voice in their education (Baumgart & Giangreco, 1996; Sapona, Bauer, & Phillips, 1989). As Sapon-Shevin (1999) notes, cooperation can be conceptualized broadly as decision making on everything that happens in the classroom. This means providing input on the arrangement and decoration of the environment, the classroom rules, and the topics that might be studied in given areas.

Aspects of Curriculum. A classroom that meets the needs of all learners must embrace the notion that instructional strategies and curriculum will need to be individualized for learner needs. Central to all models of inclusive practice is the selection and adaptation of appropriate strategies and curricula for individual learners. This approach is a foundation of this text. Throughout we provide you with a set of general principles as well as examples of specific adaptations for a variety of learners with moderate to severe disabilities.

Inclusive practice is more than simply individualizing assessment and instruction for individual learners. It involves a paradigm shift as well. As Baumgart and Giangreco (1996) point out, it involves moving from the concept of viewing the child with disabilities as someone who is different and who, therefore, must "fit into the curriculum" to, instead, looking from the viewpoint of associated needs. When making adaptations for learners with different needs, the viewpoint of associated needs requires the teacher to ask, "Who else needs this?" When we examine any classroom closely, we discover that students with disabilities are not the only ones who need adaptations and changes in the instructional strategy, materials, or curriculum. When we look at change from the "associated needs" perspective, we can see clearly the relatedness among all learners. This viewpoint allows the teacher to adapt the instruction to *all* who need it, not just those with the identified disabilities. The example of Andrew provides an application of this principle.

EXAMPLE OF ASSOCIATED NEEDS

Andrew is in a second-grade class. He has difficulty remembering transition times and staying on task when working alone. When the teacher looks at the needs of his entire class, he realizes many other students have these difficulties as well. Therefore, instead of designing materials for Andrew, he designs them for the entire class. The materials he makes for Andrew help many other students. To help Andrew and others remember transition times, he places pictures of clocks showing the time for each transition on the wall in the front of the room. To help students get ready for transitions, he uses a signal of three claps. When he claps three times, students are to stop what they are doing and begin the transition for the next activity. To increase on-task behavior, he develops a motivational system in which random checks are made during seatwork time. All children who are on task receive a sticker. Stickers can earn free time or be redeemed for privileges. Picture prompts of students working independently serve as reminders as well.

As we discussed earlier, for inclusion to be effective, it must include curriculum revamping. For the needs of all students to be met more effectively, we must make the curriculum more relevant and the activities that we use more meaningful for everyone. We discuss this aspect in greater detail later in this Chapter.

Factors Important to Implementation

Many factors contribute to a school that embraces individual differences. Certainly class size, greater operating budgets, and increased staff are desirable for quality education. However, these are not necessary or sufficient for inclusive practice. We have witnessed many schools that have implemented successful inclusion programs without increased expenditures. Factors that do appear critical to successful implementation are attitudes and preparation of the professional staff (Villa, Thousand, Stainback, & Stainback, 1992). Three factors discussed in this section are providing staff development, creating a vision for the school, and ensuring staff supports.

Provide Staff Development. One of the most critical components is the need for staff development for both regular and general education teachers (Malarz, 1996). The paradigm shift of the inclusive model requires learning new ways of teaching as well as assuming new roles. It is well known that many preservice and inservice general education teachers feel ill equipped to teach students who have disabilities (Taylor, Richards, Goldstein, & Schilit, 1997). Because in many cases they did not receive what they consider adequate formal training in this area, this attitude is understandable (Everington, Hamill, & Lubic, 1996). In addition, in the past, special educators have given general educators a hands-off message indicating the special educator is the only professional qualified to work with students with learning problems.

An important approach is to provide training for teachers through inservice or through college course work. Although this is an important component of preparing teachers for inclusion, achievement of inclusive education presumes that no one teacher can be or should be expected to have all of the expertise to meet all the needs of the children in his or her class (Lipsky & Gartner, 1998). Teachers must have support systems that enable them to collaborate on a regular basis (Lipsky & Gartner, 1998). Giving general and special education teachers common time to discuss shared students and to prepare lessons jointly provides excellent opportunities for learning new skills (Everington, Stevens, & Winter, 1999). Common planning time provides teachers the opportunity to share their expertise and to inform each other through discussions around shared students. As general and special education teachers engage in collaborative problem solving around shared students, they informally share information about their disciplines.

Giving teachers opportunities to have increased interaction with persons with disabilities assists in this process as well. We know that teachers may initially have negative views toward students with disabilities, especially students with emotional or behavioral issues (Coleman & Gilliam, 1983; Wilczenski, 1992). However, as teachers' experience with persons with disabilities increases, their attitudes toward persons with disabilities become more positive and their level of confidence in their abilities increases (Everington et al., 1999). With increased contact, teachers are more willing to work with students with disabilities and express a desire to gain the skills needed to teach these students (Giangreco, Dennis, Cloninger, Edelman, & Schattman, 1993). These experiences with persons with disabilities can be either through having them as students in their classes or through experiences outside of the school environment. In sum, experience appears to lessen fears and increase understanding, thus making teachers more amenable to diversity in their classroom.

Evidence also indicates that experience working with students with disabilities helps general education teachers meet needs of typical stu-

dents in their classroom. Teachers who have more experience working with students with disabilities make more modifications and adaptations for all students in their classroom (Stevens, Everington, & Kozar-Kocsis, 1999).

Create a Vision. Leadership is key in any systems change project. When we think of leadership, we think of the school administrator. The administrator plays a key role in school change. In fact, the administrator must be an integral part of initiating and maintaining the change for it to be successful (Huberman & Miles, 1984; Snell, 1998). A leader must set the tone and the vision for the group.

The administrator cannot carry the weight of the change alone. The teachers must share the desire for change and be active participants in creating a vision of what they believe is important about teaching and schooling. The vision needs to encompass a philosophical base and commitment that is articulated and shared by all instructional staff and the administration.

Research on inclusive education indicates successful programs have created a "culture of inclusion," meaning the school is anchored in a sense of community and values diversity (Janney & Snell, 2000). This requires a paradigm shift in which the school culture changes teaching for diversity into the norm rather than teaching for the group (Turnbull, Turnbull, Shank, & Leal, 2000). To create the change to this environment, school staff, students, and community members must have a mental image of this reality.

A part of that vision is to create a common ideal or desired state (Sapon-Shevin, 1999). Webster's *New World Dictionary* (1974) defines the term *vision* as "(a) a mental image, especially an imaginative contemplation; (b) the ability to perceive something not actually visible, as through mental acuteness or keen foresight; or (c) force or power of imagination" (p. 1588).

When creating a vision, these questions must be asked: (1) What do we want our school to look like? (Example: "We want to provide the best education for all students."); (2) What are our most commonly held values? (Examples: "All children can learn." Or "Teaching is an important endeavor.") And (3) How can we achieve those ideals? (Sapon-Shevin, 1999).

Creating shared understandings does not always happen easily or quickly. Time must be provided for this process and the values must be revisited frequently. All stakeholders and everyone in the school community must be involved in discussing the values, norms, and mission of the school (Solomon et al., 1992). This means teachers, office staff, custodians, cafeteria workers, students, parents, and community members must participate. For results to emerge, these discussions must be facilitated and time must be devoted to this process. One principal described using school assemblies to discuss school norms and values (Solomon et al., 1992).

Surveys of successful inclusive schools indicate that some promote and maintain their innovation through decision-making teams or task forces that assist in determining the school's policies and procedures (Schaffner & Buswell, 1996). In this model, the task force must be composed of representatives of all stakeholder groups. The task force can assist in enacting the vision by implementing a strategic plan (Schaffner & Buswell, 1996). For vision to become reality, someone must monitor and ensure the community is staying the course.

Change is not without discomfort and stress for all involved (Villa & Thousand, 1992). We must acknowledge that discomfort is a necessary and vital part of the change process. The administrator must provide support for all involved. The change process can be particularly difficult for the change-makers. One way to combat this is to ensure that those involved are publicly rewarded and acknowledged (Villa & Thousand, 1992).

Provide the Necessary Supports for Teachers. Effective teaching is never easy. Good teaching takes time and effort. The teacher's need for support does not decrease with experience. In

fact, the more experience that teachers have with inclusion, the more they realize they need supports (Everington et al., 1999). Supports include incentives for change, planning time, consultative support, and smaller classes (Roach, 1995). Teachers must know their administration values innovation and good teaching. Like their students, teachers need positive feedback and incentives from both their peers and their superiors. As we have discussed, successful inclusive programs are characterized as warm, caring, collaborative school environments (Janney & Snell, 1996).

 APPLIED CURRICULUM AND SCHOOL-TO-WORK INITIATIVES

In the previous discussion of inclusive practice, we addressed issues regarding where and how teaching should occur. Equally as important is what is taught—the curriculum. Applied academic, community-referenced programs emphasize hands-on activities that students find meaningful (Atkinson, Lunsford, & Hollingsworth, 1993). These kinds of curricula may be particularly valuable not only for students with moderate to severe disabilities but also for typical students because the content is presented in a way that directly connects with the student's experience. This approach enhances generalization and prepares students for skills they need as adults. This section addresses characteristics of applied curricula, provides an overview of some of the primary applied curricular models, and discusses how applied curricula can be linked to inclusive practice.

Characteristics of Applied Curriculum

Applied curricula make a direct connection between the content and the context where that content is used in the real world. Using authentic activities gives students those real-world connections and also allows the teacher to observe the student's actual level of skill acquisition. The student's performance provides a valuable assessment tool for determining how the student is progressing in an applied curriculum. Chapter 5 gives a detailed description of performance assessments. Authentic activities use real materials to construct the activities as they would actually occur in real-life circumstances. They can help students learn practical information to develop competencies that will be useful to them as they access various community settings. These competencies enhance the students' ability to negotiate school life successfully, and because of the likely transfer of these competencies to other settings, provide the students with many of the same skills they need to handle their adult lives effectively. For example, learning how to design and maintain a personal budget gives students the academic skills they need to master math concepts while developing the consumer skills they will need to function successfully as adults.

Authentic learning experiences like personal budget and recipe math activities can give students an opportunity to practice using their knowledge in real situations that may lead to greater independence in the community (Hughes, Rusch, & Curl, 1990). Providing academic instruction in authentic learning environments can further enhance the acquisition of practical knowledge for all students.

Applied instructional methods connect course concepts, materials, and activities to the contexts in which the skills being learned are used. Instruction through authentic learning activities can enhance the experiences of all students in general education classrooms. As you learned earlier in this chapter, if teachers make little attempt to frame instruction in a manner that can actually be used by the students, the students may be unable to make use of the information they receive in school in other environments.

On the other hand, teachers can use an applied curriculum to emphasize the knowledge and skills students need in their personal, social, daily living, and occupational adjustment

(Clark, 1994). Because these kinds of authentic learning experiences offer all students a more meaningful education by making direct connections between the academic content and real-life experiences, they increase the likelihood that those students will make a smooth adjustment to adulthood.

The Classroom Environment. The classroom environment in an applied, community-referenced program promotes academic learning that emphasizes functional, hands-on activities. For example, first graders might learn principles of physics by actually making and flying paper airplanes to understand the concepts of lift, inertia, gravity, and friction (Hagerott, 1997). First graders may not be ready to understand these concepts in depth, but they can begin to investigate the effects of differences in air pressure with this kind of activity. They learn that the plane flies because the air pressure on top of the wings is less than the air pressure below the wings. As they continue their investigation of air pressure, the students discuss how it affects the weather. The students explore related concepts, such as the increased possibility of rain with a low air pressure weather system and that a high pressure system usually indicates sunny weather. They learn to make wise decisions about their daily activities based on that information. For students with moderate to severe disabilities, the teacher might emphasize the need to recognize changes in the weather and choose appropriate clothing for the different conditions. The environments and activities in a classroom that uses an applied approach to learning can encourage students to develop problem-solving skills which allow them to take responsibility for their actions. Students should be encouraged to question the reason for their actions. Whenever possible, individualized learning should take place within a group setting so students develop socialization skills.

Role of the Teacher. If students are to value the information they acquire in school and retain and use that knowledge in their adult lives, we as teachers must place instruction in a framework that allows students to see the practical benefit of what they are being taught. Facilitate learning by taking a role that challenges students, allows them to risk, and enables them to think for themselves (Diem & Katims, 1991). In other words, students should know "why" they do things. As they develop the self-esteem that comes from making responsible decisions, they can internalize and generalize that information to future situations for greater independence. For example, you can show a video that presents a classroom dilemma, such as distractions that interfere with on-task behaviors. After viewing the video, the student can identify and role-play appropriate solutions to determine if they work and why. The students learn they can make good choices and their actions can have beneficial outcomes (Wehmeyer, Agran, & Hughes, 1998). You can build on the students' confidence by prompting them to incorporate the behaviors they practiced during their role play into similar situations they experience in the school and in the community.

Whenever possible, help students interact with peers. Encourage students to take an active role in their education and to draw on their experiences to make learning more meaningful (Hamilton, 1980). Support the students through the learning process and help them realize their potential by building self-esteem through self-directed activities. For example, create a self-monitoring checklist for the student to follow and complete during independent class activities (Wehmeyer et al., 1998). The checklist should contain written directions or pictures of the sequential steps in the activity with a place for students to check each step as they complete it. Students can then refer to the lists and see what they have finished and which step they need to do next without teacher assistance. This kind of support lets the students see what they have accomplished on their own. As students become more self-reliant, they are able to recognize their personal value and feel good about

their accomplishments. In addition, you can avoid giving instruction through traditional approaches such as seatwork by providing hands-on learning experiences whenever possible. You will find many examples of these kinds of learning experiences in Section III of this text.

Role of the Students. Students should not spend most of the school day in their seats. Instead, they should be actively engaged in individualized learning experiences that take place in group settings that will help them develop social and communication skills. In a classroom that utilizes applied curricula through authentic, hands-on activities, it is anticipated students

In a classroom that utilizes applied curricula through authentic, hands-on activities, students will take responsibility for their learning.

will take greater responsibility for their learning. They will become active partners in the learning process and their personal interests and experiences can be recognized and valued. The environments and activities of an applied program will encourage students to develop problem-solving skills, interact with other people, take responsibility for their actions, make good decisions, and experience greater independence.

Applied Curriculum Models

Applied curriculum models have been developed for students with and without disabilities at both the elementary and secondary levels. Some of the formats, such as vocational education courses and school-to-work programs, fall under the umbrella of career education and focus on developing skills for the workplace. Other types of applied curricula may address work competencies but also emphasize non-employment skills such as leisure activity, consumerism, personal development, and volunteerism. These curricula include community-based instruction, service learning, and self-determination programs. We discuss each of these models in this section.

Career Education Curricula. The career education model introduces and prepares students to enter the world of work. It spans the entire school experience, beginning in early grade school and proceeding to high school. Wehman and Kregel (1997) have noted the importance of addressing each of the different stages of career development at specific points. At the elementary level, students should be taught career awareness and begin career exploration. In middle or junior high school, they should continue the career exploration process and begin career preparation activities. High school students need to concentrate on career preparation with job placements at graduation.

Life Centered Career Education (LCCE) is one example of a commercially available career education curriculum based on the competen-

cies that students with disabilities need to develop in order to function as independent adults in the community (Brolin, 1989). The LCCE curriculum offers a systematic effort for integrating academic content with career development and community living skills by identifying necessary competencies and offering applied lesson plans and curriculum materials. Over 1,100 commercially prepared lesson plans are available to accompany the LCCE curriculum (Brolin, 1995). For example, a wide variety of lessons cover topics such as purchasing and cooking foods, marriage and child rearing, recreational activities, and personal finances (Brolin, 1992). Specific examples of career education curricula also are detailed in this text. They include The Kids' Kitchen in Chapter 11 and The Breakfast Place and Classy Cleaners in Chapter 13.

Vocational Education. Vocational education is one kind of career education that typically prepares older students for employment. Many secondary education programs include practical courses such as auto mechanics and home economics. These courses are commonly clustered in a vocational education program. Students taking vocational education courses develop technical skills for a specific industry. These often involve operating the same kind of equipment they will use in the workplace. Some high schools have discontinued many of their on-site vocational education programs. Those offerings are often provided in a different geographic location at a county vocational school. This may present an issue for students with moderate to severe disabilities because, to participate in these programs, they have to leave their supportive home community to attend the county vocational high school.

Vocational teachers can collaborate with general and special education teachers to make curricular connections between their programs and the general curriculum (Beck, Copa, & Pease, 1991). Integrated academic and vocational courses can give students another opportunity to see connections and understand how academic information can be helpful in work settings (Stern & Rahn, 1995). For example, the industrial arts teacher in the vocational program might collaborate with the literature and social studies teachers to present a thematic unit on housing to relate academic course work to the professional knowledge a worker in the construction industry needs. So students interested in becoming architects could learn drafting techniques while students learning carpentry might learn how to use the tools of their trade safely in the vocational program. The students also might make a community excursion to observe a new house being built to explore costs and building materials. At the same time, they discover the locations of significance in social studies classes, such as low-cost housing or historic buildings. In literature classes, they can read biographies of famous Americans in the construction industry, such as John Henry, who helped build the country's railroads, and Frank Lloyd Wright, who was one of America's premier architects.

In another case, students interested in becoming horticulturists and working in a flower shop could develop the technical skills they will need for flower arranging and preservation in the horticulture program. In biology class, they could learn about different types of plants and what conditions are required to maximize plant growth.

We expand this discussion of vocational education for elementary students in Chapter 12 and for secondary students in Chapter 13. These chapters describe specific examples of school projects that combine vocational and academic instruction.

School-to-Work Programs. Another career education model is the school-to-work initiative. In 1991, Lynn Martin, the former secretary of labor, established the Secretary's Commission on Achieving Necessary Skills (SCANS), which produced a report identifying five competencies and three foundations students must acquire to

---

FIGURE 4–2   Workplace Skills Identified in the SCANS Report

Competencies—effective workers can productively use:
- **Resources**—allocating time, money, materials, space, and staff;
- **Interpersonal skills**—working on teams, teaching others, serving customers, leading, negotiating, and working well with people from culturally diverse backgrounds;
- **Information**—acquiring and evaluating data, organizing and maintaining files, interpreting and communicating, and using computers to process information;
- **Systems**—understanding social, organizational, and technological systems, monitoring and correcting performance, and designing or improving systems;
- **Technology**—selecting equipment and tools, applying technology to specific tasks, and maintaining and troubleshooting technologies.

Foundations:
- **Basic skills**—reading, writing, arithmetic and mathematics, speaking, and listening;
- **Thinking skills**—thinking creatively, making decisions, solving problems, seeing things in the mind's eye, knowing how to learn, and reasoning;
- **Personal qualities**—individual responsibility, self-esteem, sociability, self-management, and integrity.

Source: Secretary's Commission on Achieving Necessary Skills. (1991). *What work requires of schools. A SCANS report for America 2000.* Washington, DC: Department of Labor. (ERIC Document Reproduction Service No. ED 332 054)

be successful workers in the modern workplace (Secretary's Commission on Achieving Necessary Skills, 1991) (see Figure 4–2). That report spawned the School-to-Work Opportunities Act of 1994 (P.L. 103–239). It calls for a combined school and work-based initiative with schools and business collaborating to prepare students in kindergarten through postsecondary programs for the world of work in the 21st century (Brolin, 1995).

The curriculum in a school-to-work model would integrate academic and vocational learning and relate that knowledge to segments of a particular industry (Hudelson, 1994). Teachers using the school-to-work approach identify the content and process that students need to learn so they can become competent in the workplace, and then they develop a set of strategies to assist students in learning that information. Students explore career options and learn the needed skills. With help from teachers and counselors, they can create a "career portfolio" that can be used to assess their efforts (Wacker, 1995). The portfolio would profile their employability skills with items such as documentation from work experiences, achievement records, and extracurricular activities. A school-to-work program is an approach to career education that also involves counselors and workplace mentors in helping students determine their career interests, abilities, and goals (Brolin, 1995). This counseling component of school-to-work can be enhanced through the activities of the MAPS process and personal futures planning, which you will learn about in Chapter 5.

Service Learning. Service learning offers another kind of applied approach to learning. It teaches students to be active participants in their communities both as contributing citizens and as productive workers (Hamilton & Hamilton, 1997). Service learning projects have four major components: (1) learning, (2) service, (3) reflection, and (4) celebration. Students provide a needed service without pay to their community that also meets specific curricular objectives and

develops their sense of moral responsibility and community connection as they consider what they have done and celebrate their accomplishments (Gent & Gurecka, 1998). In a service learning curriculum, academic content is applied and connected to providing assistance in the community. Students actively participate in an organized, coordinated effort between the school and the community to provide a service that addresses an identified need in the community ("Service Learning," 1998). Learning actually takes place in community settings, giving students the additional hands-on experience of providing help to those who need support. For example, students might volunteer to shop and run errands for persons in a nursing home (Everington & Stevenson, 1994). Not only do the students gain experience in learning functional community skills through shopping but they also provide companionship to elderly citizens who may have limited access to family and friends. At the same time, the students develop a feeling of competence and self-worth as they reflect on the value of their efforts to help others. Additional examples of service learning activities that take place in community settings are provided in Chapter 14.

Apprenticeships. Apprenticeships can give students a mentoring experience that provides guidance and supports to the students as they actively participate in the workplace to identify and understand their individual vocational interests and skills (Hartoonian & Van Scotter, 1996). Apprenticeships provide the opportunity to give students rigorous and systematic work-based learning experiences that can help them gain specific skills to meet actual industry standards (Hamilton & Hamilton, 1997). The apprentice studies the needed technical skills under the supervision of an expert while learning from and modeling that expert's work behaviors. Apprenticeships can be developed as individual or group experiences. For example, an individual student might work with a professional stage manager as an assistant or a team of students could work with a professional theater set crew to study set design and construction (Miller, Shambaugh, Robinson, & Wimberly, 1995). For additional information on apprenticeships, see Chapter 14.

Community-Based Instruction. Community-based instruction (CBI) refers to teaching students practical skills in the real settings where those skills are actually used (see Figure 4–3). Instruction occurs in the actual environments the student uses at the present time or is anticipated to use in the future. Although it is sometimes thought of as a special education curriculum, community-based instruction can be an effective model for providing a meaningful inclusive curriculum to all students (Beck, Broers, Hogue, Shipstead, & Knowlton, 1994). In community-based integrated instruction, for example, all the students in an economics class might visit a local plant that manufactures electronic equipment. Some of the students might shadow various workers to learn what skills they need to work in that industry, and other students could investigate the production process from raw materials to finished product. At the same time, another group of the students would collect data on factors such as the cost of materials, salaries, and other expenses as well as the gross sales, net profits, and other revenues for later analysis in class. As you will note, both service learning and apprenticeships are examples of projects that involve community-based instruction because they are both learning experiences that take place in community settings. Chapter 14 addresses community-based instruction in depth.

Self-Determination Curricula. Another applied approach is a self-determination curriculum that would address the practical skills needed for successful interactions with co-workers as well as in personal relationships. A self-determination curriculum should address issues related to problem solving, self-reliance, and involvement in the community. Self-determination refers to a person's ability to make re-

FIGURE 4–3   Goals of Community-Based Integrated Instruction (CBII)

1. Students with disabilities have opportunities to model typical peers in structured learning experiences in community settings.
2. Every student has opportunities to practice learned skills in natural settings at his or her own ability level.
3. Teachers collaborate to make meaningful connections for all students with the general education teacher integrating applied curriculum in the classroom and the special education teacher providing instruction in the community.

Source: Beck et al. (1994). Strategies for functional community-based instruction and inclusion for children with mental retardation. *Teaching Exceptional Children, 26*(2), 44–48.

sponsible choices and to act as independently as possible to achieve his or her desired goals (Wehmeyer, 1992). All students need to learn to communicate their needs and wants effectively. As they learn to voice personal choices and solve problems, they will gain a positive sense of themselves. This confidence also will allow them to rely on the internal knowledge they have gained through previous experiences as a basis for understanding new information. Consequently, a self-determination curriculum should teach students to make good personal decisions and communicate them effectively. To accomplish this, self-determination curricula would contain as many of the following components as possible: (a) choice and decision making; (b) goal setting and attainment; (c) problem-solving; (d) self-evaluation, observation, and reinforcement; (e) self-advocacy; (f) self-directed IEP programs; (g) relationships with others; and (h) self-awareness (Test, Karvonen, Wood, Browder, & Algozzine, 2000). Self-determination is covered in greater detail in Chapter 15.

Linking Applied Curricula and Inclusive Practice

Because many applied approaches—service learning, vocational education, and community-based instruction—are generally thought to take place outside of the general classroom environment, some consider these approaches in opposition to inclusive practice, which is assumed to embrace the general classroom curricula and setting. In fact, some have gone as far as advocating that approaches such as community-based instruction occur only after school because this form of instruction segregates persons with disabilities from their general classroom peers (Stainback & Stainback, 1996). We do not see these approaches as incompatible. *It is our position that neither applied curricula approaches nor inclusive practice are special education initiatives.* That is, we believe *all* students can benefit from both and that both are compatible with other initiatives in school renewal.

As we discussed in Chapter 1, we believe general classroom curricula can benefit from a more applied orientation and this instruction can be delivered in inclusive environments. This form of delivery may mean that the place and type of curricula the general education students participate in changes. Examples of this shift are classroom or schoolwide curriculum projects such as the school restaurants described in Chapters 11 and 13.

◆ LINKING INCLUSIVE PRACTICE AND APPLIED CURRICULA WITH EDUCATIONAL REFORM

School districts that are most successful with inclusive practice make special education part of the restructuring process, not a separate agenda (Roach, 1995). As Baumgart and Giangreco (1996) state, "Inclusive education is not a disability issue" (p. 89). It is part of school improvement that seeks to provide meaningful education to a range of students. Therefore, inclusion is very compatible with many current reform and restructuring movements. We briefly review some of the current reforms in education today. As a teacher, you need some understanding of the foundations for current educational reforms so you can visualize and facilitate inclusive practice and applied curricula within those agendas.

The first wave of contemporary school reform started in the 1980s with the *Nation at Risk* (U.S. Department of Education, 1983) report and focused on external factors: higher standards, new curricula, strengthened teacher certification requirements, and increases in funding (Lipsky & Gartner, 1997). However, educational services for students with disabilities were excluded from this movement (Kochar et al., 2000). Further, this emphasis on achieving higher academic levels has made teachers feel overwhelmed and overburdened with the concept of inclusion, and thus they are more likely to be resistant to adopting inclusive practice (Kochhar et al., 2000).

The second wave, which began with the *Goals 2000* in 1993, centers on what Lipsky and Gartner (1997) term a "focus on adults," that is, the parents and teachers. This movement includes teacher empowerment, school-based management, charter schools, parental choice, and vouchers. Many, including Gardner and Lipsky (1997), have called for additional reforms and school restructuring that focuses on learner needs. It is this last call for reform or renewal where inclusive practice fits the most comfortably.

Over the past decade, there has been an increasing awareness of the inadequacy of schools to meet the needs of many learners, particularly those who are culturally, racially, or economically different from the norm (Goodlad, 1994). Many contend that we have simply failed to educate poor and minority students (Goodlad, 1994). This is evidenced by the higher dropout rates and lower achievement of these groups (Orland, 1994). As a result, there has been a strong call for educational renewal (Smith &

Fenstermacher, 1999). Within this context, there have been many areas of suggested change. Three areas of focus are increasing access to knowledge for all students, preparing students to function in a democracy, and creating caring, nurturing communities of learners.

Providing Access to Knowledge. Many believe children and youth who differ culturally, racially, and economically from the norm do not receive the same educational benefits (Oakes & Lipton, 1999). Some contend that this is an access to knowledge issue (Goodlad & Keating, 1994). That is, some groups do not have the same opportunities for a good education. Students from impoverished backgrounds are more likely to be at risk of failure in the educational setting and thus are possibly the most in need of a good education. That is, the achievement of students from minority and economically deprived backgrounds has been historically lower than students from the norm (Lipsky & Gartner, 1996). Hodge (1994) acknowledges those who

are in the most need of excellent curriculum and good teachers are the least likely to get it. It has been shown repeatedly that schools in urban and lower socioeconomic areas are unlikely to get the best trained teachers or to have the best curricula or resources (Darling-Hammond, 1994; Hodge, 1994; Oakes & Lipton, 1999). Therefore, as educators, we must dismantle the barriers for achievement and increase the opportunities for all students.

To compensate for inequities in educational opportunity that children of urban and lower socioeconomic backgrounds face, many have called for changes in school structure, resources, and curriculum. Some of these changes include abandoning ability tracking in schools (Slavin & Braddock, 1994), changes in assessment of student achievement, and differentiated curriculum.

The first aspect, ability tracking, refers to the practice of grouping children by perceived ability. Many researchers contend that tracking is harmful to students who are placed in "lower tracks" because expectations are lower and

TABLE 4–1 Group-Related Differences in Learning Opportunities

Higher-Group Advantages	Lower-Group Advantages
*Curriculum emphasizing concepts and problem solving	Curriculum emphasizing low-level facts and skills
*More time on instruction	More time on discipline
*More active and interactive learning activities	More worksheets and seatwork
*More qualified and experienced teachers	More uncertified and inexperienced teachers
*Extra enrichment activities and resources	Few enrichment opportunities
*More engaging and friendly atmosphere	More alienating and hostile atmosphere
*Hard work as classroom norm	"Not working" as classroom norm

Source: Oakes, J., & Lipton, M. (1999). Access to knowledge: Challenging the techniques, norms, and politics of schooling. In K. Sirotnik & R. Soder (Eds.), *The beat of a different drummer: Essays on education renewal in honor of John I. Goodlad* (pp. 131–150). New York: Peter Lang.

curriculum is less challenging (Oakes & Lipton, 1994). In Table 4–1, Oakes and Lipton (1999) list examples of disparities commonly observed in classrooms based on ability grouping. Laski (1994) argues that the segregated education of people with disabilities is similar to that of minority groups. If you examine the table that highlights low and high ability groups, you will see parallels to the segregated special education classroom. The "low track" of the school is the special education classroom.

The position of inclusive practice is one of increased equity in education for all groups. Inclusive practice is incompatible with tracking because the assumption of inclusion is that the curriculum is differentiated and students are educated in heterogeneous groups. Further, as we have discussed, inclusive models typically employ cooperative learning approaches.

Second, many contend that the standardized assessment practices used to measure educational achievement unfairly penalize students who come from culturally different or minority backgrounds (Ysseldyke, Algozzine, & Thurlow, 2000). In response to this charge, many are calling for a refocusing of assessment practices to using more authentic forms of assessment (Lipsky & Gartner, 1996). Authentic assessment falls under the umbrella of applied curriculum because it employs the evaluation of the student's skill level in the actual performance of a real life task (Sprenger, 1999). Authentic assessment facilitates inclusive instruction because it provides more options in determining student gains. Authentic assessments can more closely measure desired educational outcomes in work, social/interpersonal skills, and independent living. For example, an authentic assessment might involve any of the following: (a) demonstrate understanding by role-playing an interview with an employer, (b) perform the task (operating the cash register in the school store), or (c) provide a portfolio of work samples collected over a period of time that illustrate the development of a particular skill (Knowlton, 1998). For a more detailed description of authentic assessments, see Chapter 5.

Third, the way that students are taught and the expectations of their teachers are important factors in access to knowledge. Hodge (1994) contends that the best strategy for teachers to meet the needs of all students is by becoming skillful in dealing with individual differences, the effects of socioeconomic circumstances, and other factors affecting student learning. This notion implies that teachers must learn to accommodate for individual differences in learning and to be sensitive to differences brought by cultural and socioeconomic factors. This is certainly compatible with the agenda of the inclusive school (Lipsky & Gartner, 1996).

Providing Democratic Educational Environments.   For many, the growing problems in the schools are an outgrowth of the growing problems in our society. This concern highlights the importance of educating our children and youth to be active participants in a democratic society. Preparing citizens for democracy has implications for curricula as well as for school and classroom organization. Implications for curricula include teaching students to think critically, to voice their opinions, and to make and act on their own decisions. The notion of the school's responsibility for preparation of its citizenry for democratic participation is not new. It was espoused by John Dewey early in the 20th century (Dewey, 1959). In a democracy, citizens must learn to behave themselves in a civil manner. This includes learning consideration for the opinions of others and expressing their own needs in socially appropriate ways. Democratic ideals include teaching children to responsibly balance their interests and the collective interests—those of others around them. Certainly, these ideals are best learned in heterogeneous school and classroom environments. How are students to learn how to negotiate effectively in diverse society if they have no experience with others who differ from themselves? Inclusive environments provide this as well as they support values of social justice.

In an applied approach to education, students and teachers are actively engaged with each other. Teachers facilitate learning for students who take greater responsibility by actively participating in the learning process. Students sitting in rows doing isolated tasks and taking written tests do not learn to get along with others or make decisions for themselves. Individualized learning should take place within a group setting so students develop skills in democratic participation (Bauer & Sapona, 1991; Dewey, 1959).

To provide students with experience in democracy, schools must be run in a more democratic fashion. That is, students should be given opportunities to have choices, voice their opinions, and to make decisions in issues relevant to their learning. One such approach is to have class meetings (Glasser, 1986). A democratic group process can provide experiences in problem solving and conflict resolution (Schniedewind, 1993). This type of classroom environment provides applied experiences that should enhance communication and self-determination skills for the workplace and independent living as well as prepare a democratic citizenry.

Providing Caring, Nurturing Environments. An important aspect of school renewal and reform efforts is the realization that schools must become more nurturing and caring environments (Noddings, 1992). Caring and high expectations are essential ingredients for effective education (Wasley, Hample, & Clark, 1997). This means that teachers must care enough to spend time to get to know the students and families in their class, demonstrate genuine concern about their welfare, and have the patience to effect learning in difficult-to-teach students. Caring also means having high expectations. Teachers must believe all students have the capacity to learn and push them to achieve their best (Wasley et al., 1997). By its focus on individual needs and valuing of diversity, the inclusive classroom should lend itself toward a more caring and nurturing environment.

 SUMMARY

This chapter provided an overview of inclusive practice and applied curriculum. Schools that operate with an inclusive philosophy are better able to meet the needs of *all* students. Applied curriculum makes learning relevant to the students and enhances connections with post-school outcomes. Instruction is most effective when it takes place in inclusive classroom, school, and community settings where the teachers make direct connections to the world beyond through activities where experiences are practical and hands-on. Inclusive practice and applied curricula are compatible with educational reform that seeks to make schools more democratic, caring environments that provide access to all learners.

 CHAPTER EXTENDERS

Key Terms and Concepts

1. *Inclusion* refers to providing educational services with the needed supplementary aids and support services in age-appropriate general education classrooms in neighborhood schools.
2. *Associated needs* viewpoint requires that when making modifications and adaptations for individuals with disabilities, the teacher uses the same modification or adaptation for all students in the class who have a similar need.
3. *Applied curriculum* refers to a curriculum that directly relates course concepts to their real-life application.
4. *Authentic environments* are those learning environments situated outside of the classroom or school building.
5. *Authentic activities* include learning in real-life situations and involve the use of real materials.
6. *Community-based instruction* refers to teaching skills in the community settings where those skills are actually used.

7. *Service learning* takes place in community settings and applies academic content to providing assistance to members of that community.
8. *Ability tracking* refers to the practice of grouping children by perceived ability.

Study Guide

1. Discuss the characteristics of an inclusive classroom. What are the roles of the teachers? The students?
2. Discuss the characteristics of an applied curriculum. What is a classroom that implements the approach like?
3. Name three aspects important to implementing an inclusion model in a school.
4. Why is inclusion referred to as a paradigm shift? How is this approach different from traditional models of instruction?
5. List some contemporary educational reforms. What commonalities does inclusive practice have with these current educational reforms?
6. Describe how implementing an applied curriculum enhances an inclusion program.

Small Group Activity I

Break into a small groups. List the skills you think would be necessary to participate in a democracy. What are some ways to teach these skills? What are some strategies to make your classroom more democratic? Generate specific examples of ways students can participate in the decision making.

Small Group Activity II

Break into small groups and discuss ability grouping. Have any of you had personal experience being in a low-ability or a high-ability group? If so, how did it feel? Was it beneficial? What are the advantages of ability grouping? What are the disadvantages?

Small Group Activity III

List the qualities of the best teacher(s) each person in the group has encountered. Break into small groups to compare those qualities and develop a list of the most commonly mentioned characteristics. (It is likely you will identify many personality characteristics that apply to caring, nurturing, and high expectations.) How do we develop these characteristics in our fellow teachers? How can you support other teachers to approach their work with students in a more caring and effective manner?

Field Experience

Visit an inclusive school. Interview the following: (a) the building administrator, (b) at least one special education and general education teacher, and (c) at least one support person (e.g., speech/language pathologist). Address the following in your interview:

1. What is the approach used to serve *all* learners in the general classroom? (Do teachers use differentiated, individualized instruction and cooperative learning?)
2. What is the mission statement of this school? Does it include mention of *all* students?
3. What is the role of the special educator and the support personnel in this model?
4. How was the change process initiated in this school?
5. Was there resistance? If so, how was it addressed?
6. What kind of training did the teachers have?
7. What ongoing supports are present to enable the innovation to continue (e.g., do they have common planning time and access to outside consultation?)?
8. What is the climate of the school? What has been done to promote community?
9. What evidence of accommodations do you see used?

chapter 5

Authentic Assessment in Inclusive Environments

John Clark is a general education teacher. He has just welcomed Marcus, a student who has severe disabilities, is nonverbal, and has some difficulty with ambulation and fine motor skills, into his class. John panics because he knows Marcus will not fit easily into the standard fifth-grade curriculum. What should he do? How can he teach Marcus these skills on the IEP and teach the rest of the class? How can he include Marcus in the curriculum/activities the rest of the class is doing? Can this kid learn anything? Maybe having students like Marcus in the general classroom is a crazy idea after all . . .

John Clark's dilemma exemplifies a situation in which assessment information can be critical. The term *assessment* can have different implications, depending on its use. Luckasson et al. (1992) list four purposes of assessment: (1) eligibility for services, (2) IEP development, (3) instructional evaluation, and (4) identifying supports and evaluating their effectiveness. In this chapter, we address each of these types of assessment and their relevance to teachers.

Regarding eligibility, special education federal legislation (P.L. 94-142 and IDEA) requires nondiscriminatory evaluation for identification and placement in special education. Individual states specify guidelines on the types of assessments required to determine eligibility for special education services. These types of assessments are typically *norm-referenced* instruments that have been standardized on large population samples (Pike & Salend, 1995). There are many types of norm-referenced instruments. The two measures commonly used to establish eligibility for persons with cognitive disabilities are intelligence measures and measures of adaptive skills. Although these instruments have little utility for the teacher

for instructional planning, they can provide useful benchmark information (Pike & Salend, 1995). We briefly discuss some of the more common instruments used for this purpose in the first section of this chapter.

Assessment for IEP development and evaluation of instruction are two critical needs for the classroom teacher that are addressed in depth here. We review various approaches, but this chapter focuses on strategies that are functional and authentic. We describe various approaches to assessment and how information gained from these approaches can be used for instructional planning and evaluation. Then we examine ways you can document student progress on a daily or weekly basis.

A final important function of assessment is to identify and evaluate support needs. To ensure maximum independence, you need to be mindful of strategies for identifying supports for students with disabilities. In the final section of this chapter, we address assessment approaches for identifying natural supports.

NORM-REFERENCED AND TRADITIONAL FORMS OF ASSESSMENT

Norm-referenced tests refer to measures that have been standardized on a large population sample. Their purpose is to compare an individual student's progress to a larger, more typical group. Norm-referenced measures are typically used for determining eligibility for special services. They have been designed to measure many things: intelligence (IQ tests), academic achievement, language ability, adaptive behavior, and human growth/development (developmental scales). Two types of norm-referenced instruments you will surely encounter in your work with persons with cognitive disabilities are intelligence tests (IQ tests) and measures of adaptive behavior. We concentrate on those in this section.

Intelligence Measures

Intelligence measures are designed to provide an indication of the individual's learning ability and intellectual capacity (Brown & Snell, 1993). For classification, individually administered IQ tests are recommended. The current IQ tests provide a global score of intelligence (full scale IQ) as well as measures on verbal and performance domains (Bryant, 1997). The Wechsler scales, including the *Wechsler Preschool and Primary Scale of Intelligence-Revised* (WPPSI-R) (Wechsler, 1989); *Wechsler Intelligence Scale for Children—III* (WISC—III) (Wechsler, 1991); and *Wechsler Adult Intelligence Scale—III* (WAIS—III) (Wechsler, 1998), are the IQ tests most commonly used for eligibility decisions. The Wechsler scales provide a full scale IQ score as well as verbal and performance IQ scores. The full scale score is used for determination of mental retardation.

Additional scales for assessment of intelligence include the *Kaufman Assessment Battery for Children* (K-ABC) (Kaufman & Kaufman, 1983); and the *Stanford-Binet Intelligence Scale—Fourth Edition* (SBIS-4) (Thorndike, Hagen, & Sattler, 1986).

The application of IQ test results for students with moderate to severe disabilities is problematic for several reasons. First, students with moderate to severe disabilities are often not included in the norming samples of many tests; and, second, many students with moderate to severe disabilities do not score on these tests (Brown & Snell, 1993; Snell & Brown, 2000). For example, the lowest score on the *Wechsler Intelligence Scale for Children—III* (WISC—III) (Wechsler, 1991) is 40. Many persons with moderate to severe disabilities may be functioning in an intellectual range below 40. Therefore, the test does not provide accurate information on student functioning.

Second, the very low score that a person with a moderate to severe disability receives does little to predict skill acquisition and later learning potential. At worst, it dampens expectations.

To identify and classify students with moderate to severe disabilities, assessment of adaptive skills is required. Adaptive behavior is composed of two main skill areas: personal independence and social responsibility (Boan & Harrison, 1997). Personal independence are those skills necessary to live independently and to take care of oneself. Examples of skills in this area include community mobility, housekeeping, shopping, food preparation, self-care, employment, and money management. Skills related to the area of social responsibility focus on getting along with others and coping skills. Examples in this area include skills related to socialization, friendships, interpersonal dynamics, and self-control.

Adaptive skills are typically assessed using adaptive behavior assessments. These instruments are given in an interview format to an individual who knows the student well—parent, teacher, or other caregiver. They typically address the adaptive skill areas of communication, domestic skills, self-care, social skills, and functional academics.

Numerous adaptive behavior measures are on the market. Four commonly used adaptive behavior measures you are likely to encounter are *Vineland Adaptive Behavior Scale* (Sparrow, Balla, Cicchetti, 1984); *Scales of Independent Behavior—Revised* (Bruinicks, Woodcock, Weatherman, & Hill, 1996); *AAMR Adaptive Behavior Scale: Residential and Community Scale, Second Edition* (Nirhira, Leland, & Lambert, 1993); and the *AAMR Adaptive Behavior Scale: School 2* (Lambert, Nirhira, & Leland, 1993).

When the adaptive skill interview is completed and the test scored, you will often receive a report similar to Table 5–1, which summarizes the *Vineland Adaptive Behavior Scales* information for Alex, an 18-year-old with moderate disabilities. The first column lists the test domain. In the second column, you see the standard score. The standard score is a converted score that enables comparison to typically

TABLE 5-1   Summary of Alex's Performance on the Vineland Adaptive Behavior Scales

Domain	Standard Score	Percentile Ranking	Adaptive Level	Age Equivalent
Communication	32	<0.1%	Low/Severe	6 yrs 10 months
Daily living skills	45	<0.1%	Low/Severe	7 yrs 3 months
Socialization	36	<0.1%	Low/Severe	6 yrs 0 months
Adaptive composite	38	<0.1%	Low/Severe	6 yrs 8 months

functioning individuals of the same age. Like IQ measures, the standard score is based on a mean (or average) for the general population. As you can see from the table, the standard scores for Alex are well below the population mean of 100. They range from a low of 32 in Communication to a high of 45 in Daily Living Skills. In the next column, you see the percentile ranking, which tells you the percentage of persons who score higher than Alex on this test. As you can see, he is in the first percentile, which means 99% of the general population will score higher on this test than Alex.

The next column, adaptive level, provides another indication of Alex's performance in relation to others. You can see he is listed in the low/severe deficit range.

The final column, age equivalent, references the age typical individuals perform that skill. As you can see from the profile of Alex, his skill level is generally comparable to a 6-year-old. Some of the norm-referenced information presented—percentile rankings, adaptive levels, age equivalents—are not particularly helpful for a teacher of someone like Alex who is 18 years old. In fact, this information can be misleading and stigmatizing because it could result in lowered expectations for Alex.

If we look at Alex's performance on the test domains, we can gain more useful information. You can see Alex has a relative strength in daily living skills. Subdomains within the Daily Living domain include Personal, Domestic, and Com-munity Domains. Alex, his family, and his teachers have worked very diligently to teach him skills in self-care, housekeeping, and community mobility. He continues to have needs in these areas, particularly in relation to community skills such as shopping, banking, and employment.

However, as you can see from his profile, his greatest areas of need are in Communication and Socialization Domains. Subdomains within the Communication Domain are Receptive, Expressive, and Written. Alex is continuing to work on literacy skills, but handwriting is difficult for him. He has begun to use prostheses such as a rubber name stamp in place of a signature. Within the Socialization Domain are the subdomains of Interpersonal Relationships, Play and Leisure Time, and Coping Skills. Alex has been participating with peers in leisure activities—board games and sports—but continues to have more difficulty with interpersonal relationships and coping skills. He experiences problems in controlling his anger or hurt feelings and weighing the consequences of his actions. He has friends, but has difficulty in initiating and maintaining conversations and in expressing his feelings.

Alex's profile of greater needs in communication and socialization areas is common for many persons with cognitive disabilities (Greenspan, 1999). The information gained from his adaptive behavioral profile can be helpful for team and family members because it suggests they pay special attention to making sure that communication and socialization skills are stressed in all environments. In addition, this information suggests the team will want to conduct additional testing in these areas.

Although adaptive skill measures provide some information regarding the individual's functioning relative to others in his or her peer group, they are not considered the best source for IEP development or for evaluation of instruction (Allinder & Siegel, 1999). Because many teachers may receive a report similar to Alex's that summarizes individual performance, referencing instruction to individual skill items is difficult. In addition, adaptive behavior measures are less effective for planning or evaluating instruction because they have too few items, are not tied to the student's curriculum, and often do not directly measure performance (Shinn, 1995).

More recent conceptualizations of adaptive skill assessment focus on functional assessment of the individual within his or her environment (Shalock, 1999). This form of assessment is more useful for the teacher because it focuses on the individual's interests, challenges, assets, and needs within his or her context (Allinder & Siegel, 1999). We discuss this form assessment in depth in the next section. Should evaluations for identification begin to focus more on this type of information, reports may be more useful for teachers in the future.

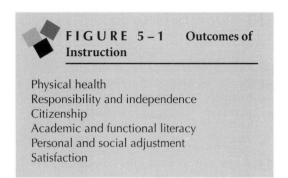

FIGURE 5–1   Outcomes of Instruction

Physical health
Responsibility and independence
Citizenship
Academic and functional literacy
Personal and social adjustment
Satisfaction

What Is Authentic Assessment?

In an attempt to increase accountability for instruction, many states are focusing on outcomes of instruction (Ysseldyke, 1996). Stakeholders—parents, school administrators, community members, legislators, and members of advocacy groups—want clearer definitions of educational goals (outcomes) and better documentation of student progress toward those outcomes. Figure 5–1 presents educational outcomes identified for students with disabilities by the National Center on Educational Outcomes (Ysseldyke, 1996; Ysseldyke et al., 2000).

As you can see from examining the skills listed in the figure, many reflect the adaptive skill domains we discussed earlier: responsibility and independence, academic and functional literacy, and personal and social adjustment. Skill areas that may differ from other taxonomies developed for persons with moderate to severe disabilities are "citizenship" and "satisfaction." Citizenship skills reflect those considered important for participation in a democratic society such as voting, awareness of civic and community issues, conformance to laws and regulations, and involvement in community service or organizations. The inclusion of citizenship as an outcome area for persons with disabilities is in keeping with the reforms in general education, which call for an increased emphasis on democracy (Goodlad, 1994). Many believe that for our democracy to survive, schools must concentrate more on teaching the

AUTHENTIC ASSESSMENT FOR PLANNING AND EVALUATION OF INSTRUCTION

We address four approaches to authentic assessment in this section: (a) curriculum-based assessment, (b) functional and environmental assessment, (c) collaborative, person-centered approaches, and (d) portfolio assessment. We begin by defining authentic assessment and by providing some background on this movement.

skills necessary for citizen participation (Smith & Fenstermacher, 1999).

The area labeled "satisfaction" refers to the relative degree of satisfaction the students and parents have with the education the student has received in the system. This skill area is intended to bring more accountability to the school system.

An outgrowth of the outcomes movement is the emphasis on *authentic assessment,* which is an attempt to link assessment more closely to classroom instruction (Engel, 1994; Pike & Salend, 1995). Authentic assessment differs from traditional forms of assessment because it examines individual growth and performance in relation to a set criteria or standard rather than in relation to population norms (Darling-Hammond & Falk, 1997). This form of assessment focuses on observable and measurable outcomes of learning—the demonstration of learning and the products of learning (Darling-Hammond & Falk, 1997). Because this type of assessment employs multiple forms of evidence, many approaches could be used to determine progress. We examine several types of authentic assessment approaches you can use for both planning and evaluating instruction.

Curriculum-Based Assessment

One form of authentic assessment is *curriculum-based assessment* (CBA), a procedure for determining the instructional needs of a student based on his or her ongoing performance within the current course content (Salvia & Ysseldyke, 1998). This type of assessment generates instructional objectives by focusing on the individual's functioning in relation to the current academic curricula of the classroom or school district (Shinn, 1995). CBA focuses on core academic curricular areas—reading, spelling, writing, and math. This approach is becoming increasingly popular because assessment results are directly related to what is being taught. We can categorize this form of assessment as "authentic" because it relies on measuring the stu-

dent's ability in relation to the grade-level curriculum used in the classroom (Shinn, 1995).

CBA is useful for determining IEP objectives as well as for evaluating the effectiveness of instruction. To determine where to begin instruction, students are assessed on the current curriculum. The many ways to do this vary from informal reading inventories to end-of-unit mastery tests. The information gained from these informal assessments enables the teacher to individualize instruction for students in the class. For example, the reading inventory indicates students are functioning at various grade levels in reading. Teachers can choose materials and activities appropriate for each student's level.

Curriculum-based measurement (CBM) is a form of CBA that generates standardized scores (local norms) on current curriculum for the classroom, building, or district (Shinn, 1995). Because it is norm-referenced, CBM is similar to the traditional testing formats we discussed earlier. CBM differs in that the student is referenced to the present school curriculum rather than to a norm-referenced measure such as an adaptive behavior scale or achievement test. After the testing is complete and results analyzed, the student receives a global score indicating level of proficiency within the curriculum (Fuchs, Fuchs, Hamlett, Phillips, & Bentz, 1994). CBM is an ongoing form of measurement and designed to test fluency—accuracy and speed. Examples of testing strategies for CBM for each content area include the following: (a) reading—read orally for 1 minute; (b) spelling—write dictated words at specified time intervals, (c) writing—write a story for 3 minutes after being given a story starter, (d) math—write answers to problems for 2 minutes (Shinn, 1995).

Curriculum-based measurement has been effective in increasing student achievement in academic areas (Fuchs et al., 1994). It is advantageous for an inclusive classroom because it allows you to individualize instruction more effectively and to enable each student to work at his or her own pace. In addition, CBM and other forms of CBA are excellent ways to monitor students' progress. The timed strategies for CBM are relatively quick to implement.

However, CBM does have some limitations for use with students with moderate to severe disabilities. One disadvantage of CBM is that it is designed to measure fluency—accuracy and speed. Many students with moderate to severe disabilities may remain at the acquisition stage of learning for an extended time period, and thus they may be unable to perform in a test of fluency or speed. Should you use the CBM model for assessment, you will need to make some testing accommodations for these students.

Testing accommodations should be individualized according to student need. For example, for a timed test, the time limits could be extended, particularly if the student is not at the level of fluency on the given skill. If a written response is required and the student has difficulty with handwriting or expression via a written mode, other modalities—use of a computer or an oral response—could be used. For math tests requiring reading (story problems), the problems could be read to the student or recorded on tape. For the student you know cannot read the grade-level text, the text material could be modified or a lower grade level text provided. For example, if it is a schoolwide CBM program and the student is in third grade, a first-grade text could be used for the CBM test.

For modifying the text, the portion used for testing could be rewritten at a lower level of difficulty. We discuss strategies for modifying grade-level text in Chapter 10.

As we indicated earlier, the purpose of CBM is to generate norms for the classroom or the school. When accommodations are made in the testing material or response requirements as discussed here, do not include the test results for that particular student in the class norms. However, the information you have gathered on student performance will be helpful in designing academic objectives.

Finally, as we have learned, students with moderate to severe disabilities have instructional needs in many other adaptive skill areas besides academics, and therefore they require additional means of assessment. For these students, other forms of assessment—functional and environmentally referenced strategies—need to be conducted in addition to the CBA.

Functional and Environmentally Referenced Assessment

Functional or environmentally referenced assessment strategies are sometimes referred to as *ecological assessment.* This type of assessment has been the most common with persons with severe disabilities during the past decade. It can be classified as *environmentally-referenced* because it focuses on what might be termed the *person-environment* match of the individual within the context of his or her current environment and culture (Shalock, 1999). It moves beyond curriculum-based assessment and examines the individual's total needs within the environment, with academics being only one domain of focus. Ecological assessment examines the individual's functioning on important activities in the domains of domestic (home), school, leisure, vocational, and community (Brown & Snell, 2000). It differs from traditional norm-referenced assessment because it shifts the emphasis from what people *are,* which results in establishing an eligibility label, to what they *need,* which focuses on curriculum and supports (Shalock, 1999).

Ecological assessment has several advantages for persons with complex needs. First, it focuses on skills needed in the immediate and future environments. Because students with disabilities have a great deal of difficulty with generalization, there must be a good match between the curriculum and student needs (Dowdy & Smith, 1991; Smith & Dowdy, 1992). Ecological assessment has an advantage over a prepared curriculum because it is referenced to the immediate culture and context. For example, learning to ride a bus is commonly considered functional for many individuals with disabilities. However,

Juan's small town does not have any public transportation. It is not anticipated that Juan will leave his area when he graduates from high school. Therefore, bus riding will not be targeted as a skill for assessment or for instruction. However, if Juan's teacher were using a prepared curriculum guide assessment as her reference of instruction, this skill, which is not important for Juan, might be taught.

Consider another case. Although an art activity—making pottery or baskets—may be considered by some to be a nonfunctional activity, for Tina it was targeted as an important current and future vocational skill. Tina's parents live on an Indian reservation and make their living weaving baskets and making pottery for sale. She has shown an interest in this work, and they would like her to live in their community and work with them. Tina can enhance her skills in this area through taking art classes, and her teacher can work with her to integrate artwork as a means of expression in her academic instruction.

Conducting the Assessment. Ecological assessment is particularly effective for targeting goals for IEP development. One approach frequently used is the ecological inventory (Brown et al., 1979; MacFarlane, 1998). There are several steps for this process. We go through each of the steps and then provide you with some examples. Remember that in the process of assessment, both current and future needs must be considered. Brown et al. (1979) emphasize that the teacher should consider the requirements of independent adult functioning in each domain.

First, identify desired instructional domains— school, domestic (home), leisure, community, and vocational. These domains and the amount of emphasis placed on each will differ according to student needs. For the student who is in a full-time inclusion general education class, the community and domestic domains may receive less attention. The exception would be if applied approaches advocated in this text are used with all students. Then community and domestic domains become integral parts of the instruction plan for the student with disabilities as well. As we have learned, applied curricula incorporates functional community-based curricula for all students.

The age of the student is an important consideration. For an older student, the vocational, community, and domestic domains may receive a stronger emphasis because these are important for transition.

Second, examine in detail the individual's most common current and future environments within each domain. Typical environments for the elementary school domain might include the classroom, cafeteria, playground, restroom, and library. Environments for the community domain would focus on those areas where the class spends the most time and where the student and her family spend the most time out of the school environment.

To determine important skills needed in environments outside of the school environment, parents and caregivers should be surveyed (Brown & Snell, 2000). Environments outside of the school context for a young student might include the neighborhood park and a friend's house. For an older student, this might include the grocery store, movies, a fast-food restaurant, and the mall as well as a friend's house and the neighborhood park.

Third, identify critical activities within each environment. "Critical activities" are the main activities that take place in the given environment. For example, critical activities for Marcus in the school lunchroom include the following:

Lunchroom Activities:

1. Order food.
2. Eat meal.
3. Socialize with others.
4. Use appropriate table manners.
5. Clean up area.
6. Return tray.
7. Line up and return to classroom.

Fourth, assess the individual's performance on the skills required for the activities listed. Once those activities have been targeted, the skills required to perform the activity are identified. For students who lack requisite skills in many of these activities, you may wish to concentrate instruction on only one or two activities. In choosing the activities to examine for a given student, refer to Figure 5–2 on p. 115, to help narrow your focus. For Marcus, we chose to concentrate on activity 1, ordering food, because elements of this activity are compatible with other skills he is learning. Ordering food allows him to use communication skills he is learning in other settings. Making choices enhances self-determination goals on his IEP. In addition, Marcus's family and peer support group has expressed a desire for him to be more independent and have preferenced this activity. For Marcus, we might also concentrate on activity 3, socializing with others. For both activities 1 and 3, we perform a task analysis. The task analysis for ordering food is presented here.

The task analysis is a common approach for identifying skills to complete an activity such as ordering food in the cafeteria. For example, for the activity of ordering food in the cafeteria, the following skills might be identified:

Skills for Activity 1, Ordering Food

1. Stand in line.
2. Get tray.
3. Get napkin and silverware.
4. Wait turn in line.
5. Order food.
6. Get plate of food.
7. Put plate on tray.
8. Move down line.
9. Order drink.
10. Place drink on tray.
11. Select dessert.
12. Place dessert on tray.
13. Retrieve lunch ticket from wallet.
14. Give ticket to cashier.
15. Place ticket in wallet.
16. Pick up tray.
17. Walk with tray.
18. Locate seat with friends/class.
19. Carry tray to seat.
20. Place tray on table.
21. Sit down at seat facing tray.

Depending on the student's needs, a more in-depth analysis may be required. Students who do not have any of the requisite skills in the sequence or who do not reach acquisition quickly may need skills broken down into smaller steps than this example.

Assessment of specific skills can be accomplished by a combining of direct testing and an interview (for the home environment). For direct testing, develop a check sheet listing the required skills and observe the student performing the task. It is sometimes necessary to record the level of assistance that a student needs with each step. The example of Jonelle includes such an approach (see Figure 5–3 on p. 116). The final step is the analysis of performance, which we discuss in the next section. For this, the individual is compared to the performance of typical peers in this area.

It may not be possible to observe student performance on some targeted activities in the home and community domains. In these cases, you can interview a parent, caregiver, sibling, peer, and/or employer or provide them with an ecological inventory to complete.

The Example of Jonelle. The example of Jonelle displays the activities that could be addressed in two environments in her school. To complete the inventory, it would be necessary to examine activities in all of the frequently encountered environments within the school domain: content area classes, restroom, gym, cafeteria, auditorium, library, athletic field, and so on. The rule of thumb in choosing environments is to focus on those where the most time is spent. There may be other environments she occasionally encounters—office of guidance counselor—that would be unnecessary to inventory.

In addition, as we discussed earlier, there are environments outside of the school in which Jonelle spends time—home, leisure, and community. It would be important to gather information from family members on the priority skills needed in those areas. We discuss ways to integrate that information into your planning later in this chapter. However, because Jonelle spends all of her day in the general educational environment, that should be the primary area of focus for skill development.

As you can see from the example, Jonelle can complete activities in each environment, but certain areas need to be addressed for her to function more independently. From the assessment, you can see her performance varies greatly depending on the activity. Some activities—greeting others—she can perform with only a verbal reminder. Others, such as hanging up her coat, she can perform with gestures and partial assistance on a few steps. Still others, such as opening her locker and copying down the information for the day, she is unable to perform without full physical assistance from her teacher.

For instruction, you may wish to target a few skills for direct instruction and provide supports for Jonelle to perform other activities, thus delaying instruction on those. For example, based on Jonelle's performance on the assessment, you might suggest to the team that Jonelle work on the following: greeting others, hanging up her coat, and taking the attendance slips to the office. She was able to perform each of these skills with minimal prompting. There would be other skills you might suggest that instruction be delayed on. We might determine that you can provide supports for her to perform the skills of opening her locker and copying the information from class. You might determine that a peer could assist with opening the locker and might arrange for the teacher to provide a list of important information, thus removing the need for direct instruction on those activities at this time. Decisions regarding what to teach and the amount and type of support

are complex and should be considered carefully by the individual and the team. As we discuss in the next section, the skills identified by the teacher will likely be prioritized by the team.

Determining Priorities for Instruction. Information generated from this type of assessment can be overwhelming. A multitude of needs will become apparent. How do you as a teacher prioritize needs? One of the most critical aspects on which to base priorities are the desires of the individual and his or her family. For example, when you look at the skills the teacher identified for Jonelle, taking attendance to the office was a skill determined to be most critical for the family because this type of skill increases her independence. In addition, from observation, it is apparent that Jonelle really enjoys this; so she is likely to make more rapid progress.

A student's performance can vary, depending on the activity.

Next you may wish to examine the frequency of use. How often does this skill occur during the day? As we know, the more opportunities to teach a skill, the more likely the individual will acquire and maintain the skill. Does the skill contribute to the individual's social acceptance? As we know, acceptance within one's peer group is an important consideration. If you look at the skills the teacher identified for Jonelle, "greeting classmates" is an important skill that would likely result in her increased acceptance. Finally, what are the future needs of this student and how does this instructional goal contribute to those needs? Figure 5–2 provides some guidelines the team may find helpful in determining where to begin instruction.

Disadvantages of the Ecological Approach. When examining activities needed in a given environment, you may tend to focus on the more obvious skills such as self-care, domestic, and academic skills. In many cases, essential communication and social skills may be easily overlooked. As we know, persons with moderate to severe disabilities have critical needs in these areas. Therefore, when conducting an ecological analysis of an environment, be watchful for relevant communication and so-

cialization skills and opportunities to perform those skills.

Strategies for targeting communication skills include examining the communicative demands of the environment, the vocabulary needed, the opportunities presented for teaching communication skills, and the most effective communication modes for the environment or activity (Brown & Snell). If we use the previous example of the cafeteria with Marcus, you can identify the following communication skills in that environment: (1) request food, (2) speak to the cashier, and (3) engage in conversation with peers. All of these skills have specific vocabulary and response requirements and can be adapted for students who use a variety of communication modes. For example, Marcus may not have oral communication but he can point to food he wants, gesture to the cashier, and answer yes/no questions posed by peers during mealtime. For another student who may also be nonverbal, these skills may be addressed through another mode such as a picture book.

Within this activity, you can also identify natural cues for eliciting responses. Teaching the individual to respond to the natural cue alleviates the need for teacher prompt and ensures that the skill will be more likely maintained. If you

F I G U R E 5 – 2   **Suggestions for Prioritizing Instructional Needs**

1. Is the skill important to individual and/or family? (If yes, make high priority)
2. Is the skill relevant to the projected future needs of the individual? (If yes, make high priority)
3. Will the skill enhance social interactions/acceptance with others? (If yes, make high priority)
4. Are there medical or physical limitations that would make acquisition of this skill difficult? (If yes, consider prosthesis or other supports)
5. Are there many opportunities to perform the skill in the current environment? (If yes, make high priority)
6. Is this skill compatible with other skills addressed in other environments? (If yes, make high priority)
7. Is there a history of previous unsuccessful instruction on this goal? (If yes, make *low* priority)
8. Does the student express disinterest or dislike for learning the skill? (If yes, make *low* priority)

Source: Browder, D. M. (1991). Assessment of individuals with severe disabilities: An applied behavior approach to life skills assessment (2nd ed.) (p. 53). Baltimore: Paul H. Brookes Publishing Co.. Adapted with permission.

FIGURE 5-3   Sample of Ecological Assessment for Jonelle, a Middle School Student

CODE: FP = Needs full physical prompts to perform
      PP = Needs partial prompt to perform
      VP = Needs verbal prompt (reminder) to perform

Domain	Environment	Activities	Performance
School	Hallway	Locate locker	✓
		Open lock	FP—cannot do
		Hang up coat	PP
		Deposit unnecessary materials	✓
		Get books needed for class	VP
		Ask for help if needed	✓
		Greet classmates	VP
		Walk through crowded hall	✓
		Find classroom before bell	FP
	Homeroom	Locate seat	✓
		Greet friends	VP
		Sit quietly during announcements	✓
		Sit quietly during Pledge	VP—sings
		Copy down needed information	FP—cannot do
		Perform assigned job—take attendance to office	PP
		Work on seat activity until bell rings	✓—takes out book

look at the communication skills identified for Marcus, you see several natural cues. The cafeteria worker asking, "What do you want?" is a natural cue for providing food names. The cafeteria worker returning his change provides a natural opportunity for Marcus to say or gesture, "thank you." A peer asking a question provides a cue for conversation.

Futures Planning for Older Students. There are times when the current curriculum may not meet the future needs of the student (Dowdy & Smith, 1991; Smith & Dowdy, 1992). Students with disabilities have great difficulties in transitioning to postsecondary employment and independent living. Transition issues are especially crucial for older students. As students get closer to exiting school, you must think more about the future and become more realistic in planning their goals (Dowdy & Smith, 1991; Smith &

Dowdy, 1992). In looking at the future, you should consider postsecondary training as well as employment. In futures planning, all information—including performance on norm-referenced tests—is considered.

Collaborative, Person-Centered Approaches to Assessment and Planning

Ecological approaches to assessment are helpful and the information gained from such assessment strategies is critical for identifying skill areas and strengths. However, this is not the last step in assessment. You must translate that information into IEP goals, curriculum, and instructional strategies. As we have discussed throughout this text, assessment and planning must be a collaborative process centering on the needs of the individual. Several structured approaches have been developed to enable teams to work in ways that are more collaborative and *person centered*. These approaches tend to differ from traditional assessment and planning in three ways:

1. They focus more on the *process* of generating the student's needs. The composition of the team and the process they use for generating goals is very important. As you will see, each approach has a prescribed list of steps the group should follow in targeting goals for instruction.
2. They have an increased focus on the individual and his or her family and friends. Hence, they are person centered (Knowlton, 1998). Focusing on the vision for the individual is an important part of this type of approach (Jorgensen, 1992).
3. These approaches tend to be more informal. Creating an atmosphere of comfort and cooperation is important. For example, the team might meet at a restaurant or a home (Knowlton, 1998).

This is not to discount the information gained from teacher-made assessments such as ecological inventories and CBM. This information is very valuable for the team in the decision-making process for the educational plan.

Two person-centered approaches that have been used are *MAPS* (Vandercook, York, & Forest, 1989) and *PATH* (Pearpoint, O'Brien, & Forest, 1993). We discuss each one and compare the approaches.

MAPS. *McGill Action Planning System* (MAPS) (Vandercook et al., 1989) is probably the first approach of this type. MAPS is a form of futures planning that focuses on inclusion in regular education settings. The team composition and group planning are critical elements. The team is generally composed of the individual, family members, teachers (general and special education), and peers (friends). Friends are an integral

---

FIGURE 5-4   Steps of MAPS

1. What is *(student's)* history?
2. What are your dreams for _____?
3. What is your nightmare?
4. Who is _____?
5. What are _____ strengths, gifts, and talents?
6. What are _____ needs?
7. What would an ideal day at school look like and what must be done to make it happen?

Source: Reprinted with permission from Forest, M., & Lusthaus, E. (1990). Everyone belongs with the MAPS action planning system. *Teaching Exceptional Children* 22(2), Copyright The Council for Exceptional Children.

---

part of this process so much so that the authors do not recommend having the MAPS meeting until the individual has been in the general education environment for a few months. This allows time for friendships to form and to identify peer members of the planning team.

The planning should occur after school so siblings and other family members who might not typically attend can be present. The process used should be similar to the one presented in Figure 5–4. One of the purposes of this process is to identify a vision for the individual.

The MAPS approach is good step in generating natural supports among family, peers, and other adults in the building. The student should emerge from the MAPS planning meeting with general goals identified and persons responsible. The steps for "Suggestions for Prioritizing Instructional Needs" in Figure 5–2 might be useful as a follow-up activity because it provides a framework for narrowing goals and objectives for the IEP.

PATH. PATH stands for *Planning Alternative Tomorrows with Hope.* The authors, Pearpoint et al. (1996), explain it is an expansion of the MAPS approach. PATH provides a framework

MAPS PLANNING EXAMPLE FOR MARIA, AGE 10

Present at the meeting: Maria, her mother (Perfedia), the school principal (April Dawn), the special needs teacher (Dan Poythress), general education teacher (Sue Clover), and three of Maria's circle of friends: Juanita, Julie, and Peggy.

1. **What is Maria's history?**

Maria had been placed in segregated school run by the county board of mental retardation for grades 1–2. She has been in her neighborhood school for the past 2 years. She was in a segregated special education classroom for the first year and has been in the fourth-grade general education classroom this year. Maria's teacher has started a circle of friends program for Maria, and there are five students that are very involved with Maria. Maria's parents are from Central America, and Spanish is the primary language spoken in the home. Maria's parents are very involved in her program.

2. **What are your dreams for Maria?**

Maria's mother wants her to get married, to have children, and, most of all, to be happy. Maria wants to learn how to read better. Her friend Juanita wants her to be able to talk to people better (Maria interrupts and goes off topic frequently). Julie wants Maria to be able to defend herself when the class bully teases her. Dan, the special needs teacher, wants her to improve her social skills with other students and to stay on task longer. Sue, the general education teacher, would like to find ways for her to participate more in the regular curriculum.

3. **What is your nightmare?**

All agreed that their worst nightmare was for Maria to be taken advantage of by others. They worry that she is too friendly and trusting.

4. **Who is Maria?**

A variety of descriptors were supplied by the participants. Among them were cute, silly, crazy, happy, stubborn, friendly, a hard worker, dedicated, funny, and fun.

5. **What are Maria's strengths, gifts, and talents?**

Many agreed that Maria's good nature was one of her greatest strengths. She is friendly and outgoing. She is not afraid to try new things. She is on the girl's soccer team and a member of a Girl Scout troop. Maria's teacher shares some of the strengths she identified in her ecological assessment. She found that Maria is good at domestic and community skills and works hard at jobs in the school.

6. **What are Maria's needs?**

Maria needs some support in all areas. She particularly needs support with academic, social, self-care, and communication skills as identified by the teacher. She takes medication and will need some health care assistance. She needs help from the special needs teacher for assistance in adapting the class curriculum. She needs her friends to provide support during the day in various activities. She needs the assistance of a speech and language pathologist for improvement of her communication skills. She has hemiplegia and, therefore, does not have full usage of one side of her body. She needs an occupational therapist for adaptations for feeding and a physical therapist for improvement of ambulation.

7. **What would an ideal day at school look like and what must be done to make it happen?**

All agreed that Maria has made an excellent transition into the general education classroom. She wants to stay in the room. She will participate in all classroom activities. She will need to continue to receive therapy. The speech/language pathologist will work with her and other students who need her services within the general classroom. Maria will leave the room two times a week, during individual work time, to receive physical therapy. Her circle of friends will provide assistance with helping her to stay on task and with communication goals. Dan and Sue, Maria's teachers, will adapt her reading, language arts, and math lessons. Maria's mother will continue to involve her in after-school activities and to work on team-identified goals. The principal, April Dawn, will ensure that Dan and Sue have a common planning time so they can collaborate on Maria's program.

for the team to do a more in-depth examination of the student's current setting and needs than MAPS (see Figure 5–5). This appears to be an excellent approach to use with individuals who have very complex support needs. For example, PATH would be needed for an individual who has complex behavioral or medical needs that the team has had difficulty addressing conventionally.

The example of a PATH process for Ronnie, using the steps outlined in Figure 5–5, describes the situation of a student who has experienced significant behavioral challenges. Using the eight-step PATH process, a facilitator guided the team through an assessment of this situation. At the conclusion, the team was able to clarify its goals for him and to seek more positive solutions. Participants in the team included Ronnie, his parents, all teachers who work with Ronnie, two teaching assistants, and the building principal.

Portfolio Assessment

As we indicated earlier, states have mandated identifying learner outcomes and instituting procedures for accurately measuring student performance on outcomes. One of the assessment reforms that many districts and some states—California, Vermont, and Kentucky—have chosen to implement is portfolio assessment. A *portfolio* can be defined as a collection of products of what a person has done and, by inference, what the student is capable of doing (Salvia & Ysseldyke, 1998). This form of assessment has been traditionally used in art, design, and music areas. However, portfolio assessment can be particularly useful in displaying progress for persons with moderate to severe disabilities. This form of progress monitoring can mesh well with other approaches we have discussed. The portfolio can be used as a way to collect information on the goals and activities targeted though the MAPS or PATH planning session.

Portfolio assessment has many advantages. First, it is believed this form of assessment can show higher levels of understanding than tradi-

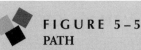

FIGURE 5–5   Steps for PATH

1. Touching the dream
2. Sensing the goal
3. Grounding in the now
4. Identifying people to enroll
5. Recognizing ways to build strength
6. Charting action for the next few months
7. Planning next month's work
8. Committing to the first step

Source: Stainback, S., & Stainback, W. (Eds.) (1996). *Inclusion: A guide for educators* (p. 80). Baltimore: Paul H. Brookes. Adapted with permission. Available from Inclusion Press, www.inclusion. com.

tional assessment because the creation of final products requires synthesis and application of the learned material. Second, portfolio assessment offers multiple indicators of performance. Most portfolios contain samples of different types of materials. Third, some believe this form of assessment displays the achievement of students with special needs better than traditional forms of assessment (Carpenter, Ray, & Bloom, 1995). Finally, because portfolios display personal achievement and you can always find some artifacts for each child, this form of assessment can build confidence and self-esteem in students (Engel, 1994) and cultivate a base of support from the parents.

What Should Be in a Portfolio?   Consider the contents of a portfolio carefully so it presents an accurate reflection of the student's abilities without overwhelming the reader. Typically, portfolios contain a variety of types of student products including videotapes, photos, drawings, samples of written work, checklists, and anecdotal observations made by the teacher (Gelfer & Perkins, 1992; Wesson & King, 1996).

As part of its educational reform, Kentucky has mandated performance-based assessment for all students (Kleinert, Kearns, & Kennedy, 1997). Students with moderate to severe disabilities participate in the alternate portfolio

A PATH PROCESS EXAMPLE FOR RONNIE, AGE 8

1. **Touching the dream.** The team identified that their dream for Ronnie is to be able to attend the general education class for a full day without significant behavioral problems.

2. **Sensing the goal.** For this, the team identified a goal that was attainable within a year. The team decided that by next year, they would like for Ronnie to be back in the general education classroom full time.

3. **Grounding in the now.** The members admitted that the present situation has reached a crisis state. Ronnie is no longer being taught in the general education classroom. Ronnie blows up when requests are made and is aggressive with peers when they interact with him. Whenever, he is given independence of any kind, he "blows it." To stop the outbursts, he has been receiving instruction in a storage room all day. His behavior has further deteriorated, and he is now lashing out at others in that setting. Teachers and assistants take turns in providing individual instruction. All agree that this is not what they want for Ronnie, but do not feel they can see options at this time. Emotions have been running high. Many people no longer like Ronnie.

4. **Identifying people to enroll.** A conclusion is reached by the group that outside assistance will be necessary. There have been several suggestions. All agree that a quick fix is not the best approach and that time is needed to defuse the situation. One suggestion is to secure the services of the district behavior management specialist to do a series of observations and to work with the team over a period of time. Another suggestion is to contact the local university. A special education professor indicated that she has graduate students taking a positive behavior support class that need field hours. These students could provide additional support for the team. Another suggestion is to build a stronger base of student support for Ronnie because he has no friends. A final suggestion is to determine if Ronnie would benefit from a return to medication for his attention and impulse control problems. His parents say he benefited in the past.

5. **Recognizing ways to build strength.** To build strength, the team agreed that they need to meet more frequently, use outside help, and to keep in close contact with the family.

6. **Charting action for the next few months.** The group agreed that all suggestions: contacting the behavior management specialist and university professor, investigating medication, and starting a student support group will be tried. They have agreed to delay the referral for home-based instruction until these other avenues are investigated and suggestions tried.

7. **Planning next month's work.** All will meet on a weekly basis for the next month. The special education and general education teachers have agreed to record their interactions with Ronnie more carefully during the next weeks.

8. **Committing to the first step.** Assignments have been made for contacts. His father agreed to investigate the medication. The school principal has agreed to contact the behavior management specialist. The reading teacher has agreed to contact the special education professor at the university. The general and special education teachers have agreed to come up with a plan for a student group.

assessment project (Kleinert et al., 1997). The following six items are considered essential for every alternate portfolio for students with disabilities in Kentucky (Kleinert et al., 1997):

1. Documentation of the student's primary mode of communication.
2. A copy of the student's daily/weekly schedule (may be in picture form).
3. A student letter to the reviewer indicating why entries were chosen.
4. Samples of projects and investigations from one or more of the learner outcome categories.
5. A work resume for students in the 12th grade.
6. A letter from parents or guardians indicating the level of satisfaction with the portfolio entries.

Suggestions for Creating Portfolios. It is important to keep the portfolio work current. Whenever possible, the student should provide input on the items selected for entry. The entries should reflect the best work to date. It is preferable that there be fewer items of the best quality. Items can be saved to show growth over time. Thus you can organize the presentation to reflect current and past works. In terms of the document itself, many recommend that the teacher use an expandable file (Gelfer & Perkins, 1992) and organize items by subject area (Wesson & King, 1996).

We provide examples of portfolios for two different students. The first is Annie, a 12th-grade student with a moderate disability. Her ecological inventory identified strengths in verbal communication and primary-level academic skills. Her MAPS planning team helped her identify employment and social skills as the main areas of instruction for this year. Because Annie is able to write at a primary level, she is able to include a paragraph about herself. In addition, Annie's work-study teacher uses her portfolio when they role-play job interviews. In contrast, the second portfolio is for Dorian, an

SAMPLE PORTFOLIO FOR ANNIE, A HIGH SCHOOL STUDENT

1. A videotape of Annie working at her job busing tables at Pedro's Restaurant.
2. Sample job application that Annie has completed.
3. A resume containing Annie's work experience (includes in-school jobs), volunteer work in the community, club membership, and career goals.
4. Skill checklist for Annie for her duties at the restaurant.
5. A sample of Annie's work in her consumer math class.
6. A list of the clubs/activities that Annie has been involved in while in school and description of her role in these clubs.
7. A sample of artwork from her high school art class.
8. A photograph of Annie presenting with her group in American history class and a description of the project.
9. A brief written statement from Annie. (Title: "Who is Annie?")
10. List of current IEP goals and progress updates.

elementary student who is nonverbal. Attention is paid to work experience, but more emphasis is placed on documenting his communication accomplishments and his relationships with his peers (see circle of friends entry). These were the primary areas targeted for Dorian.

Disadvantages of Portfolios. Portfolios can be very time consuming for the teacher (Carpenter et al., 1995). Grading can be difficult. Some approaches recommend developing a rating scale or scoring rubric for rating portfolios (Kleinert et al., 1997). Using this type of system, each

SAMPLE PORTFOLIO FOR DORIAN, A THIRD-GRADE STUDENT

1. A list of Dorian's current IEP goals and performance indicators.
2. Videotape of Dorian performing two classroom jobs: handing out materials and watering plants.
3. A skill checklist displaying mastery and progress for Dorian's in-school jobs.
4. A sample of the picture vocabulary for Dorian's communication board and description of his communication modes.
5. A videotape of Dorian using his communication board with gestures.
6. A sample from an art project from this year.
7. A sample picture story that Dorian completed with a class peer in creative writing class.
8. A photograph of Dorian's circle of friends, list of their names, and description of the role that each plays.
9. A transcription of the last MAPS meeting and goals.
10. A sample counting assignment that Dorian completed in math class.

portfolio receives a score. However, studies examining how teachers score portfolios indicate it can be difficult for them to establish reliable rating systems (Kleinert et al., 1997). That is, the same teacher might give two students who have done similar work very different scores. This is a disadvantage if the portfolio is the sole means used to determine grades and progress in the curriculum. Clearly, other forms of assessment that are more objective—ecological inventories and curriculum-based assessments—are also needed to display progress and to identify goals.

DOCUMENTING INSTRUCTIONAL PROGRESS

As we have discussed, documenting instructional progress is essential. As you have learned in this chapter, there are many ways to determine instructional goals and objectives: ecological inventories, MAPS, PATH, and so on. These strategies are excellent for planning and goal setting but are not practical for more frequent—daily or weekly—assessment of student progress. Teachers frequently have difficulties in knowing when they have reached their instructional goals (Ysseldyke, 1996). For teachers who work with students with significant disabilities, finding ways to record progress is particularly critical. Often, these students may work for a long period of time on a single goal. Teachers may need to develop finite measures to show that progress has, indeed, been made. Progress documentation is not only important for accountability to the stakeholders—student, parents, school—but also for you as a teacher. You need to see that you are making a difference in your students' lives.

As we indicated earlier, authentic assessment examines the demonstration of learning and the products of learning (Darling-Hammond & Falk, 1997). This type of assessment focuses on observable and measurable student outcomes. In academic areas, traditional teacher-made tests involve multiple-choice or other objective test formats. Because students with disabilities may have difficulty taking these types of written tests, authentic assessment strategies are uniquely suited for this population. Therefore, your assessment strategies should consist of direct observation of students performing the targeted skills, whenever possible. In this section, we discuss ways to document your student's progress on his or her instructional objectives. In Chapter 8 we provide additional information on different types of recording for social skills and behavioral issues. Regardless of the measurement approach used, you must devise a system you can implement comfortably, without a great deal of effort. Otherwise, you will not use the system (Kerr & Nelson, 1998). The more you record behavior, the better your systems will become as you continually refine them.

Anecdotal Observations

Anecdotal formats involve your observations over time and are informal. For this type of recording, you write down your observations at the end of the day or during the day as you observe the target behaviors. Some strategies for anecdotal recording include the following: notebooks for each child, note cards for each child, or self-stick removable notes that are transferred to the student's file (Pike & Salend, 1995). This type of recording has the advantage of providing rich details in many areas but the disadvantage that it is not systematic. The critical aspect is to develop a system for recording on a regular basis. Otherwise you will be unable to see progress with many students.

Teacher-Made Informal Assessments

Teachers are accustomed to making their own tests. These can be paper-and-pencil tests of academic skills or performance-based measures. We discuss paper-and-pencil tests first. Students with moderate to severe disabilities will most likely be able to participate in the academic curriculum at some level (possibly not at the same level as the rest of the class). Frequently, tests given by the teacher must be modified. There are a number of testing modifications strategies you may find useful (Burns, 1998). Reading or tape-recording instructions enables you to individualize instructions for persons who may need additional information or who may have a modified test. Taped instructions can be helpful to students as well because they can play them again as needed. Using special seating or alternative testing locations, such as giving the test in another room, can assist students with attention difficulties. Prosthetic aids such as calculators can help individuals participate in tests.

Write down your observations during the day as you observe the targeted behaviors.

FIGURE 5–6 Checklist for Opening Activities for School Restaurant

Student Name ____________________

Codes: I = completed task independently

V = needed verbal reminder

D = demonstration or cue card used

FP = physical prompt needed to perform activity

Skill / Days	Comments 1	2	3	4	5
1. Turn on lights.					
2. Start coffeemaker.					
3. Wipe tables.					
4. Wipe counter.					
5. Sweep floor.					
6. Put bowl of fruit, crackers, granola bars on counter.					
7. Get out toaster tarts.					
8. Place toaster tart labels on menu.					
9. Put cups, lids, stirrers, cream, sugar, by coffee maker.					
10. Get out cash box.					
11. Put OPEN sign on the door.					
12. Open the door.					
13. Greet co-workers as they arrive.					

Tape-recording answers can be effective for students who have difficulties with handwriting. The content of the test can be altered as well. Items can be simplified or the number of test items decreased. As we discuss in later chapters when we address curriculum modifications, you are only limited by your creativity.

Performance-Based Assessment

In performance-based assessment, the student performs the skill in the training or generalization setting to determine mastery. This type of assessment is very common for persons with moderate to severe disabilities. To determine mastery, you might use a checklist similar to the ecological inventory checklists we constructed earlier. The difference is that this type of checklist is used to measure progress on a daily and weekly basis. Your checklist will change as your students expand their skill repertoire within the teaching environment. Figure 5–6 displays a checklist for one phase of the student-run restaurant—the opening. As you can see from the example, this checklist could be used for more than one student. To test more than one student on these skills, change the "days" column to insert student initials. Using this strategy, progress for five students could be recorded on this form daily.

Measures of Frequency and Duration. In many instances you will want to track the number of times (frequency) a behavior occurs during a specified time period (hour or day) or the length of time (duration) in which the individual engages in the behavior. Both of these recordings are discussed in greater detail in Chapter 8 when

FIGURE 5–7   **Number of Times Mavis Starts a Conversation with Peers and Duration of Conversation**

Activity	Date	Time began/ended	# of times	Duration	Comments
Lunch	11/5/99	11:30–12:00	1	2 min	She is having difficulty in keeping conversation going. Peers tend to talk to someone else.
			2	<1 min	
			1	2–3 min	
Freetime in class	11/5/99	2:00–2:15	1	<1 min	Peer talking to someone else. Talked to Joey about bus for 2 minutes.
			1	2 min	

we address behavioral interventions. An example of a frequency recording is the number of times a student engages others in appropriate conversation during lunchtime. An example of a durational recording is the length of time the student spends engaged in a conversation with others. For an example of a data collection procedure that measures both frequency and duration, see Figure 5–7.

Task Analysis.   Task analysis is an effective method for skill instruction. As we discussed earlier, for some students, skills from activity checklists need to be broken down into individual steps. Consider the activity checklist for the school restaurant in Figure 5–6. Starting the coffeemaker is a skill many students may find difficult. The teacher may need to conduct direct instruction on this skill or develop some adaptations so the student can perform the skill independently. Figure 5–8 shows a task analysis of this skill. Below is a task analysis for this skill using a particular brand of coffeemaker. As brands differ in the assemblage of parts, the task analyses may differ.

As you can see from the task analysis for Miron, he can perform many of the skills with only a verbal reminder. Because the skill of measuring the six scoops of coffee—step 4— was very difficult for Miron, the teacher de-

cided to make an adaptation by finding a large scoop that contained the amount needed to fill six scoops, thus eliminating the need to teach that skill. For the other skills, as Miron was nearing acquisition, she decided to make a picture sequence of the steps for making coffee. The pictures served as prompts for Miron to complete the sequence. The only skill that the teacher determined needed direct instruction was step 11, pouring the water from the pot into the maker.

Permanent Products.   Permanent products are tangible items or outcomes of instruction (Alberto & Troutman, 1999). Teachers have many artifacts they can save to display student progress over time. Permanent products teachers typically have access to are student written work and creative efforts. Tests are the most commonly used way to show progress. For students with moderate to severe disabilities, keeping samples of student daily work may provide a more sensitive picture of progress over time. Teachers can also take photographs of student work such as a student making a presentation to the class or pictures of students working together on a project. Videotapes can be considered permanent products because they can be referred to repeatedly. The portfolio assessment we discussed earlier in the chapter typically

FIGURE 5–8   **Coffeemaker Data Sheet**

Student: <u>Miron</u>   **Date:** _____
Codes: ✓ = performs independently
             V = needs reminder
             M = needs model or demonstration
             F = needs physical prompt

Skill	Performance	Teaching Decision
1. Remove the top basket from the maker.	✓	
2. Remove the lid from the coffee can.	✓	
3. Locate the coffee scoop.	V	Picture of step
4. Measure 6 scoops, putting each into the basket.	F	Make adaptation
5. Place the basket back in the maker.	V	Picture of step
6. Remove the glass coffeepot from the maker.	V	Picture of step
7. Take the pot to the sink.	V	Picture of step
8. Turn on the water.	✓	
9. Fill the pot to the red line.	M	Picture of step
10. Take the pot to the maker.	V	Picture of step
11. Pour the contents of the pot into the top of the maker, trying not to spill.	F	Practice skill
12. Return the empty pot to the bottom of the maker.	V	Picture of step
13. Push the red ON button on the maker.	✓	
14. Wait until the pot has filled before removing.	✓	

combines many forms of permanent product assessment with some observational information. For the portfolio, the best examples of each type are saved and displayed.

Self-Recording. Whenever possible, students with disabilities must take an active role in the instructional process (Carr, 1997). One of the best ways for students to take responsibility for their own learning is to encourage self-recording of their own progress. This includes setting goals for learning, recording progress, and providing self-reinforcement (Workman & Katz, 1995). In Chapter 8, we provided more detail on this process. There are many ways for students to have a more active role in instructional progress monitoring. Students can keep daily journals in which they reflect on their learning and their progress. If this is not feasible, checklists can be devised for students to record

their progress. Some students may need more concrete reminders. For example, Towanda's teacher wanted her to see her improvement in math. For each problem she completed correctly, she colored a square on a bar that had five squares. When the bar was filled, she obtained a sticker. The number of stickers earned daily were posted on a monthly chart. This served both as a nice reminder and a reinforcer for Towanda.

Figure 5–9 is an example of a self-recording data sheet for self-evaluation of class participation for a student who was having difficulties paying attention to class activities and remembering to raise her hand before speaking. This chart provided prompts for her in regard to appropriate behavior and assisted her in judging her success in meeting her behavioral goals. It must be emphasized that students must be taught to self-record.

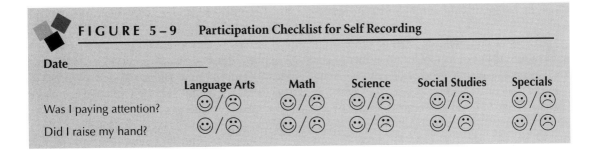

FIGURE 5–9   Participation Checklist for Self Recording

Date_____

	Language Arts	Math	Science	Social Studies	Specials
Was I paying attention?	☺/☹	☺/☹	☺/☹	☺/☹	☺/☹
Did I raise my hand?	☺/☹	☺/☹	☺/☹	☺/☹	☺/☹

STRATEGIES FOR DETERMINING SUPPORT FOR PLANNING AND INSTRUCTIONAL PROGRESS

As we have discussed throughout this book, supports are essential for maintaining persons with moderate to severe disabilities in inclusive environments. We believe that support should be an important consideration when developing goals and assessing progress. Whenever possible, we want to encourage what many call *natural supports* so the individual can function as independently as possible in the environment, with minimal intervention from the teacher or other adults. The following is a definition for natural supports:

> Natural supports are these components of an educational program—philosophy, policies, people, materials, teacher, and curriculum—that are used to enable all students to be fully participating members of school and community life. Natural supports bring children closer together as friends and learning partners rather than isolating them. (Jorgensen, 1992, p. 183).

When we think of supports, we often consider just the human supports—help from a teacher or other adult. Support means much more than that, and we must broaden our thinking to embrace a bigger picture. Heal and Tassé (1999) suggest considering the following four support dimensions when planning instruction or when conducting assessment. These dimensions are not presented in a hierarchy and should be individualized.

1. **Prosthetic:** What kinds of assistive technology or environmental changes will help the person function more independently?
2. **Motivation:** Is motivation—self-support—needed to help the individual function more independently?
3. **Supervision:** What kind of supervision is needed? Can you use peers to assist?
4. **Human Assistance:** What kind of prompts—verbal or physical—are needed?

When you consider what this means in terms of planning, it implies you may want to assess and plan in a multidimensional way. That is, you might not only ask yourself questions about the level of skill performance in a given area, but also what kind of supports are needed to enhance performance. Like the other strategies discussed in this chapter, you can integrate this information into the MAPS or PATH planning process as well as in the IEP. Support is an important component of any planning process and should be addressed.

For the first dimension, prosthetics, you can consider the design and seating arrangements in our classroom. Does seating the student closer to the door afford more independence? What assistive devices are available to aid functioning? For example, will using adapted silverware enable independent eating? If so, it will eliminate the need for instructional assistance for this skill at this time. What other support is available to assist the person in functioning more independently?

When you consider the second dimension, motivation, think of empowering students and decreasing the characteristics of learned helplessness and outerdirectedness we discussed in Chapter 2. When you assess your students, ask yourself if they are displaying those characteristics. If so, how can you address that in your plans? Teaching students to self-record and evaluate their own behavior is one way to increase motivation. Positive supports are essential. Everyone—teachers and peers—must provide positive feedback and support at a high rate. In addition, when you involve the student in the planning process, you are more likely to have increased motivation for learning.

When you consider the third dimension, supervision, reference age-appropriate peers as instructional supports whenever possible. However, when examining peer support, you need to look at the quality of the interactions that occur with nonhandicapped peers. Is the student with a disability treated as an object of pity, object of amusement, or as an infant in need of care? Is it a friendship or caretaker relationship? If appropriate student support does not exist, how can you, as the classroom teacher, encourage it? Building a classroom community that embraces diversity is one of the first steps to overcoming some of those obstacles. Some of the collaborative, person-centered, planning strategies—MAPS and PATH—discussed earlier enhance the probability of positive peer support. We discuss other strategies such as peer buddies and circle of friends in later chapters.

When you consider the final dimension, human assistive support, look at the frequency and number of prompts and cues the student is given when performing the task. As we discussed in Chapter 2, many students with severe disabilities are "overprompted." That is, we give too much physical or verbal assistance too frequently. When assessing student progress, you must measure the type and amount of prompt-

ing provided. Whenever possible, you will want to move the student from your physical or verbal assistance to more natural cues that are *not* supplied by you. For example, for some students, movement from a physical prompt to performance of the task with only a picture as a reminder is a significant step and worthy of note in a progress report and celebration.

Finally, an important consideration for implementing any dimension of support is the notion that you must use "least intrusive supports" first (Jorgensen, 1992). For example, when you look at the support dimensions, choose technology that can be easily integrated into the routine over something that is cumbersome, calls excessive attention to the student, or could only be used in a few contexts. As we discussed in Chapter 3, when you choose a mode of alternative communication, consider whether or not it can be easily transported across environments and whether it affords easy communication with many people. On that basis you *may* choose a picture board over sign language or a stationary computer. When you consider prompts and cues, you generally want to start with the least intrusive (color cue or picture) rather than physical guidance.

 SUMMARY

In conclusion, you will be using assessment information in your teaching in many ways. First, we talked about norm-referenced instruments, tests based on large population samples and typically used for classification purposes. As we indicated, the information gained from these tests can be helpful in targeting areas for curricular emphasis.

However, the majority of testing is conducted using authentic assessments. There are several types of authentic assessment, all of which you will use for different instructional needs. You may use curriculum-based assessment to target skills within the academic curriculum. To identify key adaptive skills within the student's present and future environments, you will use an ecological inventory. To assist the team in instructional planning and to develop a consistent vision for your student, you may use a person-centered approach such as MAPS or PATH. To display your student progress and talents, you will use a portfolio. To see progress on a daily basis, you will use some of the strategies for recording described here.

Finally, support is a critical component of any program. You learned some strategies for identifying different types of support and principles for using the least intrusive supports.

 CHAPTER EXTENDERS

Key Terms and Concepts

1. *Authentic assessments* measure individual growth and performance in learning through demonstration and products.
2. *Curriculum-based assessment* is based on a student's performance in current course content by measuring the student's ability in relation to the grade-level curriculum used in the classroom.
3. A *curriculum-based measure* generates standardized scores (local norms) on the current curriculum for a classroom, school, or district.
4. *Ecological assessment* is an environmentally referenced measure that focuses on the individual's functioning within the context of his or her environment and culture.
5. MAPS is a form of futures planning that enables a team of teachers, peers, and family members to identify strengths, needs, and supports.
6. *Norm referenced tests* are assessment measures that have been standardized on a large population sample.
7. PATH is a form of planning that enables a team to provide an in-depth action plan.
8. *Performance-based assessment* is an evaluation of the student's ability to actually

execute a particular skill in the training or generalization setting.
9. Person-centered approaches involve the individual, family, and friends in creating a vision for instructional and future planning.
10. *Portfolio assessment* is an evaluation of a collection of student products.
11. *Task analysis* is a strategy for breaking an activity into its individual steps.

Study Guide

1. Give an example of how you would use each of the following in your classroom: (a) CBA, (b) ecological assessment, (c) person-centered planning, and (d) portfolio assessment.
2. Compare norm-referenced and environmentally-referenced assessments. How would you use each? What are the advantages and disadvantages of each?
3. What are natural supports? Make a list of supports you use in your own life to help you to function (e.g., "To do" notes, daily planner, special color codes for different keys).
4. Identify the major characteristics of the (a) MAPS and (b) PATH processes and discuss how these person-centered approaches differ from traditional assessment and instructional planning.

Group Activity I

Take an environment common to many of the students in the group—restaurant near the university or the university classroom building. Construct an ecological assessment of that environment. Make a list of the critical activities that occur. Break the more complex activities into skills. Develop a check sheet for assessing those skills.

Group Activity II

Perform a task analysis of a simple skill such as getting a cold drink from a vending machine.

Construct a task analysis assessment sheet. Give the assessment to another group. See if they can follow the sequence you developed. Have them note steps your group omitted.

Group Activity III

Have one group member identify a critical problem that he or she would like assistance with. Use the eight PATH planning steps to assist in solving the problem. Have students reflect on the process afterward.

Field Experience

Spend a morning observing a student in a classroom. Target a skill to observe—for example, the number of times the student raises his hand before speaking. Develop a data collection sheet and record the student progress for 2 days. Summarize your information and make recommendations.

chapter 6

Designing the Instructional Program: The IEP

The written document that guides the instructional decisions for students with disabilities is called an individualized education program (IEP). According to IDEA, an IEP is written for each student who has been identified with a disability (Turnbull & Cilley, 1999). D.D. Smith (1998) has identified seven steps in the process of planning a student's individualized education program: referral, assessment, identification, analysis of services, placement, instructional decision making, and program evaluation. In Chapter 5 you learned about assessment, which is used in identifying a disability when a student is referred for special education services. Analysis of services, placement, instructional decision making, and program evaluation deal specifically with the development and implementation of the student's IEP and are addressed in this chapter.

 WHAT YOU WILL LEARN IN THIS CHAPTER

In this chapter, you will explore how special education and related services are identified in an IEP to provide the supports a particular student needs to access learning and benefit from instruction. You will learn about the IEP team and the meeting of team members to determine a course of action for addressing those issues. You also will learn about legal mandates and procedures for developing the IEP document and implementing the strategies designated in the document.

First we review the federal mandate in IDEA that addresses the development and implementation of IEPs for students with disabilities. This section also presents an overview of the IEP process. It includes a discussion about documenting special education services for the student as well as information about writing IEPs for the least restrictive environment. Then we describe the participants who make up an IEP team. This section also discusses the process team members go through as they prepare for and participate in the IEP meeting. In the third part of the chapter we detail the different components of an IEP with a description of each section of the document, including the student's present level of performance, annual goals and short-term objectives for instruction, criteria for evaluation, needed supplementary aids and related services, the location and schedule for the special education services, and other IEP concerns involving addressing student behavior, participation in assessments, and reevaluation of the disability. You will learn strategies for futures planning and for selecting curriculum goals. This section also includes a discussion of the ITP and the IFSP, individual plans similar to the IEP that are developed for adolescents and very young children, respectively. Finally, our discussion of the IEP includes methods for developing integrated programs and monitoring student progress. This section also includes a discussion of strategies for implementing and monitoring the IEP as well as strategies for promoting student and parent participation.

LEGAL FOUNDATIONS

The 1997 IDEA amendments (P.L. 105-17) mandate an IEP for each student who qualifies for special education services. They stress three major concepts for the IEP: (1) the student's progress in the general education curriculum with attention to her individual needs, (2) a collaborative planning effort among parents, special educators, and regular educators to support the student's educational success, and (3) the student's preparation for postschool life (National Information Center for Children and Youth with Disabilities, 1999).

The Law and the IEP

The process and structure for writing an IEP is specifically addressed in IDEA. Two components to the IEP requirements are listed. Section 614(d)(1)(A) of the IDEA amendments of 1997 addresses the content and structure of the IEP, and Section 614 (d)(1)(B) describes the IEP team members and their roles (Bauer & Shea, 1999).

The first component describes the establishment of a multidisciplinary team that meets to develop the student's IEP. The assessment process for identification of a disability is carried out by a prereferral team. Once a prereferral team has determined from the results of a multifactored evaluation that the student should be identified with a disability, that team is replaced with an IEP team. The IEP team consists of a group of individuals who have valuable information about the student and the professionals who will be responsible for implementing the IEP. The 1997 IDEA amendments require the IEP team to include the student's parents, at least one general education teacher, a special educator, a school or agency administrator, other individuals with valued knowledge or expertise, and the student when appropriate (Turnbull & Cilley, 1999). The various team members are equal partners who share responsibility for working collaboratively and make decisions jointly to ensure that each student has the best possible educational program. The 1997 amendments to IDEA mandate a major change in the entire IEP process to a concentration on student participation in the general education curriculum (Yell & Shriner, 1997). IDEA also now requires the IEP to have a statement of the needed services and adaptations to support the student's involvement in extracurricular and other nonacademic activities (Bateman & Linden, 1998). As you learned in Chapter 3, the 1997 amendments also specifically require the IEP team to consider assistive technology for every student with a disability. We provide a detailed discussion of the IEP team members and the meeting process later in the chapter.

The second component described in IDEA is the written IEP document. After discussing the student's present skill strengths and instructional needs and agreeing on a plan of action to support the student, the IEP team members write the IEP document to identify and guide the implementation of instructional interventions to ensure the student has that support. The law requires the IEP document to include (1) a statement of the student's present levels of educational performance, (2) measurable annual goals and short-term objectives, (3) needed special education and related services and supplemental aids and services, (4) explanation of the extent to which the student will not participate in general education activities, (5) modifications to district or statewide assessment measures or an alternative assessment plan, and (6) a schedule for reporting student progress in meeting annual goals that at least matches the timetable for reporting educational progress for typical students (Turnbull & Cilley, 1999).

The 1997 amendments to IDEA also mandate new requirements that include providing information in the IEP document that (1) considers how the student's disability affects participation and progress in the general education curriculum, (2) identifies the level to which the student will participate in assessments, (3) provides consideration of the student's language and communication needs, and (4) addresses behavior concerns (Council for Exceptional Children, 1999). For example, as Figure 6–1 illustrates, the team must discuss and address in the IEP the student's needs in developing proficiency with English, an effective mode of communication, and supports for communicating with others. Another change requires that a statement of the student's transition needs be included in the IEP by the time the student is 14 years old with specific transition goals identified by the time the student is 16 years old. Orientation and mobility services also have been added to the related services identified in the 1997 amendments (Council for Exceptional Children, 1999). The third part of this chapter describes in depth the different components in the IEP document.

Due Process.   Parents must give consent for their child to receive special education

FIGURE 6–1 Areas of Language and Communication Needs

1. Limited English proficiency
2. Mode of communication (verbal, sign, picture exchange, etc.)
3. Supports (speech and language pathologist, hearing aids, picture exchange cards, Braille materials, etc.)

evaluation and programming. They may refuse to give consent or disagree with the educational plans for their child through due process. According to IDEA, the states are responsible for providing mediation services when parents and the school disagree about how the student should be educated (Turnbull & Cilley, 1999).

In the event that the parents and school personnel cannot reach agreement in planning for a student's educational program, either party has the right to request and have outside mediation. A mediator might be brought in to resolve a conflict, for example, when the parents want their child to have a service the school feels is not necessary, is difficult to obtain, or costs too much. In such a case, an outside mediator is appointed to provide the needed arbitration. The mediator is trained in both mediation techniques and special education law and is not associated with the school district (Yell, 1997). A formal due process hearing may be necessary if voluntary mediation fails. The specific series of steps parents and the school officials go through as they try to resolve their differences through the arbitration process are structured in the following sequence: (1) an informal case conference that gives both sides the opportunity to talk through their concerns, (2) an administrative review by the superintendent in response to a written request, (3) a prehearing conference involving an outside mediator to try to resolve concerns without a

formal due process hearing, (4) an impartial due process hearing heard by an outside official who renders a decision that is binding on both parties, (5) the right to appeal the due process decision through a state-level review, and (6) the right to appeal the review by bringing a civil action in the courts (Ohio Department of Education, 1995).

Documenting Individualized Special Education Services

The purpose of the IEP is to document the specific services needed to support a student with a disability in accessing and experiencing success in school. IDEA requires the IEP to state projected beginning and ending dates as well as the frequency and duration for the identified special education services (Etscheidt & Bartlett, 1999). Those services may involve a wide range of supports that can include any of the following resources: (1) personnel, (2) modifications to the general education curriculum, and (3) assistive equipment. Some examples of special education services are listed in Table 6–1.

Placement: Least Restrictive Environment and the IEP

IDEA also states the IEP must address the location where the student will receive special education services (Etscheidt & Bartlett, 1999). The 1997 amendments to IDEA clearly emphasize placing students with disabilities in the general education classroom. The student's IEP designates the modifications and supports needed to help the student participate successfully in the general education curriculum within the general education classroom. In fact, the law requires the team to provide a written statement in the IEP to justify any plan that either calls for moving a student to a more restricted setting for any part of her school day or references a curriculum other than the general education curriculum (Yell & Shriner, 1997).

TABLE 6–1   Examples of Special Education Services

Personnel	Curriculum Modifications	Assistive Equipment
Special education teacher	Language development	Hearing aids
Para-educator	Community-based instruction	Braille writer
Occupational therapist	Taped text materials	Calculator
Physical therapist	Partial participation	Computer
Speech and language teacher		Wheelchair
Work-study coordinator		Adaptive keyboard

THE IEP TEAM AND THE IEP MEETING

The IEP Team

The IEP team is made up of a group of professionals and individuals close to the student who come together to determine the student's special education needs. At a minimum, all IEP teams must include the parent, an administrator, a special education teacher, a general education teacher, and the student when appropriate. However, a variety of other individuals also commonly serve on an IEP team when those individuals have expertise to contribute to the design of an effective educational program for a particular student. For this reason, the IEP team for a student with severe disabilities may involve a fairly large group of people.

Parent Involvement. Parents are extremely important members of their child's IEP team (Turnbull & Turnbull, 1997). Most parents have strong feelings about their child's educational experiences. They want their child to be involved in school activities and to have friends among the other students. When their child experiences difficulty in school, some parents may ask themselves, "What are we supposed to do? After all, we're just parents and we don't have any special expertise." Other parents, who may feel the school is not taking proper care of their child, might ask, "What are the teachers going to do to help our child?" Still other parents, who may feel the school is demanding too much of their child, can pose questions like, "Why are teacher expectations so high?" Whether parents are unsure, angry, or overwhelmed, it is important for them to be able to voice their concerns and desires in a forum where they can actively affect future educational expectations and experiences for their child.

Parents expect teachers to know specific information about the learning needs of their child. Sometimes they think teachers know all the right answers and so they do not feel comfortable speaking up. They even may believe teachers have all the "expert" knowledge because the teachers talk in terms unfamiliar to them. All of this can be very intimidating. It is important for the teacher to make parents feel comfortable and recognize that the knowledge they have about their child also is "expert" knowledge and essential to the IEP process (Perl, 1995). Also, education professionals need to be careful not to talk down to parents. They must listen carefully to parents and use nonjargonistic language when describing educational strategies and procedures (Kroth & Bolson, 1996).

Student Involvement. The student should be included in the IEP meeting as soon as she is old enough to participate (see Figure 6–2). Although IDEA does not state the specific age at

FIGURE 6–2   Reasons for Including Young Students on Their IEP Teams

1. *Hearing what needs to be learned and why it is important.* By being at the IEP meeting, the young student can watch the team members as they brainstorm to determine what concepts are important and why the student needs to learn them. She listens to the "experts" as they determine her present abilities and educational needs for the following year. By listening to their conversations, she will learn to recognize her strengths and weaknesses, which create the foundation for developing her own self-determination skills.
2. *Becoming a voice in the decision making process.* No one should decide entirely for another person what that person's life should be. The student's own ideas should be included in the conversation. The young child should be encouraged to start sharing her interests with the team. As she gets older and has a greater understanding of herself and how she wants to live her life her contributions to the conversation will increase.
3. *Taking ownership in the educational program.* As the student gets older, if she does not buy into what the team is trying to accomplish, she may not cooperate in learning the planned activities. However, if the student helps decide her own goals and objectives for the following year she has a piece of the ownership in her program. She is more likely to be an involved and eager student who is willing to work hard to accomplish those goals and objectives.

which the student must be included, the team certainly should begin inviting the student to her IEP meeting at a very early age. Regardless of the level of functioning or age, the student needs to get used to the idea that people come to her IEP meeting to have a conversation and decide how to plan her educational program for the next school year. This allows the student to learn what the meetings are like and to become comfortable with the process so she can begin to know what to expect, start to contribute helpful information, and ultimately participate more effectively.

Students with moderate to severe disabilities should be an integral part of the decision-making process in their IEP meetings. The IEP team needs to recognize that students with moderate to severe disabilities have valuable input that can enhance the planning process. The student can understand all or some of the interaction taking place in the meeting and can contribute insight to the plans being formulated. The other team members should never deal with the student as if she is an object to be acted upon. For example, during the meeting they should di-

rectly ask the student questions such as, "Abby, what do you think we should concentrate on next year at school? What kinds of things do you think are important for you to learn?"

The education professionals on the team should make sure to encourage the student to participate in the decisions being made at the meeting. Including the student in the IEP process helps her take ownership in her educational program. Even a student with moderate to severe disabilities can sabotage the team's plans if she is not part of the system and does not choose to cooperate. The student should be a full member of the IEP team and included in decisions to the maximum extent possible. This does not mean the student is the only voice or that she should run the entire meeting, but she should be considered an equal member of the team. The student will make valuable contributions if the adult members of the IEP team consider her an asset and value her contributions. In the same way they talk to parents, team members should be careful never to talk down to the student or use educational jargon that the student does not understand.

Students with more significant disabilities may have a limited ability to communicate verbally, so the IEP team has to find alternative ways of eliciting that student's participation. For example, they may need to use one of the assistive communication strategies we described in Chapter 3. Some professionals incorrectly assume students with moderate to severe disabilities cannot possibly know what they want. Actually, both young students and adolescents with moderate to severe disabilities have a sense of what they want, what they can do, what they have difficulty doing, and the things they strongly dislike. Unfortunately, often nobody asks them directly because they assume professionals can understand the students' needs better than the students can. In fact, including the student in the decision-making process in a meaningful way helps her develop self-determination skills and leads to greater independence (Wehmeyer et al., 1998). You will learn more about self-determination skills in Chapter 15.

Starting to involve the student in her IEP meetings early will help prepare her for the larger role she will play in the IEP process after age 18. For students over the age of 18, IDEA encourages even greater student participation by providing for the transfer of rights from parents to the students (National Information Center for Children and Youth with Disabilities, 1999). In fact, one year before her 18th birthday the IEP must include a statement that the student will be informed of her right to make her own decisions (Yell & Shrivner, 1997).

Other Team Members. The team should include the teachers who have worked with the student during the expiring IEP period and the teachers who will be working with her during the next IEP period. As explained earlier, the 1997 amendments to IDEA state that the IEP team must not only include a special education teacher who is familiar with the student, but must also include at least one regular education teacher who is familiar with the curriculum the student will be learning. The team must also include an administrator who can allocate the resources the team determines are necessary to support the student. Students with moderate to severe disabilities can need extensive services, so the team may include the professionals who provide those services, such as an occupational

Gerald turned 18 years old last month. As his IEP meeting begins, the team members describe an important change in Gerald's role. They explain that he has become an adult and he will have a greater role in deciding how his educational program will help him prepare for his life in the community. When he graduates from high school, Gerald wants to work in the housekeeping department at the local Days Inn and he wants to live in an apartment with his best friend, Paul. Gerald's parents share his dream. They encourage him to reach for the things he wants and to work toward achieving his goals. Once the team has thoroughly explained to Gerald what his new status as an adult means, his teacher writes a statement acknowledging this change on the cover page of his IEP. After all team members are sure Gerald understands his rights and his new role in the IEP educational decision-making process, he signs the statement.

> My rights as an adult have been read to me and explained. I understand my new role as an adult in the IEP educational decision-making process.
> Signed _____

therapist, school psychologist, physical therapist, assistive technology specialist, social worker, speech/language pathologist, behavior support specialist, school counselor, or school nurse. These individuals will have a great deal of valuable information about the student's progress and support needs that they can bring to the planning process. The team also should strive to make sure that what the student does in the classroom is connected to what is happening in other educational environments, such as at a community recreational program or job training site. For example, if the student is learning job skills through a work-study program, invite the job coach who goes to the work site with the student. This coordinates everyone's efforts so all members of the team are on the same page and have some ownership for a consolidated education program. Other participants may include any person who is close to the student or has relevant information to share.

Preparing for the IEP Meeting

Each member of the team should have a specific role and set of responsibilities so the meeting will run smoothly. For example, one member of the team should assume the role of chairperson. The chairperson should not be the "boss" but should take responsibility for monitoring the process. The chairperson sets meeting times, keeps the documentation together and organized, and monitors the proceedings so everyone has an opportunity to speak and share their ideas.

The chairperson should notify the other team members of the time and place for the meeting and send a written invitation to the student's parents or guardian. Written notification should be sent well before the meeting takes place to give parents enough time to respond and to suggest convenient times for scheduling the meeting. It is important to document efforts to inform parents, such as follow-up phone calls to the written invitation (Turnbull & Turnbull, 1997). Be sure to make several serious attempts

and even send a certified letter if those efforts are not successful in reaching and receiving a response from the parents. The team should be flexible in scheduling the meeting time and make every attempt to accommodate the parents (Turnbull & Turnbull, 1997). If the parents both work during the day, the meeting should be scheduled for the evening. Not only will this help parents feel welcome, but it also emphasizes their importance on the team and the value of their input in the IEP process.

> *Note:* If the teacher regularly calls to talk with parents about the student's progress, then it will be a simple task to contact the parents to invite them to the IEP meeting and schedule a time for the meeting that is convenient for the parents.

It is also important to choose a location for the IEP meeting that is convenient for the parents. For example, the intervention specialist might be responsible for going to the trailer park, picking the parents up, and bringing them to the school. The team could even hold the meeting at the trailer park in the family's home if that is the best way to include and support the parents. If it is appropriate for the student to attend the IEP meeting, the team should not only invite the student directly, but they also should encourage the parents to include her in the process.

The administrator on the team needs to arrange for substitute teachers to cover the classrooms of the participating teachers while they attend the meeting. Some school districts may have difficulty with the expense of hiring substitutes. The administration may need to find creative alternatives to overcome this problem. For example, the principal or school counselor could cover a classroom for that period of time. It is vital for the student's primary general education teacher to attend the meeting. He or she should be prepared to give information about the student's progress in class activities and provide important guidelines for the following year.

Any of the professionals who interact with the student, contribute to her education program, and want to come to the meeting should feel welcomed. They should come to the IEP meeting prepared to share helpful student information as well as learn more about the student and her parents. They should actively participate in the educational decisions being made. The team should not plan a student's program without input from the educators who ultimately will be responsible for implementing that plan because if it is to be implemented successfully, everyone involved in delivering the educational program has to support it.

All the necessary forms and supplies should be gathered and organized before the meeting begins so team members do not have to look for them at the last minute. For example, the student's primary teacher has critical information about the student's progress toward reaching the goals of the previous year's IEP, so the team should make certain he or she knows to bring relevant information about that progress, including work samples and curriculum-based assessments. The special education teacher should bring last year's IEP and the forms for writing this year's IEP. Parents also have valuable information they may want to share with the team during the meeting. The kinds of records they should bring to the meeting might include (1) a list of the student's responsibilities at home, (2) medical records, (3) a list of the things the student likes to do and things she does well, (4) information about the student's participation in community activities, and (5) any outside evaluations of the student (*You and the IEP,* 1999). The chairperson may even contact the parents by phone or send them a survey to target goals or parental preferences prior to the meeting.

Planning Approaches

It is important to develop an organized structure for the IEP planning process. This will allow the team members to follow an agenda, use their time effectively, facilitate the participation of all members, and ensure the consideration of all ideas. Several planning approaches can facilitate a highly participatory and efficient planning process. Two models particularly useful in planning for a student with moderate to severe disabilities include (1) the McGill Action Planning System (MAPS) and (2) Choosing Options and Accommodations for Children (COACH).

MAPS. As you learned in Chapter 5, MAPS is a student-centered technique for developing a vision for planning the student's educational routines in the general school community. The approach is structured to help the people close to the student identify her particular strengths and interests. A group of individuals close to the student meets for several hours to share their ideas and develop strategies for designing inclusive IEP goals and objectives (Vandercook et al., 1989). The planning strategy involves asking the family and others who know the student well a series of questions that will help the team develop a plan of action (*You and the IEP,* 1999) (see Chapter 5 for the list of questions). The team should include several of the student's typical peers and actively solicit their ideas, because they can provide a student perspective of the support their friend with a disability will need in the general education classroom activities (Vandercook et al., 1989).

COACH. COACH is another approach to identifying the family's preferred educational outcomes for their child to facilitate the IEP planning process. COACH uses a family interview designed to help parents identify the learning outcomes they want for their child during the following school year (see Figure 6–3). The family interview asks the family to respond to a series of questions and to prioritize valued life outcomes they wish to emphasize during the year. The team then restates the family's priorities for the student as IEP goals and objectives as well as identifies and includes the general

FIGURE 6–3   COACH Family Interview Questions

1. What, if anything, would you like to see change in [student's name] current health or safety that would help him/her to have a better or more enjoyable life?
2. If everything goes as you hope, do you anticipate that [student's name] will continue to live where he or she does throughout the school years?
3. Would you like to talk about where a desirable place would be for [student's name] to live as an adult? Feel free to answer "No" if you think that decision is too far in the future to discuss at this time.
4. Is there any place you would not like to have [student's name] live in the future?
5. With whom does [student's name] have relationships and friendships? With whom does [student's name] like to spend time?
6. How, if at all, would you like [student's name] relationships to change to expand in the near future?
7. What kinds of choices and control does [student's name] have now that match his or her age and family/community situation?
8. How, if at all, would you like to see [student's name] choices and control change or expand in the near future?
9. What kinds of activities does [student's name] currently do that he or she likes or values? Where does he or she spend time?
10. How, if at all, would you like to see these activities or places change or expand in the near future?
11. *Usually you ask this question only if the student is 13 years old or older.* Have you given any thought to what kinds of activities [student's name] might do or places he or she might go as a young adult? For example, in the future how might [student's name] spend his or her time that is now spent in school (e.g., competitive work, supported work, volunteering, continuing education)?

COACH Family Valued Life Outcomes

Being Safe and Healthy
Having a Home, Now and in the Future
Having Meaningful Relationships
Having Choice and Control That Match One's Age and Culture
Participating in Meaningful Activities in Various Places

Source: Giangreco, M.F., Cloninger, C.J., and Iverson, V.S. (1998). *Choosing outcomes and accommodations for children: A guide to education planning for students with disabilities* (2nd ed.). Baltimore: Paul H. Brookes. Reprinted with permission.

supports necessary to reach those goals and objectives (Giangreco, Cloninger, & Iverson, 1998).

The IEP Meeting

The purpose of the IEP meeting is to allow team members to work together to develop and write a student's IEP document. All aspects of the IEP process, including planning, implementing, and evaluating the student's skill acquisition, involve a collaborative effort, and the IEP should clearly reflect the shared accountability for that implementation and assessment. All ideas should be valued equally. For that reason, all the participants must be knowledgeable about the IEP process. It may be the first time the parent, student, or other members of the group have participated in the process, so the chairperson should begin by going through the procedures, expectations, and goals of the meeting.

If this is an initial IEP, the meeting will begin with the appropriate members of the multifactored evaluation team reporting the results of their evaluation to determine that a disability is present and then identify, from those findings, what goals should be targeted in the student's education program. To be certain all team members are fully informed, the evaluation information should be reported even if team members have received some of that information before the meeting. When reporting results, team members should always start with a positive statement in their evaluation of a student. They should begin by praising the student's accomplishments before giving constructive criticism. For example, a team member might note, "Astri really likes school. She is outgoing and wants to help others. She is eager to be involved in group activities with peers, but her efforts to participate are often unsuccessful because she does not always understand the rules for appropriate social behavior. Astri needs to learn the social expectations in the classroom and adjust her behavior accordingly."

If it is not an initial IEP meeting, the team begins the process by going through the past year's IEP and checking each item to determine if the student has mastered the identified skills. A team member, typically either the general or special education teacher, reports the skill level the student has reached for each goal listed in the expiring IEP. For example, the teacher might report that the student has accomplished one of two objectives toward her goal of communicating her choices and needs effectively. She responds to communication from teachers/peers with appropriate facial expression and/or body movement during 4 out of 5 trials which meets the criteria identified for the objective. However, she has not met the criteria for a second objective. When she is given items/events to choose from and a modeled phrase of "I want _____," she makes a choice and repeats the phrase during only 1 out of 5 opportunities rather than the 3 out of 5 opportunities called for in the criteria. The teacher supports the IEP review with written documentation that identifies when and how often the student was

evaluated and how well she was able to perform the task during the assessment. Because the student mastered the objective of responding appropriately with facial expressions and/or body movements, the team would not include that objective in the IEP for the following year. However, the student did not master modeled verbal responses so the team must decide whether or not they want to include that objective in next year's IEP.

Once the team has reviewed the student's accomplishments from the previous year, they consider which goals and objectives to include again and which ones should be eliminated either because they have been mastered or because the team no longer believes they are a high priority. Although team members may want to jot down some ideas before the meeting and they will bring review information to the meeting, the actual document for the following year should be written during the meeting to reflect input from all the team members. The team considers and writes any new goals and objectives they feel should be included for the following year. They also address evaluation of the goals and objectives, supplemental aids and related services the student may need for a successful learning experience, and other concerns we describe in detail in the next section.

The IEP should target those areas where the student shows the greatest need. Students with more severe disabilities will have more extensive needs. It may be impossible to address all of them within the 1-year time frame of a single IEP, so the team must choose those areas of need they want to emphasize during the next year. As you learned in the discussion on decision making in Chapter 5, they should focus on the most important and immediate needs.

 THE IEP DOCUMENT

The IEP team is responsible for creating the student's IEP document. It is written for every student from age 3 to 21 who has been identified with a disability. It provides the blueprint for designing an educational program tailored to the student's individual needs. Members' contributions to specific portions of the IEP may vary according to their individual expertise and knowledge of the student. However, no one person should write an IEP, and team members should not sign off on a document they have not helped to create. It should be written when the whole team is assembled so each member can discuss and respond to the ideas of other members. As you learned earlier, the team begins to create the new IEP document from their review of the multifactored evaluation or the previous IEP.

Although formats may differ from state to state, all IEP documents are constructed to include the following components: (1) a statement of the student's present level of educational performance, (2) annual goals and short-term objectives or benchmarks, (3) evaluation procedures and criteria, (4) services and educational settings, (5) the professionals responsible for monitoring student progress, and (6) a time frame for implementing the IEP. The goals, objectives, evaluation procedures, services, and learning environment all must be connected to and follow from the written statement of the student's present level of performance. So the team first describes the student's accomplishments and needs in a statement of her present level of performance from which they then write annual goals and short-term objectives for the student. To determine the student's progress in developing the skills identified in the goals and objectives, the team next chooses an evaluation procedure for determining student progress as well as the needed services and the least restrictive setting for implementing the interventions. A description of each component is provided next.

The Present Level of Performance

The present level of performance (PLP) statement provides a narrative description of the student's current functioning. It identifies skills the

student has already acquired and indicates major areas of need that require the support of special education services. To help familiarize the professionals who will be working with the student, the PLP should be written as a narrative, or "little story" which presents the student as a complete person rather than just as a series of test scores that only give a narrow view of performance. It should begin with information relevant to the student's strengths and interests. It should always start with positive comments about what the student can do before reporting areas of concern. If the PLP starts by describing the student as a happy child who loves to play games, the teacher forms an initial view of the student participating positively in the classroom rather than first seeing the student at a deficit.

Once the teacher learns about the student's strengths, he or she will need to know the areas of concern to address with the student. The team should indicate needs in the areas of cognitive, social, and physical development that are applicable to the student's education. Next, they should prioritize those needs to determine the

PRESENT LEVEL OF PERFORMANCE STATEMENT FOR LINDA

Linda is a friendly child who likes to play games and gets along well with her classmates. She is always smiling and asking other students to play with her. Linda is able to count and write single digit numbers from 1 to 5. She can write her name and many of the uppercase letters of the alphabet with assistance but has not yet learned to write lowercase letters. Linda needs to develop independent handwriting skills. Linda expresses frustration when she has difficulty correctly completing a learning task and needs to develop self-calming strategies.

most important concerns they want to address during the next IEP period. Remember, the IEP can only be written to cover one school year. Some students have multiple and extensive needs so it may not be possible to address every concern in one year. Some needs may be less important than others or can be more appropriately addressed in a future IEP when, for example, they are more in line with a later grade-level general education curriculum.

Annual Goals and Short-Term Objectives

After the IEP team writes a PLP, they formulate annual goals and short-term objectives. The team writes a different goal with short-term objectives for each major need identified in the PLP statement. For example, the team should only write goals or objectives that say the student needs to work on initiating conversations with peers if there is specific information in the PLP statement that says she needs to work on initiating conversations with peers. They should not write goals and objectives for needs that have not been stated in the PLP. Consequently, the team would not write goals and objectives for addressing money skills if there is no statement in the PLP that stipulates the student needs to learn money skills.

A student's annual goal should build on the student's previous knowledge and be connected to the general education curriculum. The short-term objectives should address a portion of the annual goal and attend to one of the sequential steps toward mastery of the goal. The team must relate the goals and objectives to the general education curriculum and identify the student's instructional needs beyond the explicit general education course of study. In other words, the team must consider what additional instructional support the student needs to participate successfully in the general education curriculum. For example, if Rosemary is in the first grade, although the team decides she needs to learn the days of the week, they would not in-

clude that as a goal because it is already part of the first grade general education curriculum. However, they might write a goal for Rosemary to learn numbers from 1 to 5 because the first grade curriculum addresses addition with the assumption that students already can recognize and count single digit numbers.

The annual goals and short-term objectives also identify how much the student might reasonably learn beyond the skill level identified in the PLP. For example, if Hank can redirect his attention to participate in a classroom activity with teacher prompts when the IEP is written, the team might decide he can reasonably learn to self-monitor to redirect his off-task behavior by the end of the next IEP period.

Annual Goals. Annual goals are statements of specific skill areas the student should concentrate on learning during the next school year. The team must decide what is a challenging but manageable learning experience. For example, if Jason is just learning to write letters of the alphabet it would be unreasonable to expect him to write full sentences by the end of the school year. On the other hand, it is important to challenge the student to learn new information at a rate that is reasonable for him. So the team might reasonably expect Jason to learn at least five letters of the alphabet during the year so he will be able to write his name.

The components of an annual goal include (1) the skill that will be targeted identified in measurable terms, (2) the projected achievement that can be expected in one academic year, (3) how the skill will help the student succeed in the general education curriculum or with other needs resulting from the disability, and (4) the intermediate benchmarks that will facilitate reaching the goal (Gibb & Dyches, 2000).

The IEP team must carefully choose goals that the student can realistically accomplish within one school year as well as identify a level of achievement the student can reasonably attain during that time. Consequently, the team would not say the student will increase his fine

Elliot is a first-grade student who is nonverbal and physically challenged. He enjoys being with his peers and engaging in gross motor activities such as being pushed on a roller wedge during gym class and standing in his prone stander.

The vision Elliot's parents have for him includes having him develop a friendship with a classmate and learning to express his needs and wants. As a result the team writes the following annual goals for Elliot:

1. By the end of the school year, Elliot will increase his gross motor ability from his present level of performance by sitting with support with peers on the floor during activities for at least 10 minutes during the school day.
2. By the end of the school year, Elliot will increase his ability to communicate his needs when asked from his present level of performance by pointing to an item or picture of an activity to identify his preferences for 3 of 5 requests.

motor skills because the category of fine motor skills is too large to cover in just one year. However, they might identify developing functional keyboarding skills as an area of fine motor development that could be reasonably addressed within the annual time frame. Next, the team must decide how much new material they believe the student can learn during the year. For example, they might designate that the student will use proper finger placement with both hands when typing on the keyboard, if they have determined (and stated in the PLP) that the student already can identify the location and push the correct individual letter key with one finger but needs to learn appropriate finger placement for two-handed typing. They must also state the level of performance they expect the student to attain and give specific criteria for measuring whether or not it was reached by the end of the year. In this case, they might decide that by the end of the year the student should be able to place both hands correctly on the keyboard and use the appropriate fingers to type five-letter words correctly 60% of the time.

Short-Term Objectives. For each annual goal the team must write at least two short-term objectives (Gibb & Dyches, 2000). Short-term objectives are the intermediate steps or benchmarks that will lead to the achievement of an annual goal. For example, if the goal is to learn the skill of subtraction without borrowing, the team might write one objective for the student to calculate single digit numbers and a second objective for the student to focus on learning to subtract a single digit number from a double digit number. The time frame for addressing the first objective might be from September to December, and efforts to address the second objective would take place between January and May. Like the annual goals, the short-term objectives are comprised of components that include (1) the conditions under which the skill will be performed and (2) a measurable student performance of that skill. To create short-term objectives, the team breaks the task to be learned into small steps that can be checked along the way.

The team should start by deciding what portion of the goal to address first and then what they want to build on from what was covered in the first portion. Consequently, if the goal is for the student to initiate verbal interactions independently with peers in 3 out of 5 attempts, the objectives might identify less invasive support structures for addressing the identified skill as the student becomes more proficient. So the objectives might include (1) when presented with the opportunity to interact with a peer, the student will say hello to the peer when given a verbal prompt by the teacher, (2) when presented with the opportunity to interact with a peer, the student will say hello to the peer when given a gesture cue by the teacher, and (3) when presented with the opportunity to interact with a peer, the student will say hello to the peer without teacher assistance. The team can project the first objective to be met in 4 out of 5 attempts by December, the second objective to be met 4 out of 5 attempts by March, and the final objective to be met 3 out of 5 attempts by June.

The short term objectives provide teachers with the basis for developing individualized instruction and assessing student progress (Gibb & Dyches, 2000). The team also must carefully design the annual goals and short-term objectives so they can be evaluated. If the goals and objectives are not measurable, it will be impossible to determine if the student has developed the targeted skills.

Evaluation Criteria and Procedures

Evaluation allows the team to determine the extent to which the student has made progress toward mastering her goals and objectives for the year. To identify the student's instructional needs for the following year, the team not only must learn exactly how much, and in which areas, the student has made progress but also where the expected progress did not occur. The evaluation criteria should describe what, how much, and how the student's performance will be measured as well as who will evaluate the student's progress and how often that evaluation

---

PARTIAL IEP FOR FRITZ

PLP Statement

Fritz is a really eager student. He works very hard to learn new skills. Fritz is very proud of the alphabet letters he has learned in school this year. He really likes to sing the alphabet song, although he sometimes gets confused about the names of some of the letters. Fritz can consistently identify 9 capital letters and 4 lowercase letters in the alphabet when the teacher names a letter and asks him to point to it or when the teacher points to the letter and asks Fritz to name it.

Annual Goal

By May, Fritz will increase letter recognition from present levels of performance by identifying 15 capital and 8 lowercase letters of the alphabet with 75% accuracy.

Short-Term Objectives or Benchmarks

- By December, when the teacher names different letters in the alphabet, Fritz will correctly point to 15 capital letters 70% of the time.
- By March, when the teacher points to different letters in the alphabet, Fritz will correctly name 15 capital letters 60% of the time.
- By January, when the teacher names different letters in the alphabet, Fritz will correctly point to 8 lowercase letters 70% of the time.
- By April, when the teacher points to different letters in the alphabet, Fritz will correctly name 8 lowercase letters 60% of the time.

Note: The goals and objectives are measurable because the teacher can observe Fritz's performance and determine if he is actually able to identify specific letters either visually or verbally.

will take place. The team needs to find an objective, nonbiased procedure for deciding whether or not the previous instruction has been effective. They must identify a procedure appropriate for the method and content of the instruction to determine the level of success for each of the IEP objectives. In other words, the team decides whether progress should be assessed with a test, an observation form, a worksheet, or through some other measure. They should avoid simply designating "teacher observations" as the procedure for evaluating student progress. This type of evaluation is too subjective because the results can easily be biased by the evaluator's personal feelings toward the student rather than the student's actual achievement. In other words, just writing "teacher observation" does not provide the objectivity that a more structured evaluation instrument, such as a checklist, can offer.

The IEP team also should designate how much of each skill the student is expected to master. In order to determine whether or not the student has learned what was expected, the team must stipulate the specific tasks the student will perform to demonstrate her proficiency and state the expected proficiency level in objective, measurable terms. For example, "When shown a picture of the materials needed to complete an assigned task, Anne will gather the correct materials" identifies the skill to be obtained but it does not indicate the level of competency. However, if the team writes, "When shown a picture of the materials needed to complete an assigned task, Anne will gather the correct materials 70% of the time," they indicate a skill level required for mastery.

Finally, the team must identify a specific person who will be responsible for monitoring the student's progress for each objective. They should state the extent of that individual's responsibility including how and when to review the student's progress. For example, the team may feel a particular objective should be evaluated every week or once a month. They might decide that for certain tasks, such as reading comprehension, the general education teacher

EVALUATION CRITERIA FOR ONE OF BERNIE'S IEP GOALS

One of Bernie's IEP goals for this year is to follow three-step directions in completing an assigned task. To learn this skill, he has to be able to follow directions correctly when the teacher shows him the directions in a sequenced set of pictures, when the teacher models the directions for him, and when the teacher explains the directions verbally. To show mastery by the end of the IEP period, Bernie will perform activities with three step directions by (1) correctly following a sequenced set of pictures 4 out of 5 times, (2) correctly following a step-by-step demonstration 3 out of 5 times, and (3) correctly following verbal directions 3 out of 5 times.

should have primary responsibility, but the intervention specialist should be responsible for evaluating the student's progress for tasks such as personal care management. For other tasks, they may designate primary responsibility to the physical education teacher or the occupational therapist. In any case, the intervention specialist should not be the only professional responsible for monitoring the student.

Supplementary Aids and Related Services

The IEP team also identifies the specific educational aids and services that the student needs to accomplish the annual goals and short-term objectives. Related services, such as physical therapy, assistive technology, orientation and mobility services, behavior support, counseling, or medical services, refer to resources that help the student benefit from special education (Turnbull & Cilley, 1999). Supplementary aids and services refer to resources that facilitate each student's ability to participate in the general education program (Etscheidt & Bartlett, 1999). Supplementary aids and services can include a co-teacher, para-educator, calculator, communication board, or other support that will allow the student to access the general educational experience successfully. For example, if the student is learning to add single digit numbers, a calculator is a support that can help her perform this task as she learns the new skill. The IEP team can write one objective for the student to add single digit numbers using the calculator followed by another objective for the student to add single digit numbers without the calculator. For a student with a more severe disability, the team might only write the objective that allows the student to use a calculator but break the objective into smaller pieces. In that case, a first objective might call for the student to add single digit numbers from 1 to 5 with a calculator followed by a second objective that targets adding single digit numbers from 1 to 10 with a calculator. By including this kind of information in the IEP document, the team can protect the student's opportunity to use a calculator in the classroom if the teacher does not generally allow students to use calculators. However, if the team does not write it in the IEP, there is no guarantee that the student will be permitted to use a calculator in math class.

Location and Schedule for Services

As you have already learned, IDEA mandates serving students with disabilities in the least restrictive environment. That means students receive instruction in the general education classroom where they learn the general education curriculum with the supports they need to make their access to that education effective. The IEP must indicate how the student's needs will be met in connection with the general education curriculum (Yell & Shriner, 1997). The IEP team must make every effort to ensure the student has

the supports she needs to participate to the maximum extent possible in this typical school experience. In those rare instances when the IEP team feels the general education setting is not the least restrictive environment for addressing certain goals or objectives, the team must make a case for placing the student in an alternative environment for that instruction. Before a student can be pulled out of the general education classroom or curriculum, the team has to give a written justification for why the student cannot have an effective and successful educational experience with that content and in that setting even with the proper supports.

The team also must determine the projected beginning and ending dates for implementing the IEP. They decide when the services start and how long they will last. An IEP is typically written for one school year, but the team may choose to write the document for a shorter period of time if they anticipate major changes will be necessary more frequently; however, they may never extend the time frame beyond one school year. Finally, it is particularly important to identify needed assistive technology supports in the supplemental aids and services in the IEP because those supports often are crucial for maintaining placement in general education settings for students with moderate to severe disabilities (Parette & Murdick, 1998).

Addressing Other Issues in the IEP

Behavior Plans. A behavior plan that identifies proactive intervention strategies must be instituted for any student who exhibits inappropriate behaviors that interfere with her learning (Katsiyannis & Maag, 1998; Zirpoli & Melloy, 2001). A behavior plan is included in the IEP if the student has behavior issues even if those issues are not significant enough to constitute an identified behavior disability. As you will learn in Chapter 8, to decide the best structure for that plan with the most appropriate strategies for addressing the behaviors, a functional behavioral assessment should be conducted to determine the triggering events, the manifested behaviors, and the resulting consequences (Zirpoli & Melloy, 2001). Once the functional behavior assessment uncovers the relationship between the student's problem behavior and the learning environment, the IEP team members can create a plan that will reduce those environmental pressures and the resulting behaviors. The team should write the behavior plan to include the following components: (1) a description of the student's behavior, (2) a description of the events that trigger the behavior, (3) the behavioral expectations for the student, (4) strategies for achieving the expected behavior, (5) a plan for evaluating the student's behavior, and (6) a description of the supports needed to achieve the expected behavior (Myles & Simpson, 1998). This topic is discussed further in Chapter 8.

Students with disabilities generally cannot be excluded from the education placement identified in their IEP for more than 10 days each school year as a result of inappropriate behaviors that occur because of their disability. If the administration wants to change the student's placement or suspend or expel the student during the year for more than the 10-day period, they first must conduct a review known as a "manifestation determination" to decide if the offending behavior is connected to the student's disability (Yell, 1997). They can proceed beyond the 10-day period only if they determine the student's disability is not a contributing factor.

Participation in Assessments. According to the 1997 amendments to IDEA, students with disabilities are expected to participate in district or statewide achievement testing; they may participate fully, with accommodations, or take an alternative assessment (Elliott, Ysseldyke, Thurlow, & Erickson, 1998). If a student is not able to participate fully, the IEP must include a statement designating any adjustments needed for

 Karen's IEP includes a behavior intervention plan (BIP) because the IEP team has determined that her confrontational behavior interferes with her learning (Bateman & Linden, 1998). She frequently responds to teacher directions or requests with angry verbal outbursts. On Karen's IEP, the team has identified the need to address this behavior with a plan that includes using a social script. They have developed a script for the teachers and Karen to use as an intervention tool to help Karen calm down and handle herself appropriately in the situation. When she becomes confrontational, they calmly redirect her to a safe and quiet location. They tell her she can stay in the quiet place until she has calmed down and thinks she is ready to return to the classroom.

When Karen becomes upset, Mr. Gagne asks her politely to go to one of two classrooms (depending on the time of day) to calm herself or, if necessary, to get assistance in calming down from Mr. Wayne, the para-educator. Mr. Gagne does not shout or try to intimidate her in any way. He follows the script by verbally reminding her that (1) she is angry and (2) she needs to calm down before she can deal with her anger. He tells her (3) when she is calm, they can talk about what is bothering her.

When Karen gets to the quiet room, she says the same script to herself that Mr. Gagne used when he asked her to come to the quiet room. She says, "(1) I am angry, (2) First, I need to calm down, and (3) Then, I can tell Mr. Gagne what's wrong." She repeats the script until she has collected her emotions. She then returns to class and calmly tells Mr. Gagne why she was upset.

the student to engage in the testing. If the student is unable to do this even with modifications, the team writes a statement describing why the assessment is inappropriate for the student and identifies an alternative method of assessment. Alternative assessments are usually arranged for a student with significant cognitive disabilities whose education program focuses solely on life skills (Elliott et al., 1998). For example, the student might be given a functional living skills assessment such as the Brigance Employability Skills Inventory or the Checklist of Adaptive Living Skills (Gibb & Dyches, 2000).

Reevaluation of Students. IDEA requires a reevaluation at least every 3 years to determine if the student continues to have an identified disability and, therefore, still qualifies for special education services. Before the reevaluation can be administered, parents must give permission for the testing. However, the 1997 amendments state that the reevaluation does not have to be conducted if the IEP team determines it has sufficient documentation that the disability still exists. In that case, the team reviews the existing information and gathers any additional data they need to determine the student's continuing disability status. Still, a reevaluation must be conducted if the parents request it even when the team believes it already has the necessary data (*You and the IEP,* 1999).

The ITP and the IFSP

As you now know, the IEP is the document that maps out an individual student's instructional plan. Educational teams also write two other documents that are similar to an IEP: the individual transition plan (ITP) and the individual family service plan (IFSP).

The ITP. The ITP focuses on the transition process from school to adulthood. The IEP team must begin to consider transition needs in the IEP by the time the student reaches the age of 14 and must incorporate an ITP into the IEP by the

time the student is 16 years old. When the student is 14 years old, the IEP must have a statement that identifies how transition is addressed in her educational program. The statement should concentrate on how the student's course of study will facilitate her eventual move to adult life (Yell & Shriner, 1997). The IEP team should ask, "What concepts and information are being addressed in the course work the student will be studying that will help her transition to adult life?" Then they should state the need to concentrate on that material in the student's IEP. When the student is 16 years old, an ITP must be written to identify needed transition services and any interagency linkages and responsibilities (Turnbull & Cilley, 1999). The ITP is developed with the IEP and designed to address the student's needs in preparation for adult life. Adult life refers to employment, living arrangements, personal management, leisure pursuits, postsecondary education, and other activities in the community. In other words, the ITP focuses on the next stage in life for that student. The ITP represents a long-range plan that is started and worked on during the student's secondary education career. It coordinates the efforts being addressed in the school with the student's future needs in the outside world.

When it is relevant, the ITP goals should be coordinated with adult service providers. For example, the IEP team should invite a representative from vocational rehabilitation services to participate in the IEP process during the final year of high school for a student who will need assistance in employment or living arrangements after graduation. By connecting the student, school, and adult service provider *before* the student actually enters the adult system, the team facilitates the student's smooth transition and avoids the possibility of a long waiting period before acquiring adult services. The ITP is discussed in depth in Chapter 15.

The IFSP. An IFSP is written for children from birth to age 3 and, at the discretion of the state, the school district, and the parents, it also may be used instead of an IEP for students in pre-school programs (Council for Exceptional Children, 1999). An IFSP is family centered rather than school centered. It maps out an instructional and support plan for both the child and her family developed from (1) a multidisciplinary family-directed assessment leading to services that benefit the family, (2) and a written plan developed by a multidisciplinary team (Turnbull & Cilley, 1999). The members of the team include the parents and other relevant family members, the service coordinator, the individuals involved in assessments, the people who will provide the intervention services, and other advocates the parents want to include (Turnbull & Cilley, 1999).

The major components of an IFSP are similar to those in an IEP. The plan must identify the (1) supports and services that help the family meet the developmental needs of the child, and (2) must be evaluated at least once a year with reviews at least every 6 months (Turnbull & Cilley, 1999). IFSP goals and objectives should focus on the skills that (1) are needed for coping successfully in daily environments, (2) represent a general concept that can be adjusted to meet individual needs in a variety of settings with different people, (3) occur in the regular routines of the child's natural environment, (4) are directly measurable, and (5) include a hierarchical, and increasingly complex, progression of short-term objectives toward reaching long-range goals (Nortari-Syverson & Shuster, 1995). The IFSP interventions should be provided in a natural environment, such as the child's home, with the team justifying in writing any deviation from delivering services in the appropriate natural environment (Council for Exceptional Children, 1999). The IFSP also must address the child's transition from early intervention services to preschool or another appropriate environment. A transition meeting must take place at least 90 days before the child can enter preschool (Council for Exceptional Children, 1999). We

discuss transition to preschool programs further in Chapter 9.

STRATEGIES FOR IMPLEMENTING THE IEP

You must remember two important principles when implementing an IEP. First, students can learn more than you might expect. Students may need support, but they will amaze those who believe they are capable with how much they can do. Each student has individual preferences and special talents that give teachers a starting point for exciting the student and engaging her in new learning experiences. Second, all the adults who work with a particular student are responsible for that student's education. Educating a student is not only the responsibility of teachers but also of family and community members who interact with that student. Students learn in different ways, so providing them with different views of the concepts they are learning will increase the probability of reaching everyone.

Developing Integrated Programs

Any information the team puts in the IEP must be addressed in the student's education program. The teachers who work with the student must be able to develop and implement instruction for and evaluate the tasks identified in the student's goals and objectives. To illustrate, the teacher may develop a social studies activity that involves producing a model of a covered wagon to help a student whose IEP identifies a need to improve manual dexterity and follow multistep directions. Things that do not appear in the IEP also can be addressed when the teacher feels they would be beneficial for the student. For example, the teacher may feel a student needs to work on making eye contact with other people when she is in a conversation with them even though the IEP does not identify this as one of her goals and objectives.

Implementing and Monitoring the IEP

Many different individuals may have responsibility for implementing the student's education program. An administrator, such as the school principal, may be in charge of coordinating the student's program and supervising the implementation of the IEP (*You and the IEP,* 1999). However, the student's teachers and other personnel who provide instructional support are responsible for the day-to-day instructional planning. They might include not only general education and special education teachers but also a para-educator, a physical therapist, a speech/language pathologist, the school nurse, and others.

 Ms. Chapland is a para-educator who supports students in physical education and art classes. One of her responsibilities during those classes is to monitor Candy's progress on her IEP goals and objectives. The goals on the IEP for that school year that Ms. Chapland monitors include having Candy (1) actively listen when spoken to by keeping her eyes open until the interaction is completed 80% of the time and (2) correctly follow two-step directions 3 out of 4 times. Ms. Chapland uses a checklist to monitor Candy's behavior during class. She charts Candy's interactions and tallies the results to determine how often Candy exhibits the appropriate behaviors.

Any teacher can use the student's identified abilities and interests from the PLP statement to build new competencies in areas where weaknesses have been recognized. This gives the teacher a starting point for instruction and helps identify the kinds of activities that will stimulate the student and engage her in learning the specific skills in the areas pinpointed in the annual goals and short-term objectives. He or she can create instructional activities that emphasize what the student likes to do and can reduce the student's frustrations with difficult content.

The goals and objectives will be teachable if the team has considered how the student will perform the particular skill and has included observable criteria for evaluating performance. For example, an objective that states "Frank will initiate one peer interaction during a 15-minute group activity" provides a structure for teaching the skill of initiating social interactions. The teacher can plan learning activities for the whole class that are situated in a small group format and then teach the student to engage her peers in a variety of ways, such as using verbal prompts from the teacher or a peer buddy.

However, structuring the IEP objectives to teach particular skills does not ensure those skills will be taught. Writing teachable annual goals and short-term objectives only provides a reference point. The teacher must actually implement the appropriate instruction thoroughly and consistently in the classroom. Even when information is clearly stated in the IEP, teachers do not always provide the specific instruction called for in the goals and objectives (Gelzheiser, McLane, Myers, & Pruzek, 1998). The teacher must consistently integrate that instruction into his or her daily teaching practice. Developing a schedule can help the teacher monitor the instructional coverage of the student's objectives. The schedule should include the interventions described in the IEP listed according to the time period for instruction of each objective as well as ideas for instructional activities appropriate for teaching the identified concepts.

PARTIAL INTERVENTION SCHEDULE FOR MALIK

The PLP in Malik's IEP indicates he enjoys going to school and interacting with his friends. He can initiate conversations with his peers and adults. Malik can write his name and copy all the letters of the alphabet. He knows a few survival words, but needs to learn additional words to be more independent and successful in the community.

One of Malik's IEP goals states, "Malik will develop independent living skills by correctly reading 10 information signs commonly found in the community." The IEP identifies two short-term objectives toward reaching that goal. The first objective states, "By the end of the first semester when given the following survival words on flash cards, Malik will correctly name 5 of the 6 words: *walk, don't walk, stop, exit, poison, go.*" The second objective says, "By the end of the school year when given the following survival words on flash cards, Malik will correctly name 7 of the 10 words: *walk, don't walk, stop, exit, poison, go, danger, do not enter, open, closed.*"

Intervention Schedule

week 6   survival word activities to introduce *poison, go*/review *walk, don't walk, stop, exit*

week 12 survival word activities to introduce *danger*/review *poison, go, walk, don't walk, stop, exit*

week 18 survival word activities to review *danger, poison, go, walk, don't walk, stop, exit*

week 24 survival word activities to introduce *open, close*/review *danger, poison, go, walk, don't walk, stop, exit*

week 30 survival word activities to introduce *do not enter*/review *open, close, danger, poison, go, walk, don't walk, stop, exit*

week 36 survival word activities to review *do not enter, open, close, danger, poison, go, walk, don't walk, stop, exit*

Suggested Activities

1. Board game cards with survival words
2. Bingo cards with survival words
3. Work box with survival word flash cards, stencils, and blank cards
4. Community excursions to locate survival words in natural settings

Remember, if it is on the IEP it must be addressed. If it is not mentioned on the IEP, it can still be taught.

As you have already learned, the responsibility for implementing the IEP is shared. All the annual goals and short-term objectives are not necessarily addressed in every class or during every part of each school day. Every teacher is not necessarily responsible for addressing all of the student's IEP. To clarify the responsibilities of the different individuals implementing the student's educational program, a matrix can be developed and distributed to provide an easy reference (see Figure 6–4). The matrix can be used as a tracking or planning tool to ensure the student's IEP goals are addressed during instruction (Power-deFur & Orelove, 1997).

Student and Parent Participation

As you have seen, the student must be engaged in learning the goals and objectives for the IEP to be useful. The instructional activities you design to attend to the student's IEP should be

FIGURE 6–4 **IEP Instructional Matrix**

Routine	IEP Goals				
	interpersonal communication *(will initiate conversation with peers using 3–5 word sentence)*	functional reading/ survival words *(will use common sight vocabulary and decoding skills to complete reading tasks)*	money skills *(will use calculator to check accuracy of money exchanges)*	personal care *(will attend to personal hygiene needs and maintain a neat appearance)*	behavior plan *(will recognize and respect others' personal space)*
7:30–7:45 homeroom	X			X	X
7:50–8:40 math			X		X
8:45–9:35 English		X			X
9:40–10:30 computers		X			X
10:35–11:25 work study	X	X	X	X	X
11:30–12:00 lunch	X		X	X	X
12:05–12:55 social studies		X			X
1:00–1:50 PE	X			X	X
1:55–2:45 family life	X	X	X	X	X

functional and relevant to the student's daily life. The more meaningful the learning experiences are to the student, the more likely she is to have a successful experience. If the student can make personal connections with the activities taking place in the room, she is more likely to remember them and integrate them into her own knowledge base.

It also is important to invite parents into the implementation phase of the IEP. You need to value their contributions about instructional options and make certain they are equal partners who can effect changes when they feel there is a need (Pruitt, Wandry, & Hollums, 1998).

The more parents participate, the more consistency there will be between the school and home environments, which also facilitates the generalization of skills across settings. The team can designate that the parent and the intervention specialist will implement and monitor a coordinated effort between school and home. For example, they might collaborate on a behavior plan for the student so the student learns certain social expectations are consistent across environments.

You also can show support for parents and concern for the student by calling them on the phone or inviting them to meet face to face. You can share notes on the student's interactions in school and have the parents share their notes on behaviors at home.

Student Progress

Parents must be informed of their child's progress in meeting IEP goals at least as often as the parents of typical students are notified. This can be done through a variety of different activities. For example, you can make notations in a parent-teacher interactive diary, document scheduled conferences or phone calls, or create an IEP report card. An IEP report card would list each short-term objective identified in the student's IEP and show the progress to date on a scale that includes (1) not yet addressed, (2) some progress, (3) good progress, and (4) completed (Gibb & Dyches, 2000).

Do not expect the student to meet unrealistic benchmarks. For students with moderate to severe disabilities, it is beneficial to do a task analysis of the skill and target parts of the skill as objectives so the student might reasonably accomplish them during designated intervals within the IEP timetable. These smaller expectations can be evaluated frequently to determine when the student has mastered a task and is ready to learn the next piece in the sequence. For example, you might formally observe or quiz the student every 2 weeks and determine that the student has met the standard identified in the first objective after 8 weeks. You will then know that the student is ready and you can begin to address the second objective.

 SUMMARY

This chapter discussed the individualized education program mandated in the 1997 amendments to IDEA for each student with a disability. We investigated the process for meeting and developing the IEP document and learned about the members of the IEP team and their responsibilities. We also considered the various com-

ponents of the IEP document and discovered strategies for implementing instruction to address the student's goals and objectives in the classroom.

 CHAPTER EXTENDERS

Key Terms and Concepts

1. A *behavior plan* is written for students who exhibit inappropriate behaviors that interfere with learning and describes the student's inappropriate behaviors, the events that trigger them, behavioral expectations, intervention strategies, an evaluation plan, and needed supports.

2. *Choosing Options and Accommodations for Children (COACH)* is an approach to facilitate the IEP process by discovering the family's desired student outcomes.

3. *Individualized education program (IEP)* is the document that maps out an educational program tailored to meet an individual student's special education needs.

4. An *IEP meeting* is the meeting held to develop and write a student's IEP document.

5. The *IEP team* is a group of professionals and individuals close to the student who work together to determine the student's special education needs.

6. *Individualized family service plan (IFSP)* is a document similar to an IEP that is a family-centered plan for children with disabilities from birth to age 3 that focuses on the needs of the family in meeting the goals identified for the child through instruction and supports for both the child and her family.

7. The *individual transition plan (ITP)* is written to address the student's needs in preparation for adult life, including employment, living arrangements, personal management, leisure pursuits, postsecondary education, and other activities in the community.

8. *LRE* stands for "least restrictive environment" and describes the location where stu-

dents with disabilities are to receive special education services.

9. The *McGill Action Planning System (MAPS)* is a student-centered method of planning for a student's instructional program in general education settings.

10. *The present level of performance (PLP)* is a statement in the IEP document that provides a narrative description of the student's present skills and needs.

11. *Annual goals* are statements in the IEP of specific areas of need the student should concentrate on during the school year.

12. *Short-term objectives* are the intermediate steps or benchmarks in the IEP that will lead to achieving an annual goal.

13. *Supplementary aids* are the resources that facilitate the student's ability to participate in the general education program.

14. *Related services* are those services that support the student's special education needs.

Study Guide

1. List and briefly describe the major components of an IEP.

2. Name four individuals who would typically serve on a student's IEP team and explain the role and responsibilities for each one.

3. Discuss why annual goals and short-term objectives need to have measurable evaluation criteria.

Field Experiences

Visit a local school and interview the teachers (special education and general education) who participate on IEP teams about their experiences. Here are some questions you might want to ask:

1. When and where do you hold your IEP meetings?
2. How frequently do you have meetings?
3. Who are the people who typically attend your meetings and what are their responsibilities?
4. Do you ever have other people come to an IEP meeting? If so, why?
5. What procedures do you follow during the meeting? Can you describe them?

Small Group Activity I

Work in small groups of three or four students to discuss the following questions and then present your findings to the whole class:

A. What issues might make it difficult for a parent to attend an IEP conference? How might the IEP team alleviate those difficulties?

B. Why is it important for the student to be present/invited to an IEP meeting?

C. What insight might an agency representative bring to a conference that would benefit the student?

D. What are some of the teacher's main purposes for meeting with a parent to discuss the IEP?

Small Group Activity II

Work in small groups of three or four students to develop IEP goals and objectives as well as evaluation procedures and criteria. Each group should use a different one of the following PLP statements as a guide:

PLP STATEMENT 1

Nadja is a 9-year-old student at Rising Hills Elementary School. Her strengths include being able to match pictures and objects with minimal physical assistance. She uses an inexpensive talk communication device at lunchtime to indicate her wants. She can follow one-word commands. She points to some pictures at verbal request. She is able to prepare snacks and water plants with assistance. She uses the toilet with minimal assistance. She likes to vacuum. She likes to ride a bike and use a trampoline but is restricted due to her brace.

Nadja's academic level is pre-kindergarten. She has a full range of needs including socialization, behavior, academic, motor, communication, self-help, vocational, and other functional living skills (such as those used in the community). Nadja's support needs include increasing social interaction, improving behavior, increasing involvement in regular education classes, and improving her vocational and functional living skills. Her needs in language arts include learning to recognize community signs, using a name stamp with less assistance, and listening to a story with headphones. Her math needs include learning to request "more" and sorting items. Her social studies needs include recognizing teachers and people in her school community. Her science needs include learning to prepare a snack and learning the life cycle of plants.

General evaluation concerns include fitness, weak response to verbal requests, socialization skills, fine motor skills, and self-care. In general education classes, Nadja does not look at the teacher or peers. She does not appear to attend or look at the speaker in a group setting. She will attend one-on-one. She does some parallel activities with physical assistance. At times, she gets out of her seat or cries out and needs to be removed from the classroom if she cannot be redirected. She had been pinching other students but that behavior has been reduced since the implementation of a positive behavioral support project.

Nadja needs assistive technology including augmentative communication devices and TouchWindow. She is nonverbal. Her communication needs include learning signs and using communication devices in more settings. She has begun to point to pictures this year at verbal request but needs to learn to use picture exchange to communicate. She has had seizures and takes a seizure medication at home. She has scoliosis and wears a brace to school. She was absent a lot this year due to recurring ear infections.

PLP STATEMENT 2

José is a 14-year-old student at Jamestown High School. He enjoys being with peers and teachers and participating in schoolwide activities. He is friendly and has a strong desire to communicate with his peers by using some signs, pointing to pictures, and using a communication device. Other strengths include following simple directions, responding to yes/no questions with gestures, and using a picture shopping list to find grocery items with minimal assistance. José also can match items by color. He can make a sandwich for his lunch at school with physical assistance.

José functions at a kindergarten level in all academic areas. He needs one-on-one support throughout the day. In general education classes, José can pass out supplies, activate tape recordings, and perform other classroom management tasks. He can partially participate in some activities by pressing a button to activate a prerecorded message or point to the answer on a card. José has difficulty focusing on his work in a group setting. He can move from one class to another with the support of a peer. He can indicate the need to use the bathroom by signing. His language arts include learning to use his communication cards more independently and to recognize more signs and symbols in the community. In math, he needs to learn to match items that are the same and to identify different coins and bills. In social studies, José needs to learn to identify places in the community. He needs to learn to order, pay, and eat at a fast-food restaurant with less assistance and to purchase snacks from a vending machine. José's vocational needs include completing class activities and assigned errands during his work-study assignment in the school office. He also needs to respect the personal space of others and use appropriate behavior when meeting a new person.

General evaluation concerns include the need for José to learn functional activities that lead to independent adult life skills as well as increased socialization skills, good health habits, and community participation. He sometimes makes vocalizations at inappropriate times or gets up from his desk during class, but he is easily redirected and his behavior does not usually interfere with his learning.

José uses a communication device (pocket talker). He is learning to use a calculator and a touchscreen window on the computer. He is allergic to milk and should avoid eating too much corn. José needs to further develop his communication methods such as vocalizations and pointing pictures, signing, and using augmentative communication devices. He receives speech services for 30 minutes twice a week to increase his verbalization skills.

PLP STATEMENT 3

Kenny attends a general education third grade class at West Street Elementary School. He is a quiet, well-mannered student who always appears to listen carefully when instructions are given. Although Kenny's athletic skill level is quite low, he likes sports of all kinds but he is particularly interested in football. He relies on a walker for mobility and struggles with pencil-and-paper activities that require fine motor skills. Kenny particularly likes to sing in music class and learn in social studies about people who have done important things. He interacts extremely well with adults, although he tends to demand their constant attention. He constantly seeks approval by asking the teacher how good his work is after each step of an activity.

Kenny has a speech impairment and has difficulty expressing himself both in class discussions and in social situations with his peers. He rarely initiates interactions with his peers, and he has trouble establishing ongoing relationships with children in his age group. He also avoids participating in extracurricular activities. Kenny is often impatient in class and does not function well in situations that involve whole class activities. He has difficulty waiting for his turn during group activities.

PLP STATEMENT 4

Betty is a student in a fifth grade general education classroom at Bakerton Elementary School. Betty is a quiet, well-mannered student. She always appears to listen carefully when instructions are given, but never seems to understand them well. She always asks the teacher to explain directions again or "show" her how to do the activity. She attempts to complete academic work correctly, but has a lot of difficulty both with paper-and-pencil activities as well as with strenuous physical activity. Not only does she have difficulty keeping up with her classmates during physical activities like those in physical education class, but her teacher reports that she frequently puts her head on her desk and quits working before she finishes an academic task.

Betty attempts to get attention from the teacher by constantly asking how good her work is after each step of an activity. In the past, she has spent most of her day with her special education teacher, but this year she is fully included in the general education classroom. Betty recognizes about 50 sight words and reads some simple sentences. She can add single digit numbers. She is beginning to add a single digit and one double digit number when there is no carrying involved. Betty also is beginning to learn subtraction of single digits with a value of less than 5.

Betty's parents report that Betty would rather play with her 6-year-old sister and her sister's friends than with the other children in the neighborhood who are her own age. Betty also likes to play "house" with an imaginary friend.

PLP STATEMENT 5

Marc is a 16-year-old male with Down syndrome who attends Howard High School. He is outgoing and friendly. Marc likes to go to school and enjoys interacting with his friends. He has several good friends among the other students in his classes. He can initiate conversations with his peers and adults. He is well liked by his teachers and works very hard in school. He enjoys getting positive, verbal feedback from adults and likes to please others. He has increased his gross motor skills and lost weight this year due to his involvement in extracurricular activities. Marc particularly likes his classes in physical education, life science, and introduction to computers.

Marc can write his name and copy all letters of the alphabet. He can write the numbers from 1 to 10 and count from 1 to 15. He can sort coins according to their value. He knows some survival words, including *walk, don't walk, stop,* and *exit,* but needs to learn additional words to be more independent and successful in the community. He also knows the universal signs for *telephone* and *bathroom.* Although he initiates conversations with staff and peers, he has difficulty speaking in full sentences, naming the letters of the alphabet, and recognizing basic sight words. Although he can identify individual coins and their value, he continues to have difficulty counting money. He needs to improve his counting skills as well as learn to combine coins and round up to the next dollar.

Marc participates in a work-study program at the school. He likes to work and enjoys spending the paycheck he receives. Marc's teacher uses modeling, one-on-one coaching, and community experiences as the primary methods of instruction. She would like him to work more independently and develop greater self-management. Marc is expected to participate in group activities in the classroom and likes to play games with his peers. Marc's mother would like him to learn to make simple sandwiches for himself.

PLP STATEMENT 6

Shawanda is a senior at Belkay High School. Although she is unable to see details, she can easily distinguish shapes and can immediately recognize people with whom she is already familiar. Shawanda has a great deal of difficulty working with written material, so she relies on class discussions and help from peers in order to pick up pertinent information. She also has difficulty taking written tests. Shawanda can read some words if they are written in very large print. Although she has difficulty sounding out words she does recognize about 25 sight words.

Shawanda has exhibited behavior difficulties. She seems to have a hard time paying attention during structured activities and sometimes talks during quiet class time. She often interrupts instruction, makes fun of other students, and complains about the work being both too hard and "dumb." Shawanda often comes to class late. She does not appear to listen when instructions are given, and she often asks out loud to have them repeated. She does not complete assignments. She often is found out of her seat and off task during those times when the students are doing individual work. Shawanda does not seem to have many friends and antagonizes other students with frequent verbal put-downs.

chapter 7

Supporting Inclusive Environments Through Collaboration

Thomas B. Pierce and Caroline Everington

Ana's annual IEP meeting was held to determine her goals, objectives, and benchmarks for the coming year. The meeting was one of many, because Ana's family was not satisfied with the services she was receiving. They had an attorney attend the meeting, and the school district had 14 professionals in attendance who worked with Ana. The professionals included an occupational therapist (OT), speech/language pathologist (SLP), teacher, teacher assistant, general education teacher, principal, psychologist, district due process manager, nurse, outside expert, technology specialist, social worker, special education facilitator, and a special education administrator. The IEP team met across numerous days, resulting in a total of over 15 hours of meetings. Tensions were high, and distrust between parties was obvious. Imagine the confusion, and imagine getting anything accomplished. This was the result of no collaboration. How did things get this far? How did a simple IEP meeting get to a point that more time was spent in planning than in a day's teaching? This situation probably occurs everyday across the country. Anger, resentment, distrust, and blame started fires that burn out any attempt to collaborate.

Teachers blamed parents for not following through with Ana's school program at home. Parents stated they were unable to be teachers at home. They did not feel competent or trained to do the "programs" prescribed by the teachers, and in some instances did not agree with the programs. Teachers were certain they could not help the student unless the parents worked harder. This resulted in a stalemate.

Collaboration is one of those terms that many people use but few understand. Special educators have long collaborated, but most often it was with each other. The changing roles of special educators have brought about new constituents and new partners with whom to discuss, share information, and interact. These new stakeholders are often trained in ways unfamiliar to those in special education, but more importantly, they require a common language. If each constituent speaks his or her own language, some individuals will be excluded from the conversation. For example, individuals from England and the United States both speak English, but certain words are not common between the two speakers (e.g., *petrol* for gasoline, *bumbershoot* for umbrella, *bonnet* for car hood). If words are not understood, it makes it very difficult for communication to be meaningful.

 ## WHAT YOU WILL LEARN IN THIS CHAPTER

This chapter suggests ways to develop collaborative skills for interacting among all partners on behalf of children. We begin by defining collaboration. Second, we address strategies for collaborating with the various team members in your school: colleagues, specialists, administrators, teaching assistants, parents and families, and therapists. Third, we present models of effective team collaboration. The ideas here will help you to develop a style that is comfortable for you and that facilitates conversation.

 ## WHAT IS COLLABORATION?

Consulting may be very different than calling in a consultant. The art of consulting infers that communication is occurring. The term *consultant* suggests there is an individual from whom you are requesting expertise. Historically, consulting with regular education teachers and other school personnel was the method used to communicate ideas and strategies for students with disabilities (Cramer, 1998; Rainforth & York-Barr, 1997). This method did not provide for adequate problem solving between the consultant and the consultee. A consultant who *tells* a teacher what to do is not a consultant, but rather someone who believes he or she has power and authority. The consultant develops a strategy for a person with a problem and is not necessarily collaborative (Friend & Bursuck,

1999). The individual seeking a consultant can then absolve the person of the responsibility for the problem (Jorgensen, Fisher, Sax, & Skoglund, 1998). Effective consultation occurs when neither party relinquishes his or her role. Collaboration, in contrast, implies two or more people sitting down and sharing information, expertise, and strategies. If a general education teacher abandons participation in the consultation, the student may not receive effective instruction.

Collaborating with others about students with more severe support needs is critical. Most people with moderate to severe disabilities have complications in their lives that are supported by a host of professionals. Physical therapists, mobility specialists, occupational therapists, teachers, counselors, speech/language pathologists, and advocates are just a few of the people interested in the student's growth. Each of these individuals comes into the picture with a different agenda, expectations, and expertise. Often the teacher is faced with sifting through information from a variety of disciplines and expected to make educational decisions. Many times, this is difficult, if not impossible, and dangerous for all involved if assumptions are made based on a lack of information, thus ultimately providing services that are harmful.

The teacher is placed in a situation of choosing the route rather than assisting in the development of the route. For example, a speech therapist may want to introduce sign language into the student's repertoire of skills. The parent may want her child to speak words. The physical therapist is concerned that the student may not have the manual dexterity to use sign language. The teacher does not know sign language. In this situation, what should the teacher do?

If you believe the teacher is responsible for making these decisions, you may be making judgments that are not collaborative. It is as if the teacher is the president and all of the cabinet secretaries are giving advice. Eventually, the president must make a decision. Some will be seen as winners and some will be seen as losers.

This does not promote healthy team building, nor does it allow for collaborative ventures to strengthen. Imagine if you were the speech therapist and the teacher said she was not going to choose sign language. The speech therapist may feel she was not listened to or her professional opinion was not valued. What might be some better ways to make educational decisions in a more collaborative fashion? Remember, the individuals you are communicating with have special expertise that should not be ignored. Decisions should be made in context (i.e., the place in which learning will occur, generalization, culture, and needs for technology). For example, we worked with a family from Korea whose child is in the transition to the world of work stage of his schooling career. The professionals have stressed the need for independence and living on one's own. The family, as many Korean families believe, do not think that moving far away from home or having an independent residence is a positive idea. The team needs to put concepts in context so all members of the team agree on final goals and objectives. All of these need resolution before implementation.

 COLLABORATIVE MODELS

Several variations of collaborative models are available in the literature (Dettmer, Dyck, & Thurston, 1999; Friend & Bursuck, 1999; Idol, Paolucci-Whitcomb, & Nevin, 1986). These models build and diverge from each other in the depth, breadth, and function of collaboration. As with most models, many teachers have their own variations that are developed to meet the needs of their students and school structure. The important point is that collaboration must occur and must be meaningful. Collaboration cannot occur in a vacuum; without regular communication, the student with a disability will suffer.

Before our discussion of various models, we must understand the team approach. *Team decision making* is one of the foundations of special education. Teams are used to develop programs and strategies as well as identify responsibilities, priorities, and future directions. The team in special education is often erroneously thought of as the IEP team. The IEP team is a legal requirement to satisfy federal regulations set forth in IDEA. This is one component of the total team for a student with a disability. The team is also a structure for program planning, evaluation, and identification of student supports. Teams should meet regularly to discuss the progress of the student and what is needed to support the student, the teacher, the classroom, and the other students. Teams need to communicate regularly to fine-tune and update the student's program. Later on in this chapter, we discuss individual student support teams.

Team Structures

The essence to any collaborative venture in today's schools starts with the team. The team is the center of how collaboration will be accomplished. Just as curricula change, so does the approach in which we develop individualized programs. Since the passage of P.L. 94-142, the team process has gone through many changes, all of which build on previous approaches and move toward the goal of more coordination, cooperation, and functional implementation of goals and objectives. The three major team approaches are multidisciplinary (MDT), interdisciplinary (IDT), and transdisciplinary (TDT).

Multidisciplinary (MDT). Based on the medical model (Hart, 1977), the MDT organizes professionals from various disciplines to assess, plan, and implement services and programs based on an individual's disciplinary specialty. Team members submit their program for the student at the team meeting, resulting in an isolated approach to treatment services. For example, the physical therapist (PT) brings to the meeting the student's strengths, needs, goals, and objectives in regard to gross motor development and movement. The PT reports her program to the team

and then implements it as written. Each team member does likewise—no input is given or sought. The MDT members merely report on their proposed programs. The MDT has been criticized for its isolation and for its lack of meaningful input from other team members (Orelove & Sobsey, 1991; Peterson, 1980). In addition, the MDT may not provide needed coordination of the student's goals, objectives, and strategies.

Interdisciplinary Team (IDT). As the team process matured, parents and professionals became disenchanted with the lack of coordination of the MDT. The IDT adds a more cooperative process in which consensus is reached for a student's needs, goals, objectives, and strategies (McCormick & Goldman, 1979). The IDT provides more discussion between parents and professionals about individual programming elements. However, discussions of objectives continue to emphasize a discipline-specific approach. For example, all members of the team may agree the student needs to learn to walk, but strategies may not be consistent across disciplines. This isolated therapy model may not provide for learning in the natural environment, and students may receive skill training only during the specific time allotted to that discipline.

Transdisciplinary (TDT). Originally developed to promote a comprehensive planning strategy for high-risk infants (Hutchison, 1978; United Cerebral Palsy, 1976) and based on comments from parents and professionals, the TDT grew out of dissatisfaction with the previous approaches. The TDT approach empowers individual teams to develop cooperatively the IFSP, IEP, or ITP at the meeting (Orelove & Sobsey, 1991). On the basis of the student's needs, the team prioritizes goals and objectives. Those goals and objectives with the highest priority are implemented across each discipline. For example, if a team agrees that communication skills are the student's greatest need, then each team member determines how communication will be integrated into his or her discipline. The physical therapist develops a communication program as part of the activities delivered during the physical therapy session. Parents also develop and reinforce programs at home. Perhaps most unique about the TDT is that the therapists and other team members become collaborators and practice role release (Nietupski, Scheutz, & Ockwood, 1980).

The TDT approach can be meaningful for students with moderate to severe disabilities. Those with disabilities may have difficulty generalizing skills across people, settings, time and materials that may be lessened by the TDT approach. Parents become participants in the TDT rather than observers. Professionals focus on an individual's needs and incorporate their areas of expertise. This approach requires, however, that all people work together, rather than supporting a "role" in which they have investment. Finally, students with disabilities have their needs addressed in a cooperative effort.

Meaningful Collaboration

Friend and Bursuck (1999) have developed a list of characteristics that promote meaningful collaboration. Remember, collaboration is a process developed within the structure of the team and the culture of the school. Each team collaborates differently, but with the characteristics listed in Figure 7–1, the outcomes should create meaningful changes to the lives of students with and without disabilities.

COLLABORATING WITH TEAM MEMBERS

A variety of people are involved in the team process. In order to be an effective collaborator, communicating and understanding each of these individual's agenda, training, and expertise is important. In the following sections we suggest strategies for working with a variety of people to promote a collaborative transdisciplinary team.

FIGURE 7–1
Characteristics of Collaboration

- Collaboration is voluntary.
- Collaboration is based on similarities and shared expectations.
- Collaboration requires a shared goal.
- Collaboration includes shared responsibility for key decisions.
- Collaboration includes shared accountability for outcomes.
- Collaboration is based on shared resources.
- Collaboration is emergent—it is a process that matures with practice.

Source: From Friend, M., & Bursuck, W. D. (1999). *Including students with special needs: A practical guide for classroom teachers* (2nd ed.). Copyright © 1999 by Allyn & Bacon. Reprinted/adapted by permission.

Collaborating with Colleagues. Effective collaborators understand the variety of people that comprise a team. Here we offer suggestions to assist collaboration with various stakeholders. Some of the suggestions require systemic change (Gartner & Lipsky, 1997), and some require personal introspection. As you will see throughout this text, systemic change requires a resolution to change. Change takes work and commitment. Without this change, it will be business as usual and schools will continue to become more and more nonresponsive to the changing needs of society.

Collaborating with Specialists. Each school has many professionals who are teachers, even though they may not have a traditional teaching role. They may include colleagues with such titles as facilitators, coordinators, or subject matter specialists (e.g., reading teachers, math specialists, art teachers, etc.). All of these individuals provide services that are discipline-related. In addition, there are the therapists who because of their training have degrees and expertise in fields other than teacher education (e.g., occupational therapists, physical therapists, school psychologists, etc.). We discuss the therapists later in this chapter. The specialists are generally teacher educators. They do not necessarily have the same students for an entire day, nor do they teach a curriculum that transcends subjects. In cases of special education coordinators or facilitators, they may be seen in the role of troubleshooters or as people who coordinate paperwork and administrative tasks.

Collaborating with these individuals requires an understanding of their roles and responsibilities. Conflict may arise when these colleagues differ from classroom teachers when trying to understand their mutual student. They may have excellent skills in developing specific curriculum adaptations or in their subject specialty areas. Even though they may have started out as classroom teachers, they may not have the immediate understanding of how your classroom runs on a day-to-day basis. Unfortunately, many teachers have been to meetings where specialists have given advice based on a student's file and not from direct knowledge of the student.

Incorporating these individuals into the inclusive classroom is necessary, but can get in the way of effective collaboration. Their role is generally one of consultant, program developer, or problem solver. Their agenda may be different than the classroom teacher. Yet they should not be left out because they may have important strategies to provide the teacher.

The team needs to listen carefully to a specialist's expertise and, in turn, explain to him or her how the classroom operates. This is not to suggest the team uses the "yes but" strategy. That is ineffective. If you are asking for advice, and constantly challenge the advice, then collaboration is over. Statements such as "You do not understand my classroom," "I have 25 other students to teach," or "We tried that and it did not work," are all challenges to the team and never effective. If you are asking for advice, then listen to the advice. If the advice is not valuable, then why continue to seek it out? Teaming cannot work when one person has veto power or when one uses debate tactics to obfuscate the issue.

It may be more productive to seek out ways the work can be accomplished together. These include understanding the consultant's position. The team has asked for advice from someone who may not know the student very well but who may know regulations, staffing patterns, administrative routes, and so on. Prior to requesting advice, ask the individual to visit the classroom or other environments in which the student interacts. Make sure the student and the specialist have time to connect in a meaningful way. For students with more severe needs, frequent visits across multiple environments may be necessary. Remember, general education teachers may have 25 students, but the specialist may have an entire school. Schedule early, and keep in mind that multiple visits may be needed.

Specialists in education may have their own language to refer to strategies and approaches for students with moderate to severe disabilities. Teams must develop a common language. Professional jargon can confuse the listeners. Initials, acronyms, and specialized terminology can get in the way of an adequate understanding of what the specialist is asking (e.g., IST, QMRP, ATNR, ICF/MR, etc.). If at all possible, do not use these. If you must, explain what you mean. And if you are meeting with a team and a member is using professional jargon, ask him or her to explain. Teachers always tell their students, "If you do not understand, ask"—we should heed the same advice. Many times we are afraid to look ignorant or incompetent—when in doubt *ask!* Reinforce those who ask for clarification. A simple "I am glad you asked what that meant" is an excellent strategy for creating a culture of safety as well as group understanding.

Let suggestions grow on each other. When a suggestion is offered, build on it and develop it into an effective strategy. Do not expect one person to have the "magic bullet" or the "cure"—it does not exist. Always remember that collaboration is effective when the listeners and the speakers reverse roles—speaking and listening (see Figure 7–2 for a summary of suggestions).

FIGURE 7–2 **Enhancing Collaboration with Specialists**

- Make sure the team is listening to suggestions—ask for clarification or ask for examples of "how can Mary do this."
- Avoid saying "yes but" or "we have tried that before."
- Share ownership of the problem—ask "How can we do this together?" Or "How do we all have problems with this area?"
- Avoid the so-called magic bullet.
- Agree on and develop a common language.
- Encourage the specialist to observe the student in the natural environment.

Collaborating with Administrators. Another member in the team process is the building administrator, such as the principal. Many other administrators may work in a school (curriculum specialists, special education facilitators, assistant principals, etc.) but here we mainly speak of principals. Many times the administrator satisfies the legal requirement of the local education agency (LEA) representative. The principal is perhaps the best individual to sell team decisions to district administrators and thus an important part of any team. The principal, as the LEA representative, must represent the district, and conflict can ensue. Principals may adhere to a completely different set of rules and regulations for students receiving special education. There may be separate rules for discipline, expulsion, suspension, parental due process, and a host of other regulations set forth in federal statutes. Principals would probably prefer to stay out of the fray, and many times they may rely on your expertise to keep them out of lengthy and expensive confrontations. The principal will be grateful for a team that helps in this collaborative understanding of special education. The team can collaborate in a meaningful way, but at times the district's policies and the IEP may come into conflict. Remember, princi-

pals prefer to speak about the good things happening at their schools.

As we discussed earlier, resistance can come from fear, ignorance, lack of motivation, and so on. Administrators are not different. An administrator may fear direct conversations with a team because he or she lacks knowledge in special education. A team may find an administrator resistant because the strategy is out of the ordinary. A team may decide a student is in need of community-based instruction (CBI). As we discuss in Chapter 14, CBI teaches skills in naturally occurring environments (Falvey, 1989). It requires students to leave the classroom and be taught in the community. Administrators may be very resistant to CBI because it is out of the typical school routine, requires transportation, implies different daily schedules or patterns, or extends issues of liability. The team has a choice: Agree it is impossible to implement and find another strategy, or collaborate to engage the principal's support. The latter should be the team's choice because it is clearly in line with the needs of the student. If a team agrees on a strategy to meet the needs of a student with a disability, then it is the team's responsibility to make sure the strategy is implemented. Certainly, the easiest way is to simply put it in the IEP. But this can also be a destructive choice. Telling the principal that CBI is in the IEP and the IEP must be followed is not collaboration; it is confrontation. Better to engage the administrator's support rather than confront with an ultimatum. We discuss specific strategies for gaining administrative support for CBI in Chapter 14, but techniques for enhancing collaboration with administrators appear in Figure 7–3.

We have seen some administrators with laissez-faire attitudes (just keep me out of trouble) and some administrators who participate actively. Yet many times administrators do not have the special education training or are not involved because they have never been encouraged to become a member of the team. It is your job to invite and encourage their participation.

FIGURE 7–3 Enhancing Collaboration with Administrators

- Include the building administrator in your decision-making process.
- Invite the principal into the classroom.
- Make sure your students are visible.
- Revel in successes and not in defeats.
- Problem-solve with the administrator about areas of professional concern (e.g., planning time, resistance, materials, etc.).
- Avoid language that is threatening or intimidating—"the law says you have to do it."
- Develop a common language.
- Collaborate on schoolwide topics outside of the field of special education.

Collaborating with Teaching Assistants. As a group, teaching assistants may be the most uninvolved members of the team. Yet they are the individuals currently being used in greater proportion than ever before (Blalock, 1997; Olson & Platt, 2000). Teaching assistants are often left out of the collaborative process. Yet they are often the people who must carry out the decisions set forth by the team. They are also the individuals who are paid the least, have the least amount of training in special education, and are given important responsibilities (e.g., diaper changing, feeding, behavior management implementation). Imagine yourself being told what to do and never having the opportunity to engage in decision making. This situation may create animosity toward "professionals."

Many times, a team recommends additional personnel support for a student with moderate to severe disabilities. Teaching assistants are critical in the lives of many people with disabilities, but teaching assistants cannot be the only people responsible for the implementation of a student's IEP. Sometimes the teaching assistant appears to be attached like Velcro to the student, and the teacher and other students never interact with the student. For example, we have seen general education students interact more with

the teaching assistant than the student with a disability. It seems that everywhere the student is, the teacher assistant is there. This is neither inclusion nor providing support. It is the most covert form of segregation. The student with moderate to severe disabilities appears to be included, but is in fact totally blocked from participation and interaction because the teaching assistant is hovering nearby.

Many times teaching assistants feel responsible for the success or failure of the student because they have been given total responsibility for the student. If the student does not perform well, they feel it is a reflection of their ability. This is not support. We would prefer that a student not be "assigned" a teaching assistant. Rather, the teaching assistant provides support in the classroom. In this way, the teaching assistant is a member of the classroom, supporting the teacher and the activities of the entire class. Figure 7–4 is a form used with teaching assistants to identify the roles they perform during the school day (Fox, Leo, & Fox, 1999). Without this type of collaboration, it is impossible for the student to be included in a meaningful way.

As you can see in the figure, the team has organized activities where additional support is

FIGURE 7–4 Enhancing Collaboration with Teaching Assistants

- Invite them to meetings where discussions of students are taking place.
- Invite them to eat lunch with you.
- Ask them to evaluate students' progress.
- Include them in parent meetings.
- Ask them to evaluate strategies being used.
- Have them develop instructional materials.
- Reinforce and support their efforts.
- Remind them that they are important to the entire class.
- Seek out avenues to acknowledge them publicly.

needed. In math, the teaching assistant provides instruction to the whole class, so the teacher then is free to work individually with the student with a disability. During lunch, the teaching assistant is needed to ensure the behavior management program is being carried out, as well as working on building friendships, peer supports, and assisting in the transition time to and from the cafeteria.

We have worked with many teaching assistants over the years. Many of them tell us that they do as much teaching as the certified teacher does. Teachers and teaching assistants must collaborate in the same way that a teacher and a physical therapist collaborate. Professional courtesy and respect should always be at the forefront in all professional interactions. A teaching assistant who feels he or she is "just the aide" could be a hindrance rather than a benefit.

Collaborating with Teacher Unions. As inclusion has taken on a greater emphasis in today's schools, teacher unions have become involved in some of the demands placed on their members. Collaborative efforts stop when one of the members of the team says, "That's not in my contract." When this happens it becomes very difficult for agreement to occur. Unions need to understand how to support teaching in a collaborative fashion, rather than supporting the status quo. Teacher unions are very powerful. Many teacher organizations have formed as a result of teachers being mistreated by the system. These same members have power to shape the focus of their contractual negotiations. This can include negotiating for planning time, meeting time, and professional growth. If these are issues that compromise effective collaboration, than teachers should seek out their union representatives to negotiate for these items. See Figure 7–5 for suggestions for enhancing collaboration.

Collaborating with Parents and Families. Special education has a long history of data and research on the need to involve parents and families in educational decisions for their children (Turnbull & Turnbull, 1990). Equally important

FIGURE 7–5   Enhancing Collaboration with Teacher Unions

- Become active in the issues for which negotiation is occurring.
- Become a member of a teacher union.
- Seek out planning time as a part of contractual agreements.
- Develop a position statement on inclusive schools for union support and endorsement.
- Incorporate into teaching contracts training for collaboration, team building, and problem-solving techniques.

is the legislative intent behind the IDEA to include parents and families in all decisions about the education of students with disabilities. Yet it appears that when collaborative efforts fail, it is because of a breakdown in communication between school personnel and families.

We know that for inclusion to work, partnerships and communication is critical. If parents are excluded in the decision-making process, adversarial relationships may develop. Parents and family members, especially those families with a person who has a severe disability, are the only people who know the entire child. They have seen a wide variety of professionals before they have entered school. Doctors, social workers, social security employees, neighbors, and psychologists have all given their professional opinions and prognostications regarding the life of that child. Each time the parents and family members go to one of these professionals, they hear a different story and often hear a different prognosis. They now come to school with years of information, and the school determines what is best for the child. This is not the best approach. Those who have lived with him or her are in the best position to understand the nuance of a child with a moderate to severe disability. The ways the child communicates feelings, wants, and needs are best understood by the family. The family knows what makes the child happy, what irritates him or her, how to soothe him or her, or whether the child is sick or not. For example, teachers who begin with, "Oh yes, I have worked with children who have Down syndrome before" may be walking into animosity. Experienced teachers would not say, "Oh yes, I have worked with African American children." These types of statements reinforce to a parent that their child is something other than a person. Remember, the collaboration should reinforce your competence but also should enlist the support of parents and families to explain the unique parts of *this* child.

Collaboration takes time and effort. Making meetings convenient for all parties (especially for working parents) is a critical need of effective collaboration. Teams should come to agreement early on to develop a language that is understood by all. Using professional jargon is not a strategy for including all parties in the discussion.

Figure 7–6 illustrates a form that can facilitate parent communication. It is a way in which the team can determine the preferences of parents and families and how they want to communicate with school personnel (Fox, Leo, & Fox, 1998). Such a form can be very beneficial in promoting positive strategies for working with parents and families of children with disabilities.

Collaborating with Therapists. For students with moderate to severe disabilities, therapists such as occupational therapists, physical therapists, speech/language pathologists, and behavior specialists are usually an integral part of program development and implementation. Yet these are individuals who may not have taught in classrooms and do not have curriculum development experience. Therefore, meaningful collaboration becomes very important. Rainforth and York-Barr (1997) have described the use of an integrated therapy model. They suggest the integrated therapy model also include an ecological approach that takes into account the context in which learning occurs. This model promotes therapy integrated throughout the normally occurring rhythms of the student's school day.

FIGURE 7–6
Collaborating with Parents and Families

- Avoid being the expert of someone else's child.
- Include parents and families in all team meetings.
- Include parents and families in problem-solving strategies.
- Agree on the form of communication with parents and families, and communicate often.
- Prioritize goals and which goals should be taught and reinforced at home.
- Listen! The answers you seek may be coming from the parents and families.
- Agree on a common language and avoid professional jargon.
- Make information available and accessible.
- Make meetings at convenient times for parents and families.
- Plan family gatherings at school to promote discussions with and between parents and families.

In an isolated therapy delivery system, students will receive therapy in settings outside of the classroom (Rainforth & York-Barr, 1997). For example, the student will receive speech therapy in the therapy room or an empty room. People with moderate to severe disabilities often have difficulty generalizing, or transferring, information across settings, people, and materials (Stokes & Baer, 1977). These difficulties should uniquely influence where therapy occurs. Individuals with moderate to severe disabilities should receive therapy in natural settings to enhance skill development and circumvent the problems resulting from generalization deficits (Rainforth & York-Barr, 1997). Natural settings are those environments where the student will use the skill. Thus walking on the playground or in the hallway between classes is more valuable and results in fewer generalization deficits than walking in the physical therapy room.

Another drawback of isolated therapy models is the teacher's inability to observe therapy. Many times teachers need to reinforce the therapy in the classroom. When the teacher is not in the therapy setting, however, he or she is unable to replicate and reinforce activities in the classroom. We once knew a student who was being taught sign language in isolated speech therapy while being taught words in the classroom. The student would sign to the teacher, and the teacher would have no idea what the student was saying. This is not only a problem of isolated therapy, but also a problem of a total lack of communication between team members. Integrated therapy obviates this. Integrated therapy is more than just doing the therapy in the classroom. It also involves role release and coordination among all who work with the child (Thomas, Correa, & Morsink, 2001). The PT may facilitate the walking program while also communicating with the student in sign and implementing the behavior management plan. The SLP meanwhile may be teaching sign but also reinforcing walking skills and implementing a behavior management plan. See Figure 7–7 for suggestions on enhancing collaboration with therapists.

Resistance to Collaborative Efforts

Nothing is more frustrating than for good ideas to go untested because of resistance. Many times teachers run into stumbling blocks that make change seem impossible (Kampwirth, 1998). The finesse a teacher must use to create and implement new ideas can seem overwhelming. Sometimes the teacher may not understand that certain seemingly supportive behaviors and statements are actually behaviors and statements that represent resistance. Karp (1984) wrote an excellent description of nine types of resistance people use to prevent change from occurring. Table 7–1 adapts Karp's work as it relates to teachers and the collaborative process. It also provides examples of ways to deal with the forms of resistance.

FIGURE 7–7   **Enhancing Collaboration with Therapists**

- Develop common language, priorities, and goals.
- Include specialists in meetings, planning, and curriculum modifications.
- Share in responsibilities of service delivery.
- Incorporate therapy (when appropriate) in natural contexts.
- Incorporate therapy (when appropriate) in settings outside school.
- Ask for assistance from specialists in understanding therapeutic techniques, conditions, and interventions.
- Remember, therapists have large caseloads of students. Plan time efficiently and be sensitive to the therapist's other responsibilities.
- Become aware of state regulations regarding what professionals are permitted to do with respect to reinforcing therapeutic techniques (see the licensing requirements for occupational therapy or physical therapy).

 COLLABORATION STRATEGIES

Numerous models of collaboration in the literature provide suggestions for enhancing the opportunities for people with disabilities. The models described here are used to enhance collaborative efforts for students with disabilities and promote positive interactions across professions.

Teacher Assistance Teams

Chalfant, Pysh, and Moultrie (1979) developed *teacher assistance teams* (TAT) to curb the increasing referral rate of students at risk for special education. Teachers refer students to the

TAT for interventions prior to special education referral. These teams have been effective in reducing the special education referral rate for students with milder disabilities (Chalfant & Pysh, 1989).

Team Teaching

Team teaching, or co-teaching, occurs when two teachers share in teaching the same group of students, share in leadership of the classroom, and share in the responsibility of the daily routine (Friend & Bursuck, 1999). Pugach and Johnson (1995) suggest this is the preferred collaborative model. Variations on this theme are frequently mentioned in the literature (Walther-Thomas, Korinek, McLauglin, & Williams, 2000). Generally, team teaching includes a special education teacher and a general education teacher who provide instruction to students with and without disabilities.

Co-teaching occurs when two teachers share in teaching the same group of students.

Team teaching requires great deference to personal style and relinquishing of roles. Each teacher has a unique style, and sharing a classroom with another can be daunting. The collaborative elements we have discussed in this chapter become critical. Opening lines of communication, developing common visions and goals, and sharing responsibility for all children are vital (Tiegerman-Farber & Radziewicz, 1998). Team teaching may be likened to the rite of marriage—two people sharing, communicating, and being responsible. Two people doing different things will likely result in divorce.

Decisions and agreement must be made by the team teachers on how responsibility for subject matter, behavioral issues, curriculum adaptations, consultations, and program development will be shared. A team that says, "I teach from 9 to 10 and you teach from 10 to 11" is probably not sharing responsibility. Team teaching is not half time. It is full-time teaching with support given to each other throughout the school day. It may be that one teacher is teaching a math lesson while the other is circulating around the room providing assistance to students during the lesson. It may be that both teachers are working with small groups, or one teacher is teaching the class with the other teacher helping one student adapt to the lesson. Any of these models represent team teaching and promote all children learning together. Pugach and Johnson (1995) have found the principles listed in Figure 7–8 to be effective for team teachers.

The Vermont Model

For almost 15 years, the University Affiliated Program (UAP) at the University of Vermont has worked closely with students, families, teachers, administrators, and government officials to make a systemic change in teaching students with disabilities (Thousand, Fox, Reid, Godek, Williams, & Fox, 1986). The collaborative model that was developed has paved the way for other states to include students with moderate to se-

TABLE 7–1 Karp's Model of Resistance

Type of Resistance	Illustration	Definition	Responding to Illustration
The block	"I do not want that kind of student in my class." "I prefer not to be involved."	The resister is obvious, honest, and clear about participating.	"Tell me why you feel that way." "Please explain what your objections are."
The rollover (passive resistance)	"Explain to me exactly what I should do."	An uncommon form of resistance and very difficult to work with. Based on fear and retribution of doing the wrong thing.	"Are you clear about what you are supposed to be doing?" "Do you understand that your responsibility is required?"
The stall	"I will do that next week."	The stall may be honest and forthright, so an understanding of how the person operates may be necessary.	"What is in the way so you cannot do it tomorrow?"
The reverse	"That's the best idea I have heard."	Subtle in nature and almost impossible to detect. The resister gives you what you want and then ignores it after the meeting.	"I am glad you like it. What part do you like the best?"
The sidestep	"I think inclusion should be done with kids with mild disabilities first."	This requires you to justify your actions and culminates in debate over your choices.	"I understand why you feel like this, and I would like you to help in including all students."
The projected threat	"The union will not like this, the teachers will not like this, the parents of the other children will not like this."	The threat is that some other power or entity will threaten successful implementation.	"We will call each of these groups; meanwhile we would like you to . . ."
The press	"If I include this student, you will owe me."	This is genuine resistance. The resister does not want to participate.	"I know that I will owe you, but right now I need your help. What will you be doing to help?"
The guilt trip	"You are asking me to do something that I just cannot do."	Guilt is a common tactic to change behavior. You do not own the resisters' problems.	"I am sorry this is a problem for you, but what will you be doing to include this student?"
The tradition	"We have always sent students like this to special education."	The traditional approach for personal safety and familiarity. The resister is unwilling to take risks.	"The way things were done worked for many years. How can we adapt the past to make the future better?"

Source: Karp, H. B. (1984). Working with resistance. *Training and Development Journal, 38*(3), 69–73. Adapted with permission.

FIGURE 7–8 **Suggestions for Team Teachers**

1. Team members challenge themselves to improve their teaching.
2. Team members share responsibility for all students.
3. Team members share responsibility for instruction.
4. Team members communicate regularly about the progress of their work.
5. Teachers who team teach support their partners.
6. The team teaching agenda requires working actively to include all learners.

Source: Pugach, M.C., & Johnson, L.J. (1995). *Collaborative practitioners, collaborative schools,* (pp. 179–185). Denver: Love Publishing. Adapted with permission.

vere disabilities in regular classrooms. In the United States, the average percentage of students with mental retardation whose primary placement is the regular class is only 10% (Twentieth Annual Report to Congress, 1998). In Vermont, placement of students with mental retardation in regular classes is over 75%. A primary reason for this high rate of general class placement is the commitment to collaborative efforts from the entire spectrum of education constituents. The next section outlines the components and characteristics that support this program.

Individual Student Support Teams. The Vermont model has been frequently described by a variety of authors (Thousand et al., 1986). From 1993 to 1999, the UAP conducted training sessions for individual teams from states across the country. Individual teams received instruction in the Vermont model and incorporated the concepts to meet the needs of their individual states, schools, and communities. The model emphasizes that inclusion and collaboration for students with moderate to severe disabilities is a process for changing existing systems rather than a cookbook approach for exact replication. For a

team to be effective, it must agree on a common set of goals, beliefs, and priorities. Without these agreements, the team will be at odds with itself regarding focus, direction, and vision. On those areas where consensus cannot be reached, team members understand there are issues on which they cannot agree but these issues should not prohibit the important work yet to be accomplished.

The Vermont model has provided some essential elements for meaningful collaboration. The single most important element is the *student support team.* This group consists of people who interact with the student on a regular (daily) basis. Typically, the student support team includes the special and general education teacher, teaching assistant, parent, and appropriate therapists. The team may meet weekly to problem-solve or plan for the week. After the team is communicating with ease, weekly meetings become bimonthly or as the team's needs warrant collaboration. Planning issues may include curriculum accommodations, behavioral issues, changes in the student, and student successes.

Organization of this model can appear daunting, but its purpose is to change how the team does business. Team members are assigned roles at each meeting. The roles of meeting facilitator, timekeeper, jargon buster, and note taker are filled by team members and rotated on a schedule to ensure the sharing of roles and responsibilities. Team members follow a prescribed agenda with time allotments for each item because time is a valuable commodity. Should further time be needed, the team decides how to deal with the need for more discussion time. This keeps the team on track and focused on the issues at hand.

Critical to any team functioning is the efficiency with which the team operates. The *facilitator* keeps the team on track and limits extraneous conversation. *Jargon busters* are used to keep communication at a common understanding for all team members. The *timekeeper* lets team members know when discussion time has concluded. Team responsibilities and roles may vary depending on the number of people at the meeting.

The support team is responsible for the daily completion of goals, objectives, and priorities. During the team meeting, updates are given, and when appropriate, modifications are suggested. For some teams, the general education teacher may be showing lessons for the coming week and asking for assistance in making curricular accommodations for the lessons. For other teams, it may be a time to plan how to include a student for more time in the general classroom. The agenda depends on the needs of the student. Teams are for individual students, not groups, and it is important that a team does not use individual student planning time as a shortcut for group special education planning.

The individual student support team process challenges some schools to look carefully at teaching assignments and scheduling. Finding time to plan in a busy school day is essential (Mostert, 1998). Many teachers have multiple commitments before the start of the teaching day. Some schools have teacher committees, school meetings, and school functions, so there may be little time for meaningful planning during the morning. It may be necessary for the school to revisit all of these committees and other nonteaching-related assignments and evaluate whether or not the school needs them or whether the particular teachers need to be members. Administrators, unions, and teachers should jointly develop opportunities to commit to the process of collaboration. It will take systemic change for outdated models of inclusive collaborative efforts to be successful. Thousand and Villa (1995) have developed some excellent ideas for increasing time to plan (see Figure 7–9).

Schoolwide Support Teams. Schools can also develop collaborative teams across school environments, grades, and activities. Schoolwide teams may include administrators, subject specialists, coordinators, union representatives, and so on. This team develops solutions to problems faced by individual support teams. For example, it may be necessary to plan transition activities

for a student to be successful in the next grade. Scheduling opportunities, class coverage, and training will need to be resolved by the school team. Individual teams may also need assistance in locating resources or determining policy issues for program implementation. The school-wide team should also be a proactive team. It should anticipate problems that may arise on a school level and reach consensus on solving potential barriers to meaningful collaboration. Yet problems cannot be solved if there is not a common purpose or common outcome.

School personnel may need to have a candid conversation with each other about their visions for their school. Many times you walk into a school and the school has developed a motto for its environment. A motto such as "Our school celebrates all children" is a powerful statement and takes vigilance to accomplish. If students are not in their home school, or are segregated from their siblings or friends, it is unlikely that meaningful celebration is going on.

School teams must seek out the vision and mission of their school and work toward that goal. It should be as if the school is making an IEP for itself. What is the school's present level, and what goals and objectives do you plan to accomplish? It will be a challenge, but worth it. As more teachers feel increasingly alienated from their profession, having a say in the vision may make participatory collaboration an attainable goal.

 ## PUTTING COLLABORATIVE TEAMS INTO PRACTICE

The 1997 amendments to IDEA have added a new focus to collaborative efforts. The IEP must now include conversations about assessment modifications, student achievement test participation, and participation with students without disabilities. These requirements make it important to ensure that the IEP collaborates in a fashion that makes the student's educational program valuable and meaningful.

FIGURE 7–9   Strategies for Expanding Time for Collaborative Planning, Teaching, and Reflection

- Ask staff to identify with whom and when they need to collaborate, and redesign the master schedule to accommodate these needs.
- Hire "permanent substitutes" to rotate through classrooms to free up teachers periodically to attend meetings during the day rather than before or after school.
- Institute a community service component to the curriculum; when students are in the community (e.g., Thursday afternoon), teachers meet.
- Schedule "specials" (e.g., art, music), clubs, and tutorials during the same time blocks (e.g., first and second period), so teachers have 1 or 2 hours a day to collaborate.
- Engage parents and community members to plan and conduct half-day or full-day exploratory, craft, hobby (e.g., gourmet cooking, puppetry, photography), theater, or other experimental programs. Partner with colleagues and universities; have their faculty teach in the school or offer TV lessons, demonstrations, on-campus experiences to free up school personnel.
- Rearrange the school day to include a 50- to 60-minute block of time before or after school for collaborative meeting and planning.
- Lengthen the school day for students by 15 to 30 minutes per day. The cumulative "extra" student contact hours each month allow for periodic early dismissal of students and time for teachers to meet.
- Earmark some staff development days for collaborative meetings.
- Use faculty meeting time for small group meetings to solve problems related to issues of immediate and long-range importance.
- Build into the school schedule at least one "collaborative day" per marking period or month.
- Lengthen the school year for staff but not for students, or shorten the school year for students but not staff.
- Go to year-round schooling with 3-week breaks every quarter; devote four or five of the 3-week intersession days to teacher collaboration.

Source: From Managing complex change toward inclusive schooling. In *Creating an inclusive school* (p. 67) by Thousand, J.S. & Villa, R.A. Alexandria, VA: Association for Supervision and Curriculum Development. Copyright © 1995 ASCD. Reprinted by permission. All rights reserved.

   The next section outlines some of the positive steps you can take in your classroom, school, and community to promote collaborative interactions. Remember, these are suggestions and by no means an exhaustive list. Reflect also on some areas you would add.

Make a Schoolwide Commitment to a Team Model

Many schools today are developing mission and vision statements that reflect their philosophy. A team approach model can be a first step in developing a mission and vision to work collaboratively. At a general meeting of the faculty and staff, it would be appropriate to detail those specific areas that inhibit effective teaming. Strategies can be developed and reinforced to promote a healthy environment that supports team process and team decision making.

   MAPS (McGill Action Planning System) was developed to assist in developing appropriate strategies and supports for people with severe disabilities (Forest & Lusthaus, 1990). As you have learned in previous chapters, the MAPS team discusses an individual's dreams, fears, needs, and priorities for a successful educational program. In addition to individual student planning, this process can be used at the school level to elaborate on the school's mission and vision.

By asking a series of questions about what we hope (dreams), what will get in the way (fears), and what it is we need for appropriate implementation (needs), a school can develop an appropriate mission and vision that promotes successful team planning models. Once the MAP of the school is completed, it becomes the faculty and staff's responsibility to implement the strategy.

Collaborative teams may not be effective without the support of the entire school. Having a philosophy that focuses on individualized team planning will result in more appropriate strategies for students with *and* without disabilities.

Develop Opportunities for Collaboration

Even if the school has agreed on a common vision for planning and team decision making, the implementation could be difficult. For example, many teachers state they do not have enough time in the day for meetings. If the school is serious about its mission, what are some of the opportunities that can be implemented to restructure time commitments of teachers? Some committees at schools have been together for a long time. They may not be needed as much anymore. Perhaps student-planning teams can replace some of these outdated committees. Teachers could develop team support structures whereby teachers team teach for a small part of the day so student teams can meet. Lengthening the school day so teachers have time to plan is another way to promote team meetings. Note that teams do not have to meet for a lengthy period of time. In many cases a very structured, highly organized meeting can take place in only 15 minutes. By keeping to the agenda and staying on task, a team can generate excellent ideas and strategies.

Teachers need opportunities to share effective strategies, materials, and ideas with other teachers. Schedule a teacher-sharing opportunity that specifically addresses topics relating to collaborative teams such as these:

How I adapted materials for students with reading problems
How to work with teams that are having scheduling difficulties
How to work with parents
How to work effectively with the special education teacher

All of these topics can lead to productive solutions to issues surrounding teams. Through thoughtful disclosure, sharing information builds trust and respect between colleagues. The information is shared rather than dictated.

Provide Resources for Training and Support

Many times we have heard teachers complain there are not enough resources to meet their needs. Sometimes, those of us who provide resources to teachers are told we do not understand the unique needs of their school. This can lead to an impasse. Numerous resources are available to teachers who want to develop effective teams. The resources cited in this chapter are a good place to start. The bottom line, however, is for teachers to develop a trust in each other to investigate their own solutions. Outside experts can be very effective to start the discussion, but the ultimate responsibility for determining effective strategies will be up to the faculty.

Depending on your state, you may look to your local state university for assistance. Many universities have subject area specialists as well as those who specialize in system change. Every state also has a University Affiliate Program (UAP). This federally funded program is designed to assist in areas of mental retardation and developmental disabilities. Their primary purpose is to assist in their local states. UAPs also have many contacts with their colleagues in other states. They may be an excellent resource to collaborate with other schools throughout the nation. Developing a solid working relationship with your state's UAP can be of great benefit to you, your school, and to the children you serve.

In special education we have always believed that evaluating practice leads to better outcomes for children. The same is true for collaborative teams. Teams must evaluate and make recommendations on how to make their structure at their school more effective and efficient. Teams should be fluid enough in structure to make appropriate modifications. Completing periodic needs assessments keep the school responsive to the team's needs. Inquire about what the team needs with respect to support, resources, logistics, and training. Evaluating the team's effectiveness will be the ultimate outcome for an effective team.

Acknowledge the Uniqueness of Individual Teams

Throughout this chapter you have seen how collaborative teams can function. It is critical, however, that the team is not bound to convention that prohibits creative problem solving. Each team may do its business in a different way. There should be outcomes that are expected from any team (e.g., individualized goals and objectives, bridging general and special education curricula, family involvement, etc.). Because each team will have different members and personalities, teams should develop a comfort zone for their work.

Troubleshooting potential problems can be the responsibility of a variety of individuals at the school. The administrator, a special education facilitator, and a general education teacher all can assist teams that are not reaching their outcomes. Members should develop norms for their team. What kind of behavior is expected? When do we meet? What are our goals? All of these should be agreed on and revisited to update and amend as needed.

 **SUMMARY**

This chapter introduced you to the fast growing body of literature on how to collaborate in schools. Consider several points when developing collaborative efforts. The school must be-

lieve in your efforts, and if not, you must work toward educating those who are resistant. Collaboration is an effective tool for solving many of the issues and concerns seen in today's schools. Parents, teachers, teacher assistants, specialists, and therapists all make up the complex web of people who work with students. Without their input and cooperation, there will be little on which to collaborate. Remember, there is no proven way of effective collaborating. Certainly we have learned that developing a mission and seeking out answers for one individual student at a time is an effective start.

 CHAPTER EXTENDERS

Key Terms and Concepts

1. *Collaboration* is the act of sharing information and resolving problems using consensus.
2. *Individual student support teams* are teams set up to promote individualized education which meet regularly to problem-solve, evaluate, and reflect on the effectiveness of the student's education plan.
3. *Team decision making* is the process in which a group of individuals makes decisions based on discussion and consensus, ensuring that team members are comfortable and agree with implementation of goals and objectives.
4. *Interdisciplinary teams* are made up of members who continue to emphasize their individual disciplines but cooperate to reach consensus on the student's program.
5. *Multidisciplinary teams* are made up of members who take responsibility for providing student information related to their own specialties.
6. *Transdisciplinary teams* are made up of members who work together to promote comprehensive planning across their different disciplines in a cooperative effort to meet the student's needs.

Study Guide

1. Compare and contrast two types of collaboration models.
2. Describe and give an example of each of the team approaches, and include the strengths and weaknesses of each.
3. Select four of Karp's resistance categories, and identify how you would deal with a person displaying this type of resistance.
4. Identify three strategies for communicating effectively with unions, parents, specialists, and administrators.
5. Discuss how to find time during the school day to meet regularly as a team.
6. You have a teacher in your school who is not willing to allow a student with a moderate to severe disability in his class. Discuss what you will do to resolve this situation.
7. A parent of a student in the general class does not want a student with a disability in the class. She has complained to the principal and the school board. Describe how you would respond.

Small Group Activity I

In a small group, role-play Karp's resistance model. Each student takes the resister role and the resolver role. Use scenarios developed by your teacher. Resolving the problem is just as important as identifying the type of resistance.

Small Group Activity II

Develop scenarios about students with moderate to severe disabilities. Discuss how to implement general and special education activities during the school day.

Small Group Activity III

Develop a team teaching plan for use in a general education class. From dyads, and after the plan is completed, share the plan for evaluation and reflection with another dyad.

Field Experience I

After receiving permission from the school, attend an IEP meeting. Observe and reflect on the team approaches used. Do they collaborate? What type of team approach (IDT, MDT, TDT) do they use? Do all members contribute? How is the parent involved? Are decisions being made for people who are not in attendance? If you were the teacher, would you be able to implement the plan?

Field Experience II

Interview the parents of a student with a moderate to severe disability. Discuss with the parents their experiences with IEP meetings, involvement in classrooms, and teacher communication. What do they identify as strengths and weaknesses of the process?

chapter 8

Positive Behavioral Supports in Inclusive Settings

One of the areas of greatest concern for many teachers is behavioral intervention, particularly if the individuals they are working with have difficulty communicating their needs. The focus of this chapter on behavioral intervention is *proactive* and *positive*. Our approach is proactive; we emphasize strategies for preventing or minimizing of behavior difficulties through designing environments that are structured and provide sufficient support for persons with complex needs. Our approach is positive for two reasons. First, we concentrate on building appropriate behaviors that are more adaptive for the individual in the situation. Second, when we do employ strategies for reducing behavior, we employ a model that uses the least intrusive alternative. This model mandates that you, as a teacher, must always begin your intervention with positive approaches (Walker & Shea, 1999). More restrictive approaches that employ methods considered punishment—for example, time-out and removal of privileges—are only used after other approaches have been systematically tried and failed.

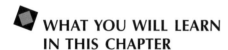

WHAT YOU WILL LEARN IN THIS CHAPTER

Behavioral intervention is a critical component of the 1997 amendments to IDEA (P.L. 105–17). The IDEA reauthorization requires that if behavior impedes the student's learning, behavioral intervention strategies and supports be part of the IEP (Council for Exceptional Children, 1997). In this situation, the teacher must do the following: perform a functional assessment, determine and implement intervention strategies, and evaluate those strategies (Council for Exceptional Children, 1997). In this chapter, you will learn some basic strategies for addressing challenging behaviors. First we discuss methods for pinpointing the problem and analyzing the context. Then we address strategies for determining the function of behavior. You will learn ways to identify both the critical

events that may trigger the behavior and the consequences in the environment that may maintain the behavior. Third you will learn how to use the information from the earlier sections to implement successful interventions. You will learn strategies for building new, more functional behaviors through reinforcement and shaping as well as strategies for prevention through environmental rearrangement and communication training. As you will learn in this chapter, many behavioral issues are related to problems in communication. Finally, we address strategies for decreasing inappropriate behavior and for developing crisis intervention plans.

 PINPOINTING THE PROBLEM AND ANALYZING THE CONTEXT

Pinpointing the Problem

Define the Behavior. The first question you must ask is, "What is the problem?" This is a critical step. In this process, the general complaint, "Mario is disruptive," "Maggie is off task," or "Sol is noncompliant," is transformed into a measurable, observable description. This can be accomplished in many ways. One way is to describe the situation. What is Mario actually doing? In this case, the problem is that he is yelling at his peers and the teacher and taking items from his peers. Another student, Sol, does not follow directions and resists prompts to follow through with requests. Sometimes, you may need to observe the student in the classroom to gain a clearer definition. You know Maggie does not complete independent seatwork, but what is she doing instead? An observation reveals that Maggie is looking away and humming when she should be working independently. Keep in mind that this initial definition of the problem may change as you observe and gain more information about the behavior and its relationship to environmental events.

Pinpoint Temporal Patterns in Behavior. As you define the behavior, you will also determine the best time for a closer look. When does the behavior occur the most frequently? You may wish to use a checklist called a *scatterplot* to determine if there are temporal patterns in the behavior. If you are consulting with a classroom teacher, give a scatterplot to him or her to complete a few days before you come for an observation. In this type of recording, you arrange the time in blocks of 15 to 30 minutes and check if the behavior occurred during that time. If you wish to get more precise information, you can note the number of times the behavior occurred during the time block. When making this recording, note the activity and any other information associated with the behavior. A scatterplot generally will not give you as much information as other methods of recording we review, but it does give you a rough representation of the rate and an indication if there is a time of day or activity that appears to trigger the behavior.

In the example shown in Figure 8–1, Maureen, a student with autism, screams periodically for no apparent reason. As you can see from the scatterplot, Maureen screams primarily during the time blocks from 8:30 to 9:00 and from 10:00 to 10:30. Therefore, it would be advantageous to observe her more closely at those times to determine the possible causes for the increase in behavior. In Maureen's case, those times are for individual work on academics. You

may ask these questions: "Are the assignments appropriate?" "Does Maureen need more support to complete her work?" "Can the assignment be simplified so she can work more independently?"

Note that although you will be observing for occurrence of the behavior, you should also consider the circumstances when the inappropriate behavior does *not* occur. What conditions are in effect at those times? Closely examining environments where the behavior is not occurring gives you useful information for interventions. For example, you can see Maureen rarely screams from 9:00 to 10:00. During this time, students are working in cooperative groups and are more actively engaged. You could hypothesize that either the active engagement and/or the peer support tend to decrease screaming.

Observing and Recording Behavior

Anecdotal Recordings. When you have established a good definition for the behavior, continue observations and recording to gain more information. Information is key in understanding behavior, so do not underestimate the value of careful observation. For difficult, complex, and long-standing behavioral problems, the time you take to observe and analyze the behavior will pay off in more successful intervention and prevention efforts. The richest source of information is an anecdotal recording.

FIGURE 8–1   **A Scatterplot for the Morning Incidences of Screaming**

Time	Day 1	Day 2	Day 3	Day 4	Day 5
8:30–9:00	2	4		3	2
9:00–9:30			1		
9:30–10:00		2			
10:00–10:30	1	5	1	2	
10:30–11:00			1	2	

FIGURE 8–2   Sample Observation

Code: T = Teacher, S1 = Maurice, S2 = Jane, + = teacher praise , × = teacher correction
Time: 8:30–40 group
T begins morning group
S1 leaves seat
T 3 S1 (brings back to group)
S1 sits appropriately
S2 answers question
T 1 S2 (good job)
S1 still seated appropriately
S1 sings song with group
T calls on S2
S2 answers question
T 1 S2 (good job)
S1 leaves group
T 3 S1 (brings back to group)

To truly capture the relationships between the environmental events and the behavior, sit back and take note of as many variables as you can: (1) the activity or instructional task, (2) the student's behavior, (3) the behavior exhibited by the teacher and/or peers, and (4) the events following the exhibition of the behavior. Many people find it difficult to record all the events in a sequence and use codes or abbreviations for certain people or behaviors. Figure 8–2 provides an example of a coded observation. You will find coding especially helpful if you find it difficult to collect observational information while you are teaching.

From the figure, you can see that S1 (Maurice) may have a problem sitting in the group. He gets out of his seat twice during the 10-minute group. Further, you can also see the teacher's attention was only directed to Maurice's inappropriate behavior during this observation.

ABC Analysis. The antecedent-behavior-consequence paradigm is one of the most useful tools for understanding behavior (Redmond, Bennett, Wiggert, & McLean, 1993). The *antecedent*

(A) refers to antecedent events, those that immediately precede the behavior. Examples are an instruction given by a teacher, comments made by a peer, bell ringing for change of class, bus arriving at the school, or worksheet or reading material assigned. The *behavior* (B) refers to the behavior the student exhibits in response to that event, (e.g., peer makes a comment → Ronette screams and flaps her hands around her head). The *consequence* (C) refers to the specific action or event that follows the behavior, (e.g., when Ronette screams and flaps her hands around her head, peer walks away). When viewed in a sequence, ABCs can provide an excellent picture of the nvironmental events influencing the behavior and the function the behavior serves for the individual. For example, if you look at the previous situation with Ronette, the comment by the peer appeared to trigger the outburst by Ronette. The peer left as a result. If you see this pattern repeated, you may conclude that Ronette is using this behavior to escape from interaction with peers. However, you may want to look more closely at the verbal and nonverbal actions of peers toward Ronette as well. If peers are making derogatory remarks to Ronette, it

TABLE 8-1   ABC Analysis for Juanita

Antecedent	Behavior	Consequence
J. is playing alone.	J. yells at peer for Kleenex.	Peer gets Kleenex.
Peer picks up toy.	J. yells at peer that she wants toy.	Peer gives J. toy.
Teacher gives attention to peer.	J. demands to comb teacher's hair.	Teacher lets J. comb her hair.
Teacher tells class to clean up.	J. tells peers to clean up.	Peers clean up; J. does too.
Teacher takes peer to restroom.	J. demands to go to restroom.	Teacher takes J. to restroom.
Peer shows pebble to teacher.	J. knocks pebble out of peer's hand.	J. is reprimanded.
Peer picks up pebble again.	J. asks to have pebble.	Peer gives J. pebble.
All students go to get coats.	J. yells for peers to move.	Peers hurry to get coats.

will be necessary to plan an intervention with the peers too.

Read the examples of ABCs in Tables 8–1 and 8–2. What pattern do you see? In the first ABC, you can see that Juanita's yelling and demanding behavior has been very effective in meeting her needs. Others give her what she wants when she yells. In the second ABC, recorded by a sibling in the home setting, you see that Minnie's use of "I'm sorry" serves as a means of keeping her place in the conversation. In both cases, you can see how these behaviors will be maintained if you do not intervene. That is, they enable the individual to meet her needs. In addition, the second ABC was taken in the home setting. This information provided the teacher with information on the behavior of the student in other settings.

In addition to providing insights regarding the *antecedent events* preceding the behavior and the possible *function of the behavior*, the ABC can give you information on new behaviors that need to be taught. From the examples discussed, you can see Juanita needs to learn to make requests in more appropriate ways and to share with others, and Minnie needs to acquire some basic conversation skills.

Frequency Recordings. There are many ways to capture behavior. The choice of recording depends on the type of behavior and your constraints. Possibly the most common and easiest type of recording is *frequency recording*. This type of recording lends itself to behaviors that are discrete such as hits, talk-outs, or refusals. Frequency data is helpful because it provides you with information on how often the behavior is occurring. Having this information early on is important. In some cases, your perception may be that the student engages in a particular behavior *all the time* because it really irritates you. When you complete a frequency recording, you determine that in fact he or she only engages in the behavior once or twice a day. This information may change your decision on whether or not to plan an intervention.

For frequency recording, simply note each occurrence of the behavior. You may be working in the classroom as you collect your information, so user-friendly, easy methods of recording

TABLE 8–2   Analysis of Thanksgiving Dinner Conversation

Antecedent	Behavior	Consequence
Group discussion on Kara's college choice.	Minnie is quiet but grows restless.	Group continues discussion.
Kara drops her napkin.	Minnie says, "I'm sorry."	Kara tells Minnie not to worry.
Katie asks for turkey.	Minnie says, "I'm sorry," and passes the turkey.	Katie says she likes turkey.
Dad starts a political discussion.	Minnie says, "I'm sorry."	Kara says, "We are all sorry." (She does not like these discussions.)
Mom spills her water.	Minnie says, "I'm sorry."	Mom says, "It is not your fault."
John says he has a 15-page paper due.	Minnie says, "I'm sorry."	John says, "It is not your fault."
Mom talks about a neighborhood child who got in trouble.	Minnie says, "I'm sorry."	Mom says, "It is not your fault."

are preferable. You can use wrist counters commonly sold for tallying groceries or golf shots or stitch counters designed for knitting (Alberto & Troutman, 1999). Simple daily check sheets can be posted in a convenient place. You are limited only by your creativity. For example, some teachers employ a strategy of transferring a bean from one pocket to another each time the behavior occurs (Alberto & Troutman, 1999).

Frequency data can be summarized in many ways. Often, a total of the occurrences for the time period is sufficient. However, you may have observation times that are not equal. Examine the observation log for Chaquille's hand biting in Table 8–3. The teacher counted hand biting the first day for 1 hour, the next day for 2 hours, and the third for 1.5 hours. If you only examine the total for the day, you will think Chaquille's hand biting is increasing daily. Because the observation times are not equal, this would not be accurate. For a more accurate estimate, the teacher would need to convert this data to a *rate per minute*. To do this, you convert hours to

minutes and then divide the number of occurrences for the day by the number of minutes. For example, for the first day, this is the computation: $24 \div 60 = .40$ per minute. When we convert the data this way, we see a different pattern. The rates per minute for each day in succession are .40, .23, and .36. From the converted data, we can see the behavior is declining somewhat.

Percentage is another form of conversion for frequency data. You compute percentage when you have a set number of responses or opportunities to respond. For example, you want Nick to give you eye contact when you address him. You approached Nick 15 times during the course of the morning. He gave you eye contact on 5 of those occasions. You can say he gave you eye contact 33% of the opportunities ($5 \div 15 \times 100$). Because opportunities may vary each day, recording a daily percentage would be preferable to just the total of the correct responses.

Durational Recordings.   For some behaviors, such as out of seat or tantruming, the amount

TABLE 8–3   Summary of Frequency of Hand Biting for Chaquille

Date	Observation Time	Total Occurrences
3/21/00	10:00–11:00	24
3/22/00	10:00–12:00	28
3/23/00	9:30–11:00	33

of time the person engages in the behavior is a very important piece of information for you to know. For example, Jim's mother thinks he spends too much time with the game PlayStation. You ask her to record the number of times he plays the game each day for 5 days. She completes a frequency recording indicating he plays the game three times a day each day for 3 days. This does not really seem to be a problem. However, his mother insists it is a serious problem. When you ask her to record the amount of *time* he spends each day on Play Station, you arrive at a very different conclusion. He spent 5 hours on Monday, 3 hours on Tuesday and 8 hours on Friday for a total of 16 hours over 5 days. From this, you can see the duration gave you better information.

In addition, some behaviors such as hand flapping or face slapping occur in such rapid succession that they cannot be measured easily by frequency recordings. *Durational recording* is the preferable method for these types of behaviors.

A stopwatch is the most accurate way to record duration. If you do not have one available, counting seconds or marking beginning and ending times can give good approximations of behavior.

You can summarize durational data in many ways. You may wish to total the time for each observation day or session as you did for Jim. When you are viewing behavior over a period of time, for example a week, you may wish to compute an average. You can see from Jim's data that he spends an average of 5.33 hours a day with PlayStation.

Permanent Product Recordings.   *Permanent products* are tangible items or outcomes of behavior (Alberto & Troutman, 1999). These are very easy to count. Examples of permanent products are the work produced by the student—written or creative efforts—or changes in the environment the student has made—amount of carpet shredded, the amount or number of pieces of trash left around desk area, amount of food on the counters or floor. Permanent products can also include such occurrences as wet or soiled pants.

Collecting Information on Behaviors

Records. If the behavior is longstanding, chances are there are many records of this behavior you can access. These records give you information regarding previous interventions, but use caution in interpreting success or failure of a given approach. You must look closely at how systematically the approach was implemented and over how long a time period the approach was used. Remember, just because an approach has not worked in the past does not mean it will be unsuccessful in the present. You may be able to employ the same method more systematically and consistently and enjoy great success.

In addition, note that these records are important in documenting the least restrictive alternative, which we discuss in greater detail later in the chapter. The records can indicate what approaches have been used in the past and if those approaches have been positive. For example, a more restrictive approach cannot be used unless positive approaches have already been tried systematically and proven ineffective.

Interviews. In all cases, interview the parent, team members, previous teachers, peers, and other persons who have had frequent contact with the student. Useful information can be gathered not only on the rate and frequency of the current behavior in other settings, but also on previous intervention strategies and potential reinforcers. When gathering information from others, do not become discouraged by thinking all approaches have been already used. Questions to ask include these: "How long did you do this? How often did you do this? What problems did you have when you did this?" An in-depth examination will usually reveal that persons making such remarks typically did not employ comprehensive or thorough interventions. In other words, do not listen to behavioral naysayers.

◆ DETERMINING THE FUNCTION OF THE BEHAVIOR

Understanding *why* the behavior is occurring is the key to a successful intervention. In this section, you will learn to recognize some of the basic functions of misbehavior, to determine the influence of outside events (setting events) on behavior, and how to conduct functional assessments.

Examining the Relationship Between Function and Behavior

More recent approaches to behavior management have moved away from concentrating on eliminating inappropriate behavior in favor of determining the function the inappropriate behavior serves for the person and developing replacement behaviors to meet that need (Bishop & Jabala, 1995). The function of the behavior is the probable reason the person performs the behavior (Redmond, Bennett, Wiggert, and

MacLean, 1993). Some of the more common functions that have been observed are the following: (1) to escape from an unpleasant event or person, (2) to gain attention from teachers or peers, (3) to provide sensory stimulation, (4) to gain tangible items, and (5) to communicate needs.

Because human behavior is complex, it is reasonable to assume other factors motivate behavior besides these five categories (Reiss & Havercamp, 1999). Even within the framework of these functions, an individual may perform a behavior for more than one reason. For example, an analysis of a student's acting-out behavior may reveal he acts out in class for peer and teacher attention. Further analysis may indicate this student does not have appropriate ways to communicate when he needs teacher or peer attention. It could be determined that a secondary function of this behavior is communication.

There are many ways to determine the probable function of the behavior (see later in this chapter). The basic premise in determining the function is to look at the effect of the individual's behavior on the environment. Remember that the same behavior can perform more than one function for the individual, and therefore you must examine the context.

Escape as a Function. One common function, especially in school environments, is escape. If the behavior causes the activity to stop or the person to go away, it is likely the function is escape. For example, every time you present Jerry with a seatwork task such as writing his name, he begins to hit himself. As a result, you usually halt the activity. You can then conclude the function of his hitting is most likely escape. Once you have determined the function, the next step is to look more closely at that activity to determine what changes you can make. Why is Jerry trying to escape these seatwork tasks? Does he escape all seatwork tasks? We examine these issues in more detail when we discuss antecedents to behaviors.

Attention as a Function.   If the behavior frequently results in attention from others—even if it is a verbal reprimand—generally the function is attention. Attention includes remarks made by the teacher or peers, touches, or even just glances. Because social recognition and affiliation are basic human needs, attention is one of the most common functions. Many persons develop aberrant social behaviors in an effort to have some form of socialization, recognition, and attention from others (Reiss & Havercamp, 1999). The example of Tawanda illustrates a behavior serving this function.

Sensory Input as a Function.   Many behaviors may be exhibited by the individual for self-stimulation or sensory feedback. One way to determine if a behavior is sensory is to determine if it continues to be displayed when the individual is alone or without environmental consequences. If so, it is most likely sensory in nature and functions as sensory input or feedback (Iwata, Dorsey, Slifer, Bauman, & Richman, 1982). Both self-injury and self-stimulation can be sensory in nature. Such repetitive movements may serve to ease anxiety or to stimulate the individual.

Tangible Gain as a Function.   We perform many behaviors for tangible gain. Certainly one of the functions of work is to gain a paycheck. People may steal for personal gain, although they may steal for other reasons as well. For example, when peers in the preschool initiate play with a new toy, Tony frequently attempts to take the toy from his peer by grabbing the toy or hitting the peer.

Communication as a Function.   In many cases, behavior is a form of communication. Because many students with moderate to severe disabilities have limited communication repertoires, you must examine the social context and determine what the student may be attempting to communicate with his or her behavior (Donnel-

lan, Mirenda, Mesaros, & Fassbender, 1984). Persons with disabilities may have inadequate means to communicate basic needs—thirst, hunger—in conventional ways. One poignant example is of a young man in a classroom who kept running and sticking his head in the toilet. The teacher was horrified at this behavior and made many attempts—in vain—to stop it. A closer analysis revealed that he was, in fact, drinking from the toilet—even more upsetting to the teacher. A contact with the parent revealed he had been put on a new medication that caused increased thirst. He had no means of telling anyone in the environment he was thirsty. For the intervention, the teacher provided frequent opportunities to have liquids and also began teaching a gesture to communicate thirst.

Communicative functions are often observed in combination with other functions. For example, the student may be acting out to escape frustrating work. The main function of the behavior may be escape, but the student is also unable to communicate frustration and, therefore, may have a second need to communicate. You must try to understand the individual and to make available many different forms of communication so students have greatest opportunity of communicating their wants and needs to you. If students are unable to communicate effectively, all types of behaviors will surface as they try new ways to communicate their needs. The stories of Tawanda and Mona provide examples of cases in which the students had resorted to inappropriate behaviors to communicate some basic needs to their classmates.

You can see just from these two examples how an outsider can misinterpret a behavior as an act of aggression. The initial way each girl chose to communicate was successful, but, unfortunately, not appropriate. In the first case, Tawanda wanted attention from her peers, and pulling hair did, indeed, slow down the peers to interact with her. In the second case, Mona

TAWANDA: AN EXAMPLE OF A BEHAVIOR WITH BOTH ATTENTION AND COMMUNICATION FUNCTIONS

When on the playground, Tawanda, a first-grade student, would grab and yank the hair of her classmates. At first, the students and the teacher jumped to the conclusion that she was being aggressive and attacking or lunging after her peers. But when the team began to problem-solve, they realized that Tawanda was beginning to initiate interactions with peers for the first time. One of her strategies was to reach out and tap or touch her peers. This worked well in class, but her peers moved so quickly on the playground that she was unable to get their attention gently. By the time she saw her friends, moved toward them, and reached out to them, the peers were long gone. She had to grab their hair and hold on tight to get them to stay. This immediately stopped the girls, and they had to stay with her until their hair was untangled. Tawanda had found a way to slow down her peers long enough to initiate some type of interaction.

Realizing she needed a more appropriate strategy, the team requested the peers' assistance in solving the problem. The students decided that whenever they saw her coming toward them with her arms out, they would take her hand and ask her, "What do you want to show me?" The peers practiced it in the classroom and on the playground. In the beginning, Tawanda was shocked and amazed and didn't quite know what to do with this newfound interaction. When the children would take her hand and ask, "What do you want to show me?" she began to lead the peer to a favorite place on the playground. As a result, this behavior had been deciphered and developed to become a bridge to build two-way friendships among the children.

Example adapted from Joy Garand-Nichols, 1998.

wanted to escape situations in which she felt overwhelmed. Biting did stop the peers from taking her where she didn't want to go and provided her with some personal space. The examples also demonstrate that classmates can assist in solving behavior issues for their classmates. The classmates were not told by a teacher what to do but designed a program they thought would help the student communicate in a different way and still get her needs met.

Examining the Relationship Between Setting Events and Behavior

To this point, we have examined the interaction of the variables within the classroom or school environment and the behavior. As every teacher knows, many events occur outside of the classroom that greatly influence the student's behavior and the effectiveness of the reinforcement or punishment used (Horner, Vaughn, Day, & Ard, 1996). These events (lack of sleep, medication change, a family move, fight on the morning bus ride) have been termed *setting events* (Dadson & Horner, 1993). The following displays the influence of the setting event on behavior:

Setting event → antecedent event → behavior → consequence.

Having information on setting events can greatly enhance your success with students. Information on setting events can enable the teacher to have the appropriate supports in place in the school environment. Keeping in frequent contact with parents and caregivers in other environments can provide crucial information in these areas.

MONA: AN EXAMPLE OF A BEHAVIOR WITH BOTH ESCAPE AND COMMUNICATION FUNCTIONS

Mona became included in a full day middle school setting in a block with 23 students. She had been in a special class with only 5 students, all of whom had special needs. The peers in the new general classroom were very excited to teach and help her with everything. This was especially evident in the lunchroom and hallway where the students pulled Mona with them. At times, many students surrounded her to the point that it was difficult for the teacher to spot her in the halls between classes. The students were just excited, but Mona was slowly building up frustration and becoming overstimulated. Soon, Mona began biting the students when they would surround her or take her hand. It wasn't long until many of the students had been bitten at least once.

The class met as a group to try to determine what Mona was trying to tell her friends by biting them. None of the peers thought that she did not like them. The class worked as a team and developed a solution. They decided to teach Mona that when she didn't want to go where her friends were taking her or when her friends were getting too close, she should give the sign for *stop*. The students modeled and role-played this with her. Because the students designed the plan themselves, they were eager for success. It took a while for the students to teach the sign, but it turned out to be very successful as Mona began using the sign appropriately rather than biting her classmates.

Example adapted from Joy Garand-Nichols, 1998.

Influences From Other Environments. Many students with behavioral issues experience considerable stress and disruption in their home environments. The teacher can often do little to change these conditions, but it is of critical importance that he or she be apprised of situations occurring outside the classroom. In some cases, environmental setting events are predictable. For example, Juan rides on a bus 45 minutes to school. He hates the bus and arrives at school agitated and angry. This agitation can linger all morning. Some changes could be made for the bus ride to be more pleasant, but the teacher must also address this behavior in the classroom. For example, the teacher found that if he gives Juan 10 minutes of relaxation, "cooldown" time, as soon as he arrives, the agitation quickly diminishes, and he is ready to engage in classroom events.

Many students appear to have "bad" days or arrive at school in a "bad mood" (Horner et al.,

1996). These students may live in homes where there is frequent disruption and inadequate emotional support. Students may display a higher rate of inappropriate behavior at these times. Giving students opportunities during the school day to discuss home events in the school setting is one way to address this issue.

For students who are unable to communicate frustrating events in their home or community environments—parental divorce, change in staff or schedules—the teacher must stay in frequent contact with the family or caregivers. If this information is available, the teacher can act on it by making sure the school environment is consistent and very positive.

Medical Issues.   As we noted in Chapter 2, many students with moderate to severe disabilities have complex medical and physical needs. Sometimes, these issues can be mistakenly interpreted as behavioral problems. Therefore, the teacher must maintain frequent contact with parents, caregivers, and medical professionals.

As we noted in Chapter 2, many students take medication. Because medication can cause many changes in behavior, it is critical that the teacher be aware of the medications the student is taking and the possible side effects of those medications (Kerr & Nelson, 1998).

Persons with limited communicative abilities are often unable to tell others when they are ill or not feeling well. If possible, the student's communication system should incorporate the signs, pictures, or symbols for communicating illness or discomfort. If this is not possible, the teacher must make careful observations. For example, Keoni appeared to display self-injurious behavior sometimes more than others, and these behaviors seemed independent of the interventions tried. Keoni did not have adequate communication skills to tell others how he was feeling. The team collected all records on Keoni's behavior and graphed the occurrences for a 3-year time period. When they studied the graph, they saw a higher rate of the behavior in the late summer and fall. One of the team members suggested allergies. Keoni was tested for allergies and found to be highly reactive to certain pollens present during that time. He was put on medication and the behavior decreased dramatically.

For some students, lack of sleep can be a setting event that influences performance. In a case such as this, it is often possible to work with the home setting to ensure changes are made so the individual arrives at school rested (Horner et al., 1996). In other cases, the teacher may need to arrange for a time for the student to rest in class.

Determining the Function of Behavior

Use Observational Information. The information you gather through scatterplots, ABCs, and anecdotal recordings gives you a rich picture of the relationships between the behavior and the environment (Redmond et al., 1993). For example, for escape behavior, look very closely at the antecedent events preceding the behavior. When you examine curricular antecedents, frequently you will determine that the assigned task needs modification. Several aspects of instructional tasks may need modification. Watching how the student reacts to the antecedents (instructional materials, the manner of presentation, instructional content), you can gain valuable information (Alberto & Troutman, 1999).

Frustration can be caused by instructional materials that are too difficult. For example, the material given to the student can be the antecedent that occasions the disruptive escape behavior. In this case, you may determine the worksheet is written at a difficulty level far beyond the student's reading level. For example, if the questions on the sheet are written at grade 3 and the student reads at a preprimer level, he or she will not be able to work independently on the sheet. Rather than constantly ask for help, he or she may act out. *One way to remedy this situation is to make sure the materials are at the appropriate instructional level.* This can include making sure the reading level is appropriate for the student's level. Another way is to break the material down into smaller units or steps that will ensure success for the student.

Boredom can be caused by instructional tasks that are too easy or too familiar for the student. A particular teaching routine could be the antecedent for a problem behavior. Often, students with moderate to severe disabilities may have the same objective on their IEP for *years.* For example, a student may have been working on a self-care skill, shoe tying, for several years. The student may not have mastered the skill completely, but has become bored with working on the same task every day. If you observe a behavior issue arising around the instruction of that skill, you may wish to discontinue instruction and encourage the parent to purchase shoes with Velcro fasteners or slip-on loafers. In another case, the teacher may be presenting the same task repeatedly (puzzle completion) to the student to keep him or her occupied during free times. In this case, the teacher needs to be

FIGURE 8–3   When Do You Eat?

Think about when you eat between meals. Each item is about a time you might eat. Decide how much you eat at that time.

Circle one of the answers for each item:	Eat a lot	Eat some	Eat a little	Don't eat
1. After school	Eat a lot	Eat some	Eat a little	Don't eat
2. When you are bored	Eat a lot	Eat some	Eat a little	Don't eat
3. When out with friends	Eat a lot	Eat some	Eat a little	Don't eat
4. When you are angry	Eat a lot	Eat some	Eat a little	Don't eat
5. When you are sad	Eat a lot	Eat some	Eat a little	Don't eat
6. When you watch TV	Eat a lot	Eat some	Eat a little	Don't eat
7. When you are nervous	Eat a lot	Eat some	Eat a little	Don't eat
8. When you help make dinner	Eat a lot	Eat some	Eat a little	Don't eat
9. When you want to relax	Eat a lot	Eat some	Eat a little	Don't eat
10. When you want to cheer up	Eat a lot	Eat some	Eat a little	Don't eat
11. When you are hungry	Eat a lot	Eat some	Eat a little	Don't eat
12. When you are frustrated	Eat a lot	Eat some	Eat a little	Don't eat

more creative in looking for meaningful activities in the immediate environment.

The *lack* of specific antecedents can also give you information on the function of a behavior. If a student engages in a particular behavior (rocking) across settings, people, and activities with no apparent pattern, you might conclude the function of the behavior is sensory-stimulation. The person engages in the behavior because it makes him or her feel better. In this case, the surrounding events have less importance.

Use Functional Assessment Scales. You can complete several published scales to gain information on the function of the behavior. One scale, *The Motivational Assessment Scale* (Durand, 1988), provides a profile in each of the following areas: sensory, escape, attention, and tangible. Another scale, the *Problem Behavior Questionnaire* (Lewis, Scott, & Sugai, 1994), is designed for classroom use and provides a profile for the following functions: teacher attention, peer attention, escape from the teacher, escape from peers, as well as another category—setting events (causes external to the school environment).

You can create your own interview profile by listing questions such as those in the teacher-made assessment in Figure 8–3 designed to determine reasons for between-meal eating. These types of questionnaires can be given directly to the individual to complete or given during an interview with an informant such as a parent. Responses to the questionnaire can display patterns of potential causes of overeating. For example, if an individual answered that she eats more when she is frustrated, nervous, or bored, eating may serve a sensory function. In this case, the intervention should include some form of replacement behavior to reduce anxiety such as walking or relaxation exercises.

 IMPLEMENTING STRATEGIES FOR INCREASING DESIRED BEHAVIORS

Three aspects are critical to any successful intervention: (1) teach replacement behaviors that address the desired function; (2) make changes in the environment to support appropriate behaviors; and (3) use reinforcement contingently and responsibly. We address each of these aspects in this section.

One of the first steps is to develop a hypothesis about the behavior (Redmond et al., 1993). From that, you develop your plan for building new behaviors and, if necessary, eliminating inappropriate behaviors. Keep in mind that intervention plans are only that—plans. The continuation of any given approach depends on its success in creating a more positive environment for the student. If the behavior does *not* change, you *must* modify your approach. Behavior change is an ongoing process and often takes persistence and creativity on your part. *Remember that most interventions involve changing many elements—reinforcement, instructional materials, environmental supports* (Horner et al., 1996). If success is not achieved within a short period of time, you must continue to problem-solve with the team until you discover the right combination of reinforcement and environmental supports to enable the student to be successful.

Teach Replacement Behaviors

When working with a student who may be exhibiting an undesirable habit or behavior, teaching the absence of the habit is not going to work. A student needs to be taught a new way to communicate or have his or her needs met.

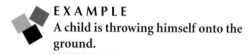

EXAMPLE
A child is throwing himself onto the ground.

Not a solution: The child must stop throwing his body on the ground and everyone is going to make the student stop the behavior.

*Solution: The team needs to assess the situation and determine what is being communicated and what the child can do **instead** of throwing his body on the ground.*

Target Desired Behavior. In determining replacement behaviors, look to the function of the behavior. For attention, you want to enable the individual to gain the attention he or she desires from others in a better way that will be naturally reinforced in the environment. Replacement skills could include teaching any of the following: ways to get the attention from others, greeting skills, conversation skills, hand raising in the classroom, and/or ways to express feelings. For the student who needs significant amounts of adult attention, he or she may be taught to elicit praise from the teacher (e.g., ask, "How am I doing?") (Alber, Heward, & Hippler, 1999). For acquiring tangible items, you may need to teach the student request behaviors. For example, the student may be taught to ask for favorite toys rather than taking toys from other students.

For behaviors that provide sensory stimulation for the individual, one approach is to give the student a tangible item he or she can hold. For example, if the student appears to be nervous in the crowded school hallways or in other high traffic areas, he or she can hold a soft ball such as a Koosh ball while walking. In the vignette about Dorian, you can see how he was taught a more appropriate method for gaining the supervisor's attention.

Use Response Building Strategies to Teach New Behaviors. In some cases, the individual does not have the new replacement skill in his or her repertoire. In those cases, you will need to teach a new skill(s). In other cases, the individual may display the behavior, but at a very low level. For your intervention to be successful, you need to increase the behavior. In Chapter 2, you learned that some skills are easier to learn when you break the skill into small steps or stages and present the steps incrementally. This strategy, known as *shaping*, is important in behavioral intervention programs.

One of the most important decisions in beginning a shaping program is where to begin. The information you recorded on the duration and frequency of the behavior will give you guidelines. For example, when you observed Roxanne in the morning group, you noted that she only sits for less than a minute before she becomes restless and tries to leave. Based on this information, begin providing reinforcement for sitting approximately 1 to 2 minutes (initially, prompts to sit may be needed). If she stays longer, continue to deliver the reinforcement. Once the student is sitting for 2 or more minutes without prompts, the criteria for reinforcement would be changed to 4 minutes. Shaping is frequently a very rapid process with criteria changing in response to student gains in behavior.

Make Environmental Changes

In addition to teaching new behaviors, proactive teaching involves structuring the environment and the teaching materials so the students are more likely to have success. The antecedent events triggering the behavior need to be examined closely and, in many cases, changes need to be made there as well.

Adapt Instructional Materials.   As we noted, especially in regard to escape behavior, the antecedent events are very relevant. Students act out because they are frustrated with the learning experience as it is arranged. As we discussed in Chapter 2, you want to design programs that minimize error. Often this involves changing the difficulty level of the material, adding cues or prompts, or even abandoning the lesson. The instructional modifications you will learn about in Chapters 10 and 11 will provide you with more tools for this approach.

Use Picture Schedules.   Changes in schedules—school assembly, teacher absence—are often antecedents for problematic behavior (Horner, Neill, & Flannery, 1993). There are many ways to prevent problems through the use of picture schedules. For many students, a picture schedule is an effective strategy for intro-

A PROGRAM FOR TATTLING

Dorian is a student in a secondary vocational classroom. In this environment, the students are expected to do their janitorial jobs with minimum supervision. The vocational teacher noted that Dorian was coming to him on an average of six times a day to complain about one of his coworkers. When this happened, the teacher acknowledged the remark and sent Dorian back to his station, telling him he would handle the situation. As Dorian walked away, the teacher frequently heard him remark, "I don't do that." Because this strategy was not changing the behavior, the teacher decided to conduct a functional assessment. The teacher determined the function of the behavior was for teacher attention and for recognition. For the intervention, the teacher set aside about 10 minutes each morning for Dorian to talk with him about his personal problems. In addition, he made sure to give Dorian specific descriptive praise on his work at least one time every 30 minutes. He decided to ignore the tattling behavior should it occur. The intervention was so successful that the behavior dropped to zero occurrences by the second day and did not reoccur. The teacher and the team decided to maintain the program but to reduce talk time to about 5 minutes each day and to fade the descriptive praise to at least one time per hour. It was stated by the team that descriptive praise should always be a part of every student's program.

ducing structure into a day (Earles, Carlson, & Bock, 1998). It gives the student an opportunity to be aware of the routine daily events and to prepare for changes. Schedules can also assist in preventing behavioral problems. To prepare for changes, the teacher can hand the picture of the new activity to the student, and the student can physically change his or her own schedule. As the two pictures are exchanged, the student is the one making the change in the schedule. This can make the transition easier. In addition, schedules are very valuable tools to help build independence, time management, and organizational skills. In the appendix of this chapter, you will find detailed descriptions of three types of picture schedules that can be adapted for individual and classroom use.

To enhance coping with unforeseen schedule changes, establish a system of communication so you can prepare the student for the change. One way is to provide a concrete marker for the student using a picture or symbol. Choose a relevant picture or symbol for the student that will be placed on the board each time a change is about to happen. For some students, it might be a big picture of the sun, a lightning bolt, or an alarm clock. Place the picture in sight of the student 3 to 5 minutes before the change is going to occur. This gives the student time to prepare for the transition. You may wish to take a few moments to discuss the change with the student as well.

Use Proactive Classroom Management Strategies

Organize Your Environment. Proactive teachers anticipate problems before they occur and structure the classroom environment to minimize their occurrence (Gettinger, 1998). When examining the antecedents to the behavior, consider manipulating the classroom environment, such as making changes in seating arrangements, removing distracting materials, or decreasing noise levels (Zirpoli & Melloy, 1997, 2001). These are easy changes to make and can frequently preclude the need for intervention. For example, Jamal was displaying considerable agitation in his fifth-grade class during the day—screaming, rocking, and getting out of his seat. A closer examination of the environment revealed he was seated in the highest traffic area of the class—next to the book shelves. Students had to go to the shelves several times daily to get and return books for each subject. Students would frequently brush against Jamal, who would become even more agitated. The chaos that ensued with each change made Jamal nervous. A change in seating arrangements and the imposition of transition rules for all students drastically reduced Jamal's agitated behavior.

In another case, Isabel was throwing objects. Each time she threw an object, she laughed hysterically. The behavior was reduced by removing all objects from her reach and by controlling the objects she worked with. The teacher provided

A picture schedule is an effective strategy for introducing structure into the day

physical prompts for her to hold objects and provided immediate and strong reinforcement for holding without throwing. By using systematic reinforcement strategies, time holding objects was gradually increased and objects were gradually introduced in the surrounding environment.

Employ Good Teaching Strategies. Teacher proximity can improve student behavior (Gunter, Shores, Jack, Rasmussen, & Flowers, 1996). Teachers who use "proximity control" move effectively about the classroom and have frequent interactions with students. If the teacher is standing near a student, he or she is less likely to act out. Effective teachers provide frequent positive reinforcement and attention to other students, which also has the effect of decreasing inappropriate behavior (Gunter et al., 1996). Teachers who communicate awareness of student behavior and who are able to maintain momentum of instruction have fewer behavioral problems as well (Evertson & Harris, 1992).

There are other principles of effective classroom management that are proactive and act to prevent behavioral problems. These include establishing rules and procedures, providing lessons that engage students, and communicating student expectations clearly (Evertson & Harris, 1992). Effective teachers establish a management system at the beginning of the school year and monitor the system consistently during the year to ensure its effectiveness.

Use Student Performance Data to Make Program Changes. As we discussed earlier in this chapter, keep good records on student behavior and on your interventions. It is important to examine and evaluate student progress on an ongoing basis. If after a specified period of time, several days or a week, the student is not making sufficient progress, change part of your intervention. For example, change the reinforcer, the instructional materials, the instructional setting, the procedure for correcting errors or misbehavior, and/or the rate or pace of materials pre-

sented. Careful examination of the conditions of the intervention should yield information on the best aspect to change. When considering variables to change, look again at the function of the behavior and make sure the intervention as you designed it is meeting the identified function effectively.

Rarely is it appropriate to change more than one or two aspects of the intervention or to discard the intervention. Once the change has been made, continue to monitor progress and make additional changes, if needed. Do not become discouraged. On first interventions, it is common to make several changes before the right combination of environmental, curricular, and reinforcement variables is present.

Build and Maintain Behavior with Reinforcement

Understand the Principles of Reinforcement. Reinforcement is one of the most important aspects of any intervention. Let's first define reinforcement. A *reinforcer* is a consequence that causes an increase in the target behavior. You judge the effectiveness of the consequence by the observed change in behavior. This underscores the importance of observation and data collection. For example, if the consequence you apply—teacher praise—does not result in an increase in the target behavior—student following requests—you can say that consequence is *not* a reinforcer. In this case, you need to try other potential reinforcers—access to a preferred activity or removal from a nonpreferred activity—until you achieve an increase in this behavior.

Finding effective reinforcers and applying them contingently and consistently can be difficult for the beginning teacher (Kerr & Nelson, 1998). This section outlines some ways to choose and apply reinforcement. Generally, social reinforcers—positive descriptive feedback and praise—are the most powerful reinforcers. For many students, however, social reinforcers must be paired with other types of reinforcement. Categories of reinforcers can include activities (computer time or free time), tangibles (edible items, tokens, and objects), and social interactions (time with a teacher or friends).

Choose Effective Reinforcers

Observe in the Context. One of the best ways to determine what is valuable to a student or classroom of students is to observe the actions of the students in your class (Maag, 1999). Where do the students go during their free time? What are the events or objects that cause disputes? With whom does the student prefer to spend the most time? For students who have severe disabilities, you may conduct some experiments by placing objects or food items out for the student and observing the frequency with which he or she interacts with these items.

Selection of reinforcement for some students requires considerable creativity. In some cases, the inappropriate behavior can be used as the reinforcer. For example, for the student who likes to run, playing chase can be an effective reinforcer. For the student who spends his or her days talking in class to peers, talk time can be a good reinforcer.

Use Reinforcement Inventories. Giving preference or reinforcement lists to parents or students can be a very efficient way to determine reinforcers (Walker & Shea, 1999). In making your inventory, you can use information gained from observations to construct the items on your list. For example, you may make a list of classroom activities that many students like— line leader, computer time, group leader—and ask students to rate their preference for these. You may ask them to tell you their favorite foods or musical groups. There are many ways to approach this. The important aspect is that you have a wide variety of reinforcers to use with each student. See Figure 8–4 for a sample reinforcement menu.

 FIGURE 8–4   Sample Reinforcement Menu

Circle the activities or things you like best:

1. Free time for games

2. Computer time

3. Cash for school store

4. Gift from surprise bag

5. Special jobs

6. Listening to music

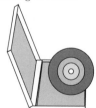

FIGURE 8–5   Ellen's Participation Contract

Ellen's Participation Contract

When Ms. Everington asks the class a question, I, Ellen, agree to raise my hand and answer questions at least two times a day. I will tap my fingers on my desk to let her know that I know the answer.

I, *Ms. Everington*, agree to call on Ellen only when her fingers are tapping. That means that she knows the answer.

We will review this contract at the end of the week. ☺

Ellen	*Ms. Everington*
Ellen	Ms. Everington

Apply Reinforcement Correctly

Apply Reinforcement Contingently. The *contingency* is the planned systematic relationship between a behavior and its consequence (Kerr & Nelson, 1998). Reinforcement must be applied consistently and immediately. The behavior that earns reinforcement must be made clear to the student. For some students, this can be accomplished by a simple contract. You can see the simple contract for Ellen and the teacher in Figure 8–5. This contract tells what both Ellen and the teacher will do. Ellen's reinforcement is to have an opportunity to give the correct answers in class. Note that the contract should include a beginning and an ending date.

For other students, the contingency is made clear through making sure the desired behavior is exhibited at a rate high enough to gain frequent reinforcement. You may need to make changes in the environment or prompt the behavior so the desired behavior will occur at a higher rate. You may also need to reinforce successive approximations of behavior. For example, Terrance did not know appropriate greeting behaviors and displayed inappropriate hugging when he met his friends in the school hallway. The teacher began with prompting him to gesture hello. To teach the new behavior, the teacher needed to stop or interrupt the inappropriate behavior (hugging) and physically prompt a hand gesture or handshake. Terrance was initially reinforced (praise and a pat on the back) for cooperating with the physical prompting sequence. When he began to show signs of initiation of the new gesture, the reinforcement was given only for independent behavior.

Use Differential Reinforcement Strategies. When reinforcement is applied with the focus of increasing positive alternatives, this process is called *differential reinforcement* (Webber & Scheuermann, 1991). You can apply differential reinforcement in several ways. One way we have already discussed is to reinforce a functional alternative. This approach is sometimes called *differential reinforcement of alternative behavior* (DRA). Because students may not be initially motivated to perform the new, alternative behaviors, the teacher must maximize the reinforcement for these new behaviors (Horner et al., 1993).

For example, if you return to Minnie who says "I'm sorry" constantly in all conversations, you determine she uses that phrase to initiate and stay in the conversation. You can generate some functional alternative behaviors for her. You can begin by teaching Minnie questions to start conversations and ways to reply to statements made by others.

Another approach is to reinforce behaviors that are incompatible with the inappropriate behavior, *differential reinforcement of incompatible behaviors* (DRI). For this type of reinforcement, you choose a behavior to reinforce that makes it impossible to display the inappropriate behavior. Some examples of incompatible behaviors include (1) out-of-seat →in-seat, (2) off-task → on-task, (3) hitting face with hands →keeping hands folded or occupied holding objects. Be aware that sometimes the incompatible behavior (being quiet) is not the most functional behavior. Care should be taken to refer back to the functional assessment when choosing behaviors to reinforce.

Two other examples of differential reinforcement include *differential reinforcement of low rates of behavior* (DRL) and *differential reinforcement of other behaviors* (DRO). In DRL, the student is reinforced for exhibiting a lower rate of behavior. The idea is to get the behavior to a rate that is more acceptable in the typical population. To determine a desired rate, you may wish to observe the class for a day. For example, an observation of five students in the class shows an average of three times out of seat during the hour. You may gradually reduce the number of times a student gets out of seat from 10 times per hour to 1 to 2 times per hour. One to 2 times per hour is within the range of the other students. In some classes that may use a more student-centered approach, out-of-seat behavior is a common occurrence for all students. You would not want to penalize the student with disabilities by making him or her sit continuously.

In the second example, DRO, you reinforce the person for *not* exhibiting a behavior for a period of time. This type of reinforcement is good for behaviors that cannot be tolerated in the environment—hitting, destruction of property, cursing, running away. For DRO, the student is reinforced for going for a specified time period without exhibiting the behavior. For example, the student is reinforced for each 10-minute time period that he or she does not display ag-

gressive behavior toward other students on the playground. The time intervals for reinforcement are determined by the initial information (baseline) you collected.

Use caution with these two approaches—DRL and DRO—because they do not consider the function of the behavior and do not involve training new behaviors. As a result, you may get what is called *symptom substitution*—other behaviors will arise. For example, reinforcing not hitting on the playground may *not* address the reason the student was hitting—she needed a means to communicate needs to her peers. If these approaches are used, they need to be combined with functional assessment and DRI or DRA.

Use Self-Management and Cognitive Behavioral Strategies

Self-Management Strategies. Because the goal of your efforts is to teach students to manage and to take responsibility for their own behavior, self-management strategies must be an integral part of the positive behavioral support program. Whenever possible, persons with disabilities must be collaborators in the intervention process (Carr, 1997; Fox, Vaughn, Dunlap, & Bucy, 1997). This means participating to the maximum extent in all stages of the intervention process including recording one's own behavior, setting goals for desired behavior, and reinforcing oneself (Workman & Katz, 1995). Self-evaluation is an important part of this process (Zirpoli & Melloy, 2001). To do this, you must provide the student with criteria by which he or she can compare his or her performance. For students with moderate to severe disabilities you need to provide concrete models. You might provide a sample of a finished product (folded napkin) or a picture (clean room). Upon completion, students should rate their performance. Graphics, such as the faces ☺ used in the self-charting example in Chapter 5, can be helpful.

Students need specific instruction and feedback on each of the self-management strategies.

FIGURE 8 – 6   **Problem-Solving Sequence for Mia**

1. What is the problem? (Students tease me in the cafeteria)
2. What can I do? (Call them names back, hit them, walk away, ignore them, tell the teacher)
3. What will happen if I (hit them)? (Generate consequences for the alternatives)
4. What is the best choice for now? (Mia decides to tell the teacher because she can't ignore them)
5. How will I do this? (Mia and the teacher make a plan)
6. How did it work? (Mia and her teacher discuss the results the next day and the plan may be revised)

In addition, there are many ways you can incorporate peers into interventions. Peers can assist one another in monitoring behavior and can be trained to administer reinforcement—positive comments—for one another.

Cognitive behavioral interventions are critical components of any plan. These approaches focus on changing the "unobservable" portions of behavior: thoughts, private speech, and emotions (Harris, 1982). One cognitive behavioral approach that has been very effective in this area is self-instruction or self-guidance. The prompting strategies we discussed in Chapter 2 can be taught to students enabling them to provide their own prompts to regulate their behavior. Through self-guidance, students can use strategies of self-talk or self-presented images to regulate behavior (Workman & Katz, 1995). Self-talk has been used effectively in many ways. Students can learn to regulate their anger by learning to tell themselves calming statements: "Take it easy" or "Calm down" (Kellner & Tutin, 1995). They can increase academic performance by developing positive self-statements such as "I can do it" and "I've got it" (Harris, 1982). Students can be taught to imagine themselves being successful or calm in a situation prior to the event (Workman & Katz, 1995).

Problem Solving.   Problem solving is particularly difficult for students with moderate to severe disabilities. Teaching the students approaches to identify the problem, think of alternatives, and identify potential consequences is

important and must be addressed systematically (Zirpoli & Melloy, 2001). Figure 8–6 provides an example of steps that can be used in a problem-solving sequence for a student named Mia who is experiencing difficulty with teasing from students in another class. It would be important for the teacher to review each of these steps with Mia as often as possible.

Anger Management Training.   Emotions and feelings are difficult for many students to change. Using an approach such as *anger management training,* students with cognitive disabilities are taught to identify triggers for anger and methods for addressing feelings of arousal (Benson, 1992; Kellner & Tutin, 1995) (see Figure 8–7). The following sequence adapted from Yell, Robinson, and Drasgow (2001) can be used for teaching anger control to students.

1. Identify triggers. In this first step, students are taught to identify situations that make them angry. One approach is to have students think of all the things that make them angry. This can be done as an individual or group activity. Kellner and Tutin (1995) advocate keeping a "trigger list." In this case, students keep a log of things that make them mad. The trigger list is complied from contributions of all students. The list helps students learn to identify and verbalize anger.

Some students may need instruction on identifying feelings prior to this activity. The teacher may need to help them identify how

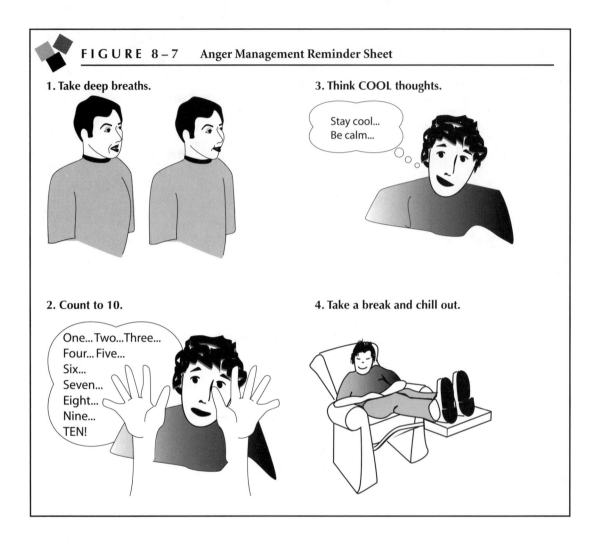

FIGURE 8–7 Anger Management Reminder Sheet

1. Take deep breaths.

3. Think COOL thoughts.

Stay cool...
Be calm...

2. Count to 10.

One...Two...Three...
Four...Five...
Six...
Seven...
Eight...
Nine...
TEN!

4. Take a break and chill out.

they feel in reaction to various situations at the time of the occurrence.

2. Prepare for the provocation. In this stage, students are taught to plan strategies for preparing for situations in which they are likely to become angry. One approach that has been very effective is role play (Kellner and Tutin, 1995). Using role play, students act out a potential situation of conflict (student is excluded from the activity). The preparation should include more appropriate ways to address the situation in the future (ask others if he or she can join the activity).

Self-talk can be helpful at this stage. A student can be taught to use statements that will help with self-control. For example, "I know I can do this." "Those kids are not going to make me mad." "I am going to keep my cool."

3. Address feelings of arousal. An important step in controlling anger is to teach students to identify when they are angry and to control the arousal feelings. Strategies for addressing feelings of arousal include relaxation training, deep breathing, counting exercises, and self-talk. In initial training stages, many students find it helpful to use supports such as squeezing a small ball or by taking voluntary time-outs. A voluntary time-out is when the student leaves the situation to go to another area of the room or to another room. We discuss voluntary time-out later in this section.

One approach that has been effective in self control and arousal reduction is to teach students to *stop and think*. This simple message can assist students with impulse control. To help students remember this, signs reading STOP AND THINK can be posted in the classroom or on desks.

4. Reflect on your behavior. As part of any self-managment program, students must learn to self-evaluate. In anger control training, this includes evaluation of their behavior after the incident. One way to do this is to have students keep a *hassle log* (Kellner & Tutin, 1995). In this approach, students write down the situation and how they handled it. For students who have difficulty with self-evaluation, faces ☺ can be used.

IMPLEMENTING STRATEGIES FOR DECREASING INAPPROPRIATE BEHAVIOR

At times you will need to provide direct intervention to decrease an inappropriate behavior. The strategies discussed in this section use the least restrictive treatment alternative. A consequence is known as a *punisher* if it weakens the occurrence of the behavior (Smith, 1993). Punishers are identified by their *effect* on behavior (Alberto & Troutman, 1999). For example, if the consequence—time-out—does not decrease the behavior, then it is *not* a punisher. This underscores the importance of recording and continuously evaluating the progress of your intervention programs.

Punishment can be effective, but there are many negative side effects. These can include (1) escape or avoidance of the situation or the person administering the punishment; (2) emotional effects—fear, anger, agitation; (3) aggression—especially toward the punisher; (4) mod-

eling of the aggressive behavior of the punisher; and (5) suppression of other behaviors (Smith, 1993). Therefore, in all cases, *implement positive approaches systematically before attempting punishment strategies.* When considering any intervention, apply the principle known as the *least intrusive alternative* (Alberto & Troutman, 1999). That is, select the procedure having the least intrusive effect on the individual. We present and discuss strategies in a hierarchy. Four approaches are commonly used to decrease or eliminate problematic behavior: *extinction, time-out, response cost,* and *overcorrection.* Of the strategies we discuss, extinction is the least intrusive and, as a result, most commonly used. When using time-out, response cost, or overcorrection, parental permission is suggested. In addition, a program review or human rights committee should be established to review reduction programs that are restrictive such as exclusionary time-out, response cost, and overcorrection (Zipoli & Melloy, 1997). We discuss each of these strategies in this section.

Although there is a fifth category, contingent use of aversive stimuli—yelling, physical restraint, spanking, verbal reprimands—that has been shown to be effective in reducing or eliminating behavior, these approaches are not considered an ethical or appropriate practice for the classroom teacher (Meyer & Evans, 1989). Physical restraint is one such approach that warrants further discussion. With persons with severe disabilities, physical restraint is sometimes used in classrooms to maintain individuals in their seats or as a consequence for aggressive or self-injurious behavior. These applications of physical restraint are not appropriate because they do not teach new skills. An example is the teacher who straps the wandering student into her chair so she does not disrupt the class. If the student has difficulty sitting in a chair, the teacher must begin teaching in-seat behavior and make the appropriate environmental modifications that will promote easy acquisition of sitting behavior. Strapping a child in a chair does not promote skill acquisition and is considered an aversive approach. The same would be true for using physical restraint to prevent a child from hitting himself.

Having said that, there are emergency situations where the student presents a danger to self or to others in which physical restraint may be appropriate. The difference in this type of application is that it is an *emergency* procedure. As soon as the situation is stabilized, the team should meet and develop a positive program to address the problem.

Using Extinction and Time-Out

Extinction. Extinction can be defined as "the discontinuation or withholding of the reinforcement of a behavior that has previously been reinforced" (Walker & Shea, 1999, p. 185). One of the most common uses of extinction is planned ignoring. In this approach, the teacher removes attention from the individual during the time the individual is displaying the inappropriate behavior. This approach can be very effective *if positive reinforcement is frequently provided for appropriate behavior.* Here are several caveats to keep in mind when using this approach:

1. Behavior change can be slow at first.
2. The problematic behavior may increase before it decreases, displaying what is known as an *extinction burst* (Malott, Whaley, & Malott, 1997).
3. This approach only works if the main function of the behavior is attention.
4. It is hard to ignore a student effectively.
5. If you inadvertently give the student attention, the behavior will most likely be maintained.
6. Many students are very creative and will do something you cannot ignore—run out of the room, hit another student, destroy property.

If you have a student you fear may display a strong reaction to ignoring or may push the limits, have a contingency plan for those events in advance or do not employ this strategy with that student.

Time-Out. Two types of time-outs can be appropriate for classroom use: *nonexclusionary* and *exclusionary* (Alberto & Troutman, 1999). A third type, *seclusionary time-out,* involves the removal of the student and placement in an especially constructed time-out room; we do not believe this is an appropriate approach for public school settings.

The most important aspect of time-out is its definition—time away from reinforcement. *Remember, time-out does not work if you do not have a classroom environment rich with reinforcement and a curriculum the student finds engaging and inviting.* If these elements are not present, time-out can have the opposite effect: It can positively reinforce escape from class activities.

Nonexclusionary Time-Out. The first type of time out, nonexclusionary, should be the approach of choice for the general classroom because it can be easily implemented with little risk to the teacher or student. In this type of time-out, the student is *not* removed from the setting, but rather, he or she is denied access to materials or reinforcers for a short period of time contingent on specified misbehavior (Zipoli & Melloy, 1997). There are many possible applications of this approach. One way is to remove materials. For example, when Tobias begins to use the art materials inappropriately, the teacher removes them for approximately 2 minutes. At the end of this time, she asks him if he is ready to work with the materials.

A second application of nonexclusionary time-out is the removal of the ability to earn reinforcement for a specified time period. An example of this procedure is the ribbon technique (Salend & Gordon, 1987). In this approach, each child wears a ribbon on his or her wrist. As long as students wear the ribbon, they can earn reinforcements—tokens, praise, or edibles. When a specified misbehavior occurs, the ribbon is removed for a specified time period during which the individual cannot earn reinforcement. The remainder of the class continues to earn reinforcers during this time. Another application of this approach is to create small signs—red or green lights—that can be placed on the students' desks. When a misbehavior occurs, the teacher flips the sign to red and the student cannot earn reinforcement for a specified time.

Exclusionary Time-Out. The second type of time-out that can be effective is exclusionary time-out. In this approach, the student is physically removed from the immediate instruction or peers. This is more restrictive because physical removal can cause disruption and involve injury to the teacher or to the student. One approach of this type is *contingent observation*. In this approach, the student who misbehaves is removed from the activity, but can still observe the others (Maag, 1999). This approach is frequently used in early childhood settings. This is effective if the student will stay seated without intervention and you can prevent the student from continuing to receive attention from the other students (Maag, 1999).

A second application of exclusionary time-out is to remove the student to an area that obstructs his or her view of the class such as placement behind a partition, in the hallway, or in a study carrel. For this to be effective, you must be able to prevent the student from accessing reinforcement in the other area (Maag, 1999). Hallways can provide a welcome escape from class and invite attention from other classmates. Study carrels can provide opportunities to engage in other misbehavior—scribbling on the walls and property destruction (Maag, 1999).

Voluntary Time-Out. An approach that can be effective with students who have problems with impulse control and aggression is voluntary time-out. In this approach, when the student shows signs of agitation, he or she removes himself or herself from the group until composure is regained and then returns to the class setting. This technique can be a first step in teaching self-control. Remember, a staff member must be able to monitor the student's behavior in the other area. In addition, voluntary time-out is subject to the problems discussed in relation to exclusionary time-out. That is, it can serve as a reinforcer and the inappropriate behavior will continue or escalate.

Using Response Cost and Overcorrection

Response Cost. Response cost is the removal of a specified amount of reinforcement contingent upon misbehavior (Maag, 1999). Fines are response-cost measures. We see response cost frequently in programs that use token economies. Other uses of response cost include removal of preferred activities such as recess, lunch in the cafeteria with classmates, or free time. This approach is relatively easy to implement, but be careful to provide many opportunities to earn reinforcements. Otherwise, if students are continuing to receive fines or penalties without the ability to earn rewards, they will become disenfranchised with the system and continue to display high rates of misbehavior.

Overcorrection. A final approach that can be effective in reducing behavior is overcorrection. This approach is considered the most restrictive of the ones discussed thus far. In overcorrection, correct behavior is taught through an exaggeration of the experience (Alberto & Troutman, 1999). There are two types of overcorrection—positive practice and restitutional overcorrection. In positive practice, the student practices the correct behavior an exaggerated number of times. For example, if students are loud returning from lunch, they must practice walking from the lunchroom to the classroom quietly several times in succession. If a student inappropriately hugs others, she is required to display a more appropriate greeting—handshake—many times with each person. The exaggeration of the experience makes this approach more intrusive and unpleasant.

For restitutional overcorrection, the environment is not only restored to the original condition, but beyond that (Alberto & Troutman, 1999). For example, a student who places chewing gum under her desk is required to clean the bottoms of all desks in the classroom. The student who throws and spills a milk carton is required not only to clean the spill, but also to mop the entire floor around the cafeteria table.

Crisis Intervention

Always have a crisis management plan in place (Dwyer, Osher, & Hoffman, 2000). If you know you have a student who is likely to have outbursts that are dangerous to him or her, to others, or to property, have a plan for handling the situation. In order to maintain safe schools, each building should have a behavior support team in place that is ready to respond to dangerous situations (Skiba & Peterson, 2000). This team should have prepared and rehearsed plans for a variety of situations. The team must have a mechanism for initiating an immediate response. A contact person, like the office secretary, can be responsible for alerting the group. To get assistance, you might use another student to notify the office, or you may have a code signal that alerts other teachers you need the team's assistance. You may be able to prevent team intervention by talking to the student until he or she is calm. Even in those cases, the team should be alerted and ready (possibly waiting out of view of the student).

Team interventions can involve briefly restraining the student until he or she is calm or taking the student to a safe place. If implementing such procedures, team members should have training in crisis intervention techniques to avoid injury to staff or to the student. The team must practice the techniques as a group. *It is very important to remember that restraint should not be used as an intervention.* Restraint is only to be used in emergency situations. When you restrain or isolate a student, make sure to allow time for the student to cool down (Kaufman, Mostert, Trehut, & Hallahan, 1998). If you release the student too soon, injury to staff, other students, or property can occur.

When you notice a behavior escalating, try to intervene—by redirecting the student, talking calmly to the student, and removing the provoking stimulus (dangerous objects or other students). When the situation has become more dangerous, avoid actions that will cause the behavior to escalate further—touching the student, correcting the student (Kaufman et al., 1998)—and initiate contact with the behavior support team. As with any intervention involving potential conflict, the teacher and team members should avoid showing anger, frustration, or fear (Abrams & Segal, 1998).

 **SUMMARY**

In this chapter, you learned the importance of pinpointing and defining behavioral problems and conducting intervention-based assessments. You learned how to examine observational data and to determine the impact of environmental events in many settings on the behavior. You learned the various functions that inappropriate behavior serves for individuals and how to conduct functional assessment. Intervention involves hypothesis generation and testing and generally requires teaching new behaviors, making changes in the environment or instructional demands, and applying positive consequences more consistently. More restrictive approaches involving behavior reduction should only be used after positive approaches have been systematically implemented and have failed to produce results. In most cases, positive interventions are sufficient to effect the needed changes.

◆ CHAPTER EXTENDERS

Key Terms and Concepts

1. *Antecedent* refers to the event that immediately precedes a behavior.
2. *Behavior* refers to the student's response to the antecedent event.
3. *Behavioral interventions* are proactive and positive strategies for preventing or minimizing behavioral difficulties.
4. *Cognitive behavioral interventions* are strategies that focus on changing unobservable behavior through self-guidance.
5. *Consequence* refers to the specific action or event that follows a behavior.
6. *Contingency* is the planned and systematic relationship between a behavior and its consequence.
7. *Differential reinforcement* refers to strategies that focus on increasing positive alternatives.
8. *Duration recording* provides data on how long a behavior occurs.
9. *Extinction* is the discontinuation of a previously used reinforcer of a behavior.
10. *Frequency recording* provides data on discrete behaviors.
11. *Permanent products* are the tangible results of behavior.
12. A *reinforcer* is a consequence that increases the target behavior.

Study Questions

1. Name five functions of behavior and give examples of each.
2. Define ABC. Provide an example of an ABC for one of your own behaviors that you find troubling.
3. Define and provide examples of each of the following types of recordings: frequency, duration, permanent product, and anecdotal.
4. Define setting events and provide two examples of setting events that influenced your performance at work or school this week.
5. Define the following types of reinforcement and provide an example of each: DRO, DRI, DRA, DRL.
6. What is the least intrusive alternative treatment model? Arrange the following in a hierarchy: response cost, differential reinforcement, extinction.
7. Define the following and provide examples: response cost, extinction, time-out, and overcorrection. Which is easiest for general classroom use? Why?

Group Activity I

Earl is a 6-year-old who does not have oral communication. Some mornings when he arrives in school, he is cooperative and willing to follow instructions. Other morning, he sulks, cries, and refuses to participate. His limited language ability prevents him from telling you what is happening. What might be some of the factors influencing his behavior? How will you investigate this? What might be some changes you could make to address some of the possible causes you have identified?

Group Activity II

Devona is a fourth-grade girl who is frequently out of her seat and inattentive during cooperative learning group times in class. What might be the function(s) of her behavior? How will you investigate this problem? Identify two possible functions of Devona's behavior and strategies for addressing each.

Field Experience

Conduct a 2-week behavioral intervention with a school-aged student. Include the following in your intervention: (1) a 3-day observation of the behavior, (2) an ABC analysis, (3) an analysis of the function of the behavior, (4) a reinforcement survey, and (5) an intervention plan. Your intervention plan should include (1) changes in the environment and the curriculum, (2) a strategy for reinforcement of appropriate behavior, and (3) a strategy for teaching new replacement behaviors. Run your program for at least 2 weeks. Keep daily records on your progress. If you do not see progress within 5 days, change part of your program. Analyze the effectiveness of your program and share the results with teachers, parents, or other caregivers.

Using Picture Schedules to Assist Students in Participating in the General Education Classroom

Joy Garand-Nichols

This appendix reviews the use of picture schedules to structure the environment and enable students with disabilities to function more independently. Picture schedules can be made with the written word, Mayer Johnson Picture Communication Symbols, or actual objects. Use whatever is most meaningful for your student. The following presents some examples of schedules that begin with simple left-right sequences and moves to those that include multistep activities. The last example is a schedule for an entire class. The class schedule would be placed in the front of the room and students could take turns assuming responsibility for changing the activities.

Example 1: A Simple Left-to-Right Sequence

Each square contains a picture. The pictures are small laminated cards that are put on the schedule board with Velcro. The Velcro allows the board to be easily changed when needed. The schedule is placed with pictures in a row so the students begin to learn to read from left to right. The Velcro also allows students to remove the picture when they have finished the activity and to place it in a basket. This allows students to immediately look to the next picture to see what the following activity will be. For some students, placing a number below the picture helps them move sequentially across the board.

Example 2: A Schedule That Includes Directions for Activities

This schedule is for a student who can read left to right, top to bottom, and can follow a multiple-step request. The student begins with number 1 and follows each step in the routine. For example, the first row displays the morning routine: Hang up your coat and backpack, get your

1			
2			
3			
4			
5			

materials from your box, and begin independent work. The numbers can also be used to name a task and then break it down. For example, number 1 would start with a picture of the backpack and then continue with pictures of things that need to be taken out of the backpack (lunch money, homework folder, and gym shoes). Usually, the front of the schedule addresses activities before lunch and the back, the afternoon schedule. A plastic page slide holder may be used to allow the pictures to slide easily in and out. As students become successful with the weekly schedule, they can change to a weekly schedule.

Example 3: A Schedule for the Entire Class

A large schedule can be a pocket chart card holder with enlarged Mayer Johnson pictures. Schedules can also be made in the same formats by replacing pictures with words or sentences.

As students continue to be successful with their daily schedule, they can work up to a weekly schedule. For students who need more time to process change, a calendar in or on their desk is helpful to remind them of the change that will be occurring this month. Special activities—field trips or assemblies—should be included on the calendar.

chapter 9

The Preschool Classroom

Young children are energetic and anxious to make new friends. They are naturally curious and eager to learn. Preschool programs that emphasize student-initiated learning experiences can engage and nourish these attributes. The curriculum should emphasize motor, social skills, and language development as well as provide family support and involvement (Smith & Luckasson, 1995). A typical preschool is filled with hands-on materials that encourage students in the development of these skills. Large Lego and wooden building blocks; puzzles and books; drawing, coloring, cutting, and pasting materials; and play phones, cars, and dolls are common items in preschool classrooms. There also are usually several different play areas in the room, which may include a sand or water table, a dramatic play area, computers with age-appropriate software (Wright & Shade, 1994), and an open area for building blocks. Providing these different learning centers offers a wide variety of choices for students to explore. Using a small group structure for activities can encourage the development of friendships. At the same time, the curriculum must be responsive to the individual needs of each student and his or her family.

Early childhood education is critical for many young children to attain their maximum development. It provides the foundation that elementary and secondary education programs can build on (McDonnell et al., 1995). P.L. 99-457, the 1986 amendments to P.L. 94-142, mandated appropriate special education and related services for children with disabilities from 3 to 5 years old and authorized the establishment of public school preschool programs or programs contracted with outside agencies (McDonnell et al., 1995; Westling & Fox, 2000). New mandates added to the 1997 IDEA amendments allow professionals to delay identification of a specific disability category until the child is 9 years old. Children with developmental delays from age 3 to 9 can now receive special education and related services under the term *child with a disability* (Turnbull & Cilley, 1999). Another

change calls for preschool programs to take place in fully inclusive classrooms and offer young children a well-planned curriculum with individualized interventions when needed (Cavallaro & Haney, 1999). Preschool programs should be based on language and social skill development framed in a problem-based curriculum where children learn new skills through a variety of play activities (Malloy & New, 1994).

WHAT YOU WILL LEARN IN THIS CHAPTER

This chapter addresses curriculum and adaptations for inclusive preschool classrooms. First, we describe the most popular general education and special education curricular philosophies and how the two approaches can be combined to provide an effective inclusive environment. This section also highlights adaptations to the way students receive instruction, the materials they use, and the content they learn. Second, we provide information about developing self-care, language and communication, motor, and social skills. This section also discusses the beginning of career education. Third, we present approaches to developing peer relationships including peer tutoring, teaching students to be peer buddies, and supportive friendships.

ADDRESSING THE CURRICULA OF THE PRESCHOOL CLASSROOM

Preschool classes often are half-day programs that meet 4 or 5 days a week. Many programs are designed to serve 3- to 5-year-old children with and without disabilities. Preschool curricula should be developmentally- and age-appropriate for typical students and then modified for students with disabilities so they can be successful learners in that general education curriculum.

The teacher should plan developmentally- and age-appropriate exploratory play activities and events that emphasize cognitive, language, social, and motor development. To integrate these developmental areas into the instructional schedule, weekly lesson plans could be developed around a theme or topic. Student-directed learning stations, such as a painting easel, sensory table, and creative play area, would be designed around the weekly theme or topic. Daily plans for opening exercises; teacher-facilitated emergent literacy skills or career education activities; and endeavors that address fine motor and gross motor skills, language development, and social skills should incorporate the weekly theme or topic. Lesson plans also need to address any modifications necessary for students with disabilities to be successful learners. For each student with a disability, notations should be made that identify the activities to be modified and describe the specific adaptations needed (see Figure 9–1).

A variety of curricular approaches have been developed both for general education programs and for special education students. Among them are two philosophies that provide the strategies most commonly practiced in today's preschool classrooms. Developmentally appropriate practice (DAP) is the predominant philosophy used in general education classrooms, whereas special education programs commonly ascribe to early childhood special education (ECSE) methods.

Developmentally Appropriate Curriculum

DAP is the general education method of instruction recommended by the National Association for the Education of Young Children (NAEYC) (Bredekamp & Copple, 1997). It is based on the premise that children typically develop at different rates but in a similar sequence. As development progresses, skills become more complex. Early learning experiences have long-term benefits and can best be achieved through socially situated, individualized student-directed exploratory activities.

Guidelines include student-initiated activities facilitated by the teacher and highlight play that is exploratory and interactive (McDonnell et al., 1995). As a teacher using this method, you develop the curriculum from an understanding of the way young children develop and learn as well as from your knowledge of the social and cultural context of your students and the individual differences they exhibit (Bredekamp & Copple, 1997). Your role is that of a facilitator, promoting students' independence and self-esteem by building on the students' interests and encouraging student-initiated social interactions and play (Cavallaro, Haney, & Cabello, 1993). For example, you can encourage students' imaginative interactions during dramatic play activities with comments such as, "I see you are dressed as a ____. What are you doing? What is ____ doing?" This is an excellent way to stimulate the development of both language and cognitive skills.

A DAP curriculum typically emphasizes the development of motor, language, cognition, and social skills. In the motor domain, activities are designed to target both fine and gross motor skills. To illustrate, activities such as rolling a ball on the playground emphasize gross motor development; stringing beads in the classroom increases fine motor skill. Activities that concentrate on the language and cognitive domains stress functionality. For example, students discuss the seasons, holidays, and daily weather as well as practice number recognition as they count the dates on the monthly calendar. Social skill development is fostered by situating motor, language, and cognitive instruction in a social context. For example, students build friendships through informal peer interactions during daily snack time as they pass and help themselves to various food items. At the same time, you might use this time to teach the students about unfamiliar foods or give them nutritional information about the different foods they are eating. You also can use snack time to teach students pragmatic language skills such as saying "please" and "thank you" at the appropriate times. This

FIGURE 9-1   Daily Lesson Planner

Theme or Topic _____   Week _____

Easel:
Sensory Table:
Creative Play:

	Monday	Tuesday	Wednesday	Thursday
Warm-ups and opening				
Directed activity (emergent literacy skills or career education)				
Language				
Fine motor				
Gross motor				
Snack/Social				

Adaptations

Student	Activity(ies)	Description of Adaptation(s)
(Name)		
(Name)		
(Name)		
(Name)		
(Name)		

integrated approach to curriculum allows the students to learn skills in multiple developmental domains at the same time.

Family and Cultural Diversity.   DAP also stresses the importance of integrating the students' family and cultural backgrounds in the learning experience. Preschool is usually a young child's first experience away from home and family. Each student's home and family background is unique, and some students' family experiences may be very different from that of their classmates. You must value the diverse family and cultural backgrounds of all the students. Develop classroom activities that encourage the whole group to learn about and celebrate the different traditions and experiences of each student (Cavallaro & Haney, 1999). For example, a Native American student in Oklahoma may attend weekend powwows with his family, where he wears specific traditional regalia and participates in social and contest dances. Encourage the student to share his experiences with his classmates and maybe even teach them the dances he has learned and performed in the tiny tots category at the powwows. You also can incorporate the child's language or customs into the classroom by reading stories that highlight that child's culture and use survival vocabulary in the child's own language. Note that although some characteristics may be common among families from similar ethnic backgrounds, you should always be careful not to stereotype students and their families.

Parents define their child's behavior and emerging identity, so collaborate with parents to provide language-rich environments and frame behavior in the classroom and at home for later school success. In addition, help parents develop positive discipline techniques as well as a positive self-image in their child. Develop a "posture of reciprocity" to create a collaborative relationship with parents by (1) identifying issues of conflict, (2) recognizing how your beliefs impact your position, (3) determining how the beliefs of the family impact the issues, (4) bringing each

of those belief systems clearly into the discussion, and (5) finding an intersection of shared beliefs to begin to resolve conflicts (Harry, 1997).

Students also should be encouraged to recognize and accept other differences in positive ways. For example, encourage them to ask questions about the children with disabilities in the classroom to understand that the ways in which they do class activities are just another kind of diversity that brings richness to the learning experience for everyone. One way to encourage this kind of acceptance is to read stories that show preschool children with and without disabilities learning together and enjoying the same things (Brown, Ortiz, & Morris, 1984). Including materials in the classroom that promote diversity and relating those materials to the students' own feelings and experiences should be an important part of the preschool program (Appl, 1996). Some examples include switch-operated toys and modified computer software and keyboards.

Special Education Curriculum

A DAP curriculum may not fully meet the needs of students with disabilities without additional considerations (Odom & McLean, 1993). Students with disabilities have special needs that can best be met in a program that includes appropriate and frequent individualized interventions as well as opportunities to develop friendships with typical peers in inclusive settings (McDonnell et al., 1995). Early childhood special education (ECSE) strategies use an adult-directed format aimed at improving the students' ability to function in future environments; they emphasize direct instruction of specific skills in teacher-arranged activities and limited informal peer interactions (Cavallaro et al., 1993). Children with moderate to severe disabilities may need to be shown how to play. You can facilitate these interactions through direct instruction by modeling the desired performance or giving verbal prompts. One advantage of inclusive preschool education is that typical peers can provide good role models for students with moderate to severe disabilities during play activities. You also can facilitate the development of peer social interactions during play with modeling or verbal prompts.

Udell, Peters, and Templeman (1998) have identified five basic principles of ECSE, including (1) focusing interventions on functional goals, (2) providing family-centered services, (3) monitoring and adjusting interventions regularly, (4) using a multidisciplinary approach to providing services, and (5) planning for transition to the next school setting. Functional goals are aimed toward assisting students in learning to interact more effectively and independently with their peers and the environment. Functional goals also target helping students acquire independent self-care skills. A transdisciplinary team should plan and institute instruction based on those goals. As you learned in Chapter 7, the team should include the parents, general educator, special educator, and other relevant professionals, such as the speech pathologist, occupational therapist, and physical therapist. The team should frequently measure the student's progress toward mastering those goals, systematically and

in a variety of settings, and make adjustments when needed to assure the student's successful progress. The professionals on the team should make sure the family plays a significant role in designing the student's school program as well as helping connect them to community resources. They also should plan and prepare the student to transition smoothly to the next school level. We discuss transition from preschool to elementary school in detail in Chapter 15.

Although DAP and ECSE curricula approach the learning environment from different perspectives, they can be combined to provide an effective inclusive educational experience for students with and without disabilities. In this approach, the transdisciplinary team would collaborate to ensure a student's individual IEP objectives are addressed using tasks organized around the student's interests and in activities he or she chooses and initiates (Cavallaro et al., 1993) (see Figure 9–2).

In a program that utilizes a combined DAP and ECSE approach, you will need to make additional specific adjustments to the curriculum to allow all students, including those with moderate to severe disabilities, to participate fully in

FIGURE 9 – 2 **Blending DAP and ECSE Strategies**

1. Emphasize materials that are conducive to social play and cooperation.
2. Promote interaction with play activities based on individual objectives and needs or by assisting in developing student-initiated play and then fading assistance.
3. Use visual prompts to provide limited and clearly defined choices; fade prompts and increase the number of choices as the students become more proficient in choice making.
4. Facilitate opportunities for peer modeling by providing multiple sets of materials and designing class spaces and activities for small groups of students.
5. Use modeling to demonstrate targeted behaviors, to provide verbal cues that encourage student problem solving, and to assign verbal labels to help students understand and express their feelings.
6. Give verbal, gestural, pictorial, and partial physical prompts as well as full physical manipulations when more directive strategies are needed.
7. Offer feedback to encourage appropriate or desired student behavior and match adult responses to student's specific ability and functioning level.
8. Situate peers near students with disabilities, prompt students with disabilities to observe and imitate their peers, train both groups to initiate interactions, and praise them when they do.

Source: Cavallaro, C. C., Haney, M., & Cabello, B. (1993). Developmentally appropriate strategies for promoting full participation in early childhood settings. *Topics in Early Chidlhood Special Education, 13*, 293–307. Copyright 1992 by PRO-ED, Inc. Reprinted with permission.

the various classroom activities. Adaptations may involve adjustments to the way instruction is delivered, to the materials being used, to the content being presented, and for some students, to the extent a particular student participates in an activity.

Instructional Adaptations

You can create an accessible learning environment in the preschool classroom for all students by making instructional adaptations for those students who need them. You can modify verbal directions, provide visual cues, or give physical support when necessary to assure every student's active involvement in the class activities.

Modify Verbal Directions. As part of the preschool program, students learn to follow directions, take turns, and share with their peers. To illustrate, you could use the end of the school day to instruct students in listening and following directions. Have the students take turns going to their "cubbies" to get their coats by first saying, "If you have Velcro on your shoes, you may go to your cubbie." Next, you might say, "If you have buttons on your shirt, you may go to your cubbie." After the students with Velcro on their shoes or buttons on their shirts have gone to their cubbies, you would continue to give these kinds of instructions until all the children

have a turn to go to their cubbie to get their belongings. For the student with moderate to severe disabilities, you might adapt verbal directions in one or more of the following ways: You can speak slowly and simplify the words, question the student for understanding, break directions into small steps and repeat them after each step, repeat directions in a different way, and face the student when talking (McCormick & Feeney, 1995). For example, you can give verbal cues to alert the student to the end of one activity and the beginning of the next event. So you might say, "When Raffi sings 'watermelon,'" the song will be over and you will come join us" rather than, "As soon as Raffi's song is over, it will be time to join us for a story." Or you may say, "When Raffi sings 'watermelon,' come join us," the first time and then, "Yes, you will come join us after you hear Raffi sing 'watermelon'" when you repeat the directions.

Present Visual Cues. Verbal cues alone might not be sufficient. Young students may need additional prompts to understand fully what is expected of them. Give a demonstration at the beginning of each activity to illustrate what the students are expected to do. Other visual cues you might use to provide instructional support for students who need additional assistance include providing pictures or other symbols, using facial expressions and gestures, situating the

Mr. Rodriguez asks all the students to come sit on the rug in a circle for story time. Tory does not always listen carefully when Mr. Rodriguez gives directions. She frequently is distracted and today is no exception. She is absorbed with rubbing off the glue she has gotten on her hands while she pasted shapes during an art activity. Mr. Rodriguez notices that Tory is not responding, so he reminds her that it is time to join the group. He repeats his request, saying, "Tory, please come sit with us.

We are going to hear a story about a little girl and her puppy." Tory still doesn't respond. Mr. Rodriguez goes to where Tory is sitting and gently takes her hand. He then leads her to the circle area to listen to the story and praises her for coming to the group.

Mr. Rodriguez reminds Tory to pay attention by asking her to give verbal feedback. When they arrive at the rug, he asks, "Tory, why are we sitting in the circle?" Tory says, "Story time." Tory is learning to observe her environment and to attend to directions.

student to watch and copy the actions of the other students, or placing the applicable items closest to the student (McCormick & Feeney, 1995).

Provide Physical Support. Some students also may need extensive physical support to participate in classroom activities. You may need to place the student in close proximity to an activity or other students to maximize his or her participation. As you learned in Chapter 3, students with cerebral palsy may require adaptive equipment and environmental adaptations to enhance their involvement in class activities. You can use adaptive equipment such as wedges to prop the student up during activities on the floor, a stander or modified chair during activities at the table, or a wheelchair for mobility (McCormick & Feeney, 1995).

Materials Adaptations

Preschool classrooms are typically filled with a wide variety of colorful age-appropriate and developmentally-appropriate items. Students work with a variety of toys, such as blocks, cars, and dolls. They create with different art materials like crayons, Play-Doh, construction paper, and scissors. They play using equipment, such

as slides, swings, and a sensory table that uses either sand or water. They explore their world with materials like books and puzzles. Sometimes these materials need to be adapted for students with disabilities. For example, students who have difficulty with fine motor skills or eye-hand coordination can use puzzles with large pieces and pegs for easy grasping. Using scented modeling clay can help students identify colors.

 Max likes to choose the yellow Play-Doh when he goes to the art table. Max is visually impaired and uses his sense of smell to identify the different colors of Play-Doh available at the table. Max's teacher, Ms. Kennedy, has scented the different Play-Doh colors. She put lemon scent in the yellow one, mint scent in the blue one, and cherry scent in the red one. After picking up two different containers, he happily discovers the yellow Play-Doh because it is the one that smells like lemons.

 Ms. Laurette, the occupational therapist, rubs Dallas's limbs with a foam brush to stimulate him. At the same time, she supports his head, reminding him not to push it back against her hand, to help him develop the muscles he needs to control its movement. This activity takes place on the floor among the other students while they play with trucks and building blocks.

After a while, Ms. Laurette puts the brush away and places a hard foam wedge under Dallas's chest and pulls his arms over the top of the wedge. With his arms extended above the wedge, he is able to push with his hands to raise his head a bit higher to look around to watch the other students or grab a shiny truck when a friend hands it to him. While they play, the other students show Dallas the different trucks and the buildings they have made and they hand him some of the materials they are using to hold. This helps Dallas develop his motor skills while he also participates in the social interactions. Dallas lets his friends know he is enjoying the play activity by responding with sounds and smiles. Dallas's classmates always make sure he is included in some way in whatever activity the group is doing.

Drawing and Cutting. Young students are naturally curious and eager to explore. Providing students with creative activities addresses their inquisitiveness and provides opportunities for personal expression. Drawing and cutting activities can give students the chance to show their individual creativity as well as refine or develop fine motor skills.

Students use a variety of drawing materials to illustrate their ideas, including pencils, crayons, markers, chalk, paints, and brushes. They can use these drawing tools to demonstrate their understanding of concepts in creative ways. For example, when asked to draw a picture of something yellow, one student might draw a sunflower, another student might choose to draw a lollipop, and a third student might draw a moon and stars. However, some students may need support to accomplish this. In that case, you might ask the student to identify a yellow object and draw the outline of the selected object(s) for the student to fill in. Then you can show the student a selection of three colors of crayons or markers and ask the student to choose the yellow one to color her picture.

You also can adapt drawing materials in other ways. For example, use a very thick black marker to give the student a completed outline with a broad border as a boundary to stay within or draw a dotted outline of the shape for the student to trace before filling in the shapes with color. Make a cardboard template of the items being colored and place the template over the shape while the student colors to prevent the drawing instrument from going beyond the edges of the shape, or attach a raised material such as yarn or crushed uncooked pasta pieces to the outline of the shapes. You also could outline the shape with glue and let it dry to provide a raised edge.

Attaching a soft plastic grip may help some students keep the crayon, marker, paint brush, or pencil from slipping in their hands. For students with more significant needs, you may need to make additional adjustments such as clamping the pencil to the student's hand with a Velcro band, having the student draw or paint with fingers or feet, attaching the drawing paper to the floor or other easily accessible surface, and letting the student move a funnel of paint over a large piece of paper while the paint drips out (Sheldon, 1996).

 Ms. Frankel is teaching her students about shapes and colors. The students are having fun while they develop fine motor skills. Ms. Frankel puts paper circles, squares, and triangles of different colors and a variety of crayons on the table. She also gives each student a piece of paper with a circle, a square, and a triangle already drawn on one side. Ms. Frankel asks the students to color their shapes. Some students choose the color they want each shape to be, and they color in their shapes. Other students choose to trace or draw their own shapes and then color them. Some students also choose and paste different shapes on the other side of their papers. While the students create their pictures, Ms. Frankel asks them to describe their work. As one young student picks a large circle and glues it on her paper, she asks, "What shape is that?" She asks another student, "What color is your triangle?"

Ms. Frankel has adapted papers for some students. She gives Li a paper with the shapes drawn with very thick lines. For example, the outline of the circle is drawn in blue. She asks Li, "Can you color your circle with the same color?" She gives Hank a paper with the shapes drawn with a very thick black line, and she has made an additional adaptation for him. She has glued uncooked rice around the outside edges of each shape so he not only can see the shape but he also can feel the edge of the shape with his finger or crayon.

Cutting activities also can be adapted for a student who has limited physical control. Use a very thick black line to draw the shape so the student has a wider border to follow when cutting. If a student needs additional support, cut out the most difficult portion of the shape ahead of time so the student can be successful in accomplishing a smaller amount of cutting. Also, students can use adapted scissors with large loops instead of finger holes or scissors with teacher holes and student holes.

Books. Story time is usually a daily event in the typical preschool classroom. It provides a rich medium for language and literacy development. Use story time to familiarize students with lots of different topics as well as to introduce and practice emergent literacy skills and appropriate social behaviors. Story time often involves the teacher reading books that highlight different colors or letters in the alphabet. For example, you might show the students pictures in the book you are reading about a flower garden and ask, "How many red flowers can you count on this page?" To assist a student with disabilities in participating and accessing the information, include textured books or stories that allow you to use individual sounds or different voices for different characters (Sheldon, 1996). Also use oversized books with large pictures and print that are commonly found in preschool classrooms.

Equipment. Most preschool playgrounds are equipped with swings and slides that encourage the students to engage in cooperative play and gross motor skill development. The preschool classroom also may be equipped with special swings that have wide platform seats and safety

Mr. Sidky's students are making "F" books. He gives each student a blank book that consists of two pieces of paper folded in half and stapled at the top and bottom on the fold. On the cover of each book, he has drawn a capital letter F and lowercase letter F. He and the students then practice saying the sound that the letter F makes and identifying things whose name begins with that sound. Mr. Sidky points to a small fort the students have built out of blocks and asks the students to say "fort" with him. They then discuss the sound of F that starts the word. They brainstorm other words that start with F, such as *family, flower, friend,* and *fork.* Next, Mr. Sidky asks the students to open their books to their blank second and third pages.

Mr. Sidky has the students cut pictures out of old magazines of things whose name begins with F and then glue them on the second and third pages of their books. With his encouragement and suggestions, some of the students also draw pictures of frogs, flowers, furniture, fish, fruit, and flies. On the last page, the students cut out or draw pictures of helpful people whose jobs begin with the sound of the letter F. This time, Mr. Sidky encourages the students to find firefighter, farmers, family members, and friends.

Mr. Sidky makes modifications to the books for several students. Shanda glues precut pictures on each page of her book. Mr. Johnson, the para-educator, draws an outline of an 'F' picture that Noah has chosen to color. Britney chooses a sticker of a fan and a feather and puts them in her book. After Mr. Sidky writes the dotted letters, Frank traces his name and Bobby traces the word for each picture he has drawn on his paper.

After the students make their pictures on each page, Mr. Sidky asks them to circle the letter, say the name of the letter, and make its sound. Mr. Johnson helps Britney and any other students who need assistance with circling the correct letter or with pronouncing the letter and its sound.

straps. The safety straps let students who have low muscle tone sit up comfortably while they prevent them from falling away from the seat. The swing also allows you to help students develop coordination. It provides peers with the opportunity to interact with each other and give encouragement and support. Swinging activities can be leveled to meet the individual needs of the students. For example, one student may be able to swing independently while you help her count each time she goes back and forth by saying, "One, two, three, ... ten." Another student might need you to provide the additional support of verbal cues to make the swing move back and forth. As this student rocks back and forth with his legs raised above the ground, help him develop greater control by saying, "Scoot forward and put your feet down and push to make the swing move." For a third student who requires physical assistance, you might say, "Hold on to the ropes. Use both hands." While you closely supervise and encour-age the student to practice grasping skills, you can encourage friendships by asking the student's peers to push the swing. This peer support also can provide an additional opportunity for peers to improve their motor skills. For example, you might remind the peer how to make the swing move by saying, "Use two hands and push hard."

Content Modifications

Recognizing patterns, shapes, and sizes, identifying colors, counting numbers, and learning the letters in the alphabet typically are cognitive development skills addressed in preschool classrooms. Students are taught to recognize different sizes of circles, squares, rectangles, and triangles with activities like making shapes in whipped cream or making pictures of buses after singing "The Wheels of the Bus Go Round and Round;" identify series of objects in a pattern, such as large and small teddy bear shapes

Students explore cognitive concepts such as numbers from 1 to 10.

FIGURE 9–3   Portable Leveled Learning Centers

For each activity, the student follows the picture directions in his or her box to assemble the materials inside.

Stringing Beads in a Pattern
Each box should contain a photograph or illustration that shows the beads strung in the desired pattern and the following:

In the first box, put:
    20 jumbo wooden beads in 2 colors and 1 long piece of sturdy thread attached to a large blunt-tipped needle

In the second box, put:
    36 very large wooden beads in 4 colors and 1 long piece of sturdy thread attached to a large blunt-tipped needle

In the third box, put:
    48 large wooden beads in 6 colors and 1 long piece of sturdy thread attached to a large blunt-tipped needle

Sorting Items by Size
Each box should contain a photograph or illustration that shows the items already sorted into piles and the following:

In the first box, put:
    5 large paint brushes, 5 medium paint brushes, 5 small paint brushes

In the second box, put:
    8 jumbo black markers, 8 large black markers, 8 regular black markers, and 8 thin black markers

In the third box, put:
    12 extra long white shoelaces, 12 long white shoelaces, 12 medium white shoelaces, 12 short white shoelaces, and 12 very short white shoelaces

Note: A further adaptation for this activity might be for the student to place actual beads on the corresponding picture of each bead. Another adaptation would be to touch or point to the bead that a peer or other assistant would then string. One other additional adaptation for this activity might be to place a model in front of the student with the correct items glued to the bottom for the student to follow.

Source: Adapted from Hamill, L., & Dunlevy, A. (1999). *Work boxes* (Rev. ed.). San Antonio, TX: PCI Educational Publishing. Reprinted with permission.

while the teacher helps one student create a pattern for another student to identify; name the numbers from 1 to 10 and their amounts when, for example, students count raisins at snack time; identify letters of the alphabet and understand those symbols represent sounds through activities such as saying the sound their names start with while tracing the sandpaper letters with their fingers; and recognize basic colors when they discuss a story the teacher is reading or when they bring their favorite things to school to show their friends.

These skills are often integrated into many different classroom routines and activities. Students explore cognitive concepts in both play and structured activities. Adaptations may be needed to include the student with moderate to severe disabilities in these activities. For example, as part of learning to count and practice number recognition, some of the students might fill in the day's date on their individual monthly calendar worksheet. At the same time, the student with a disability might trace a broken line image of the number that already appears on his calendar or match the date with a card that shows the same number.

Learning Centers. Instructional activities are commonly placed in learning centers in the preschool classroom (Cavallaro & Haney, 1999). Learning centers allow students to choose activities that interest them and to work independently. Students learn through discovery with materials that stimulate their natural curiosity. Learning centers can be designed so they are portable, which allows you easily to rotate or exchange a variety of different activities periodically, and they can be leveled so children with differing abilities can successfully participate in each activity (Hamill & Dunlevy, 1999) (see Figure 9–3). For example, each center can be stored in a series of three boxes. Each box would contain similar materials organized around a particular skill, but the task level would become progressively more difficult. In other words, the task in the second box would be more difficult than the task in the first box and the third box would be even more complicated than the second box. Different learning centers might include materials for stringing beads in a pattern or sorting items by size.

You can even turn the snack table into a math learning center (Meriwether, 1997) (see Figure 9–4). Snack time provides a natural opportunity to learn counting skills. To do this, draw a menu card that shows the predetermined amounts of various foods that each student should take for snack that day. The student would then collect and count the designated amounts of each item. This activity could be adapted so while some students collect their food by looking at the drawings, a student who needs additional support could match each food item by actually placing the food item on the corresponding drawing of that item on the menu card until the card is filled with the correct snack portions.

Learning Through Play. Play is an important part of any preschool program. It provides an excellent vehicle for letting students explore their own interests without adult direction being imposed, and the students develop friendships as they learn to share (Cavallaro & Haney, 1999).

Young children learn to understand different facets of their world through play. They often observe the activities their parents and other adults are engaged in and imitate those activities in their own play. In other words, young children like to pretend they are cooking or driving a car. To encourage pretending real-life events, design a variety of play areas, such as one space with a play kitchen, another area with a pretend garage, and a third place that is a make-believe fishing hole.

Bruce (1993) has identified eight ways teachers can facilitate students' learning through play. These strategies include (1) helping students discover and explore their world in a wide variety of role playing activities, (2) helping students understand and make up their own rules for play, (3) helping students remember and value the experience and process of their play, (4) respecting students' ownership and control of their own learning, (5) encouraging students to pretend and joining in their play without controlling it or imposing adult ideas, (6) adjusting activities to accommodate students' skill levels and the technical competence and control used in play, (7) providing opportunities for solitary and group play because students need both, and (8) allowing time for students to experience ideas, feelings, and relationships in their play so they become whole individuals.

FIGURE 9-4   A Snack Time Math Center

The teacher draws the pieces of the foods on a "menu card" in the portions the students will eat. For example, the teacher might draw one white circle to represent one cup of milk, four brown squares to represent four saltine crackers, and two yellow rectangles to represent a slice of American cheese that has been cut in half. The students match the number and type of actual food pieces using the menu card as a guide. The menu cards can be leveled to accommodate individual ability levels.

For one student, the menu card would look like this:

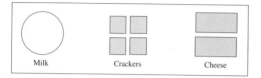

For a second student, the menu card would look like this:

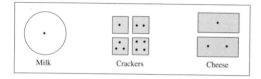

For a third student, the menu card would look like this:

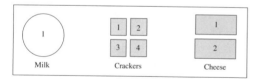

For a fourth student, the menu card would look like this:

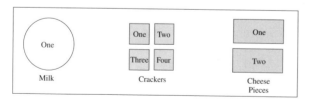

Note: This activity can be further adapted by having the student put the food items directly on the menu card rather than on a separate plate or napkin.

Source: Adapted from Meriwether, L. (1997). Math at the snack table. *Young Children, 52*(5), 69–73. Reprinted with permission from the National Association for the Education of Young Children.

Play can be difficult for young students with moderate to severe disabilities because it is compounded by cognitive, physical, and/or communication weaknesses. The classroom environment can be adapted with accessible tables and materials. Teaching some sign language to all students can assist children with hearing impairments communicate with their peers at school.

Before her students begin a dramatic play period, Ms. Yoon discusses their options for play materials, equipment, and activities with them. She asks the students to talk about how they plan to use the materials and equipment in their chosen play activities.

Ms. Yoon helps Josh, who is blind, engage in make-believe activities by guiding him into his chosen play activity. Today, he has expressed an interest in being a doctor just like his aunt Grace. When his friend Hannah hears that Josh wants to play doctor she says, "I want to be the patient!" Ms. Yoon guides Josh with specific instructions such as, "Josh, since you chose to be the doctor and Hannah wants to be the patient, go to where we always keep the dress-up clothes and Hannah can help you find the doctor's coat. Inside the coat pocket you will find a stethoscope. Can you tell me what the doctor uses a stethoscope for?"

One student with a physical disability may use a special board to help her stand at an art easel while another student may use large blocks for building so they are easy to manipulate. Many of the assistive technology and augmentative communication devices we described in Chapter 3 can support young students with physical disabilities.

Play also can add a fun component to adult-facilitated learning. You can create an environment that encourages learning through play by incorporating instructional lessons into students' pretending activities. For example, construct a fishing activity that teaches students information about colors or numbers (see Figure 9–5). Draw a simple fish shape to use as a template. Next, use the template to produce as many fish as needed. Then draw or write a piece of information on one side of each fish in a set. To make all the information on a particular topic easily identifiable, color the other side of all the fish in that set the same. For example, to teach math concepts, one side of each fish in one set would be colored blue and some of the blue fish would be oversized and others would be small. A second set of fish would have pictures of big things, such as a tree, and little things, such as a flower, and the other side of all those fish would be colored orange. A third set of fish would all have one side colored green but the other side of each one would have a picture of up to three items on it. For example, one fish might have a picture of three crayons. A fourth set could be colored yellow on one side and have a number of dots from 1 to 10 drawn on the other side. For a student who has a visual impairment, the dots could be cut out of sandpaper. A fifth set might all be colored red on the back side with a numeral from 1 to 10 written on the front side of each fish.

Make the fishing poles from a short thick dowel. Tie a long piece of thick string around one end of the dowel and attach a piece of magnet tape (which can be purchased inexpensively at an art supply store) to the other end of the string to create fishing poles. With a piece of clear tape, secure a large paper clip to each fish. When the student guides the end of his fishing line onto a fish and then pulls the pole up, the paper clip attached to the fish will stick to the magnetic tape, letting the student catch the fish.

For students who have difficulty with fine motor skills, make oversized materials for easier handling, such as an extra thick dowel for the

FIGURE 9–5 Fishing for Numbers: A Leveled Cognitive Development Play Activity

The students hold their fishing poles over a group of fish and drop the magnetic ends of their lines onto the top of fish. When they pull their pole up, they have a fish attached to the line. They then identify the information on the fish and throw it back in the imaginary pond. Each student goes fishing for the color of fish that addresses the concepts he or she is learning.

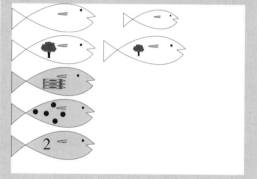

fishing rod with an extra large magnet on the end of the line. Create oversized fish for a student with a visual impairment. Attach a pair of soft Velcro straps to the fishing rod and secure them around the arm of a student who has difficulty grasping or using his hand to hold on to objects.

Parallel or Partial Participation. It may be necessary for some students with moderate to severe disabilities to participate in only part of an activity or engage in a parallel task. For example, assembly tasks provide an opportunity for students to interact with materials in a variety of ways so all students enjoy the activity and each student can work at his or her individual skill level. To illustrate, students develop language, social, and motor skills and they learn to be independent workers while they put Cooties to-

gether. Cooties are commercially made large plastic buglike characters that come disassembled in a box. Although Cooties is really a game, the bugs can be assembled without actually playing the game. The students have to plug the legs into holes on each side of the main body piece. They also plug in a head that has holes where they attach the eyes, mouth, and antennae. A student with limited physical control can enjoy partial participation in this activity by (1) holding the plastic pieces in her lap for a classmate and handing each part of the Cootie to the friend, (2) helping the friend put the parts into the body and helping take them out once the Cootie is assembled, and (3) helping put the body parts back in the box at the end of the activity. Another toy that students can assemble

Herbert likes to help his classmates put Cooties together. He lies on the rug next to them supported by a large bright blue wedge. He holds his head up to reach for and grasp the brightly colored Cooties that his friend, Carlos, holds out for him to grasp. Ms. Brookstone, the para-educator, models for Carlos how to help Herbert put the Cootie together with a hand-over-hand method of support. Carlos then guides Herbert's hand to plug in the different body parts until they have worked together to assemble the whole Cootie.

When it is time to finish the activity, Ms. Brookstone asks Herbert, "Are you finished with the Cootie? Can you put him in the box?" Using hand-over-hand support, she then helps Herbert put the Cootie part that he is holding back in the box.

Herbert is increasing his motor skills. He also is participating with his peers in the informal social interactions taking place in the classroom.

is Mr. Potato Head. With Mr. Potato Head, students explore facial features while they attach the different parts, such as the nose and eyes.

ADDRESSING INDEPENDENT LIVING SKILLS IN THE GENERAL EDUCATION CLASSROOM

Independent living skills such as toileting, dressing, self-feeding, and self-control are skills young children need to function effectively. Developing independent living skills is an important part of the educational experience for young children. Preschoolers also should begin to develop and practice self-determination skills so they can advocate for the supports they will need to be able to function as independently as possible in the future (Brown & Cohen, 1996). You can help students develop self-determination by encouraging them to make choices, solve problems, try new things, and be self-reflective to begin a process that will lead to developing their own internal loci of control (Wehmeyer et al., 1998). We discuss teaching self-determination in detail in Chapter 15. Both self-determination and independent living skills will help young students function effectively when they are in the community both now and in the future. Preschool teachers should help their students develop these functional skills in the areas of self-care, language and communication, motor, social, and career development.

Self-Care Skill Development

Dressing. The dressing skills typically taught in preschool classrooms include learning to button, zip, and put on coats and other clothes independently. Students with moderate to severe disabilities may have difficulty performing some dressing tasks. Many of the regular preschool routines lend themselves to teaching dressing skills within the natural context of the class-

room and without making large adjustments to the normal classroom routine (Young, West, Howard, & Whitney, 1986). For example, students practice taking off their coats and hats when they enter the classroom and practice putting them back on again when they leave. They also button and unbutton, zip and unzip, or snap and unsnap various pieces of clothing when they go to the bathroom or play dress-up during a free-choice period. Functional adaptations may be needed to allow students with moderate to severe disabilities to perform the tasks as independently as possible. One adaptation includes replacing buttons or zippers with Velcro straps.

Toileting. Mastering toileting skills is an important accomplishment for preschool students. Many children gain the physical control needed for this skill when they are 2 or 3 years old. Toileting should be taught as part of the preschool curriculum for those students who are ready to learn but have not yet mastered the skill. Westling and Fox (2000) have identified a plan for teaching toileting that can be summarized in four major steps: (1) collect data, (2) teach independent toilet use, (3) teach associated skills, and (4) teach generalization of the skill. Using this model, the teacher and parent should collaborate to collect data to determine the student's elimination pattern before beginning instruction. They will need to make frequent inspections to determine when the student is most likely to need to use the bathroom, and, at the same time, they should be attentive to the private nature of the behavior. For example, school personnel should partition off the area when they change students. Once a pattern has been determined, as Westling and Fox (2000) have elaborated, establish a classroom routine that includes (1) putting the student on the toilet at designated times, (2) praising successful toileting, (3) praising successfully staying clean and dry between toileting, and (4) allowing the student to remain on the toilet for a sufficient period of time. Teach the associated skills necessary for successful independent toileting behavior, such as traveling to and from the bathroom, pulling pants down, and washing hands. Finally encourage generalization of the skill by making sure the student has lots of opportunities to use a variety of different bathrooms.

Language and Communication Skill Development

Helping young children develop effective communication skills is a vital part of any preschool program. Take every opportunity to encourage student communication. For instance, begin activities by asking students to describe what they plan to do and ask them to review their interactions as the activity ends (Cavallaro & Haney, 1999). Story time, snack time, and play time provide excellent opportunities for you to encourage student communication. The following sections provide examples for each of these activities.

Use Story Time. Story reading is a common routine in most preschool classrooms and provides an excellent environment for encouraging language development. You can use several strategies to expand the students' skills, including (1) praising their talk, (2) expanding their words, (3) asking open-ended questions, and (4) pausing for them to initiate conversation (McNeill & Fowler, 1996). You can praise students' verbal skills with comments such as, "I like the way you said that!" You can help students expand their vocabulary by naming unfamiliar items or events and by rephrasing the students' remarks in a more complex structure. For example, while you are reading *I Was So Mad* (Mayer, 1983), a student might say, "No frogs." You can rephrase and expand the student's statement by responding, "That's right. Mom says, 'No frogs in the bathtub.'" You also could ask an open-ended question, such as, "Why doesn't the mother want frogs in the bathtub?" Finally, you might encourage students to initiate conversation if you stop reading after a particularly interesting part of the story and

look expectantly at the students to encourage them to share their ideas about the story.

Use Snack Time. Snack time is another daily routine that offers a natural environment for developing the pragmatics of language. Snack time allows you to observe student behavior patterns, listen to casual conversations between students, praise appropriate language, and redirect those interactions when they become inappropriate. When the students gather in the snack area to eat, encourage them to develop appropriate social language skills. For example, prompt them to use the appropriate words when asking for food or drink items. A student might hold up her cup or simply say, "More juice." Model the correct language by responding, "I want more juice please." When the student repeats what you said, you fill the student's cup with juice while praising her for asking in such a nice way. Snack time also may offer opportunities to discourage peers from correcting each other inappropriately or tattling to adults.

Use Play Time. Students also develop and sharpen their language skills through the casual conversations they have with each other during collaborative play times. The Cootie assembling activity discussed earlier is an example of play that gives students the opportunity for informal verbal interaction. As the students attach the Cooties' various body parts, they talk with each other about their Cooties. They might invent and share stories about where their Cooties live, what they eat, and the kinds of things their Cooties do to take care of their families. You can develop more appropriate language during play activities. For example, you may want to facilitate social play with verbal cues or by modeling verbal interactions for students who have moderate to severe disabilities.

Use Augmentative or Alternative Communication Systems. As you learned in Chapter 3, some students with severe disabilities do not have the skills necessary to communicate verbally. They need to use augmentative or alternative communication systems to make their needs and interests known. One easy-to-use, inexpensive method of providing communication support is the Picture Exchange Communications System (PECS) (Schwartz, Garfinkle, & Bauer, 1998). To illustrate, a nonverbal student can take a picture from her word box, which has a variety of pictures including one of a book, and give it to you to let you know she wants to hear a story. You then can say, "You want to read a book. Will you please get me a book to read to you?" PECS uses simple picture symbols to represent a wide variety of topics such as common activities, body parts, foods, requests for assis-

tance, emotions, clothing, holidays, and so on. The picture symbols are available in 1- and 2-inch sizes in print form (Johnson, 1994) or they can be generated with computer software (King, 1998). The PECS system can provide communication support in many different settings in the school, home, and community. Another way to do this is to use magazine or newspaper pictures or actual photos of the items. Using photos has the added advantage of being more meaningful to the student because they make a specific connection to the student's own experience.

Once students have learned to trade the picture of what they want for the real item, they can learn to combine pictures to communicate whole sentences. This allows students to enter into social interactions with their peers. In fact, because PECS pictures are so simple to interpret, it is easy for the student to initiate a social interaction with just about anyone.

Motor Skill Development

Students increase their fine motor coordination as they write letters or numbers during cognitive development exercises, color and cut to make art projects, or use a variety of toys during play times. For example, a group of students might use blocks to build a community of houses and streets and then move little cars and trucks along the roads.

Students also develop their motor skills when they play on the swing or throw a ball during outside play and when they do stretching exercises or sing songs during whole group activities. Songs like "The Ittsy Bitsy Spider" let students practice fine motor coordination while they have fun singing favorite tunes. While they sing, they move their fingers and arms to illustrate what the words are saying.

Some students may need specific training to develop the muscle control and physical strength needed to produce functional motions. The "Ittsy Bitsy Spider" activity presents an opportunity for the physical therapist (PT) or occupational therapist (OT) to work in the natural

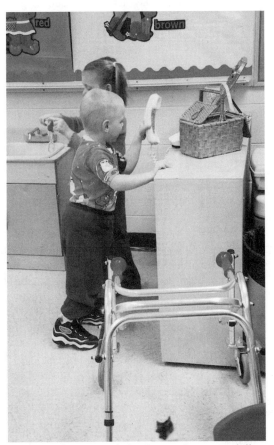

Playing with toys can help sharpen language skills.

environment to support a student who needs to develop muscle control and physical strength to produce functional motions. For example, the PT can guide the student's arms or use hand-over-hand to push the student's fingers gently together at the appropriate points during the song. The PT or OT and the classroom teacher also can work collaboratively during other activities that take place in the classroom to teach students who need this kind of additional assistance. For example, the OT might develop an instructional plan for a student who has difficulty opening her own milk carton at snack time. Then the teacher or the OT, if she is available during snack time, would deliver the instruction within the natural routine of the classroom.

Social Skill Development

An inclusive preschool classroom offers many opportunities for students with moderate to severe disabilities to develop social skills. Some strategies include (1) creating a classroom environment that facilitates peer interaction such as pairing peers so those less skilled can observe and imitate the positive behaviors of their more socially competent peers, (2) identifying and pairing students with common interests and similar play styles to encourage friendships, (3) teaching socially competent students to coach their peers in learning social skills, and (4) teaching students the characteristics of good friendships, which include students who differ from them in physical appearance, gender, skill level, and cultural background (Bergen, 1993). You should encourage students' social interaction in a variety of both structured and unstructured classroom activities.

Use Role Play Activities. You can encourage students' socialization by providing opportunities for them to participate in unstructured child-directed role play activities, such as grocery store or veterinarian office. As students pick from several options, you can help those who have difficulty choosing by questioning them about their preferences or even guiding them toward a particular activity. Some students with moderate to severe disabilities may have difficulty getting involved when there are too many

Most of the students in Mrs. Goldstein's class can pass the food plate without spilling anything and open their own milk cartons during snack time. However, Betsy slides the food plate to the student sitting next to her because she has trouble holding it up in the air. She also has a lot of difficulty opening her own milk carton.

Mr. Kelly, the OT, has devised a plan for helping Betsy develop the fine motor skills she needs to open her milk carton independently. First, he gently squeezes and pulls Betsy's finger to imitate the pinching and pulling motion of opening the spout of a milk carton. Next, he has Betsy squeeze and pull his finger in the same manner. Betsy practices on Mrs. Goldstein's finger to build the muscle strength and learn the physical movements necessary for opening a small milk carton.

Mr. Kelly also has Betsy perform another exercise several times during the school day to increase the muscle strength in her hands. He has given Betsy two small spongy balls. She puts one in each hand and repeatedly squeezes both of them at the same time. In a short time, Betsy develops enough physical strength and motor control to open her own milk carton with only verbal assistance and a little physical help getting started. Mom also helps at home by having Betsy open the Pringles, which is her favorite snack. Before long, Betsy is able to open her milk each day without any physical support.

choices or may always want the same activity or toy. You may need to (1) limit the choices to one or two and have the student make a selection from a picture or representative object, (2) save the student's special toy or project until she has participated in a different play activity for a short while, or (3) organize materials and activities for role play around the student's interests (Cavallaro & Haney, 1999).

Use Games.   Structured adult-facilitated play activities also can promote social skills development. Games provide an excellent play environment that give young students the opportunity to practice interpersonal skills such as turn taking and good sportsmanship while they develop cognitive skills. There are commercially produced games that you can use with preschool students, such as Candyland or Chutes and Ladders. Teacher-made games also can help students develop these skills and they have an added advantage because they can be built to target specific instructional concepts. For example, you can produce a simple card game that makes learning directional concepts fun. You write directions for the students to act out on large unlined index cards. The students then pick cards you read and the students act out. For example, cards might say things such as hop *between* two chairs, take crayon *out of* the box, walk *around* Billy, hold a toy *over* your head, or *close* your eyes. An adaptation for a student with a motor related disability would be to change words like *hop* or *walk* to *move* or *wiggle*.

Teacher-made games can even be designed to correspond with the different holidays and seasons. The theme focus adds an extra element to the fun and provides an additional instructional feature (see Figures 9–6 and 9–7).

Leveling the game cards individualizes the activity so each student can participate successfully. Some students with moderate to severe disabilities may need the support of more extensive modification to participate effectively. Some additional adjustments might include large

markers weighted on the bottom, larger game cards made of heavy cardboard that may prove helpful for students with physical challenges, and stickers or other incentives placed on the game card that may prove helpful for students with behavioral or attention issues (Raschke, Dedrick, Heston, & Farris, 1996). Also, playing partner bingo can allow two students to work together and provide peer support as the structure for partial participation rather than adult intervention.

Game playing also provides a vehicle for beginning career education (Hamill & Dunlevy, 1994). As young students learn to follow directions, they are starting to develop employability skills that will eventually help them succeed in the workplace.

Career Education

The beginning of a student's educational experience marks the start of his or her trip along the road to work. Although it will be some time before students actually enter the work force, learning gross and fine motor, self-care, communication, and appropriate social skills are important for success in the workplace. For those reasons, preschool teachers need to begin teaching career awareness. During this early phase of career education, introduce students to the world of work in a many different ways and in a variety of environments (Razeghi, 1998). Teaching self-awareness skills to help students become knowledgeable about themselves as well as understand how others view them also should be part of a career awareness program (Wehmeyer et al., 1998).

Learn About Workers in the Community.   The environments young children typically frequent, such as the family kitchen, the preschool classroom, and the local grocery, provide the optimal settings for learning and generalizing career awareness information. Active, hands-on projects and integrated lessons about community workers can foster young students' natural

FIGURE 9–6   **Leveled Valentine Color Bingo**

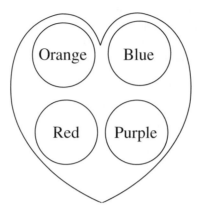

Student 1: This student would place a cover marker on the circle containing the color that the caller names. This student also could be designated the caller, using a set of call cards with a different color circle painted on each card.

Student 2: This student would place a cover marker on the circle containing the color with the color word written in black ink that the caller names. This student also could be designated the caller using a set of call cards with a different color circle with the color words written in black ink on each card.

Student 3: This student would place a cover marker on the circle containing only the tinted color word circle that the caller names. This student also could be designated the caller using a set of call cards with a different color word written in the corresponding tint on each card.

Student 4: This student would place a cover marker on the circle containing only the untinted color word that the caller names. This student also could be designated the caller using a set of call cards with a different untinted color word written on each card.

Note: A student who needs further support could place the call card on the equivalent color picture on the bingo card or matching colored button corresponding to the corresponding colored circle on the bingo card. This student also could be designated the caller using a set of call cards with a different color circle painted on each card and with verbal prompts from the teacher, aide, or a peer. Another student who needs additional help could point to the color picture on her bingo card. This student also could be designated the co-caller, using a set of call cards with a different color circle painted on each card and with verbal support from the teacher, aide, or a peer.

eagerness and energetic inquisitiveness. For example, combine teaching students about nutrition with a school visit from the manager at the local grocery during a food preparation activity for snack time. A follow-up field trip to the grocery store can provide students with a second experience. The students develop new language as they talk with store employees about different food items and learn which items can be combined in a balanced diet that provides good nutrition. You also might design a matching activity using a picture grocery list. Let the students take the list with them to the store and match the pictures to the actual food items.

You can help students practice skills in school that will help them become good employees in the future. For example, they can pick up

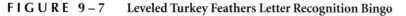
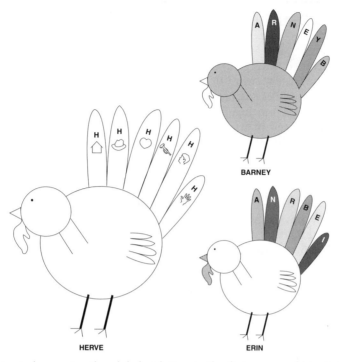

The teacher creates turkeys using the alphabet letters in the first names of his students to focus on uppercase letter identification. He gives each student his or her own turkey. For example, the tail feathers for one of the students has the different letters of his first name written on them. The teacher also has a set of feathers with the corresponding letters on them. He picks a feather and reads it to the players, who then cover the appropriate feather on their turkeys. An example of a feather the teacher might pick would be, "H. Can you make the sound that H makes with me? H is the first letter in Herve's name . . . and H is also the first letter in house. Can you find the feather with the H on it?" (and to Herve also say, "Can you find the picture of the house?") Each student has his or her own turkey with the following information:

Herve's feathers:

       Each feather has a capital letter H for Herve's name and a different picture that starts with the letter H (example: H and a picture of a house)

Barney's feathers:

       Each feather is a different color and has a different one of the following capital letters: B A R N E Y

Erin's feathers:

       Each feather has a different capital letter of the alphabet that is not necessarily in Erin's first name.

Note: Adaptations for students with more severe disabilities might be for the student to point to the corresponding feather after the teacher uses hand-over-hand to trace the letter made out of sandpaper.

MILKSHAKE CHEFS!

The students in Mr. Romano's class are making milkshakes for snack today! Mr. Romano has made a chef's hat for each student by gluing a slightly pinched piece of white tissue paper to a band of white cardboard. He tapes the ends of the cardboard band together to fit around the student's head after he writes that student's job title on the front. Three hats say, "Fruit Person," three hats say, "Milk Person," three hats say, "Ice Cream Person," and three hats say, "Blender Person."

The students are excited as each one puts on a chef's hat. They take turns performing the tasks listed on the giant brightly colored recipe card Mr. Romano has made on a sheet of poster board. Jake is one of the blender people. Mr. Romano uses hand-over-hand to help him push the large red button that has been hooked up to the blender. The blender runs each time Jake pushes the button.

When each student has had a turn to help, and they have made enough milkshakes for everyone to enjoy, they sit at the snack table to review their "cooking" process and responsibilities while they enjoy the rewards of their work. Mr. Romano says, "You are really hard workers and you did a great job. Maybe someday, you could work at the Braums' ice cream store!"

Strawberry Milkshake Recipe

1. Ice Cream	– fill blender
2. Milk	– pour into blender
3. Strawberries	– add while blender is running
4. Blender	– mix ingredients in blender

garbage or twigs on the school playground. They also should clean up their own materials at the end of each class activity as well as help classmates who need assistance putting materials away.

Develop Self-Awareness. As students learn their birthdate, home address, and other personal information, they become self-aware and understand how they are connected to their community. As they learn about themselves, they also can develop a sense of self-worth that gives them confidence in their interactions with others. Students gain a positive self-image as they get to know who they are and see how others see them. For example, the Talk About Your Life Game can help young students learn how they are viewed and how they relate to the lives of those around them (see Figure 9–8).

FIGURE 9–8   The "Talk About Your Life" Game

The students take turns answering general information questions on a variety of personal topics. The questions are written on blue, green, or red large question mark-shaped pieces of paper and placed in three different bowls to identify the inquiries at three levels of difficulty. Each student takes a turn by picking a question out of the bowl that the teacher designates and handing it to the teacher to read.

(Below are three lists with some possible questions for students to answer. You may want to add to the list or change the questions to fit the individual needs of your students.)

Blue List	**Green List**	**Red List**
1. What is your name?	1. What is your first name?	1. What is your last name?
2. Are you a girl?	2. How old are you?	2. Where do you live?
3. Are you a boy?	3. What is your teacher's name?	3. What is a food you like to eat?
4. Are you happy?	4. What is your favorite toy?	4. How do you spell your first name?
5. Are you tired?	5. Do you have a sister?	5. What is your phone number?
6. Where is your teacher (student can point to teacher)	6. Do you have a brother?	6. What number should you dial in an emergency?

Source: Adapted from Hamill, L., & Dunlevy, A. (1994). *Playing to learn: Classroom games for content area, social, and living skills.* Portland, ME: J. Weston Walch.

PEER SUPPORTS FOR INDEPENDENT FUNCTIONING

Establishing positive peer relationships is important in a preschooler's life because those early interactions commonly provide the first social experiences outside of the student's own family (Erwin & Schreiber, 1999). Even at such an early age, peers can offer friendship and natural support that will facilitate the successful participation of students with disabilities in the preschool community. Successful peer support, like other forms of assistance, (1) secures the student's effective involvement, (2) promotes membership in the peer group, (3) generates positive outcomes, and (4) is harmonious with the natural setting (Erwin & Schreiber, 1999).

Teach Peer Interaction. Brown and Odom (1995) have identified steps that teachers can employ to support students who need intervention to engage in social interactions and to maintain and generalize those interactions during classroom activities. Their eight step process includes (1) identify students who seldom initiate or respond to peers, (2) observe those students to determine which materials and activities interest them, (3) identify peers who would be good social interaction partners for them, (4) earmark daily routines appropriate for teaching social behavior among peers, (5) map out a variety of methods for prompting and encouraging peer interactions, (6) monitor and encourage positive peer interactions while redirecting negative behaviors, (7) exhibit interest in the circumstances and individuals with which the students are involved taking advantage of opportunities to coach or encourage peer interactions, and (8) acknowledge and praise the students for their positive social interactions.

FIGURE 9–9 Sample T-Chart

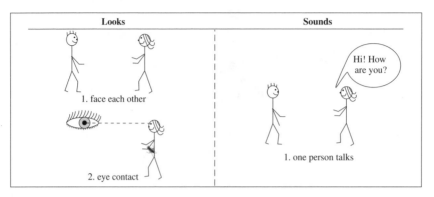

You also can teach students appropriate social interactions through instructional activities, such as creating a T-chart (see Figure 9–9). For example, draw a large T on the chalkboard. On top of the left side of the T, write the word *sounds* and above the right top of the T write the word *looks.* Ask the students what an interaction between two people sounds like and then ask them how it looks. As the students identify and describe those behaviors, list or draw the students' ideas on the T-chart. To illustrate, the list of how a social interaction looks might include bodies facing each other and making eye contact, and the list of sounds might include one person talking at a time (Kagan, 1992).

Typical peers can provide the encouragement and support that students with disabilities may need to participate in the activities and social interactions occurring in the classroom. They can be taught to direct social initiations, such as inviting a peer with special needs to play until the student responds, or to encourage and reward acceptable play behavior with verbal praise (Lowenthal, 1996).

Peer Buddies. Developing friendships is one of the rewarding experiences of preschool for young students. Often these relationships develop naturally, but sometimes you may need to encourage students with and without disabili-

ties to become friends. Assigning a student without disabilities and a student with disabilities to work together as "buddies" can promote meaningful participation in the various events that take place in the classroom (Drinkwater & Demchak, 1995). For example, you might assign peer buddies to collaborate during an event like the Cootie-assembling activity we described earlier. The buddies would support each other by providing both verbal support and physical help when it is needed. They might ask each other, "Can you help find an eye?" or "Can you put the mouth on for me?" Some students may need more support to participate in the activity. For example, one of the students might physically put the Cootie together with a student with significant physical limitations while the student points to or touches different body parts and then holds the assembled Cootie when the peer hands it to him.

Student Aides. If the preschool classroom is located in an elementary school building, older students can provide support to the preschool teacher while they practice the skills they are learning in their own classroom. For example, a second grader might read a story to some of the students that allows him to practice his reading skills and, at the same time, releases the teacher to work with a small group of students doing a

Mrs. Smith reads a story about a big red fish to the students. Then she has the students work in small groups to make a "fish" picture. She gives each group a large piece of paper that has a large fish drawn on it and pieces of red and blue construction paper. The students tear small bits off the construction paper and paste them on their pictures to fill in the fish and the water.

Mrs. Smith has asked Robert and Jon to be peer buddies. They help each other decorate their fish picture. Robert tears the bits of construction paper and hands them to Jon. Jon glues the pieces to the paper with some support from Robert. Sometimes, Jon gets confused about where to glue the bits of paper and asks for Robert's help. Robert shows him how to put the red pieces inside the fish shape and the blue pieces outside to

different activity. This type of "reading buddies" program can benefit both the preschool students who receive support in learning through reading activities with an older peer and the second grader who gets additional reading opportunities and the increased self-esteem that comes with providing a needed service to others (Rowley, 1997).

SUMMARY

This chapter has shown you a view of how to create a successful inclusive preschool classroom. You have learned how early childhood special education strategies can be blended with a developmentally appropriate general education curriculum to create learning experiences for all students. Using this approach, you were given a variety of ways to present and adapt instruction, materials, and content. You were pro-

vided ideas for shaping the learning process and student interactions to allow all students, including those with moderate to severe disabilities, to learn and flourish in a supportive preschool environment.

Thank you to Ms. Marty Cheek and to Ms. Diane Perry and the preschool students at Marshall School in Oxford, Ohio, for sharing their classroom.

 CHAPTER EXTENDERS

Key Terms and Concepts

1. *Developmentally appropriate practice* refers to a general education preschool curriculum that emphasizes student-initiated activities facilitated by the teacher and highlights exploratory and interactive play.

2. *Early childhood special education* describes teacher directed curriculum strategies for preschool students with special needs aimed at improving students' ability to function in future environments and emphasizes direct instruction of specific skills in teacher-arranged activities and limited informal peer interactions.

3. *PECS* is an augmentative communication system made up of simple picture symbols that allows students to communicate nonverbally by exchanging a picture of a desired item for the real item and combining pictures to express themselves in social interactions.

4. P.L. 99-457, the 1986 amendments to P.L. 94-142, federally mandated appropriate special education and related services for 3- to 5-year old children with disabilities.

5. The 1997 IDEA amendments allow educators to use the term *child with a disability* rather than identify a specific disability category for students who are under the age of 9.

Study Guide

1. List five characteristics of developmentally appropriate practice (DAP).
2. List five characteristics of early childhood special education (ECSE).
3. Discuss differences and similarities in the DAP and ECSE approaches to curriculum.
4. List and describe three advantages of stressing child-directed activities in the preschool classroom.
5. Describe the role of the teacher as a facilitator of student-directed learning in preschool classrooms.

Small Group Activity

In a small group of 3 to 4 students, develop a list of four or five student-directed, role-play activities for preschool students. For each of the activities, list two modifications that would allow a student with moderate to severe disabilities to participate successfully in the activity. One modification for each activity should allow a peer to provide the support needed for the student with a disability to participate in the activity and one modification should be teacher facilitated. Once the activities and adaptations are compiled, complete the exercise with each group sharing their lists with the whole class.

Field Experience

Visit an inclusive preschool in your community. Watch the students interact with the curriculum and with each other. Afterward, write a description of the classroom environment and students. Describe the adaptations to materials and activities or other accommodations for students with disabilities that you observed during your visit. In your write-up, also discuss the peer interactions you observed. Be sure to pay particular attention to diversity in your descriptions of the students, materials, and activities.

chapter 10

The Elementary Classroom

Caroline Everington, Lee B. Hamill, and Joy D. Garand-Nichols

The elementary classroom is a rich and vibrant environment both for the typical student and the student with challenges. It is a place where education is more than preparation but actual experiences for the students in the classroom. So it is crucial that the special educator and the regular educator work together with the team to create an environment in which all students in the classroom are thriving and successful individuals. One of the important aspects of an inclusive classroom environment is that it is responsive to the needs of *all* students, not just those with identified disabilities (Lipsky & Gartner, 1997). As we discussed in Chapter 4, for inclusive practice to be effective, we must improve the quality of instruction for all students (McDonnell, 1998). The approaches discussed in this chapter can be applied to all students in your classroom who are experiencing difficulties with the standard curriculum.

With all students with identified disabilities, the IEP should help determine how to apply the curriculum to the individual student. As we discussed in Chapter 6, the IEP process should identify students' learning styles, strengths, and areas of instructional emphasis. In determining instructional objectives and activities, always first reference the general education curriculum and identify the general education teacher's desired outcomes for the entire class (Ryndak, 1996). Next, determine how these goals and instructional activities apply to the student with challenges.

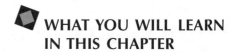

WHAT YOU WILL LEARN IN THIS CHAPTER

This chapter focuses on the general classroom. In Chapter 5, you learned strategies for assessment and progress monitoring. Chapter 6 addressed strategies for designing and implementing IEP objectives. In this chapter we look at how to adapt the general education curriculum and classroom to accommodate the student's IEP objectives and to identify other (non-IEP) teaching outcomes based on the lessons for the general education students. We not only address strategies for identifying curricular needs of students with disabilities within the general classroom environment, but also for providing support for independent functioning and social adjustment. Figure 10–1 displays the format for instructional intervention we present in this chapter. As you can see, step 1 is to make no changes. Step 2 is to adapt the general education instructional strategies, materials, or response requirements.

In this chapter we first address approaches for adapting the general education curricula. However, in some cases, the established general curricula cannot be adapted to the student with severe disabilities or it may not meet his or her immediate needs. Step 3 is to alter the content. In the second section of this chapter we suggest strategies for altering the curriculum for students who are unable to function with the adap-

---

FIGURE 10–1   **Decision-Making Process for Instructional/Curricular Changes**

1. Leave the general education content and instructional strategy as is.
   ▼
2. Adapt the general education instructional strategies, materials, or response requirements.
   ▼
3. Alter the content through leveling or by using applied curriculum.
   ▼
4. Use curriculum overlapping by teaching related independent living skills.

Source: Adapted from Neary, T. (1992). Student specific strategies: Designing an individualized program. In T. Neary, A. Halverson, R. Kronberg, & D. Kelly (Eds.), *Curriculum adaptations for inclusive classrooms* (pp. 56–125). San Francisco: San Francisco State University.

tations discussed earlier. These alterations include making the curriculum more applied for *all* students. Further, for most students with disabilities, functional skills in the areas of language, socialization, career education/employment, and self-care are identified by the team. For maximum generalization, these goals must be integrated into the daily classroom routine. Step 4 is to address these independent living skills through an approach, sometimes known as curriculum overlapping (Giangreco & Putnam, 1991). We address curriculum overlapping in the third part of the chapter.

Finally, students with disabilities need supports to function independently as members of the classroom community. We discuss using peers for enhancing classroom participation in the final section.

ADAPTING THE STANDARD CURRICULA OF THE GENERAL CLASSROOM

Standard curricula can be defined as "locally determined state-approved general education curricula from which non-disabled students are instructed"(Knowlton, 1998, p. 99). Adaptations can be defined as modifying or supplementing the curriculum to meet the needs of the individual students (Hoover & Patton, 1997). Whenever possible, the student with disabilities should participate in the same activities as the rest of the class (Giangreco, 1996). Therefore, adapt the environment and the instructions before altering the content (Ryndak, 1996). When making adaptations to curriculum content, effective practice focuses on adaptations that enhance functioning, rather than on teaching developmental prerequisites that may be skills intended for younger students (Knowlton, 1998). For example, a student in fifth grade is unable to spell the words assigned for the grade level. A content adaptation to enhance functioning would be to assign vocabulary words important to her. A less appropriate

content adaptation would be to assign the first grade spelling book. The first-grade text book could stigmatize the fifth-grade student and may not contain vocabulary relevant to her needs in the fifth grade class.

Where Do You Begin?

One of the key elements in creating a successful classroom is being able to truly understand the needs of the student with challenges. It is important to know strengths and weaknesses, learning styles, likes and dislikes, and to have a firm grasp of how the challenge or disability is affecting the student. Adaptations will be different for every student in your classroom. As we discussed in Chapters 5, 6, and 7, decisions regarding adaptations are the result of a collaborative effort among the team members. For most teams, frequent meetings are necessary to ensure that appropriate adaptations and proper supports are in place for success. Some teams meet at the beginning of each unit, at the start of each week, or when needed. It is important to meet at a regular time to make sure everyone on the team is kept current and the work is truly collaborative. It may be the special educator who initially develops ways to adapt a lesson, but all members of the team have expertise in their areas and can add greatly to the support for the student. The team will find that quickly all members are adapting lessons and everyone is beginning to truly understand how to teach and work with the particular student.

When deciding on adaptations and goals for the student, first clarify learning outcomes (Giangreco, 1996). As mentioned previously, some skills are part of the general curriculum and some are not. One way to assist with this process is to create a profile for the student that can be shared by the team. With this information in hand, the team can begin the process of creating that successful environment where all students can thrive and grow. The team should formulate a checklist or quick screen (Hoover & Patton, 1997) and use it to ensure all aspects for

FIGURE 10–2   **Checklist for Learning Outcomes Adaptations**

- What is the general curriculum assignment or activity?
- Can the student participate as is?
- Is assistive technology needed for the student to participate?
- Does the assignment or activity need to be simplified?
- Does the student need to use a different response mode to demonstrate knowledge?
- Does the pace of the lesson or activity need to be increased or decreased?
- What kind of supports are needed for the student to participate?
- How can other students be involved?
- How can we make this as concrete as possible?
- Who is going to do the adapting?
- Who is going to do the implementing?
- Are the IEP goals incorporated?
- Who will do the documenting?

the student have been addressed. The checklist in Figure 10–2 can serve as a starting point to help teams identify outcomes and relevant adaptations.

Once the quick screen has been completed, conduct a more detailed analysis of needs regarding instructional strategies, materials, response requirements, and content (Hoover & Patton, 1997). All of these areas are key to a successful lesson. At first, this may seem time consuming, but after several lessons have been adapted for a particular student you will see a repetition in techniques, materials, and adaptations that work not only for one student, but for many others as well, *including students who have not been identified as having a disability.* That is, the strategies you develop for a student with moderate to severe disabilities are useful for many others who have difficulties in your class. As we discussed in Chapter 4, when you view adaptations from the associated needs perspective, you improve instruction for all students. The process will actually begin to save time as you prepare adaptations in advance. In this section, we address adaptations to the standard curriculum in the following areas: (1) instructional strategies, (2) materials, and (3) response requirements. As you read this section, keep in mind that these three types of adaptations are

not mutually exclusive. That is, you may employ more than one modification for any given lesson, particularly if your student has complex needs.

Instructional Adaptations

When deciding on adaptations, you might look first to changes in the way you deliver instruction (Janney & Snell, 1998). Modifying directions or creating more structure in the lesson are often all that is necessary to enable the student to participate in the lesson. These types of adaptations are not time consuming or intrusive and assist in building independence because the student will not have to ask for assistance as readily. Like the other adaptations we discuss in this chapter, these can be used with any student in the classroom who is experiencing difficulty.

Modify Directions. For some students, directions can create an auditory or visual overload. Simplification of instructions is an easy modification. Either black out the unnecessary directions or rewrite them in simpler terms or use pictures as cues. Highlighting key words can also help students to interpret the directions and to remember them as they proceed through the lesson. You can also prepare students for listening by providing an outline (Wood, 1998). Such advanced organizers can assist many of the students in the class.

Use Auditory or Tactile Cues. When presenting material to students, it is always helpful if the presentation can be multisensory (Wood, 1998). Multisensory presentations could be any of the following examples used for different students. For example, counting can be introduced with a metronome, while bouncing a ball, or while tapping on the blackboard. This makes the counting have a rhythm and highlights the critical aspects of the task. Students can also use this technique on their own when learning to count.

A second example of an auditory presentation would be to change intonation as you teach (Wood, 1998). Highlight important information by using a whisper, a chant, or a song. Providing information in a chant or a song can assist the student in recalling the information. The more ways an idea is presented, the greater probability of retention and generalization. Acting out a word or making up a sign to accompany the new word can function as an aid in retrieving that word.

Tactile cues can bring attention to critical components of a task and can enhance understanding. For example, the Touch Math (Bullock, Pierce, & McClellan, 1987) program uses tactile cues and has been successful with students with moderate to severe disabilities. In this program, students touch dots attached to each numeral as they learn to identify the numeral and amounts. For students having problems with discrimination, you can add a dimensional aspect to the dots by gluing material or using textured paint.

Tape-Record Directions. Tape recordings can be useful supports to encourage independence (Stainback, Stainback, Stefanich, & Alper, 1996). For students who may experience difficulties with attention and memory or for those who make frequent requests for teacher assistance, you can tape-record the directions for the lesson. This way, the student can refer back to them instead of asking you to repeat the instruction. Tape recordings have been used effectively to cue appropriate behaviors in students with severe disabilities in many settings (Alberto & Troutman, 1999). To make the adaptation unobtrusive, the student can wear a small headset.

Structure the Lesson. Many students experience frustration in understanding the scope of the work. Address this challenge by establishing clear expectations. This includes enhancing the discrimination between the beginning and the end of the child's work. For example, when Tamika is presented with worksheets that are copied front and back, it is often difficult for her to understand when she finishes the front of the work, she needs to turn it over and complete the back. She becomes frustrated because she believes she is finished when she completes the front. Oral directions from the teacher do not seem to help. Remedy this by photocopying both sides of a paper. A second approach is to provide a folder that, when opened, has the labels "start" on one side and "end" on the other.

Another method of structuring the lesson is to supply summary notes or outlines of the lesson for students (Falvey, Givner, & Kimm, 1996). Provide notes to students individually or write them on the board for the class. If you prepare the outlines on a word processing program, the future preparation is minimized.

Materials Adaptations

Materials adaptations are relatively easy to make and help many students, including those without disabilities, understand and participate in the lesson. Materials can be changed in many ways such as enlargement of print or positioning, which requires minimal teacher effort. Supports such as cue cards, pictures, or manipulatives can be added to any lesson and can greatly increase understanding and retention of material. In the next section we provide examples of eight adaptations to the standard curriculum.

Use Pictures. Pictures can be used to support instruction in many ways. They can assist the student in organizing the relevant information in the lesson. For example, to enhance attention and participation in a group setting, you can photocopy pictures from the story. Students can either follow the pictures in sequence during the reading of the story or have their own copy of the story. These picture cues can later be used for instructional practice, allowing students the opportunity to sequence the events of the story with the cards or can be used by the students as response cards during class discussions.

Pictures can assist in comprehension. In spelling, it is often helpful to introduce a new word with an accompanying picture (Blenk & Fine, 1995). For example, when introducing a new lesson on the life of a ladybug, pictures of a ladybug, where it lives, and what it eats will help students with moderate to severe disabilities participate with the class and understand the content. These approaches help students make associations and build more pathways for retrieval.

Pictures can assist students in understanding directions for an activity. For example, students can have a picture of each activity for a given lesson. As they complete each activity, they remove the picture from their picture list. This provides concrete reminders of the sequence of events.

Use Cue Cards. Cue cards can help students participate independently in seatwork. Cue cards are index cards used to provide reminders of instructions or classroom rules. For example, use a cue card to remind students that after two worksheets are completed, they are finished with their work. For other students, a written list telling them exactly what will be introduced will help them follow you and the class discussions that follow. For example, if you only want the students to complete the first two problems of a lesson and then have a whole class discussion, you will probably have to give these cues in a written form for some students. You literally may have to write the word *stop* on the papers of other students so they know when to end and wait.

Cue cards can also be used for vocabulary development and to enhance participation in class discussions (Falvey et al., 1996). New vocabulary or key concepts can be put on cards for the student. Encourage students to refer to these cards for written assignments or class discussions.

Use Enlarged Print. Certainly students with visual impairments benefit from enlarged print, but others can too because it assists in highlighting the critical attributes of the task. The enlarged paper or print can be used in many ways. Teachers have always used this strategy for posting classroom rules or other critical information. Bigger paper can be used for individuals as well. For the individual, words and pictures on worksheets can be enlarged. This can help focus attention.

USING PICTURE CARDS TO ENHANCE INDEPENDENCE IN THE CLASSROOM

Chevonne could not follow verbal directions given by the teacher. As a result, the classroom teacher or assistant had to lead her to each activity, like circle time. To enable her to do this independently, the teacher made a line drawing of the circle time on an $8\frac{1}{2} \times 11$-inch paper that he posted in the area. He gave Chevonne a smaller picture (4×5-inches) that she could carry and instructed her to match her picture to the one in the area when asked. When she began to come to the circle independently, the picture in the circle area was reduced and finally eliminated. This same strategy was used successfully to teach Chevonne to go to the nurse's office, cafeteria, and the bathroom.

CUE CARD ASSISTS IN PREPARATION FOR ACTIVITY CHANGE

Freddy, a second-grade student, found it hard to make the transition from classroom work to lining up and leaving for lunch and recess. Even when a card was handed to him several minutes before the transition would occur, he still had difficulty. Verbal as well as visual reminders did not assist him through this difficult transition. Eventually, what the teacher did was to hand him five cue cards that had the word "lunch" or "recess" on them. Freddy would then walk around the room to the different centers. He would stop at each center and hand the students a card for lunch or recess. By the time he had handed out all his cards, he was ready for the transition to lunch or recess. This repetitive action not only provided the support Freddy needed for the transition, but it also helped to ready the rest of the class for the next activity.

Position Material for Ease in Viewing. Positioning can be crucial when presenting material to students. For students with visual difficulties, the easiest adaptation is to move the student to a location near the teacher, chalkboards, and other visual displays. For many students, particularly those who may have difficulty with head control, material presented in an upright display may be easier to see. An easel is a piece of equipment commonly used in classrooms to present important information. For the child with visual difficulties, the easel can be moved closer to the individual and still provide benefit to the class. This is particularly helpful if it is not possible to move the child closer to the board or center of instruction.

Use Color Coding. Often presenting material on different colored paper helps the individual organize work, recall information, and function more independently. You can organize different subject matter according to different colors. Color coding can also assist in addressing the discrimination problems we discussed in Chapter 2. In this approach, all materials and paper are color coded for a given subject area. For example, you can put a blue piece of paper on the board with the word *math* on it. You can then go over and hand the student a blue piece of paper with the word *math* on it. The student can go over to her storage space and retrieve her blue math folder and the blue basket with the math manipulatives in it. Helping students to begin to make connections among objects teaches them to organize the world around them. For example, students learn that for math, they need the blue basket that has a ruler, blocks, number cards, and a pencil in it.

Colored paper can help students focus on the work or on the manipulatives they are working with at their table (Dalrymple, 1995). As we discussed in Chapter 2, persons with autism have difficulty in attention. Creating boundaries for tasks assists them with attention (Earles, Carlson, & Bock, 1998). A colored piece of paper placed behind the regular worksheet or under the manipulatives helps pull students' attention to the work placed in front of them and provides boundaries for the task. Putting students' work in a manila folder with the front cut out helps give them boundaries.

Use Manipulatives. Hands-on material helps assist all students in constructing meaning (Wood, 1998). In spelling or reading students may need to have the words made into something concrete they can manipulate. Using a movable or magnetic alphabet can be very beneficial for some students. Using Magnetic Poetry can also be another way to begin helping students put together words to form sentences. Magnetic Poetry is a commercially available product consisting of small magnets with words on them. You can make your own magnetic poetry by writing words on index cards, laminating them, and gluing a magnet to the back of each card. If the student is very interested in blocks, you can increase his interest in words and reading by taping words on blocks and arranging them to give a three-dimensional effect. If the student is interested in cars, tape the words to cars and allow her to move the cars around to form sentences and phrases.

Incorporate a Permanent Model of the Finished Product. Some students need to visualize the finished product (Wood, 1998). Being able to see, touch, and handle an example of what you are expecting the class to create assists in understanding and thus creates the likelihood they will be able to complete the task without assistance. Often, the example shown to the class can be placed near the student who has difficulty visualizing completed projects. Even a simple activity like lining up cubes in a pattern will be easier for a student if a model of the finished product is provided. For example, students will be much more successful if you lay six blocks out and ask them to build a pattern like the one before them than if you place a bucket of blocks out and ask them to build a pattern like the one in the picture.

Use Learning Centers or Learning Boxes. Many general education teachers use learning centers to supplement or enhance class content. For students who may need more time with the material, learning centers can be placed in boxes that the students can take to their desks or even home (Hamill & Dunlevy, 1999). One advantage of placing content enhancement activities in boxes is their portability. Students can use a learning box for an extended period of time wherever they are most comfortable doing an activity. This also allows you considerable versatility in assigning activities and provides flexibility in times for working on them.

Learning boxes also give you an opportunity to use alternative forms of homework and make valuable connections with parents. You can make this kind of content enhancement activity accessible for all students by leveling the materials in the learning centers or learning boxes (see Table 10–1). We discuss leveling more in the next section.

Response Requirement Adaptations

Some students may not be able to complete the lesson as assigned to the class, even with modifications in directions or in materials. In these cases, you may need to modify the response

---

PERMANENT MODEL MODIFICATION

Morgan was having extreme difficulty in art class. The only activity he would engage in was drawing cowboys. When the art teacher started a new project, he would get very upset and continue to draw his pictures. The teacher was very understanding, but she wanted to expose the student to new media. The team decided to give him a model to work from. The art teacher always created an example in front of the class so the students knew what was ex-

pected of them. In this case, what she did was to take her example and place it in front of Morgan and ask him to create the same piece of artwork. It was amazing. Morgan began to copy, to the best of his ability, the teacher's product. In the beginning, he even copied the colors and materials the teacher used. After several weeks of success, the teacher began to suggest a different color or different piece of material for a part of the project. Soon Morgan was able to use the example as a frame of reference and create works of art that had unique aspects.

TABLE 10–1 Leveled Learning Boxes for Sorting by Food Groups

Contents of Box 1	Contents of Box 2	Contents of Box 3
1. Ten pictures of different grocery items, either cut out of magazines or commercially prepared photographs.	1. Twenty pictures of different grocery items, either cut out of magazines or commercially prepared photographs.	1. Thirty pictures of different grocery items, either cut out of magazines or commercially prepared photographs.
2. Two 5 × 7-inch manila envelopes, each with one of the following words written on the front:	2. Four 5 × 7-inch manila envelopes, each with one of the following words written on the front:	2. Six 5 × 7-inch manila envelopes, each with one of the following words written on the front:
• Food • Non-food	• Meats and Milk • Fruits and Vegetables • Breads and Cereals • Sweets and Fats	• Meat, Poultry, Fish, Dry Beans, Eggs, and Nuts • Milk, Yogurt, and Cheese • Vegetables • Fruits • Bread, Cereal, Rice, and Pasta • Fats, Oils, and Sweets

Source: Hamill, L., & Dunlevy, A., (1999). *Work boxes* (rev. ed.) San Antonio, TX: PCI Educational Publishing. Reprinted with permission.

requirements (Janney & Snell, 1998). That is, the student may do less work or may demonstrate mastery of the material in other ways such as speaking or drawing rather than by a written product. In this section, we discuss several alternative ways that students can display mastery. As with making other adaptations, you are limited only by your creativity.

Reduce Response Requirements. For many students, breaking down the task into smaller units is very effective (Kochhar, West, & Taymans, 2000). For example, reducing the number of problems on a worksheet enables some students to participate successfully. Other students may need to set a different pace to complete their work. They may not be able to finish a whole set of problems in one lesson. To address this, you can break up the assignment into smaller units and provide a break in between.

When worksheets are overwhelming for a student, there are different ways to accommodate the student. The worksheet can be cut up in strips, and the student can complete one strip at a time. For example, on a math worksheet, students can also cut off the problems as they finish them. For some students, taping the strips back onto a solid piece of paper can provide a reinforcing activity that signals completion of the lesson.

Use Oral or Taped Presentations. For written assignments such as reports or journals, students can give oral presentations (Wood, 1998). Audiotapes can provide good support as well. One adaptation is for the student to tape-record a homework assignment for you to review at a later date.

Use Pictures and Artwork as an Alternative Response Mode. For science, social studies, and language arts, allow some students to use pictures or artwork to demonstrate understanding of the material. These areas are often easier to adapt because hands-on materials can be easily worked into the lesson. For example, when studying a unit on fish, a student can create a collage of pictures of fish. Another student may make different fish out of clay and put labels on them. When you use these formats, you may want to have the students describe the contents of the pictures or models to ensure comprehension.

Use Computers as an Alternative Response Mode. Don't forget the versatility of the computer (King, 1999). Often, the computer can simply be used to help students type answers they are unable to write. If students are unable to participate in the assigned activity on the computer, they can practice typing their name or work a program related to the unit the class is studying. We discuss parallel tasks such as this in greater detail in the next section.

Many adaptive devices can both assist the student in responding and create access to course materials (Blenk & Fine, 1995). Many different alternative keyboards and software programs are available to make the computer more accessible to students with varying challenges. As we discussed in Chapter 3, word processors such as Intellitalk or Write: OutLoud have simplified screens and can read written text back. TouchWindows that fit over the screen can enable a student who cannot manipulate a mouse to interact with many software programs (Blenk & Fine, 1995). Intellikeys is a large flat keyboard that can be very useful for students who may have trouble isolating a finger to hit a key. There is also a delay that can be programmed for students who have difficulty lifting their finger after they have pressed a key. Intellipics (1995) is a computer software program that can be adapted for a variety of uses in the classroom. You can use the program to create stories, teach sequencing, and do picture match-

ing. There are multiple ways this program can be adapted to accommodate students who function at different levels. For example, one student can create a story using the software text. A second can assign pictures to the story. A third can sequence the events. A fourth can use a switch to click on pictures for learning cause and effect. Other software companies that produce products for special needs populations include Don Johnson, Broderbund, Judy Lynn Software, Laureate Learning, and R. J. Cooper (Pugliese, 1999).

Use Calculators as an Alternative Mode. For mathematics, calculators have become an integral part of the classroom environment. For students who may not be achieving at the same level as their classmates, calculators can serve as an alternative or can supplement instruction on computation (Browder & Snell, 1994).

 ALTERING THE CONTENT

When the student cannot perform the tasks in the standard curriculum, even with modifications in instruction, materials, or in responses, it may be appropriate to identify an alternative, related task within that content area or to alter the content (Janney & Snell, 1998). If you employ the associated needs perspective, this is true for *all students* in the classroom. The next section discusses two approaches to content modification: identifying alternative, related goals for students whose ability level does not match the standard lesson and changing the content for all students in the class to be more applied and meaningful.

Using Leveled Instruction to Alter Content

In some cases, students will be unable to perform the task, even with modifications. This does not mean students cannot participate in the activity. In this case, a related skill is identified in the content area, thus enabling students to progress at their own rate and, at the same time, work with others (King-Sears, 1997; McDonnell, 1998; Stainback, Stainback, & Stefanich, 1996). An example of a related skill in language arts would be a student who is working on writing simple sentences while the other students are writing essays. This student may use index cards and possibly a movable alphabet. Like her peers, this student will be working on writing skills, but at a different level of difficulty. This content adaptation enables the student to continue to participate in the language arts curriculum.

When making this type of adaptation in academic skill areas, refer to the student's measured level of academic functioning. For example, if standardized inventories indicate the student has reading skills on a first-grade level or computational skills on a second-grade level, the alternative task must be appropriate for his or her ability. For preparation of teacher-made reading materials, use a readability formula periodically such as that developed by Fry (1977) or by Raygor (1977) to check difficulty levels. When the materials are appropriate for the student's academic level, he or she is more likely to complete the work independently and to display greater comprehension.

A second example of a parallel assignment in math could take place when the class is working on division and multiplication. This same student could work with sandpaper numbers and matching numerals to amounts. Have the student work within the same framework of the classroom so she does not become alienated. When possible, involve the other students. Encourage collaboration because it is easy for such a student to feel she is not an active part of her classroom.

Within any classroom, you will find students who may need parallel assignments. Many of these students may not have identified disabilities. Therefore, teachers in inclusive classrooms

frequently adjust or level their curricula to meet the needs of learners with differing abilities (Giangreco, Cloninger, & Iverson, 1993). One way to meet the need of a diverse learning community is to create lessons for individuals on many levels (see Figure 10–3). That is, all students work in the same content area—reading—but some students work at different levels (Giangreco, 1998).

Science is a content area that easily lends itself to multilevel instruction (Blenk & Fine, 1995). In a science experiment, you can assign tasks of differing levels of difficulty, especially if students work in cooperative groups. For example, one student can act as a recorder, another can read the directions, and a third can hold the materials. As a result, each student has a meaningful role and can make a valuable contribution to the success of the experiment.

You can use the concept of leveled instruction to enhance participation in class discussions. Questions differing in difficulty can be used for selected students to enable them to participate in the discussion (Wood, 1998). For example, before the class discussion, you can identify specific topic areas the student with a moderate to severe disability can answer and subsequently arrange to call on the student at those times. To elicit responding from students with significant cognitive disabilities, ask a specific structured question rather than an open-ended question. For example, students will more likely respond appropriately to the question, "Whose birthday is it today?" than to the question, "Why is this a special day?"

Using Applied Content

One effective way to create greater access for the general education curriculum for students with disabilities is to use applied content. When you do this, many students benefit. There are many approaches to make the curriculum more meaningful to the student.

FIGURE 10–3
Leveled Curriculum

Goal: Write Sentences Using Basic Sight Words

- Student A matches photos that have the sight words written on them.
- Student B matches the words to the pictures.
- Student C points to words as the teacher says them.
- Student D fills in the correct sight word to finish a sentence. (Bob carries his books to *school* each day.)
- Student E writes sentences using the sight words.

Use Personal Experiences. When presenting material to individuals with challenges, particularly those with moderate to severe disabilities, it often helps to make the work meaningful and applicable to their personal lives (Hoover & Patton, 1997; Sapon-Shevin, 1999). One way to accomplish this is by using a modified language experience approach (Bock, 1991). In this approach, you incorporate themes and topics relevant to the child's life. One approach is to incorporate the names of familiar people and objects in stories and math problems. Another approach is to use personal photographs of people or actual objects to enhance the material for the student. A third approach is to incorporate the experiences of the student or others in the classroom into the lesson. The example illustrates an adaptation for the morning writing activity in which the subject of the sentence has been changed to incorporate a real experience, in this case, the teacher. The objective of capitalization and punctuation is still addressed, but relevant information has been substituted for the workbook example. In addition, examples such as this help prepare students for changes in their routine. In this case, the routine change involves the teacher leaving on her honeymoon.

EXAMPLE
Goal: Capitalize names, days of the week, and countries, and use punctuation.

Example from workbook: *jane and bill will be in canada for their vacation on Monday of next week*

Personalized example: *miss garand will not be here on Monday because she will be on her honeymoon in jamaica*

Make Your Curriculum Applied. One of the best ways to connect learning to the students' personal lives involves teaching an applied curriculum as an overarching approach to instruction. Connecting classroom activities to experiences outside of school can help students understand how what they learn in school can help them be part of the community. As we discussed in Chapter 4, there are many ways to weave applied material into the standard curriculum. In the next section we present examples of ways that games and worksheets can be used to introduce applied curriculum into the general classroom.

Teach Applied Content Through Games. Games provide a good vehicle for reinforcement of curriculum. They also provide a means of integrating applied curriculum concepts into the general classroom.

Bingo games can address applied skills such as money recognition and traditional academic content such as number identification. For number identification, you can level the game by putting dots of varying amounts on cards of one color for some students, numerals on different cards of another color for other students, and number words on the last set of still different colored cards for a third group of students. For money recognition, you can glue photocopied pictures of coins or realistic pictures of coins cut out of an elementary math workbook and place one coin on each card of one color for some students, simple combinations of coins on other cards of another color for other students, and complex combinations of coins on the third set of cards in a different color for the last group of students.

The entire class can play life-skills games together and the students with a moderate to severe disability can work on their IEP goals while they play the games (Hamill & Dunlevy, 1994). You can create board games using a wide variety of game cards interchangeably with the various game boards. The game cards should cover a range of skill levels and subject matter to meet the needs of the students' different interests and ability levels. Game cards can address functional curriculum such as places in the community for the social studies curriculum. You can make game cards of photographs of community sites that are familiar to the students, such as the school, McDonald's, hospital, farm, or bank.

This type of activity can be easily leveled for students with differing IEP objectives. For example, some students can play the game by identifying the sites. Other students can read cards that list the words for those places, such as campground, movie theater, and bus station. A final group of students can identify community sites through descriptions. For example, a hotel card might say, "This is a place with lots of rooms. Most of the rooms have beds in them," and a grocery store card might say, "This is a place with lots of different kinds of food in it. Some of the food is in cans and some of the food is frozen." In the same way, you can develop sets of game cards for the math curriculum that would involve a range of skills from coin recognition to making change. For more information on how to make board games, refer to Figure 10–4.

Incorporate Applied Content Into Seatwork. You can develop worksheets that teach academic skills using real-life activities and materials from the everyday experiences of the students. For example, develop leveled worksheets that ask students to find information in the TV Guide magazine or the TV section of the local newspaper. Elementary and middle school students are likely to have some familiarity with these media. Worksheets such as those using a TV Guide (see Figure 10–5) can help students contextualize reading and writing skills through their interest in this typical out-of-school activity.

Connect classroom activities to experiences outside of school.

FIGURE 10–4 **How to Make Board Games Using Applied Curricula**

You can easily develop and produce inexpensively a variety of board games. They are made on 11 × 14-inch manila file folders. Design a trail made of small commercially made stickers or colored dots made with markers that begins with the word *start* and ends with the word *finish*. Make each space on the trail have equal value or give special value to certain spaces by identifying them with the following designations: "go back one space," "move ahead two spaces," "roll again," and "miss a turn." The length of the trails on different game boards should vary to accommodate the amount of time available for playing a game and the attention span of the students. You also can develop game boards with different themes by using special stickers or drawings to identify a holiday, sport, or other event. You can even make a trail using a simple coloring book page and marking dots along the outline on the commercially made picture.

Sample Board Game Configuration

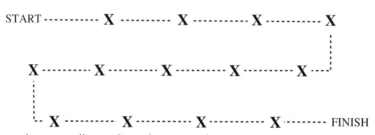

The students take turns rolling a die and moving a button, coin, or erasers along the game trail to the finish line. The winner is determined randomly by the roll of the die rather than by the number of correct responses.

You can make game cards by printing words on the cards or by cutting pictures out of magazines and pasting them on cards. For each set of cards, choose a topic or subject area and make cards at several different skill levels. Using different colored paper for each skill level will help keep them separate from one another. The sets of cards can be used interchangeably with different game boards, and individual students can use different sets of cards while playing the same game. For example, one game might include a student using cards with social skills questions, another student using sight word cards, a third student using cards that require the student to complete partial sentences, and a final student using time-telling cards showing pictures of clocks.

For students with physical disabilities, it may be necessary to modify the game materials. To stabilize the board, secure it or place it in a tray. Larger game pieces may be needed if your student is unable to pick up a button. To make game pieces easier to move, make a border on the trail by gluing string on either side. Magnet boards can be very easy for many students to use.

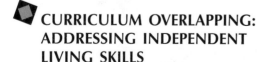 **CURRICULUM OVERLAPPING: ADDRESSING INDEPENDENT LIVING SKILLS**

As you learned in Chapter 4, applied curricula involve teaching skills considered important for the individual's independent functioning. These skills, sometimes called functional skills, include but are not limited to skills in the following domain areas: self-care, mobility, language/communication, socialization, and career/vocational. Generally, goals and objectives in these skill areas are identified on the student's IEP (Ryndak, 1996). For maximum generalization, all of these goals should be addressed in the class-

FIGURE 10 – 5   Reading the *TV Guide* for Information

Name _____

Use the *TV Guide* to answer the following questions:

For one student:
1. Write the name here. _____
2. What picture is on the cover? _____
3. What is your favorite show on TV?_____
4. Circle the things you can find in the *TV Guide*.

         movies   comics   stories   puzzles

For another student:
1. On what day of the week does the *TV Guide* begin? _____
2. What is the name of the first TV show listed on Monday evening at 6 p.m.? _____
_____What channel(s) is it on? _____
3. Pick a movie whose name begins with the letter [   ] in the movie guide section of *TV Guide*. What is the name of the movie you chose? _____
4. What is the picture about on the cover of the *TV Guide?* _____
_____
5. Name one of the channels listed in the *TV Guide*. _____

For a third student:
1. What dates does the *TV Guide* cover? _____
2. What is the name of the TV show that is on channel ___ at 11:30 on Saturday morning? _____
_____
3. Pick a movie whose title begins with the letter [   ] in the movie guide section of the *TV Guide*. Answer the following questions about the movie you chose:

      What day of the week will it be on TV? _____
      What time of day will it be on TV? _____
      What channel will it be on? _____
4. What is the title of the cover story shown on the front of the *TV Guide?* _____
What page does the cover story begin on?_____
5. Name one of the *cable* channels listed in the *TV Guide*. _____
6. What is the name of the TV show that is on channel [ ] at 6 o'clock on Tuesday evening? _____

For a fourth student:
1. What date is the Wednesday that is covered in the *TV Guide?*
2. Find a TV show on Thursday afternoon you would be interested in watching. Answer the following questions about the show you chose:

      What is the name of the show?_____
      What time is it on? _____
      What channel(s) is it on? _____
      What does the *TV Guide* say about this week's episode of the show? _____
3. Pick a movie whose title begins with the letter [ ] in the movie guide section of the *TV Guide*. Answer the following questions about the movie you chose:

      What day of the week will it be on TV? _____
      What time of day will it be on TV? _____
      What channel will it be on? _____
      What TV rating is it given?_____
      What is the movie going to be about? _____

continued

FIGURE 10–5   **continued**

4. Name one of the premium channels listed in the *TV Guide*. _____

What abbreviation is used to indicate the channel you named? _____

5. Find a TV show on Monday evening you would be interested in watching. Answer the following questions about the show you chose: ·

      What is the name of the show? _____

      What time is it on? _____

      What channel(s) is it on? _____

      What does the *TV Guide* say about this week's episode of the show? _____

6. What is the title of the cover story shown on the front of the *TV Guide*? _____

Read the cover story in the *TV Guide* and describe what or who it is about.

7. Pick a movie whose title begins with the letter [   ] in the movie guide section of the *TV Guide*. Answer the following questions about the movie you chose:

      What day of the week will it be on TV? _____

      What time of day will it be on TV? _____

      What channel will it be on? _____

      What TV rating is it given? _____

      What is the movie going to be about? _____

Source: Adapted from Hamill, L. B., & Dunlevy, A. (2000). *Members of the community: Worksheets for transition activities in the community and the classroom.* Verona, WI: IEP Resources. Reprinted with permission.

room daily. These skills can be incorporated into the typical classroom day with a little ingenuity and imagination. Adjusting the general education curriculum to find or enhance the functional connections between the content and its use in everyday life offers the best way to make the curriculum accessible to students with moderate to severe disabilities without lessening its value for general education students or detracting from its academic benefit. Placement in a typical classroom gives students with moderate to severe disabilities many role models to help them acquire functional skills at a much quicker rate.

As you learned in Chapter 5, you will use the ecological approach in identifying the critical skills needed in each class routine. This approach of using ongoing classroom routines for instruction has been termed *naturalistic teaching* (McDonnell, 1998). As we discussed in Chapter 2, teaching skills within the natural context enhances skill retention and generalization. Naturalistic instruction has been very effective in inclusive settings (Haring, Neetz, Lovinger, Peck, & Semmel, 1987). Although it is most desirable to teach skills within the ongo-

ing routine, sometimes this is not possible due to limited time or infrequent opportunities. Some teachers have found that the downtime before and after recess and lunch can be a good time to provide additional instruction on these skills (Hamre-Nietupski, McDonald, & Nietupski, 1992). In this section, we delineate some of the more common areas of applied curriculum—self-care, career education, language, and social skills—and provide examples of strategies for integrating these skills into the daily classroom routine of the elementary general classroom.

Self-Care Skills. Often on an IEP, a student will need to develop more independent skills related to grooming, dressing, hygiene, or eating. Daily routines all the students participate in provide excellent opportunities for teaching these skills. As we discussed in Chapter 2, for skill acquisition and retention, students with moderate to severe disabilities need many opportunities to practice skills. Opportunities for teaching dressing and grooming skills occur several times daily. When the students come into the room, they need to unzip their coats, take them off, and hang them up. This is a perfect chance to work on zipping, buttoning, tying, and snapping. Every time the students go out to recess is also another wonderful time to work on this skill.

Many elementary classrooms are equipped with a sink. Handwashing often occurs before lunch and snack and after art or science activities. These routines provide opportunities for not only working on handwashing, but also for instruction on related activities such as waiting in line or cleaning up.

Elementary school students often need to work on tying their shoes or putting them on the correct feet. For example, many classrooms make the reading area a carpeted or loft area where students may be required to take off their shoes. This gives students a good opportunity to practice this skill in a practical situation that is meaningful to them.

Skills related to eating may also be part of a child's IEP. Working on snacks in the classroom can be a good time to concentrate on specific skills such as self-feeding, chewing, or swallowing as well as more advanced skills such as table manners, table setting, and the preparation of simple foods. Because food is highly motivating for most students, mealtimes are also an excellent time to teach language skills. Gestures, pictures, or signs can be used to request food items. Conversational skills can be addressed informally with peers at these times.

Career Education. All students have a need to begin to develop skills that will enable them to function independently in work environments. Often, these skills are embedded throughout the child's day. Opportunities for addressing personal responsibility occur throughout the day. Expectations for the general education students can provide a reference for these skills. For example, in most classrooms, all students are responsible for gathering their personal materials needed for specific tasks or assignments. These skills should be addressed with students with moderate to severe disabilities as well.

As you learned in Chapter 4, school-to-work concepts bring the working world into the classroom. Adapting the elementary school classroom to infuse school-to-work concepts in the curriculum makes connections between academic concepts and their real-life use. In the classroom, students can learn about different jobs in the community and how their schoolwork relates to those jobs.

Classroom jobs provide all students with informal work-related experiences. Students can take turns with their peers completing classroom jobs such as handing out papers, turning off the lights, picking up different sections of the room, cleaning off work tables, sorting classroom materials, collecting lunch money, and taking paperwork to the office. Jobs can even be created specifically to work on a desired skill for a particular student.

Sax, Pumpian, and Fisher (1997) provide an example of a creative modification of a classroom job for a student who had a physical disability. For climate control, students took turns misting the room with a spray bottle. To enable the student with disabilities to participate, a switch-operated spray bottle was created. The student with disabilities regulated the amount of spray with his switch and the peers helped point the sprayer.

Language/Communication. Communication should be a skill embedded throughout the student's entire day. It is the thread connecting all aspects of the student's educational experience from academics to friendships. The naturistic teaching and milieu teaching procedures discussed in Chapter 3 are very effective for language acquisition and can be integrated easily into the classroom routine (Westling & Fox, 1995). All different levels from simple requests to conversational skills can be woven into the daily routine.

Classroom peers can be effective in providing support for language instruction (Sax et al., 1997). They can act as models as well as facilitators. Peers in the environment must be aware of new and ongoing language goals so they can provide support and assistance (Kaiser, 1993).

We discussed the role of assistive technology in depth in Chapter 3, but note here that when creating overlays and choice boards, students' individual preferences, and the norms of their peers and the school community should be strong considerations in selecting the vocabulary choices on the board. For example, if all the students in the class raise their hands and ask to use the bathroom, then the student's augmentative device should not say, "I need to use the lavatory." Make sure the team is aware of the phrases and lingo the students use in the school and classroom. Often asking peers' help to program the overlay used for social time proves to be very beneficial. Remember, this overlay is for a student and not an adult.

Social Skills. When working with the peers to build a supportive community, remember that the student usually needs help learning how to form friendships. Skills that frequently need to be addressed include appropriate forms of interaction with peers, initiating and maintaining conversations, greetings and departures, eye contact, and skills related to cooperation. As we discussed in Chapter 2, many students—including those without disabilities—often have difficulty discriminating the verbal and nonverbal cues that accompany social interactions.

There are many opportunities for teaching social skills throughout the day in the general classroom. Many classrooms use cooperative learning models that require considerable interpersonal interaction (King-Sears, 1997). Teaching students to work together effectively is central to the success of any cooperative learning model (Hoover & Patton, 1997). Although cooperative learning can be composed of small groups or pairs, in a setting in which there are many students with disabilities, pairs

may be preferable (Hoover & Patton, 1997). We provide a more detailed description of cooperative learning models in Chapter 11 when we discuss inclusive practice in the secondary classroom.

There are many approaches to teaching social skills. Role play can be a valuable tool. Another technique used to help individuals increase their responsiveness to social cues are "social stories" (Gray & Garand, 1993). The stories do not encourage the student to memorize what to do in social situations but, rather, teach them to be able to read social cues occurring in a social situation. Social stories are short written stories created with and without pictures, depending on the needs and learning style of the student. The stories describe a social situation, dictate social responses, and explain social perspectives. The stories are written in response to the student's needs. The needs for the student can be determined by a social skill assessment, observations of situations that are difficult for the student, or through discussions that follow after watching a videotape of a particular situation. Social stories can be written, audiotaped, videotaped, put on index cards, or placed on a poster that hangs next to the student (Gray & Garand, 1993).

For example, Vicki has difficulty waiting, especially when food is involved. The class had a birthday ritual in which cupcakes were given to each student. Students had to wait for the song to be sung and for the "birthday boy/girl" to take the first bite before eating their own cupcakes. Rather than changing the ritual, the teacher decided to use this opportunity to teach Vicki to wait. She wrote the story and used the pictures in Figure 10–6.

PEER SUPPORTS FOR INDEPENDENT FUNCTIONING

The general education classroom can be a fast-paced confusing experience for students who have disabilities. Independent functioning is

In Room 2, we celebrate birthdays.
First, the birthday (girl/boy)
hands out the treat.

Sometimes we get cupcakes.

Sometimes we get a
different treat.

Everyone must wait for the treat.

I sit and wait with my hands in my lap.

We sing the birthday song.

I sing the song with my class.

Next the birthday person takes a bite
of cupcake and we wait.

I need to wait.

Now it is my turn to eat
the birthday treat.

critical for success. In this section we discuss support for persons with disabilities in the general classroom through the use of peers.

Friendships are so important to a student's education. The most important thing that we do in our lives is make relationships. Whether students are preschool age or adults, their relationships and friendships are key for a satisfactory quality of life (Halpern, 1993). No matter the severity of the challenges of the individuals you work with, never underestimate the power of a smile or touch of the hand by a friend and a peer. Students listen many times more readily to their peers than to their teachers. But these friendships do not build themselves automatically. Often it takes planning and systematic intervention to foster these relationships between students and their peers. This section discusses two approaches used in the elementary classroom for building friendships: "circle of friends" and "peer buddies."

Circle of Friends

The first step is to build an understanding and awareness among peers about the student, his or her challenges, and the type of supports needed. There are many techniques, but one common approach used in inclusive classrooms is circle of friends (Pearpoint, Forest, & O'Brien, 1993). This is a program designed to help build a social support community for a student with disabilities. It begins with an activity that encourages all students in the classroom to examine the support they have in their lives, compare it to the support in the student's life with a challenge, and problem-solve ways to make the circles look similar. It is not just a onetime project but an opportunity to create a support network for the student.

Begin the activity by creating a series of concentric circles such as those shown in Figure 10–7. The students can create their own circles

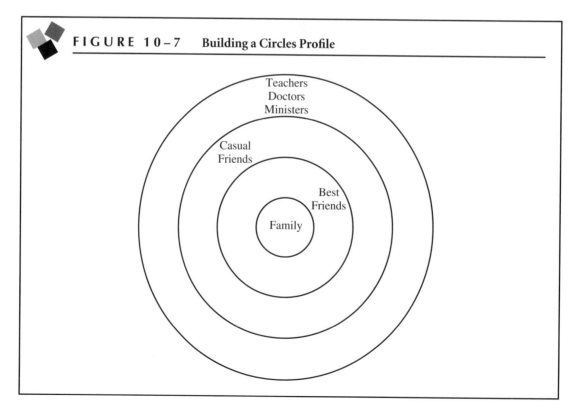

FIGURE 10–7 **Building a Circles Profile**

Teachers
Doctors
Ministers

Casual
Friends

Best
Friends

Family

profile. The interior circle contains family. The second circle contains best friends, the third casual friends, and the fourth, persons who might be paid to assist with the individual such as teachers, doctors, or minister. Not all circles will be the same (Forest & Pearpoint, 1992). Students can use this time to examine the role of family and friends in their lives. Encourage students to discuss their circles profile. For the students with a disability, their circles may not be as full as those of others. Although this must be handled delicately, it can create the window of opportunity for volunteers to become part of the circle of friends for this individual. Remember, this approach is not limited to persons with disabilities. Other students in the classroom may be in need of a support circle as well, and this provides a forum for discussion of community too.

After the initial activity, allow many opportunities for the students to understand the student with challenges. An overview of disabilities during this time helps the students understand areas of needed support. For example, if the student uses any form of augmentative communication, the device can be demonstrated. Be open and allow the students to ask questions about behaviors or needs of the student. Remind the peers that all behavior is a form of communication and sometimes we need to act like sleuths to try and figure out that Jimmy is trying to communicate. "Can we put words with Jimmy's actions? No, but we can guess and try to see if we are correct by working with Jimmy." Role-playing with the students is also important. "How would you communicate anger if you were unable to talk?" "How would you tell the teacher you needed a break if you couldn't talk?"

Frequent meetings with typical peers are crucial learning tools to ensure that alienation does not occur when the student with a disability behaves differently. These meetings give students opportunities to discuss what happened, problem-solve a solution, and role-play it with the student, if possible. Students need to talk through situations and feel as though they are a vital link to the solution. Reading books regarding different challenges that students face can be helpful in preparing students for diversity in their classroom. In addition to helping students gain a greater understanding of disabilities, the process used in circle of friends can give typical students more insight into their own attitudes and behaviors as well (Falvey, Grenot-Scheyer, Coots, & Bishop, 1995).

Remember that you, as the teacher, must model acceptance for diversity. How you interact with any student with differences serves as a model for the students (Jubala, Bishop, & Falvey, 1995). Stand back and watch a miniature version imitate you.

After the introductory presentations, individual adaptations begin. For every student, the program will evolve into a support system specifically designed for the individual student's needs. As the student is introduced, strengths and likes of the student can be shared. In some cases, you can share areas that will pose a potential challenge for the student and let the class brainstorm ideas to support the student. Work with students in appropriate ways to provide support for the students with disabilities (Janney & Snell, 1996). Typical students may need guidance on the amount of assistance needed. The students must learn not to provide too much assistance and to give feedback for accomplishments.

As students grow throughout their school career, you may want to continue to build support and develop long-range goals with the group. *MAPS* and *PATH* (Forest & Lusthaus, 1990; Vandercook et al., 1989) discussed in Chapters 5 and 6 as part of the assessment and IEP process, can be used in this context to assist a circle of friends in developing these plans.

With the primary grades, circle of friends can turn into a weekly meeting in which the class discusses issues and problems in their classroom community. If this proves successful, eventually students can become facilitators of the small groups. This is a very exciting process but it also requires ongoing support and facilitation from you and other adults in the setting.

Peers can be effective in building and modifying curriculum. Often in groups of five to seven students, a circle of friends or curriculum team can help modify required projects, plan field trips with accessibility in mind, or suggest new learning activities related to instructional objectives.

When considering peer support, keep in mind that persons with disabilities can provide support to their nondisabled peers. Typical peers in inclusive classrooms experience personal growth through their experiences with friends with disabilities (Evans, Salisbury, Palombaro, Berryman, & Hollowod, 1992). As we discussed earlier in the text, everyone needs a variety of types of support, from assistance with daily living tasks to support with social and emotional issues. Persons with disabilities can assist in all areas. When an applied curriculum and leveled instructional approaches are used, differentiated roles will be designed for students on many cooperative tasks. There will be natural opportunities to arrange for the student with a disability to assist his or her nondisabled peer on a given task. Social and emotional supports are important as well. The person with a disability may be a person who makes the typical student feel good through his or her sunny disposition and encouragement. The person with a disability may be a good listener or a friend the typical peer can depend on to be there. Highlight these forms of mutual support in class or group discussions.

Peer Buddies

For some students, circle of friends may not be an appropriate form of support. Some students may feel uncomfortable having the entire class or a group discuss their disability and plan for their support needs. Another strategy to foster relationships among the students is peer buddies. In this approach, a small number of students—sometimes only one—volunteers as a friend or buddy. Peer buddies enable students to learn appropriate expectations from someone their age (Barnett, 1995). Like circle of friends,

FIGURE 10–8 **Using Peer Buddies for Support with Transitions**

Daily, at the beginning of group time, you play music (auditory cue), tell the students it is time to come to group through a song, and take a picture of the group and place it on Freddy's desk. Suzie would go over to Freddy's desk and hand him the picture. "Look, Freddy, it's time for group. Let's go to group." Suzie would take Freddy's hand and lead him to group. This peer buddy was helping Freddy through the transition of seatwork to group time. Eventually, Suzie went to Freddy's desk, handed him the card as a reminder, and Freddy took Suzie's hand and led *her* to group.

peer buddies can provide support in a variety of ways: be a class friend, assist with teaching, and act as a tutor. Peer buddies not only help develop relationships with peers, but they also decrease the amount of adult support given to the student. Peer buddies have been found to be particularly effective in providing support for instruction on functional skills such as self-care, language, and socialization (Hamre-Nietupski et al., 1992). Figure 10–8 provides an example in which a peer buddy assists a student prepare for transitions during the day.

 SUMMARY

In this chapter, you learned several approaches for adapting the standard curricula in the general classroom. As you discovered, there are many ways to include students with disabilities as well as typical students who are experiencing difficulty with the general curricula. One way is to modify instructions by changing directions, adding cues, and adding structure to the environment. Another way is to adapt materials.

Usage of pictures, cue cards, and manipulatives are among the materials strategies. Response requirements can also be altered to increase participation. Students can show mastery of material in a variety of ways including speaking or drawing instead of writing. Responses can be shortened or other modalities—pictures or computers—used. For students who cannot achieve with those modifications, you learned how to take a lesson and identify a parallel-related task and how to deliver leveled instruction to a group of students.

We discussed how to address applied curricula within the routine of the general classroom. The daily routine provides abundant opportunities for teaching skills in independent living, socialization and communication. Finally, you learned approaches for increasing independence through creating peer support systems. Circle of friends and peer buddies are two approaches for creating a network of support and for bringing the student into the classroom community.

 ## CHAPTER EXTENDERS

Key Terms and Concepts

1. *Circle of friends* is a group of individuals who create a support network for a student.
2. *Curriculum overlapping* refers to integrating functional skills instruction into the normal routine of the classroom.
3. *Learning boxes* are portable learning centers that provide versatility for individualization and flexibility in when and where they are used.
4. A *peer buddy* is an individual who volunteers to provide support to a student his or her own age who needs functional, social, or academic assistance.
5. *Social stories* teach students to read the social cues in a situation by describing the situation, explaining social perspectives, and prescribing appropriate responses.

Study Guide

1. Explain what standard curriculum, applied curriculum and leveled curriculum are and how they compare with one another.
2. Make up a social story for a student who has difficulty keeping her hands to herself in class.
3. Provide an example of applied curricular objective.
4. Compare and contrast the two approaches: circle of friends and peer buddies.
5. Provide *two* examples of each of the following types of adaptations for a first-grade reading lesson: instructional strategies, materials, response requirements, and content adaptations.
6. Provide examples of functional skills and ways to integrate them into a routine.
7. Provide an example of a way to adapt a math lesson for three different levels of difficulty.
8. Describe the procedure for implementing circle of friends.
9. Applied curriculum has typically been associated with students with academic difficulties. Discuss the benefits of applied curricula for *all* students in the general classroom. Brainstorm ways that the standard curricula can be made more applied for *all* students.
10. Circle of friends is an approach frequently used to assist persons with disabilities in becoming part of the classroom community. The approach has been criticized because it singles out the student with disabilities as a topic of discussion by the class, thus possibly stigmatizing him or her. Discuss the pros and cons of this approach. If you feel this is happening, what could you do?

Small Group Activity I   *Identifying Functional Skills in the Daily Routines*

1. Create a morning schedule for a typical elementary classroom day.

2. Take two or three of the routines (taking attendance, going to recess) and generate a list of critical skills a person with moderate to severe disabilities may need assistance with.
3. Generate some ideas for teaching those skills using peers for support.

Small Group Activity II   *Adapting a Lesson*

The students in math class are learning basic multiplication facts. You have several students who need modifications. Amy has difficulty in working independently—she constantly asks questions and will not stay on task. Generate three ideas for instructional adaptations to enable her to complete the lesson independently.

Billy (who is in the same class) is still learning his basic math facts—addition and subtraction. Generate the following types of adaptations for him: (1) content modification using a parallel skill and/or (2) a response requirement change.

Field Experience

Spend a day observing in an inclusive classroom. Interview the teacher and note for the following: What adaptations are made for the individuals with identified disabilities? For other students who appear to experience difficulty with the curriculum? Look for the following types of adaptations: changes in materials, different instructions, changes in response requirements, and content modifications. What is the nature of the interaction of the student with disabilities with the other students? Does the student appear to be accepted in the classroom? Who makes the majority of the adaptations—the general education teacher, the special education teacher, or the para-educator? Are the students with disabilities actively engaged in what appear to be appropriate learning activities for their ages and needs?

chapter 11

The Secondary Classroom

As you learned in Chapter 10, standard curricula are general education curricula in which typical students are instructed. Before addressing standard curricula at the secondary level, let's look at how they differ from the standard curricula at the elementary level. First, the course content is more abstract. At the elementary level, instruction is usually presented with close connections made to the students' personal experience. For example, you might introduce the social studies concept of multiculturalism by discussing different people from the students' hometown. A high school anthropology teacher would more likely describe the concept by introducing the students to distant peoples who live in places very different from the local community. Second, the course content is presented with greater specificity at the secondary level than it is in the elementary classroom. Instruction has moved beyond basic concepts to a more in-depth discovery of a particular topic. Elementary teachers concentrate on providing basic information and general concepts. In contrast, secondary teachers delve into the specificity of the course content and concentrate their attention on examining the different facets of the subject matter in great detail. These kinds of changes create challenges for inclusion at the secondary level.

Students with moderate to severe disabilities and their parents also may have many questions about the kind of secondary education experience that will best meet the individual needs of the student. For example, they may need to decide whether or not the student should attend the local high school or a vocational high school if the local high school does not offer a vocational program appropriate to the student's interests and needs. Parents may be faced with the dilemma of having to choose between making sure their daughter has good training for her future career or has the daily involvement of a local peer group. Even after the students and parents choose inclusion in the local secondary education program, they have decisions to make. For example, they must decide how many

and what major subjects the student should participate in during each semester. They must consider how much time the student should spend in academic classes and how much time in community-based instruction. If they want the student to complete the necessary course work and graduate with a high school diploma, they need to discover which courses are required as well as to make sure the student is enrolled and properly supported in successfully completing those required courses. They must also find out if their state mandates participation in competency testing designed to determine whether or not a student will receive a high school diploma. If so, they may want to investigate modified or alternative testing and determine how those adjustments would affect the student's graduation status.

 ## WHAT YOU WILL LEARN IN THIS CHAPTER

This chapter presents strategies for including students with moderate to severe disabilities effectively in general education academic classrooms at the secondary level. Note that some states now require separate middle childhood licensure to teach fourth through eighth grades. Some portion of the education program in those settings may more closely resemble the experience found in elementary schools. For guidance in techniques appropriate for those settings, refer to Chapter 10. This chapter focuses on teaching students in junior high and high school programs as well as the middle school programs designed for sixth through eighth grades.

The secondary classroom is the platform from which students will launch their adult lives. Therefore, it is an important vehicle for providing the information and skill development adolescents need to prepare for their impending move into adulthood. Secondary education programs should provide inclusive general education classes so students with disabilities can interact regularly with nondisabled peers to develop the academic knowledge, interpersonal skills, and natural supports that will allow them to function successfully in the community when they become adults. Consequently, the chapter highlights those strategies that not only work well in secondary education core academic classrooms but also help students develop practical knowledge and skills.

First, we describe adaptations and modifications for supporting student learning of the typical academic curriculum in general education courses. You will learn how to adapt the mode of instruction and method of student response. You also will discover ways to adapt the course content, classroom materials, and evaluation criteria. As earlier chapters have shown, students with disabilities likely will experience the greatest success when teachers provide an applied approach to the curricular content. In this section, you will learn how applied course content in inclusive secondary classrooms ultimately facilitates successful secondary education experiences for all students.

Second, we provide strategies for developing increased independence through instruction in daily living skills in secondary education academic settings. This section addresses topics in self-care, communication, and social skills.

Finally, the third section offers strategies for facilitating peer support to increase the ability of students with moderate to severe disabilities to access the academic content in secondary education course work and, at the same time, enhance their interpersonal skills. We describe a variety of support roles for secondary education students including student aides, peer tutors, circle of friends, and peer buddies.

◆ ADDRESSING THE STANDARD CURRICULA OF THE GENERAL EDUCATION CLASSROOM

The specificity of the content with greater attention to abstract concepts as well as the move away from the personal experiences of the students typical of secondary education curricula poses a challenge for many students. Students who have difficulty generalizing and transferring information may find this increase in content intensity particularly taxing. In addition, each state requires its high school students to complete a specific number of credits, sometimes referred to as Carnegie units. To illustrate, a student would have to complete a total of 22 credits to fulfill the graduation requirements in a school where a one-semester course is worth half a credit. The student would have to spread those credits among different subject categories in the following configuration: 4 in English; 3 in social studies; 3 in math; 2 in science; .5 in health; .5 in physical education; 1 in business, technology, fine arts, or foreign language; and 8 in elective courses.

Although these issues may pose difficulties for students, other changes that occur at the secondary level may increase learning opportunities. For example, course offerings at the secondary level expand to accommodate the more in-depth level of detail in the subject matter, which gives students greater choice in the courses they can take. Within each general subject area, students can choose from several different courses. Thus students could meet the requirement for English by taking any one of a variety of courses. In this way, students can pick courses that make connections with their personal interests. At the same time, students can meet graduation requirements in courses that would likely be more accessible because that content would be closely related to the student's present personal experiences and future life in the community. Courses that emphasize concrete information would meet the same requirements as courses that deal with more abstract material. For example, students could satisfy their math requirements by taking courses like consumer math instead of more abstract courses such as calculus. See Table 11–1 for examples of course offerings at the secondary level.

TABLE 11–1 Examples of Course Offerings at the Secondary Level Organized by Subject Area

Social Studies	Math	English/ Language Arts	Science	Health
American History [b]	Algebra [b]	American Literature [b]	Anatomy and Physiology [a]	Coping in a Changing World [a]
Anthropology [b]	Business Math [a]	Creative Writing [a]	Botany [b]	Family Life [a]
Current Affairs [a]	Calculus [b]	English Composition [a]	Chemistry in the Community [a]	First Aid [a]
Federal Government [a]	Computer Applications [a]	Interpersonal Communication [a]	Earth Science [a]	Principles of Health Science [a]
Psychology [a]	Consumer Math [a]	Pleasure Reading [a]	Introductory Biology [a]	Wellness and Nutrition [a]
Sociology [a]	Economics [a]	Shakespeare [b]	Life Sciences [a]	
U.S. Geography [a]	Geometry [b]	Speech [a]	Physics [b]	
World Cultures [b]	Integrated Math [a]	Technical Writing [b]	Zoology [b]	

Note: These particular course offerings may not be available in all secondary education programs.
[a] Course with content that offers opportunities for a focus on concrete information.
[b] Course with content that primarily emphasizes abstract concepts.

The variety of choices offered at the secondary level allows students to take courses that meet the requirements for graduation and still deal with the everyday concepts with which students can easily connect. Consumer math may be particularly interesting to students because of the practical, applied academic nature of the content. Consequently, the course offerings traditionally listed by subject area also can be arranged according to the major life domains. As well as considering the subject area requirements for completing a secondary education program successfully, students can consider scheduling courses that will attend to their future needs in the important life domains (Cronin & Patton, 1993; Dever & Knapczyk, 1997). These important life domains can be broadly categorized into four major areas: (1) career/education, (2) home life/personal management, (3) community participation/consumerism, and (4) health/leisure. For example, students in physical education classes develop interests and skills that can enhance their participation in leisure activities. The home life and personal management domain are addressed in courses about wellness and nutrition. Students learn about community participation and consumerism in economics and current affairs classes. A computer applications course can help students develop skills in the career/education domain. Table 11–2 illustrates how subject area courses can be organized by life domains to help families and educators focus on the student's transition needs while still attending to academic subject area requirements.

Within the broad subject categories, students in many secondary schools can make course choices according to their personal interests. Because students are interested in the content, they may be more engaged with the material and more attentive to instruction. Having and making personal choices is an important component of being independent. This is helpful in preparing students for the transition from school to adult life, which is mandated at the secondary level (see Chapter 15). Consequently, students

	Life/Personal	Participation/	
Career/Education	**Management**	**Consumerism**	**Health/Leisure**
Algebra [b]	Anatomy and	Consumer Math [a]	Anatomy and
Business Math [a]	Physiology [a]	Coping in a Changing	Physiology [a]
Computer	Botany [b]	World [a]	Botany [b]
Applications [a]	Chemistry in the	Current Affairs [a]	Coping in a Changing
Economics [a]	Community [a]	Economics [a]	World [a]
English	Computer	Federal Government [a]	Creative Writing [a]
Composition [a]	Applications [a]	Interpersonal	Current Affairs [a]
Geometry [b]	Consumer Math [a]	Communication [a]	Earth Science [a]
Integrated Math [a]	Earth Science [a]	Sociology [a]	Pleasure Reading [a]
Interpersonal	Economics [a]	Speech [a]	Principles of Health
Communication [a]	Family Life [a]	U.S. Geography [a]	Science [a]
Speech [a]	First Aid [a]		Psychology [a]
Technical Writing [b]	Introductory Biology [a]		Wellness and Nutrition [a]
	Psychology [a]		Zoology [b]
	Wellness and Nutrition [a]		
	Zoology [b]		

TABLE 11–2   Examples of Secondary Level Course Offerings Organized by Life Domain

Note: These particular course offerings may not be available in all secondary education programs.

should be encouraged to schedule courses in the academic subject areas that will attend to both their personal interests and their future needs in the four life domains (Helmke, Havekost, Patton, & Polloway, 1994). The guidance counselor can assist students in making choices that meet these criteria as well as the school's graduation requirements.

Some schools now offer only fundamental academic courses, such as first-year English and sophomore English. Those schools may not give students as many choices as schools that provide topical core courses, but both types of instructional programming offer elective courses. Electives can provide valuable opportunities for students to have successful learning experiences that prepare them in useful ways. For example, creative writing or pleasure reading courses offer experiences that students may want to pursue in their leisure time both in the present and in the future. Students may find the material in many elective courses easily accessible because it

makes direct connections through hands-on activities to bridge the gap between school and community. The practical nature and experiential component of the material makes few or less extensive adaptations necessary and makes the classroom environment least restrictive for all students.

Determining the Need for Adaptations

Adaptations that allow students with moderate to severe disabilities to participate in typical curricular activities have many parallels between the elementary and secondary levels. Some examples would include attending to different learning styles, developing experiential events, having peer buddies, and creating cooperative learning activities. However, many adaptations, although similar at both the elementary and secondary levels, may need to be presented differently to attend to age appropriateness and the structure of the secondary education classroom environment. Also, the complexity of the material and high academic expectations are important considerations at the secondary level (O'Shea & O'Shea, 1998).

Although secondary classrooms, especially at the middle school level, make use of instruc-

Last year, Brent graduated with honors from high school. Although he has a moderate developmental disability, he earned a 3.51 grade point average during his high school experience. He took the same general education classes with the same course content as his typical peers. Throughout high school, Brent's classmates regularly provided support and his teachers adjusted their instructional methods and made the necessary content and evaluation adaptations that allowed him to be so successful.

tional strategies such as experiential learning in cooperative formats as well as projects and hands-on activities that have an applied focus, some students need additional accommodations (Field et al., 1994) (see Figure 11–1). Accommodations involve adjusting the delivery of instruction, the content taught, the materials used, and the evaluation expectations to improve the learning experiences for students who would otherwise have difficulty participating effectively in the general education classroom. For example, you could expect the student with a moderate to severe disability to put drops of water from a dropper on different paper towels until the towel tears as her contribution to a class project. She participates in the small group activity and has individual responsibility. The student is developing skills toward her IEP goal of increasing her fine motor skills while she participates in a portion of the general education science curriculum that addresses designing an

FIGURE 11–1   **Framework for Designing Instructional Accommodations**

1. A different format.
2. The same content, but less of it.
3. Streamlining of the sequence of content.
4. Partial participation by the student with disabilities.
5. Instruction targeting the same skills, but using different materials.
6. Instruction geared toward a different skill level but using the same materials.
7. The same activity, but targeting different skills.
8. Skills embedded in the activity.

Source: Field, S., LeRoy, B., & Rivera, S. (1994). Meeting functional curriculum needs in middle school general education classrooms. *Teaching Exceptional Children, 27*(2), 40–43. Copyright The Council for Exceptional Children. Reprinted with permission.

experiment. Other students in the group gather materials to set up the experiment, count the number of drops needed to tear different towel brands, and record and analyze the data.

When you design instruction, consider the need for these individualized adaptations and incorporate the adaptations directly into your written lesson plans. Developing a lesson plan for general education classroom that includes adapting the curriculum for students with moderate to severe disabilities requires making adjustments to the typical lesson plan. You not only have to consider the procedures, content, and materials of the standard lesson, but you also must attend to the individual's learning objectives and need for adjustments in evaluation. (See Figures 11–2 and 11–3 for an inclusive lesson plan template and a sample plan.)

Steps in Designing a Lesson Plan with Adaptations for Students with Disabilities for Use in the General Education Classroom:

1. Define the setting, students, and time frame for the lesson.
2. Describe the content you will cover and the individual objectives you will address both

for the typical students and the students with disabilities.

3. Identify the materials you will need to teach the lesson and any assigned tasks as well as any adaptations needed for the students with disabilities to use the materials effectively.

4. Identify the strategies you will use to teach the content and summarize the sequential steps in the planned instruction. Be sure to note any adjustments you will make in in-

structional delivery so the students with disabilities will be able to access the content.

5. Describe the method for evaluating student work and the effectiveness of the lesson. Again, be sure to list any evaluation criteria modifications needed to determine accurately the accomplishments of the students with disabilities.

6. List any follow-up activities with the appropriate adaptations.

FIGURE 11–2   Inclusive Lesson Plan Template

Subject/Grade: Group Size: Time Available:

Learning Objective(s):

* Functional Application of Learning Objective(s) (connection with real-life context):

> * Individual Objective(s):

Materials:

> * Adaptation(s) to materials:

Procedure:

> * Adaptation(s) to Procedure:

Student Evaluation:

> * Modified Student Evaluation:

Self-Evaluation:

Possible Follow-up Activities:

FIGURE 11–3 **Example of an Inclusive Lesson Plan**

Subject/Grade: 9th grade   Group Size: 23   Time Available: 45 minutes

Learning Objective(s): Celebrating Diversity: Understanding and dealing appropriately with individual differences

* Functional Application of Learning Objective(s) (connection with real-life context): Making good first impressions: Monitoring and evaluating initial interactions with people you meet for successful interactions. Recognizing the impact of our actions on others and adjusting our behavior to fit the situation.

> * Individual Objective(s): Maggie will correctly choose and use appropriate behaviors when initiating interactions 4 out of 5 times.

Materials: Text: *To Kill a Mockingbird,* paper, pencils, several identical sets of 10 pictures of teens showing appropriate and inappropriate behaviors

> * Adaptation(s) to Materials: visual response cards ([card 1] YES—Appropriate, [card 2] NO—Inappropriate)

Procedure:

    1. In small groups, students will describe at least 6 events that changed Scout's & Jem's feelings (toward trespassing, Boo Radley, etc.) and how they handled them. (written synopsis)

    2. Students then note and discuss similar experiences in their own lives and describe how they dealt with them. (written synopsis)

    3. Next, the students describe the teens in the set of pictures and determine what effect their behaviors are liable to have on others. (written synopsis)

    4. The students choose and demonstrate strategies for dealing effectively with diversity by role-playing their solutions to the situations depicted in the pictures.

> * Adaptation(s) to Procedure: Maggie will be assigned to a small group and listen to the descriptions from the text and she will contribute one personal experience. When the other students list their descriptions of the pictures, Maggie will sort the pictures onto visual response cards. (She will participate in the role-play activity.)

Student Evaluation: The students will show understanding of diversity through written descriptions (1, 2, and 3 in the Procedures) and role-playing demonstrations.

> * Modified Student Evaluation: Maggie will correctly sort 8 of the 10 pictures. With teacher prompts, she will choose one inappropriate behavior shown in the pictures and identify an appropriate response with verbal prompts from the teacher.

Self-Evaluation: (Teacher considers completed lesson and identifies strategies that might improve similar lessons in the future.)

Possible Follow-up Activities: Make a video of student interactions in various school settings (cafeteria, hallways, etc.). Students watch video to evaluate students' interactions to determine positive examples and develop strategies for those interactions that could be improved.

Instructional Adaptations

You can use a variety of strategies to modify the way you deliver instruction. These kinds of changes might consist of modifying directions, using auditory or tactile cues, tape-recording directions, or structuring the lesson to provide the student with additional supports.

Modify Directions. You can give test directions and questions orally rather than in a written format and you can shorten the item choices or simplify the words you use (O'Shea & O'Shea, 1998). For example, ask the student to use the computer mouse to find and click on a choice of two possible answers without expecting the student to use the correct hand positions to type short essay answers.

Use Written or Pictoral Cues. One strategy that may cue a student to the steps needed to complete a task is the cognitive credit card (Edmunds, 1999) (see Figure 11–4). A cognitive

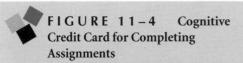

FIGURE 11–4   Cognitive Credit Card for Completing Assignments

1. Do I have all the materials I need?
   —paper or computer disk
   —pencil or pen
   —worksheet and/or textbook
2. Do I need help in reading the assignment?
   —Who should I ask to help me?
   —How should I ask for help?
3. What is this assignment about?
   —What are the most important points?
   —What am I having trouble understanding?
   —Who should I ask to help me?
   —How should I ask for help?
4. Have I checked my work before I turn it in?

Source: Adapted from Edmunds, A. L. (1999). Cognitive credit cards: Acquiring learning strategies. *Teaching Exceptional Children, 31*(4), 68–73. Copyright The Council for Exceptional Children. Reprinted with permission.

credit card is a laminated piece of paper the size of a credit card that can fit in the student's wallet. If covering the relevant information requires additional space or the student needs enlarged print, the card can be made bigger and designed to fit in the student's notebook. The card contains an individualized list of the steps the student needs to take to complete a learning task successfully. For example, written or pictoral prompts would identify the questions the student would ask when having difficulty understanding the verbal directions the teacher typically gives during a class activity.

Use Instructional Scaffolds. You can use many of the same instructional scaffolds at both the elementary and secondary levels. You can apply many of the techniques we described in the elementary classroom chapter in the secondary education classroom. They include providing summary notes, outlines, or tape recordings of the lesson. Students also can try a system that allows printed material to be scanned and then displays the material including pictures while it reads the text aloud with synthetically generated speech (Kurzweil 3000, n.d.).

Videotaping provides another instructional scaffold. You either make or purchase a commercially made videocassette that demonstrates the academic or social skill to be learned. The student then watches the tape, which provides a visual model to emulate. This use of video has several advantages, including (1) allowing the student to review the content as often as necessary by pausing or replaying the tape, and (2) encouraging family involvement by sending the tape home to share information and help the parents participate in teaching particular skills (Salend, 1995).

Materials Adaptations

The strategies described in Chapter 10 for adapting materials, such as using cue cards, enlarging print, positioning material for ease in viewing, and color coding, also work well in the secondary classroom. Although the process is similar at both the elementary and secondary levels, the actual product may look different to fit appropriately with the secondary setting. To illustrate, color coding might be used to support the needs of the secondary education student differently than it would be handled in the elementary classroom. Because secondary students take a wide variety of courses each semester, they may have difficulty keeping track of their materials. This can be frustrating and time consuming for all students and especially challenging for students with moderate to severe disabilities. Color coding can help the students find and organize those materials (Williamson, 1997). For example, a student might have one large notebook for a semester with different colored dividers to separate each subject or the student might have a separate notebook of a different color for each subject. Regardless, the student could cover the corresponding textbook in the same color; that is, both the math notebook (or notebook section) and the math text cover would be red and both the English notebook (or notebook section) and the English text cover would be green. You also might put a colored dot on other needed materials. For example, a red dot could be attached to the calculator the student needs to bring to math class.

Use Manipulatives and Models. You can develop your own manipulatives or use a wide variety of commercially made materials. In an algebra class, you could use paper clips to represent x and pencil tip erasers to represent y to help students understand like terms such as $2x + 3y$. To help students understand regrouping, use base ten blocks. To provide the model, set the base ten blocks on a colored mat that allows the student to organize and count the blocks easily into the appropriate groups (see Figure 11–5).

Use Learning Centers. As you already learned in Chapter 10, individual learning centers contain materials placed in small sturdy boxes that can be presented at different skill levels. To make the concept accessible for all students in the class, the materials in a group of boxes address a particular concept but each box in the group contains age-appropriate materials at a different skill level. The boxes are portable so they can be easily stored when they are not being used by a small group of students at a classroom table or an individual student at his or her desk.

All students in the classroom can work with the learning centers at the same time. When all students are engaged in learning center activities, you can provide individual help to those students who may need additional support to understand a particular instructional concept. Small groups of students can work together to complete the tasks in an individual learning center or, if enough centers are available, each student can work in a different box. Each box contains inexpensive age-appropriate materials that provide hands-on practice to help students contextualize the concepts addressed in almost any course. As Figure 11–6 shows, measurement is a math concept that lends itself to an individual learning center activity.

Another advantage of portable learning centers is the opportunity for students to improve their self-discipline and ability to follow directions (Hamill & Dunlevy, 1999). Students take responsibility for getting their assigned materials, reading the instructions (a tape recording of the instructions can be placed in the box for nonreaders or the student can ask a peer to read the instructions), requesting help if necessary, and completing their work as independently as possible.

FIGURE 11–5
Regrouping Mat

Hundreds	Tens	Ones

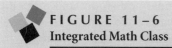

FIGURE 11–6 Portable Leveled Learning Centers for Measuring Objects in an Integrated Math Class

Container 1: Calculate Areas. Include the following directions in container 1:
1. Use the ruler in the container to measure the length and width of the objects in the container.
2. Now find the area of each object (length × width = area)
3. Record your findings on the worksheet.
4. Continue to work until you measure all the objects in the container or until the time available to do the job is over. If you finish with extra time, measure some objects in the room.

Name _____ Date _____
Start time _____ End time _____ [Total time worked _____]

(Put the following items in the container and list them on the worksheet:)

paper _____ envelope _____ computer disk _____
napkin _____ file card _____ game board _____

(Note: To reduce the level of difficulty, have the student measure the items in container 1 using a flexible ruler that identifies only the full inch place markers and determine the area using a calculator.)

Container 2: Calculate Volumes. Include the following directions in container 2:
1. Use the ruler in the container to measure the dimensions of the objects in the container.
2. Now find the volume of each object (for rectangles: length × width × height = volume)
                             (for circles: [write symbols for πr^2] × height = volume)
3. Record your findings on the worksheet.
4. Continue to work until you measure all the objects in the container or until the time available to do the job is over. If you finish with extra time, measure some objects in the room.

Name _____ Date _____
Start time _____ End time _____ [Total time worked _____]

(Put the following items in the container and list them on the worksheet:)

book _____ art gum eraser _____ this container _____
videotape _____ wood block _____ small jewelry box _____
napkin ring _____ piece of pipe _____ small soft drink can _____

Container 3: Calculate Densities. Include the following directions in container 3:
1. Use the ruler in the container to measure the dimensions of the objects in the container in centimeters.
2. Use the scale in the container to weigh the objects to determine their mass in grams.
3. Now find the density of each object (for rectangles and circles: mass divided by the volume = density)
(Remember: for rectangles: length × width × height = volume
             for circles: [write symbols for πr^2] × height = volume)
4. Record your findings on the worksheet.
5. Continue to work until you measure all the objects in the container or until the time available to do the job is over. If you finish with extra time, predict whether each object will float or sink and then put the object in water to test your hypothesis. **(Remember:** Objects that have a density of less than 1 will float)

Name _____ Date _____
Start time _____ End time _____ [Total time worked _____]

(Put the following items in the container and list them on the worksheet:)

full legal pad _____ pencil box _____ small packet of tissues _____
piece of chalk _____ prescription bottle _____ individual cereal box _____
pencil _____ wedding ring _____ tape cassette case _____
plastic straw _____ roll of pennies _____ straight-sided beaker _____

Source: Adapted from Hamill, L. & Dunlevy, A. (1999). *Work boxes* (Rev. ed.). San Antonio, TX: PCI Educational Publishing. Reprinted with permission.

Mr. Fitch has made a tape recording of his written instructions and placed it with a tape recorder in the learning center box that provides practice in measuring length, width, and height. Javier is able to listen to the tape and follow the directions for measuring the various items he finds in the box and recording his information. He also wraps a Velcro band he finds in the box around his left wrist. He uses it to secure each item he takes from the box. Each item in the box also has a small piece of Velcro attached to it so Javier can attach it to the strap and hold it securely while he measures it.

Response Requirements Adaptations

The methods typically used in secondary education classrooms for obtaining student responses are difficult for some students to follow. If the teachers of these students want to access the knowledge the students have acquired, they may need to adjust their expectations. This section describes some of the many ways you can make adaptations to the response modes you ask students to use in secondary education classrooms.

Alternative or Reduced Requirements.   The adaptations for alternative or reduced requirements that secondary education teachers make are often the same as those used by elementary teachers. We have already addressed many of these kinds of adaptations. For example, teachers at all levels can ask students to complete a portion of the class assignment or break work periods into smaller units. They also can allow students to provide verbal or tape-recorded information rather than requiring written responses.

Use Pictures and Artwork as an Alternative Response Mode.   You can adjust adaptations typically used at the elementary level to fit the struc-

ture of the secondary classroom and make the activity appealing to adolescents. In a social studies class, students can work together in cooperative learning groups to make their own political cartoons. This would allow the group to utilize the different skills of group members to design the layout, draw the figures, and write the script. You can modify student assignments for this project to focus on individual strengths. For example, a student who likes to use the Internet could be the "explorer," who researches the information the group will need to write the text. A socially adept student could be the "encourager," who gives positive feedback to the group and keeps everyone on track. A talkative student could be the "reporter," who presents the group's project to the whole class.

Use Dictation as an Alternative Response Mode.   Have a student who struggles with writing dictate his written work to a peer, the teacher, or the classroom aide. The designated scribe would copy the student's words verbatim. Before turning in the work, the student could check the transcript by either reading it himself or having the scribe read it to him and then correcting any errors (Mahony, 1997).

Use Computers as an Alternative Response Mode.   Many schools are now equipped with TVs, laser discs, and computers for classroom use. These kinds of technology can support students in having successful learning experiences. Numerous computer software programs and hardware attachments offer a variety of support options. Touch screens and customized keyboards or switches are a few examples of the many devices available to support students who have difficulty using a mouse or standard keyboard. Software programs, such as Write Out Loud and Intellitalk, offer an effective alternative response mode for students who have difficulty providing written responses and need the support that a talking word processor can provide (Roblyer, Edwards, & Havriluk, 1997). Also, speech recognition systems like Dragon

Naturally Speaking reproduce words on a computer screen as those words are spoken by an individual (Dragon Naturally Speaking Preferred 3.0, 1998). This software can give students with limited fine motor skills a way of generating written assignments independently.

Computers also can provide an interactive experience for students. A computer video is a visual database that motivates and individualizes learning by giving the student flexibility and control of the material (Heide & Henderson, 1994). For example, students in history class can follow Magellan while he describes his trip around the world. Students click the onscreen map to choose different sites to investigate along his route (Explorers of the New World, 1995).

Use Calculators as an Alternative Response Mode. Handheld calculators are a tool many adults commonly use to solve the math problems that arise in their daily lives. For example, it is not unusual for a contractor to use a calculator to figure the cost of remodeling as she walks around a building site with the homeowners or for an automobile salesperson to pull a calculator out of his pocket and figure the monthly payments for prospective buyers as they look at different cars on the dealer's lot. Many large supermarkets even attach calculators to their grocery carts for their customers' convenience. Teaching students in secondary education math classrooms to use a calculator to solve math problems provides them with opportunities for practice as they develop skills that give them the necessary competency to function effectively as they move into adulthood.

Alternative Response Mode for Assignments. You need to encourage students to participate in partial ways and allow them to present their assignments in a variety of modes. For example, students in a speech class might be expected to turn in a written copy of the speech they read in class. Because the ability to communicate effectively is the more important skill being addressed in the course, students who have diffi-

culty with the writing portion of the assignment could prepare for their class presentation by turning in a list of key points or an outline rather than providing a complete written text of their speech. The students could talk from their notes rather than give a verbatim reading of the full text. Instead of using an outline as a guide, a student with a more severe disability could have picture cards to follow when giving her speech.

At the secondary level, allow alternative response modes in completing in-class and homework assignments for those students who need this level of support. For instance, encourage students to use handheld pocket spell checkers or co-writer software that provides more assistance than the typical spell checker. Some talking word processors for writing assignments include a talking spell checker that gives the students both visual and auditory cues for misspelled words (Write: OutLoud, 1999). Be willing to give students full credit for assignments prepared and presented in alternative modes. To limit the amount of work required of a student at one time, collaborate to stagger the due dates for completing out-of-class assignments (O'Shea & O'Shea, 1998). An assignment tracker can be used to monitor student work in inclusive classrooms (see Figure 11–7). The tracker also provides an excellent opportunity to make connections between school and home.

Content Modifications

The emphasis on applied academic content should increase at the secondary level. A significant application component in the academic content will aid students in developing the skills they need for career and adult life. Secondary education curriculum can facilitate the student's ability to negotiate successfully the next stage in life through hands-on, applied academic activities (Hamill & Dunlevy, 1993; Wilcox, 1987; Wilcox & Bellamy, 1987). As you already discovered in Chapter 4, one excellent approach to preparing students for careers and successful

FIGURE 11–7   Daily Assignment Tracker

Name _____ Date _____

Target Behaviors: 1. Work on task during in-class assignments.
2. Take home assignment information and needed materials.
3. Do assignment with parent guidance.
4. Bring finished assignment to class.

Class Period	Assignment Information	Behavioral Expectations	Parent/Teacher Initials		Goal Reached	
1		1. On task in class.	1.	/	YES	NO
Introduction		2. Materials taken home.	2.	/	YES	NO
to Computers		3. Assignment completed.	3.	/	YES	NO
Mrs. Green		4. Assignment returned.	4.	/	YES	NO
2		1. On task in class.	1.	/	YES	NO
PE		2. Materials taken home.	2.	/	YES	NO
Mr. Frank		3. Assignment completed.	3.	/	YES	NO
		4. Assignment returned.	4.	/	YES	NO
3		1. On task in class.	1.	/	YES	NO
Speech		2. Materials taken home.	2.	/	YES	NO
Mrs. Thomes		3. Assignment completed.	3.	/	YES	NO
		4. Assignment returned.	4.	/	YES	NO
4		1. On task in class.	1.	/	YES	NO
Business Math		2. Materials taken home.	2.	/	YES	NO
Mrs. Grey		3. Assignment completed.	3.		YES	NO
		4. Assignment returned.	4.	/	YES	NO
5		1. On task in class.	1.	/	YES	NO
Current Events		2. Materials taken home.	2.	/	YES	NO
Mrs. Page		3. Assignment completed.	3.	/	YES	NO
		4. Assignment returned.	4.	/	YES	NO
6		1. On task in class.	1.	/	YES	NO
Earth Science		2. Materials taken home.	2.	/	YES	NO
Mr. Daley		3. Assignment completed.	3.	/	YES	NO
		4. Assignment returned	4.	/	YES	NO

lives in the community is the school-to-work initiative, which emphasizes providing an applied curriculum in secondary education academic classrooms (Hoerner & Wehrley, 1995). Learning academic concepts embedded in life skills, including job training and consumer choices, offers increased opportunity to give meaning to students' experiences (Manzone, 1987). These experiences will support students developing an academic foundation that will allow them to navigate employment and daily living routines effectively.

Teach a Parallel Skill. In some instances, you may need to make significant adaptations to the course content to ensure a successful learning experience for the student with moderate to severe disabilities. You can accomplish this by

FIGURE 11–8   Library Book Report

Choose a book from the library and read it carefully. Fill in this worksheet when you finish reading the book.

One student would answer the following questions:

1. What is the name of the library? _____
2. What is the name of the book? _____
3. Who wrote the book? _____
4. How many pages are in the book? _____
5. Who are the main characters in the book? _____
6. Did you like the book? If so, why? _____
If not, why not? _____

A second student would answer the following questions:

1. Where is the library located? _____
2. How long can you keep the book? _____
3. What is the title of the book? _____
4. Who is the author of the book? _____
5. List the main characters in the book. _____
6. Write a paragraph telling what happens in the book. _____
7. How did the book end? _____ Was it happy or sad? _____
What issues were left unresolved? Explain how they might be resolved and give your reasons.
8. What was your favorite part of the book and why? _____
_____

A third student would answer the following questions:

1. What is the call number on the book? _____ Where in the library did you find it? _____
2. Give a complete citation for the book. _____
_____
3. If there is an index, what kind of information does it contain? _____
4. If there is a glossary, what kind of information does it contain? _____
5. Who are the main female characters in the book and why are they important to the story? _____
_____
6. Who are the main male characters in the book and why are they important to the story? _____
_____
7. What was the most important thing that happened in the book? _____
Who did it happen to and why was it important? _____
8. What kind of person do you think would enjoy reading this book and why? _____
_____
9. What did you like best about this book and why? _____
_____
10. What did you like least about this book and why? _____
_____
11. How do you think the author hoped to change the reader's point of view ? Explain. _____

(Note: A student who has difficulty writing could dictate the answers to a peer scribe. Tape-record books and worksheet directions for a nonreader. Have the student use headphones to listen to the story and circle the correct answers on the worksheet. To reduce the level of difficulty, further present the worksheet questions in picture form and answer them by matching correct pictures. The student would answer the following questions:

1. Did you like the story?   **YES   NO**   (Circling or matching faces with happy or sad expressions could be substituted here.)
2. What kind of story was it?   **HAPPY   SAD   SCARY**   (Faces also could be substituted here.)
3. Who was the main person in the story?   **MAN   WOMAN   BOY   GIRL**   (Again, faces could be substituted.)
4. Draw a picture about your favorite part of the story.

Source: Adapted from Hamill, L., & Dunlevy, A., (2000). *Members of the community: Worksheets for transition activities in the community and the classroom.* Verona, WI: IEP Resources. Reprinted with permission.

developing parallel lessons that meet the student's individual needs but are related to the general class activity (Westling & Fox, 2000). For example, a student with a moderate to severe disability in a high school American history class might work on identifying the steps he would need to follow for accessing the fire or police department at the same time other students in the class are researching and reporting on the history of public assistance programs, police and fire departments, and the social security system in the United States. Although the activities are somewhat different, they both deal with understanding government-run institutions.

Use Leveled Assignments. Leveling assignments can make the course content in secondary education classrooms accessible to all students even though they may have differing degrees of skill. In a literature class, for example, students could choose books on topics of interest to them and prepare reports for presentation to the class. Reporting on the material that they read can be leveled so everyone in the class can successfully share the information they have learned. Figure 11–8 gives an example of a leveled assignment for library book reports.

Make the Content Meaningful and More Applied. Make your curriculum applied. In order to generalize and transfer learned skills, students need to understand the function of the information they learn so they can determine how they will use it in their own lives. This becomes particularly relevant in the secondary classroom as students approach adulthood and need to put school learning to practical use. Many students, including students with moderate to severe disabilities, need to make direct connections between learning concepts in the classroom and using them in the community. This can best be accomplished through an applied curriculum.

Take advantage of any applied curriculum that can be found already imbedded in the general education core curriculum (see Figure 11–9). For example, students studying surface

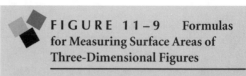

FIGURE 11–9 Formulas for Measuring Surface Areas of Three-Dimensional Figures

Square:	A (area) = s^2 (a side $\times$ itself)
Rectangle:	A = l w (length $\times$ width)
Circle:	A = $\pi\, r^2$ (pi $\times$ radius $\times$ radius)
Triangle:	A = $\frac{1}{2}$b h (half of the base $\times$ the height)

areas of three-dimensional figures in an algebra or geometry class could use rulers to measure cereal boxes and the labels on cans of vegetables. To help students understand the connection this kind of measurement makes to a real-life context, introduce the activity as preparation for designing a container cover that will help market the product. Remind them that the manufacturer needs to know the volume needed for the product to fit inside and what goes on the outside surface area to encourage consumers to buy it. Before the outside can be prepared, container designers need to know the surface areas of the box so they can design printed information and artwork that will fit properly in the space available.

Students could even make their own boxes (see Figure 11–10). Using three different shapes allows you to provide practice at various levels of difficulty. To illustrate, the cube would involve the least complex computation because all sides are equal in size, and the cylinder would involve the most complex computation because both equations for a rectangle (label) and for a circle (top and bottom) are needed. Before students assemble their boxes, they use a ruler to measure the sides of their model and write their answers on one of the sides.

For additional practice learning this skill, they could measure the sides of various commercial containers. For variety, students could make their measurements in centimeters. All students should be encouraged to use a calculator for computation, and those who need addi-

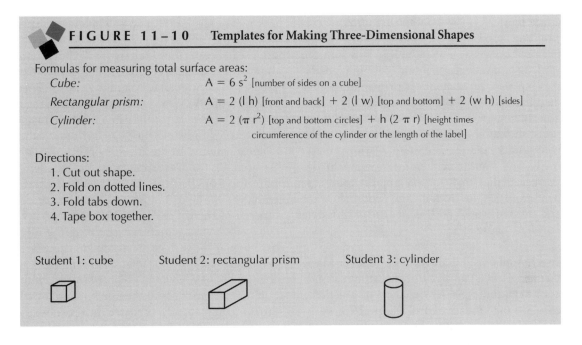

FIGURE 11–10   **Templates for Making Three-Dimensional Shapes**

Formulas for measuring total surface areas:

Cube: $\quad\quad\quad\quad\quad\quad$ A = 6 s^2 [number of sides on a cube]

Rectangular prism: $\quad\quad$ A = 2 (l h) [front and back] + 2 (l w) [top and bottom] + 2 (w h) [sides]

Cylinder: $\quad\quad\quad\quad\quad$ A = 2 (π r^2) [top and bottom circles] + h (2 π r) [height times
$\quad\quad\quad\quad\quad\quad\quad\quad\quad\quad\quad\quad$ circumference of the cylinder or the length of the label]

Directions:
1. Cut out shape.
2. Fold on dotted lines.
3. Fold tabs down.
4. Tape box together.

Student 1: cube $\quad\quad\quad$ Student 2: rectangular prism $\quad\quad\quad$ Student 3: cylinder

tional support should work with a peer buddy (see more information on peer buddies later in this chapter).

Also, many commercially prepared application materials are available that would logically accompany and enhance the academic content already being taught. For example, the students in an economics class can participate in the Stock Market Game (Mann, 1999). Not only do students have the fun of participating in a contest and the opportunity to work together in small learning groups, but they are exposed to connections outside of the abstract confines of the classroom and can generalize the information to how individuals sometimes use money. You even can add a technology component to the experience by having the students use the Internet to play the Stock Market Game with students in other schools. They can follow their stocks in the newspaper or use the Internet to get stock quotes and market information. This activity can be modified to give a student with moderate to severe disabilities the opportunity to participate by having the student follow the stock of one company in the newspaper to de-

termine if her company is increasing or decreasing in value. Help the student identify a local company's stock or a stock in which the student might have a personal interest. For example, the student might follow the stock of McDonald's restaurants if she works as part of a work-study program or after school job. This activity also provides an opportunity for you to encourage students to be responsible with their financial resources by addressing the need to budget income, including money received from work, savings, and investments.

Taking advantage of the naturally occurring application activities and commercially available application materials will help students understand their connections to abstract concepts, but some students may need to have additional opportunities to understand the relationship fully. It also will be important to develop activities and materials that can help students understand how ideas learned in the classroom can be used to enhance their lives in the community. So, just as students playing the Stock Market Game have the opportunity to see the associations between the stock market and financial effect, they can learn about the use of money on a different level when they work on developing a personal budget (Mann, 1999). In this way, the students not only learn about economic principles but also can relate those principles to their own lives at a level they actually use every day. You could draw on the students' personal affiliations, such as employment opportunities in the community, as well as costs of various apartments and houses in the area. You might develop activities that, for example, require students to price the clothing and food they want and need to work and live a particular lifestyle they have chosen.

Teach Applied Content Through Teacher-Made Games. Games can give students at the secondary level a more pleasant method of practicing concepts than the usual drill and practice worksheet format typically seen in academic classrooms. Board games, bingo games, and team games provide opportunities for reviewing and drilling previously learned course content. They provide an excellent way to extend an academic lesson and create an atmosphere of social interaction and active student participation.

In Ms. Ikegami's American history class, the students often play board games that Ms. Ikegami has made to reinforce the course concepts she has taught. Winston and Franny enjoy playing the games together and supporting each other so they all can be successful. Winston reads well but sometimes has difficulty comprehending the meaning of what he has read. Franny has trouble reading certain words but she understands the meaning when the cards are read to her. Winston reads the words that are hard for Franny and Franny helps Winston understand the meaning of what he has read.

Leveling the game materials allows all students to participate fully. To illustrate, students can use the cubes they built in the algebra lesson on calculating surface areas in a game that broadens the original lesson and gives students an opportunity to practice the newly learned concept. To prepare for the game, students make a die out of the cube they cut out during the original activity. To do this, they print or color the numbers (or dots representing the numbers) from 1 to 6 on their cube before they assemble it with the clear tape. A different number is placed on each of the six surfaces. Once the students' cubes are put together, they become the dice used to play the surface measurement game (see Figure 11–11).

Meanwhile, you would prepare file cards with questions that ask about the information found on the commercially prepared boxes the students had previously measured. The questions could be sorted and placed on different colored file cards according to their level of difficulty.

To play the surface measurement game, students line up on the side of the classroom using their desks as the game board. Each student has a turn to roll the die and move the appropriate number of desks until arriving at the desk that corresponds to the number rolled. The student sits in that desk if it is empty or occupied by another student, but moves to the next available desk if two students are already sitting at the designated desk. Next, the student answers one of the questions on the teacher-prepared file cards. The students continue to move up and down the rows of desks until a student wins the game by reaching the last desk in the room.

Incorporate Applied Content into Seatwork. Worksheets are commonly used as a tool for providing students with opportunities for practicing newly learned material. They also are used as a means for evaluating students' progress in mastering the course content. As you have already learned, connecting course content to a practical context can motivate students. For example, reading the newspaper in a current af-

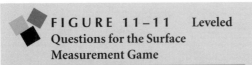

FIGURE 11–11   Leveled **Questions for the Surface Measurement Game**

Possible green file card questions:

1. How many inches long is the front on box 3?
2. What shape is the top of canister 1?
3. How many surfaces are there on box 5?

Possible pink file card questions:

1. How many sides do you have to measure when you want to figure the surface measurement of a square?
2. What is the surface area of the label on canister 2?
3. What is the surface area of the top of box 2?

Possible white file card questions:

1. What is the combined surface area of the front and back of box 4?
2. What is the formula for figuring the surface area of a square?
3. What is the surface area of the Nutrition Facts panel on the side of box 5?

Possible blue file card questions:

1. What is the area of the top half of the side panel of box 1?
2. How many sides do you have to measure when you want to figure the surface measurement of a cylinder?
3. What is the combined surface area of the top and bottom of canister 1?

fairs class can engage students' interest because it informs them about the people and events taking place in their own community. You can assess the students' ability to read for information and their knowledge of the people and events described in the newspaper by having them fill out a worksheet as they read the local newspaper (see Figure 11–12). By leveling the worksheet questions, you give every student the opportunity to participate effectively in the activity.

In a wellness and nutrition class, you might address consumer issues related to product la-

beling through topics such as ingredient information, consumer protection, and making wise personal choices. At the same time, students increase their functional reading skills. While they read various food labels, they learn to be aware of the product knowledge available on package labels so they make informed choices that lead to a healthy lifestyle (see Figure 11–13). They also can learn the value of doing cost comparison by matching the ingredients, amounts, and prices of two or more different brands of the same product. They learn they can make better choices if they know both nutritional and cost information before they choose a particular product. They also can consider the need to buy foods they, and the other people they live with, will actually eat so they avoid spending money on items they eventually would have to throw away.

Incorporate Applied Content into Small Group Activities. After the class becomes familiar with important facts available on a variety of different product labels, the students form small groups to decide on the consumer benefits of particular products. Together, they locate information on the labels of real products that have been brought into the classroom. The group investigates the benefits and potential problems for each product by looking at label information. Each member of the group takes responsibility for a different role in alerting the group to potential benefits and concerns for each of the products the group is asked to assess (see Figure 11–14).

Using cooperative learning groups can facilitate access to the application of content during labs in science courses or vocational programs. For example, during labs in science, students with moderate to severe disabilities can participate effectively if you modify the labs to include real-life, hands-on explorations that are multisensory and organized so students work in pairs or small groups to model more accomplished peers and use alternative ways of showing their accomplishments. The cooperative group for science lab that requires performing

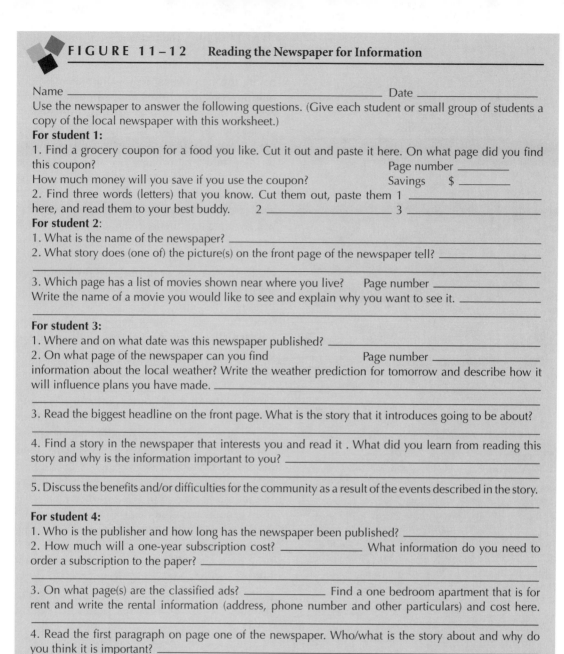

FIGURE 11–12   Reading the Newspaper for Information

Name _____ Date _____

Use the newspaper to answer the following questions. (Give each student or small group of students a copy of the local newspaper with this worksheet.)

For student 1:

1. Find a grocery coupon for a food you like. Cut it out and paste it here. On what page did you find this coupon?   Page number _____

How much money will you save if you use the coupon?   Savings $ _____

2. Find three words (letters) that you know. Cut them out, paste them 1 _____
here, and read them to your best buddy.   2 _____   3 _____

For student 2:

1. What is the name of the newspaper? _____

2. What story does (one of) the picture(s) on the front page of the newspaper tell? _____
_____

3. Which page has a list of movies shown near where you live?   Page number _____
Write the name of a movie you would like to see and explain why you want to see it. _____
_____

For student 3:

1. Where and on what date was this newspaper published? _____

2. On what page of the newspaper can you find   Page number _____
information about the local weather? Write the weather prediction for tomorrow and describe how it will influence plans you have made. _____
_____

3. Read the biggest headline on the front page. What is the story that it introduces going to be about?
_____

4. Find a story in the newspaper that interests you and read it . What did you learn from reading this story and why is the information important to you? _____
_____

5. Discuss the benefits and/or difficulties for the community as a result of the events described in the story.
_____

For student 4:

1. Who is the publisher and how long has the newspaper been published? _____

2. How much will a one-year subscription cost? _____ What information do you need to order a subscription to the paper? _____

3. On what page(s) are the classified ads? _____ Find a one bedroom apartment that is for rent and write the rental information (address, phone number and other particulars) and cost here.
_____

4. Read the first paragraph on page one of the newspaper. Who/what is the story about and why do you think it is important? _____
_____

5. Find a story in the newspaper that reports on someone in your local community and read it. What is the most important thing you learned from reading this story and why? How does this information impact your own life? _____
_____

6. Identify an event in history similar to one of the events described in the newspaper. Compare and contrast the two events. _____
_____

Source: Adapted from Hamill, L., & Dunlevy, A. (2000). *Members of the community*: *Worksheets for transition activities in the community and the classroom.* Verona, WI: IEP Resources. Reprinted with permission.

FIGURE 11–13
Important Facts/Information to Know About Product Labels

1. **The largest ingredient is the first item listed and the smallest ingredient is the last item listed.**
2. **The nutritional facts, such as fat 3 g (grams) or 4% DV (percent daily values), are given for a single portion of the product that is identified as per serving.** (Note: Pay attention to serving size information to avoid unintentional overeating and possible weight gain.)
3. **Check the expiration date and consider how quickly you plan to eat the product before making a purchase to assure freshness and avoid spoilage.** (Note: Expiration dates may be listed in one of two ways: *Sell by:* or *Use by:* so it is safe to use a product for a few days after the sell by date but not after the use by date.)
4. **Scanning the UPC code (Universal Product Code) tracks the sale and updates the store's inventory records. The UPC code also provides the customer with proof of purchase.** (Note: Scanning allows the store clerk to check the current price of a product. The scanned price may be higher than the price listed on the store's shelf tag but the clerk should honor the lower price if you remind the clerk of the shelf tag price.)
5. **To make a claim of reduced fat or calories, a product must have 25% less fat or calories than the same regular product.** (Note: Limit the amount of fast foods you eat to avoid the high fat content of fried foods. Also, counting the number of calories you consume each day can help you maintain a healthy weight.)

an experiment might include the following responsibilities: an equipment manager who gathers the needed materials and cleans up; the executer, who conducts the experiment; a

recorder, who logs the group's findings and writes the report; and a presenter, who gives the report to the whole class. The student with a physical disability might have the role of presenter and can give the lab report using voice recognition software (Dragon Naturally Speaking Preferred 3.0, 1998).

FIGURE 11–14 **Small Group Activity for Learning About a Product by Reading Label Information**

Individual Assignments Within the Group
1. Student 1 (Project Manager): This student's responsibilities include writing down the group's findings.
2. Student 2 (Financial Adviser): This student's responsibilities include locating information about cost information.
3. Student 3 (Marketing Adviser): This student's responsibilities include keeping track of marketing information such as whether or not the group members have used or expect to use a particular product, and why.
4. Student 4 (Health Adviser): This student's responsibilities include locating information about nutritional values.

Note: This lesson on labels could be extended by developing and implementing an accompanying ecology lesson. Students could learn the benefits of recycling by putting the various containers they have studied during the lesson in a class recycling bin. The students could even design a system of recycling bins for the used glass, paper, plastic, and metal containers. They also could use the bins to dispose of old papers and other trash that accumulates in the classroom!

Evaluation Modifications

Grades. Teachers use a variety of grading systems to evaluate individual student progress in the classroom. Rojewski, Pollard, and Meers (1990) list six common methods used for grading students (see Figure 11–15).

In some situations, you may find using alternative criteria is most appropriate for judging an individual student's progress. Because career preparation is an important consideration at the secondary level, one alternative might be to assign a grade based on the student's progress in developing the skills necessary to function ap-

FIGURE 11–15 **Commonly Used Grading Methods**

1. Traditional grading (letter or numeric grading)	Most commonly used and familiar type of grading system. Includes two common variations: (a) *letter grades* (A-B-C-D-F) and (b) *numeric grades* (1-2-3-4-5). Grades are used to demonstrate relative levels of student performance ranging from excellent to failing. Percentage ranges can also be used, which are then converted to letter or numeric grades.
2. Pass/Fail	A criterion-based measure used to demonstrate whether a student has met predetermined standards. Several variations of this method include (a) Satisfactory/Unsatisfactory and (b) Credit/No Credit.
3. Checklists	A criterion-based measure used to monitor progress against predetermined standards. Checklists have also been referred to as *skill reports*.
4. Contract grading	An agreement for a predetermined grade by student and teacher on successful completion of work by student, as specified in the contract.
5. Letters/Conferences with parents	Narrative information provided regrading performance, offering more detail and specificity to the individual student. *Written evaluations* are also used, which are similar to letters and conferences but usually contain greater detail.
6. Blanket grades	All students receive a predetermined grade at the end of a course of study.

Source: Rojewski, J. W., Pollard, R. R., & Meers, G. D. (1990). Grading mainstreamed special needs students: Determining practices and attitudes of secondary vocational educators using a qualitative approach. *Remedial and Special Education, 12,* 7–28. Copyright 1990 by PRO–ED, Inc.. Reprinted with permission.

propriately in the workplace. In this case, you would assess the level of workplace skills the student exhibits. For example, a letter grade would be determined by calculating how often the student meets a predetermined standard on a set of tasks that have been identified in his IEP. Those tasks might include arriving in class on time, staying on task, working appropriately for a specified period of time, or completing assigned

 Mr. O'Reilly, Tanja's American history teacher, calculates 75% of Tanja's grade for the course according to the transition skill criteria stated in Tanja's IEP and 25% for correctly completing her class assignments. Tanja is working on (1) being ready when the bell rings at the beginning of class, and (2) learning not to disturb her classmates during in-class activities. Each class, Mr. O'Reilly determines whether or not Tanja has performed her work habit tasks sufficiently well in each of the two categories to receive the full three points for each task or if she should receive only one or two points in either task category. The answer represents a percentage that corresponds to a letter grade.

At the end of the grading period, Mr. O'Reilly counts the accumulated points and divides that number by the number of points possible for Tanja to have earned. There were 40 class meetings during the 9-week term. Tanja was in class every day and earned a total of 192 of the possible 240 points. In other words, she performed the tasks at an 80% skill level. She also correctly completed 40% of her class assignments. When Mr. O'Reilly combined the two percentages $[(.80 \times .75) + (.40 \times .25)]$, he determined that she had an overall record of 70% [60% + 10%] and had earned a letter grade of C for the term.

in-class work. You could further individualize the grading process by assigning greater or lesser weight to each identified skill.

Authentic Assessment. As you learned in Chapter 5, one form of assessment particularly valuable in determining student progress is authentic assessment. You can replace or supplement traditional test grading with an assessment of the student's hands-on performances or actual work products. Evaluating students on how well they can actually use the information they are taught more closely approximates the way they will be evaluated as employees in the future when they are in real-world on-the-job settings. Students can show skill competency through written and oral reports as well as video and live demonstrations. You also can obtain valuable input from student self-evaluations as well as peer reviews (Bottoms & Sharpe, n.d.).

 ADDRESSING INDEPENDENT LIVING SKILLS IN THE GENERAL EDUCATION CLASSROOM

This section addresses skills that students need to acquire in order to manage their personal needs and the daily interactions they will encounter as adults. The purpose is to help students develop maximum independence in the community.

Self-Care Skills

Many of the self-care skills we discussed in Chapter 10, such as grooming and eating, also apply to students with moderate to severe disabilities in secondary education classrooms. One self-care issue in middle/junior high and high school settings that warrants additional attention is the onset of menstruation in young women. Often students develop an understanding of menstruation and the practical techniques for managing the related personal hygiene through sex education instruction in middle/junior high and high school health education courses. Menstruation is a private and often sensitive event for young women. Use care and discretion when supporting students in managing their personal hygiene needs during menstruation. You not only need to pay close attention to maintaining a high level of comfort for the individual student, but you also should follow the school policy for addressing issues related to sex education.

Saieda finds personal care during her menstrual cycle difficult to master but she is learning new skills to understand and manage this monthly routine. During that time each month, Ms. Romano, the para-educator, accompanies Saieda to the rest room to provide support so Saieda does not overuse the bathroom tissue and clog the toilet. She also helps Saieda dispose properly of her soiled sanitary pads.

In addition, Ms. Romano uses this private time with Saieda to reassure her that menstruation is a natural occurrence that lasts about a week out of each month. She teaches Saieda that when she is menstruating she needs to protect her undergarments but it is all right to soil the sanitary pads.

Other personal care issues also become important considerations for all secondary education students, including students with moderate to severe disabilities. In health and family life classes, students learn vital information about sexual responsibility. Students should learn about pregnancy and sexually transmitted diseases such as AIDS and how various birth control methods can help prevent them. They should be taught how to make wise choices and when to say "no." Students with moderate to severe disabilities often are easily influenced, so it is particularly important to teach them these skills. Scenario activities such as role playing or class discussions about particular situations allow students to learn the skills in a safe environment.

Career Education

In Chapter 4, you learned that career education should be part of all elementary and secondary education programs and that career education at the secondary level should use applied content in academic course work to emphasize specific daily living and occupational skills (Brolin, 1995). This greater emphasis on applied academic content provides students with the direct connections to the skills they will need to function effectively as they become adult members of their community. In Chapter 13, you also will learn about schoolwide programs that provide a range of career education opportunities for secondary education students, such as school-based enterprises and vocational education courses.

Language/Communication

Not all students have well-developed methods of communication by the time they enter the secondary education system. Communication continues to play a major role in some students' IEPs.

Some students who use little or no language have learned how to make their wants and needs known to the people around them. When the strategies they have developed are difficult to interpret or disruptive, you can redesign those strategies into more sophisticated and effective ways for the students to communicate. Ostrosky, Drasgow, and Halle (1999, p. 58) recommend a set of four guidelines for developing those strategies. First, use the student's present skills as a starting point for developing new methods of communicating that will be better understood and more socially acceptable. Next, choose methods of communicating to increase independence that the student finds appealing, and determine the best situations for addressing those new competencies. Then, support the student in using the new methods of communicating in a wide variety of interactions. Finally, make certain that using the new skills easily provides the desired result so the student will continue them.

Whenever he wanted to get help from a classmate or his language arts teacher, Frank pounded his hand on the table or desk in front of him. His teacher, Ms. Fernandes, taught him to replace the prolonged disruptive pounding with a brief gentle tap on the shoulder of the target person. She modeled the new skill and used hand-over-hand to help Frank replace the old behavior with the new one. As Frank began to use this new method of communicating in class, he got the help he wanted more quickly and without unpleasant consequences.

Ms. Fernandes and the other students encouraged Frank to use shoulder tapping in other school settings, such as the cafeteria. His parents also taught him to use shoulder tapping to get their attention at home. This gave Frank the opportunity to generalize his newly learned skills to lots of different environments. As a result, he learned to substitute pounding for tapping in a variety of situations and enjoyed more appropriate and satisfying interactions with many different people.

As you learned in Chapter 3, augmentative communication devices also can help students communicate effectively in the classroom. One example of an augmentative device that provides communication support for individuals with severe physical disabilities is the Eyegaze System (Lahoud & Cleveland, 1994). It involves a computer and a video monitor that tracks an individual's eye movements across a series of images on the computer's monitor. The video monitor then sends that information to special computer software, which processes it and provides the person's message in synthesized speech. If a student is using an augmentative device, remember to use vocabulary that is age appropriate for the student's social and academic needs.

Social Skills

There are additional challenges for students at the secondary level, such as changing classes and meeting the expectations of several different teachers during the day. Class rules should remind students of the greater personal responsibility they have for academic work and appropriate interpersonal behavior (see Figure 11–16).

Using cooperative learning groups is an excellent strategy for teaching students interpersonal skills in secondary education classrooms and can also help prepare them to interact effectively with co-workers in the future. As you have learned in previous chapters, grouping students

FIGURE 11–16   Make Wise Choices

1. Be prepared and on time.
2. Show respect for yourself and others.
3. Respect your and others' property.
4. Take responsibility for your area.
5. Follow the directions of those in authority.

heterogeneously rather than by ability level gives all students the opportunity to participate in class activities. To maximize the learning experience for all students, design the cooperative group so each member is assigned a specific role. Those roles could include the leader, who keeps the group on task; the recorder, who writes down the group's ideas; the presenter, who shares the group's product with the whole class; the facilitator, who makes sure all group members are actively involved; the timekeeper, who monitors the time available; and participants, who create new ideas and help solve problems (Jones & Carlier, 1995). Each student should be assigned a role that accentuates that student's strengths. For example, a student with good verbal skills could take the role of presenter and a less vocal student could keep track of time. To accommodate students who may have difficulty fulfilling all of the responsibilities of a particular role, divide that assignment between two students. The role of recorder could be shared by one student with good handwriting skills and another student who has artistic ability.

PEER SUPPORTS FOR INDEPENDENT FUNCTIONING

Providing natural supports for students with moderate to severe disabilities can be a complicated and challenging task at the secondary level. Because the student changes classes, the teachers and other students available to provide support change several times throughout the school day. Using a natural support matrix can provide a systematic way of managing support for the student. The educational team should develop the matrix by identifying (1) the general goals and activities, (2) the student's general objectives, and (3) the supports for each period during the day and then developing one grid that covers the

entire school day (Ryan & Paterna, 1999). Several types of natural supports can be provided in secondary general education classes. They include peers who act as student aides, peer tutors, circle of friends, and best buddies.

Student Aides

In secondary schools, students frequently provide classroom support to both teachers and other students as student aides performing duties such as grading, filing, and making copies of worksheets. Rather than having a study hall in their daily schedule, the students volunteer to work for a teacher in a particular content area. In addition to performing administrative tasks

Jeff is a typical student in his junior year of high school who works during third period as a student aide in Mr. Heston's sophomore economics class. His duties include providing academic support for students in the class when they have difficulty understanding either course concepts or class activities.

In October, the class started a project that included investigating rental costs in the local housing market. They researched rental prices in the classified ads of the local newspaper. Jeff did not know what many of the newspaper abbreviations meant but the students he usually tutored did because they had learned to read newspaper abbreviations in a family living course they had previously taken. Fortunately, Jeff was able to get the support he needed to understand the rental information from Beth, a student with a disability he often tutored.

Peer tutors can be classmates of the student with disabilities.

that assist the teacher, the student aide also might be asked to help students in the class who are having difficulty understanding course concepts or class activities. The student aide receives a letter grade and elective credit for independent study. The grade is based on how well the student aide meets his or her obligation to the teacher, the students, and to the course material (Staub, Spaulding, Peck, Gallucci, & Schwartz, 1996).

Students with disabilities also can act as student aides. They might be assigned tasks to perform as a helper for the teacher or as a friend or support to another classmate. Students who participate in a student aide program develop an increased sense of responsibility and self-esteem

as they are included in a larger social network and valued by both teachers and classmates (Staub et al., 1996).

Peer Tutors

Student aides can be assigned the role of peer tutor. They work with all students who could use help, showing them another way to understand the material. They can help individuals or small groups of students. Students in a particular course who have done well in the past make excellent peer tutors. For example, a senior in calculus could provide student support in a sophomore geometry class.

Peer tutors also can be classmates of the student with disabilities. As members of the class, they can participate in a variety of ways. They can support the teacher in monitoring student progress in understanding course concepts. They can modify and adapt classroom activities as well as help students with disabilities complete the academic work and follow class routines (Staub et al., 1996).

Circle of Friends

The circle of friends strategy you learned about in Chapter 10 also can provide important peer assistance for students with moderate to severe disabilities at the secondary level. For example, they can be trained to act as conversation partners to support their classmate in learning skills such as initiating and turn taking in conversation while, at the same time, they enlarge the classmate's social arena (Hunt, Alwell, & Goetz, 1991). Because students at the secondary level participate in many different classrooms during the school day, their circle of friends is made up of various peers who are in their different classes and activities. Find those students who are both interested in being in the student's circle of friends and are naturally in the same settings with the student during the course of the school day.

FIGURE 11–17   Social Scan Exercise

Directions

1. Draw four concentric circles.
2. Put yourself right in the middle and then take a few minutes to fill in the people in each of your four circles.

First circle:	The people most intimate in your life—those you cannot imagine living without
Second circle:	Good friends—those who almost made the first circle
Third circle:	People, organizations, and networks with whom you are involved (work colleagues, the church choir, the square dance club, softball team, etc.)
Fourth circle:	People you pay to provide services in your life (medical professionals, tax accountants, mechanics, teachers, etc.)

Source: Adapted from Thousand, J. S., Villa, R.A., Nevin, A. I. (Eds.), *Creating and collaborative learning: A practical guide to empowering students and teachers* (pgs. 347–368). Baltimore: Paul H. Brookes. Reprinted with permission.

A teacher who is a member of the student's educational team could coordinate the diverse group of peers who have volunteered to be in the student's circle of friends and to help the student with program orientation, friendship development, and problem solving (Field et al., 1994). First, you bring together a group of students, including the student with a disability, whose schedules overlap. Next, you facilitate the development of a circle of friends for the student with a disability by leading an entire group of students in a social scan exercise to identify their own circle of friends (Falvey, Forest, Pearpoint, & Rosenberg, 1994) (see Figure 11–17). During the discussion that follows completion of the students' circles, you ask the students to consider becoming involved in the lives of those students whose circles indicated they were not socially well integrated. Finally, those who volunteer to be involved become the student's circle of friends.

Peer Buddies

As you learned in Chapter 10, peer buddies can provide support as a class friend or assist with teaching as a tutor (Hughes, Guth, Hall, Presley, Dye, & Byers, 1999). At the secondary level, they can support their buddy with a disability through a variety of strategies. To help with note taking, the peer buddy could take notes on a double sheet of carbon paper and give the student with a disability the second sheet. This would not entail additional effort for the student taking the notes and would allow a student who has difficulty writing to stay focused on the lesson being taught. The peer buddies could even use the notes as a study guide for reviewing the lesson together. They also can be a special friend by walking from one class to the next with their buddy or walking to the cafeteria and sitting with him or her during lunch (O'Shea & O'Shea, 1998).

 SUMMARY

Students in secondary education programs are developing the skills they need as they prepare for the transition to adult life. Teachers can facilitate this preparation in academic classes through the use of application-oriented content and materials. You have been shown different ways to ensure that students with moderate to severe disabilities participate fully and have effective learning experiences in inclusive general education classrooms. You have learned how to modify the standard delivery, response, and evaluation methods. You also have learned to create activities that let all students contribute in a manner that benefits the group they are working in and highlights their interests and strengths. Finally, you discovered a variety of opportunities for classroom peers to offer friendship and support to each other.

 CHAPTER EXTENDERS

Key Terms and Concepts

1. A *cognitive credit card* is a laminated cue card that contains a list of the steps the student needs to take in completing a learning task.
2. *Natural supports* at the secondary education level are peers who are part of the student's circle of friends or a best buddy as well as peers who support the student as a student aide or peer tutor.
3. *Peer tutors* work with individuals or small groups of other students who need help in understanding course concepts or support in completing class activities.
4. A *social scan exercise* consists of placing the individuals in a person's life in enlarging concentric circles with those individuals most intimate in the person's life in the smallest circle and those who are paid to provide services to the person in the largest circle.
5. *Student aides* provide classroom support both to teachers (by performing duties such as grading, filing, and making copies of worksheets), and other students (by explaining course concepts and helping with class activities).

Study Guide

1. Discuss how you would identify and allocate responsibilities for the peer buddies of an eighth grader with cerebral palsy.
2. List and describe three instructional adaptations that would be appropriate to use in a secondary education academic classroom.

3. Plan a one-semester schedule for a sophomore with a moderate cognitive disability. List the courses you would recommend and give your rationale for suggesting each of them.
4. Identify two materials adaptations and describe how you would integrate them into a particular secondary general education academic course.

Have a Class Debate

Some teachers are resistant to including students with moderate to severe disabilities in their secondary general education core academic courses. They think these students will have difficulty managing in their classes because the course content often deals with abstract concepts and they expect students to be self-sufficient, independent learners. First, debate the pros and cons of these teachers' positions. Next, brainstorm ways to facilitate a change in these teachers' attitudes.

Small Group Activity

In a small group of 3 to 5 students, choose one of the topics described here (Part 1) and develop an *applied* instructional lesson (Part 2) for teaching that topic. Each group should share its lesson plan with the whole class.

Part 1

Choose one of the following topics:

Course:	Introduction to Business
Topic:	To read and understand financial statements
Course:	American Literature
Topic:	To read for information skills
Course:	Federal Government
Topic:	To develop good citizenship skills
Course:	Health and Nutrition
Topic:	To develop skills for choosing an appropriate diet

Course: Algebra
Topic: To understand fractions
Course: English Composition
Topic: To perform letter writing skills correctly

Part 2

Describe the criteria for your lesson:

1. Circle the primary type of instructional method you will use:
   lecture
   audio/visual
   cooperative learning groups
   discussion
2. List the specific objective(s) to be taught.
3. List the materials that will be used (both ready-made and teacher-made).
4. Describe the procedures for teaching the concept (instructional plan).
5. Describe the activity(ies) that students will perform to learn/practice the skill.
6. Describe what assessment will be used to determine the lesson's effectiveness.

7. List any future activities that will use the acquired skill for periodic reinforcement.
8. List any other comments or ideas that will be helpful.

Field Experiences

Visit an inclusive secondary education academic classroom. During your observation, focus on one or two individuals in the classroom who have moderate to severe disabilities. After your visit, write a reflection about your experience. In the first part of your write-up, use the interactions of your focus students as examples when you describe the activities taking place in the classroom. Describe the students' (1) accomplishments, (2) needs, (3) academic learning, and (4) social experiences. In the second part of your paper, reflect on your observations. Be sure to describe how you will use the knowledge you have gained in your own teaching.

chapter 12

The Elementary School Environment

Elementary students participate in many activities during the school day that occur outside their classrooms. These out-of-class activities are part of the natural rhythm of any elementary school. Students spend part of the school day in the hallways, in the cafeteria, on the playground, in the bathroom, and so on. It also is common for schoolwide activities and projects to be part of every elementary student's learning experience. In other words, students have a wide variety of out-of-class experiences at school, some of which occur daily (e.g., recess and lunch) and others only occasionally (e.g., a guest speaker). These kinds of schoolwide formal and informal interactions provide students with opportunities to learn both academic and social skills.

WHAT YOU WILL LEARN IN THIS CHAPTER

In Chapter 10 you learned about the elementary curriculum and routines in the general education classroom for students with moderate to severe disabilities. This chapter demonstrates how the larger school setting also can provide an appropriate learning environment. You will learn how to develop and implement schoolwide projects and activities that allow all students to participate in applied learning experiences that will begin to give them the skills they need to function effectively when they become adults. The examples described in this chapter detail learning experiences designed to help students develop academic competencies as well as appropriate social behaviors.

First we describe ways to create community in the elementary school through activities such as mock elections, environmental improvement efforts, preparation of a communal meal, and a disability awareness program. This section also covers vocational education at the elementary level by addressing career education, school-to-work projects, and work study programs. Then we give detailed explanations of two entrepreneurial efforts that can be run by elementary students. One enterprise is a bakery and the other endeavor is a school supplies store. Finally we address student interactions in nonacademic settings, including the restroom, playground, cafeteria, and school bus. This section also covers school- and community-sponsored extracurricular activities that take place at school.

FORMAL INSTRUCTIONAL PROGRAMS AS A SOURCE OF APPLIED CURRICULA

As you will learn in Chapter 15, the 1997 amendments to IDEA emphasize preparation of students with disabilities for postschool life including employment or postsecondary education. By the time they are 14 years old, students' IEPs must include a statement describing their transition needs and how those needs will be addressed in their secondary education program. By age 16, students' IEPs must address needed transition services with an individual transition plan (ITP) that identifies long-term objectives for community experiences, employment, and adult living arrangements. It also should specify the need for a functional vocational evaluation, identify needed related services, and include a plan for instruction in the acquisition of daily living skills and community experiences (Bateman & Linden, 1998).

This preparation to become productive and valued citizens can begin even earlier, as students participate in a variety of activities in their elementary school community. They interact with each other in many different school settings outside of the classroom. In this larger school environment, they participate in a variety of instructional programs that include both formal and informal learning experiences.

Creating Community in the School

Community building supports all students and gives them practical experiences in citizenship. They have the opportunity to share their personal experiences and learn to celebrate diversity (Bryant, 1999). The students can then use those skills in their interactions in the larger community outside the school.

Many schoolwide projects can teach students citizenship skills as they learn to support and value each other. Students learn to work together to create a warm and supportive community sharing both the responsibilities and accomplishments that come from collaborative efforts (Krall & Renck, 1998–1999). It is important for students to work together so they will be prepared to function effectively in the real world. A supportive school environment encourages good citizenship and creates an atmosphere in which all students are fully accepted regardless of their disability, race, gender, religion, or ethnicity (Sapon-Shevin, 1992). Some examples of these kinds of activities include schoolwide projects such as voting in a mock election, caring for the school environment, preparing and eating a communal meal, and learning acceptance of others through a disability awareness program.

Voting in a Mock Election. Young students can begin to learn civic responsibility and how to make their voices count in the community by learning about government elections. As you have learned in Chapter 4 and will study in greater detail in Chapter 15, students need to develop the self-determination skills of making choices and actively pursuing the things they want and need if they are going to become successful adults. One project that can help students begin to exercise personal choices, and at the same time learn civic responsibility, is a mock election. Students can learn how the voting process works and actually vote on the same slate of candidates as their parents.

School personnel can use the Kids Voting curriculum to teach students about the political process and voting procedures as well as how to vote alongside their parents on Election Day

The town of Appleton hosted the seventh annual Appleton Action Day. Some of the scheduled activities included (1) a beautification project with groups of community members volunteering to pick up trash and planting flowers and small shrubs to beautify the community, (2) information booths on the town square with local business owners and government service employees passing out information packets, and (3) a parade with participation and some short presentations by various individuals and organizations such as the local fire company, the high school band, members of the community softball team, the mayor, and a local barbershop quartet.

Mr. Garfleis's fourth-grade class from Appleton Elementary School went to the celebration. Mr. Garfleis paired the students for their walk to and from the center of town. Sophia and Silvester were partners. Sophia pushed Silvester in his wheelchair and he held both of their information packets as they returned to school. They helped plant flowers in hanging baskets and learned about the resources and activities available in their community. They particularly enjoyed watching the parade and listening to the band music.

When the students returned to school, Mr. Garfleis asked them why they thought Appleton was a good place to live. Then the students brainstormed how their school community was like the town. They thought of ways they could be good school citizens and participate in making Appleton Elementary School a place that welcomes and supports all the members in its community. Because he and Sophie had really enjoyed making the hanging baskets, Silvester thought the class should plant flowers by the school's front door.

(Kids Voting USA, 1995, 1998). The process works as follows: (1) a local Kids Voting advisory committee, made up of community volunteers, organizes and sets up the student voting process in the regular polling location in the school; and (2) the students go with their parents to the polls where a volunteer meets them with a special ballot sheet for the student. The student ballot lists the same candidates the parents will be considering as they vote in the real election. For example, the students can vote for president and compare the election results in their school with the actual results in their state and in the entire nation. In this kind of school-wide project, students have the opportunity to learn about the democratic process and the political system, and they discover they can have a voice in their government (Haas, Hatcher, & Sunal, 1992).

You can encourage students to voice their community concerns and interests during a class discussion, and the students can identify and vote for the local candidates who have made campaign promises that address those concerns and interests. Various adaptations can be made that allow students with moderate to severe disabilities to participate in the voting. For example, a picture of each candidate can be placed next to his or her name on the ballot sheet for students who have difficulty reading. Students who need additional support can point to the candidates' picture while a volunteer reads the name and/or marks the student's choice.

Caring for the School Environment. Recycling is a way to create a sense of community in an elementary school. It also provides an excellent opportunity to teach children to care for the environment. For example, students can learn to care for their school grounds by participating in litter collection or recycling projects (Burgie, 1991). One elementary school in North Carolina developed a schoolwide recycling program and used the money they received from recycling aluminum cans to fund and maintain a life science courtyard. The students, teachers, and

parents worked together to turn the school's central courtyard into a nature center where the students then participated in a variety of science, language arts, and social studies activities (Elliot, 1994).

 Rodney and Talia are groundskeeper buddies. They work together with other students, their teachers, and the school custodians to help keep the outside of their school beautiful. Talia walks along the fence near the edge of the playground looking for pieces of trash. Rodney follows Talia in his wheelchair helping her locate the trash. Rodney also holds open a plastic trash bag where Talia puts the trash she gathers. They are both very proud that they have collected more trash than any of the other student groundskeepers.

Preparing and Sharing a Harvest Meal. Many elementary schools schedule activities around a seasonal or holiday theme (Kuersten, 1998). For example, students might prepare and share a harvest meal during the month of November. The meal preparation and celebration can be part of an integrated language arts, social studies, math, and art unit that focuses on the arrival of the colonists and how they settled in the United States. This is an excellent project for an entire grade level to undertake. For instance, as a culminating activity to the various academic lessons designed around this theme in the different third-grade classrooms, all the third-grade students could collaborate to prepare and eat a harvest meal in honor of the first Thanksgiving shared by the colonists and Native Americans. You can integrate activities into the students' math and language arts lessons such as writing invitations to the principal and office staff to invite them to the meal or reading a recipe and calculating how much of each ingredient is needed after determining how many guests are expected. Also, specific connections to academic standards in the curriculum can be addressed. For example, address social studies standards related to cultural diversity and participatory citizenship by teaching students about the contributions of Native Americans to the survival of the newly arrived colonists. To illustrate, the local Native Americans provided the food that got the colonists through the first winter and taught them subsistence technologies that are still used today.

Each student should have at least one job to do. The students should work collaboratively and support one another in completing their assigned jobs.

The main item on the menu is a harvest soup, served with dinner rolls and pumpkin cobbler.

 Carmen wants to take charge of the preparation work at the third-grade food center. She announces, "I'm going to cut all the potatoes up and put them in the pot." Then she says to her co-worker, "Steve, you put the beans in the pot when I tell you." Steve says, "No. I want to mix."

Mr. McKenna, one of the third-grade teachers, listens to the interaction without interfering. He wants to allow the students time to resolve the issue among themselves. When the students are unable to resolve the issue after a few minutes, he intervenes by asking, "How can we do this so everyone is happy with their job even if it isn't their first choice?" With Mr. McKenna's help, the students decide that everybody gets to cut up one potato. Carmen will cut the carrots, Jimmy will add the beans, and, while Steve stirs the pot, the other three workers will add the vegetables from the cans. Everyone will help clean up.

The week before the harvest meal is scheduled, classes are given different assignments. For example, all the students in several of the third-grade classrooms make the soup. When they have finished preparing it, the soup can be refrigerated and reheated later. The students responsible for making the soup take a letter home asking for donations of specific vegetables. Check for students who may be vegetarians and make one pot of soup with water rather than beef broth to accommodate them. When the vegetables arrive at school, some students have the job of separating the cans so all the tomatoes are together, all the beans are together, and so on. When it is time to cook the soup, assign different students in the classroom to work in groups to prepare the soup. They stock each area with the necessary equipment and ingredients and then they prepare the soup. They use pumpkin carving knives that do not have the sharp edge of a regular knife to cut the vegetables.

These food preparation activities provide an opportunity to teach students proper public health and hygiene procedures. Before they begin any food preparation, students wash their hands and tie back long hair. Remind them that when food falls on the floor it must be thrown away, and that they need to turn away from the food, cover their noses and mouths, and wash their hands before they return to food preparation if they cough or sneeze.

A different group of third-grade classes makes the dinner rolls. This activity presents an additional academic opportunity. Before the students make the dough, you can give a science lesson about the interaction of different substances in the fermentation process that makes dough rise (Markle, 1990). Sprinkle some yeast in a small bowl and add water with a little pinch of sugar to demonstrate how yeast works. Talk about how the sugar acts as a catalyst and why the water must be warm. Then the students add water and sugar to their yeast and watch for the same reaction you generated. Once they have accomplished that task, they mix several batches of the dough, which they place in large bowls, cover, and put in a warm place to rise. If the school has a large number of third graders, additional groups of students can repeat the entire process after the previous group of students cleans up the work space.

After the dough rises, a new group of students forms the dinner rolls. They wash and grease their hands and then shape the dough into small balls and put them in large muffin pans to rise once again. Another group of students can carry the muffin pans to the school cafeteria to be baked. You or the cook from the cafeteria put the rolls in the oven and take them out when they have finished baking. Once the rolls have cooled, the students can put them in plastic bags and refrigerate them until the day of the harvest meal when they should be warmed in the oven just before they are served.

A new group of third graders makes pumpkin cobbler, which consists of a firm custard with a crumb crust made in big sheets and cut into individual pieces for serving. First, the students figure out how many individual pieces of cobbler are needed for everyone to have a dessert. Then they calculate how many baking sheets they will need to fill so there will be enough dessert for everyone to have a piece. Next, they make and press the crumb crust mixture into baking sheets and mix and pour the custard over the crumb crust. Once the cobbler is baked, they cut it into enough individual squares of equal size. (See the appendix at the end of this chapter for some easy harvest meal recipes.)

A final group of students prepares the tables for the harvest meal. They calculate the needed

CUTTING A PIECE OF PUMPKIN COBBLER FOR EVERYONE!

Ronald, Hank, and Peggy have to figure out how many pieces of pumpkin cobbler they will need to feed the entire third grade! They work together and pool their math skills to solve the problem. First, Peggy counts the number of trays full of cobbler while Hank goes to the office to ask how many third graders go to their school. They find out that there are 199 students in the third grade and there are 12 trays of cobbler. Ronald calculates that 12 goes into 199 16 times with 7 pieces left over. But Peggy says, "We won't have enough for all the teachers." Hank says, "The principal says there are 7 third-grade classes so we have enough for the 7 teachers." But Ronald says, "No we won't, because we have to count the special education teachers, Mr. Rolands and Ms. Harper, and that makes 9 teachers." Then Peggy adds, "Don't forget there are 3 classroom aides! We should cut a piece for the principal and office secretary, too! That makes 5 more people." "And we should give pieces of cobbler to the 3 cooks in the cafeteria to thank them for letting us cook there," added Ronald. "So, how many pieces do we have to have?"

The students add 199 + 9 + 5 + 3 and decide they need to cut 216 pieces of cobbler. Next, they divide the 216 pieces by 12 to determine that they need to get 18 pieces of cobbler out of each tray. Then, they figure they could divide the tray into 3 equal parts in one direction and 6 equal parts in the other direction to get 18 pieces that were all the same size. They determine that if they cut the cobbler in each tray the same way, they will have exactly 216 equal pieces of cobbler!

Mary is also using math skills to help with the project. She helps her friend Vanessa count the number of paper plates needed to put a piece of cobbler at the place settings for each third-grade class. Then Mary puts a piece of cobbler on each plate and Vanessa places each cobbler plate on the top left corner of each place at the table.

Students get to eat the results of their hard work.

materials and make silverware packets by wrapping spoons and forks in napkins. They can create seasonal tablecloths by drawing pictures of colored leaves, pumpkins, or turkeys on the newsprint or butcher paper. They cover enough tables in the cafeteria with the decorated tablecloths and the silverware packets to accommodate all the harvest meal participants.

Whether the students prepare the tables or the food for the harvest meal, they each make an individual contribution while they work together to create a group celebration. This project not only provides good instructional opportunities, it has a positive built-in natural consequence. Everyone learns collaboration skills and they get to eat and enjoy the results of their hard work.

Connections with General Education Academic Classes. You can make academic connections with the harvest meal project through a variety of classroom activities. For example, stu-

dents can read a story in language arts about the arrival of the pilgrims. As part of a science lesson, students might grow carrots or onions for the harvest meal soup in classroom window pots or do the yeast experiment described earlier. Also, activities such as measuring ingredients and calculating the amount of food needed for the number of people who will be eating the meal (described earlier) present opportunities for classroom math lessons. The general education curriculum also can offer opportunities to encourage understanding and acceptance of diversity.

Teaching Disability Awareness. Disability awareness can be taught through the health or science curriculum. Students learn about the effects of specific disabilities as well as possible accommodations and supports. For instance, characteristics such as dietary concerns or safety issues related to mobility might be addressed through the health curriculum, and assistive technology and augmentative communication devices can be explored through the science curriculum. You can encourage class members with disabilities to be the "speakers" and talk about their own experiences. This may begin to help reduce the stigma of disabilities and encourage typical students to accept and celebrate differences.

There also are commercially prepared curricula to teach tolerance of disability, such as the Everybody Counts program (Kayes, 1996). Everybody Counts is a program designed to teach all students about disabilities and increase their awareness and sensitivity toward individuals who have disabilities. The program is intended to give students in kindergarten through the eighth grade an understanding of nine disability categories (Kayes, 1996). A different disability is highlighted at each grade level. To illustrate, students receive a general introduction to disabilities in kindergarten, first graders learn about individuals with visual impairments, and second graders study hearing impairments. Third graders learn the basics and sixth graders have a more in-depth experience about individuals with mental retardation. Fourth graders study motor impairments and fifth graders learn about learning disabilities. Seventh graders study chronic conditions and eighth graders learn about individuals with serious illnesses. Parents or other volunteer members from the community come into the school to teach the Everybody Counts curriculum. Each unit includes a 90-minute lesson with information about the causes and characteristics as well as simulation activities (Kayes, 1996). All of the activities in each unit are designed to help students understand the highlighted disability.

Still, awareness of disability is not enough to create acceptance of individuals with special needs. Acceptance grows out of prolonged and sustained interactions between students with and without disabilities (Sapon-Shevin, 1992). Schools must schedule activities frequently and consistently to promote acceptance, such as those described in the second section of this chapter.

Vocational Education

Although formal vocational education programs are typically found at the secondary education level, elementary school students also can explore the beginnings of a general employability curriculum. Some schoolwide projects that combine academic and vocational education and are appropriate for students at the elementary level include a school store, baking cafe, and school bank (Zollers, Henderson, & Savage, 1998). These kinds of activities give students assigned responsibilities and teach important general work skills.

Career Education. As you learned in Chapter 4, students should experience career education at all school levels. During the elementary years, the career education curriculum emphasizes career awareness. Typically, students learn about various workers and the kinds of jobs those workers perform as the students go on field trips

into the local community (Swengel, 1992). We address the subject of instructional field trips in detail in Chapter 14. Students also may be exposed to other careers as they read stories in language arts and social studies classes that describe individuals who have made important contributions to their communities through work or civic activities.

Some elementary programs also offer a schoolwide career education curriculum. In this kind of program, all the students in the school have an opportunity to meet workers from their community. The workers visit the school to talk with the students about their own careers and they also help the students learn more about different career options in which the students have a personal interest (Richards & Merker, 1997). For example, a schoolwide grade-level career day can give all the students the chance to investigate several careers during a one-day speaker series. A specific group of guest speakers is assigned to speak to the students at each grade level. So the first graders might have an opportunity to hear a police officer, dentist, veterinarian, or custodian talk about their jobs and the fourth graders might listen to a firefighter, judge, bank teller, or waiter describe their jobs. To keep the student groups small enough so the students can ask the speaker questions, each speaker could repeat the same 30-minute talk with three different groups of students.

In advance of the schoolwide career day, a list of the speakers who have agreed to talk about their careers is distributed to all the students at the designated grade level. Each student then prioritizes his or her list and identifies a first, second, and third choice. The lists for first graders, and any other students who need supports, also have pictures that identify the speaker's job. For example, next to the word *veterinarian* is a picture of a woman in a white lab coat with a dog sitting on a table. Depending on their ages and skill level, the students could rank or color code their choices. Some students circle and number their choices in pencil, writing a 1, 2, or 3 next to the circled items, and other students color their choices with different color crayons, filling in their first choice with a red crayon, their second choice with a green crayon, and their third choice with a blue crayon.

On career day, each student is assigned to visit with three different speakers. The name of the careers as well as an enlarged version of the picture representation for those same jobs could be placed outside the rooms where the speakers are located. Nonverbal students or students who need the support of a visual representation could have a card on a string around their necks with small versions of the pictures that represent their choices. This allows them to find the correct room independently. The student simply flips his card up to look at it and matches his picture with the corresponding picture outside the correct room. If older students are designated to act as aides in the halls, they also can use the picture cards as a reference to guide lost students to the correct location.

The speakers should be prepared to talk about their jobs so the students gain an understanding of what those careers entail but they also should share information related to their work that can be useful in the students' present lives. For example, a judge could have the students participate in role-playing situations to learn to make good choices in solving problems. A dentist might demonstrate the correct way for students to brush and floss their teeth, give the students toothbrushes and dental floss, and then have the students practice brushing and flossing skills. The teacher can use hand-over-hand to support a student who has difficulty with fine motor coordination. Not only do the students learn, but they also have an opportunity to practice functional skills that are beneficial in their present lives. A follow-up activity to Career Day might involve a trip to the dentist's office or a visit to the city courthouse. Students could learn about other kinds of jobs at the guest speaker's

Emmet Yazee's mother, who is a Navajo weaver, was one of the guest speakers on Career Day at Borego Pass Elementary School. Mrs. Yazee talked about raising sheep and making rugs from their wool. She brought several things with her including a small rug she had just finished making.

Mrs. Yazee told the students how she makes a Navajo rug and demonstrated several of the steps in the process. First, she described how she sheared the sheep to collect the wool. Then, she explained how she washed and dyed the wool. Next Mrs. Yazee described the process of *carding*. She told the students that carding is used to remove any knots in the wool. She explained how she places a clump of clean wool between two paddles that each have one flat surface made of short comblike teeth and pulls the paddles in opposite directions to smooth away the knots. While she talked, she asked Emmet to demonstrate carding.

Emmet showed the students how he helps his mother card the wool. Because Emmet has difficulty using his left side due to cerebral palsy, Mrs. Yazee has adapted the carding paddles for him. One of the paddles was clamped to a wooden arm attached to the right side of his wheelchair and extended in front of him. He held the other paddle in his right hand and pulled it across the clamped paddle where his mother had placed a clump of the uncarded wool.

After Emmet's demonstration, Mrs. Yazee showed the students how to spin the wool into thread that could be woven. Finally, she showed the students how she weaves the wool thread into a rug by running the thread horizontally through an open space between the vertical threads that are separated by moving a section of the loom. Several of the students in the audience got to try carding, spinning, or weaving.

workplace and observe the functional skills they practiced actually being used in the community. For example, they can watch a dental hygienist cleaning patients' teeth or help the dog walker exercise the pets at the veterinarian's office. You will learn more about community-based instructional activities in Chapter 14.

School-to-Work Projects. Schoolwide projects can connect in-school activities with the world of work by teaching students the value of good work habits, which will ultimately allow them to participate effectively in their future place of employment. For example, the entire school can implement a token economy. This kind of program emphasizes school-to-work tenets and also teaches all students in the building functional skills in counting and budgeting money (see Table 12–1).

Students earn play money in their classes for doing work-related tasks, such as having the necessary supplies and being ready to work, doing their seatwork neatly, turning in assignments on time, keeping themselves and their personal belongings organized, completing assignments, not disturbing other people's possessions, staying on task during independent work time, and working cooperatively with peers. The students are paid for achievement in any or all of the categories. You can make the play money by photocopying real coins and enlarging the pictures so they will be easy for students to keep. Color coding the photocopies, with nickels copied on light gray paper and pennies copied on pale yellow paper, can also help students keep

track of their play money. Students can even exchange money for more valuable coins, such as quarters or dollar bills.

However, students cannot earn more than a predetermined limit in each category during one school day. The categories and daily limits should be the same for all students. You are responsible for determining when your students earn pay in a particular category and for giving them the pay they have earned. You can choose to pay students in several increments during the day, so you might pay a student only one penny when he turns in neat seatwork but pay him for doing neat work two or three different times during the day. Students learn some simple economic concepts and they develop important personal management skills that will be important in successfully handling the responsibilities in their future jobs.

Students save their play money to purchase items at the school's redemption center. A nonverbal student might participate in this project by using picture exchange to identify her choice. Another student might be paired with a peer buddy who can help him determine which selections he can choose based on the amount of money he has earned.

When they have earned enough money to make a purchase, the students can choose from a variety of items that the school has purchased or had donated from the community. The items might include children's books, crayons, markers, or toys from local stores, food coupons for discounts at local restaurants, or tickets to a special showing at the local movie theater. The

TABLE 12–1 School-to-Work: Token Economy

Amount	Category	Amount	Category
$.05	turning in assignments on time	$.05	personal tidiness
$.05	completing assignments on time	$.10	neat seatwork
$.10	respecting the property of others	$.10	ready with supplies
$.15	working cooperatively with peers	$.15	staying on task

school administrators or teachers might even be able to write and obtain grant funding for the project.

Work-Study Programs. Work-study programs are typically found at the secondary education level (see Chapter 13). Still, a simplified form of the program can create schoolwide applied activities for elementary school students. For example, filing library cards or stacking, carrying, and reshelving books are tasks that an elementary school student library worker could perform (see Figure 12–1). A student worker also might deliver overdue book notices to the appropriate students in different classrooms in the building. Although young students only work for a short time period each week, their job responsibilities can be structured to teach a variety of work habits as well as to give them the opportunity to practice academic skills. For example, the students could clock in for work by signing their names and reporting the time. They could then clock out by writing their initials and the time when they have finished their 15-minute shifts. Consequently, they are increasing their academic skills in math and handwriting while, at the same time, they are learning the importance of being on time and

following a work schedule. They also practice math skills when they look at the clock to be sure they arrive at work on time and to determine what time their shifts will be over. They practice skills such as reading and finding information in alphabetical order when they locate their names to sign in and out for their work shifts.

Another work-study project might be to have students work with the school custodian on a variety of jobs, such as painting four square or hopscotch boards on the blacktop area of the playground. They can help the custodian measure the space, make a stencil for painting, and do the actual painting. Assign the students to work in pairs so they can support each other. For example, one student could hold the tape while her partner does the actual measuring of the area to be painted. Some other tasks the student workers might perform are identifying the materials that will be needed, gathering those materials, and bringing them to the work site. These tasks also have academic components such as reading the labels on the paint cans to determine the color and learning how to use and store the paint correctly as well as measuring the squares and computing the area of the court to determine how much paint is needed.

FIGURE 12–1   Leveled Work-Study Activities for the Elementary School Library

1. One student's job is to put the books on the cart to be reshelved.
2. Another student's duties involve alphabetizing the books that need to be reshelved by the first letter of the author's last name.
3. A different student is responsible for pushing the cart while another student puts the books on the shelves where they belong.

INCLUSIVE SCHOOLWIDE APPLIED CURRICULUM PROJECTS

Elementary students also can learn employability, social, and academic skills by operating a real business in their school. For example, fifth-grade students in New York run a bookstore in their elementary school that sells inexpensive children's books (Winik, 1998). This kind of project involves student participation in all aspects of a business from selling a product to keeping inventory records, managing money, and getting along with co-workers (Maselow, 1995).

The Kids' Kitchen

The Kids' Kitchen is an ongoing project that provides an applied curriculum for students to learn work habits as well as academic and social skills. Profits from this project also can provide money for field trips and special cooking activities like the harvest meal we described earlier in this chapter. In the Kids' Kitchen, students make and sell a variety of baked goods, such as bread, rolls, and cookies. Usually they bake plain breads and cookies, but during certain times of the year they also bake specialty items such as pumpkin bread, hot cross buns, or Valentine cookies.

The Kids' Kitchen typically operates bimonthly with student workers performing a variety of tasks, such as keeping the inventory records, mixing bread dough, and filling out product labels. However, the bakery also could open for special occasions. For example, the bakery's student workers could prepare and even serve cookies and punch to parents or community members who are visiting the school for events such as the Career Day or Kids Vote programs we described earlier (Zollers et al., 1998). Additionally, the students might op-erate the bakery every Friday in December when the number of orders increases to accommodate holiday entertaining.

Bimonthly Bakery Activities. At the beginning of each week the Kids' Kitchen will be operating, place a notice in the main school office announcing that student workers will bake on Friday. The notice specifies the kind of bakery item(s) that will be made and how much the items will cost. Also post a sheet in the office listing the jobs needed and requesting workers for those jobs so the students interested in participating can sign up or teachers can sign up one or more of their students to work in jobs that target specific skills they want the students to learn. For that reason, the sign-up sheet should indicate the specific skills that each job emphasizes (see Figure 12–2). For example, a student with cerebral palsy who is learning to sort and group items and needs to increase fine motor skills can work at the bakery as a labeler gathering the correct baked goods to fill an order and placing them in a package for the customer. All Kids' Kitchen jobs also address a variety of daily living skills such as cooking, cleaning or personal management tasks, and dealing with inter-

---

FIGURE 12–2 Kids' Kitchen Student Sign-Up Sheet

Job Title	Job Description	Skills Addressed	Student Worker
1. ORDER CLERK	Write customer invoices	Reading and writing	_____
2. STOCKER	Lay out ingredients/utensils	Taking direction and vocabulary	_____
3. MEASURER	Put ingredients together	Reading and measuring	_____
4. MIXER	Mix ingredients	Gross motor and cooperation	_____
5. DOUGH MAKER	Knead dough	Gross motor and strength	_____
6. TRAY CARRIER	Carry baking trays	Strength and agility	_____
7. DISHWASHER	Wash and store equipment	Daily living and gross motor	_____
8. CLEANER	Clean tables and floor	Daily living and gross motor	_____
9. LABELER	Package and label	Sorting, writing and fine motor	_____
10. DELIVERY PERSON	Deliver baked goods	Counting and reading	_____
11. CASHIER	Make change	Addition and subtraction	_____
12. BOOKKEEPER	Keep sales records	Reading, addition and subtraction	_____
13. PAYROLL CLERK	Keep salary records	Addition and telling time	_____
14. INVENTORY CLERK	Keep supplies records	Reading and subtraction	_____

personal skills including collaborating with peers and taking directions from a supervisor.

Students with and without disabilities work together, sharing responsibilities and supporting each other. Usually different students work each time; however some students may choose to participate on several occasions. If their teachers believe they will benefit, specific students may even participate on a regular basis. The number of students who work each time the bakery is in operation can be adjusted for a larger school or when the number of interested students is high. If a large group of students participate, some of the jobs can be assigned to more than one student. Another way to accommodate a large number of student workers is to divide the responsibilities of a single job into two different jobs. For example, the stocker position could be divided into a food stocker and an equipment stocker with one worker only handling food items and the other worker only organizing the equipment. Jobs also can be split

to give a particular student an increased level of responsibility, to encourage peer support in performing certain tasks, or to provide an oppor-tunity for a student whose needs can best be served by partial participation in the activity. For example, the cashier position could be split into head cashier and assistant cashier to allow a knowledgeable and highly skilled student to help a student who is learning coin and bill recognition or practicing counting skills.

Once the students have indicated their interest by signing up to participate in the Kids' Kitchen, they receive a job application to fill out (see Figure 12–3). The application already has the student's name written at the top of the form as well as a check mark placed next to the job the student requested. The students fill out their applications in the general education classroom with help from their teacher. After students have returned their completed applications and they have been assigned specific jobs, a note is sent to

FIGURE 12–3 Sample Job Application

(student's name)

Job wanted:	___Order Clerk	___Stocker	___Measurer
	___Mixer	___Dough Maker	___Tray Carrier
	___Dishwasher	___Cleaner	___Labeler
	___Delivery Person	___Cashier	___Bookkeeper
	___Payroll Clerk	___Inventory Clerk	

Personal Information:
Name: _____
Address: (Street) _____
(City/State/Zip) _____
Phone Number: _____
Age: _____   Birthday: _____

Work Experience (List jobs you do at school or at home):
Job #1: _____
Boss: _____   Phone Number: _____
Job #2: _____
Boss: _____   Phone Number: _____

In an Emergency:
Call: _____
Relationship: _____   Phone Number: _____

each student's classroom teacher identifying the job that student will be doing and the time the student should report to work as well as when the shift will end. For example, the note sent to the teacher of a student who has been assigned the job of stocker might indicate the stocker should report to the Kids' Kitchen at 10:30 Friday morning to gather ingredients and utensils for the bakers and should be expected to return to the teacher's classroom by 10:50.

All Kids' Kitchen student employees practice general employability skills, such as getting along with co-workers and arriving at work on time, as well as the duties identified on the student sign-up sheet. They also may perform additional tasks specific to their assigned jobs. For example, the inventory clerk might check the supplies list to identify the bakery's restocking needs and, with the teacher's help, make a grocery list and determine the approximate cost, and the order clerk keeps sales records of the total number of each bakery item purchased that day in addition to filling out the individual customer invoices. Figure 12–4 gives an example of a sheet for determining cost and sales, and Figure 12–5 and 12–6 illustrate sheets for tracking food and equipment supplies.

Preparing Bakery Items. The Kids' Kitchen student employees sign in and out on a time sheet at the beginning and end of their work shifts. You will see an example of a time sheet in Figure 12–9 later in the chapter. When the student bakers report for work, they will find the needed ingredients and cooking utensils already have been placed by the stocker at each food preparation station. There also should be teacher-made directions at a station for each baking team, including a list of all the items that should be on the table. To support any workers who may have difficulty reading some words, the supplies list and recipe directions should have both a description for each item or procedure and a corresponding picture. You also can print a copy of the recipe, with accompanying picture cues for the ingredients and directions, on a large experience chart and place it in a location where all the workers can easily see it. (See Figure 12–10 in the appendix for some Kids' Kitchen recipes.)

Record Keeping and Other After-Hours Activities. When the bakery items have been prepared and packaged, the delivery person takes them to the customers (teachers who have placed orders). Once the customers have paid

FIGURE 12–4   Sample Sales and Cost Sheet

Kids' Kitchen Sales and Cost Sheet

Individual Count (example: | | |)   Total Amount

1. Amount baked _____

2. Amount sold _____

Price per unit} × $ _____

Total sales $ _____

3. Expenses: a) Cost of food & equipment   + _____
                   Cost of supplies
              b) Wages paid   + _____
              Total expenses $ _____

4. Bakery Profits:

Total sales $
Total expenses   — _____

Net Profit $ _____

Source: Adapted from Killy, S. (1997). *Baking Up a Storm! Kramer Kids Kitchen Bakery.* [booklet]. Oxford, OH: Kramer Elementary School. Reprinted with permission.

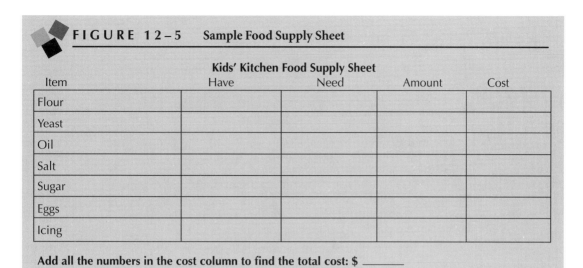

FIGURE 12–5   Sample Food Supply Sheet

Kids' Kitchen Food Supply Sheet

Item	Have	Need	Amount	Cost
Flour				
Yeast				
Oil				
Salt				
Sugar				
Eggs				
Icing				

Add all the numbers in the cost column to find the total cost: $ _____

Source: Adapted from Killy, S. (1997). *Baking Up a Storm! Kramer Kids Kitchen Bakery*. [booklet]. Oxford, OH: Kramer Elementary School. Reprinted with permisssion.

FIGURE 12–6   Sample Equipment Supply Sheet

Kids' Kitchen Equipment Supply Sheet

Item	Have	Need	Amount	Cost
Measuring cups				
Measuring spoons				
Mixing bowls				
Mixing spoons				
Pastry brush				
Baking trays				
Clean aprons				
Dish towels				
Dishcloths				
Bread bags				
Labels				

Add all the numbers in the cost column to find the total cost: $ _____

Source: Adapted from Killy, S. (1997). *Baking Up a Storm! Kramer Kids Kitchen Bakery*. [booklet]. Oxford, OH: Kramer Elementary School. Reprinted with permisssion.

FIGURE 12–7   Sample Self-Evaluation Sheet

Kid's Kitchen Employee Self-Evaluation Sheet

Name _____ Date _____

Job(s) I did today: _____

Time: I started work at _____ . I finished work at . _____

Money: Today, I earned _____ .

_____ I came to work with clean hands and face.

_____ I came to work with neat and clean clothes.

_____ I came to work on time.

_____ I got along with my co-workers.

_____ I helped my co-workers.

_____ I followed directions from my boss.

_____ I finished all my work.

_____ I left my work area neat and clean.

Signed _____

for their purchases, the delivery person returns with their payments and gives the money to the cashier. The cashier has the money tray ready with starting cash that includes an assortment of coins and some single dollar bills. He takes the payments and gives the correct change to the delivery person who returns with it to the customer. The cashier also collects money and makes change for any customers who come to the Kids' Kitchen to pick up and pay for bakery items, and he takes the collected money to the office for safe keeping.

The inventory and payroll clerks help the bookkeeper keep the Kids' Kitchen records up to date. They calculate salary expenses and supply reductions, and the bookkeeper checks their calculations and pays those expenditures. The bookkeeper also calculates bakery profits.

Evaluation of Work. Each worker might be paid 50 cents each day she works in the Kids' Kitchen for doing all her assigned tasks as well as for fulfilling the criteria for good general work habits. Before a student worker can receive the salary, she must fill out a self-evaluation form (see Figure 12–7). The worker is paid once she has reviewed the form during a brief evaluation con-

ference with the teacher. However, if a worker has not performed all the necessary tasks or has had difficulty in one or more of the identified work habits, she may be docked a portion of her salary. For example, students who forget to sign

FIGURE 12–8   Sample Flyer

Enjoy Homemade Bakery Products

The
KIDS' KITCHEN BAKERY
Will Be Baking Up a Storm This Year!!

- We will be baking homemade breads and cookies on the first and third Friday of each month.
- A loaf of bread costs $1.50 and a dozen cookies costs $1.75.
- Reserve your baked goods anytime during the week by signing the order sheet in the school office or come to the bakery to purchase items on a first come, first served basis beginning at 3 p.m. on Friday.

Source: Adapted from Killy, S. (1997). *Baking Up a Storm! Kramer Kids Kitchen Bakery.* [booklet]. Oxford, OH: Kramer Elementary School. Reprinted with permission.

in on the time sheet when they report for work could lose a nickel of their salary and they might lose another nickel if they forget to sign out at the end of their work shift. A worker might lose 10 cents if she came to the food preparation table before washing her hands or lose as much as 20 cents for fighting with a co-worker.

Advertising. Flyers can be put in the teachers' mailboxes announcing the dates the Kids' Kitchen will operate during the semester (see Figure 12–8). The flyers also should list which bakery items will be available on each of those dates and what each item will cost. In a small school, or when there is limited interest among the staff in the building, flyers could be sent to other schools in the district to attract additional business. A student-made poster could be placed in the school office to remind potential customers that the bakery will be open on a certain date or to announce unusual or special bakery items that will be available for a particular holiday or event.

Connections with General Education Academic Classes. When students work in the Kids' Kitchen, they learn vocational skills and consistent work habits, such as being on time and staying on task, following directions and performing work correctly, and getting along with co-workers and supervisors. While they are practicing basic vocational skills, the student workers are also learning both academic and independent living skills. Students develop language arts skills as they decipher recipes as well as read and fill in job applications and self-evaluation sheets. They practice math skills as they measure ingredients, fill in amounts on inventory sheets, identify work time, and calculate costs, profits, and wages. They learn independent living skills in cooking, kitchen safety, and personal care.

Peer Supports. Student collaboration and peer support are an integral part of the Kids' Kitchen experience. Workers' responsibilities often over-

lap so there are natural opportunities for sharing and helping each other. For example, the measurer and mixer decide together when to add the next ingredient and the mixer should consult with the dough maker to determine when the dough mixture is ready for kneading.

The "Super Stuff" Supplies Cart

Another example of a schoolwide project that uses an applied curriculum is a student-run school store (Zollers et al., 1998). At the elementary school level, this kind of store could easily operate twice a week on a roll-out cart. A "Super Stuff" supplies cart project is ideal for third- or fourth-grade students. The project should be organized to give all the students in the designated grade level an opportunity to run the supplies cart at least once during the school year.

Preparation and Planning. A sign-up sheet that lists all the supply cart dates for the fall and spring semesters should be passed to each of the

Customers choose from a variety of items on the supply cart.

FIGURE 12–9 Sample Work Schedule

"Super Stuff" Fall Work Schedule

Date	Name	IN	TIME	OUT	TIME
October 15: Tuesday	Frankie Smythe	_____	_____	_____	_____
	Emilio Lobos	_____	_____	_____	_____
October 17: Thursday	Katie Tobias	_____	_____	_____	_____
	Elsworth Love	_____	_____	_____	_____
October 22: Tuesday	Peggy Begay	_____	_____	_____	_____

appropriate grade-level classroom teachers (see Figure 12–9). The teachers fill in the names of their students to make sure all their students have the opportunity to work sometime during the year. This also allows the individual teachers to decide which dates they prefer to have their students participate in the "Super Stuff" supplies cart project.

Pair the students into teams so they can learn to work together and provide support if a co-worker has difficulty performing a particular task. For example, one student might hand out the supplies while the other student collects the customer's money. Depending on the size of the school, students can work in pairs serving one or two lines of customers or they might even have supply carts in two different locations.

The "Super Stuff" Activities. The store operates twice a week for approximately half an hour as the students are arriving at school. Before it opens, the student employees are responsible for making sure all the supplies specified on the price list are actually on the cart, making sure the appropriate adult is there to open the money box and supervise the operation, and taking the supplies cart out of the office to the selling location.

While the store is open, a teacher stands to the side of the supplies cart and only intervenes when the workers are clearly floundering. The student workers read the items and what they cost on the price list, which is posted on poster board next to the supplies cart. The customers

identify the items they want. Once a customer decides to purchase a particular item, a student worker hands the customer the item and collects the payment. The kinds of items typically available for sale on the "Super Stuff" supplies cart can include regular pencils, notebook paper, erasers, pencil grips, pocket folders, and pencil top erasers. Specialty items, such as Halloween or Valentine pencils, can be offered at a slightly higher cost at different times during the year.

Revenues from the sale of "Super Stuff" supplies can be kept in a money box and locked in the school office when the store is closed. Set the price of each item for sale by rounding up to the nearest 5 cents from its "wholesale" cost. For example, the "Super Stuff" store should charge customers 10 cents for pencils if the pencils cost the store 7 cents each. Although this practice will result in a fairly small profit, sufficient money should be available to pay employee wages. The student employees each earn 10 cents for working. Workers can choose to keep the dime or use it to buy something from the supplies cart at the end of their work shift.

After the store closes, the workers are responsible for restocking the supplies cart. They should begin by taking an inventory of the items they sold that day. Keep a chart in the office for the student workers to refer to that lists how many of each item should be on the supply cart when it is fully stocked. The workers count the actual items left on the cart and subtract that number from the number on the inventory chart.

Evaluation of Work. The student workers sign in and out on the master list that had originally been filled out by the teachers. They put a check mark next to their name on the master list when they arrive for work. When they finish working and have been paid, they write their names in the blank line next to the spot where the teacher had signed them up. The student workers also write down the time when they sign in and again when they sign out.

Peer Supports. A system of natural supports is already in place because all the student employees are assigned to work in pairs. Put students together who can provide each other with the support they need to be successful "Super Stuff" employees. That will allow each student to emphasize her strengths and, at the same, get help from her peer partner when she needs some assistance. For example, an outgoing student who works well with people and a shy student can work as a team, or someone who knows how to count money could be paired with somebody who is just learning money skills.

Connections with General Education Academic Classes. The "Super Stuff" project can tie into academic activities in the classroom. You can develop math worksheets that feature problems that relate to inventory or wages for the supplies cart business or have students read stories about young entrepreneurs.

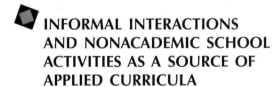 **INFORMAL INTERACTIONS AND NONACADEMIC SCHOOL ACTIVITIES AS A SOURCE OF APPLIED CURRICULA**

Informal interactions take place between students in many different school settings at the elementary level. Students participate in a variety of school-sponsored events as well as community-sponsored activities that take place on school grounds after the regular school day ends. Some examples of these kinds of activities

are a student concert or a Little League baseball team. Students also interact during the school day in various nonacademic locations in the school including the playground and school cafeteria.

Nonacademic School Settings

Students regularly play with classmates at recess, eat with their grade-level peers at lunchtime, and ride the bus to and from school each day with friends from their neighborhood. They even have brief occasions to socialize in the hallways and during rest room breaks. These different settings also provide opportunities for teaching daily living skills in the natural environment where the skills are used.

The Restroom. The restroom provides an excellent setting for teaching personal hygiene. For example, students should wash and dry their hands after using the toilet. If a student is just learning this skill, have a peer buddy help give her the verbal or physical assistance she needs. The student who is being toilet trained should go with the class to the restroom. Even if the student is not ready to use the toilet, she can wash her hands with the other students. To maintain her privacy, the student can have her diaper changed once the others have returned to the classroom. Students also can learn and practice some dressing skills during restroom breaks. They have to pull clothes on and off when they use the toilet, which often requires buttoning and unbuttoning or zipping and unzipping pants. A student who is learning these skills can benefit from observing and modeling her peers.

The Playground. The playground is a focal point for many of the informal social interactions that take place between elementary students during the school day. Students should have a variety of play options from which to choose. For instance, examples of activities that typical students and students with mobility challenges might choose to play together include stationary games like tether ball or "plastic" horseshoes. Adults supervise the environment to maintain safety and to ensure students treat one another appropriately. However, the students can choose the peers and activities they want to pursue. As you learned in Chapter 4,

 Mary is a second-grade student in a classroom of 23 typically developing students. She recently came from a classroom of 5 students with special needs. Mary's typical peers were happy to have her in their class. They were excited about teaching and helping her with everything they were doing.

Mary's circle of friends began taking her to different parts of the playground, but she became frustrated and overstimulated. She began to bite the students when they tried to take her hand. Mary's circle of friends met to determine what she was trying to tell them by biting. They developed a solution to the problem behavior. They decided to teach Mary to sign *stop* when she didn't want to go where her friends were taking her.

The circle of friends modeled and role-played the appropriate behavior for several days. Mary began to sign stop whenever she thought her friends were getting too close. She would sign stop when she was feeling too crowded or when she did not want to go where her friends were suggesting. Because the circle of friends designed the plan themselves they worked hard to make it successful. Before long, Mary's behavior improved and she was communicating her needs appropriately.

[We thank Joy D. Garand-Nichols for contributing the ideas that are the foundation for this story.]

having choices and making decisions like these can contribute to the development of a student's self-determination skills. Another component in being able to identify and make good choices is the ability to communicate effectively.

As you learned in Chapter 8, students must learn and practice appropriate ways of communicating. When a particular student exhibits an undesirable behavior, look at what is happening in the environment around the student. For example, the adult supervising the playground should watch to determine (1) whether the environment is too stimulating or overwhelming, (2) what precedes and follows the behavior, (3) whether the behavior always happens at the same time, and (4) what situations allow the student to communicate comfortably what she wants. Once the playground supervisor identifies the relevant factors, he can adjust the environment to create a positive setting in which the student can communicate more effectively and, as a result, interact more appropriately with her peers. For example, the supervisor might identify a peer buddy who can make sure the student gets in the correct line on time and waits quietly to reenter the building at the end of recess.

The Cafeteria. In the cafeteria, students learn both daily living and social skills. For example, they can practice money skills by paying for their lunches and then counting the change they get back. As students eat and visit with each other, encourage them to follow appropriate social behaviors and to use good table manners. As students develop these skills they build a social network and become more independent. Students also have the opportunity to observe and model their peers' mealtime behaviors. Adaptive eating equipment, such as the Winsford Feeder, which includes a bowl with a suction bottom and high rim or curved spoon, also can foster independence by supporting students who may not have the ability to feed themselves (North Coast Medical, 1999).

The student should decide what he wants to eat and drink and then ask the cafeteria workers for those items. These activities will increase his communication and self-determination skills. The student might also practice personal care skills by going to the bathroom to wash his hands before lunch and again to brush his teeth after he eats.

 Sidney was spitting food at other students when they sat near him in the cafeteria during lunch. His peers problem-solved the issue in their circle of friends meeting and realized he was trying to initiate interactions with them. What Sidney was actually doing was trying to get the other students' attention.

The circle of friends came up with a plan that they modeled for Sidney. They decided whenever they saw him get agitated and look at them with his mouth full, they would say his name and talk directly to him. Sidney would then have enough time to respond appropriately. For example, he could point to the friend he wanted to share his cookie with or to something he wanted to eat. Sidney's circle of friends helped him reshape his behavior to build friendships with his peers.

[We thank Joy D. Garand-Nichols for contributing the ideas that are the foundation for this story.]

The School Bus. As students arrive and leave school each day, they have another opportunity to interact socially without direct guidance from adults. This presents an excellent chance for peers to model appropriate behaviors and to provide support for their peers who may need extra assistance. For example, typical students and students with moderate to severe disabilities can be paired during this time as "buddies" who support each other in finding the correct bus, getting on and off, and getting from the bus to the classroom (Zollers et al., 1998). Peers also can provide support on the bus. For example, older students can act as "flight attendants" to encourage the acceptance and inclusion of all the students riding on their bus (Carns, 1996).

Extracurricular Activities at the School

As you learned in Chapter 6, IDEA now requires the IEP to address the student's involvement in extracurricular and other nonacademic activities (Bateman & Linden, 1998). There are many extracurricular school-sponsored activities and events for elementary school students. Some common events include activities connected to the academic curriculum, such as school plays and student exhibitions (Zollers et al., 1998). Other activities build interpersonal competencies, such as scout meetings and team sports. Although these endeavors take place on the school grounds, they are often community sponsored.

School-Sponsored Events. There are various regularly scheduled inclusive extracurricular activities in elementary schools in which students can choose to participate. Some examples include band and chorus. Occasional events such as plays, concerts, and art exhibitions also offer opportunities for students to participate in school life. Students can demonstrate their achievements with an authentic performance of their skills. These experiences allow students to develop a sense of self-worth and value to others (Schanche, 1998). After-school enrichment programs offer chances to explore art through activities, such as weaving and pottery, or learn computers applications, such as the Internet and multimedia. Other after-school programs offer physical fitness activities, such as tumbling and tennis, or participation in special interest clubs, such as science and drama.

Community-Sponsored Events. Many elementary students belong to community organizations such as the Cub and Boy Scouts, Brownies and Girl Scouts, 4H Clubs, Royal Rangers, or Boys and Girls Clubs. The scout troops often hold their meetings in the building at the end of the school day. Many sporting events, such as Little League or youth soccer, use elementary school playgrounds for team practices and games. Sports provide students with the opportunity to develop both physical and social skills. Elementary schools also can sponsor their own sports events such as an annual schoolwide sports day that can foster peer support and positive relationships among students with and without disabilities (Turner, Snart, & McCarthy, 1992). Many of these activities are structured in a way that allows students with disabilities to receive assistance through natural supports that are already in place. For example, parents might be their child's team coach or scout troop leader. Peers also can provide natural support by sharing responsibilities. For instance, two members of a Girl Scout troop might each take responsibility for different parts of the same project to earn a scout badge together or two ball players might share one position on the team. For example, a student who uses a wheelchair could play in the pitcher's position and bat but have a peer partner run the bases.

 SUMMARY

In this chapter, you learned about schoolwide curriculum projects and activities that are appropriate for all elementary students. As you have discovered, the formal instructional projects and informal learning experiences described in this chapter not only address academic content but they can help students start to develop daily living skills and social competencies. In the next chapter, and again in Chapter 15, you will see how students can increase and refine those skills at the secondary level as they prepare for adulthood.

Please note that the school-wide format may not always be available or appropriate in a particular school. In these circumstances, it is possible to scale down the activities such as a harvest meal, a career day, a token economy, or a student-run bakery like those described in this chapter, or for the kinds of projects which you will learn about in the next chapter, and operate those projects within a single classroom or among a few interested classrooms in the building.

NOTE: We wish to acknowledge the contributions of Ms. Suzanne Killy to this chapter. She generously shared many of the activities she developed for the students at Kramer Elementary School in Oxford, Ohio, such as the Kids' Kitchen and harvest meal.

 CHAPTER EXTENDERS

Key Terms and Concepts

1. *Everybody Counts* is a program designed to teach all students about individuals with disabilities by highlighting a different disability category at each grade level.
2. *Kids Voting* provides a curriculum for teaching the political process in schools and a mock voting experience for students who accompany their parents to the polls.
3. *Disability awareness* refers to creating acceptance of individuals with disabilities through prolonged and sustained interactions between students with and without disabilities.
4. An *employability curriculum* addresses both age-appropriate general vocational skills and academic competencies.

Study Guide

1. List and describe five daily living skills that could be taught in natural settings in an elementary school.
2. Discuss three advantages of schoolwide projects and how these kinds of projects promote positive inclusion experiences for both typi-

cal students and students with moderate to severe disabilities.

3. List and describe two academic components that can be incorporated into the activities of each of the following:
   a. a school clean-up project
   b. a grade level communal meal
   c. a school-wide career day

4. Identify and discuss four interpersonal skills students may develop as they participate in a schoolwide student-run business.

Have a Class Debate

All elementary students need to acquire a solid academic base. At the same time, early vocational education experiences can begin to prepare students for future careers and may be particularly important for students with moderate to severe disabilities. Debate the possible benefits and ramifications of teaching vocational education as part of an inclusive elementary school curriculum.

Small Group Activity

In small groups of 3 to 5 students, design a schoolwide project that addresses an applied approach to the elementary school curriculum.

The project can be a onetime event like the harvest meal or it can be an ongoing activity like the "Super Stuff" supplies cart described in this chapter. Each group should share their ideas with the entire class as well as provide each of their classmates with a written guide that briefly explains the project.

Field Experiences

Visit a local bakery or an office supply store. Take a tour of the facility. Consider the following questions and address those issues in a proposal for developing a student-run school bakery or supplies cart in an elementary school you have visited: What parts of the operation could you recreate in the elementary classroom? What adjustment would you have to make? Which jobs could the students do and which jobs could be divided into several smaller jobs so students could work together doing tasks that are manageable for their age and ability level?

Recipes

 Harvest Meal Recipes

Harvest Soup

1 bag of frozen or 2 cans of corn
1 bag of dry beans
2 cans of tomatoes
2–3 stalks of celery
1 large onion
3 large carrots
6 potatoes
Broth (dry mix and water or canned)
Salt and pepper to taste

1. Open cans and drain liquids (except for tomatoes).
2. Wash, but do not peel, fresh vegetables and cut into bite-sized pieces.
3. Put fresh vegetables into large stock pot with enough broth to more than cover the vegetables.
4. Simmer 1–2 hours.
5. Add canned vegetables to stock pot and cook 1 hour.
6. Season with salt and pepper.

Dinner Rolls

(See the Refrigerator Rolls recipe in "A Collection of Kids' Kitchen Favorite Recipes" which is listed on the next page)

Pumpkin Cobbler

Crust Mixture (per tray or 4 pieces):
4 cups flour
1 cup confectioner sugar
1 pound butter

1. Grease steam tray.
2. Cut all ingredients together until dough is crumbly.
3. Press into bottom of pan.
4. Bake 25 minutes in 350° oven.

Filling Mixture (per tray):
$4\frac{1}{2}$ cups pumpkin
9 eggs, beaten
$4\frac{1}{2}$ cups hot milk
$1\frac{1}{2}$ cups sugar
$1\frac{1}{3}$ cups brown sugar
$\frac{1}{3}$ cup flour
$1\frac{1}{2}$ tsp. salt
$1\frac{1}{2}$ tsp. cinnamon
1 tsp. nutmeg
1 tsp. allspice

1. Mix eggs and pumpkin with milk.
2. Blend in other ingredients.
3. Pour on top of crust and bake 45 minutes in 325° oven.
4. Cool and cut into 48 equal squares.

Source: Adapted from Killy, S. (1997). *Baking Up a Storm! Kramer Kids Kitchen Bakery.* [booklet]. Oxford, OH: Kramer Elementary School. Reprinted with permission.

FIGURE 12–10 **A Collection of Kids' Kitchen Favorite Recipes**

Kids' Kitchen Bread (makes 3 loaves)

1. Dissolve 1 package yeast in 3 cups warm water.
2. Add 1 tablespoon oil and 1 tablespoon salt.
3. Fold in about $\frac{1}{2}$ of a 5-pound bag of all-purpose flour.
4. Mix and then knead lightly and place in a bowl to rise.
5. Cover and put bowl in warm environment.
6. After mixture has risen, PUNCH DOWN.
7. Shape into 3 loaves (or divide into 9 pieces and braid each three for fancy bread).
8. Cover and let rise again.
9. Brush with a beaten egg and 1 teaspoon of water.
10. Oil baking sheet and sprinkle with cornmeal. Bake in 400° oven for 30 minutes.

Refrigerator Rolls (makes 3 dozen rolls)

1. Dissolve 2 packages of dry yeast in 2 cups of warm water.
2. Stir in $\frac{1}{2}$ cup of sugar, 2 tablespoons salt, $\frac{1}{4}$ cup soft shortening, and 1 egg.
3. By hand, mix in 6 to 7 cups of flour.
4. Cover in a bowl in the refrigerator (can be left for up to 2 days).
5. Shape and let rise $1\frac{1}{2}$ to 2 hours until doubled and cut dough into 3 balls.
6. Roll each ball and cut into 12 pieces and place in greased muffin pans.
7. Cover with towel and let rise $1\frac{1}{2}$ to 2 hours (until doubled).
8. Bake in 400° oven for about 10 minutes.

Cut-Out Cookies (makes several dozen cookies)

1. Beat 1 cup of shortening, 1 cup of sugar, and 1 egg with a mixer.
2. Add $\frac{1}{2}$ cup of milk and 1 teaspoon of vanilla.
3. Mix 2 teaspoons cream of tartar and 1 teaspoon baking soda into $3\frac{1}{2}$ cups flour.
4. Add flour mixture to other ingredients and beat again.
5. Cover and put in refrigerator for 1 hour.
6. Roll dough with rolling pin until thin.
7. Cut with cookie cutter.
8. Bake on cookie sheets in 350° oven for 10 to 12 minutes.
9. Frost if you like.

All these bakery items freeze well! Enjoy!!!

Source: Killy, S. (1997). *Baking Up a Storm! Kramer Kids Kitchen Bakery.* [booklet]. Oxford, OH: Kramer Elementary School. Reprinted with permission.

chapter 13

The Secondary School Environment

Adolescents place great emphasis on belonging to their peer group (Santrock, 1996). They want their peers to recognize them as valued members of the school community. One of the ways students become valued members of the school community is by participating with their peers in school activities. These activities meet a wide range of students' interests, talents, and aspirations. For example, students who like athletics can play on varsity or intramural teams, aid coaching staff as student managers, or express school spirit as cheerleaders. School-sponsored social events, such as dances after home football games and the prom, rely heavily on student participation in planning, setup, and cleanup. All schools have extracurricular student organizations, such as the art club, AFS (American Field Service), and Key Club, where interested students can pursue their academic interests outside the formal constraints of the academic program.

Students with moderate to severe disabilities are no exception. They want to belong in a peer group and be recognized as valued members of the school community. This can be a problem when teachers and administrators overlook students with special needs in these school experiences that occur outside of the general education core academic classroom. Sometimes, it appears as though having a developmental disability prevents students from enjoying sports or going to school dances with other students. They need to have opportunities to participate in school organizations and events with their nondisabled peers (Bender, Brannan, & Verhoven, 1984). As a teacher, you need to know how to make the full range of school experiences available to all students.

WHAT YOU WILL LEARN IN THIS CHAPTER

In this chapter, you will learn how to include secondary education students with moderate to severe disabilities in the school community. The chapter covers both formal instructional programs and informal interactions that take place in secondary schools. You will discover some of the academic and nonacademic activities available in the larger school environment.

The first section details applied curricula in the formal instructional programs typically found at the secondary level. In this section, you will learn how academic skills are addressed in a variety of models of applied curricula appropriate for all students at the secondary level and how to teach students in these contexts. The models discussed in this section include vocational education, work study, Tech Prep, and in-school service learning.

Second, we describe applied curricular projects that can be developed for all students in secondary schools. You will learn how to develop and implement two such projects: a restaurant and a laundry service. The section provides an extensive discussion about how to run the actual businesses in the school.

Finally in the third section we address school-sponsored social activities commonly provided for secondary students. These offerings include supervised and nonsupervised extracurricular activities that take place at school. The activities described in this section include school clubs, sports, lunch, and special events. Throughout this chapter, you will learn to integrate instruction in the areas of communication, behavior, social adjustment, mobility, and personal independence into academic and nonacademic school activities.

FORMAL INSTRUCTIONAL PROGRAMS AS A SOURCE OF APPLIED CURRICULA

There are several formal instructional programs for students outside of the traditional academic general education classroom in the school. As you learned in Chapter 4, applied curriculum can be taught through activities and projects implemented in the school. You also learned about the School-to-Work Initiative push to implement project-based learning. At the secondary level, a variety of projects incorporate the school-to-work tenets (Lindstrom, Benz, & Johnson, 1997). These types of projects, found in career development programs, use applied instruction to connect what students learn in school with the workplace in order to create a link to business and to the students' future employment (Brolin, 1995; Wolfe & Harriot, 1997).

Some examples of activities and projects that can prepare secondary students in schools for the future could include building bookshelves for the school media center or publishing a school newspaper. Students building bookshelves learn measurement skills while they practice carpentry. Students working on the newspaper develop language arts skills as they write stories and interpersonal skills as they conduct interviews with members of the school community. Projects like these allow students to learn functional academic and employability skills.

> Remember, an applied curriculum places content in the context in which it will be used!

In Chapter 11, you learned about applied activities in general education classrooms, such as gaining knowledge about the stock market in economics or political campaigns in social studies. There are also several programs offered in schools at the secondary level other than the traditional academic programs such as English, math, and science. They include activities that allow students to engage in applied academics in the larger school community.

School programs that deal with curriculum outside of the context of the traditional general education academic classroom are applied and emphasize teaching functional skills as well as academic content. In these programs, concepts are taught through hands-on practice using real-life work experiences. For example, students in a business program who work in a school store learn skills that help them handle dissatisfied customers in a professional manner, keep track of inventory, and develop marketing strategies. At the same time, they learn math skills to be able to balance a spreadsheet, to collect money and give change, and to develop a store budget.

The applied activities students engage in might be organized through any of the career education programs that prepare students to transition from school to work (Brolin, 1995; Wehman, 1997b). As you learned in Chapter 4, part of career education at the secondary education level involves exploration and preparation for work and life in the community through in-school activities. Vocational education, Tech Prep, work-study, and service learning projects all offer hands-on applied academic experiences that allow students to explore options and prepare for work and community life. In the following paragraphs, we discuss each of these models in greater depth.

> Remember, career education includes applied academic and career development components in all aspects of school life.

Vocational Education

The most common and well-known applied programs in high schools, vocational education programs offer a series of courses that give students academic knowledge as well as general and specific work skills to prepare them for community membership and occupations other than those requiring a baccalaureate degree (Ohio Rehabilitation Services Commission, 1997). The vocational education programs in many schools address one or more core areas, such as computer technology, office education, media, electronics, welding, diversified health, cosmetology, auto mechanics, marketing education, graphic design, and travel. The Carl D. Perkins Vocational and Applied Technology Education Amendments of 1990 support vocational education programs with federal funds and require participating schools to provide students with disabilities equal access to the programs.

Vocational education uses functional curriculum to prepare students for employment and independent living (Wircenski & Sarkees, 1990). For example, the auto mechanics teacher creates a garage to teach students how to repair actual cars that are brought in to the school to be fixed. In a commercial art program, students learn drawing and layout techniques that also increase their geometry skills by measuring the area of a wall to know how much paint is needed. A student with more severe disabilities might focus on recognizing the basic shape of different furniture pieces and placing them within the room space using a computer software program. The practical application of concepts with hands-on experiences and the support students give each other through teamwork make learning both concrete and meaningful. This approach to instruction makes learning accessible for students with moderate to severe disabilities and provides an excellent opportunity to include these students in the vocational education program (West & Taymans, 1998). You can provide support both to the students with moderate to severe disabilities as they participate in vocational classes and to the vocational teachers as they make curricular adaptations for those students (Hazelkorn & Lombard, 1991).

Work-Study Programs

Another model that focuses on teaching functional skills at the secondary level is work study. Both typical students and students with disabilities participate in work-study programs (Miller & Bragg, 1985; Wisniewski, Alper, & Schloss, 1991). Students who participate in a work-study program in the school usually work for at least one period each day. They have jobs in various

locations around the school such as washing dishes in the cafeteria, reshelving books in the library, sorting mail and answering the phone in the main office, or sweeping and emptying trash in the hallways under the supervision of the custodial staff. Sometimes these students work with classroom teachers as student aides. They may also hold jobs in the community.

Sarah, a student with moderate to severe disabilities, works in the school library. She dusts the shelves and straightens the books. She also is responsible for logging out all the computers located in the library that are not being used. She is a friendly student who is eager to participate in any way she can.

Francie is a typical student whose job in the library is checking out books. Sarah often asks Francie to help her straighten the high shelves because she has difficulty reaching them from her wheelchair. This collaboration has led to a growing personal relationship between the two girls. They have discovered that they both like to listen to the music of 'N Sync and the Backstreet Boys. They also have the same lunch period and are spending time together in the cafeteria. Next week, they plan to go to the mall together with some other friends.

In an inclusive work-study program, students with disabilities and typical students can work alongside each other while they meet the responsibilities of their own job descriptions or they can work collaboratively as a partnership to share the work. For example, a typical student and a student with a disability might share student office worker duties. During the first period of the school day, they collect and record all the attendance slips and teacher messages. They collect the slips together, or in a large school, each student collects slips in a different wing of the building. In that case, a student with a moderate to severe disability could use cards with teachers' pictures and room numbers on them to recognize the teachers and rooms where she is assigned to collect slips. After the slips are collected, one student reads the names of absent students listed from the collected slips while the other student marks the names on the master list.

Tech Prep

Tech Prep is one more example of the applied programs offered at the secondary level to both students with and without disabilities (Lombard, Hazelkorn, & Miller, 1995). The Tech Prep Education Act (Title III of the Carl D. Perkins Vocational and Applied Technology Education Amendments of 1990) authorized the funding of Tech Prep education programs. Tech Prep is a planned course of study that leads either to an associate of arts (AA) degree or 2-year certificate from a postsecondary vocational school. The program begins in the last 2 years of high school and continues for 2 years of postsecondary education. The curriculum includes technical preparation and applied academic course work in a specific career area, such as agriculture or health (Dutton, 1995). It focuses on in-school experiences that develop students' critical thinking and problem-solving skills through hands-on activi-

---

OCCUPATIONAL WORK ADJUSTMENT (OWA) AND OCCUPATIONAL WORK EXPERIENCE (OWE) PROGRAMS IN OHIO

An example of a work-study program can be found in Ohio's Occupational Work Adjustment and Occupational Work Experience (OWA/OWE) programs. At the middle school level, the entire OWA program takes place in the school. At the high school level, the program has two components. In the 9th grade, the OWA program adds community work sites to the school experiences. OWA is replaced by the OWE program for 11th- and 12th-grade students who are at risk of dropping out of school (Ohio Rehabilitation Services Commission, 1997). The OWE program is similar to the OWA program, but it offers a wider range of job experiences to its students and those jobs are always in the community.

If a student wishes to participate in the OWA program, both the student and parent must give signed permission. Students must be at least 14 years old because they need a work permit from the state. They work one or more hours a day on the school grounds, or in the community if they are at the high school level, get paid hourly for the time they work, and can have their own bank accounts in which to deposit their earnings. The in-school work component includes jobs such as custodial worker, cafeteria worker, teacher's aide doing clerical jobs and peer tutoring, and media center or office helper. The community-based components of the OWA and OWE programs are described in detail in Chapter 14.

Both the OWA and OWE programs also have a classroom component. Although students take reading, languages arts, and other core academic classes in the general education program, they have at least one vocational class with the OWA teacher. Typical activities in the vocational class include writing applications, conducting job searches with the newspaper, participating in mock interviews, and practicing other employability skills. Students receive academic credits as well as credits for the work experiences. (M. Julian, OWE Coordinator for Bulter County Joint Vocational School at Talawanda High School, personal communication, July 27, 1998)

ties and group work as well as workplace experiences that ultimately lead to employment. Tech Prep programs, like other federally funded programs, are open to and provide supports for students with disabilities (Dutton, 1995). However, the academic component in Tech Prep programs can be highly technical, so participation may be more limited for some students with moderate to severe disabilities. Through partial participation, those students may be able to concentrate on only certain aspects of the course work. To illustrate, a student might participate in only part of a high school business education program. The vocational education teacher and the special education teacher collaborate to determine the portions of the curriculum the student needs to learn in order to develop skills as a file clerk in an office. They create a program for the student that is a modified version of just the filing component of the business education curriculum. One of the activities might be to learn how to file papers by sorting color-coded pages in a preliminary breakdown by subject and then placing them in the corresponding color-coded file folders for a co-worker who then does more extensive filing by specific name, company, or other descriptor. For example, the filing work for student paperwork or yearbook pictures first might be color coded by first-year students, sophomores, juniors, and seniors and then sorted by each student's homeroom number.

Vocational education, work-study programs, and Tech Prep are examples of career education programs. Students with moderate to severe disabilities can be integrated into the school community through participation in any of these programs. Because all three programs are functional and emphasize teaching students employability skills, they offer an excellent opportunity for including these students.

In-School Service Learning

Service learning provides another opportunity for students with moderate to severe disabilities to participate in school activities with typical students. As you learned in Chapter 4, the traditional service learning model involves projects that take place in community settings. You will learn more about community-based service learning in Chapter 14. Projects implemented within the school community also can utilize some of the service learning strategies. Although service learning within the school does not represent a specific instructional program, it does represent an approach to learning that is application-based and can be implemented in almost any curriculum. An in-school service learning project allows the participants to provide a service to members of the school community while they practice skills identified in the academic curriculum. For example, the curriculum in a marketing education class supports activities for the benefit of the school community as they produce and disseminate a school newsletter or type the labels and prepare the envelopes for mailing graduation diplomas. At the same time they address concepts connected to the academic content areas such as current events (social studies); writing and organizational layout for conveying information (English); issues of distribution, use, and conservation of resources and cost of production (economics). Some of those components also can be found in the breakfast and laundry service projects we describe later in this chapter. For example, students deal with the cost of materials and distribution of resources as well as organizational skills while they make a quick breakfast option available for students and staff during the early morning rush of getting ready for the school day. Not only do they meet the learning objectives in the academic curriculum, but they also have the satisfaction of knowing they are helping others start their day efficiently and effectively.

> Remember, service learning is an educational experience that provides a service to others as well as social interaction between the students and the individuals they serve.

As you learned in Chapters 10 and 11, service learning can take place in the classroom in the form of activities like peer tutoring, but service learning can also involve the larger school community. Service learning in this form involves a project that provides a service to the entire school rather than a benefit to just one group of students in only one classroom. For example, in schools that offer an in-school educational channel, a group of interested students from different classes can provide a video news service for the school. The students develop writing skills and improve oral communication skills while they learn to write concise but informative news copy. They edit and post club announcements, sports teams schedules, and homework assignments for individual teachers. They videotape the announcements in the morning so they can be broadcast later in the day whenever it is convenient or appropriate in the school schedule. The students also can use the video to critique their speech delivery techniques as well as the content and quality of the news they are disseminating to the school community. They can even put together a "bloopers" tape to enjoy and learn from or a "greatest highlights" tape to celebrate their achievements.

Another example of a service learning project appropriate for secondary education students that could take place in the school community might be an educational campaign to prevent drinking-related accidents during prom activities. In this case, the student members of the honor society and Students Against Driving Drunk (SADD) club in one high school might work together with their faculty advisers to develop and distribute posters, present a school assembly, and give educational announcements over the public address system during the week before the prom.

Students with moderate to severe disabilities can make significant contributions to the school community through participation in schoolwide service learning projects. Service learning offers an excellent opportunity for these students to give something back to the school community (Everington & Stevenson, 1994). One of the advantages of participation in service learning projects is that the contributions students with moderate to severe disabilities make can change the perceptions of others about their capabilities and the supports they need. An added benefit from this kind of activity is an increase in the status level of the students with moderate to severe disabilities. As they provide a valuable service to the school, members of the general school community value them. As others treat them as valued members of the school community, their self-esteem increases (Dever & Knapczyk, 1997).

 INCLUSIVE SCHOOLWIDE APPLIED CURRICULUM PROJECTS

A variety of inclusive schoolwide applied curriculum projects incorporate some service learning strategies with the employability skills preparation component of the school-to-work initiative. They use a zero exclusion approach in which general education and special education teachers work together to create projects for *all* students who want to participate (Schleien & Green, 1992). These projects allow both typical students and students with moderate to severe disabilities to develop interpersonal skills, improve their academic knowledge, and prepare for a career while they provide a valuable service to other members of the school community.

The Classy Cleaners and the Breakfast Place are examples of this kind of in-school project that embraces much of the school-to-work and service learning philosophies. The Breakfast Place is a restaurant that serves the entire high school community (Hamill & Dunlevy, 1993). The Classy Cleaners is a laundry service that operates for the benefit of interested faculty, staff, and various school programs. Additionally, the Classy Cleaners might increase its service component by providing cost-free support to a local thrift center that collects and distributes clothing to needy families, and the Breakfast Place employees might use the skills they learned in the school setting to volunteer at a local food bank. Both projects are school-based enterprises known as customer service labs where students serve the school community through hands-on learning experiences in all aspects of the business (Hoerner & Wehrley, 1995).

The Classy Cleaners and the Breakfast Place also provide excellent examples of school-based applied curricula for secondary students with and without disabilities. The students have an opportunity to apply their academic learning in a real job setting. As you will discover in the following section, these projects operate in much the same way as the school store commonly found in most secondary schools. Descriptions of the two projects will give you concrete examples of inclusion at the secondary level by showing you how to bring students with and without disabilities together as employees who then regularly interact with a diverse group of customers. Typical students also can provide peer support that will enhance the instructional benefit for students with moderate to severe disabilities (Ryndak & Alper, 1996).

Credit for Participation

Any student can choose to take part in the restaurant and the laundry projects. Each project is offered as a business education course or other elective that best fits one of the school district's specific course descriptions. Students are given the appropriate letter grade and course credit for each term they participate. The grade is based on an average of the points students accumulate for how well they meet the teacher's expectations related to being on time and on task at work, executing the responsibilities of their job description, collaborating effectively with co-workers, and interacting effectively with customers (Staub et al., 1996). Students also can develop an employment résumé that highlights these experiences. The résumé may increase the

student's opportunities for having a part-time after-school job and gaining full-time work after graduation. They also can be connected to the students' school-to-work career portfolios that you learned about in Chapter 6.

Scheduling

At the secondary level, scheduling schoolwide applied curriculum projects can present some challenges. The traditional model of scheduling a class each day for less than an hour may mean either (1) dividing every class period so the first part is devoted to providing the service and second part is allotted to record keeping functions or (2) providing the service on certain days of the week (Monday, Tuesday, and Thursday) and doing the record keeping on other days (Wednesday and Friday). The most advantageous circumstance would be to provide the service and do the related record keeping during the same period of time.

Many schools have replaced the traditional model of scheduling with block scheduling, which allows a class to be offered only on certain days of the week but for longer periods of time than a class using the traditional scheduling format (Queen & Gaskey, 1997). This is the optimum situation because it provides a sufficient period of time for each class to both offer the service and attend to record keeping.

Whether schoolwide applied curriculum projects operate on a daily or block schedule, rotate the students' jobs on a scheduled basis so all students have an opportunity to learn new skills as well as experience all aspects of the project. By rotating all of the jobs every few weeks, each student gets to participate fully in the learning experience.

The Breakfast Place Restaurant

Although it takes place in the school rather than in the community where you would find most restaurants, the Breakfast Place actually operates like a real restaurant where the employees provide food, exchange money, and serve customers. As a result, it provides a secure environment in which student workers, both typical students and those with moderate to severe disabilities, can learn employability skills. The students get support to develop those skills while they work at a speed and difficulty level appropriate to their own needs.

The purpose of the restaurant is to integrate academic learning with real-life experience in order to teach students skills needed to live independently as well as to get and keep employment in the community. For example, the money management skills that the students learn in the restaurant as they make change for customers will generalize to skills needed in community settings, such as making change for the bus ride to work. In addition to having this functional emphasis, the restaurant project focuses on working as a group while meeting the needs of each individual student. Therefore, the organization of the restaurant and the restaurant jobs are defined so all students can make meaningful contributions to the functioning of the restaurant at their particular ability levels.

They must work cooperatively with each other and interact appropriately with their customers.

Restaurant employees punch a time clock or sign a log-in sheet and perform specific jobs according to their abilities and interests. Tasks include filling orders, operating the restaurant appliances, handling money and supplies, cleaning, maintaining inventory and payroll records, and dealing with customers. The student workers also record, fill, and deliver orders from charge customers throughout the school. Items for sale might include coffee, tea, hot chocolate, milk, juice, fresh fruit, donuts, bagels, toaster tarts, snack crackers, and granola bars.

The Breakfast Place operates for the benefit of the entire school. Customers may be students or staff members. They come to the Breakfast Place to purchase their food or staff members may choose to have orders delivered regularly to their own classrooms or offices and to pay weekly. Student employees accept the weekly order, deliver the food, present the staff member with a weekly bill, receive payment, and deliver change.

The restaurant can be located in a classroom or in the school cafeteria. Unfortunately, the

---

Marie uses an assistive device to help her work in the restaurant. The device is a special tray with three bins attached to the lap tray on her wheelchair. Marie's mother made it out of three plastic storage containers that she nailed to a thin plywood board. The board is fixed to Marie's wheelchair tray with clamps.

Marie uses the device in several ways. When a customer needs an item, such as a granola bar, delivered to his table from behind the serving counter, Marie brings it to him using her special tray. She also can assist in stocking the display with this device. For example, Marie can help Samuel, a typical student who is the supplies stocker, keep the serving counter display full. Either Samuel can place the needed items in the containers on Marie's chair or Marie can use her motorized chair to get the supplies. In the supply room, food supplies are kept in elevated bins purchased from a grocery supply company. The supply bins have chutes at the bottom and are situated so Marie can maneuver her chair beneath them. Marie can open the chute with a lever, and a controlled amount of the restaurant supplies will drop into the plastic storage containers attached to her tray. When each of her containers is full, Marie returns to Samuel, who can then place the materials in the display counter. With the support of her assistive device, Marie is improving her fine motor skills and developing competencies in the areas of independence and mobility.

school cafeteria is not the most ideal location. Conflicts may arise over issues such as when the space can be used as a restaurant, where to store the inventory items for each operation, and how to keep the money for each operation separate. Consequently, the best location for the restaurant would be in its own room with facilities not generally found in a typical classroom such as a refrigerator, toaster oven, and tables for seating. A large school even may allow the restaurant to operate in two locations at the same time.

Preparation and Planning. Much of the success of a restaurant project depends on thorough preparation before its opening. Students who will become employees, the staff and other students in the school who are the potential customers, and the physical and logistical requirements of the restaurant must be considered in the planning. For example, be sure to contact the health inspector prior to opening any food service. Because no food will actually be cooked in the restaurant, a phone conversation with the inspector about how food items will be stored, dated for freshness, and discarded according to expiration dates will probably be sufficient. If an on-site inspection is still needed, it could be conducted in conjunction with the normal inspections of the school cafeteria.

Preparing the students is an important task. The restaurant environment should encourage students to be as independent and responsible as possible. If independence and personal responsibility have not been stressed, you will want to help your students develop these qualities so they will have a positive and successful experience (see Chapter 15 for a detailed discussion on developing self-determination skills). The students should be well trained and confident enough to perform their duties without constant intervention from you or your assistant. They feel valuable when they have accomplished something through their own efforts. However, some students may need some level of ongoing support. For example, job shadowing experiences give students an opportunity to observe

an employee's responsibilities and contribute to the work. Assistance can fade as students are able to perform the tasks independently or with the aid of assistive devices.

When students are ready to begin specific preparation, post want ads on a bulletin board outside the restaurant. In the context of problem-solving activities, discuss the available positions and their requirements with the potential student employees. The students then make decisions about applying for the jobs that interest them and they fill out job applications (see Figure 13–1).

After you conduct interviews and aptitude tests for jobs, students are hired for jobs based on their interests and skills. For example, you interview a student interested in working as a cashier to determine that he is friendly and has good communication skills. You also test the prospective cashier to determine whether she has the coin recognition and counting skills necessary to collect money and give change or if she will need the support of a peer buddy while she learns those skills.

The specific jobs will vary from one setting to another, depending on the items to be sold, the number of customers anticipated, and the availability of students who can fill various kinds of positions. You should ensure that both typical students and students with disabilities are employed in the program. One way to do that might be for a typical student to provide support by sharing a job with a student who has a disability.

Daily Restaurant Activities. The Breakfast Place is open for approximately an hour at the beginning of the school day, starting as students and staff arrive at school. Daily activities begin as soon as the teacher arrives at school. For example, the teacher receives the donut delivery that the student employees have already placed with a local bakery for a daily delivery. The number of donuts needed each day will depend on the average daily sales potential. This presents an excellent opportunity for teaching functional math, such as estimation and calculation.

FIGURE 13–1   Sample Employment Application

Employment Application

Position being applied for: _____

Personal Information:
Name _____ Date of Birth _____/_____/_____ Sex _____
Address: Street _____
         City/State/Zip _____
Phone No. _____ Social Security No. _____-_____-_____

Employment Record:
Job Held _____ Address _____
Employer _____ _____

Job Held _____ Address _____
Employer _____ _____

References:
Name _____ Address _____
Phone No. _____ _____

Name _____ Address _____
Phone No._____ _____

In Case of Emergency:
Call _____ Relationship _____ Phone _____

When the student employees arrive, they clock in using individual time cards, wash their hands, and perform a variety of setup tasks. This is an opportunity for you to teach functional health skills, such as personal hygiene and food handling. Because the employees do not all arrive at the same time, you may need to help perform some of the following duties until everyone is at work.

Possible Setup Tasks:

1. Start the coffeemaker.
2. Wash tables the eat-in customers will use.
3. Sweep the floor in the restaurant area if it is not thoroughly clean from the previous day.
4. Put fruit, snack crackers, granola bars, and other foods where the customers can view them.

5. Put toaster tarts by the toaster and indicate the available flavors on the menu board.
6. Put disposable cups, lids, stirrers, cream, sugar, tea, hot chocolate, and artificial sweetener packets by the coffeemaker.
7. Get the cash box and receipt box out.

During the hour the restaurant is open, an outside maintenance person patrols the corridors in the vicinity of the restaurant and cleans up any debris left by the customers. As customers begin to arrive, an employee can act as the restaurant greeter in similar fashion to the job performed by employees who work for businesses such as Wal-Mart.

One or two delivery people take orders to teachers, administrators, and other staff members who have placed routine charge orders. For

Each morning, Susie greets customers as they enter the restaurant and thanks them when they leave. For her own reference, she has a sign with the words "hello" and "thank you" written on it to help her remember what to say. Her sign also has a picture of a cheerful face to remind her to smile and make eye contact with the customers as she talks with them. Susie is developing competencies in the areas of communication and interpersonal skills.

example, a teacher might order black coffee delivered to his classroom every morning. Another teacher might order tea with artificial sweetener delivered to her classroom each day with an apple delivered only on Tuesday and Thursday. Other employee duties include filling out order forms, toasting tarts as they are requested, preparing hot drinks, delivering juice or milk, and making certain the restaurant remains clean.

After customers receive their food, the cashier takes their payment and gives them appropriate change. The cashier then puts the money in the cash box and the order form (which now serves as a receipt) in the receipt box until they are used for calculating the daily sales. Duties like these give students the opportunity to learn and practice academic skills.

While the restaurant is open, the restaurant student manager encourages the employees to take responsibility for the restaurant operation. The manager creates a realistic work environment by enforcing explicit work rules and providing support when needed. The work rules should be prominently posted with visual cues for employees to reference (see Figure 13–2).

Record Keeping and Other After-Hours Activities. The after-hours duties begin when the CLOSED sign is posted on the restaurant door. Employees take inventory, count earnings and rectify them with the cash box, and complete various forms (see Figure 13–3). After-hours duties can also include cleaning tables, counters, and floors, storing food items, and washing

Students perform a variety of setup tasks.

FIGURE 13–2   Sample Work Rules

The Breakfast Place Work Rules

1. Employees who are not doing their work and/or are disrupting the smooth functioning of the restaurant will clock out. They will not receive pay for time they do not work.
2. Employees who forget to clock in or out sacrifice one fourth of the day's wages.
3. Employees who ruin food items through negligence are expected to pay for them out of their wages.

Source: Hamill, L., & Dunlevy, A. (1993). *The Breakfast Place.* Portland, ME: J. Weston Walch. Reprinted with permission.

dirty utensils. As with any other instructional activity, these after-hours duties can be leveled and adapted to meet the individual abilities of the students. When their after-hours responsibilities are completed, the employees clock out.

Some record keeping activities may occur regularly but not every day. For example, each Friday students collect payment from the charge customers and add those customers' weekly re-

ceipts to the inventory count. Every other Friday, the payroll clerks will complete payroll forms and on the following Monday they distribute paychecks. The paychecks are prepared by a student treasurer with support from the student accountant and signed by the teacher. The student accountant is responsible for supervising the activities of the payroll clerks and the treasurer. The accountant periodically checks their work to make sure they are preparing all of the paychecks and payroll forms correctly. If you have students prepare a cost/profit analysis sheet or a supply needs analysis sheet, those forms should be completed regularly, perhaps once or twice a month.

An additional after-hours restaurant activity for both typical students and students with disabilities would be to develop, or update, a résumé highlighting their work experience. The student résumés can be connected to the student's school-to-work career portfolio that you learned about in Chapter 4. They also can be connected to other transition from school activities you will learn more about in Chapter 15.

Evaluation of Work.   Each day, all student employees complete self-evaluations of their restaurant work. You, or those student workers

FIGURE 13–3   Inventory Objectives

Inventory Objectives for Students Functioning at Four Levels

1. Students working in group 1 count items such as apples, oranges, milk and juice containers, and granola bars. They count items such as tea bags, coffee pouches, and sugar packets and put a specified number of each in a container to be the initial supply for the following day.
2. The students in group 2 count the number of each item sold according to the receipts and compare these amounts with the count of the actual food items to make certain the amounts are correct.
3. The group 3 students count the money in the cash box and remove any amount above $20.00 (ten $1.00 bills, $5.00 in quarters, $3.00 in dimes, and $2.00 in nickels) needed for the next day. (The cash box is then locked and stored in a locked closet or cabinet or the school safe. Any money not needed for the next day's cash is placed in a school account that has been designated for use in the restaurant.)
4. The students working in group 4 total the sales indicated on the receipts and check the total against the amount taken from the cash box.

Source: Adapted from Hamill, L., & Dunlevy, A. (1993). *The Breakfast Place.* Portland, ME: J. Weston Walch. Reprinted with permission.

> Note: Banking at a local bank adds another dimension to this activity. It allows students to learn to make deposits and to interpret monthly bank statements (which can be sent to the school). Learning to rectify their bank accounts will assist students in generalizing personal money management skills.

who have finished their own evaluation forms, can assist students who have difficulty or are unable to read the forms. Review all the evaluations as they are turned in and point out any observed discrepancies.

You should also assess the students' job performance. You may want to ask other staff members who have regular contact with the restaurant employees to evaluate them. These evaluations are done by periodic direct observation or written summary of the quality of work performed.

Advertising.   Periodic advertising can help generate interest in the restaurant. Announcing the introduction of weekly billing is one way to attract new customers and remind people about the restaurant. Student employees can post advertising flyers on bulletin boards and distribute them to the staff several times each semester. Restaurant information can be included in the regular morning announcements. In addition, advertising flyers and announcements can be posted on a Breakfast Place Web site, which also could be used for taking orders over the Internet. Various coupons can be made available to students and staff. Both students and teachers can purchase and give coupons as gifts, and teachers can give coupons to deserving students in their classes as incentives or rewards.

Connections with General Education Academic Classes.   General education academic classes also can have opportunities to participate in the restaurant project. Academic classroom activities could provide support for restaurant activities. For example, an economics class might aid in a restaurant advertising campaign. The economics students could determine consumer trends by developing, implementing, and analyzing a market survey that asks students about the food items they prefer and why they use the restaurant. Vocational education classes also could participate in activities that support the restaurant project. For example, a home economics class might design and make aprons for the employees to wear, and a commercial art class could design and produce advertising posters to place around the school.

Dealing with customers in the restaurant also can help students develop social skills. They talk with customers when they take and deliver food orders. The students can then generalize those skills to the interactions they have with students in other settings and increase their opportunities to develop friendships.

 Hank delivers coffee and an apple each morning to Ms. Franklin, the math teacher. Hank always says hello to Ms. Franklin, who usually takes a minute or two to have a friendly conversation with him. After several weeks, Ms. Franklin gets to know quite a bit about Hank. During one of their morning chats she discovers that Hank wants to learn how to use the computer his family has at home. She asks him if he would like to participate in her Introduction to Computers course. Hank thinks he would enjoy her class, so the following semester he enrolls in the course.

Hank is developing competencies in the areas of communication and interpersonal skills. His restaurant position also has provided him with the opportunity to enroll in a course that will allow him to develop computer skills and add to his employability.

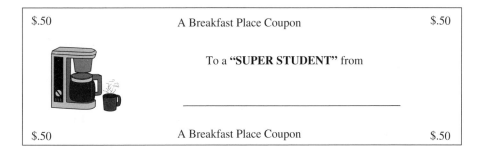

| $.50 | A Breakfast Place Coupon | $.50 |

To a **"SUPER STUDENT"** from

_____

| $.50 | A Breakfast Place Coupon | $.50 |

| $.50 | A Breakfast Place Coupon | $.50 |

A holiday gift for you from

_____

| $.50 | A Breakfast Place Coupon | $.50 |

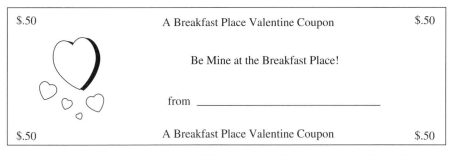

| $.50 | A Breakfast Place Valentine Coupon | $.50 |

Be Mine at the Breakfast Place!

from _____

| $.50 | A Breakfast Place Valentine Coupon | $.50 |

Source: Adapted from Hamill, L., & Dunlevy, A. (1993). *The Breakfast Place*. Portland, ME: J. Weston Walch. Reprinted with permission.

Peer Supports. The restaurant, like the other career development programs discussed in this chapter, provides an opportunity for students to support their peers. Because many of the activities are repetitive and hands-on, the restaurant is an excellent environment for peer teaching. For example, a student who has some money skills and has learned to operate the cash register can teach money math to a less skilled student while he supports that student in learning to operate the cash register.

Note: We wish to acknowledge the contributions of Ann Dunlevy to the section about the restaurant project. She helped develop and wrote much of the text for the J. Weston Walch publication of *The Breakfast Place: A Group Activity for Individual Needs* (Hamill & Dunlevy, 1993). A large portion of that text is reproduced in similar form here.

After the restaurant customers placed their orders, Penny brought them their food from the refrigerator. She learned job skills like saying hi to the customers and asking them if they had everything they needed. Roxanna was a typical student who came to the restaurant nearly every morning and always chatted with Penny. After Roxanna had gotten to know Penny in the restaurant, she sat down with her in the lunchroom. Roxanna continued to sit with Penny during lunch for the next few weeks. Then she invited Penny to join her to eat lunch with her friends who were sitting at a different table. The social skills and self-esteem that Penny developed working in the restaurant helped her feel comfortable joining Roxanna's group and building these new friendships.

Penny is developing competencies in the areas of communication and interpersonal skills. She also is learning to handle food properly and to perform her duties in a timely manner that will increase her employability skills.

John is the restaurant cashier. He takes the customers' payments and gives them change. He also supports Bobby, the assistant cashier, who is learning how to count change. During a slow time in the restaurant when there are only one or two customers, Bobby collects and counts the money while John checks and encourages him. Bobby then gives the customer change after John helps him count out the correct amount.

John and Bobby are developing their math skills in the areas of computation and problem solving. They also are developing competencies in the areas of communication and interpersonal skills when they interact with customers, and they are developing employability skills as they learn to cooperate as co-workers.

The Classy Cleaners Laundry Service

Another example of a schoolwide curriculum project is the Classy Cleaners laundry service. If there are washers and dryers in the school, they can provide students with a different business that offers students another opportunity to provide a service while they experience school-to-work preparation and learn specific job skills in a supportive instructional environment at the secondary level. The laundry service, like the restaurant project, also can provide an excellent in-school placement for work-study students. If the school has both the Breakfast Place restaurant and the Classy Cleaners laundry in operation, it may be preferable to house both the washers and dryers and the restaurant equipment in one place. The washers and dryers can even be purchased with profits from the restaurant, and a restaurant employee can be assigned periodically to clean the aprons, towels, and other washable items.

Preparation and Planning. Preparation for the Classy Cleaners laundry service project is similar to the preparation we described for the Breakfast Place. Like the restaurant employees, the laundry service employees should be well trained and confident to perform their duties as independently as possible. Bulletin board postings and class discussions can inform students about the requirements of available laundry service jobs. Students can fill out the same application form as the one used for the Breakfast Place. Conduct interviews and any needed aptitude tests before hiring the students. The laundry, like the restaurant, should include both typical students and students with disabilities in all aspects of its operation from keeping payroll records to picking up and delivering laundry. A typical student can provide natural support by sharing job responsibilities with a student who has a disability. For example, a typical student and a student in a wheelchair might work together to fold a customer's clean clothes after they are washed. However, the typical student might be responsible for moving the customer's clothes through the washer and dryer because the student in the wheelchair has difficulty reaching in and out of the machines. At the same time, the student in the wheelchair records the order on a computer spreadsheet to ensure that no items are forgotten and it gets delivered to the correct person.

Daily Laundry Service Activities. Students run the laundry business as a service to faculty and to other school programs. The Classy Cleaners can wash the gym clothes the physical education faculty has available for students to use when they forget to bring their own clothes for gym class or the aprons and dishtowels used by the cafeteria staff. Interested faculty and staff members also can bring in their laundry from home to be cleaned. They would either drop off their laundry at the Classy Cleaners when they arrive at school in the morning and pick up their cleaned clothes at the end of the school day or they would schedule the day before they want to have a laundry service employee pick up their dirty laundry and return it cleaned.

Laundry service employees clock in and out and perform the duties needed to run a laundry service. They accept the dirty laundry from customers before first period begins in the morning and they return the cleaned laundry during the final period of the school day. Although they only interact with customers at the beginning and the end of school, the employees operate the laundry several periods during

Mr. Fredrick, the social studies teacher, and Ms. Banks, the French teacher, bring their sheets and towels to school with them every Thursday morning. Betty, a student employee of the Lakeview Middle School Classy Cleaners, goes to Mr. Fredrick's classroom each Thursday, picks up his laundry, and takes it to the laundry service where students sort, wash, dry, and fold the laundry. Ms. Banks usually drops off a load of sheets and towels and her children's play clothes at the laundry on her way to her classroom. Frank, another student employee, returns Ms. Banks's clean laundry to her classroom and collects the $2.15 per load fee. Frank also returns Mr. Fredrick's clean laundry each week but, because Mr. Fredrick prefers to be billed once a month, Frank only presents a bill and collects money from Mr. Fredrick on the third Wednesday of each month.

Betty and Frank are gaining competencies in the areas of functional academics and independent living. Frank is developing math skills as he sorts laundry loads, measures detergent, and prepares customer bills. They both are developing independent living competencies as they learn to operate a washer and dryer. Reading competencies are addressed as they read clothing labels, directions on the detergent box, and special cleaning requests.

the school day. They sort, wash, dry, and fold clothes during the time they are assigned to be in the laundry facility until all the laundry is finished. Because different small groups of students are in the laundry each class period, individual students may perform only some of these tasks.

Tamika is a laundry sorter. She frequently asks others what to do. The teacher developed a set of pictures that show a pile of white clothes, a pile of light-colored clothes, and a pile of dark clothes. Tamika can use the pictures as a guide when she sorts the laundry into the appropriate piles for washing. The teacher and peers praise her each time she looks at the pictures instead of asking for help.

Tamika is increasing her math skills in the area of matching and problem solving. She is acquiring both life skills and employability skills as she learns how to do laundry. She is developing competencies in the areas of independence and self-management when she uses the set of pictures to determine what she should do rather than asking others to solve the problem for her.

FIGURE 13–4 Sample Work Rules

The Classy Cleaners Work Rules
1. Employees will use laundry equipment according to the directions in the operator's manual.
2. Employees will use detergents and other laundry chemicals only according to the directions on the containers.
3. Employees who are not doing their work and/or are disrupting the smooth functioning of the laundry will clock out. They will not receive pay for the time they are not working.
4. Employees who forget to clock in or out sacrifice one fourth of the day's wages.

If more laundry is brought in than can be accommodated in one day, the employees start with previously scheduled service and tell the customers who bring in unscheduled laundry that they are very busy and will clean the unscheduled laundry as soon as possible but it might not be ready until the next day.

Safety is an important issue in the laundry because employees use chemicals and work with heavy machinery. Consequently, post a list of rules prominently with visual cues. Like the restaurant rules, keep the rules for laundry service employees simple but explicit (see Figure 13–4).

 Delbert picks up and returns laundry to the middle school cafeteria staff and physical education faculty. The middle school is a big place and Delbert frequently gets lost or misses some of the rooms on his route. To help him become more independent, the teacher gives Delbert a map of the building with the delivery rooms marked. Charisa, the laundry's student manager, has taught him to follow the same pattern each day and to check off each room on his map as he collects or returns the laundry. The faculty and staff on his route give him positive feedback whenever he arrives independently.

Delbert is developing social studies skills in the use of maps. He also is developing employability skills as he learns to take direction from his supervisor and then begins to function independently. Charisa is developing both interpersonal and employability skills in the area of effective leadership. She learns to take personal responsibility and interact effectively while she provides appropriate support to co-workers.

FIGURE 13–5 Sample Financial Transaction Objectives

Financial Transaction Objectives for Students Functioning at Three Levels

1. Group 1 students count and record the money for the laundry that is brought into the Classy Cleaners.
2. The students in group 2 count and record the money for laundry that the employees pick up and deliver to customers.
3. The students in group 3 check the counts made by the students in groups 1 and 2 against the receipts and record the totals in the laundry service ledger book.

Other Laundry Service Activities. The laundry service employees also can contract with other school programs to provide a routinely scheduled service. For example, the cafeteria staff's aprons and towels could be cleaned every Tuesday and Friday, and the gym clothes from the physical education department could be cleaned every Monday.

Because the laundry service operates throughout the school day, there are no after-hours activities at the Classy Cleaners. However, employees do need to perform some routine duties when there are slow times during the day. For example, they need to collect and count the money received from customers (see Figure 13–5).The employees also need to keep the laundry service records up to date. These duties may not be necessary on a daily basis but they need to be performed regularly.

Possible Record Keeping Responsibilities:

1. Prepare charge customer bills and record payments.
2. Check supplies and, when necessary, fill out a request for new supplies.
3. Update records after restocking supplies.
4. Check time cards and prepare payroll checks.
5. Update bookkeeping records.

Evaluation of Work. Evaluate the employees of the Classy Cleaners laundry service in the same way the restaurant employees are evaluated. Employees fill out a self-evaluation form at the end of each work period and you routinely observe them and summarize the quality of their work (see Figure 13–6).

Advertising. An excellent way to let faculty and staff know about the availability of a student-run laundry service is to put an announcement in the morning bulletin to describe the various service options and costs (see Figure 13–7). For example, the cost of a load of laundry might be $2.00 if they drop it off and pick it up, but the same load costs $2.15 with the additional pickup and delivery service.

Peer Supports. Use the same kinds of peer supports in the Classy Cleaners that we described for the restaurant project. Knowledgeable employees can help less skilled workers develop competencies and they can model and encourage appropriate work behavior.

Both the Classy Cleaners and the Breakfast Place are nonacademic school environments where students come together in informal ways. They provide social meeting places for all students, like the hallways between classes where students visit with their friends. Like the hallways, these schoolwide applied curriculum projects provide casual atmospheres that are conducive for friendships to develop between typical students and students with moderate to severe disabilities. Although students should be encouraged to socialize with friends and acquaintances during slow periods, they need to learn to keep socializing to a minimum on the job during peak demand periods. You can perform a task analysis of the work demands during the period of restaurant or laundry service operation and then model the appropriate work and social behaviors to support those demands. Give students repeated opportunities to practice those behaviors and provide them with corrective feedback when necessary.

FIGURE 13-6   Sample Work Evaluation Form

Work Evaluation Form

Name _____ Date _____

_____ I was on time for work today.   _____ I was clean and well dressed.
_____ I worked the whole time.   _____ I did neat and careful work.
_____ I did what my supervisor told me.   _____ I kept my work area clean.
_____ I asked questions when I did not   _____ I got along with my co-workers.
         understand how to do the job.   _____ I worked quickly.
_____ I did not ask for help when I   _____ I finished the job I started.
         could do the job on my own.

I did the best job I could do at work today. Tomorrow I will be sure that I _____
_____ so I can do a good job and be a valued employee.
                                          Signed _____

(Note: Add picture cues, such as those produced by Mayer Johnson, for students who are limited- or nonreaders.)

Source: Adapted from Hamill, L., & Dunlevy, A. (1993). *The Breakfast Place.* Portland, ME: J. Weston Walch. Reprinted with permission.

FIGURE 13-7   Sample Advertising

Attention Faculty! Staff! Administrators!
Are you tired of doing laundry after working hard all day?

Let the Classy Cleaners laundry service do your laundry while you work. Bring us your laundry when you arrive at school and we'll have it ready for you at the end of the school day. The laundry is open for drop-off and pickup during the first and last periods of the day each Tuesday, Wednesday, and Thursday. The Classy Cleaners is located in room _____. For a small extra fee, we'll even pick it up and return it to your room.

        Cost per load:
            $2.00 when you bring it to us
            $2.15 when we pick up and deliver

If you would like to schedule laundry service or you would just like more information, please fill out the form below and place it in the box marked "Classy Cleaners" on the secretary's desk in the main office. We will get in touch with you as soon as possible. Thank you for your support!

Name _____ Room No. _____ Date _____

_____ I would like to schedule laundry service.
_____ I would like more information about the laundry service.

Maurice has a great deal of difficulty interacting with others and expressing himself when he is frustrated. He keeps track of inventory and stocking supplies that requires minimum interaction with customers. When he gets frustrated, he lashes out and has been known to strike others or destroy property. Maurice's co-workers are aware that difficulties in communication cause some of his outbursts. As a result, they are encouraging him to use more appropriate means to express his preferences and feelings.

Maurice is developing competencies in the areas of communication and interpersonal skills. With help from his peers, he is learning to control the reactions he has to the events and people around him.

 ## INFORMAL INTERACTIONS AND NONACADEMIC SCHOOL ACTIVITIES AS A SOURCE OF APPLIED CURRICULA

Informal student interactions at the secondary level are somewhat different than they are in the elementary school. Socialization in the elementary school occurs in all environments, including the classroom. For example, students in an elementary classroom typically sit on the rug together and share their favorite belongings. That kind of interaction does not happen in secondary classrooms, but students do have many opportunities to interact socially with one another outside of classes. Students spend time together in the hallways between classes, on the school bus, and in the cafeteria during lunch.

There are many nonacademic activities, such as school-sponsored clubs, sports, and other extracurricular events, that can make important contributions to the leisure time education of all students whether or not they have disabilities. An important part of being an adult involves enjoying leisure time activities that include social relationships. Many of the extracurricular activities sponsored by the school offer secondary education students the opportunity to learn how to enjoy their leisure time and to share in social activities with friends. For example, they often attend, or at least sit, with their peers rather than their families at school plays, pep assemblies, concerts, and sporting events.

> Remember, the 1997 IDEA amendments compel the IEP team to make sure the student is involved in extracurricular and other nonacademic activities (Bateman & Linden, 1998).

The interactions that take place in nonacademic settings in secondary schools not only promote friendships, but they also place demands on students to act appropriately (Knapczyk & Rodes, 1996). Like all students, students with

Students can often socialize with each other while working.

moderate to severe disabilities need to develop friendships and learn how to have rewarding social relationships (Westling & Fox, 2000). They need to have opportunities to be in nonacademic settings with their typical peers so they can develop the necessary interpersonal skills. Consequently, it is important for students with moderate to severe disabilities to participate in the social interactions that take place in the school hallways and during the lunch period. They also need to participate in organizations that fit their interests such as the wrestling club, the pom-pom corps, or the school play.

Social Life and Supervised Extracurricular Activities at the School

Students enjoy many school-sponsored activities and events that are not part of the formal academic curriculum. School-sponsored sports are particularly important for many adolescents. Being a member of the football team, the basketball team, or the cheerleading squad gives students prestige among their peers. These teams can easily include students with moderate to severe disabilities. One way to include a student would be as the team's equipment supervisor. The student gets a chance to participate in a sport she likes and, at the same time, she builds self-esteem by being associated with a prestigious group. This could be accomplished easily by enlisting the help of the team coach. With the coach's support, it also might be possible to work out an arrangement in which a typical student and a student with disabilities share the team manager's position. The students could work together, each taking responsibility for part of the manager's duties. As co-managers, each one could do the activities they are most able to perform well and they would have the opportunity to become friends.

School clubs provide another excellent opportunity for students with moderate to severe disabilities to build friendships with typical students who share similar interests (Sodac, 1997). For example, a student who joins the school weight lifting club can improve his body tone and strength in an environment where students do not compete against one another but each person works on developing his own skill level. Although performance is measured by individual improvement, the students do support each other. Consequently, the student with a disability might spot a typical student using a weight bar. In this case, the student not only gives support to someone else, but he also has the opportunity to develop a friendship.

Students with moderate to severe disabilities also can get involved in school events that occur on special occasions. For example, they can par-

Greg is a somewhat physically clumsy student with a moderate disability who loves baseball and dreams of being a major league player. Although it might be unrealistic for Greg to play professional ball, he can participate in an adult community baseball team for recreation. Being the manager on the high school baseball team gives Greg the opportunity to learn about the game and feel comfortable being part of a team. He can become friends with other members of the school baseball team who later might be Greg's teammates on a community team. Greg's high school friendship with them could ease any uncertainty he might feel about joining and participating on the community team.

Greg can develop competencies in interpersonal skills while he is learning how to foster physical wellness and enjoy leisure activities. As part of his responsibilities as team manager, Greg works on the schedules of game times and dates and team members' statistics, thus developing math skills as well.

ticipate in schoolwide fund-raising projects like selling holiday wreaths to raise money for the prom or working in the athletic boosters' concession stand during home football and basketball games. School assemblies also provide an opportunity for students to interact socially with the other students who sit near them.

Hank and Bobby both work as volunteers in the athletic boosters' concession stand during home football and basketball games where they use the skills they have developed working in the Breakfast Place Restaurant during school. Hank hands the customers the food they have ordered and Bobby collects their money with support from a booster who is the mother of one of the cheerleaders. Hank and Bobby are not only developing competencies in the areas of math computation and problem solving, communication and interpersonal skills, and cooperation with co-workers, but they are learning that those skills generalize to other settings as they transfer what they have learned in the restaurant to their work in the concession stand.

Social Life and Nonsupervised Activities at the School

Small group discussions and role playing allow you to illuminate authentic situations relevant to the student's personal experience (Antonello, 1996). You can provide instruction and model desired behaviors and then let the students problem-solve possible solutions and actually practice the appropriate social skills. For example, participating in role-playing scenarios helps adolescents understand how their nonverbal behaviors may interfere or reduce the success of their social interactions.

Sally, Josh, and Kara participate in a scenario to explore how standing too close to another person might create an uncomfortable situation.
Josh and Sally talk about an upcoming school dance and Kara tries to join them and enter the conversation. In her eagerness to be friendly, she stands too close to Sally and immediately begins talking to her. Josh is cut off in midsentence and Sally can no longer see him clearly because Kara is standing between them obstructing her view. After Kara becomes frustrated because the other two students try to move away from her and ignore what she is saying, they discuss and then recreate the scenario to practice more appropriate ways to enter a social conversation. Kara learns that when she stands back a little bit, the other person is more likely to want to include her in the conversation.

You also can develop individualized social stories to guide a student through appropriate social interactions. When the related situation occurs, the student reviews the written script, which should be composed of specific directions with accompanying picture cues, and acts out the actions identified in the social story to reinforce and practice the appropriate behavior (Turnbull et al., 1999).

The cafeteria, the school bus, and the hallways are places where students have opportunities to interact with each other without being organized or directed by adults. These unstructured settings in secondary schools are important social environments where adolescents establish their own peer groups and priorities. Students meet at their lockers before and after school, in the restrooms between classes, and eat together during lunch. They sit with their friends during assemblies and athletic events. Students use these less structured times during the school day to discuss their personal lives with one another. This is a time when they share their present plans and dreams for the future. They talk about clothes, music, and other important aspects of adolescent culture. Students with moderate to severe disabilities need to have these same kinds of opportunities to interact with their peers beyond the scrutiny of adult supervision. Unstructured school settings offer important opportunities for students with moderate to severe disabilities to form friendships. Successful interactions in social environments can foster self-esteem and ultimately greater independence (Knapczyk & Rodes, 1996).

Still, students with moderate to severe disabilities often miss social cues and may have difficulty understanding the appropriate use of some of the behaviors they observe. They need to observe their peers' habits and learn how to use those behaviors in the appropriate situations so they will fit in and be accepted (Dever & Knapczyk, 1997). Help your students learn to observe their social environment and make meaning out of what they see. You can facilitate this through a special friends program.

A schoolwide program in which typical students volunteer to be special friends with students who have moderate to severe disabilities can facilitate inclusive social interactions (Westling & Fox, 2000). For example, many high schools sponsor a peer buddies program, which we described in Chapter 11. This kind of program brings interested students with and without disabilities together on a regular basis. Typical students who volunteer to become special friends also learn how to provide support, when it is needed, for their friends with disabilities. They learn to share their own experiences and perceptions with their friend who has a disability when they get together. The special friends share their experiences and feelings about the everyday events in their lives when they eat together during lunch or walk through the hallways between classes. At the same time, special friends can provide guidance or coaching in social situations that may pose difficulties. For example, they share their insider knowledge about the latest clothing styles and social etiquette when they get together with their friends who have disabilities.

Acting and dressing like their typical peers will enhance their opportunities to participate in many of these school-sponsored social events. Adolescents often assist one another in finding a date for the prom as well as providing essential information on what to wear and how to act. Special friends can plan to meet and sit together at school assemblies, dances, and basketball games. These kinds of interactions reflect the sense of community that occurs in inclusive schools when everyone involved accepts and embraces individual differences and provides support for diversity.

However, before you can effectively encourage these peer interactions, you need to become knowledgeable by observing typical student behaviors to understand their interests. Spend time in the hallways between classes listening and watching the interactions of the general education students.

> Note: Do not forget to share what you learn with your students' parents. Encourage them to help their sons or daughters get involved in out-of-school activities such as the church youth group or a 4-H club.

One way to help your students be part of social life in the school with their typical peers is to see that they are equipped with the same things as those peers. Make sure they get their own lockers mixed in among the lockers of the typical students. Teach your students how to use a combination lock. The students can keep a card with their locker number and combination written on it in their wallets to help them remember the numbers. In addition, you may need to review lock combinations with students periodically to ensure skill maintenance, but it is well worth the effort.

As you already have learned, the hallway between classes is an important place to meet and talk with friends. To increase opportunities, assist the students in decorating the inside of their lockers with the kinds of items used by the typical students, such as pictures of their favorite rock stars. This provides the students with disabilities the opportunity to talk to their peers about the rock stars they have on the inside walls of their locker or the pictures they see in their neighbors' lockers.

Lockers also can offer opportunities for working on grooming skills. Typical students comb their hair and/or apply makeup at their lockers between classes. The student with moderate to severe disabilities may wish to have these items—and a mirror—in their locker as well. This is another example of a situation in which special friends are good sources of natural support. Clearly, lockers are an important resource for giving students with moderate to severe disabilities many informal opportunities for making social connections with peers.

 **SUMMARY**

In this chapter, you learned how to develop a variety of schoolwide formal and informal curriculum projects and activities at the secondary level. The learning experiences described use an applied approach to academic content while providing students with instruction in the daily living skills and social competencies they will need as they become adults. At the same time, students are given general preparation for future employment while they participate in projects like the Breakfast Place Restaurant and Classy Cleaners Laundry Service. Like the schoolwide curricular ideas for elementary students we described in Chapter 12, the projects and activities in this chapter are appropriate for all students.

 CHAPTER EXTENDERS

Key Terms and Concepts

1. *Special friends* are typical students who volunteer to befriend students with moderate to severe disabilities during extracurricular and other social activities sponsored by the school.
2. *Tech Prep* is a planned course of study that includes career preparation and applied academic course work in a specific technical field.
3. *Vocational education* courses prepare students for employment through real hands-on activities.
4. *Work-study* programs are secondary education programs in which students learn functional skills in a curriculum that combines academics with work experiences.
5. *Block scheduling* refers to a format for holding the classes for a particular course only on certain days of the week, but having each class meeting last for a longer period of time.

Study Guide

1. Discuss how in-school service learning projects can benefit the students who are involved and the members of the school population they serve.
2. List two school-to-work strategies and describe how they can be incorporated into school-based activities.
3. List and describe three strategies for addressing the competencies needed in everyday life in nonacademic school environments.
4. List and detail five ways to promote the successful inclusion of students with moderate to severe disabilities in after-hours school activities and discuss the benefits to students with and without disabilities.
5. Describe two strategies that help students with moderate to severe disabilities develop appropriate social skills in school.

6. Discuss the advantages and disadvantages of inclusive instructional programs through schoolwide service projects.

Have a Class Debate

Pressure from peers to be like everybody else sometimes causes adolescents to be cruel to people who look or act differently than they do. Debate the value of students belonging to the group versus being their own persons and the consequences of each position.

Small Group Activity

Form groups of 3 to 5 students for this activity. Each group should identify a club that one or more of the group members participated in during high school. If the club included students with disabilities, describe the inclusive activities and supports that took place. If the club did not include students with disabilities, brainstorm some ways the club could have included these students. Ask the following question: As a teacher, how would you encourage students in the club to implement the inclusive ideas you have developed in your discussion? How would you adapt the club activities for persons with more severe disabilities? Each group should have a few minutes at the end to share their ideas with the whole class.

Field Experiences

Visit a local restaurant or laundry. Tour the facility and discover how the business is organized: work schedules, employee responsibilities, the compensation plan, and so on. Write a paper discussing how a school business could be similar to the community business and what activities would have to be done differently in a school-based project.

chapter 14

Community-Based Instruction

Laura Owens-Johnson and Lee B. Hamill

Jeanette just completed a year of high school geometry but has no idea how to calculate how much carpet she needs to cover the floor of her bedroom. Cameron is pulled out of his middle school language arts classes to work on basic reading skills, but he is not able to read the menu at a local restaurant. Students drop out of schools at alarmingly high rates because they do not see the relevance in what is being taught in school to their everyday lives. These scenarios demonstrate the importance of implementing innovative and creative instructional approaches in schools today. Community-based instruction is one such approach.

Both general and special education have utilized the community as an extension of the classroom for many years. However, since special education became its own system of education for students with disabilities with the passage of P.L. 94-142 (reauthorized in 1990 as the Individuals with Disabilities Act, or IDEA), community-based instruction has been seen as a separate form of instruction for students with disabilities (Kluth, 2000). Community-based instruction was developed as a reaction to the traditional readiness model imposed on individuals with moderate to severe disabilities. Individuals with significant disabilities were often relegated to the task of proving their readiness to live, work, or play prior to actually participating in community environments. Support for using community-based instruction was based on studies indicating that they had difficulty generalizing skills learned in simulated environments such as classrooms and that teaching in actual environments in which the skills were utilized would increase the generalization of these skills (Stokes & Baer, 1977). The readiness philosophy has changed in schools, and community integration is now viewed as an individual's right rather than a privilege to be earned.

Today's classrooms serve a diverse group of students including students with disabilities, students from various cultural backgrounds, and non-English-speaking students. The traditional curriculum and instructional practices used in classrooms today are not meeting the needs of this diverse student population, and, as a result, creative instructional methods must be implemented (Simmons & Kameenui, 1996). Effective inclusive education requires that teachers use a variety of instructional strategies and multilevel curricula in order to meet the diverse needs of learners in today's classrooms. Community-based instruction is one type of instructional approach that allows teachers to design lessons that are meaningful, relevant, active, and interesting for all students. Sufficient evidence in the literature suggests that information presented in

CLASSROOM-BASED INSTRUCTION VERSUS COMMUNITY-BASED INSTRUCTION

Doug, a student with significant cognitive disabilities, was deemed ready to participate in the community apartment program. He was able to explain correctly to his teacher what to do if a stranger came to the door of the apartment. However, while at the apartment learning independent living skills, a stranger came to the door. Doug opened the door and let the stranger in without asking any questions. When asked why he let the stranger in, Doug said he did not know. However, after the incident, he was able to verbalize once again what he should have done. Providing instruction at the apartment initially, rather than using worksheets or question/answer problem solving in the classroom, would have allowed Doug to practice the skills in a meaningful way, and thus he would have acted on his knowledge of not allowing a stranger to enter the apartment.

meaningful contexts is retained longer and the value of learning is enhanced when instruction takes place in natural environments (Christ, 1995; Cox & Firpo, 1993; Miller et al., 1995). Some studies have stated that classroom-based learning may actually interfere with a student's ability to problem-solve in the natural setting. Instruction provided in the community provides students with the opportunities to inquire about broader social issues such as social justice, politics, and civics, which are objectives of quality inclusive education (Kluth, 2000; Peterson, 1996).

 ## WHAT YOU WILL LEARN IN THIS CHAPTER

This chapter provides background information on community-based instruction as a curricular approach. You will learn why this approach is, and has been, effective for many years. This section also addresses what community-based instruction is and is not. Finally, you will learn strategies for implementing community-based instruction in inclusive environments with all students.

 ## A HISTORICAL PERSPECTIVE

Community-based instruction is not new to either general or special education. Booker T. Washington (1969) promoted physical work and the acquisition of occupationally useful skills as a part of quality education. The Cardinal Principles of Secondary Education in 1918 also advocated a practical approach to education identifying its main objectives as health, the mastery of fundamental processes, worthy home membership, vocation, citizenship, worthwhile use of leisure, and ethical character (Lazerson, 1987). John Dewey (1938), educator and philosopher, led the progressive education movement. Progressives believed that students must be active participants in learning socially useful skills (Knapp, 1994; Spring, 1989).

After World War II, the United States turned back to the traditional basic skills model that breaks life skills into discrete units and does not apply them to practical use (Brown, Collins, & Duguid, 1989; Kluth, 2000). This model promoted learning as a matter of decoding skills in reading, computation skills in math, and memorizing various facts in science and history. Higher order thinking skills are desirable only after students master the basics (Jones, 1990). However, with new academic standards set by school districts for students to move from grade to grade and graduate, the bar continues to be raised in terms of learning academics. Students are now being required to pass various proficiency or statewide assessments that generally focus on verbal-linguistic or logical-mathematical knowledge acquired in classroom settings. Further, traditional curriculum focuses on learning academic skills in artificial settings without a focus on future outcomes for students. Skills are typically taught in contexts unrelated to their use in professional or everyday life. This is not to say that academic subjects such as English, math, science, and history are not functional, but they need to be learned in ways that are purposeful and meaningful to students' lives (Peterson, LeRoy, Field, & Wood, 1992). Curriculum should be expanded to include daily living, vocational skills, and community problem solving for all students. Students must graduate from school with the ability to apply the skills learned to real-life environments that range from home management to political activism in the community (Peterson et al., 1992). Education must offer opportunities for students to learn and practice critical thinking and problem-solving skills and provide them with more than a superficial exposure to skills. Teaching basic skills without focusing on problem solving and critical thinking often results in students learning a little about a lot of different topics as opposed to gaining a deep understanding of a few key concepts they can use in different situations (Porter, 1989). It is not enough for students to simply be able to propagate information. They must be able to apply this information to the world in which they live in order for continued prosperity and success.

Community-based instruction in special education has been considered a best practice for students with moderate and severe disabilities since the 1970s (Brown, Nietupski, & Hamre-Nietupski, 1976, Brown, et al., 1979; Falvey, 1995). The main factors influencing community-based instruction for students with disabilities include deinstitutionalization, the emergence of philosophies such as normalization, legislation mandating educational opportunities for students with disabilities, studies indicating lack of skill generalization from simulated to real environments, and the desires of individuals with disabilities to live and work independently in the community (Csapo, 1991; McCombs, 1993; Stokes & Baer, 1977). Community-based instruction allows teachers to move students with moderate and severe disabilities from self-contained, segregated classrooms into the community. The expectation is that students acquire skills more quickly and maintain and generalize those skills across a variety of environments (Hamre-Nietupski, Nietupski, Bates, & Maaurer, 1982). Over the years, the benefits of community-based instruction for student with disabilities have been demonstrated (e.g., Anderson, Hiebert, Scott, & Wilkinson, 1985; Brown et al., 1976; Brown et al., 1983; Jones, 1990; Rainforth & York, 1987). Students learn practical skills in real rather than simulated environments and thus the experiences are more meaningful.

The recent dilemma with regard to community-based education for students with disabilities involves removing students from general education classrooms to provide instruction in the community (Tashie & Schuh, 1993). Many educators feel they need to make a choice between educating students in general education classrooms alongside their peers or providing community-based instruction. Educators must find a balance and begin to address ways in which community-based instruction can benefit all

students. Inclusion of students with moderate and severe disabilities in general education classes should not preclude their participation in community-based experiences. At the same time, students with moderate and severe disabilities should not be denied in-school experiences in order to participate in community-based experiences (Falvey, 1995). Instruction for students with moderate and severe disabilities should not be an all-or-nothing approach. The involvement of students with and without disabilities in both school and community instruction merges the best in education.

COMMUNITY-BASED INSTRUCTION FOR ALL STUDENTS

Jasmine is a middle school student with severe cognitive disabilities. Shopping, locating and purchasing items in a grocery store is a goal on her IEP. She is included in general education classes. In her math class, students are learning estimating and averaging. Jasmine and her cooperative group of two peers without disabilities go to three local grocery stores. The goal for Jasmine is to locate the cereal aisle and the three different types of cereal from the coupons. The goal for her nondisabled peers is to write down the price and weight of the cereal in each store to determine which store has the best price.

 ## WHAT IS COMMUNITY-BASED INSTRUCTION?

Community-based instruction is also called community-referenced instruction, field experience, or life skills instruction (Falvey, 1995; Kluth, 2000). Simply said, community-based instruction is teaching meaningful or functional skills in natural or real-world environments.

Community-based instruction can take the form of mobility training, participating in community recreational activities, working in the community (paid or volunteering), or shopping at local stores. In understanding what community-based instruction is, we must also recognize what it is not (see Table 14–1). Community-based instruction is not a field trip, but rather an instructional strategy that challenges the adequacy of classroom-based instruction and advocates for using the community as a classroom (Thompson, 1995). It is essential for educators to understand that community-based instruction is a curricular approach that allows teachers to design lessons with multiple roles, challenges, and opportunities for learning (Kluth, 2000).

When evaluating traditional curricula and instruction, proponents of community-based instruction argue that the question many students ask, "When are we going to need this?", should be taken seriously (Christ, 1995).

TABLE 14–1   Community-Based Instruction versus Field Trips

Community-Based Instruction	Field Trips
Functional instruction/skills	Pleasurable
Individual needs Specific skills Specific environments	Part of school or whole class activity
Practice life skills	Exposure
Clearly defined instructional objectives	Fun trips May have some defined instructional objectives
Based on IEP	Culmination to activity or unit
Systematic, organized	Systematic, organized
Daily/weekly experience	Sporadic
Active participation by students	Participation through observation
Part of student's schedule of instruction	Not part of regular schedule of instruction
Learning over time	One-day learning event
Planned learning trip	Casual learning
Small group (2–3 students)	Large group (whole class)
Structured experiences/activities	More social, looser structure
Lower student to teacher ratio	Higher student to teacher ratio
Paid by school system, parents, grant money	Paid by parents or grant money
Liability issues	Liability issues
Consistent—provides primary educational setting for student	Episodic—reinforces learning
A curricular method to teach lifelong skills	A curricular method to enhance learning and a source of recreation

Source: Adapted from *Community-Based Instruction: Technical Resource Manual.* Bureau of Education and Exceptional Students, Florida Department of Education, 1993. Reprinted with permission.

Students applying skills in nonschool, real-world settings that have some relationship, relevance, and purpose to their lives now or in the future characterize community-based instruction. Typically community-based instruction relates to vocational, daily living, community, or recreation curricular domains involving the use of natural environments and teaching functional skills.

Natural Environments

Natural environments refers to those settings in which students generally use the skill being taught and are places frequented by peers without disabilities (Brown et al., 1976; Falvey, 1989; Sailor & Guess, 1983). Instruction for students should occur in a variety of natural environments reflecting the natural proportion of the population (Brown et al., 1976). In other words, students with disabilities should not consist of more than 1% to 3% of the total number of individuals in that environment (Falvey, 1989). Further, community-based instruction should occur in the natural environment of the student's community and neighborhood. Natural environments can be identified in four domains, vocational, daily living, community, and recreation, that directly affect the independent living and quality of life of individuals with moderate and severe disabilities.

Access to the natural environments is a critical consideration when determining where to teach certain skills. As we discussed in Chapter 5, prior to implementing community-based instruction, conduct an ecological inventory that looks at attitudinal and physical accessibility (Falvey, 1989). Figure 14–1 provides an ecological inventory format that can be completed for community environments chosen for instructional purposes to ensure both attitudinal and physical accessibility. Attitudinal accessibility refers to environments in which individuals are supportive, or not opposed to, the idea of teaching students with disabilities in their place of business or recreational facility. Physical accessi-

bility refers to environments that do not pose physical barriers or obstacles for students with a significant disability (Falvey, 1989). Environments in which physical barriers are not present or are easily eliminated characterize physical accessibility. With the passage of the Americans With Disabilities Act in 1990 (ADA), physical accessibility is less of an issue than it was in the past. However, it is still important to look for environments that pose the fewest barriers. For example, although a building is considered accessible, students may need to enter using the service elevator rather than the main elevator. This environment may not be optimal to begin instruction, but may be chosen later. Look at the accessibility of the environment as well as the skills you could teach in each environment.

Along with accessibility, Falvey (1989) suggests other considerations for choosing instructional environments. These include environments that (1) are frequented by the student and his or her family, (2) would be frequented if the student learned the skills necessary to participate, (3) are frequented by peers without disabilities, (4) are preferred by the student and his or her family, (5) involve skills preferred by the student and his or her family, (6) involve skills needed in a variety of community settings, and (7) would be accessible to the student outside of school.

Another type of informal assessment strategy to help you identify instructional environments is the life space analysis (Figure 14–2). The life space analysis combines parent and student interviews and direct observations to determine appropriate environments to utilize with students (Brown et al., 1984). *Life space* refers to all the experiences and activities that occur in an individual's life, 24 hours a day, 7 days a week. The life space analysis can be used to answer the following questions: (1) How do the number of environments compare to those of peers without disabilities? (2) How could the number of functional and appropriate activities be increased? (3) What kinds of social interactions/relationships occur and how could these be

FIGURE 14–1 Ecological Inventory

Domain: Community
Environment: Grocery Store

Subenvironment	Subenvironment	Subenvironment
Entrance	Aisles	Checkout	Exit

Subenvironment Entrance	Subenvironment Aisles	Subenvironment Checkout	Subenvironment Exit
Activities: ☐ Read sign on door ☐ Enter through correct door ☐ Hold door for others ☐ Get cart	Activities: ☐ Identify correct aisle from list ☐ Push cart in straight line without running into things or people ☐ Say "excuse me" when needing to get around someone ☐ Ask for assistance	Activities: ☐ Pushing cart into checkout ☐ Waiting ☐ Putting items on conveyor belt ☐ Giving cashier correct money ☐ Putting change in wallet	Activities: ☐ ☐ ☐ ☐ ☐
Priority Activity/Skill: Reading Physically taking cart	Priority Activity/Skill: Asking for assistance Identifying correct aisle from list	Priority Activity/Skill: Waiting Putting items on conveyor belt Money identification	Priority Activity/Skill:

FIGURE 14–2 Life Space Analysis

Life Space Profile Chart

Student: _____
Date: _____

Day of the Week: _____
Person Completing Form: _____

Time	Domain	Environment	Sub-Environment	Activity	People Present	Integrated with non-disabled peers	Functional Nonfunctional	Other Information
6:00 a.m.								
6:30 a.m.								
7:00 a.m.								
7:30 a.m.								
8:00 a.m.								
→								

improved? (4) How could personal choice be increased? and (5) Are there any large gaps in the student's day/week that may negatively affect his or her learning or performance? A life space analysis is essentially an ecological assessment that allows both general and special educators to identify the current environments and skills in a student's repertoire prior to implementing changes or determining instructional strategies. For example, as Figure 14–3 shows, it is clear that the student spends the majority of his time at home or in school with either family or people paid to be with him. When analyzing this life space analysis, potential changes in the student's instructional environments could include general community environments and interactions with peers.

Functional Skills

Functional skills refer to those skills needed to increase a student's interdependence and quality of life. This notion of teaching students skills necessary to participate in a variety of integrated community environments is not new. Annie Inskeep, in 1926, delineated curriculum development strategies for teaching functional skills to individuals with disabilities in her book *Teaching Dull and Retarded Children*. When determining if an activity or skill is functional, ask the question, "If the student does not learn the skill or activity, would someone else have to do it for him or her" (Brown et. al., 1979). If the answer is yes, the skill/activity is more likely to be functional. Given this definition, however, do not assume that general educational curriculum is not functional for some students. Although all students may not be able to learn the same amount or the same things in all academic areas, any knowledge gained is of value to enhance an individual's overall quality of life (Stainback, Stainback, & Moravec, 1992). At a Wisconsin high school, a student with autism was included in a civics class. One activity included daily presentations by students on a current event from the newspaper or television. The student en-

joyed looking at photographs or pictures, and thus identified a current event from the local newspaper based on this criteria (i.e., the article had a photo he liked). The family worked with him at home highlighting key words from the article. He presented his article to the class by reading the highlighted words and showing the picture from the article. This was a functional activity for this student for several reasons. First, he was becoming more aware of his community; second, he was increasing his vocabulary; and third, he was learning to participate with others, which enhanced his ability to develop relationships with his nondisabled peers.

Also consider the "criterion of ultimate functioning" when determining what functional skills to address (Brown et al., 1976). That is, where will the student ultimately be working, living, and recreating next year, in the next 5 years, or as an adult? As we discussed in Chapter 5,

WHAT WOULD YOU DO?

Ling is a Hmong student with significant disabilities. When talking with Ling, she indicated she would enjoy participating in the work-study program at the high school. She was interested in working with children. Because many of her peers also worked with children through babysitting, this was considered an appropriate functional activity for Ling. However, her parents were opposed to any type of vocational planning with Ling. The teacher was told that Ling would not be going to work after graduation and would stay at home helping the mother take care of the household. The cultural differences between the teacher and the family with regard to a young woman working in the community needed to be bridged. How would you handle this situation if you were the teacher?

FIGURE 14–3 Sample Life Space Analysis

Time	Domain	Environment	Subenvironment	Activity	People
6:00 a.m.	Domestic	Home	Bedroom	Getting out of bed	Mom
6:30 a.m.	Domestic	Home	Kitchen	Making toast	Mom/Dad
7:00 a.m.	Domestic	Home	Bathroom	Brushing teeth/ toilet/ dressing	Dad
7:45 a.m.		Home	Front porch	Wait for bus/ ride bus	Mom/Peers with disabilities
8:30 a.m.	Community	School	Locker/classroom	Take off coat/ get supplies	Instructional assistant
8:40– 11:40 a.m.	Community	School	Classroom	Instruction 1-1 assistance	Instructional assistant/ Peers with and without disabilities
11:45 a.m.	Community	School	School cafeteria	Eating lunch	Instructional assistant
12:15 p.m.	Community	School	Bathroom	Toileting	Instructional assistant
12:30 p.m.– 3:00 p.m.	Community	School	Art class Chorus	Pottery Assist in handing out music	Instructional assistant/ Peers with and without disabilities
3:15 p.m.	Community	Yellow bus	Seat on bus	Riding home	Peers with disabilities
4:00 p.m.	Domestic	Home	Bathroom	Toileting	Mom
4:30 p.m.	Leisure	Home	Family room	Watch TV	Alone
5:30 p.m.	Domestic	Home	Kitchen	Eating dinner	Mom/Dad
6:30 p.m.	Domestic	Home	Bedroom	Listen to music	Alone
7:00 p.m.	Leisure	Home	Family room	Talk with family member on phone	Mom/Dad
8:00 p.m.	Domestic	Home	Bathroom	Toileting/get ready for bed	Dad
8:45 p.m.	Domestic	Home	Bedroom	Go to bed	Alone

in deciding whether or not to teach a skill or activity, consider the following: (1) student and family preferences, (2) age appropriateness—what and where individuals without disabilities are or will be working, living, and recreating, and (3) cultural factors.

It is the school's charge to provide a variety of opportunities for individuals with disabilities rather than limiting opportunities based on the disability. In other words, you should not consider the criteria of ultimate functioning for students with moderate to severe disabilities to be sheltered workshops or group homes. Further, you should not be considering limited competitive employment opportunities such as the fast food or janitorial industries. Students with moderate and severe disabilities must be provided with a variety of experiences in different environments so they can make informed choices in their lives. Too often a student's disability or the severity of the disability is used to determine future instructional environments rather than focusing on what the student wants. For example, a young man with significant disabilities has been included in general education business classes (e.g., keyboarding, data entry) and earning B's and C's with no support other than nondisabled peers and the general education teacher. He has clearly demonstrated this is an area of interest for him. However, despite scoring the highest on an entrance test, using the computer, he was denied access to a computer training program because his reading scores were too low. Because all of his work experience in high school revolved around cleaning, it was suggested he enter a janitorial program at a local adult service agency. This young man's future was not based on his skills or interests, but on his disability.

It is essential to provide students with moderate to severe disabilities a variety of experiences, despite their disability. As we will discuss in Chapter 15, students must be given the tools to advocate for themselves by becoming self-determined individuals. Schools should not place barriers on students based on their disability, but provide them with numerous opportunities to experience areas of interest. You must also consider that a student's interests will change over time. For example, in elementary school Charlie wanted to be a teacher; in middle school he wanted to be a firefighter; and in high school he wanted to be a veterinarian. Too often students with moderate to severe disabilities are not given opportunities to dream or try out these dreams. In middle school Charlie toured a firehouse, participated in the organization of fire safety week at school, and talked about fire safety to the local elementary students with a firefighter and a nondisabled peer. In high school Charlie was provided opportunities to visit various veterinarians; he interviewed veterinarians and toured their clinics for class projects, participated in a job shadowing experience, and worked as an assistant (not just cleaning cages!) in a veterinarian's office in a work-study capacity.

When providing opportunities for students, educators must work together. Collaboration between general education business, work-study, and school-to-work staff is crucial to provide effective and meaningful opportunities for all students. At a local high school, the special educator and general education work-study coordinator worked together to provide semester-long experiences for students with and without disabilities in various industries. Using the general education teacher's business contacts, the special educator would go in and identify jobs for the students. For example, at a local

---

How Did You Get Where You Are Today?

Think about your school career. What were your interests and skills? Did they change over time? How did you become interested in your career goals? Who helped you develop your career goals? Who set up barriers? Who helped you overcome these barriers? How could you help your students reach their dreams?

insurance company, the nondisabled students worked as a file clerk and receptionist while two students with moderate to severe disabilities inserted material into packets and labeled envelopes for distribution. The job was further developed for one student into a messenger position.

Ask the following questions to help prioritize the skills and activities to begin working on with a student: (1) Does the skill enhance the quality of life for the student—is it functional? (2) Is the skill required in future environments—criterion of ultimate functioning? (3) Is the skill chronologically age appropriate? (4) Can the skill be used across environments? (5) Does the skill increase or have the potential to increase interactions with nondisabled peers? and (6) Is the skill a student and/or family preference? Community-based or community-referenced models drive the delivery of functional skill instruction due to the nature of the environments. It would be difficult to teach nonfunctional skills in community environments (e.g., teaching students to put together nuts and bolts at the local laundromat).

You must consider *both* age appropriateness and the functionality of skills being taught. For example, opening a checking account at a bank

is clearly functional. However, it is not age appropriate for a 6-year-old. Further, learning the names of all the presidents may be age appropriate for an eighth-grade student, but may not be functional. Another important consideration is to ensure that embedded skills such as language and social skills, which are often overlooked, be incorporated throughout all instructional environments.

 APPLICATIONS TO INSTRUCTION

Community-Referenced Applications to Instruction

Traditional curricula and school structures seem to embrace academic performance in artificial settings with little regard to future outcomes for students (Peterson et al., 1992). In contrast, many educators and members of the community believe that schools should provide students with the skills necessary to function as effective adults in their communities (Jones, 1990). Due to this belief, a growing movement in education is to shift from the traditional classroom-based model of instruction to a more community-referenced model (Thompson, 1995). The question becomes, what should teachers teach and students learn? Many believe that learning in schools should focus on meaningful outcomes for students in their adult lives—fulfilling employment, community participation, developing and maintaining relationships, obtaining and maintaining a home, and becoming involved in recreational and cultural activities (Peterson et al., 1992).

There are a variety of learning experiences that provide challenging opportunities for all students. Objectives must be established for all students involved in community-referenced instruction and lessons planned around the needs of all students in the classroom (Kluth, 2000). This section discusses the issues and logistics of implementing community-based instruction.

 IS THE SKILL FUNCTIONAL?

Pero is a high school student with moderate to severe disabilities and is learning to sort colored blocks in class. If Pero did not sort the colored blocks, would someone need to do it for him? No. However, if Pero were not taught to sort the mail by department for his community job, would someone else have to do it for him? Yes. Therefore, sorting colored blocks would not be a functional skill, but sorting for the purpose of distributing mail would be. What are some other functional and nonfunctional skills?

General Education Models of Applied Curriculum in the Community

Community-based instruction may very well result in unanticipated benefits for general and special educators as well as students with and without disabilities. Collaboration among all professionals and collective responsibility in designing and implementing this kind of instruction will promote the sharing of resources, creative and dynamic instruction, and active learning for all students (Kluth, 2000). Four types of community-based instruction provide challenging experiences for all students in general education settings: community service learning, research teams, community work-based learning, and community-referenced instruction.

Community Service Learning. It has been said that students are not acquainted with society and the world because educators typically teach *about* these topics without teaching *how* to become active participants in living (Martin, 1995). Community service learning is an approach that responds to this criticism. It can be defined as "an approach to experiential learning, and *expression of values*—service to others, community development and empowerment, reciprocal learning—which determines the purpose, nature and process of *social and educational* exchange between learners (students) and the people they serve, and between experiential education programs and the community organizations in which they work" (Stanton, 1990, p. 66). Service learning has clear roots in traditional volunteerism (Kraft, 1996). Ohio's Occupational Work Adjustment and Occupational Work Education (OWA/OWE) programs are examples of community-based curriculum to help nondisabled students transition from school to work. The Detroit public schools now have a graduation requirement of 200 community service hours and students in Maryland between their 8th- and 12th-grade years must volunteer 75 hours prior to graduation (Lozada, 1998;

Markus, Howard, & Kling, 1993). A list prepared by the National Youth Leadership Council identifies service learning activities such as participating in projects like Big Buddies, blood drives, board membership, environmental cleanup, Meals on Wheels, public media, tutoring, victim aide, voter education, crisis centers, recycling, and building projects such as Habitat for Humanity (Cairns & Kielsmeier, 1991). The ultimate goal of service learning is to integrate what is learned in the classroom into the community (Lozada, 1998). Research has shown that community service learning is beneficial to students with and without disabilities (e.g., Gent & Gurecka, 1998; Kraft, 1996; LaGreca & Stone, 1990; Shumer, 1994; Yoder, Redish, & Wade, 1996).

Research Teams. Students with and without disabilities can be grouped into heterogeneous research teams in which students conduct their research in the community. Rather than utilizing the school library, students collect information about topics by exploring artifacts, conducting interviews, and observing people and things in their communities (Kluth, 2000). Students who conduct community research gain confidence in communication skills by interviewing and answering questions from the community (Miller et al., 1995). Investigative team research allows students to obtain information visually, auditorily, and kinesthetically, and provides numerous experiences unable to be simulated in the classroom setting.

Research teams include not only academic learning, but also embedded skills such as communication and social skills. Students might develop a research plan; gather and organize information; develop interviewing skills; and operate communications equipment such as video cameras, tape recorders, and computers.

Community Work-Based Learning. General education has recently been revitalized with youth apprenticeship programs, work-study programs, mentorships, and business partnerships (Hamilton & Hamilton, 1997). Special education has always considered work an important component in a student's educational plan. The School-to-Work Opportunities Act (STOWA) passed in 1994 was established for general education programs to provide work-related opportunities for all students. As you can see in Table 14–2, this act closely parallels the Individuals With Disabilities Act of 1990 (IDEA) transition components.

Work-based learning can be grouped into three categories: (1) visits to businesses either

---

TABLE 14–2 Similarities Between IDEA and the School-to-Work Opportunities Act

Individuals with Disabilities Education Act	School to Work Opportunities Act
Career/Transition Curriculum Component	**Career/Transition Curriculum Component**
☐ Includes instruction, community experiences, development of employment and other adult living objectives; acquisition of daily living skills and functional evaluation (if appropriate)	☐ Includes career awareness and exploration; counseling to identify interests and goals
	☐ Career major selected by 11th grade
☐ Annual planning and review meetings (IEP) for each student beginning no later than age 16	☐ Integration of academic and vocational learning
	☐ Regularly scheduled student evaluations
☐ Functional vocational assessment; assess student needs and interests	☐ Entry into postsecondary education
Experiential Component	**Experiential Component**
☐ "Transition services"; coordinated set of activities, outcome oriented, promotes movement from school to postschool activities	☐ On-the-job work experiences
	☐ Relevant job training experiences
	☐ Workplace mentoring
	☐ Instruction on general work competencies
Integrating Activity Component	**Integrating Activity Component**
☐ Development of employment and other adult living objectives/interest based	☐ Match student interest with employers
☐ Provision of related services	☐ School site mentor as liaison
☐ Transition statement in IEP	☐ Provide technical assistance to employers when integrating school and work-based learning
☐ Student participation	☐ Encourage employer participation
☐ Graduation assistance	☐ Collect and analyze information on student outcomes

through field trips or job shadowing experiences; (2) worklike experiences such as service learning, paid or unpaid internships, school-based/student-run businesses; and (3) employment in the community through subsidized training, paid internships, or apprenticeships (Hamilton & Hamilton, 1997). Work-based learning can occur in school or in the community.

Community-Referenced Curriculum.   When the home economics classroom, the Breakfast Place Restaurant described in Chapter 13, or the Kids' Kitchen Bakery described in Chapter 12 is not in operation, those spaces could be utilized for other community-referenced activities. To illustrate, members of one of the extracurricular clubs at school could use the restaurant or bakery facilities to plan and prepare a community pancake breakfast to raise money to fund club projects. Those facilities also could be used to implement problem-solving activities for an upcoming community excursion and the follow-up project in the school. In this case, the students might be engaged in a curriculum to learn the skills needed for personal money management, proper nutrition and food preparation, and functional reading. As you learned in Chapter 12, the focus activity might be to plan and cook a holiday meal. Students would work together looking through cookbooks to plan a well-balanced menu. They could then use the newspaper to identify and price the necessary ingredients. Once they develop the appropriate list and cost of needed items, they go to the store to make their purchases. When they return from the store, they store their purchases and later prepare, eat, and clean up after the meal.

In addition, the restaurant and bakery facilities could be used in conjunction with career development activities. For example, work-study students could use the restaurant's time clock to punch in and out as part of their work experience just as they would do in the community.

Students with moderate disabilities may take a slightly different direction in job training ex-periences and living skills development than those with more significant disabilities. Because students with moderate disabilities will enter more independent living arrangements and employment situations, they may benefit from educational circumstances and learning situations involving less supervision. For example, they could have paid community work experiences supervised by the employers as part of their education.

Students with significant disabilities need extensive training experience and some level of support throughout their lives. For example, shopping for food at a local store with a nondisabled peer tutor affords the student practice dealing with grocery shopping. Experiences like this give students an opportunity to use their knowledge in real situations which may lead to greater independence through the use of natural supports in the community (Hughes, Rusch, & Curl, 1990).

 ISSUES AND LOGISTICS

In designing and implementing effective community-based instruction, several issues offer new challenges for educators and schools. Each of these issues must be addressed based on the individual needs of students and the local district policies and procedures. Next we look at some of the most salient challenges involved in community-based instruction as well as possible solutions.

Transportation and Mobility

Utilizing the community as the classroom requires getting to and from the various environments. In addition, transportation is embedded in other issues such as funding, liability, safety, and scheduling. Keep in mind that the ultimate goal of community-based instruction is to teach students to maximize their participation in the community. Therefore, students must learn various modes of transportation. In sum, transportation is a pivotal issue and it is necessary to think about various methods of transportation as well as which modes of transportation enhance community functioning.

A variety of transportation modes may be available for students. One method is walking or using wheelchairs, or riding a bike. These are natural forms of transportation that will be used by most of the students throughout their lives. Another method is public transportation such as buses, taxis, and subways. Many public transportation departments provide training for faculty and students if requested. When using public transportation, other embedded skills such as communication (asking for directions or calling for a ride) and reading/telling time (looking at the bus schedule and determining when to be at the bus stop) can also be taught. Using specialized transportation for individuals with disabilities may be another option for students.

It is difficult to discuss transportation without mentioning funding. Creativity is the key when identifying ways to provide funding for transportation. Examples of possible transportation and funding options include, but are not limited to the following:

- Tapping into the classroom supply budget
- Applying for grants (Department of Public Instruction discretionary grants or through local organizations such as the Lions or Kiwanis Clubs)
- Establishing a carpool of parents or local volunteers (make sure to work out liability with your school or district)
- Utilizing existing transportation (e.g., senior citizen or religious organization vans, carpool with co-workers)
- Arranging school transportation to drop off/pick up at community site in the morning rather than at school
- Using bus tickets donated by local businesses or organizations
- Utilizing volunteers such as retired bus drivers or service club members (make sure to work out liability with your school or district)

- Coordinating with community-based instruction at other schools or with trips with other classes in the school
- Requesting parents/students pay for transportation
- Obtaining donated vehicles from car dealerships or auctions
- Using profits from applied curriculum projects such as the Kids' Kitchen Bakery, "Super Stuff" supplies cart, the Breakfast Place Restaurant, or the Classy Cleaners Laundry

If you choose to drive students, several factors must be taken into consideration. First, ensure that the school district and student's parents are aware and appropriate releases are signed. Second, contact your automobile insurance company to discuss expanded coverage options (find out from your school district if it would pay for the additional cost). Third, you may want to obtain your commercial driver's license (CDL) for liability reasons. This option is the least preferred because of liability issues and continued dependence on you to provide transportation.

Staffing

Staffing patterns is another issue that must be addressed when implementing community-based instruction. Adequate coverage in the community is logistically more difficult to manage than providing instruction in the traditional school setting. Traditional staffing arrangements often need to be altered in order to provide appropriate instruction in community settings. Creativity and flexibility are keys to successful staffing for community-based instruction.

One option for addressing staffing in the community is to use other staff members such as occupational therapists, physical therapists, speech/language pathologists, social workers, counselors, educational assistants, or other specialty teachers (e.g., reading specialists). Ideally, these types of services should be offered in integrated rather than isolated settings. It would be more beneficial for the speech/language pathologist to work with a student while ordering at a restaurant than in a small room in the back of the school or for an occupational therapist to work with the teacher and student on developing appropriate adaptations on a community job. By utilizing current staff, they become an integral part of community-based instruction by teaching skills in meaningful settings to ensure the student generalized the skills in other environments.

Another option is to use a team teaching approach with general or special education teachers. Special education teachers can enhance topics being learned in general education classes by taking small groups of students into the community to practice what was learned. For example, a middle school general and special education teacher were team teaching. The subject was science and the topic was water pollution. The special education teacher took a small group of students, one of whom had a significant disability, to various water sources (ponds, rivers, swamps) and to the water purification plant. The goal for the student with a disability was to follow directions and assist in collecting the various sources of water for analysis. The goal for the students without disabilities was to provide directions on how to collect the water samples, interview the water purification employee, and analyze the results from the water samples collected.

Volunteers are another staffing source for implementing community-based instruction. Volunteers can be obtained through a variety of sources such as universities, retirement groups (including teachers!), service organizations, or local businesses. In addition, peers can also be used as volunteers. At a local high school, the teacher solicited the cheerleaders and athletes to volunteer in her classroom. Initially the students volunteered during their study halls. After a year, the teacher approached the principal and asked if students could earn credit. A mini course was developed in which the teacher trained the peer volunteers and students earned a half credit per semester for volunteering with

students who had moderate to severe disabilities. Note that if volunteers, peers or community, are utilized, training must be provided to ensure goals and objectives are being addressed within the community.

Scheduling

Implementing community-based instruction creates challenges in scheduling students and staff. Ford and colleagues (1989) suggest a step-by-step guide to developing schedules that ensure appropriate staffing as well as addressing student goals and objectives:

Step 1: Create a master list of each student's major instructional goals.
Step 2: Determine staff, volunteer, and other personnel resources availability.
Step 3: Schedule integrated general education classes and unstructured parts of the day (e.g., lunch, recess) and determine where staff are needed.
Step 4: Schedule remaining community-based and functional activities optimizing heterogeneous groups of students.

When scheduling, student goals and objectives must drive the schedule, not the professionals. It is up to the professionals to be creative and flexible in order to meet the needs of all students based on their individual goals.

Liability

Liability of school personnel and safety procedures are crucial components to consider when implementing community-based instruction. School districts may vary on how they cover liability. For example, in some districts, teachers are covered under the district's policy, but instructional assistants may not be covered. Parents should be made aware of what community-based instruction their child will be participating in and should sign a release. Be sure to obtain a copy of the district's liability policies and talk with the risk management personnel.

As we mentioned, community-based instruction is not just a field trip. Therefore, each community-based experience must be documented and data collected. This documentation is helpful not only for liability, but essential for tracking student progress. Provide alternative activities for substitutes to replace planned community experiences. Not many substitutes are trained or have the knowledge in implementing community-based instruction and this could turn into a liability concern for the district. It is also crucial that instructional assistants be trained for community-based instruction.

To ensure safety, give students and staff personal identification cards while in the community. Let the office secretary know when community-based instruction is occurring—where you will be and when you will return. It may be helpful to have portable phones or walkie-talkies while in the community to ensure safety.

Funding

Funding may be an issue, not just for transportation, but also for general programming. A local high school has written a discretionary grant with the state Department of Public Instruction to obtain money for additional staff to provide community-based instruction. A middle school has created a student-run popcorn business and students sell popcorn during lunch, after school, and at various school events. After the purchase of the popcorn, oil, and bags, the profits are used to fund community-based activities. Other schools have utilized shopping services for parents or school staff in which students are provided with a list of items and money. A local elementary school developed a postcard company and students create holiday and event-related cards (e.g., birthday, Valentine's Day) to sell to family and staff. The students choose stencil designs and create various packages of 5 or 10 cards per pack.

ADAPTATIONS FOR COMMUNITY-BASED INSTRUCTION

Determining the Need for Adaptations

Regardless of the severity or type of disability, all individuals have the right to participate in all activities. If students are unable to acquire or perform certain skills in order to participate in community activities, they should not be excluded. The principle of partial participation (Baumgart et al., 1982; Ferguson & Baumgart, 1991; York & Rainforth, 1991) states that it is better for students with moderate to severe disabilities to participate to the extent possible than to be denied access and opportunities. An individual does not have to have all the skills in order to participate in an activity with others. For example, Toni, a student with significant disabilities, can go to the mall after school with a group of nondisabled friends and purchase a snack at a fast-food restaurant. The fact that Toni cannot read and has limited verbal and fine motor skills should not exclude her from this experience. Her peers could take out the communication cards identifying various food items and assist Toni in deciding what to order. Toni can stand in line with her peers and hand the order card to the cashier. A peer could assist Toni in opening her wallet and taking out a dollar. Toni can hand the cashier the money while her peer assists in putting the change back in the wallet. Toni can also carry her tray to the table with her peers.

In addition to partial participation, individualized adaptations can be developed for students with moderate and severe disabilities to assist them in participating rather than excluding them from activities in the community. Educators must never assume the need for an adaptation and never use adaptations as substitutes for teaching. Four faulty assumptions are often made with regard to adaptations:

WE *ALL* "PARTIALLY PARTICIPATE"!

Partial participation should not be viewed as "less than."

From time to time, we all partially participate in activities. Diane, a nondisabled individual, won tickets to a football game and was very excited about going. The following week, I asked Diane how she liked the game. She said it was the best time she ever had. Knowing Diane knew nothing about football, I asked her where her seats were located. Her response was "I'm not sure, somewhere near the 65 yard line" and then added, "The team made a lot of great plays, especially when the team made a home run!" (For those non-football fans like Diane, a football field only goes up to 50 yards and the team makes touchdowns, not home runs!) Despite the fact that Diane did not always know what was happening, she "partially participated" in attending the football game and had a great time!

1. The goal of teaching is to achieve "normal" performance. This assumes an individual cannot be viewed as successful unless he or she can perform an activity in the same manner as someone without a disability. Through the principle of partial participation, we know that an individual with a disability does not have to be able to perform all the skills involved in an activity in order to gain experience and knowledge.

2. A core set of skills must be mastered before a student can participate in the community. This readiness concept or the need to attain certain prerequisite skills is detrimental to students with moderate and severe disabilities. If we think about our own lives, how many of us were truly ready for anything we accomplished in our lives? Most of us learned how to be ready by learning as we did activities and making mistakes. The same holds true for individuals with moderate and severe disabilities.

3. The same skills should be learned by everyone. This assumes that priority should be placed on the completion of a specific sequence of skill acquisition. We need to remember that we are all individuals and not all sequences make sense when taught in a certain manner.

4. The goal of instruction is independence. The presumption that an individual's participation is contingent on ability to perform certain tasks without assistance is a dangerous one. As human beings, we are dependent on one another, we are *interdependent* versus independent. When we insist that individuals with disabilities must be independent, we are in essence setting them up for failure. We need to begin teaching *interdependence*.

Adaptations can target a change in the environment (physical or social) or in the person (cognitive or sensory). Five types of individualized adaptations can assist students in participating in community and inclusive settings: (1) adapting skill/activity sequences, (2) adapting rules, (3) utilizing personal assistants, (4) creating or altering materials or devices, and (5) changing attitudes and social expectations (Baumgart et al., 1982; York & Rainforth, 1991). Table 14–3 includes examples of possible adaptations to facilitate a student's participation in community settings.

When deciding whether or not to use an adaptation, or what type of adaptation to use, first determine the discrepancies in performance. Use a discrepancy analysis, another informal assessment tool that can identify what skills are needed in a certain activity and where the potential discrepancies may be specifically in regard to a student with a moderate to severe disability (see Table 14–4 for an example). This assessment technique differs significantly from traditional evaluations because it requires a detailed examination of the actual skills needed to

TABLE 14–3   **Adaptation Possibilities**

Area of Need	Possible Adaptations for Job Accessibility
Mobility	✔ Doorways: minimum of 36″ wide to allow standard-sized wheelchair to pass through (as well as people using crutches, walkers, etc.). Doors should be automatic or easy to open. ✔ Paths: Ideally, the same 36″ width could be used for paths between desks or other areas within the workplace. Halls and other pathways should not have tables, chairs, tools, or other equipment narrowing the width of the path. One side of the path could be kept free of any items for people using wheelchairs or who have limited vision and use the wall as a guide. ✔ Handrails: If possible, handrails should exist along frequently used paths for people with difficulty seeing. Bright tape could mark the handrails as well. Handrails should be placed along ramps and in restrooms.
Grasping	✔ Handles: If doors are not opened electronically, large handles or handles that can be secured with an entire hand may be helpful. Levers can also fit over standard doorknobs. ✔ Built-up devices: Handles and controls can be made bigger or easier to manipulate. A drop of hot glue can be used to help identify the correct button to push or levers can be attached to the button. Foam or moldable plastic can be built up on tools for easier gripping. ✔ Switches: Many of the built-up devices and switches can be found commercially in catalogues (occupational therapy or physical therapy) or at local Radio Shacks. ✔ Increased steadiness: Dycem (found in occupational therapy catalogues) or Scoot Guard (found in hardware or carpet stores) are great for holding items in place. ✔ Replace traditional fasteners: Velcro or attachments to zippers (e.g., key chains).

This is not an all-inclusive list of adaptations, but may serve as a guide when making adaptations for individuals with disabilities.

perform a certain activity and does not focus solely on the individual's intellectual or physical competencies. Obtain information with regard to the skills needed to perform a certain task (a skill inventory of an individual without a disability) and compare it to an inventory of the skills the student with a disability has for that activity. Analyze this information to identify patterns or points of disparity in the skill performance and then list possible reasons for the discrepancies. Often, these discrepancies are not evident until you analyze the entire skill sequence. Figure 14–4 provides an example of a completed discrepancy analysis.

Area of Need	Possible Adaptations for Job Accessibility
Cognitive	✔ Picture cues: written instructions, directional/emergency signs, and other printed material can be reformatted into pictures. Pictures can be actual photos, drawings, or cutouts from magazines. ✔ Audio tapes: Prerecorded instructions/directions or reinforcement can be provided on audiotape for individuals to listen to either on a headset or a handheld tape player. ✔ Variety of instructional formats: It may be helpful to provide directions in a variety of formats (e.g., verbal and demonstration). ✔ Color coding: Organizing or providing information using specific colors (e.g., colored dots, colored folders, a red mark on the clock) may help individuals who cannot read or tell time. ✔ Peer/community member supports.
Sensory	✔ Noise reduction: Turn off machinery or equipment when not in use; place equipment/machinery in an isolated location. ✔ Increased contrast: Use of contrasting colors (e.g., walls are white and doors are outlined in blue), edge of stairs painted bright orange or yellow, computer screens, warning/informational signs. ✔ Alternative formats: Training and informational material should be made available in alternative formats (e.g., large print, on tape, Braille). Sans serif font should be used if possible (sans = without; serif = the little dots at the bottoms or tops of some letters). ✔ Use of personal guides: Sighted or helping dogs, peers to assist using sighted guide technique.

Prior to making any adaptations, ask the following questions: (1) Can environmental modifications eliminate the discrepancy? (2) Can other skills be taught to minimize the discrepancy? (3) Can restructuring or redesigning the skills sequence or activity eliminate the missing skill(s)? (4) Can the missing skill be compensated with a device or a modification of materials? (5) Do all skills involved in the activity need to be completed to participate?

Worksheets for Community Excursions

Functioning effectively and comfortably in the mainstream of community life involves more than academic and vocational skills. It involves skill in leisure pursuits, consumerism, getting from one place to another, and accessing community services, all of which lead to greater independence. Community-based worksheets can

TABLE 14–4 Job Adaptation Analysis

EMPLOYEE: Jennifer
JOB/TASK: Photocopying

Major Step	Description of Difficulty	Possible Adaptations
Get originals from secretaries and take to machine, then return copies to secretary.	Each secretary has photocopying in various locations on their desks. It will be difficult for Jennifer to (1) locate photocopying items from different locations and (2) remember which information goes to which secretary.	1. Each secretary can have a basket labeled "copy basket" placed in specific location. 2. Each secretary could have a color-coded circle to identify who they are and their materials.
Code machine with copy key number, the number to be copied, and collate/staple if needed.	It may be difficult for Jennifer to (1) keep track of the numbers to be copied and copy codes and (2) remember the collate/staple codes on machine.	1. The order forms could be adapted; copy key number, pictures of what to do (e.g., staple), and typed numbers would be circled by the secretary. 2. A red sticker could be attached on forms for collating (with a red sticker on the copier "collate" code), and a blue sticker could be attached on forms for stapling (with a blue sticker on the copier "staple" code).

provide curricular support to learn these skills during excursions into the community (see Figure 14–5).

As you have learned in previous chapters, the worksheets can be designed at different levels of difficulty to allow nondisabled students and students with moderate and severe disabilities to participate in the same excursion activity at their own skill levels. For each set of worksheets, the questions and tasks are asked at several levels, which vary in the number of questions asked as well as in the degree of complexity of those questions. Each level should address different information rather than simply watering down the information presented at a more difficult level. The box on p. 373 identifies the steps to follow when creating leveled worksheets. You always can vary the number of difficulty levels when you create the worksheets to accommodate the needs of a particular student or group of students (Hamill & Dunlevy, 2000).

Community-referenced worksheets used in the classroom can help students prepare for community excursions, and other worksheets can bring closure after the experience. Creating community-referenced worksheets for the

FIGURE 14-4   Discrepancy Analysis

Student: _____   Environment: _____
Domain: _____   Activity: _____

Inventory of a Person without a Disability	Inventory of a Person with a Disability	Reason for the Discrepancy*	Instructional Solutions Possible Adaptations
Skills:			
1. Goes to file on desk labeled "To Copy"	S: — Cannot read words on file T: Told what words said	L, I	Put color marker on file
2. Gets packets of material from file	S: — Forgets what he should do T: "What do you need to do?"	L, I, M	Picture sequence cards
3. Gets pencil or pen from counter			
4. Writes date and initial at top of each work order	S: — Forgets what he needs T: "You need a pencil"	L, I, M	Attach pencil to desk
5. Brings material to copy room	S: — Cannot write date from memory T: "The date is _____"	L, I	Have student use a date watch
6. Takes first group to file and unclips papers	S: + T:		
7. Enters copy code from work order	S: + T:		
8. Enters number to be copied	S: Cannot match numbers from paper to copier key pad T: Holds paper above key pad and points to numbers	L, I	Highlight code in yellow Use template over key pad
9. Gathers copies	S: Cannot match number for copy number T: Holds paper above key pad and points to number	L, I	Highlight number in blue Use template over key pad
10. Puts copies on shelf by name of order	S: + T: S: Cannot match name with order T: Points to name on work order and name on shelf	L, I	Preorder work in order Names on shelf

*Reasons for the discrepancy can be coded in the following manner:

I= instructional issues   P= physical, motor,
L= student learning issues   or sensory factors
E= environmental factors   M= motivation

369

F I G U R E 1 4 – 5   **Hospital Visit Worksheet**

Name_____   Date _____

During your tour of the hospital you will learn many important things that will be helpful to know if you ever need to go to the hospital. Listen carefully and ask questions when you do not understand something you see or hear. Fill in the worksheet as you tour the hospital. If you are not sure how to answer any of the questions, please ask the tour leader to help you.

For Student 1:

1. What is the name of the hospital? _____

2. What is the phone number of the hospital? _____

3. What number should you call if you forget the hospital number and you need medical help right away? _____

Touring the Hospital Lab

1. What does it feel like to have your blood taken? _____

2. What is the name of the place in the hospital where you go to have your blood taken?_____

_____

Touring the Hospital X-Ray Department

1. What is the name of the picture that looks inside your body?_____

2. On what floor is the hospital x-ray department? _____

Touring the Hospital Family Care Unit

1. Name a reason you would go to the family care unit. _____

_____

2. On what floor is the hospital family care unit? _____

---

classroom can inform students about what they will experience during a future excursion into the community. For example, leveled book reports about the different characteristics and habitats of animals can prepare students for a trip to the zoo. Other worksheets such as writing thank you letters can be completed in the classroom after a trip to the community. Some community-referenced worksheets can be used either in the school or in the community. For example, a worksheet can be created for students to use in the school library as well as the local public library (see Figure 14–6).

SUMMARY

In order for effective learning to occur for all students, the classroom must extend beyond the confines of four walls. This chapter described

For Student 2:

1. What is the name of the hospital? _____

2. On what street is the hospital?_____

3. What is the phone number of the hospital? _____

4. What is the name of the person who is showing you the hospital? _____

    What is that person's regular job in the hospital? _____

Touring the Hospital Lab

1. Why would you go to the hospital lab? _____

2. On what floor is the hospital lab? _____

3. Why might a doctor need to test your blood? _____

Touring the Hospital X-Ray Department

1. Name a reason that you might have an x-ray. _____

2. What does an x-ray show the doctor? _____

Touring the Hospital Family Care Unit

1. What are two reasons that might cause you to go to the family care unit?

    a. _____

    b. _____

2. How would you make an appointment at the family care unit? _____

3. On what floor is the hospital family care unit? _____

Source: Hamill, L., & Dunlevy, A. (2000). *Members of the community: Worksheets for transition activities in the community and the classroom.* Verona, WI: IEP Resources. Reprinted with permission.

what community-based instruction is and what it is not. We suggested ways to fund, staff, and schedule community-based activities. You learned about tools such as the life space analysis, ecological inventory, and discrepancy analysis charts to assist in assessing the needs of students and community environments. You were shown different ways in which community-based instruction can be incorporated into general education settings to benefit all students. Finally, this chapter provided sample work-sheets at varied levels for use in community-based instruction.

 CHAPTER EXTENDERS

Key Terms and Concepts

1. *Attitudinal accessibility* refers to settings where merchants and other providers of community services support the idea of

FIGURE 14–5   continued

For Student 3:

1. What is the full name and address of the hospital? _____
   _____
   _____

2. What is the phone number of the hospital pharmacy?_____

3. Name two reasons for which you might need to go to the hospital?
   a. _____
   b. _____

4. How can you find out which department you need to go to when you get to the hospital? _____
   _____

5. Where do you pay your hospital bill?_____

Touring the Hospital Lab

1. Name two things that happen in a hospital lab.
   a. _____
   b. _____

2. What kind of test uses what looks like a long cotton swab rubbed on the back of the throat? _____
   _____

3. What kind of instrument does the lab technician look into to make cells appear large enough to
   see? _____

4. What color is your blood? _____

5. Name a body fluid other than saliva or blood that might need to be looked at in the hospital lab.
   _____

Touring the Hospital X-Ray Department

1. What kind of doctor looks at x-rays? _____

2. What do you think doctors did to find out what was wrong inside a person's body before there
   were x-rays? _____

   Now that there are x-rays, do they still have to do this sometimes? _____
   Why? _____

Touring the Hospital Family Care Unit

1. Why would you choose to go to the family care unit instead of another department in the
   hospital?_____

2. Who would take care of you at the family care unit? _____

3. What does a visit to the family care unit cost? _____

4. Name a reason that the family care unit would not be the right place to go if you needed medical
   care. _____

Leveling Worksheets

How do you level worksheets? The worksheets should be structured so all the students are working on the same concepts even though they are actually solving different problems or answering different questions.

1. Decide which concepts/information you want to address.
2. Consider how each bit of information might be presented in a simpler form and which information can be assigned greater detail.
3. Sort the information, turned into questions/problems, by difficulty into several levels.
4. As each worksheet becomes more difficult, the number of questions/problems should increase as well as the difficulty of the questions/problems. The questions at each level of difficulty should address different information rather than contain the same questions in a watered down form.

Source: Adapted from Hamill, L., & Dunlevy, A. (2000). *Members of the community: Worksheets for transition activities in the community and the classroom.* Verona, WI: IEP Resources. Reprinted with permission.

teaching students with disabilities in their businesses or recreational facilities.

2. *Community-based instruction* refers to one type of instructional approach in which teachers design lessons that teach meaningful or functional skills in natural or real-world environments rather than simulated environments.

3. *Community-referenced curriculum* refers to instruction that takes place in the school but is directly related to activities that typically occur in the community or to activities for upcoming community excursions or follow-up projects in the school.

4. *Community service learning* is an instructional approach in which students provide service to others, increase community development and empowerment, and experience reciprocal learning with the people they serve.

5. *Community work-based learning* refers to workplace excursions, paid and unpaid work-like experiences, and paid work training.

6. *Ecological inventory* combines observation of community environments with physical and attitudinal accessibility with the activities for instruction and student priority goals.

7. *Discrepancy analysis* is an informal assessment tool used to identify what skills are needed in a certain activity and where the potential divergence may be specific for a student with a moderate to severe disability. It analyzes the information to identify patterns or points of disparity in the skill performance followed by listing possible reasons for the discrepancies.

8. *Functional skills* are the skills a student needs to increase interdependence and quality of life.

9. *Life space analysis* combines observations and interviews with the parents and student to discover the experiences and activities that occur in all aspects of the student's life and thus determine the current environments and skills in his or her repertoire prior to implementing instructional strategies or changes.

10. *Natural environments* are the places where both students with and without disabilities commonly use the skills they are learning.

11. *Physical accessibility* refers to environments that do not pose barriers or obstacles that prevent students with disabilities from entering or moving around in the setting.

12. *Research teams* group students with and without disabilities together to collect information on a particular topic by interviewing and observing the relevant people and things in their community.

FIGURE 14–6 Library Worksheet

Name _____ Date _____

For Student 1:

Using the Library

1. What is the name of the library? _____

2. What day(s) of the week is the library closed? _____

3. Who can you ask to help you find a book? _____

4. Where do you return the books you borrow from the library? _____

_____

5. What do need before you can check out a library book? Circle the answer.

   a. money   b. library card

Getting Help

1. Ask for help to find a book about *(topic of interest to the student)*. Write the name of the book you find here.

_____

_____

Study Guide

1. Discuss the advantages as well as the disadvantages of providing students with moderate to severe disabilities with community-based instruction.

2. List and discuss five considerations to take into account when choosing instructional environments.

3. Identify and describe at least two possible problems that might arise for each of the following areas for community-based instruction: (a) transportation, (b) staffing, and (c) scheduling.

4. What are the advantages and disadvantages of community-based versus community-referenced curriculum?

5. List and discuss three ways a program of community-based instruction can be effectively combined with inclusion in the general education classroom.

Small Group Activity

In small groups of 3 to 4 students, complete the following activity. Each group should read one of the scenarios given on pp. 377–378 and answer the following questions to develop an appropriate community-based instructional lesson. Then share the activities with the whole class.

1. What specific objectives do you plan to address and why do you believe they can better be achieved in the community than the classroom?

2. What academic content will be addressed during the excursion and how does it relate to the community environment you will be investigating?

For Student 2:

Using the Library

1. Where is the library located? _____

   _____

2. What days of the week is the library open? _____

   _____

3. Answer the following questions about borrowing library books:

   a. How many days can you keep a library book? _____

   b. What happens if you keep the book longer? _____

   c. What happens if you lose the book you've borrowed? _____

4. Use the computer terminal to find *(title of a book the student will enjoy reading)*.

   a. What is the name of the book's author(s)? _____

   b. Where is it in the library? _____

Getting Help

1. Are there any special events that sometimes take place at the library? _____ If so,

   what are they? _____

2. Where can I return books when the library is closed? _____

   _____

Source: Hamill & Dunlevy, (2000). *Members of the community: Worksheets for transition activities in the community and the classroom.* Verona, WI: IEP Resources. Reprinted with permission.

3. What methods of instruction/materials will you provide before, during, and after the excursion? How will you provide the instruction/materials during the excursion?

4. How will you assess student understanding of the lesson?

5. List any future excursions/activities that will provide periodic reinforcement of the skills that students acquired during the original excursion.

Field Experience

Visit a local service provider (police/fire/utilities) and investigate how you could develop a class excursion. Ask questions about accessibility, information materials, and any educational tours/lectures that might be available. Use the information you acquire to develop a plan for providing a community-based instructional lesson at that location for a class of students (including students with moderate to severe disabilities).

FIGURE 14–6 **continued**

For Student 3:

Using the Library

1. What is the library call number on the book? _____

2. In what section of the library did you find the book? _____

3. What can you borrow from the library in addition to books? _____
    _____

4. a. What are the library's usual hours of operation? _____

    b. Are there any days of the week when the library is open during different hours? _____

    c. If so, what day(s) and what are those hours of operation? _____

5. How much is the daily fee for each book that is overdue? _____

6. Pick a subject that interests you. _____ Use the computer terminal to find a book on that subject.

    a. What is the title of the book? _____
    _____

    b. What is the author's name? _____

    c. Now find another title by the same author. _____
    _____

Getting Help

1. Ask the librarian about story times/lectures you can attend. With the information you learn from the librarian, answer the following questions:

    a. Do they happen on a regular basis? _____

    b. If so, what are they and when are they offered? _____
    _____

    c. What is the next event that is offered? _____

    d. What date and time is the next scheduled event? _____

2. Can I renew a library book without going to the library? _____ If so, how can I do it? _____

Group 1: **Take a community excursion to:**
   The local grocery store
You have the following teaching assignment:
   A second-grade health class made up of 26 students, including one student with severe mental retardation and one student with cerebral palsy who has a visual impairment
Plan community-based instruction to teach the following general skill:
   To develop skills for choosing proper nutrition
The following conditions exist:
   The grocery store is only three blocks away but there are two very busy intersections between the school and the store.

Group 2: **Take a community excursion to:**
   The local courthouse
You have the following teaching assignment:
   An 11th-grade government class made up of 21 students, including one student who has mild mental retardation and a significant hearing impairment and one student with a physical impairment who uses a wheelchair
Plan community-based instruction to teach the following general skill:
   To develop skills for voting
The following conditions exist:
   The school is unable to provide a school bus for transportation but there is public transportation available in your town. The courthouse is located about a mile from the school.

Group 3: **Take a community excursion to:**
   The local zoo
You have the following teaching assignment:
   A third-grade science class made up of 24 students, including one student who has autism and one student with a hearing impairment who uses a hearing aid and who also wears braces and uses a walker
Plan community-based instruction to teach the following general skill:
   Environmental awareness
The following conditions exist:
   The school is unable to provide a school bus for transportation but public transportation is available in your town. The zoo is located several miles from the school and will require changing buses.

Group 4: **Take a community excursion to:**
   The local bank
You have the following teaching assignment:
   A ninth-grade business math class made up of 22 students, including one student who has Down syndrome and one student who has muscular dystrophy
Plan community-based instruction to teach the following general skill:
   Simple and compound interest on loans
The following conditions exist:
   The school is unable to provide a school bus for transportation and there is no public transportation available in your town. The bank is located six blocks from the school.

Group 5: **Take a community excursion to:**

To see a play at the local theater

You have the following teaching assignment:

A seventh-grade language arts class made up of 26 students, including one student with a significant health impairment who has a tracheotomy and uses a wheelchair and a student who has a severe visual impairment

Plan community-based instruction to teach the following general skill:

Character and plot development in writing

The following conditions exist:

The school is able to provide a school bus for transportation. The play is located 3 miles from the school.

Group 6: **Take a community excursion to:**

The local hospital

You have the following teaching assignment:

A fifth-grade health class made up of 25 students, including one student who has cerebral palsy and one student who has moderate mental retardation

Plan community-based instruction to teach the following general skill:

Gaining and maintaining a healthy body

The following conditions exist:

There is no public transportation available in your town and the school is unable to provide a school bus for transportation. The hospital is located on the far side of town about seven blocks from the school.

chapter 15

Educational Transitions

Transition is the process of moving from one place to another. Although entering a new situation can be exciting, the experience also may be accompanied by a good deal of uncertainty and stress. The transition process is part of all students' school experience. Students go through several transitions during their school careers. As they enter school, each time they move from one level to another, and again as they exit school, students and their families experience the excitement, uncertainty, and stress associated with transition. Times of transition may be particularly difficult for students with moderate to severe disabilities and their families. Careful planning can reduce the uncertainty and stress and help create successful transitions.

WHAT YOU WILL LEARN IN THIS CHAPTER

In this chapter, you will learn how to support students with moderate to severe disabilities and their families as the students enter school, move from elementary to secondary education, and leave school for adult lifestyles. You will discover how the collaborative efforts of a group of individuals organized into a transition team develop and implement a written plan that facilitates the student's inclusion into the next stage of his or her life. You will learn about various kinds of situations and events that students and their families should investigate as they prepare for each transition, and you will explore different instructional activities that can help prepare students to meet the challenges that face them in their next environment.

After a brief general overview of the components of the transition process, the chapter is divided into four major sections. First we describe the transition process for young children as they enter preschool programs and elementary school. The transition team, planning process, and specific skills a young child will need to adjust successfully in the next stage of the educational experience are discussed. Then

we address the transition from elementary to secondary education programs where school places emphasis on specificity in academic content and students change classrooms and teachers throughout the school day. Again, the particular transition team, planning process, and skills the student will need to move effectively to the secondary level are presented. In the third section we show how to create successful transitions for students as they leave school. Again we describe the transition team, planning process, and skills students will need to negotiate adulthood effectively. Finally, we provide information about how adults with moderate to severe disabilities connect to life in the community. Topics discussed in this section include postsecondary education, employment, lifestyles, and community participation.

WHAT IS TRANSITION?

IDEA requires schools to address transition for students with moderate to severe disabilities as they enter school and as they prepare to leave it (Bowe, 1995; Wehmeyer et al., 1998). In addition, ADA and the Rehabilitation Act amendments of 1992 mandate access to the community for these individuals (Hamill, 1994). A transition team meets to plan a student's move to the next level of education or the next stage of his or her life.

Transition Team

The transition team should facilitate the flow of relevant information between the individuals involved in the student's transition to ensure success without an interruption of services. The team is made up of those individuals who have information that will help define a transition plan to best suit the student's needs. The student and parents are critical members of the transition team. The parents provide the team with pertinent information about the family's strengths and what they want their child to accomplish. In addition, they identify skills and resources they have to support the student in attaining those goals. The student gives the team valuable insights into out-of-school interests and skills, such as community activities and neighborhood friends. He or she also informs the team about preferences and issues of concern at school. For example, the parents might share their desire for their child to live independently and the student can identify course selections and career aspirations. The team needs to be sensitive to the family's desire to get involved and encourage them by offering a variety of ways the family can participate in making transition decisions (McNair & Rusch, 1991). The student's present teachers, as well as the teachers he or she will have during the following year, also are vital members of the team. Other members of the team might include general education teachers, vocational coordinators and other relevant school personnel who know the student's education accomplishments, and service providers and others who know about programs and services available in the community.

Transition Planning

Transition planning involves developing a written transition plan (see Figure 15–1). The team works together to develop a vision of the outcomes they hope to help the student attain. Educational goals for all students, including students with disabilities, should address the development of self-esteem and independence to give students the tools necessary to take control of their lives. Often students with disabilities do not have the skills or the opportunity to exercise personal choices. As you have learned in the previous chapters, an applied curriculum encourages students to participate actively in projects that can present them with real-life problems. That kind of participation provides students with opportunities to make personal choices and develop problem-solving skills as they attempt to work through those problems. The student's strengths, interests, and needs

should guide the team in developing related transition goals and objectives that will be put into the written plan. To illustrate, Beth is a 16-year-old student who has both hearing and cognitive impairments. She is learning to be a banquet server in the work-study program at her high school. Beth's vision is to be employed, and she hopes to become a floor manager after graduation in the banquet service department of a major hotel. Beth particularly enjoys the setup and decorating aspects of banquet services. At the present time, Beth is able to read and understand restaurant floor plans and directions for banquet setups. Beth is friendly and eager to please. Her IEP states that Beth needs to develop language skills so her IEP team has noted that her language skill instruction should target specific restaurant and banquet terminology. The planning process should identify resources and the necessary supports to help students reach their goals (Institute for the Study of Developmental Disabilities, 1995).

It is important to keep records. Students and their parents should develop a system for keeping track of accomplishments and other personal milestones. The family might create a transition portfolio, which documents critical information about a student, and put in information such as personal information, documents, and contact persons relevant to various aspects of the student's life (Demchak & Greenfield, 2000) (see Figure 15–2). Well-kept records can prevent the loss of valuable information and avoid redundancy.

TRANSITION TO SCHOOL

Entering school is a giant step in the life of any young child. For young children with moderate to severe disabilities and their families, it can be a particularly stressful time. The children and their families need preparation as well as support during the transition process (Chandler, 1993). Educators need to help students and their parents develop the necessary skills to facilitate

FIGURE 15–1 **Writing Transition Plans**

All transition plans should include the following components:
1. A vision statement of the desired long-term outcomes for the student in the following areas:
   - employment and postsecondary education
   - adult living arrangements
   - community participation
2. A description of the activities and services needed to meet the desired long-term outcomes, the time frame for administering those activities and services, and the party responsible for monitoring progress.
3. A description of the next placement options and programs that will support the student in attaining the desired long-term outcomes.
4. A description of the annual goals and strategies needed toward achieving those long-term outcomes reflected in the student's IEP.
5. Identification of the appropriate course work in the secondary education program that will support the student in attaining the desired long-term outcomes.

the student's smooth transition from early intervention services to the preschool program and again as the student prepares to enter elementary school (Fowler & Hazel, 1996). This section discusses these transitions in the early years of school for young students with moderate to severe disabilities.

Transition Team

The transition team is made up of the various interested individuals and those who have relevant information to help plan for the successful transition of the child into formal schooling. The 1997 IDEA amendments stipulate that the transition process from early intervention to preschool must be a cooperative interagency effort between early intervention and early childhood education personnel (Turnbull & Cilley, 1999). Agency personnel include the early intervention specialist, social worker, medical professionals, or other professionals who have provided services and supports identified in the child's IFSP, and early childhood education personnel include the teachers, physical therapist, school nurse, speech/language pathologist, and/or other professionals who will provide the student's preschool instruction. The team also

must include the child's parents. No one knows the child's needs or can provide a bridge to the next stage in his life better than his parents. They have been an integral part of his life from the time he was born and they will continue to be important advocates for him the rest of their lives. For students transitioning from preschool to elementary school programs, the team again includes parents, the preschool and elementary school general and special education teachers, and any other individuals who may provide relevant insights. The other team members should include the professionals who work with the child now as well as those who will be working with the student during the following year. Depending on the particular needs of the individual child, the team also may include a school administrator, the child's doctor, a physical therapist, and other individuals.

Transition Planning

IDEA mandates transition planning from early intervention programs to preschool programs for students with disabilities by their third birthday (Turnbull & Cilley, 1999). During the final year of preschool, many states implement a formal transition process for a student who has

FIGURE 15–2

Keep Track of Accomplishments and Personal Milestones in a Transition Portfolio
1. Personal information:
    *   demographic data
    *   friends
    *   favorite things
    *   out-of-school activities
2. Records:
    *   financial records
    *   medical records
    *   copies of IEPs
    *   work history
    *   other reports
3. Contacts:
    *   names (agency and contact person)
    *   phone numbers
    *   brochures

Source: Adapted from Osborn, K., and Wilcox, B. (1992). *School to community transition: A planning and procedures handbook for parents and teachers in LaPorte County.* Bloomington, IN: Institute for the Study of Developmental Disabilities. Reprinted with permission.

received preschool special education services even if the teacher suspects the child will not qualify for school-age special education services. The following details the steps frequently taken in the transition process to the school-age program (E. Esber, personal communication, April 12, 1998).

Steps in the Transition to the School-Age Program:

1. (Usually in the Fall): The elementary special education coordinator gets referrals from preschool teachers and meets with the student's parents on a home visit. The home visit allows the transition process to begin in an environment most comfortable for the family. During the visit, a MAPS program is planned. As you learned in Chapter 5, a MAPS program is a valuable tool that can help articulate what the family hopes for in their child's education program.
2. (Usually in the Winter): The IEP team meets to review the IEP and begins to prepare for the student's transition into a school-age program. At the meeting, they fill out a transition referral form and determine what evaluation process is needed. The evaluation process takes place and the team develops and discusses a MAPS for the child. This allows the parents to determine their vision for the child. That vision is used to guide the team as they write a transition plan based on the child's present and future needs and determine what supports and services the child will need during the next year.
3. The intervention specialist visits different general education classrooms and then takes parents to look at the various possibilities.
4. (Usually in the Spring): The IEP team meets again for the annual IEP review. The team includes school teachers and therapists who will be involved in the child's education program for the coming year. The team will review the evaluation results and determine eligibility for school-age special education services. If the child qualifies for services, the team will determine the appropriate general education classroom and write an IEP with

goals and objectives as well as needed supports and services.

5. The child and the parents visit the elementary classroom to meet the teacher and become comfortable with the new environment as well as to give the teacher an opportunity to become familiar with the child's strengths and weaknesses. Personal contact between parents and future staff beyond the IEP meeting is very important because parents often fear leaving the security of their child's current staff and setting.

Transition Skills

Teach Students to Make Choices. Children who have good transition skills are prepared to enter elementary school. For example, children who possess skills such as taking turns appropriately and following directions are better prepared than children who have not mastered those skills (Chandler, 1993). Preschool students need to develop skills that will help them when they transition into elementary school. The demands made on students in elementary school are greater than they are in preschool. Students are expected to be able to do many more things on their own (Rule, Riechtl, & Innocenti, 1990). They must learn to be more independent so they can meet the increased demands and greater expectations in elementary school. For example, developing toileting skills often is one of the biggest achievements in preschool, and independent toileting typically is an expectation of students in elementary school.

One important aspect teachers need to make a part of their classrooms, whether they are supporting individuals with challenges or just typically developing children, are opportunities for personal choice. All children need opportunities

 Victoria is a 5-year-old with cerebral palsy who is nonambulatory. She enjoys preschool and interacts well with her peers during group activities. She will be attending a new school in her neighborhood next year. Victoria's transition team includes her parents, her preschool teacher, the special education teacher, the kindergarten teacher she will have next year, the occupational therapist, the physical therapist, the speech/language pathologist, and the school nurse. Because Victoria is medically fragile, the nurse will need to provide needed medical services.

Victoria's parents report that she has enjoyed her preschool experience. The feel their daughter has progressed emotionally as well as cognitively. They tell the team she has gained better trunk control and can sit independently for short periods of time. They want Victoria's occupational and physical therapy to continue to increase her independent sitting skills and strengthen her upper body to improve her range of motion. Victoria's parents also want to make sure the speech/language pathologist continues their daughter's speech therapy. Victoria has begun to use the picture exchange system this year and her parents want her to increase her use of the pictures to identify choices. The occupational therapist, the physical therapist, and the speech/language pathologist all agree with the parents' assessment of Victoria's progress and her needs for the following year.

The team discusses the parents' vision as well as the team members' recommendations. They then write new IEP goals to address those decisions. They also organize a series of scheduled visits to the kindergarten room so Victoria can become comfortable with her next school environment in advance of the new experience. The special education teacher and the kindergarten teacher agree to coordinate those visits and make the arrangements with the parents.

to express their choices as they grow and prepare to become as self-sufficient and independent as possible. For the child with moderate to severe disabilities, opportunities for personal choice are extremely important because much of the time he may need to be assisted by others. Like all children, he needs to have opportunities to feel independent and have some input in the decisions that impact his life. You can incorporate choice into the school day by scheduling activities that involve the student making choices about what kind of work he wants to do, what food he wants to eat, or the peers with whom he wants to interact. Some students may need you to do more than give a list of choices verbally. For example, you can give a nonverbal student several different foods to taste and observe the reaction to determine the student's preferences. These types of opportunities help build self-esteem and may defuse disagreements before they begin. Choice is a powerful tool in the classroom because it gives the student personal control over his life and allows him to act independently.

Guidelines for Giving the
Preschool Student Choices:

1. **Allow the student to make choices and make sure those choices can be carried out.** For example, do not give the student the option of going outside to play as a choice on a rainy day.

2. **Use choices that can easily be part of the classroom routine.** For example, have the student decide which activity he wants to do first or let him arrange the order in which he will complete a set of activities for that day. Remember to put out only the work or activities that are the choices available for that day.

3. **Incorporate choice into the informal activities that take place during unstructured school time.** For example, play period can be a time that allows for student choices. You can help the student choose an activity such as putting a puzzle together or using blocks to make a road for toy cars. Even when the student has a severe disability, he can make choices by either using picture cards or by pointing to either the puzzle or the blocks. You or the para-educator can hold up two of the items and ask, "Do you want to make a road with the blocks or put a puzzle together?"

4. **Provide opportunities for choice in social interactions.** For example, riding the bus to and from school can provide an opportunity for the student to make choices. Ask the student who he wants to sit with on the bus and encourage the chosen peer to participate. For a student with a severe disability, use a photo board that has several photographs of students in the class. Ask the student to point to or pull off the pictures of the student he chooses. If a photo board is too difficult for the student to use, have him choose while his peers are waiting in the classroom for dismissal by asking, "Can you go stand by, or point to, the student you want to sit with on the bus today?" Some children may need to use a yes and no board and be asked, "Do you want to sit with John today?"

Present choices in a way that allows the student to give an accurate answer. If he always chooses the last thing you say, word or picture cards may help him make his own preference known. Another way to alleviate this problem may be to repeat the question after giving all the choices so the names are not the last thing the student hears. For example, you might ask, "Who do you want to sit by today? Do you want to sit next to Michael or Stephen? Who do you want to sit by today?" Students who have echolalia, automatic speech, and other speech difficulties may need this additional support. This choice of sitting next to a peer can also be used throughout the day.

Teach Skills Needed in Future Environments. Not only should a transitional preschool curriculum provide students with opportunities for choice making, but it also should offer instruction that encourages and supports the development of other skills needed for a successful adjustment to an elementary school program. Students must be able to learn to work appropriately both in groups and independently, to complete seatwork in the manner prescribed, and to transition into, between, and out of activities. Help the preschooler develop these competencies by providing him with a variety of activities that address these skills. As the student nears the end of the preschool experience, the curriculum should increasingly focus on this kind of instruction to prepare students for the more intense level of these kinds of activities in elementary school (Rule et al., 1990). To learn what specific skills the student will need in the next setting, visit the classroom and survey the future staff. As you learned in Chapter 5, you can use an ecological inventory to assess that environment and determine the student's future needs.

TRANSITION FROM ELEMENTARY TO SECONDARY SCHOOL

The transition process from elementary to secondary education is less formal than the transition either into or out of school. Although IDEA requires schools to address transition for students with disabilities into school-age programs and from school to adulthood, no such mandate deals with transition between the different program levels in school. Nonetheless, recognize the importance of giving it formal consideration because the move from elementary school to middle school or junior high, and again when the student prepares to enter high school, can involve a good deal of change and adjustment. At the secondary level, students have to deal with a more complex curriculum and school environment as well as larger numbers of teachers and peers (Kaiser, 1997). This section describes transitions during the middle school years for students with moderate to severe disabilities.

Transition Team

The transition team that will help a student move to the next level of schooling always should include the parents and the sending and receiving teachers. The student should provide input about his preferences and should be included as a full participating member of the team. The team also may include other interested individuals as they become involved in the student's educational experience, such as the occupational therapist, a school administrator, respite care provider, job shadow coach, or other community members.

Transition Planning

During the final year of the student's elementary school experience, the student's teachers should get together with the middle school or junior high teachers who will be working with the student. These two groups of teachers need to communicate directly with each other to ensure an effective transition for the student (McKenzie & Houk, 1993). Whenever possible, also involve the student's parents and the student in the process (Kaiser, 1997). The school district can allow the teachers to meet during scheduled inservice time or provide substitute teachers and release them from a half day of teaching responsibilities. Before the meeting, the elementary school teachers should prepare a portfolio of the student that provides information beyond what can be found in the IEP. The portfolio should contain samples of the student's work that illustrate areas of strength and weakness as well as educational programming suggestions including effective instructional techniques and adaptations, the student's preferred methods of participation, positioning strategies, behavior plans and strategies for reinforcement, communication methods, and/or any other needed supports (Demchak & Greenfield, 2000). The teachers also should include a profile of peers who are important in the student's school day. For example, they might include information about the typical students and other students with disabilities who are friends of the student or who have interacted with the student in informal school settings such as sitting together at the same lunch table or playing with each other on the playground during recess. The family also should prepare a profile of the student's current friends or other students with whom their child is familiar from their church group, neighborhood, or other out-of-school setting. That kind of information can help the transition team place the student in secondary settings where there are other students with whom he is already comfortable.

At the meeting, the elementary teachers and the family members who are present share the profile they have compiled. They describe and discuss the student's personal and educational strengths and needs. They offer any strategies they used and found successful as well as those strategies that were unsuccessful and should be avoided. When the teachers and family members have shared the student profile, they help the middle school or junior high teachers construct the student's new program. They need to "establish a firm transition plan between elementary and middle school that provides direction and focus for academic achievement and emotional and social growth" (Kaiser, 1997). Together, they brainstorm to determine how they can support the student as he encounters new surroundings and adjusts to new demands such as changing classes during the school day. The meeting participants also decide the most appropriate structure for the student's education program. For example, they consider issues such as inclusion, course scheduling, and curricular adjustments. They also should be aware of adolescents' need for social relationships and develop a plan to help the student cultivate a circle of friends (Kaiser, 1997). To begin this process, they can plan a series of visits to the new middle/junior high school before the transition takes place to help the student become comfortable with the new setting and students. The sending and receiving teachers can even develop collaborative activities with the elementary and middle/junior high students to encourage familiarity among the two groups of students and begin a peer buddy relationship.

Address transition again as the student prepares to enter high school. Repeat the same process undertaken at the end of the student's elementary school experience during the final semester of the student's middle school or junior high experience. Just as the meeting to address transition from elementary school involved the family and the relevant individuals from both the student's present and future school programs, this meeting should include the sending and receiving school personnel as well as the student and his parents.

Transition Skills

Teach Students to Make Choices. Like the preschool teacher, the elementary school teacher needs to help students develop skills that will enable them to become more self-sufficient and independent when they enter the secondary school environment where such behavior is typically expected of students. Follow the same simple guidelines for providing students with choices for elementary students as you would for preschoolers. For example, lunch can present opportunities for the elementary student to incorporate choice into the informal activities that take place during unstructured school time. The parents can help the student pack his own lunch at home or the cafeteria staff can help him pick a lunch from among the items available in the lunch room. Even when the student has a severe disability, he can make choices by either using picture cards ahead of time and simply handing the card to the cafeteria helper or choosing what he wants to eat first on his tray. The teacher or para-educator can hold up two of the items on the tray and ask, "Do you want to eat your cheese sticks or your hot dog first?" Recess can provide opportunities for choice in social interactions. Ask the student who he wants to play with and encourage the chosen peer to include the student. Remember, you may have to use strategies such as a yes and no board or a board with classmates' photographs to support choice making for a student with a severe disability. You may even have to ask the student to choose from his actual classmates while they are standing in the line for recess. Remember to make sure to present choices in a way that the student can be successful in answering. Success allows him to build self-esteem and gives him the confidence to risk making more choices for himself.

Teach Skills Needed in Future Environments. A well-designed pretransition program that directly prepares students to move from one school level to another also is an important component of the transition process (McKenzie & Houk, 1993). A curriculum that focuses on the specific skills the transition team's receiving teachers have identified as important in their curriculum will help the student handle the increased expectations he will encounter at the next school level. Consequently, if the middle or high school program has an inclusive applied curriculum, such as the Classy Cleaners we described in Chapter 13, the preceding elementary program should provide similar inclusive activities, such as the "Super Stuff" cart described in Chapter 12. An underlying goal in each program is to give students opportunities to build friendships and collaborative skills that will prepare them to interact effectively with co-workers as well as learn basic workplace routines and build expectations for the future. To ensure connections are made between those programs so students can move smoothly from one to the other, a formal structure for communicating on a regular basis about each program's activities and expectations should be developed and include the teachers at both levels. For example, a portion of the time allotted for regularly scheduled districtwide inservice activities or cross-grade level subject area staff meetings could be designated for teachers to exchange this kind of information.

Another important transition occurs for students with moderate to severe disabilities during their secondary education experience when they leave the junior high or middle school building and enter high school. Students need to be prepared for new expectations and increased demands. They may have greater academic responsibilities, such as more homework and more complicated schedules. They will have new extracurricular activities and social opportunities, such as dating and school dances. These new experiences can be both exciting and sometimes overwhelming. The sending and receiving teachers should meet with the student and his parents to address these issues and ease the student's transition into high school. Then during the high school years, the student's team members focus their efforts on preparation for the final transition out of school and into adult life.

 TRANSITION FROM SECONDARY SCHOOL TO ADULTHOOD

Transition to adulthood is an important time in the life of a student with moderate to severe disabilities. Issues such as accessing the community, additional schooling, gaining employment, and adult lifestyle choices can be particularly complicated issues for the student and his family. The student may require either intermittent or ongoing support to participate fully in these activities.

Postschool adjustment studies have found that adults with moderate to severe disabilities have greater difficulty than their typical peers attaining and maintaining a reasonable quality of life (Blackorby & Wagner, 1996). They are frequently isolated in the community, leaving them feeling lonely (Chadsey-Rusch, DeStefano, O'Reilly, Gonzalez, & Gollet-Klingenberg,

1992). They may lack knowledge of the appropriate behavior needed to participate in everyday interactions with acquaintances, the general public, co-workers, and supervisors. They also may have limited job-related skills, awareness of appropriate jobs, and ability to obtain and maintain employment (Sitlington, Frank, & Carson, 1992). Although family members and friends help many individuals with disabilities find postschool employment, they often work in jobs that pay low wages (Love & Malian, 1997). Individuals with moderate to severe disabilities also have greater difficulty than their typical peers in seeking and maintaining housing; accessing community services and recreational activities; maintaining personal health; and planning, buying, and preparing food (Chadsey-Rusch, Rusch, & O'Reilly, 1991; Edgerton, 1967; Edgerton & Bercovici, 1976).

At the secondary education level, the school should create an environment and a curriculum that promotes preparation for successful transition from school. As you learned in Chapters 11 and 13, the student's secondary education program should help him develop the skills necessary to negotiate adult life successfully. Teachers should provide instruction in identifying career and lifestyle goals, using self-advocacy skills, and developing friendships with same-age typical peers. This section addresses these issues for students with moderate to severe disabilities as they prepare to transition from school to adult life.

Transition Team

At the secondary level, the transition team should address all aspects of the student's future life, such as postsecondary education placements, employment, community resources, and service options. Team members should represent not only the environments in which the student will be involved in the future, but also the various environments in which the student is presently involved (Steere, Wood, Panscofar, & Butterworth, 1990). They should include the student, parents, friends, and the student's present teachers and other service providers as well as future service providers such as adult service agency personnel and potential employers. No one knows the student's desires more than the student does. His wishes, with support from his parents, should guide the planning process. The team must also identify and include agency personnel who are presently involved in the student's life and adult service providers who will help the student access and navigate the community, work, and home settings in his adult life. For example, a respite care provider or behavioral consultant who provides support to the family outside of school can offer another perspective that provides valuable data and insights. In addition, a representative from the Bureau of Vocational Rehabilitation must be invited to the student's team meeting in the final year of high school to ensure that supports will not be interrupted when school services cease and need to be replaced with adult services. The team helps the student and his parents develop and implement his transition to adulthood.

Planning and the Individual Transition Plan (ITP)

The team should administer a variety of formal and informal assessments to determine the student's aptitudes and interests. These instruments help team members narrow their focus and target the student's real interests and strengths (Kapes & Martinez, 1999). For example, a formal vocational assessment given prior to the meeting can reveal that the student will likely be most successful in a job that involves sorting materials but does not require a good deal of physical stamina or upper body strength. In addition, informal assessments also provide useful information and can be simple to administer. For example, you can observe and chart the student's performance during typical school routines. The student will indicate interests and reveal strengths as he participates in school activities and engages in authentic assessments in the classroom. Interviewing the student and his family also will help determine their desires for the student's future. For example, the student and those close to him may participate in the COACH family interview or the MAPS process you learned about in Chapters 5 and 6. The student also may identify interests during the discussions that take place in the ITP meeting.

Planning for the transition from school to adulthood means helping a student have choices and make personal decisions about where he will work, where he will live, and what kinds of social life he wants. The purpose for this planning is to ensure that the student has a high-quality and successful adult life at home, work, and in the community (Wehman, 1996). In other words, planning should focus on supporting the individual with a moderate to severe disability as he makes his choices known.

Use a Person-Centered Approach. Person-centered planning is often used to refer to the process of personal futures planning. This method of transition planning empowers students and their families to take an assertive role in planning for the future (Miner & Bates, 1997). It is a consumer-oriented approach that focuses on placing the person with the disability at the center of the decision-making process (Hagner, Helm, & Butterworth, 1996). For example, the student should help decide the time and location of meetings and provide input in the choice of transition team members. He should be asked to determine appropriate postschool interests and goals, and then should help identify appealing strategies for attaining those goals. To help in making those decisions, the student must consider his strengths and interests. Here are some questions that may assist students in this process:

1. How independent am I, and what supports do I need to be as independent as I want to be?
2. What are my strengths and weaknesses, and how can I accommodate them?
3. What are my goals and how can I accomplish them?

Implementing the ITP.   When the student graduates from high school, he should be able to live in a home with people he chooses, work in a job he likes, and share in community activities with friends. The transition team incorporates an individual transition plan (ITP) into the IEP to ensure that will happen. As you learned in Chapter 6, the IEP must contain a statement about how the student's curriculum addresses transition by the time the student reaches age 14. An IEP/ITP that identifies needed transition services must be written by the student's 16th birthday, but it may be written earlier for students with extensive disabilities who need additional time to make adjustments and learn needed skills (Turnbull & Cilley, 1999). The ITP should focus on the student's successful integration in the community. It includes a statement of the student's desires and needs for his future life, identifies strategies and supports for attaining those goals, and connects the student with the appropriate service system providers (Institute for the Study of Developmental Disabilities, 1992). (See Figure 15–3 for a sample IEP form.)

The ITP not only guides the transition efforts focused on postschool strategies and outcomes, but it also guides the student's secondary education program. The ITP is included with the IEP and links the identified skills the student will need to function effectively in his workplace, home, and community to specific IEP goals and objectives (Bateman & Linden, 1998). Consequently, if the ITP notes that a student's postschool strategy for independent living is to be able to manage personal finances, the student's IEP should have a goal linked to developing those skills. For example, the team members may determine that the student should learn to rectify a monthly bank statement in preparation for this transition. To address this transition need, they can put an annual goal in the IEP that states the student will reconcile his checking account statement with his personal check record and use a calculator to correct all errors. The goal could be addressed while learning basic accounting techniques in a business math class.

F I G U R E   1 5 – 4   Ohio IEP/Secondary Education Transaction Form

Discuss and Document a Statement of Needed Transition Services

Name of Student _____ Date _____ Person(s) Responsible for Coordinating Transition Services _____

Write a statement of transition service needs that focuses on the student's courses of study during his/her secondary school experiences (beginning at age 14 or younger, if appropriate).

- Long-term Outcomes—What is the vision for the student exiting education?
- Activities and Services—What needs to be accomplished in one year to support the student in meeting long-term outcomes?
- Activities and services must include community experience.
- If activities and services are instructional-based, they must be reflected in goals/objectives of IEP.
- The courses of study during the student's secondary school experiences must support the student's long-term goals.

For 16 Years and Older		Completed After IEP Development

Employment and Postsecondary Long-Term Outcome: _____

Current Year Activities and Services	Responsible Person/Provider	Initiation/Duration (Specify Date)	Goals/Objectives that Support Activities/Services

Postschool/Adult Living Long-Term Outcome: _____

Current Year Activities and Services	Responsible Person/Provider	Initiation/Duration (Specify Date)	Goals/Objectives that Support Activities/Services

Community Participation Long-Term Outcome: _____

Current Year Activities and Services	Responsible Person/Provider	Initiation/Duration (Specify Date)	Goals/Objectives that Support Activities/Services

Vocational Evaluation ☐ Needed ☐ Not Needed Date Completed _____
Functional/Daily Living Evaluation ☐ Needed ☐ Not Needed Date Completed _____

Source: Ohio Department of Education (2000). *Model policies and procedures for the education of children with disabilities.* Columbus, OH: Author.

As you learned in the previous chapters, school programs that include applied academics and work experiences help prepare students to be successful adults. Students who have been given a curriculum that emphasizes a school-to-work philosophy and provides maximum opportunities for education with typical peers will have the best chance to make a successful transition to adulthood. For example, students who have participated in projects like the Breakfast Place during high school gain real work experience in jobs that they can do successfully and exist in the job market, thus easing their transition from school to the community. Likewise, students who have attended classes with their typical peers and who have gained acceptance in the school community will be better prepared for the social challenges of adulthood.

Transition Skills

Teach an Applied Curriculum. The increased focus on preparing students with moderate to severe disabilities for transition from school to postschool life means that all educators must find instructional approaches and make adaptations to the curriculum. The secondary curriculum should provide a foundation that will shape the student's ability to negotiate his or her future life successfully (Manzone, 1987). The curriculum not only should give students a solid applied academic foundation but also should provide them with functional living skills to give them many of the tools they will need for a successful adult life. A curriculum that attends to the social and vocational needs of students creates links between school and adult life and can provide meaningful experiences as the students prepare to enter adulthood (Udvari-Solner, 1992; Weaver, Landers, & Adams, 1991).

Teach Students Independence with Choices. Students who lack the skills to become as independent as possible will find their entrance into adult life a difficult experience with few rewards. Helping students develop skills that will enable them to become more self-sufficient and independent by giving them choices is essential at the secondary level. Earlier in this chapter, you learned that elementary school programs need to provide students with choices. Secondary education programs also need to offer students lots of opportunities for making choices. As with younger children, integrate opportunities for choices into both the classroom routine and unstructured school time. The same general guidelines for working with preschool and elementary students will provide secondary students with valuable opportunities to make choices.

Teach Self-Determination Skills. Presenting students with choices is one way to help them become self-determined individuals who can create an adult life they find personally satisfying. The term *self-determination* refers to the ability to make choices, set personal goals, and take initiative in achieving those goals (Martin & Marshall, 1995). Individuals who are self-determined make their own decisions and are in control of their lives. They act autonomously, in a psychologically empowered manner, with self-regulated behavior, and are self-realized individuals (Wehmeyer et al., 1998).

To be self-determined, students need to develop an understanding of who they are and learn to advocate for themselves. They must be aware of their strengths and weaknesses. They have to know what their needs are and what interests them. Students should recognize their personal worth and their value to others. They also need to become personally accountable and take responsibility for their actions.

Once students understand themselves, they can learn to act on their own behalf. To become effective self-advocates, students must be able to communicate their needs and desires to others. They must have choices and learn to make their own decisions. Students also need to learn to set priorities and have realistic goals. They should know and understand their civil rights.

To give students with disabilities the maximum opportunity for success in their adult lives, the curriculum should address issues related to self-determination. The purpose of teaching self-determination is to foster independence and self-esteem. An ideal curriculum is one in which self-determination is thoroughly integrated throughout the student's curricula and daily interactions and emphasizes the application of instructional concepts to real-life situations (Cronin & Patton, 1993). Your stance in this process should be one that promotes active student participation in the learning process (Nunn & Nunn, 1993).

Teaching self-determination as part of the applied and inclusive curricula you learned about in this text involves two major components: (1) self-knowledge and (2) self-advocacy. The self-knowledge component involves teaching the student to understand and accept his or her strengths and weaknesses, needs and interests, personal worth and importance to others, and personal accountability and responsibility (Wehmeyer et al., 1998). Teachers who try to shield the student from the realities of his disability or from negotiating the difficulties that everyone must face in life only *handicap* the student and add to the problems he will have to face when he leaves school. The self-advocacy component involves teaching the student to communicate his needs and desires, have choices and make decisions, learn to set personal priorities and have realistic goals, develop skills that allow for the greatest degree of independence, and protect personal interests by knowing his civil rights (Wehmeyer et al., 1998).

The stance you take in delivering instruction and encouraging students to become self-determined is equally as important as what you teach about self-determination. If a student is to learn self-determination, you must approach the student as if he is capable of taking control of his life. As much as possible, take the role of a facilitator who aids the student and guides him in developing the skills necessary to take responsibility for himself. Respect the student, encourage the student's personal growth, and encourage him to participate actively in the learning process. Create an environment where the stu-

dent has choices and makes meaningful decisions. Encourage parents to provide a similar experience for the student when he is at home.

Guidelines for Developing
Self-Determination Skills:

1. **Promote interpersonal skill development.** Frequently, the reason employers give for firing an employee is not that he was unable to perform the required tasks but that he was unable to get along with co-workers or supervisors. Students should learn to follow directions, recognize the difference between good and bad advice, and handle constructive criticism from those in authority.

 Beth has regular opportunities to receive and respond to verbal feedback on her academic and behavioral performance in school during periodic individual conferences with her teacher, Mr. Beal. The regularly scheduled meetings provide a forum for learning and practicing appropriate responses that will help Beth deal effectively in her future interactions with an employer or supervisor.

2. **Encourage communication skill development.** Students should learn to ask for help when it is appropriate. They need to practice expressing themselves to make their choices known and their opinions heard.

 During a school outing, Frank goes into a clothing store and tries to find an item he has been assigned to locate and price. Frank initiates the search for the item and asks a clerk for assistance when he is unable to gather any necessary information.

3. **Teach civil rights.** Students should learn that they have certain civil rights and understand the laws that protect those rights. For example, they should know that the Rehabilitation Act amendments and the Americans With Disabilities Act (ADA) will protect their rights throughout their lives. The curriculum should address an individual's specific rights and an individual's recourse if those rights are violated. Teaching these civil rights laws could easily be infused into a federal government or civics curriculum (Hamill, 1993).

As part the of the curriculum in a U.S. government class, Barbara and her classmates learn about the Americans With Disabilities Act. The students work in cooperative groups to research and write reports on the accessibility of various local business and activities in their community. Barbara's assignment is to call several places, ask what accommodations they provide, and report what she learns to her group.

Not only can you promote self-determination through your instruction considerations, but you also can promote self-determination with the teaching stance you take. A number of strategies are helpful.

Guidelines for Using a Teaching
Stance That Promotes
Self-Determination:

1. **Use facilitative teaching strategies.** Encourage students to participate. Provide a learning environment where students take an active role in the learning process. Instruction should be experiential and involve hands-on activities.

During a small group activity in Mrs. Welling's health class, Katie and three other students busily use one of the classroom game boards and custom-made cards to practice and reinforce their knowledge of household safety. They make up one of six different groups of students who are simultaneously playing games in the classroom. Katie has been chosen her group's leader for the activity so she both plays and monitors the game. She makes sure everyone follows the rules and makes sure all the players have the opportunity to help each other with difficult words or concepts. Mrs. Wellings acts as a facilitator by watching each of the small groups as they all play the games using different boards and cards. She only helps Katie and the other students when everyone in the group has had difficulty correctly reading a game card or when they have tried unsuccessfully to determine a particular answer.

2. **Value and respect students.** When interacting with your students, accentuate the student and deemphasize his or her disability. Recognize your students' capabilities. Have high, but reasonable, expectations for their achievements. Instruction should come from students' interests and needs. Encourage your students to express themselves and "listen" when they do.

Mrs. Hall schedules a weekly round table class discussion to allow her students the opportunity to talk about and resolve problems that occur in school. During the round-table discussions, the students also share experiences they have outside of school.

3. **Promote student growth and maturation.** Provide opportunities for your students to have positive experiences. Successful experiences build self-esteem. Students will be more likely to try new things if they have experienced success in the past. Focus instruction on the students' strengths and interests. Encourage your students to develop confidence by giving them *real* choices.

 When Mr. Williams's government class studies local government, he plans to have a guest speaker come into the classroom as well as take the class on a community excursion. He encourages his students to suggest government offices they want to visit and he lets them decide which guest speaker they want to have come to talk to the class. The students choose to have a representative from the League of Women Voters come to class to teach them proper voting procedures, after which they vote to visit the courthouse to talk with a local

4. **Promote student participation.** Make learning an active process for your students. Provide hands-on activities and apply content to the students' lives. Encourage your students to risk new situations. Allow your students to make mistakes and solve problems for themselves. Do not *fix* things for them. Expect your students to take responsibility for their actions. Help them understand and accept the consequences of those actions.

 Tanesha participates in a work experience as part of a community-based secondary education program. Her teacher, Mr. Raymond, expects her to take responsibility for any inappropriate actions.

When she showed up late for work one day last week, he did not make excuses for Tanesha with her employer. Because it was the second time Tanesha was late, she lost part of her pay for that day. Mr. Raymond expected Tanesha to deal with the results of her actions and accept the consequences her employer imposed.

5. **Ask parents to support this process.** Parents can help their child become self-determined at home. Encourage parents to have high, but reasonable expectations and recognize their child's capabilities. Help them understand that they can encourage their child to express opinions and *listen* to his ideas. Tell parents that they can help their child develop good consumer skills, ask for help when it is appropriate, express his opinions, and make his choices known.

 Mrs. Vasques, Lance's teacher, encouraged Lances's parents to give him real responsibilities at home with a routine "household job." She suggested they have Lance wash dishes, do laundry, or find some other activity he can learn and do on a regular basis that benefits the family. In return for contributing to the household, Mrs. Vasques suggested Lance's parents could provide a regular allowance. The allowance could include adequate funds to purchase school lunches and access social activities such as going to the movies that would give Lance the opportunity to learn and practice budgeting money and managing personal finances.

6. **Encourage active student participation in IEP/ITP meetings.** The IEP/ITP meeting provides an excellent opportunity to evaluate a student's level of self-determination. Look for examples of the student expressing what he wants to do after school and the plans he describes for attaining those goals. Be sure the student has choices and those choices guide the decision-making process (Hamill, 1993).

Mary has expressed a desire to work in a hospital, so the members of her IEP/ITP team have questioned her to determine how she would like to reach her goal. The team will help Mary find and make modifications to her education program so she can develop the skills she will need to work in that setting. For example, they have decided she will participate in the school's Breakfast Place Restaurant project as well as a work-study placement in the local hospital cafeteria. Her participation in the Breakfast Place will allow her to develop foundation skills and will complement her work-study placement in the local hospital cafeteria.

You may use a variety of measures to determine the extent to which teaching self-determination skills has been successful and how well the student transfers learned skills to new situations (Wehmeyer et al., 1998). Watch the student as he engages in an activity that allows him to exhibit self-determined behavior. Record descriptions of the instances of the observed behavior. Provide debriefing activities after instruction and practice that involve self-determination (see Figure 15–4).

 ## ADULT OPTIONS AND OUTCOMES

Everyone needs some level of assistance, either intermittent or ongoing, in at least some areas of their life to experience and benefit fully from adult options and outcomes. That support can come from family, friends, community services such as the local newspaper, or support agencies such as family services. These kinds of supports should be linked with the student's wishes and integrated into the transition plan. This section addresses four areas of transition for successful adjustment in adulthood: postsecondary education, employment, life style, and community participation.

 FIGURE 15–4 **Self-Determination Debriefing Activity**

Give a worksheet or have a class discussion. Questions might include the following:
1. What did you learn from this activity?
2. What did you like best about this activity?
3. What was easy for you to do?
4. What was hard for you to do?
5. What problems did you have?
6. How did you solve the problems you had?
7. What would you do differently next time?
8. What would you choose to do again?

The concept of normalization should guide all aspects of planning for successful transition to adulthood. Normalization refers to all individuals with disabilities having available everyday living routines that are as close as possible to the typical life patterns of the nondisabled population (Nirje, 1969). The principle of normalization has guided special education service delivery since it was first introduced in the United States in the late 1960s by Wolf Wolfensburger (Beirne-Smith et al., 1998). When transition team members consider appropriate community options, they should reference the lifestyles and the routines of the general public. For example, individuals with moderate to severe disabilities should live on their own or in homes and with friends or family. They should work in competitive employment settings. They should have opportunities to develop interpersonal relationships such as friendships, marriage, and families. They should have access to and control over their finances to the greatest extent possible.

Postsecondary Education Options

Section 504 of the Vocational Rehabilitation Act (P.L. 93-112) and the Americans With Disabilities Act (P.L. 101-336) have increased the opportunity of students with disabilities to participate in postsecondary education (Cole, 1995). Choosing a postsecondary institution is a challenge for all high school students and their families. Students with disabilities have to make the same choices and often meet the same standards as other students. Choosing a postsecondary institution and program of study that accommodates the interests and needs of students with moderate to severe disabilities calls for careful planning. For example, a student with a visual impairment would need to determine which institution he is interested in attending and then contact the disability support services office at that school to determine how he would access adapted computer keyboards on campus and other accommodations he might need.

Tanya is enrolled in the cooperative business education program at the local junior college. She is learning filing procedures and keyboarding skills as well as how to operate office equipment such as the fax and the copy machines. Tanya has a visual impairment that only allows her to see objects clearly with her peripheral vision. She must attend carefully to the classroom/office landscape to avoid contact with anything in the room that might have inadvertently been moved. The disability services office has provided Tanya with an adapted computer keyboard and software that enlarges print to use during keyboarding activities. Tanya's instructors have created enlarged filing labels that have been placed next to the corresponding standard materials. They also have enlarged the written directions for using the office equipment as well as the other written materials Tanya uses in her program.

The literature shows that a relatively large percentage of students with physical, health, and sensory impairments pursue postsecondary education (Turnbull et al., 1999). Although few students with cognitive disabilities participate in the academic programs on college campuses, their numbers have begun to increase (Page & Chadsey-Rusch, 1995; Hall, Kleinert, & Kearns, 2000).

High school counselors are a source of information about all kinds of postsecondary education programs. The Vocational Rehabilitation (VR) counselor is another good source of support for a student preparing to enter a postsecondary education institution. VR services may include needed supports during a student's postsecondary education program. Services may include tuition, housing, books, tutors, note takers, or other supports the student needs to be able to participate in postsecondary education programs. In some cases, the curriculum may even be modified.

James wants to work in a flower shop. He loves flowers and often helps his mother pick and arrange the flowers from their family garden. His transition team is helping James enroll in the horticulture program at the local vocational school. They also will work with the instructors at the school to implement modifications that will allow James to have a successful experience. Because James would have difficulty learning some of the skills associated with growing healthy plants, his program will be designed to meet his individual needs and interests. The math calculations related to plant food and growth cycles, knowledge of fertilizer chemistry, and plant biology are some of the components of a horticulture curriculum James would have significant difficulty mastering. Therefore, he will not take the entire course of study. Instead, his program will be designed so he will be able to focus solely on learning plant care techniques and flower arranging. When James finishes his personalized horticulture program, the vocational school will assist with his job placement as a flower arranger in a neighborhood flower shop.

Support services provided by the institution can help the student access the postsecondary education experience to attain not only improved employment options but also interpersonal rewards. Taking a reduced course load, having flexible instructors, auditing classes, working with a study buddy, or participating in a special on-campus program to develop independent living skills may allow the student to attend col-

lege (Page & Chadsey-Rusch, 1995). Many college campuses have student organizations, such as Natural Ties (Hughes, 1994), which can provide an excellent source of social connections and natural supports.

Types of Postsecondary Education Options:

1. **Four-year college or university.** These programs are designed to be completed in 4 years, but students may enroll in fewer courses at a time and take longer to finish. Students take general courses such as math, science, literature, history, and foreign languages as well as about ten courses in their major subject. Upon successfully completing the program requirements, the student receives a bachelor's degree.

2. **Two-year schools.** These schools offer programs to educate students for specific careers. There are two different kinds of programs available. The nontransferable programs offer occupational training for students who do not want to continue school after the program, and transfer programs that are 2-year academic programs that offer an associate of arts degree and can count towards a 4-year degree. Note that many of the courses taken in programs such as the vocational/technical schools may not transfer to a 4-year school.

3. **Occupational, technical, and business schools.** These programs are designed to train individuals for specific jobs. Students earn certificates in programs that take about 6 to 12 months, diplomas in programs that take about 9 to 18 months, and associate degrees in programs that take about 2 years. The longer training programs usually prepare students for jobs with more pay and responsibility. It is important to know that students in these types of programs often take a series of general education courses that may not be appropriate for all students with disabilities.

Students and their parents need to ask questions to determine the extent to which the postsecondary institution is able and willing to make necessary accommodations. The student needs to ask questions related not only to his disability and interests, but also to his strengths and weaknesses when choosing a school. The student must know what he does well and does not do well to make choices that will lead to a successful experience. Students and parents also may find it helpful to visit prospective schools and ask questions. Asking questions may help them learn important information about a school they are investigating.

Questions to Ask When Visiting a Postsecondary School:

1. What are the requirements for admission? Will I have access to priority or early registration? What are the goals and objectives of the program? What are the possibilities for financial assistance if I attend this school? What residential options are available to me?
2. What assistance services are available on this campus that will support my needs? What kind of accommodations are available to me? Is there an adapted transportation system available on campus/off campus? Who is eligible to ride on it? What are my responsibilities in assuring the services I need? Is there a charge for them? How do I obtain such services?
3. Where do I go for academic and career counseling on campus? What is the level of career placement of graduates? What is the average starting salary?
4. Are the extracurricular activities such as guest lecturers, clubs, and receptions accessible to me? Where are the major off-campus gathering spots, and are these places accessible to me? What are my responsibilities in getting access?

Employment Options

Competitive Employment. People typically get jobs by applying for advertised positions and by interviewing with prospective employers. In

Greg is working with a job coach in the dining hall at the local university to learn job skills and responsibilities. He is learning a variety of skills working in the dish room. He performs a number of tasks, such as pulling finished meal trays off a conveyer belt, sorting dirty dishes and utensils into the appropriate compartments on the washer rack, and restocking clean forks, knives, and spoons into the correct silverware containers. When Greg graduates from high school, the university plans to employ him as a full-time dishwasher with health and retirement benefits.

many instances, individuals with disabilities can secure and maintain their own employment without outside intervention. They may use generic services to locate jobs such as the classified section of the local newspaper, employment agencies, or personal connections.

However, some individuals need specialized services. These specialized services may involve time-limited or ongoing support. A time-limited service is authorized to provide assistance for a specified time period. Two time-limited options are (1) performance-based placement and (2) work force development.

Performance-Based Placement. Performance-based placement programs are generally provided and paid for by local vocational rehabilitation (VR) services. The VR counselor can locate and fund some short-term supports, such as vocational assessments, placement, and training (Osborn & Wilcox, 1992). Individual need determines the level of support provided and length of time that support is available. After the job is acquired and the person has learned the necessary skills, outside support is faded and the person must rely on his own competence to maintain the employment.

Work Force Development. Work force development programs are administered through the Job Training Partnership Act (JTPA). Among the different options available through JTPA are services for students with and without disabilities between the ages of 14 and 21 who meet the local economic need requirements (Southwest Ohio Transition Round Table, 1998). Those programs can provide time-limited supports for job training in high-demand occupations such as working with computers. Training can take place in postsecondary vocational classrooms and/or on the job. Supports offered include assessment, locating and accessing employer-administered job training, funds for items such as books, and workshops on topics involving preparing résumés, filling out applications, and career choices.

Teachers, students, and parents should investigate a variety of employment options. Most

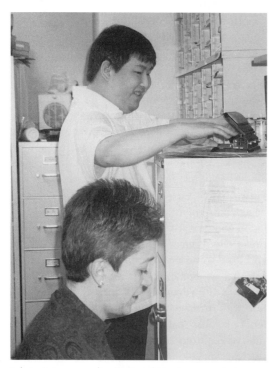

Job training coordinators and teachers can help match the jobs available to their students' interests.

cities and counties offer support through human services agencies as well as business organizations that readily employ persons with disabilities. A job training coordinator or teacher can determine what opportunities are available and match them with the students' interests and abilities. The student and the job trainer should visit the relevant area programs and ask questions. They should talk to prospective employers as well as potential co-workers to learn about the workplace environment and to discover the expectations and responsibilities for a particular job.

Guidelines for Talking With Prospective Employers or Potential Co-Workers:

1. What services do you provide? What sort of training do you offer? What is the application procedure?
2. What are the entry requirements for this job? What is the average annual wage of someone doing this job? When will this job begin?
3. Where do the employees go and what kinds of things do they do during their work breaks? Do the employees get together outside of work? If so, when do they get together and what are the kinds of activities they do together?
4. What public transportation is available and how close is it to the work site? What community services and activities are accessible from the work site? (List adapted from Osborn & Wilcox, 1992)

Supported Employment Options. Some individuals with moderate to severe disabilities may need some form of support on an ongoing basis. Supported employment options provide support as long as the individual needs it, which in some cases may be permanently. Funding for ongoing work support is provided by social service agencies, such as the Bureau of Vocational Rehabilitation, although the designated funding agency can vary from state to state. The actual supports and services may be delivered by the same agency or by another provider, such as the Board of Mental Health and Mental Retardation or Department of Human Services. The individual with a moderate to severe disability then can use those funds to purchase supports and services from the social service agency or he can purchase the needed supports and services from a private vendor.

The amount of support varies according to individual needs, with some persons requiring only a biweekly visit from the job coach and others needing daily assistance on the job site. Ongoing support should be tailored to the individual's needs and the setting requirements. Support can be provided in several ways. In some instances, a co-worker can be trained to provide the needed assistance. In other cases, a job coach may spend time on-site regularly.

Placement in competitive job settings offers the preferred employment model. When that is not possible, small groups of individuals with disabilities can work in the community in a mobile crew or they can form an enclave in a competitive industry.

Lifestyle Options

Many adults with moderate to severe disabilities, like their typical counterparts, want to move out of their parents' homes. They want to have the opportunity to choose a lifestyle that

 Chandra is an only child who recently moved out of her parents' house and into a group home. She has had to make a big adjustment to living with seven other people. For example, now she has to share the bathroom, deal with the noise of her roommate's loud music, and wait for her turn to use the telephone. Her experience is very much like that of a college student who has to adjust to the routines of living in a dormitory.

allows them to be as independent as possible. For some individuals this may mean living in their own home, and for others, it may mean living with one or more other individuals.

 Harvey learned how to shop and cook when he lived in a group home. He always practiced going to the grocery store and cooking dinner with a group of people. Once he could manage those chores on his own, he moved into his own apartment. The first time he went to the store he bought a 64 oz. can of lima beans and cooked all of it just as he had done when he lived at the group home. Harvey got sick when he tried to eat all the lima beans in one sitting. After that, he realized he had to prepare meals for one person so he only bought and fixed smaller portions.

Independent Living with Natural Supports. Some individuals with moderate disabilities are able to live on their own with little outside support. These individuals can successfully create and support their own independent community living situations. Family members, neighbors, or friends can periodically check in and help the individual with matters such as financial management.

Supported Living. Many community-living arrangements can be adjusted to persons who need varying levels of support. Individuals with moderate to severe disabilities and their families need to carefully select living arrangements that address the needs of the individual without being too restrictive. Group homes were preferred during the 1970s and 1980s, but persons with moderate to severe disabilities can enjoy a variety of living arrangements today, including owning their own homes and hiring their own personal assistants (O'Connor & Racino, 1993; Racino & Taylor, 1993).

Students and parents should visit residential providers and express their independent living option preferences. They should determine the facilities and services available in and near the various living option locations they visit. There are many questions to consider when determining which option provides the best choice.

Guidelines for Making Lifestyle Choices:

1. **What skills do I need to live on my own?** Do I know how to manage my finances and budget my money? Do I know how to do my own laundry, manage my time, make arrangements, and keep my commitments?
2. **What kind of lifestyle do I want to have?** In what kind of housing arrangement do I want to live? Do I want to live alone or with a roommate? What does a particular housing option require of me and what services does it offer? Do I want to stay near my family or be some distance away? What kinds of social and recreational activities am I interested in? Where are they located and how will I access them? What kinds of transportation, shopping, health care, and other community services will I use and how will I access those services?

Community Participation

Participation in the community is an important part of daily life for all adults. A variety of activities is available in most communities. An individual with moderate to severe disabilities can participate in both generic and specialized options.

Specialized Resources. Specialized options include programs that exclusively serve persons with disabilities such as ARC or a state Board of Mental Retardation. They offer a variety of opportunities for socialization for adults with disabilities such as dances, outings, and trips. These programs provide ample support, but the opportunities for socialization with nondisabled community members is severely limited.

Generic Resources. Generic community options are activities open to anyone. They may include restaurants, softball leagues, church groups, or art classes. Individuals with moderate to severe disabilities should be aware of what their community has to offer. Students and parents should carefully plan for community opportunities and determine participation based on the student's personal interests and desires. Neighbors are a good, and often overlooked, source of information. Once the student's preferences have been identified, the transition team should incorporate that information into the transition plan so similar activities will be part of the student's adult life.

To enhance the quality of their adult lives, students with moderate to severe disabilities need to have opportunities to try various different leisure and recreational activities (Halpern, 1993). Options in the community may include a wide variety of social and recreational resources such as libraries, parks, community classes, and entertainment programs. Being a consumer is part of daily life for all adults, including those with disabilities. Some of the choices available to consumers in most communities include shopping, banks, and legal services. All people want to feel good and be healthy. It is important to know how to access health care. Options available in the community may include doctors, dentists, clinics, and hospitals. This should be thoroughly addressed during the transition process because adults with moderate to severe disabilities often are not given high priority in the health care system although they may have a high incidence of medical care needs.

Mental health services and support groups offer more specialized services to provide assistance to individuals with moderate to severe disabilities. Counseling and mental health services offer support for solving problems in a safe environment. As you learned in Chapter 2, persons with moderate to severe disabilities have a higher incidence of mental health problems than the general population. As students with moderate to severe disabilities transition from school and home environments to begin living independently, they may have a greater need for mental health support. Unfortunately, they may have difficulty accessing these services. Some mental health providers do not serve individuals who have been diagnosed with mental retardation or a developmental disability. Team members should be aware of this issue and help in locate appropriate resources in the community.

Interpersonal Relationships. All adults need to have friends and feel valued by others in the community. Individuals with moderate to severe disabilities are no exception. Not only do they need to have rewarding interpersonal relationships to feel valued in the community, but they may have to have support to participate fully in community life. Those support needs present excellent opportunities for individuals with disabilities to establish friendships with classmates and neighbors without disabilities.

Support groups can provide encouragement for people with similar interests and concerns. Sharing feelings with others can help people solve problems and make good choices. Individuals with disabilities will experience self-empowerment though support group activities. Many adults with disabilities belong to self-advocacy support groups such as People First and Becoming Empowered (Dybwad & Bersani, 1996). Through groups like these, they develop friendships, find support, and work to gain access and improve the life circumstances in the community for all individuals with disabilities (Cone, 1997).

The need for positive intimate, interpersonal relationships also is an important aspect of adult life. These relationships can be hindered by limited opportunities or societal attitudes toward individuals with moderate to severe disabilities. For example, the community may offer few organized peer social/recreational activities and the individual may have difficulty express-

ing his feelings or needs because of limited communication skills. Still, peer relationships are an important factor in students' ability to adjust successfully in the community. Several issues associated with human sexuality must be taught to ensure the safety and security of individuals with moderate to severe disabilities. Expressing one's sexuality involves more than preferences or desires. Individuals with moderate to severe disabilities are often at risk in their interpersonal relationships with respect to sexual vulnerability. Students need to be taught how to express their sexuality through responsible adult behaviors (Westling & Fox, 2000). They need to learn about the possible repercussions of sexual activity including pregnancy, sexually transmitted diseases, and harassment. These topics and others, such as dating and marriage, birth control, and issues of privacy, should be addressed explicit in the curriculum.

Intimate relationships also can contribute to a fulfilling and successful life as well as provide social support for adults with moderate to severe disabilities. Llewellyn (1995) has found that parents with cognitive disabilities give support and receive support from their partner and from willing family members but they are less likely to rely on friends and neighbors. Getting married and raising a family of their own can be both a desire and a challenge for these individuals. For example, mothers with mental retardation may need to be taught to provide a stimulating home environment that will encourage their child's development as well as to be responsive to their child's needs (Keltner, 1994). With periodic or ongoing supports, individuals with moderate to severe disabilities also can learn how to organize the household environment so it is a safe place in which to care for their children (Tymchuk, Hamada, Andron, & Anderson, 1990).

Students and parents should collect information about each alternative as they investigate community services and activities. They should look at the advantages and disadvantages of the different options and select those options that will best help students realize their goals. They also need to consider the various options in relation to their accessibility to his place of work and his home.

Guidelines for Making Community
Options Choices:

1. Ask when services and activities are available.
2. Find out ahead of time what they cost.
3. Figure out how to get to and from them.
4. Determine what supports are available.

Financial Independence. Financial independence also is a concern for individuals with moderate to severe disabilities. Many of these individuals qualify for some assistance from government programs such as Social Security Disability Insurance (SSDI) or Supplemental Social Security Income (SSI). SSDI provides support for previously employed qualifying individuals and their dependents. SSI provides support for qualifying individuals who have not worked or are not covered under SSDI. Although they may receive some support from these kinds of entitlements, they often have less income than individuals without disabilities (Beirne-Smith et al., 1998).

Individuals with moderate to severe disabilities also may need support in budgeting their resources and managing daily expenditures. For example, paying bills and managing their income to make the money last until the next check arrives is a challenge for many adults, but it is a particularly difficult task for individuals with disabilities (Goode, 1996). They may need guidance from family members or adult service personnel. The people who provide that guidance need to emphasize the individual's voice in financial planning and focus on allocating funds in a manner that will secure those preferences.

 **SUMMARY**

As you have learned in this chapter, preparing for adult life is important for individuals with moderate to severe disabilities. At each level in the education process, transition teams that include the student and his family map out a plan designed to ensure the student's smooth move from one school setting to the next. Independent living, employment, participation in the community, and becoming a self-advocate are important components of a successful transition to adulthood. Students can best learn the skills that allow them to develop these transition competencies through knowledge they gain from applied curricula taught in inclusive education programs. To have maximum opportunities to learn transition competencies, inclusive environments and applied curricula should be the standard for students with moderate to severe disabilities throughout their entire school experience.

 CHAPTER EXTENDERS

Key Terms and Concepts

1. *Individual transition plan (ITP)* is a written plan that focuses on the student's successful integration in the community by identifying the student's desires and needs for the future, strategies and supports for reaching those goals, and connections with service system providers.
2. *Self-determination* is the ability to make choices, set personal goals, and take initiative in achieving them.
3. *Transition* is the process of moving from one place to another.
4. The *transition team* is a group of interested individuals who have relevant information to give in helping plan for the successful transition to the next stage in the student's life.
5. *Vocational rehabilitation services (VR)* provide support for individuals with disabilities in accessing employment, living arrangements, education, and other community activities.
6. *Job Training Partnership Act (JTPA)* administers workforce development programs that

provide time-limited supports for training 14 to 21 year olds who meet the economic requirements for high demand occupations.

7. *Normalization* describes the principle that individuals with disabilities have everyday routines that are as close to the life patterns that are typical for adults without disabilities.

8. *Person-centered planning* is a consumer-oriented approach to transition planning that puts the person with a disability at the center of the decision making process.

Study Guide

1. Define *transition* as it relates to special education.
2. List three ways in which families can participate in the transition process.
3. List and define the roles of team members for each of the following transitions: (a) transition to school, (b) transition between elementary and secondary education programs, and (c) transition from school to adulthood.
4. List and describe two employment options for persons with moderate to severe disabilities.
5. List and describe two types of living arrangements for adults with moderate to severe disabilities.
6. Discuss the purpose of establishing a vision in the transition process.

Have a Class Debate

Many adults with moderate to severe disabilities find most of their social opportunities through specialized programs that serve only persons with disabilities. They go to dances, shop, and take vacations with other persons with disabilities. Their parents are happy because they believe their children are safe in these environments. The individuals with disabilities are satisfied with their friendships. However, these experiences do not reflect patterns of the typical adult population. If individuals with disabilities utilize specialized services for all of their social needs, they can have an entire lifetime with little contact with nondisabled persons. Is this appropriate or should these programs be disbanded in favor of social inclusion in the greater community? Debate specialized versus generic options for socialization for adults with moderate to severe disabilities.

Small Group Activity I:

This is a role-playing activity for small groups of 5 to 8 students. Each member of the team must determine his or her (1) responsibilities, (2) rights, and (3) level of participation in the transition process. Each group can report their determinations to the whole class for further discussion and refinement of each role. Each member of the group is given one of the following roles to play on an imaginary transition team:

1. parent
2. student
3. teachers (special education teacher; regular education teacher)
4. other school personnel (school psychologist, principal, nurse, school counselor)
5. nonschool personnel (vocational rehabilitation counselor, doctor, job coach, other relevant individuals)

Small Group Activity II

List the transition activities you completed before going to college. Identify the services you used and identify the formal and informal sources of support.

Or for traditional college-aged students, list all of the decisions you will have to make when graduating, including finding a place to live and a job, moving, and making new friends in the community. Identify the services you will use and identify the formal and informal sources of support.

Field Experiences

Study community living arrangement options by visiting and then comparing and contrasting each of the following: (1) a supported independent living situation, (2) a group home, and (3) a large congregate care facility or nursing home.

Guidelines for Observing
Community Residences:

1. What services and activities are available in the neighborhood? What are the neighbors like?

2. What are the admission procedures? What agency is operating the residence? Is the facility the "least restrictive environment" for everyone living there? What is the condition of the facility?

3. What activities are available for the residents? Where do the activities take place? How do the residents view other residents and staff members?

4. What are the staff members' training and qualifications? How do they treat the residents?

5. What are the daily routines and how individualized are they? How are the residents dressed? Is it age and situation appropriate? Do the residents have their own possessions? Where do they keep them? Do they have their own money and how is it handled?

6. Are residents free to come and go as they choose? Do they have opportunities to interact with members of the opposite sex? Can they smoke and drink alcohol? Are they involved in self-advocacy groups and do they have access to advocates? What opportunities do they have to interact with family members?

7. Would you live there? Would you allow your child to live there? (Adapted from Osborn, K., & Wilcox, B. (1992). *School to community transition: A planning and procedures handbook for parents and teachers in LaPorte County.* Bloomington, IN: Institute for the Study of Developmental Disabilities.)

References

Abrams, B. J. & Segal, A. (1998). How to prevent aggressive behavior. *Teaching Exceptional Children, 30,* 10–16.

Alber, S. R., Heward, W. L., & Hippler, B. J. (1999). Teaching middle school students with learning disabilities to recruit positive teaching attention. *Exceptional Children, 65,* 253–270.

Alberto, P. A., & Troutman, A. C. (1995). *Applied behavior analysis for teachers* (4th ed.). Upper Saddle River, NJ: Merrill/Prentice Hall.

Alberto, P. A., & Troutman, A. C. (1999). *Applied behavior analysis for teachers* (5th ed.). Upper Saddle River, NJ: Merrill/Prentice Hall.

Allinder, R. M., & Siegel, E. (1999). "Who is Brad?" Preservice teacher's perceptions of summarizing assessment information about a student with moderate disabilities. *Education & Training in Mental Retardation, 34,* 157–169.

Alper, S. (1996). An ecological approach to identifying curriculum content for inclusive setting. In D. L. Ryndak & S. Alper (Eds.), *Curriculum content for students with moderate and severe disabilities in inclusive settings* (pp. 19–31). Needham Heights, MA: Allyn & Bacon.

Anderson, R., Hiebert, E., Scott, J., & Wilkinson, I. (1985). *Becoming a nation of readers: The report of the commission on reading.* Urbana: University of Illinois.

Anson, D. K. (1999). *Alternative computer access: A guide to selection.* Philadelphia: F. A. Davis.

Antonello, S. J. (1996). *Social skills development: Practical strategies for adolescents and adults with developmental disabilities.* Boston: Allyn & Bacon.

Appl, D. J. (1996). Recognizing diversity in the early childhood classroom: Getting started. *Teaching Exceptional Children, 28*(4), 22–25.

Apter, S. J. (1982). *Troubled children, troubled systems.* New York: Pergamon Press.

Atkinson, J. S. C., Lunsford, J. W., & Hollingsworth, D. (1993). Applied academics: Reestablishing relevance. *The Balance Sheet, 74*(2), 9–11.

Bailey, R. W. (1989). *Human performance engineering: Using human factors/ergonomics to achieve computer system usability.* Upper Saddle River, NJ: Merrill/Prentice Hall.

Baker, B. (1986). Using images to generate speech. *Byte, 3,* 160–168.

Barnett, D., Graney, P., Rook, J., Greene, P., Hanes, K., Heltzel, C., Duffy, C., & Smith, B. (1995). *The systems change primer: A closer look at inclusion.* Pierre, SD: South Dakota State Department of Education and Cultural Affairs.

Basham, A., Appleton, V. E., & Dykeman, C. (2000). *Team building in education: A how-to guidebook.* Denver, CO: Love.

Batavia, A. I., Dillard, D., & Phillips, B. (1991). How to avoid technology abandonment. In H. Murphy (Ed.), *Proceedings of the fifth annual conference, Technology and persons with disabilities* (pp. 55–64). Los Angeles: Office of Disabled Student Services, California State University, Northridge.

Bateman, B. D., & Linden, M. A. (1998). *Better IEPs: How to develop legally correct and educationally useful programs* (3rd ed.). Longmont, CO: Sopris West.

Bauer, A. M., & Sapona, R. H. (1991). *Managing classrooms to facilitate learning.* Upper Saddle River, NJ: Merrill/Prentice Hall.

Bauer, A. M., & Shea, T. M. (1999). *Inclusion 101: How to teach all learners.* Baltimore: Paul H. Brookes.

Baumgart, D., Brown, L., Pumpian, I., Nisbet, J., Ford, A., Sweet, M., Missina, R., & Schroeder, J. (1982). Principle of partial participation and individualized adaptations in educational programs for severely handicapped students. *The Journal of the Association for Persons With Severe Handicaps, 7,* 12–27.

Baumgart, D., & Giangreco, M. F. (1996). Key lessons learned about inclusion. In D. H. Lehr & F. Brown (Eds.), *People with disabilities who challenge the system* (pp. 79–98). Baltimore: Paul H. Brookes.

Bayley, N. (1969). *Bayley scales of infant development.* San Antonio, TX: The Psychological Corporation.

Beck, J., Broers, J., Hogue, E., Shipstead, J., & Knowlton, E. (1994). Strategies for functional community-based instruction and inclusion for children with mental retardation. *Teaching Exceptional Children, 26*(2), 44–48.

Beck, R. H., Copa, G. H., & Pease, V. H. (1991). Vocational and academic teachers work together. *Educational Leadership, 49*(2), 29–31.

Beirne-Smith, M., Ittenbach, R. F., & Patton, J. R. (1998). *Mental retardation* (5th ed.). Upper Saddle River, NJ: Merrill/Prentice Hall.

Bell, J. K., Blackhurst, A. E., & Lahm, E. A. (1999). *National survey of state Department of Education assistive technology policies.* Unpublished manuscript. Lexington: University of Kentucky.

Bender, M., Brannan, S. A., & Verhoven, P. J. (1984). *Leisure education for the handicapped: Curriculum goals, activities, and resources.* San Diego, CA: College-Hill Press.

Benson, D. (1992). *Teaching anger management to persons with mental retardation.* Chicago: International Diagnostic Systems.

Berdine, W. H., & Blackhurst, A. E. (Eds.). (1993). *An introduction to special education* (3rd ed.). New York: HarperCollins.

Bergen, D. (1993). Teaching strategies: Facilitating friendship development in inclusion classrooms. *Childhood Education, 69,* 234, 236.

Bigge, J. (1990). *Teaching individuals with physical and multiple disabilities* (3rd ed.). Upper Saddle River, NJ: Merrill/Prentice Hall.

Bishop, K. D., & Jubala, K. A. (1995). Positive behavior support strategies. In M. A. Falvey (Ed.), . *Inclusive and heterogeneous schooling: Assessment, curriculum, and intervention* (pp. 159–186). Baltimore: Paul H. Brookes.

Blackhurst, A. E. (1993). The development of special education. In W. H. Berdine & A. E. Blackhurst (Eds.), *An introduction to special education* (3rd ed., pp. 5–36). New York: Harper Collins.

Blackhurst, A. E., & Berdine, W. H. (Eds.) (1993). *An introduction to special education* (3rd ed.). New York: HarperCollins.

Blackhurst, A. E., & Lahm, E. A. (2000). Technology and exceptionality foundations. In J. D. Lindsey (Ed.), *Technology and exceptional individuals* (pp. 1–45). Austin, TX: Pro-Ed.

Blackhurst, A. E., Lahm, E. A., Harrison, B., & Chandler, W. (1999). A framework for aligning technology with transition competencies. *Career Development for Exceptional Individuals, 22*(2), 153–183.

Blackorby, J., & Wagner, M. (1996). Longitudinal postschool outcomes for youth with disabilities: Findings from the National Longitudinal Transition Study. *Exceptional Children, 62,* 399–413.

Blalock, G. (1997). Strategies for school consultation and collaboration. In E. Polloway & J. R. Patton (Eds.), *Strategies for teaching learners with special needs* (pp. 520–550). Upper Saddle River, NJ: Merrill/Prentice Hall.

Blatt, B. (1987). *The conquest of mental retardation.* Austin, TX: Pro-Ed.

Blenk, K., & Fine, D.L. (1995). *Making school inclusion work: A guide to everyday practices.* Cambridge, MA: Brookline.

Bliss, C. K. (1965). *Blissymbolics.* Sydney, Australia: Semantography Publications.

Boan, C. H., & Harrison, P. L. (1997). Adaptive behavior assessment and individuals with mental retardation. In R. L. Taylor (Ed.), *Assessment of individuals with mental retardation.* San Diego: Singular.

Bobath, B. (1963). A neurodevelopmental treatment of cerebral palsy. *Physiotherapy, 49,* 242–244.

Bock, M. (1991). A modified language-experience approach for children with autism. *Focus on Autistic Behavior, 6,* 1–15.

Bogdan, R., & Knoll, J. (1995). The sociology of disability. In E. Meyen & T. Skirtic (Eds.), *Special education and student disability* (pp. 675–712). Denver, CO: Love.

Bottoms, G., & Sharpe, D. (n.d.). *Teaching for understanding through integration of academic and technical education.* (Available from the Southern Regional Education Board, 592 Tenth Street, N.W., Atlanta, GE 30318–5790)

Bowe, F. (1995). *Birth to five: Early childhood special education.* New York: Delmar.

Bradley, V. J. (1994). Evolution of a new service paradigm. In V. J. Bradley, J. W. Ashbaugh, & B. C. Blaney (Eds.), *Creating individual supports for people with developmental disabilities* (pp. 11–32). Baltimore: Paul H. Brookes.

Bredekamp, S., & Copple, C. (Eds.). (1997). Developmentally appropriate practice in early childhood programs (rev. ed.). Washington, DC: National Association for the Education of Young Children.

Brenot-Scheyer, M., Abernathy, P.A., Williamson, D., Kimberlee, A. J., & Coots, J. J. (1995). Elementary curriculum and instruction. In M. A. Falvey (Ed.), *Inclusive and heterogeneous schooling: Assessment, curriculum and instruction* (pp. 319–340). Baltimore: Paul H. Brookes.

Bricker, D. (1993). *Assessment, evaluation, and programming system (AEPS) for infants and children.* Baltimore: Paul H. Brookes.

Bricker, D. (1997). The challenge of inclusion. In D. Podell (Ed.), *Perspectives: Educating exceptional learners* (pp. 169–179). Boulder, CO: Coursewise Publishing.

Brolin, D. E. (1989). *Life centered career education: A competency based approach* (3rd ed.). Reston, VA: The Council for Exceptional Children.

Brolin, D. E. (1992). *Life centered career education: Competency units for daily living skills* (Vols. 1–3). Reston, VA: The Council for Exceptional Children. (ERIC Document Reproduction Service No. ED 350 784)

Brolin, D. E. (1995). *Career education: A functional life skills approach* (3rd ed.). Upper Saddle River, NJ: Merrill/Prentice Hall.

Browder, D. M. (1991). *Assessment of individuals with severe disabilities* (2nd ed.). Baltimore: Paul H. Brookes.

Browder, D. M., & Snell, M. E. (1994). Functional academics. In M.E. Snell (Ed.), *Instruction of students with severe disabilities* (4th ed., pp. 442–479). Upper Saddle River, NJ: Merrill/Prentice Hall.

Brown, F., & Snell, M. (1993). Meaningful assessment. In M. E. Snell (Ed.), *Instruction of students with severe disabilities* (pp. 61–98). Upper Saddle River, NJ: Merrill/Prentice Hall.

Brown, F., & Snell, M. (2000). Meaningful assessment. In M. Snell & F. Brown (Eds.), *Instruction of students with severe disabilities* (5th ed., pp. 67–112). Upper Saddle River, NJ: Merrill/Prentice Hall.

Brown, L., Branston, M. B., Hamre-Nietupski, S., Pumpian, I., Certo, N., & Gruenewald, L. (1979). A strategy for developing chronological age appropriate and functional curricular content for severely handicapped adolescents and young adults. *Journal of Special Education, 13,* 81–90.

Brown, F., & Cohen, S. (1996). Self-determination and young children. *The Journal of the Association for Persons With Severe Disabilities, 21,* 22–30.

Brown, J., Collins, A., & Duguid, P. (1989). Debating the situation. *Educational Researcher, 18,* 10–12.

Brown, L., Nietupski, J., & Hamre-Nietupski, S. (1976). Criterion of ultimate functioning. In M. A. Thomas (Ed.), *Hey, don't forget about me! Education's investment in the severely, profoundly and multiply handicapped* (pp. 2–15). Reston, VA: The Council for Exceptional Children.

Brown, L., Nisbet, J., Ford, A., Sweet, M., Shiraga, B., York, J., & Loomis, R. (1983). The critical need for nonschool instruction in educational programs for severely handicapped students. *The Journal of the Association for Persons With Severe Handicaps, 8,* 71–77.

Brown, W. H., & Odom, S. L. (1995). Naturalistic peer interventions for promoting preschool children's social interactions. *Preventing School Failure, 39*(4), 38–43.

Brown, T., Ortiz, F., & Morris, E. L. (1984). *Someone special just like you.* New York: Henry Holt and Company.

Bruce, T. (1993). For parents particularly: The role of play in children's lives. *Childhood Education, 69,* 237–238.

Bruiniks, R., Woodcock, R., Weatherman, R., & Hill, B. (1996). *Scales of independent behavior—revised.* Chicago: Riverside Publishing.

Bryant, B. R. (1997). Intelligence testing. In R. L. Taylor (Ed), *Assessment of individuals with mental retardation.* San Diego: Singular.

Bryant, C. J. (1999). Build a sense of community among young students with student-centered activities. *Social Studies, 90,* 110–113.

Bullock, J., Pierce, S., & McClellan, L. (1987). *Touch Learning Concepts Incorporated: Touch Math.* Colorado Springs: Innovative Learning Concepts.

Burgie, P. S. (1991). A kindergartner's environmental workweek. *Science and Children, 28*(7), 40–42.

Burnett, D., et al. (1995). *The systems change primer: A closer look at inclusion.* Washington, DC: Special Education Programs (ERIC Document Reproduction Service No. ED 391 323)

Burns, E. (1998). *Text accommodation for students with disabilities.* Springfield, IL: Charles C. Thomas.

Bybee, G. S., & Zigler, E. (1992). Is outerdirectedness employed in a harmful or beneficial manner by students with or without mental retardation? *American Journal of Mental Retardation, 96,* 512–521.

Cairns, R., & Kielsmeier, J. (1991). *Growing hope: A sourcebook on integrating youth service into the school curriculum.* Roseville, MN: National Youth Leadership Council.

Calculator, S. N. (1997). AAC and individuals with severe to profound disabilities. In S. L. Glennen & D. C. DeCoste (Eds.), *Handbook of augmentative and alternative communication* (pp. 445–471). San Diego, CA: Singular.

Campbell, P. H. (2000). Promoting participation in natural environments by accommodating motor disabilities. In M. Snell and T. Brown (5th ed.), *Instruction of students with severe disabilities* (pp. 291–330). Upper Saddle River, NJ: Merrill/Prentice Hall.

Carlson, F. (1986). *Picsyms categorical dictionary.* Unity, ME: Baggeboda Press.

Carlson, F. (1994). *Poppin's cut and paste with 1000+ DynaSyms.* Arlington, VA: Poppin & Company.

Carns, A. W. (1996). School bus safety: A peer helper program with a career development focus. *Elementary School Guidance and Counseling, 30,* 213–217.

Carpenter, C. D., Ray, M. S., & Bloom, L. A. (1995). Portfolio assessment: Opportunities and challenges. *Intervention in School and Clinic, 31,* 34–41.

Carr, E. G. (1997). The evolution of applied behavior analysis into positive behavior support. *Journal of Association for Persons With Severe Handicaps, 22,* 208–209.

Carr, E. G., Reeve, C. E., & Magito-Mclaughlin. (1996). Contextual influences on problem behavior in people with developmental disabilities. In L. K. Koegel, R. L. Koegel, & G. Dunlap (Eds.), *Positive behavioral support. Including people with difficult behavior in the community* (pp. 403–424). Baltimore: Paul H. Brookes.

Cavallaro, C. C., & Haney, M. (1999). *Preschool inclusion.* Baltimore: Paul H. Brookes.

Cavallaro, C. C., Haney, M., & Cabello, B. (1993). Developmentally appropriate strategies for promoting full participation in early childhood settings. *Topics in Early Childhood Special Education, 13,* 293–307.

Chadsey-Rusch, J., DeStefano, L., O Reilly, M., Gonzalez, F., & Collet-Klingenberg, L. (1992). Assessing the loneliness of workers with mental retardation. *Mental Retardation, 30*(2), 85–92.

Chadsey-Rusch, J., Rusch, F. R., & O'Reilly, M. F. (1991). Transition from school to integrated communities. *Remedial and Special Education, 12*(6), 23–33.

Chalfant, J., & Pysh, M. (1989). Teacher assistance teams: Five descriptive studies on 96 teams. *Remedial and Special Education, 10*(6), 49–58.

Chalfant, J., Pysh, M. V., & Moultrie, R. (1979). Teacher assistant teams: A model for within building problem solving. *Learning Disabilities Quarterly, 2*(3), 85–96.

Chandler, L. K. (1993). Steps in preparing for transition: Preschool to kindergarten. *Teaching Exceptional Children, 25*(4), 52–55.

Christ, G. M. (1995). Curriculums with real-world connections. *Educational Leadership, 52(8),* 32–35.

Clark, G. M. (1994). Is a functional curriculum approach compatible with an inclusive education model? *Teaching Exceptional Children, 26*(2), 36–39.

Clark, R. W. (1999). *Effective professional development schools: Agenda for education in a democracy.* (Vol. 3). San Francisco: Jossey-Bass.

Cole, B. S. (1995). Social work education and students with disabilities: Implications of Section 504 and the ADA. *Journal of Social Work Education, 31,* 261–268.

Coleman, M. C., & Gilliam, J. E. (1983). Disturbing behaviors in the classroom: A survey of teacher attitudes. *The Journal of Special Education, 17,* 121–129.

Cone, A. A. (1997). The beat goes on: Lesson learned from the rhythms of the self-advocacy movement. *Mental Retardation, 35,* 144–145.

Cook, A. M., & Hussey, S. M. (1995). *Assistive technologies: Principles and practice.* St. Louis, MO: Mosby.

Council for Exceptional Children. (1997, November/December). Strategies to meet IDEA 1997's discipline requirements. *CEC Today,* pp. 1, 5, 13.

Council for Exceptional Children. (1999). Special focus issue— a primer on IDEA 1997 and its regulations. *CEC Today, 5*(7), 1, 5, 9,12, 15.

Coutinho, J. J., & Repp. A. (1999). *Inclusion: The integration of students with disabilities.* Belmont, CA: Wadsworth.

Cox, M., & Firpo, C. (1993). What would they be doing if we gave them worksheets? *English Journal, 82*(3), 42–45.

Cramer, S. F. (1998). *Collaboration: A success strategy for special educators.* Boston: Allyn & Bacon.

Cregan, A., & Lloyd, L. L. (1990). *Sigsymbols: American edition.* Waucouda, IL: Don Johnston Inc.

Cronin, M. E., & Patton, J. R. (1993). *Life skills instruction for all students with special needs: A practical guide for integrating real-life content into the curriculum.* Austin, TX: Pro-Ed.

Csapo, M. (1991). Community-referenced instruction. In D. Baine (Ed.), *Instructional environments for learners having severe handicaps* (pp. 15–33). Edmonton: University of Alberta.

Dadson, S., & Horner, R. H. (1993). Manipulating setting events to decrease problem behaviors. *Teaching Exceptional Children 25*(3), 53–55.

Dalrymple, N. J. (1995). Environmental supports to develop flexibility and Independence. In K. A. Quill (Ed.), *Teaching children with autism: Strategies to enhance communication and socialization* (pp. 243–264). Albany, NY: Delmar.

Darling-Hammond, L. (1994). Teacher quality and equality. In J. I. Goodlad & P. Keating (Eds.), *Access to knowledge: The continuing agenda for our nation's schools* (pp. 237–258). New York: College Entrance Examination Board.

Darling-Hammond, L., & Falk, B. (1997). Supporting teaching and learning for all students: Policies for authentic assessment systems. In A. L. Goodwin (Ed.), *Assessment for equity and inclusion: Embracing all our children* (pp. 51–70). New York: Routledge.

DATI (2000). What's for dinner? Independent living tips for cooking and dining. [On-line] Available: http://www.asel.udel.edu/dati/dinner.html.

Demchak, M., & Greenfield, R. G. (2000). A transition portfolio for Jeff, a student with multiple disabiities. *Teaching Exceptional Children, 32*(6), 44–49.

Denham, A., & Lahm, E. A. (2001). Using technology to construct alternative portfolios of students with moderate and severe disabilities. *Teaching Exceptional Children, 33*(5), 10–17.

Dettmer, P., Dyck, N., & Thurston, L. (1999). *Consultation, collaboration, and teamwork for students with special needs* (3rd ed.). Needham Heights, MA: Allyn & Bacon.

Dever, R. B., & Knapczyk, D. R. (1997). *Teaching persons with mental retardation: A model for curriculum development and teaching.* Madison, WI: Brown & Benchmark.

Dewey, J. (1937). *Democracy and education: An introduction to the philosophy of education.* New York: Macmillan.

Dewey, J. (1938). *Experience and education.* New York: Macmillan.

Dewey, J. (1959). *Moral principles in education.* New York: Greenwood Press.

Dexter, M. E. (1998, October). *Aided language stimulation: Strategies for improved verbal output for children with perva-*

sive developmental disabilities. Presentation at the Closing the Gap Conference, Minneapolis, MN.

Diem, R., & Katims, D. S. (1991). Handicaps and at risk: Preparing teachers for a growing populace. *Intervention in School and Clinic, 26,* 272–275.

Donnellan, A. M., Mirenda, P. L., Mesaros, R. A., & Fassbender, L. L. (1984). Analyzing the communicative functions of aberrant behavior. *Journal of Association for Persons With Severe Handicaps, 9,* 201–212.

Dowden, P. A. (1997). Augmentative and alternative communication decision making for children with severely unintelligible speech. *AAC Augmentative and Alternative Communication, 13,* 48–58.

Dowdy, C. A., & Smith, T. E. C. (1991). Future-based assessment and intervention. *Intervention in School and Clinic, 27*(2), 101–106.

Dragon Naturally Speaking Preferred 3.0 [Computer software]. (1998). Newton, MA: Dragon Systems.

Drew, C. J., & Hardman, M. L. (2000). *Mental retardation: A life cycle approach* (7th ed.). Upper Saddle River, NJ: Merrill/Prentice Hall.

Drinkwater, S., & Demchak, M. (1995). The preschool checklist: Integration of children with severe disabilities. *Teaching Exceptional Children, 28,* 4–8.

Dunn, L. M. (1968). Special education for the mildly retarded— is much of it justifiable? *Exceptional Children, 35,* 5–22.

Dunn, W. (1991). The sensorimotor systems: A framework for assessment and intervention. In F. P. Orlove and D. Sobsey (Eds.), *Educating children with multiple disabilities: A transdisciplinary approach* (2nd ed., pp. 33–78). Baltimore: Paul H. Brookes.

Dutton, M. (1995). The evolution of tech prep/school-to-work: Career paths for all students. *NASSP Bulletin, 79*(574), 3–13.

Dwyer, K. P., Osher, D., & Hoffman, C. C. (2000). Creating responsive schools: Contextualizing early warning timely response. *Exceptional Children, 66,* 347–366.

Dybwad, G., & Bersani, H. (1996). *New voices: Self-advocacy by people with disabilities.* Cambridge, MA: Brookline.

Earles, T., Carlson, J., & Bock, S. J. (1998). Instructional strategies to facilitate successful learning outcomes for students with autism. In R. L. Simpson and B. S. Myles (Eds.), *Educating children and youth with autism: Strategies for effective practice* (pp. 55–111). Austin, TX: Pro-Ed.

Edgerton, R. B. (1967). *The cloak of competence: Stigma in the lives of the mentally retarded.* Berkeley: University of California Press.

Edgerton, R. B., & Bercovici, S. M. (1976). The cloak of competence: Ten years later. *American Journal of Mental Retardation, 80,* 485–497.

Edmunds, A. L. (1999). Cognitive credit cards: Acquiring learning strategies. *Teaching Exceptional Children, 31*(4), 68–73.

Elders, P. S., & Goossens', C. (1994). *Engineering training environments for interactive augmentative communication.* Birmingham, AL: Southeast Augmentative Communication Conference Publications.

Elliot, I. (1994). Saying it with flowers (and wildlife, too). *Teaching Pre K–8, 25*(2), 34–38.

Elliott, J., Ysseldyke, J., Thurlow, M., & Erickson, R. (1998). What about assessment and accountability? Practical implications for educators. *Teaching Exceptional Children, 31,* 20–27.

Engel, B. S. (1994). Portfolio assessment and the new paradigm: New instruments and new places. *The Educational Forum, 59,* 22–27.

Erwin, E. J., & Schreiber, R. (1999). Creating supports for young children with disabilities in natural environments. *Early Childhood Education Journal, 26,* 167–171.

Etscheidt, S. K., & Bartlett, L. (1999). The IDEA amendments: A four-step approach for determining supplementary aids and services. *Exceptional Children, 65,* 163–174.

Evans, I. M., Salisbury, C. C., Palombaro, M. M., Berryman, J., & Hollowod, T. M. (1992). Peer interactions and social acceptance of elementary-age children with severe disabilities in certain inclusive schools. *Journal of the Association for Persons With Severe Handicaps, 17,* 205–212.

Everington, C. (with Yarasheski-Domme, S., Heckert, S., Jones, S., Pierce, T., Stith-Richards, B., Thomas, C., & Worley, L.). (1982). *The Los Lunas Curricular system: A criterion-referenced assessment for severely/profoundly handicapped* (4th ed.). Los Lunas: State of New Mexico.

Everington, C., & Fulero, S. (1999). Competence to confess: Measuring understanding and suggestibility of defenants with mental retardation. *Mental Retardation, 37,* 212–220.

Everington, C., & Luckasson, R. (1989). Addressing the needs of the criminal defendant with mental retardation: The special educator as a resource to the criminal justice system. *Education and Training in Mental Retardation, 24,* 193–200.

Everington, C., Hamill, L. B., & Lubic, B. (1996). Restructuring teacher education for inclusion. *Contemporary Education, 67,* 52–56.

Everington, C., Stevens, B., & Winters, V. R. (1999). Teacher's attitudes, felt competency, and need for support for implementation of inclusive educational programs. *Psychological Reports, 85,* 331–338.

Everington, C., & Stevenson, T. (1994). A giving experience: The use of community service for training community living skills and promoting integration with individuals with severe disabilities. *Teaching Exceptional Children 26*(3), 56–59.

Evertson, C., & Harris, A. H. (1992). What we know about managing classrooms. *Educational Leadership,* pp. 74–78.

Explorers of the New World [Interactive CD-ROM]. (1995). Cambridge, MA: SoftKey International.

Falvey, M. A. (1989). *Community based curriculum: Instructional strategies for students with severe handicaps.* (2nd ed.). Baltimore: Paul H. Brookes.

Falvey, M. A. (Ed.). (1995). *Inclusive and heterogeneous schooling: Assessment, curriculum, and instruction.* Baltimore: Paul H. Brookes.

Falvey, M. A., Forest, M., Pearpoint, J., & Rosenberg, R. L. (1994). Building connections. In J. S. Thousand, R. A. Villa, & A. I. Nevin (Eds.), *Creativity and collaborative learning* (pp. 347–368). Baltimore: Paul H. Brookes.

Falvey, M. A., Givner, C. C., & Kimm, C. (1996). What do I do Monday morning? In S. Stainback and W. Stainback (Eds.), *Inclusion: A guide for educators* (pp. 117–140). Baltimore, MD: Paul H. Brookes.

Falvey, M. A., & Grenot-Scheyer, M. (1995). Instructional strategies. In M. A. Falvey (Ed.), *Inclusive and heterogeneous schooling: Assessment, curriculum, and instruction* (pp. 131–158). Baltimore: Paul H. Brookes.

Falvey, M. A., Grenot-Scheyer, M., Coots, J. J., & Bishop, M. A. (1995). Services for students with disabilities: Past and present. In M. A. Falvey (Ed.), *Inclusive and heterogeneous schooling* (pp. 8–23). Baltimore: Paul H. Brookes.

Ferguson, D. L. (1997). The real challenge of inclusion: Confessions of a "rabid inclusionist." In D. Podell (Ed.), *Perspectives: Educating exceptional learners* (pp. 169–179). Boulder, CO: Coursewise Publishing.

Ferguson, D. L., & Baumgart, D. (1991). Partial participation revisited. *The Journal of the Association for Persons With Severe Handicaps, 16,* 218–227.

Fiedler, C. (2000). *Making a difference: Advocacy competencies for special education professionals.* Boston: Allyn & Bacon.

Field, S., LeRoy, B., & Rivera, S. (1994). Meeting functional curriculum needs in middle school general education classrooms. *Teaching Exceptional Children, 26*(2), 40–43.

Finnie, N. (1975). *Handling the young cerebral palsied child at home* (2nd ed.). New York: E. P. Dutton.

Ford, A., Schnorr, R., Meyer, L., Davern, L., Black, J., & Dempsey, P. (1989). *The Syracuse community-referenced curriculum guide for students with moderate and severe disabilities.* Baltimore: Paul H. Brookes.

Forest, M., & Lusthaus, E. (1990). Everyone belongs with the MAPS action planning system. *Teaching Exceptional Children 22*(2), 32–35.

Forest, M., & Pearpoint, J. (1992). Families, friends and circles. In J. Nisbet (Ed.), *Natural supports in school, at work, and in the community for people with severe disabilities* (pp. 65–86). Baltimore: Paul H. Brookes.

Foster-Johnson, L., & Dunlap G. (1993). Using functional assessment to develop effective, individualized interventions for challenging behaviors. *Exceptional Children 25*(3), 44–50.

Fox, L., Vaughn, B. J., Dunlap, G., & Bucy, M. (1997). Parent-professional partnership in behavioral support: A qualitative analysis of one family's experiences. *Journal of Association for Persons With Severe Handicaps, 22,* 198–207.

Fox, W., Leo, K., & Fox, T. (1997). *Activities matrix.* Presentation at the 4th Vermont Leadership Institute. Burlington: University of Vermont, University Affiliated Program.

Fox, W., Leo, K., & Fox, T. (1998). *Teacher-Family communication plan.* Presentation at the 5th Vermont Leadership Institute. Burlington: University of Vermont, University Affiliated Program.

Fox, W., Leo, K., & Fox, T. (1999). *Paraeducator/Volunteer management plan.* Presentation at the 6th Vermont Leadership

Institute. Burlington: University of Vermont, University Affiliated Program.

Fowler, S., & Hazel, R. (1996). Planning transitions to support inclusion. In K. E. Allen & I. S. Schwartz, (Eds.), *The exceptional child: Inclusion in early childhood education* (3rd ed., pp. 171–186). Albany, NY: Delmar.

Friend, M., & Bursuck, W. D. (1999). *Including students with special needs: A practical guide for classroom teachers* (2nd ed.). Boston: Allyn & Bacon.

Friend, M., & Cook, L. (1992). *Interactions: Collaboration skills for school professionals.* New York: Longman.

Fry, E. (1977). Fry's Readability Graph: Clarifications, validity, and extension to level 17. *Journal of Reading, 21,* 242–252.

Fuchs, D., & Fuchs, L. S. (1994). Inclusive schools movement and the radicalization of special education reform. *Exceptional Children, 60,* 294–309.

Fuchs, L. S., Fuchs, D., Hamlett, C. L., Phillips, N. B., & Bentz, J. (1994). Classwide curriculum-based measurement: Helping general educators meet the challenge of student diversity. *Exceptional Children, 60,* 518–537.

Fulero, S., & Everington, C. (1995). Assessing competency to waive Miranda rights in defendants with mental retardation. *Law and Human Behavior, 19,* 533–543.

Galinsky, E. (1987). *The six stages of parenthood.* Reading, MA: Addison-Wesley.

Galligan, B. (1990). Serving people who are dually diagnosed: A program evaluation. *Mental Retardation, 28,* 353–358.

Gartner, A., & Lipsky, D. K. (1987). Beyond special education: Toward a quality system for all students. *Harvard Educational Review, 57,* 367–395.

Gee, K., Graham, N., Sailor, W., & Goetz, L. (1995). Use of integrated, general education, and community settings as primary context for skill instruction for students with severe multiple disabilities. *Behavior Modification, 19,* 33–58.

Gelfer, J. I., & Perkins, P. G. (1992, Winter). Constructing student portfolio: A process and product that fosters communication with families. *Day Care and Early Education,* pp. 9–13.

Gelzheiser, L. M., McLane, M., Meyers, J., & Pruzek, R. M. (1998). IEP-specified peer interaction needs: Accurate but ignored. *Exceptional Children, 65,* 51–65.

Gent, P. J., & Gurecka, L. (1998). Service learning: A creative strategy for inclusive classrooms. *The Journal of the Association for Persons With Severe Handicaps, 23,* 261–271.

Gerry, M. H., & Mirsky, A. J. (1992). Guiding principles for public policy on natural supports. In J. Nisbet (Ed.), *Natural supports in school and work and in the community for people with severe disabilities* (pp. 341–346). Baltimore: Paul H. Brookes.

Gessell, A. (1940). *The first five years of life.* New York: Harper Brothers.

Gettinger, M. (1998). Methods of proactive classroom management. *School Psychology Review, 17,* 227–242.

Giangreco, M. (1996, February). What do I do now? A teacher's guide to including students with disabilities. *Educational Leadership,* pp. 56–59.

Giangreco, M. (1998). *Quick-Guides to inclusion 2.* Baltimore: Paul H. Brookes.

Giangreco, M. F., Cloninger, C. J., & Iverson, V. S. (1993). *Choosing options and accommodations for children.* Baltimore: Paul H. Brookes.

Giangreco, M. F., Cloninger, C. J., & Iverson, V. S. (1998). *Choosing outcomes and accommodations for children: A guide to education planning for students with disabilities* (2nd ed.). Baltimore: Paul H. Brookes.

Giangreco, M. F., Dennis, R., Cloninger, C., Edelman, S., & Schattman, R. (1993). "I've counted Jon": Transforming experiences of teachers educating students with disabilities. *Exceptional Children, 59,* 359–372.

Giangreco, M. F., & Putnam, J. W. (1991). Supporting the education of students with severe disabilities in regular education environments. In J. H. Meyer, C. A. Peck, & L. Brown (Eds.), *Critical issues in the lives of people with severe disabilities* (pp. 245–270). Baltimore: Paul H. Brookes.

Gibb, G. S., & Dyches, T. T. (2000). *Guide to writing quality individualized education programs: What's best for students with disabilities?* Boston: Allyn & Bacon.

Glasser, W. (1986). *Control theory in the classroom.* New York: Harper & Row.

Goessling, D. P. (1998). Inclusion and the challenge of assimilation for teachers of students with severe disabilities. *JASH, 23*(3), 238–251.

Goetz, L., Gee, K., & Sailor, W. (1985). Using a behavioral chain interruption strategy to teach communication skills to students with severe disabilities. *Journal of the Association for the Severely Handicapped, 10,* 21–30.

Gold, M. (1980). *Try another way manual.* Champaign, IL: Research Press.

Goode, B. (1996). It's been a struggle: Her own story. In G. Dybwad & H. Bersani (Eds.), *New voices: Self-advocacy by people with disabilities* (pp. 37–50). Cambridge, MA: Brookline.

Goodlad, J. (1994). Common schools for the commonweal: Reconciling self-interest with the common good. In J. Goodlad & P. Keating (Eds.), *Access to knowledge: The continuing agenda for our nation's schools* (pp. 1–24). New York: College Entrance Examination Board.

Goodlad, J., & Keating, P. (Eds.). (1994). *Access to knowledge: The continuing agenda for our nation's schools.* New York: College Entrance Examination Board.

Goodlad, J., Soder, R., & Sirotnik, K. A. (1990). *The moral dimensions of teaching.* San Francisco: Jossey-Bass.

Goossens', C., Crain, S, & Elder, P. S. (1992). *Engineering the preschool environment for interactive symbolic communication: 18 months to 5 years.* Birmingham, AL: Southeast Augmentative Communication Conference Publications.

Gray, C. A., & Garand, J. D. (1993). Social stories: Improving responses of students with autism with accurate social information. *Focus on Autistic Behavior, 8*(1), 1–10.

Gray, S. (1997). AAC in the educational setting. In S. L. Glennen & D. C. DeCoste (Eds.), *Handbook of augmentative and alternative communication* (pp. 547–601). San Diego, CA: Singular.

Greenspan, S. (1999). A contexturalist perspective on adaptive behavior. In R. L. Shalock (Ed.), *Adaptive Behavior and its measurements: Implications for the field of mental retardation* (pp. 61–80). Washington, DC: AAMR.

Gunter, P. L., Shores, R. E., Jack, S. L., Raumussen, S. K., & Flowers, J. (1995). On the move: Using teacher/student proximity to improve student's behavior. *The Council for Exceptional Children, 57–59.*

Guralnick, M. (1980). Social interactions among preschool children. *Exceptional Children 28*(1), 12–14.

Haas, M., Hatcher, B., & Sunal, C. S. (1992). Teaching about the president and presidential elections. *Social Studies and the Young Learner, 5*, 1–4.

Hagerott, S. G. (1997). Physics for first-graders. *Phi Delta Kappan, 78*, 717–720.

Hagner, D., Helm, D. T., & Butterworth, J. (1996). "This is your meeting": A qualitative study of person-centered planning. *Mental Retardation, 34*, 159–171.

Hall, M., Kleinert, H. L., & Kearns, J. F. (2000). Going to college!: Postsecondary programs for students with moderate and severe disabilities. *Teaching Exceptional Children, 32*(3), 58–65.

Halpern, A. S. (1993). Quality of life as a conceptual framework for evaluating transition outcomes. *Exceptional Children, 59*, 486–498.

Hamill, L. B. (1993, May). *Self-determination guidelines: For teachers of students with disabilities.* Bloomington, IN: Institute for the Study of Developmental Disabilities.

Hamill, L. B. (1994). Transition from school for students with disabilities: Policies and issues. Transition Focus: *Graduate Students Perspectives, 1*, 11–19.

Hamill, L., & Dunlevy, A. (1993). *The breakfast place.* Portland, ME: J. Weston Walch.

Hamill, L., & Dunlevy, A. (1994). *Playing to learn: Classroom games for content area, social, and living skills.* Portland, ME: J. Weston Walch.

Hamill, L., & Dunlevy, A. (1999). *Work boxes* (rev. ed.). San Antonio, TX: PCI Educational Publishing.

Hamill, L., & Dunlevy, A. (2000). *Members of the community.* Verona, WI: IEP Resources.

Hamilton, S. F., & Hamilton, M. A. (1997). When is learning work-based? *Phi Delta Kappan, 78*, 676–681.

Hamilton, S. R. (1980). Experiential learning programs for youth. *American Journal of Education, 88*, 179–215.

Hamre-Nietupski, S., McDonald, J., & Nietupski, J. (1992, Spring). Integrating elementary students with multiple disabilities into supported regular classes: Challenges and solutions. *Teaching Exceptional Children, pp.* 6–9.

Hamre-Nietupski, S., Nietupski, J., Bates, P., & Maaurer, S. (1982). Implementing a community-referenced educational model for moderately/severely handicapped students: Common problems and suggested solutions. *Journal of the Association for Persons With Severe Handicaps, 7*, 38–43.

Handley, L. M. (Ed.). (1993). Here's something for everyone! Teacher's roundtable. *Social Studies and the Young Learner, 6*, 22–24.

Hardy, L. (1998). What do you want to be? *The American School Board Journal, 185*(11), 24–29.

Haring, T. G., Neetz, J. A., Lovinger, L., Peck, G., & Semmel, M. I. (1987). Effects of four modified incidental teaching procedures to create opportunities for communication. *Journal of the Association for Persons With Severe Handicaps, 12*, 218–226.

Harper, D. C., & Wadsworth, J. S. (1993). Behavioral problems and medication utilization. *Mental Retardation, 31*, 97–103.

Harris, K. (1982). Cognitive behavior modification: Application with exceptional students. *Focus on Exceptional Children, 15*, 1–16.

Harry, B. (1997). Leaning forward or bending over backwards: Cultural reciprocity in working with families. *Journal of Early Intervention, 21*, 62–72.

Hart, V. (1977). The use of many disciplines with the severely and profoundly handicapped. In E. Sontag, J. Smith, & N. Certo (Eds.), *Educational programming for the severely and profoundly handicapped* (pp. 391–396). Reston, VA: The Council for Exceptional Children.

Hartoonian, M., & Van Scooter, R. (1996). School-to-work: A model for learning a living. *Phi Delta Kappan, 77*, 555–560.

Haslam, R. H. A. (1996). Prevention of chronic disabilities and diseases. In R. H. A. Haslam & P. J. Valletutti (Eds.), *Medical problems in the classroom* (3rd ed. pp. 27–52). Austin, TX: Pro-Ed.

Hazelkorn, M. N., & Lombard, R. C. (1991). Designated vocational instruction: Instructional support strategies. *Career Development for Exceptional Individuals, 14*(2), 15–25.

Heal, L. W., & Tassé, M. J. (1999). The culturally individualized assessment of adaptive behavior: An accommodation to the 1992 AAMR definition, classification, & systems of support. In R. L. Shalock (Eds.), *Adaptive behavior and its measurement: Implications for the field of mental retardation* (pp. 185–219). Washington, DC: AAMR.

Heide, A., & Henderson, D. (1994). *The technological classroom: A blueprint for success.* Toronto, Canada: Trifolium.

Heller, K. W., Forney, P. E., Alberto, P. A., Schuartzman, M. N., & Goeckel, T. M. (2000). *Meeting physical and health needs of children with disabilities.* Belmont, CA: Wadsworth.

Helmke, L. M., Havekost, D. M., Patton, J. R., & Polloway, E. A. (1994). Life skills programming: Development of a high school science course. *Teaching Exceptional Children, 26*(2), 40–43.

Hickson, L., Blackman, L. S., & Reis, E. M. (1995). *Mental retardation: Foundations of educational programming.* Boston: Allyn & Bacon.

Hodge, C. M. (1994). Educators for a truly democratic system of schooling. In J. Goodlad & P. Keating (Eds.), *Access to knowledge: The continuing agenda for our nation's schools* (pp. 259–272). New York: College Entrance Examination Board.

Hoerner, J. L., & Wehrley, J. B. (1995). *Work-based learning: The key to school-to-work transition.* Westerville, OH: Glencoe/McGraw-Hill.

Hoover, J. J., & Patton, J. R. (1997). *Curriculum adaptations for students with learning and behavior problems: Principles and practices.* Austin, TX: Pro-Ed.

Horner, R. H., Neill, R. O., & Flannery, K. B. (1993). Effective behavior support plans. In M. E. Snell (Ed.), *Instruction of students with severe disabilities* (4th ed., pp. 184–214). Upper Saddle River, NJ: Merrill/Prentice Hall.

Horner, R. H., Vaughn, B. J., Day, H. M., & Ard, W. J. (1996). The relationship between settings events & problem behavior. In L. K. Koegel, R. L. Koegel, & G. Dunlap (Eds.), *Positive behavioral support: Including people with difficult behavior in the community* (pp. 381–402). Baltimore: Paul H. Brookes.

Howell, K. W., Evans, D., & Gardiner, J. (1997). Medications in the classroom: A hard pill to swallow? *Teaching Exceptional Children, 29*(6), 58–61.

Huberman, A. M., & Miles, M. B. (1984). *Innovation up close: How school improvement works.* New York: Plenum Press.

Hudelson, D. (1994). School to work opportunities: How vocational-technical educators can tap the new federal legislation. *Vocational Education Journal, 69*(3), 17–19, 48.

Hughes, C., Guth, C., Hall, S., Presley, J., Dye, M., & Byers, C. (1999). "They are my best friends": Peer buddies promote inclusion in high school. *Teaching Exceptional Children, 31*(5), 32–37.

Hughes, C., Rusch, F. R., & Curl, R. M. (1990). Extending individual competence, developing natural support, and promoting social acceptance. In F. R. Rusch (Ed.), *Supported employment: Models, methods, and issues.* Chicago: Sycamore.

Hughes, P. (Ex. Dir.). (1994). *The Tieline, 3,* 1–6. (Available from Natural Ties Incorporated, 520 Davis Street, Suite 206, Evanston, IL, 60201)

Hunt, P., Alwell, M., & Goetz, L. (1991). Establishing conversational exchanges with family and friends: Moving from training to meaningful communication. *The Journal of Special Education, 25,* 305–319.

Hutchison, D. J. (1978). The transdisciplinary approach. In J. B. Curry & K. K. Peppe (Eds.), *Mental retardation: Nursing approaches to care* (pp. 65–74). St. Louis: Charles V. Mosby.

Idol, L., Paolucci-Whitcomb, P., & Nevin, A. (1986). *Collaborative consultation.* Austin, TX: Pro-Ed.

Inge, K. (1996). Cerebral palsy. In P. J. McLaughlin & P. Wehman (Eds.), *Mental retardation and developmental disabilities* (2nd ed., pp. 147–172). Austin, TX: Pro-Ed.

Inskeep, A., (1926). *Teaching dull and retarded children.* New York: J. J. Little & Ives Co.

Institute for the Study of Developmental Disabilities. (1992). *Get it in writing: Individual transition planning for youth with severe disabilities.* Bloomington, IN: Author.

Institute for the Study of Developmental Disabilities. (1995). *A family guide to transition planning.* Bloomington, IN: Author.

Intellipics [Computer software]. (1995). Novato, CA: Intellitools, Inc.

Iwata, B. A., Dorsey, M. F., Slifer, K. J., Bauman, K. E., & Richman, G. S. (1982). Toward a functional analysis of self-injury. *Analysis & Intervention in Developmental Disabilities, 2,* 3–20.

Janney, R. E., & Snell, M. E. (1996). How teachers use peer interactions to include students with moderate and severe disabilities in elementary general education classrooms. *JASH, 21,* 72–80.

Janney, R., & Snell, M. E. (1998). *Teacher's guides to inclusive practices: Modifying schoolwork.* Baltimore: Paul H. Brookes.

Jaskulski, T., Metzler, C., & Ames-Zierman (1990). *Forging a new era: The 1990 report on persons with developmental disabilities.* Washington, DC: National Association of Developmental Disabilities Councils.

Johnson, J., Baumgart, D., Helmstetter, E., & Curry, C. (1996). *Augmenting basic communication in natural contexts.* Baltimore: Paul H. Brookes.

Johnson, R. (1981). *The picture communication symbols.* Solana Beach, CA: Mayer-Johnson.

Johnson, R. M. (1994). *The picture communication symbols combination book.* Solana Beach, CA: Mayer-Johnson.

Jones, B. F. (1990). The importance of restructuring schools to promote learning. In D. Ogle, W. Pink, & B. F. Jones (Eds.), *Restructuring to promote learning in America's schools* (pp. 13–34). Columbus, OH: Zaner Bloser.

Jones, M. M., & Carlier, L. L. (1995). Creating inclusionary opportunities for learners with multiple disabilities. *Teaching Exceptional Children, 27*(3), 23–27.

Jones, M., & Carlier, L. L. (1998). Creating exclusionary opportunities for learners with multiple disabilities: A team teaching approach. *Educating Exceptional Children Annual Editions, 98/99,* pp. 146–150.

Jorgensen, C. M., Fisher, D., Sax, C., & Skoglund, K. L. (1998). Innovative scheduling, new roles for teachers, and heterogeneous groupings. In C. M. Jorgensen (Ed.), *Restructuring high schools for all students: Taking inclusion to the next level* (pp. 49–70). Baltimore: Paul H. Brookes.

Jorgenson, C. N. (1992). Natural supports in inclusive schools: Curriculum and teaching strategies. In J. Nisbet (Ed.), *Natural supports in school, at work, and in the community for people with severe disabilities* (pp. 179–215). Baltimore: Paul H. Brookes.

Jubala, K. A., Bishop, K. D., & Falvey, M. A. (1995). Creating a supportive classroom environment. In M. A. Falvey (Ed.), *Inclusive and heterogeneous schooling: Assessment, curriculum and instruction* (pp. 111–129). Baltimore: Paul H. Brookes.

Kagan, S. (1992). *Cooperative learning.* San Juan Capistrano, CA: Kagan Cooperative Learning.

Kaiser, A. P. (1993). Functional language. In M. E. Snell (Ed.), *Instruction of students with server disabilities* (4th ed.) (pp. 347–379). Upper Saddle River, NJ: Merrill/Prentice Hall.

Kaiser, J. S. (1997). Advocate for your adolescent: Encouraging special needs parents to get involved. *Schools in the Middle, 7,* 33–43, 52.

Kampwirth, T. J. (1998). *Collaborative consultation in the schools: Effective practices for students with learning and behavior problems.* Upper Saddle River, NJ: Merrill/Prentice Hall.

Kanner, L. (1943). Autistic disturbances of affective control. *Nervous Child, 2*, 217–250.

Kapes, J. T., & Martinez, L. (1999). Career assessment with special populations: A survey of national experts. Paper presented at the Annual Meeting of the Association for Career and Technical Education, Orlando, FL. (ERIC Document Reproduction Service No. ED 438 399)

Karagiannis, A., & Cartwright, G. F. (1990). Attitudinal research issues in integration of children with mental handicaps. *McGill Journal of Education, 25*, 369–382.

Karagiannis, A., Stainback, W., & Stainback, S. (1996). Rationale for inclusive schooling. In S. Stainback & W. Stainback (Eds.), *Inclusion: A guide for education* (pp. 3–16). Baltimore: Paul H. Brookes.

Karge, B. D., McClure, M., & Patton, P. L. (1995). The success of collaboration resource programs for students with disabilities in grades 6 through 8. *Remedial and Special Education, 16*(2), 79–89.

Karp, H. B. (1984). Working with resistance. *Training and Development Journal, 38*(3), 69–73.

Katsiyannis, A., & Maag, J. (1998). Disciplining students with disabilities: Issues and considerations for implementing IDEA '97. *Behavioral Disorders, 23*, 276–289.

Kaufman, A., & Kaufman, N. (1983). *The Kaufman assessment battery for children.* Circle Pines, MN: American Guidance Service.

Kaufman, J. M., Mostert, M. P., Trehut, S. C., & Hallahan, D. P. (1998). *Managing classroom behavior: A reflective case-based approach* (2nd ed). Boston: Allyn & Bacon.

Kayes, N. (1996). Everybody counts! Our goal is understanding. Cincinnati, OH: Everybody Counts, Inc. (Available from The Enrichment Tree, Inc. PO Box 40662, Cincinnati, OH 45240)

Kellner, M. H., & Tutin, J. (1995). A school-based anger management program for developmentally and emotionally disabled high school students. *Adolescence, 30,* 813–824.

Keltner, B. (1994). Home environments of mothers with mental retardation. *Mental Retardation, 32,* 123–127.

Kerr, M. M., & Nelson, C. M. (1998). *Strategies for managing behavior problems in the classroom* (3rd ed.). Upper Saddle River, NJ: Merrill/Prentice Hall.

Khemka, I. (2000). Increasing independent decision making skills of women with mental retardation in simulated interpersonal situations of abuse. *American Journal on Mental Retardation, 105,* 387–401.

Kids Voting USA. (1995). *Kids voting USA* [manual]. Tempe, AZ: Author.

Kids Voting USA. (1998). *Kids voting USA: Kid's voting 1998 curriculum update* [manual]. Tempe, AZ: Author.

Killy, S. (1997). Baking up a storm! Kramer Kids' Kitch Bakery [booklet]. Oxfrod, OH: Kramer Elementary School.

King, D. L. (1998). Boardmaker (Windows Version 1.4A) [Computer software]. Solana Beach, CA: Mayer-Johnson.

King, T. W. (1999). *Assistive technology: Essential human factors.* Boston: Allyn & Bacon.

King-Sears, M. E. (1997). Best academic practices for inclusive classrooms. *Focus on Exceptional Children 29*(7), 1–22.

Kirstein, I. J., & Bernstein, C. (1981). *Oakland Schools Communication Enhancement Center picture dictionary.* Pontiac, MI: Oakland Schools.

Kleinert, H. L., Kearns, J. F., & Kennedy, S. (1997). Accountability for all students: Kentucky's alternate portfolio assessment for students with moderate and severe cognitive disabilities. *JASH, 22*(2), 88–101.

Kluth, P. (2000). Community-referenced learning and the inclusive classroom. *RASE, 21,* 19–26.

Knapczyk, D. R., & Rodes, P. G. (1996). *Teaching social competence: A practical approach for improving social skills in students at-risk.* Pacific Grove, CA: Brooks/Cole.

Knapp, C. E. (1994). Progressivism never died—it just moved outside: What can experiential educators learn from the past? *The Journal of Experiential Education, 17,* 8–12.

Knowlton, E. (1998a). Appropriate curriculum for students with developmental disabilities. In A. Hilton and R. Ringlaben (Eds.), *Best and promising practices in developmental disabilities* (pp. 73–86). Austin, TX: Pro-Ed.

Knowlton, E. (1998b). Considerations in the design of personalized curricular supports for students with developmental disabilities. *Education and Training in Mental Retardation and Developmental Disabilities, 33,* 95–107.

Kochhar, C. A., West, L. L., & Taymans, J. M. (2000). *Successful inclusion: Practical strategies for a shared responsibility.* Upper Saddle River, NJ: Merrill/Prentice Hall.

Koegel, R. L., & Koegel, L. K. (1995). *Teaching children with autism.* Baltimore: Paul H. Brooks.

Kohoska, C. J., & Brolin, D. E. (1985). *Career education for handicapped individuals* (2nd ed.). Columbus, OH: Merrill.

Koul, R. K., & Hanners, J. (1997). Word identification and sentence verification of two synthetic speech systems by individuals with intellectual disabilities. *AAC Augmentative and Alternative Communication, 13,* 99–107.

Kraft, R. J. (1996). Service learning. *Education and Urban Society, 28,* 131–152.

Krall, C. M., & Renck, J. M. (1998–1999). Creating a caring community in classrooms: Advice from an intervention specialist. *Childhood Education, 75,* 83–89.

Kroth, R., & Bolson, M. D. (1996). Family involvement with assistive technology. *Contemporary Education, 68,* 17–20.

Kuersten, J. (1998). Safe Halloween thrills. *Our Children, 24,* 15.

Kurzweil 3000 [Computer equipment and software]. (n.d.). Waltham, MA: Kurzweil Educational Systems, Inc.

LaGreca, A. M., & Stone, W. L. (1990). LD status and achievement: Confounding variables in the study of children's social status, self-esteem, and behavioral functioning. *Journal of Learning Disabilities, 23,* 483–490.

Lahm, E. A. (1996). Software that engages young children with disabilities: A study of design features. *Focus on Autism and Other Developmental Disabilities, 11*(2), 115–124.

Lahoud, J. A., & Cleveland, D. (1994). *The Eyegaze Eyetracking System unique example of a multiple-use technology* [online]. Available:http//web.eyegaze.com/doc/ieee94.htm

Lambert, N., Nihira, K., & Leland, H. (1993). *AAMR adaptive behavior scale: School 2.* Austin, TX: Pro-Ed.

Laski, F. (1994). On the 40th anniversary of *Brown v. Board of Education*: Footnotes for the historically impaired. *TASH Newsletter, 20*(5), 3–4.

Lazerson, M. (Ed.). (1987). *American education in the twentieth century: A documentary history.* New York: Teachers College Press.

Lehr, D. H. & Brinkerhoff, J. (1996). Best practices for young children with disabilities who challenge the system. In D. H. Lehr & F. Brown (Eds.), *People with disabilities who challenge the system* (pp. 3–21). Baltimore: Paul H. Brookes.

Leppert, M. O. & Capute, A. J. (1996). Cerebral palsy and associated dysfunction. In R. H. A. Haslam & P. J. Valletutti (Eds.), *Medical problems in the classroom: The teacher's role in diagnosis and management* (3rd ed., pp. 341–360). Austin, TX: Pro-Ed.

Levin, A. V. (1996). Common visual problems in the classroom. In R. H. A. Haslam & P. J. Valletutti (Eds.), *Medical problems in the classroom: The teacher's role in diagnosis and management* (3rd ed., pp. 161–179). Austin, TX: Pro-Ed.

Lewis, T., Scott, T. M., & Sugai, G. (1994). The problem behavior questionnaire: A teacher-based instrument to develop functional hypothesis of problem behavior in general education classrooms. *Diagnostique, 19,* pp. 103–115.

Lilly, M. S. (1988, December). The regular education initiative: A force for change in general and special education. *Education and Training in Mental Retardation,* 253–260.

Lindstrom, L. E., Benz, M. R., & Johnson, M. D. (1997). From school grounds to coffee grounds. *Teaching Exceptional Children, 29*(4), 20–24.

Lipsky, D. K., & Gartner, A. (1996a). Inclusion, school restructuring, and the remaking of American society. *Harvard Educational Review, 66,* 762–796.

Lipsky, D. K., & Gartner, A. (1996b). Inclusive education and school restructuring. In W. Stainback and S. Stainback (Eds.), *Controversial issues confronting special education* (pp. 3–15). Boston: Allyn & Bacon.

Lipsky, D. K., & Gartner, A. (1997). *Inclusion and school reform: Transforming America's classrooms.* Baltimore: Paul H. Brookes.

Lipsky, D. K., & Gartner, A. (1998). Factors for successful inclusion: Learning from the past, look toward the future. In S. J. Vitello & D. E. Mithang (Eds.), *Inclusive schooling: National and international perspectives* (pp. 76–97). Mahwah, NJ: Erlbaum.

Llewellyn, G. (1995). Relationships and social support: Views of parents with mental retardation/intellectual disability. *Mental Retardation, 33,* 349–363.

Locke, P., & Levin, J. (1999). *Making connections: A practical guide for bringing the world of voice output communication to students with severe disabilities.* Minneapolis: AbleNet, Inc.

Lombard, R. C., Hazelkorn, M. N., & Miller, R. J. (1995). Special populations and Tech-Prep: A national study of state policies and practices. *Career Development for Exceptional Individuals, 18,* 145–156.

Love, L. L., & Malian, I. M. (1997). What happens to students leaving secondary special education services in Arizona? *Remedial and Special Education, 18,* 261–269.

Lowenthal, B. (1996). Teaching social skills to preschoolers with special needs. *Childhood Education, 72,* 137–140.

Lozada, M. (1998). Old hat, new name? *Techniques: Making Education and Career Connections, 73,* 29–33.

Luckasson, R. (1992). People with mental retardation as victims of crime. In R. W. Conley, R. Luckasson, & G. N. Bouthilet (Eds.), *The criminal justice system and mental retardation: Defendants and victims* (pp. 209–220). Baltimore: Paul H. Brookes.

Luckasson, R., et al. (1992). *Mental retardation: Definition, classification, and systems of supports.* Washington, DC: American Association on Mental Retardation.

Luckasson, R., & Spitalnik, D. (1994). Political programmatic shifts of the 1992 AAMR definition of mental retardation. In V. Bradley, J. W. Ashbaugh, & B. C. Blaney (Eds.), *Creating individual supports for people with developmental disabilities: A mandate for change on many levels* (pp. 81–95). Baltimore: Paul H. Brookes.

Maag, J. W. (1999). *Behavior management: From theoretical implications to practical applications.* San Diego, CA: Singular.

MacFarlane, C. A. (1998). Assessment: The key to appropriate curriculum & instruction. In A. Helton & R. Ringlaben (Eds.), *Best and promising practices in developmental disabilities* (pp. 35–60). Austin, TX: Pro-Ed.

MacMillan, D. L. (1982). *Mental retardation in school and society* (2nd ed.). Boston: Little, Brown.

Maharaj, S. (1980). *Pictogram ideogram communication.* Saskatchewan, Canada: The Pictogram Centre.

Mahony, M. (1997). Small victories in an inclusive classroom. *Educational Leadership, 54*(7), 59–62.

Malarz, L. (1996). Using staff development to create inclusive schools. *Journal of Staff Development, 17,* 8–11.

Malloy, B. L., & New, R. S. (1994). Social constructivist theory and principles of inclusion: Challenges for early childhood special education. *Journal of Special Education, 28,* 322–337.

Malott, R. W., Whaley, D. L., & Malott, M. E. (1997). *Elementary principles of behavior.* Upper Saddle River, NJ: Prentice Hall.

Mann, L. (1999, Winter). Buying into economics: Helping students invest in the future. *Curriculum Update,* pp. 4–5, 8.

Manzone, C. (1987). A call for curricular change: Bridging the gap between school and community living. *Viewpoints,* pp. 1–20. (ERIC Document Reproduction Service No. ED 289 974)

Markle, S. (1990). In the dough: Try these simple explorations with yeast and get a rise out of science! *Instructor, 99*(5), 84–86.

Markus, G. B., Howard, J. P., & Kling, D. C. (1993). Integrating community service and classroom instruction enhances learning: Results from an experiment. *Educational Evaluation and Policy Analysis, 15,* 410–419.

Martin, J. (1995). A philosophy of education for the year 2000. *Phi Delta Kappan, 76*, 355–359.

Martin, J. E., & Marshall, L. H. (1995). ChoiceMaker: A comprehensive self-determination transition program. *Intervention in School and Clinic, 30*, 147–156.

Maselow, R. E. (1995). How little tykes become big tycoons. *Educational Leadership, 52*(8), 58–61.

Matlock, B., Lynch, V., & Paeth, M. A. (1990). *Decision rules and strategies for skill generalization trainer's kit.* Seattle: University of Washington Press.

Mayer, M. (1993). *I was so mad.* New York: Western.

McCombs, L. (1993). *Community-based instruction: Technical resource manual.* Tallahassee: Florida Department of Education.

McCormick, L., & Feeney, S. (1995). Modifying and expanding activities for children with disabilities. *Young Children, 50*(4), 10–17.

McCormick, L., & Goldman, R. (1979). The transdisciplinary model: Implications for service delivery and personnel preparation for the severely and profoundly handicapped. *AAESPH Review, 4*, 152–161.

McDonnell, J. (1998). Instruction for students with severe disabilities in general education settings. *Education and Training in Mental Retardation and Developmental Disabilities, 33*, 199–215.

McDonnell, J. J., Hardman, M. L., McDonnell, A. P., & Kiefer-O'Donnell, R. (1995). *An introduction to persons with severe disabilities: Educational and social issues.* Boston: Allyn & Bacon.

McGregor, G., & Pachuski, P. (1996). Assistive technology in schools: Are teachers ready, able, and supported? *Journal of Special Education Technology, 13*, 4–15.

McKenzie, R. G., & Houk, C. S. (1993). Across the great divide: Transition from elementary to secondary settings for students with mild disabilities. *Teaching Exceptional Children, 25*(2), 16–20.

McKleskey, J., & Henry, D. (1999). Inclusion: What progress is being made across states? *Teaching Exceptional Children, 31*(5), 56–62.

McKnight, J. (1989). Regenerating community. *Social Policy, 17*(3), 54–58.

McNair, J., & Rusch, F. R. (1991). Parent involvement in transition programs. *Mental Retardation, 29*, 93–101.

McNeill, J. H., & Fowler, S. A. (1996). Using story reading to encourage children's conversations. *Teaching Exceptional Children, 28*(4), 43–47.

Melichar, J. F., & Blackhurst, A. E. (1993). *Introduction to a functional approach to assistive technology* [Training module]. Lexington: Department of Special Education and Rehabilitation Counseling, University of Kentucky.

Menolascino, F., Wilson, J., Golden, C., & Ruedrich, S. (1986). Medication and treatment of persons with mental retardation. *Mental Retardation, 24*, 277–283.

Merbler, J. B., Hadadian, A., & Ulman, J. (1999). Using assistive technology in the inclusive classroom. *Preventing School Failure, 43*(3), 113–117.

Meriwether, L. (1997). Math at the snack table. *Young Children, 52*(5), 69–73.

Mesibov, G. B., Adams, L. W., & Klinger, L. G. (1997). *Autism: Understanding the disorder.* New York: Plenum Press.

Meyer, I. H., & Evans, I. M. (1989). *Nonaversive intervention for behavior problems: A manuel for home & community.* Baltimore: Paul H. Brookes.

Meyer, L. H., Peck, C. A., & Brown, L. (1991). Definition of the people TASH serves. In L. H. Meyer, C. A. Peck, & L. Brown (Eds.), *Critical issues in the lives of people with severe disabilities.* Baltimore: Paul H. Brookes.

Miller, A. B., & Keys, C. B. (1996). Awareness, action, and collaboration: How the self-advocacy movement is empowering persons with developmental disabilities. *Mental Retardation, 34*, 312–319.

Miller, A. J., & Bragg, D. D. (1985). *Preparing Ohio's youth through occupational work adjustment and occupational work experience programs: Prospects for the future.* Columbus: Ohio State University College of Education. (ERIC Document Reproduction Service No. ED 263 324)

Miller, P., Shambaugh, K., Robinson, C., & Wimberly, J. (1995). Applied learning for middle schoolers. *Educational Leadership, 52*(8), 22–25.

Miller, R. J., Lafollette, M., & Green, K. (1990). Development and field test of a transition planning procedure—1985–1988. *Career Development for Exceptional Individuals, 13*, 45–55.

Millikin, C. C. (1997). Symbol systems and vocabulary selection strategies. In S. L. Glennen & D. C. DeCoste (Eds.), *Handbook of augmentative and alternative communication* (pp. 97–148). San Diego, CA: Singular.

Miner, C. A., & Bates, P. E. (1997). Person-centered transition planning. *Teaching Exceptional Children, 30*, 66–69.

Mostert, M. P. (1998). *Interprofessional collaboration in schools.* Boston: Allyn & Bacon.

Mundschenk, N. A., & Sasso, G. M. (1995). Assessing sufficient social exemplars for students with autism. *Behavior Disorders, 21*, 62–78.

Myers, B. A. (1987). Conduct disorders of adolescents with developmental disabilities. *Mental Retardation, 25*, 335–340.

Myles, B. S., & Simpson, R. L. (1998). Aggression and violence by school-age children and youth: Understanding the aggression cycle and prevention/intervention strategies. *Intervention in School and Clinic, 33*, 259–264.

National Commission on Excellence in Education. (1983). *A nation at risk: The imperative for educational reform.* [Online: www.ed.gov/pubs/NatAtRisk/]

National Information Center for Children and Youth with Disabilities. (1999). Individualized education programs. *NICHY Briefing Papers: LG2* (4th ed.). Washington, DC: Author.

Neary, T. (1992). Student specific strategies: Designing an individualized program. In T. Neary, A. Halverson, R. Kronberg, & D. Kelly (Eds.), *Curriculum adaptations for inclusive classrooms* (pp. 56–125). San Francisco: San Francisco State University.

Nicholson, C. (1989). Postmodernism, feminism, and education: The need for solidarity. *Educational Theory, 39*, 197–205.

Nietupski, J., Hamre-Nietupski, S., Clancy, P., & Veerhusen, K. (1986). Guidelines for making simulation an effective adjunct to in vivo community instruction. *Journal of the Association for Persons With Severe Handicaps, 11*, 12–18.

Nietupski, J., Scheutz, G., & Ockwood, L. (1980). The delivery of communication therapy services to severely handicapped students: A plan for change. *Journal of the Association for the Severely Handicapped, 5*, 13–23.

Nihira, K., Leland, H., & Lambert, N. (1993). *AAMR adaptive behavior scale: Residential and community scale* (2nd ed.). (ABS-RC2). Austin, TX: Pro-Ed.

Nirje, B. (1969). The normalization principle and its management implications. In R. Kegel & W. Wolfensberger (Eds.), *Changing patterns in residential services for the mentally retarded* (pp. 51–57). Washington, DC: U.S. Government Printing Office.

Noddings, N. (1992). *The challenge to care in the schools: An alternative approach to education.* New York: Teachers College Press.

North Coast Medical, Inc. (1999). *Functional solutions* [Catalog]. Morgan Hill, CA: Author.

Notari-Syverson, A. R., & Shuster, S. L. (1995). Putting real-life skills into IEP/IFSPs for infants and young children. *Teaching Exceptional Children, 27*(2), 29–32.

Nunn, G. D., & Nunn, S. J. (1993). Locus of control and school performance: Some implications for teachers. *Education, 113*, 636–640.

Oakes, J., & Lipton, M. (1994). Tracking and ability grouping: A structural barrier to access and achievement. In J. Goodlad & P. Keating (Eds.), *Access to knowledge: The continuing agenda for our nation's schools* (pp. 187–204). New York: College Entrance Examination Board.

Oakes, J., & Lipton, M. (1999). Access to knowledge: Challenging the techniques, norms, and politics of schooling. In K. Sirotnik & R. Soder (Eds.), *The beat of a different drummer: Essays on education renewal in honor of John I. Goodlad* (pp. 131–150). New York: Peter Lang.

O'Connor, S., & Racino, J. A. (1993). A home of my own: Community housing options and strategies. In J. A. Racino, P. Walker, S. O'Connor, & S. J. Taylor (Eds.), *Housing, support, and community: Choices and strategies for adults with disabilities* (pp. 137–160). Baltimore: Paul H. Brookes.

Odom, L. S., & McLean, M. E. (1993). Establishing recommended practices for programs for infants and young children with special needs and their families. In L. S. Odom & M. E. McLean (Eds.), *DEC recommended practices: Indicators of quality in programs for infants and young children with special needs and their families* (pp. 1–10). Pittsburgh: Division for Early Childhood, Council for Exceptional Children.

Office of Technology Assessment. (1995). *Teachers and technology: Making the connection.* Washington, DC: U.S. Government Printing Office.

Ohio Coalition for the Education of Children with Disabilities. (1999, April). *You and the IEP.* (Available from the Ohio Coalition for the Education of Children With Disabilities, Bank One Building, 165 West Center Street, Suite 302, Marion, OH 43302–3741)

Ohio Department of Education, (1995). *Whose IDEA is this? A resource guide for parents.* Columbus: Author.

Ohio Rehabilitation Services Commission. (1997). *Transition guidelines and best practices.* Columbus: Author.

Olson, J. L., & Platt, J. M. (2000). *Teaching children and adolescents with special needs* (3rd ed.). Upper Saddle River, NJ: Merrill/Prentice Hall.

Orelove, F. P., & Sobsey, D. (1991). *Educating children with multiple disabilities: A transdisciplinary approach* (2nd ed.). Baltimore: Paul H. Brookes.

Orland, M. E. (1994). Demographics of disadvantage: Intensity of childhood poverty and its relationship to educational achievement. In J. Goodlad & P. Keating (Eds.), *Access to knowledge: The continuing agenda for our nation's schools* (pp. 43–58). New York: College Entrance Examination Board.

Osborn, K., & Wilcox, B. (1992). *School to community transition: A planning and procedures handbook for parents and teachers in LaPorte County.* Bloomington, IN: Institute for the Study of Developmental Disabilities.

O'Shea, D. J., & O'Shea, L. J. (1998). Learning to include: Lessons learned from a high school without special education services. *Teaching Exceptional Children, 31*, 40–48.

Ostrosky, M. M., Drasgow, E., & Halle, J. W. (1999). "How can I help you get what you want?" *Teaching Exceptional Children, 31*(4), 56–61.

Page, B., & Chadsey-Rusch, J. (1995). The community college experience for students with and without disabilities: A viable transition outcome? *Career Development for Exceptional Individuals, 18*(2), 85–96.

Papaioannou, V. (1996). Hearing disorders in the classroom. In R. H. A. Haslam & P. J. Valletutti, *Medical problems in the classroom: The teacher's role in diagnosis and management* (3rd ed., pp. 181–208). Austin, TX: Pro-Ed.

Parette, H. P., (1997). Family-centered practice and computers for children with disabilities. *Early Childhood Education Journal, 25*, 53–55.

Parette, H. P. Jr., & Murdick, N. L. (1998). Assistive technology and IEPs for young children with disabilities. *Early Childhood Education Journal, 25*, 193–198.

Peach, W., Sanders, C., & Cobb, S. (1989). Attitudes of pre-service and in-service teachers toward behavior disorders/emotionally disturbed students. *Journal of Instructional Psychology, 15*, 180–182.

Pearpoint, J., Forest, M., & O'Brien, J. (1993). MAPs, circles of friends, & PATH: Powerful tools to help build caring communities. In S. Stainback and W. Stainback (Eds.), *Inclusion: A guide for educators* (pp. 67–86). Baltimore: Paul H. Brookes.

Pellegrino, L. (1997). Cerebral palsy. In M. L. Batshaw (Ed.), *Children with disabilities* (4th ed., pp. 499–528). Baltimore: Paul H. Brookes.

Perl, J. (1995). Improving relationship skills for parent conferences. *Teaching Exceptional Children, 28*, 29–31.

Perske, R. (1972, February). The dignity of risk and the mentally retarded. *Mental Retardation,* pp. 24–27.

Perske, R. (1988). *Circles of friends: People with disabilities and their lives enrich the lives of one another.* Nashville: Abingdon Press.

Peterson, C. P. (1980). Support services. In B.L. Wilcox & R. York (Eds.), *Quality education for the severely handicapped: The federal investment* (pp. 136–163). Washington, DC: Bureau of Education for the Handicapped.

Peterson, M. (1996). Community learning and inclusive schools. In S. Stainback & W. Stainback (Eds.), *Inclusion: A guide for educators* (pp. 271–293). Baltimore: Paul H. Brookes.

Peterson, M., LeRoy, B., Field, S., & Wood, P. (1992). Community-referenced learning in inclusive schools: Effective curriculum for all students. In S. Stainback & W. Stainback (Eds.), *Curriculum considerations in inclusive classrooms: Facilitating learning for all students* (pp. 207–227). Baltimore: Paul H. Brookes.

Pike, K., & Salend, S. J. (1995, Fall). Authentic assessment strategies: Alternatives to norm-referenced testing. *Teaching Exceptional Children,* pp. 15–20.

Polloway, E. A., & Patton, J. R. (1997). *Strategies for teaching learners with special needs* (6th ed.). Upper Saddle River, NJ: Merrill/Prentice Hall.

Polloway, E., Patton, J., Epstein, M., & Smith T. E. C. (1989). Comprehensive curriculum for students with mild handicaps. *Focus on Exceptional Children, 21*(8), 1–12.

Porter, A. (1989). A curriculum out of balance: The case of elementary school mathematics. *Educational Researcher, 18*(5), 9–15.

Power-deFur, L. A., & Orelove, R. P. (1997). *Inclusive education: Practical implementation of the least restrictive environment.* Gaithersburg, MD: Aspen.

Pratt, B. (1999). Using technology in a classroom for young children with multiple disabilities. *Learning and Leading With Technology, 26*(8), 28–31.

Pruitt, P., Wandry, D., & Hollums, D. (1998). Listen to us! Parents speak out about their interactions with special educators. *Preventing School Failure, 42*(4), 161–166.

Pugach, M. C., & Johnson, L. J. (1995). *Collaborative practitioners collaborative schools.* Denver: Love.

Pugliese, M. (1999). *Stages: Software for special needs.* Newton, MA: Assistive Technology.

Queen, J. A., & Gaskey, K. A. (1997). Steps for improving school climate in block scheduling. *Phi Delta Kappan, 79,* 158–161.

Racino, J. A., & Taylor, S. J. (1993). People first: Approaches to housing and support. In J. A. Racino, P. Walker, S. O'Connor, & S. J. Taylor (Eds.), *Housing, support, and community: Choices and strategies for adults with disabilities* (pp. 33–56). Baltimore: Paul H. Brookes.

Rainforth, B., & York, J. (1987). Integrating related services in community instruction. *The Journal of the Association for Persons With Severe Handicaps, 12,* 190–198.

Rainforth, B., & York, J. (1991). Handling and positioning. In F. P. Orlove and D. Sobsey (Eds.), *Educating children with multiple disabilities: A transdisciplinary approach* (2nd ed., pp. 79–118). Baltimore: Paul H. Brookes.

Rainforth, B., & York-Barr, J. (1997). *Collaborative teams for students with severe disabilities: Integrating therapy and educational services* (2nd ed.). Baltimore: Paul H. Brookes.

Raschke, D. B., Dedrick, C. V. L., Heston, M. L., & Farris, M. (1996). Everyone can play! Adapting the Candy Land board game. *Teaching Exceptional Children, 28*(4), 28–33.

Raygor, A. L. (1977). The Raygor Readability Estimate: A quick and easy way to determine difficulty. In P. D. Pearson (Ed.), *Reading theory, research and practice: Twenty-Sixth Yearbook of the National Reading Conference* (pp. 259–263). Clemson, SC: National Reading Conference.

Razeghi, J. A. (1998). A first step toward solving the problem of special education dropouts: Infusing career education into the curriculum. *Intervention in School and Clinic, 33*(3), 148–156.

Redmond, N.B., Bennett, C., Wiggert, J., & McLean, B. (1993). Using functional assessment to support a student with severe disabilities in the community. *Teaching Exceptional Children 25*(3), 51–52.

Reiss, S. (1982). Psychopathology and mental retardation: Survey of a developmental disabilities mental health program. *Mental Retardation, 20,* 128–152.

Reiss, S., & Havercamp, S. M. (1999). Sensitivity, functional analysis and behavior genetics: A response to Freeman et al. *American Journal on Mental Retardation, 104,* 289–293.

Reiss, S., Levitan, G. W., & Szyszko, J. (1982). Emotional disturbance and mental retardation: Diagnostic overshadowing. *American Journal of Mental Deficiency, 86,* 567–574.

Richards, B., & Merker, A. (1997). What do you want to be when you grow up? *Principal, 77*(2), 43–44.

Richardson, S. A., Koller, H., & Katz, M. (1985). Relationships between upbringing and later behavior disturbance of mildly mentally retarded young people. *American Journal of Mental Deficiency, 90,* 1–8.

Roach, V. (1995). Supporting inclusion: Beyond the rhetoric. *Phi Delta Kappa Research Bulletin, 77,* 295–299.

Robertson, G., Haines, L. P., Sandhe, R., & Biffart, W. (1997). Positive change through computer networking. *Teaching Exceptional Children 29*(6), 22–30.

Robinson, R. J. (2000). Learning about happiness from persons with Down syndrome: Feeling the sense of joy and contentment. *American Journal on Mental Retardation, 105,* 372–376.

Roblyer, M. D., Edwards, J., & Havriluk, M. A. (1997). *Integrating educational technology into teaching.* Upper Saddle River, NJ: Merrill/Prentice Hall.

Rogers, J. (1993). The inclusion revolution. *Phi Delta Kappa Research Bulletin, 11,* 1–6.

Rojewski, J. W., Pollard, R. R., & Meers, G. D. (1990). Grading mainstreamed special needs students: Determining practices and attitudes of secondary vocational educators using a qualitative approach. *Remedial and Special Education, 12,* 7–28.

Romski, M. A., Sevick, R. A., & Adamson, L. B. (1997). Framework for studying how children with developmental disabilities develop language through augmented means. *AAC Augmentative and Alternative Communication, 13,* 172–178.

Rosenthal-Malek, A., & Bloom, A. (1998). Beyond acquisition: Teaching generalization for students with developmental disabilities. In A. Hilton & R. Ringlaben (Eds.), *Best and promising practices in developmental disabilities* (pp. 139–156). Austin, TX: Pro-Ed.

Rowley, R. (1997). Service learning in the early childhood classroom. *Young Children, 52*(7), 26–27.

Rule, S., Riechtl, B. J., & Innocenti, M. S. (1990). Preparation for transition to mainstreamed post-preschool environments: Development of a survival skills curriculum. *Topics in Early Childhood Special Education, 9*(4), 78–90.

Rutter, M., Tizard, J., & Whitmore, K. (1970). *Education, health, and behavior.* New York: Wiley.

Ryan, S., & Paterna, L. (1999). Junior high can be inclusive: Using natural supports and cooperative learning. *Teaching Exceptional Children, 30*(2), 36–41.

Ryndak, D. L. (1996). Adapting environments, materials and instruction to facilitate inclusion. In D. L. Ryndak and S. Alper (Eds.), *Curriculum content for students with moderate and severe disabilities in inclusive settings* (pp. 97–124). Boston: Allyn & Bacon.

Ryndak, D. L., & Alper, S. (1996). *Curriculum content for students with moderate and severe disabilities in inclusive settings.* Boston: Allyn & Bacon.

Sacker, G. B. (1995). Enhancing career development for all students through Tech Prep/school-to-work. *National Association of Secondary School Principals Bulletin, 79*(575), 1–9.

Sailor, W. (1991). Special education in the restructured school. *Remedial and Special Education, 12*(6), 8–22.

Sailor, W., & Guess, D. (1983). *Severely handicapped students: An instructional design.* Boston: Houghton Mifflin.

Salend, S. J. (1995). Using videocassette recorder technology in special education classrooms. *Teaching Exceptional Children, 27*(3), 4–9.

Salend, S. J. (2001). *Creating inclusive classrooms: Effective and reflective practices* (4th ed.). Upper Saddle River, NJ: Merrill/Prentice Hall.

Salend, S. J., & Gordon, B. D. (1987). A group-oriented timeout ribbon procedure. *Behavior Disorders 12*(2), 131–137.

Salvia, J., & Ysseldyke, J. E. (1998). *Assessment* (7th ed.). Boston: Houghton Mifflin.

Santrock, J. W. (1996). *Child development* (7th ed.). Madison: Brown & Benchmark.

Sapon-Shevin, M. (1992). Celebrating diversity, creating community: Curriculum that honors and builds on difference. In S. Stainback & W. Stainback (Eds.), *Curriculum considerations in inclusive classrooms: Facilitating learning for all students* (pp. 19–36). Baltimore, MD: Paul H. Brookes.

Sapon-Shevin, M. (1999). *Because we can change the world: A practical guide to building cooperative, inclusive classroom communities.* Boston: Allyn & Bacon.

Sapon-Shevin, M., & Schniedewind, N. (1990). Selling cooperative learning without selling it short. *Educational Leadership, 4*(1), 63–65.

Sapona, R. H., Bauer A. M., & Phillips, L. J. (1989). Facilitative stance: Responsive teaching of students with special needs. *Academic Therapy, 25,* 245–252.

Sax, C., Pumpian, I., & Fisher, D. (1997, March). Assistance technology and inclusion. *Policy, Research Brief Issue.* Washington, DC, U.S. Department of Education. (ERIC Document Reproduction Service No. ED 408 738)

Schaffner, C. B., & Buswell, B. E. (1996). Ten critical elements for creating inclusive and effective school communities. In S. Stainback & W. Stainback (Eds.), *Inclusion: A guide for educators* (pp. 49–66). Baltimore: Paul H. Brookes.

Schalock, R. L., et al. (1994). The changing conception of mental retardation: Implications for the field. *Mental Retardation, 32,* 181–193.

Schalock, R. (1999). Adaptive behavior and its measurement: Setting the future agenda. In R. Schalock (Ed.), *Adaptive behavior and its measurement: Implications for the field of mental retardation* (pp. 209–222). Washington, DC: AAMR.

Schanche, C. E. (1998). What's behind door number three? *Voices from the Middle, 6*(2), 37–41.

Schleien, S., & Green, F. (1992). Three approaches for integrating persons with disabilities into community recreation. *Journal of Park and Recreation Administration, 10*(2), 51–66.

Schniedewind, N. (1993). Teaching the feminist process in the 1990s. *Women's Studies Quarterly, 21*(3 & 4), 17–30.

Schwartz, I. S., Garfinkle, A. N., & Bauer, J. (1998). The picture exchange communication system: Communicative outcomes for young children with disabilities. *Topics in Early Childhood Special Education, 18,* 144–159.

Secretary's Commission on Achieving Necessary Skills. (1991). *What work requires of schools.* Washington, DC: SCANS, U.S. Department of Labor. (ERIC Document Reproduction Service No. ED 332 054)

Seligman, M. E. (1975). *Helplessness: On depressions, development and death.* San Francisco: Freeman.

Service learning yields real benefits for students with disabilities. (1998). *CEC Today, 4*(6), 1, 9.

Shaw, J. A., & Budd, E. D. (1982). Determinants of acquiescence and nay saying of mentally retarded persons. *American Journal of Mental Deficiency, 87,* 108–110.

Sheldon, K. (1996). "Can I play too?" Adapting common classroom activities for young children with limited motor abilities. *Early Childhood Education Journal, 24,* 115–120.

Shinn, M. (1995). Best practices in curriculum-based measurement and its use in a problem-solving model. In A. Thomas & J. Grimes (Eds.), *Best practices in school psychology* III. Washington, DC: National Association for School Psychology.

Shrewsbury, C. M. (1987). What is feminist pedagogy? *Women's Studies Quarterly, 15*(3 & 4), 7–14.

Shumer, R. (1994). Community-based learning: Humanizing education. *Journal of Adolescence, 17,* 357–369.

Siegel-Causey, E., & Allinder, R. M. (1998). Using alternative assessment for students with severe disabilities: Alignment with best practice. *Education and Training in Mental Retardation and Developmental Disabilities, 33,* 168–178.

Sigelman, C. K., Budd, E. C., Spanel, C. L., & Schoenrock, C. J. (1981). When in doubt say yes: Acquiescence in interviews with mentally retarded persons. *Mental Retardation, 19,* 53–58.

Simon, R. I., & Dippo, D. (1987). What schools can do: Designing programs for work education that challenge the wisdom of experience. *Journal of Education, 169*(3), 101–116.

Simmons, D. D., & Kameenui, E. J. (1996). A focus on curriculum design: When children fail. *Focus on Exceptional Children, 28,* 1–16.

Sitlington, P. L., Frank, A. R., & Carson, R. (1992). Adult adjustment among high school graduates with mild disabilities. *Exceptional Children, 59,* 221–233.

Skiba, R. J., & Peterson, R. L. (2000). School discipline at a crossroads: From zero tolerance to early response. *Exceptional Children, 66,* 335–346.

Slavin, R. E., & Braddock, J. H. (1994). Ability grouping: On the wrong track. In J. Goodlad & P. Keating (Eds.), *Access to knowledge: The continuing agenda for our nation's schools* (pp. 289–296). New York: College Entrance Examination Board.

Smith, D. D. (1998). *Introduction to special education: Teaching in an age of challenge* (3rd. ed.). Boston: Allyn & Bacon.

Smith, D. D. (2001). *Introduction to special education* (4th ed.). Boston: Allyn & Bacon.

Smith, D. D., & Luckasson, R. (1995). *Introduction to special education: Teaching in an age of challenge* (2nd ed.). Boston: Allyn & Bacon.

Smith, J. D. (1998). *Inclusion: Schools for all students.* Belmont, CA: Wadsworth.

Smith, M. (1993). *Behavior modification for exceptional children and youth.* Boston: Andover Medical Publishers.

Smith, S. J., & Jones, E. D. (1999). The obligation to provide assistive technology: Enhancing general curriculum access. *Journal of Education and Law, 28*(2), 247–265.

Smith, T. E. C. (1998). Developmental disabilities: Definition, description, and directions. In A. Hilton & R. Ringlaben (Eds.), *Best and promising practices in developmental disabilities.* (pp. 7–14). Austin, TX: Pro-Ed.

Smith, T. E. C., & Dowdy, C. (1992, September). Future based assessment and intervention for students with mental retardation. *Education and Training in Mental Retardation,* pp. 225–260.

Smith, W., & Fenstermacher, G. D. (1999). *Leadership for educational renewal: Developing a cadre of leaders.* San Francisco: Jossey-Bass.

Smith, W. F., Gottesman B., & Edmundson, P. (1997). Constructing a language of collaboration. Seattle: University of Washington, Center for Educational Renewal.

Snell, M. (1998). Characteristics of elementary school classrooms where children with moderate and severe disabilities

are included: A compilation of findings. In S. J. Vitello & D. E. Mithang, (Eds.), *Inclusive schooling: National and international perspectives* (pp. 76–97). Mahwah, NJ: Erlbaum.

Snell, M. E., & Brown, F. (1993). Instructional planning and implementation. In M. E. Snell (Ed.), *Instruction of students with severe disabilities* (4th ed., pp. 99–151). Upper Saddle River, NJ: Merrill/Prentice Hall.

Snell, M. E., & Brown, F. (2000). *Instruction of students with severe disabilities* (5th ed.). Upper Saddle River, NJ: Merrill/Prentice Hall.

Sodac, D. G. (1997). Join the AMICUS club! Increasing high schoolers' social skills in an after-school program. *Teaching Exceptional Children, 29*(3), 64–67.

Sobsey, D., & Cox, A. W. (1991). Integrating health care and educational programs. In F. P. Orelove 7 D. Sobsey, *Educating children with multiple disabilities: A transdisciplinary approach* (2nd ed., pp. 155–186). Baltimore: Paul H. Brookes.

Sobsey, D., & Wolf-Schein, E. G. (1991). Sensory impairments. In F. P. Orlove and D. Sobsey (Eds.), *Educating children with multiple disabilities: A transdisciplinary approach* (2nd ed., pp. 119–153). Baltimore: Paul H. Brookes.

Solomon, D., Schaps, E., Watson, M., & Battistich, V. (1992). Creating caring school and classroom communities for all students. In R. Villa, J. Thousand, W. Stainback, & S. Stainback (Eds.), *Restructuring for caring and effective education: An administrator's guide to creating heterogeneous schools* (pp. 41–60). Baltimore: Paul H. Brookes.

Southwest Ohio Transition Round Table. (1998). *The resource guide to income and government support for Hamilton County, Ohio.* (Available from Lighthouse Youth Services Career Connections, 1501 Madison Road, Cincinnati, OH 45206)

Sparrow, S., Balla, D., & Cicehetti, D. (1984). *Vineland adaptive behavior scale.* Circle Pines, MN: American Guidance Service.

Sprague, J. R., & Horner, R. H. (1984). The effects of single instance, multiple instance, and general case training on generalized vending machine use by moderately and severely handicapped students. *Journal of Applied Behavior Analysis, 17,* 273–278.

Sprenger, M. (1999). *Learning and memory: The brain in action.* Alexandria, VA: Association for Supervision and Curriculum Development.

Spring, J. (1989). *American education: An introduction to social and political aspects.* White Plains, NY: Longman.

SRI International. (1995). *Technology and education reform: Technical Research Report.* [Online: http://www.ed.gov/pubs/SER/Technology/]

Stainback, S., & Stainback, W. (1992). *Curricula considerations in inclusive classrooms: Facilitating learning for all students.* Baltimore: Paul H. Brookes.

Stainback, S., & Stainback, W. (1996). *Inclusion: A guide for educators.* Baltimore: Paul H. Brookes.

Stainback, W., Stainback, S., & Moravec, J. (1992). Using curriculum to build inclusive classrooms. In S. Stainback & W. Stainback (Eds.), *Curricular considerations in inclusive class-*

rooms: Facilitating learning for all students (pp. 65–84). Baltimore: Paul H. Brookes.

Stainback, W., Stainback, S., & Stefanich, G. (1996). Learning together in inclusive classrooms: What about the curriculum? *Teaching Exceptional Children 28*(3), 14–19.

Stainback, W., Stainback, S., Stefanich, G., & Alper, S. (1996). Learning in inclusive classrooms: What about the curriculum? In S. Stainback & W. Stainback, *Inclusion: A guide for educators* (pp. 209–219). Baltimore: Paul H. Brookes.

Stanton, T. (1990). Service learning: Groping toward a definition. In J. C. Kendall and Associates (Eds.), *Combining service and learning: A resource book for community and public service.* (Vol. 1, pp. 65–67). Raleigh, NC: National Society for Internships and Exceptional Education.

Staub, D., Spaulding, M., Peck, C. A., Gallucci, C., & Schwartz, I. S. (1996). Using nondisabled peers to support the inclusion of students with disabilities at the junior high school level. *Journal of the Association for Persons With Severe Handicaps, 21,* 194–205.

Steere, D. E., Wood, R., Panscofar, E. L., & Butterworth, J., Jr. (1990). Outcome-based school-to-work transition planning for students with severe disabilities. *Career Development for Exceptional Individuals, 13,* 57–69.

Steinburg, A. G., & Knightly, C. A. (1997). Hearing: Sounds and silences. In M. L. Batshaw (Ed.), *Children with disabilities* (4th ed., pp. 241–274). Baltimore: Paul H. Brookes.

Stern, D., & Rahn, M. (1995). How health career academics provide work-based learning. *Educational Leadership, 52*(8), 37–40.

Sternberg, L. (Ed.) (1994). *Individuals with profound disabilities: Instructional and assistive strategies* (3rd ed.). Austin, TX; Pro-Ed.

Stevens, B., Everington, C., & Kozar-Kocsis, S. (1999). Inclusion: What teachers are doing to accommodate for special needs students. *The Electronic Journal of Inclusive Education, 1*(3).

Stokes, T. F., & Baer, D. M. (1977). An implicit technology of generalization. *Journal of Applied Behavior Analysis, 10,* 349–367.

Stokes, T. F., & Osnes, P. G. (1988). The developing applied technology of generalization and maintenance. In R. H. Horner, G. Dunlap, & R. L. Koegel (Eds.), *Generalization and maintenance: Life style changes in applied settings* (pp. 5–19). Baltimore: Paul H. Brookes.

Sturmey, P. (1995). Diagnostic-based pharmacological treatment of behavior disorders in persons with developmental disabilities: A review and decision-making typology. *Research in Developmental Disabilities, 16,* 235–252.

Sturmey, P., & Sevin, J. (1994). Defining and assessing autism. In J. L. Matson (Ed.), *Autism in children and adults: Etiology, assessment, and intervention.* Pacific Grove, CA: Brooks/Cole.

Swengel, A. (1992). Lively zoo lessons. *Learning, 20*(5), 46–48.

Tashie, C., & Schuh, M. (1993). Why not community-based instruction? High school students with disabilities belong with their peers. *Equity and Excellence, 1,* 15–17.

Taylor, R. L., Richards, S. B., Goldstein, P. A., & Schilit, J. (1997). Teacher perceptions of inclusive settings. *Teaching Exceptional Children, 29,* 50–54.

Test, D. W., Karvonen, M., Wood, W. M., Browder, D., & Algozzine, B. (2000). Choosing a self-determination curriculum. *Teaching Exceptional Children, 33*(2), 48–54.

Thomas, C. C., Correa, V. I., & Morsink, C. V. (2001). *Interactive teaming: Enhancing programs for students with special needs.* Upper Saddle River, NJ: Merrill/Prentice Hall.

Thompson, S. (1995). The community as classroom. *Educational Leadership, 52,* 17–20.

Thorndike, R., Hagen, E., & Sattler, J. (1986). *Stanford-Binet intelligence scale: Fourth edition.* Chicago: Riverside.

Thousand, J., Fox, T., Reid, R., Godek, J., Williams, W., & Fox, W. (1986). *The homecoming model: Educating students who present intensive educational challenges within regular education* (Monograph 7–1). University Affiliated Program, University of Vermont.

Thousand, J. S., & Villa, R. A. (1995). Managing complex change toward inclusive schooling. In R. A. Villa & J. S. Thousand (Eds.), *Creating an inclusive school* (pp. 51–79). Alexandria, VA: Association for Supervision and Curriculum Development.

Tiegerman-Farber, E., & Radziewicz, C. (1998). *Collaborative decision making: The pathway to inclusion.* Upper Saddle River, NJ: Merrill/Prentice Hall.

Tsai, L. Y. (1998). Medical interventions for students with autism. In R. L. Simpson & B. S. Myles (Eds.), *Educating children and youth with autism* (pp. 277–314). Austin, TX: Pro-Ed.

Turnbull, A. P., & Turnbull, H. R. (1990). *Families, professionals, and exceptionality: A special partnership.* Upper Saddle River, NJ: Merrill/Prentice Hall.

Turnbull, A. P., & Turnbull, H. R., III (1997). *Families, professionals, and exceptionality: A special partnership.* Upper Saddle River, NJ: Merrill/Prentice Hall.

Turnbull, A. P., Turnbull, R., Shank, M., & Leal, D. (1999). *Exceptional lives: Special education in today's schools* (2nd ed.). Upper Saddle River, NJ: Merrill/Prentice Hall.

Turnbull, R., & Cilley, M. (1999). *Explanations and implications of the 1997 amendments to IDEA.* Upper Saddle River, NJ: Merrill/Prentice Hall.

Turner, K., Snart, F., & McCarthy, C. (1992). Promoting integration and cooperation: The Friendship Games. *Teaching Exceptional Children, 24*(3), 34–37.

Twentieth Annual Report to Congress on the Implementation of the Individuals with Disabilities Education Act. (1998). Washington, DC: U.S. Department of Education, Author.

Tymchuk, A. J., Hamada, D., Andron, L., & Anderson, S. (1990). Home safety training with mothers who are mentally retarded. *Education and Training in Mental Retardation, 25,* 142–149.

Udell, T., Peters, J., & Templeman, T. P. (1998). From philosophy to practice in inclusive early childhood programs. *Teaching Exceptional Children, 30*(3), 44–49.

Udvari-Solner, A. (1992, November). *Curricular adaptations: Practical tools to influence teaching practices in the general education classroom.* Paper presented at the TASH National Conference, San Francisco, CA.

United Cerebral Palsy, National Organized Collaborative Project. (1976). *Staff development handbook: A resource for the transdisciplinary process.* New York: United Cerebral Palsy Association.

U.S. Department of Education, National Commission on Excellence in Education. (1983). *A nation at risk.* Washington, DC: National Information Center for Children and Youth with Disabilities.

Vandercook, T., York, J., & Forest, M. (1989). The McGill Action Planning System (MAPS): A strategy for building the vision. *Journal of the Association for Persons With Severe Disabilities, 14,* 205–215.

Vaughn, S., & Schumm, J. S. (1995). Responsible inclusion for students with learning disabilities. *Journal of Learning Disabilities, 28,* 264–270, 290.

Venkatagiri, H. S., & Ramabadran, T. V. (1995). Digital speech synthesis: A tutorial. *AAC Augmentative and Alternative Communication, 11,* 14–25.

Villa, R., & Thousand, J. (1992). Restructuring public school systems. Strategies for organizational change and progress. In R. Villa, J. Thousand, W. Stainback, & S. Stainback (Eds.), *Restructuring for caring and effective education: An administrator's guide to creating heterogeneous schools* (pp. 109–137). Baltimore: Paul H. Brookes.

Villa, R., Thousand, J., Stainback, W., & Stainback. S. (1992). *Restructuring for caring and effective education: An administrative guide to creating heterogeneous schools.* Baltimore: Paul H. Brookes.

Villa, R. A., Thousand, J. S., Stainback, W., & Stainback, S. (1992). *Restructuring for caring and effective education.* Baltimore: Paul H. Brookes.

Walker, J. E., & Shea, T. M. (1999). *Behavior management: A practical approach for educators* (7th ed.) Upper Saddle River, NJ: Merrill/Prentice Hall.

Walther-Thomas, C., Korinek, L., McLauglin, V. L., & Williams, B. T. (2000). *Collaboration for inclusive education: Developing successful programs.* Boston: Allyn & Bacon.

Warren, S., & Kaiser, A. (1986). Incidental language teaching: A critical review. *Journal of Speech and Hearing Disorders, 51,* 291–298.

Washington, B. T. (1969). *The Negro problem: A series of articles by representative American Negroes of today.* New York: Arno Press.

Wasley, P. A., Hampel, R. L., & Clark, R. W. (1997). *Kids and school reform.* San Francisco: Jossey-Bass.

Weaver, H. R., Adams, S. A., & Landers, M. F. (1998). Meeting the life skill needs of students with developmental disabilities in integrated settings. In A. Hilton & R. Ringlaben (Eds.), *Best and promising practices in developmental disabilities* (pp. 87–106) Austin, TX: Pro-Ed.

Weaver, R., Landers, M. F., & Adams, S. (1991). Making curriculum functional: Special education and beyond. *Intervention in School and Clinic, 26,* 284–287.

Webber, J., & Scheuerman, B. (1991, Fall). Accentuate the positive . . . eliminate the negative. *Teaching Exceptional Children,* pp. 13–19.

Webster's New World Dictionary of the American Language Second College Edition (1974). New York: William Collins and World Publishing.

Wechsler, D. (1989). *Wechsler preschool & primary text of intelligence—revised* (WPPSI-R). San Antonio, TX: Psychology Corporation.

Wechsler, D. (1991). *Wechsler intelligence scale for children—III* (WISC-III). San Antonio, TX: Psychology Corporation.

Wechsler, D. (1998). *Wechsler adult intelligence scale—III* (WAIS-III). San Antonio, TX: Psychology Corporation.

Wehman, P. (1996). *Life beyond the classroom: Transition strategies for young people with disabilities* (2nd ed.). Baltimore: Paul H. Brookes.

Wehman, P. (1997a). Curriculum design. In P. Wehman & J. Kregel (Eds.), *Functional curriculum for elementary , middle, and secondary age students with special needs* (pp. 1–17). Austin, TX: Pro-Ed.

Wehman, P. (1997b). *Exceptional individuals in school, community, and work.* Austin, TX: Pro-Ed.

Wehman, P., & Kregel, J. (1997). *Functional curriculum for elementary, middle, and secondary age students with special needs.* Austin, TX: Pro-Ed.

Wehman, P., Kregel, J., & Barcus, J. M. (1985). From school to work: A vocational transition model for handicapped students. *Exceptional Children, 52,* 25–37.

Wehmeyer, M. (1992). Self-determination: Critical skills for outcomes oriented transition services. *The Journal for Vocational Special Needs Education, 15,* 3–7.

Wehmeyer, M. (1996, December). Student self-report measure of self-determination for students with cognitive disabilities. *Education and Training in Mental Retardation and Developmental Disabilities,* pp. 282–293.

Wehmeyer, M. L. (1999). Assistive technology and students with mental retardation: Utilization and barriers. *Journal of Special Education Technology, 14*(1), 48–58.

Wehmeyer, M. L., Agran, M., & Hughes, C. (1998). *Teaching self-determination to students with disabilities: Basic skills for successful transition.* Baltimore: Paul H. Brookes.

Weitz, C., Dexter, M., & Moore, J. (1997). AAC and children with developmental disabilities. In S. L. Glennen & D. C. DeCoste (Eds.), *Handbook of augmentative and alternative communication* (pp. 395–431). San Diego, CA: Singular.

Wesley, P. A., Hampel, R. L., & Clark, R. (1997). *Kids and school reform.* San Francisco: Jossey-Bass.

Wesson, C. L., & King, R. P. (1996). Portfolio assessment and special education students. *Teaching Exceptional Children 28*(2), 44–48.

West, L. L., & Taymans, J. (1998). Keeping up with the new IDEA. *Techniques, 73*(4), 25.

Westling, D. L., & Fox, L. (1995). *Teaching students with severe disabilities.* Upper Saddle River, NJ: Merrill/Prentice Hall.

Westling, D. L., & Fox, L. (2000). *Teaching students with severe disabilities* (2nd ed.). Upper Saddle River, NJ: Merrill/Prentice Hall.

Wetherby, A. M., Schuler, A. L., & Prizant, B. M. (1997).Enhancing language and communication development: Theoretical foundations. In D. J. Cohen & F. R. Volkmar (Eds.), *Handbook of autism and pervasive developmental disorders* (pp. 123–147). New York: Wiley.

Whinnery, K. W., Fuchs, L., & Fuchs, D. (1991). General, special, and remedial teachers' acceptance of behavioral instructional strategies for mainstreaming students with mild handicaps. *Remedial and Special Education, 12*(4), 6–17.

Wilcox, B. (1987). Why a new curriculum? In B. Wilcox, & G. T. Bellamy (Eds.), *A comprehensive guide to the activities catalog: An alternative curriculum for youth and adults with severe disabilities* (pp. 1–10). Baltimore: Paul H. Brookes.

Wilcox, B., & Bellamy, G. T. (1987). *The activities catalog: An alternative curriculum for youth and adults with severe disabilities*. Baltimore: Paul H. Brookes.

Wilczenski, F. L. (1992). Reevaluating the factor structure of the Attitudes Toward Mainstreaming Scale. *Educational and Psychological Measurement, 52*, 499–504.

Will, M. C. (1986). Educating children with learning problems: A shared responsibility. *Exceptional Children, 52*, 411–415.

Williams, P., & Shoultz, B. (1982). *We can speak for ourselves*. Bloomington, IN: University Press.

Williamson, R. D. (1997). Help me organize. *Intervention in School and Clinic, 33*, 36–39.

Winik, L. W. (1998). The little bookstore that grew to a thousand. *American Educator, 22*(1 & 2), 82–84.

Wircenski, J. L., & Sarkees, M. D. (1990). Instructional alternatives: Rescue strategies for at-risk students. NASSP Curriculum Report, *19*(4), 1–6.

Wisniewski, L. A., Alper, S., & Schloss, P. (1991). Work-experience and work-study programs for students with special needs: Quality indicators of transition services. *Career Development for Exceptional Individuals, 14*(2), 43–58.

Wolery, M., Ault, M. J., & Doyle, P. M. (1992). *Teaching students with moderate to severe disabilities*. New York: Longman.

Wolfe, P. S., & Harriott, W. A. (1997). Functional academics. In P. Wehman & J. Kregel (Eds.), *Functional curriculum for elementary, middle, and secondary age students with special needs* (pp. 69–103). Austin, TX: Pro-Ed.

Wolfensberger, W. (1970). The principle of normalization and its implications to psychiatric services. *American Journal of Psychology, 127*, 291–296.

Wolfensberger, W. (1983). Social role valorization: A proposed new term for the principle of normalization. *Mental Retardation, 21*, 234–239.

Wood, J. W. (1998). *Adapting instruction to accommodate students in inclusive settings*. Upper Saddle River NJ: Merrill/Prentice Hall.

Woodcock, R. W., & Davies, C. O. (1969). *The Peabody Rebus Reading Program*. Circle Pines, MN: American Guidance Service.

Working Forum on Inclusive Schools. (1994). *Creating schools for all our students: What 12 schools have to say*. Reston, VA: Council for Exceptional Children.

Workman, E. A., & Katz, A. M. (1995). *Teaching behavioral self-control to students* (2nd ed). Austin, TX: Pro-Ed.

Wright, J. L., & Shade, D. D. (Eds.). (1994). *Young children: Active learners in a technological age*. Washington, DC: National Association for the Education of Young Children. (ERIC Document Reproduction Service No. ED 380 242)

Write: OutLoud [Computer software]. (1999). Wauconda, IL: Don Johnson, Inc.

Yell, M. L. (1997). Education and the law: The Individuals With Disabilities Education Act amendments of 1997. *Preventing School Failure, 41*, 185–187.

Yell, M. L., Robinson, R., & Drasgow, E. (2001). Cognitive behavior modification. In T. J. Zirpoli & K. J. Melloy (Eds.), *Behavior management: Applications for teachers* (3rd ed., pp. 200–247). Upper Saddle River, NJ: Merrill/Prentice Hall.

Yell, M. L., & Shriner, J. G. (1997). The IDEA amendments of 1997: Implications for special and general education teachers, administrators, and teacher trainers. *Focus on Exceptional Children, 30*, 1–19.

Yoder, D., Retish, E., & Wade, R. (1996). Service learning: Meeting student and community needs. *Teaching Exceptional Children, 28*, 14–18.

York, J., & Rainforth, B. (1991). Developing instructional adaptation. In F. P. Orelove & D. Sobsey (Eds.), *Educating children with multiple disabilities: A transdisciplinary approach* (2nd ed., pp. 259–295). Baltimore: Paul H. Brookes.

Young, K. R., West, R. P., Howard, V. F., & Whitney, R. (1986). Acquisition, fluency training, generalization, and maintenance of dressing skills of two developmentally disabled children. *Education and Treatment of Children, 9*, 16–29.

Ysseldyke, J. (1996). Improving teaching and learning: A thermos bottle keeps things hot and cold, but how does it know? *British Journal of Special Education, 23*, 3–8.

Ysseldyke, J. E., Algozzine, B., & Thurlow, M. (2000). *Critical issues in special education* (3rd ed.). Boston: Houghton Mifflin.

Zigler, E., & Hodapp, R. M. (1986). *Understanding mental retardation*. Cambridge: Cambridge University Press.

Zirpoli, T. J., & Melloy, K. J. (1997). *Behavior management: Applications for teachers and parents* (2nd ed) Upper Saddle River, NJ: Merrill/Prentice Hall.

Zirpoli, T. J., & Melloy, K. J. (2001). *Behavior management: Applications for teachers* (3rd ed.). Upper Saddle River, NJ: Merrill/Prentice Hall.

Zollers, N., Henderson, W., & Savage, J. F. (1998). Inclusion: A model for effective reading instruction. *The New England Reading Association Journal, 34*(3), 4–7.

Index